Disability, Intersectionality, and Belonging in Special Education

SPECIAL EDUCATION LAW, POLICY, AND PRACTICE

Series Editors

Mitchell L. Yell, PhD, University of South Carolina
David F. Bateman, PhD, American Institutes for Research

The *Special Education Law, Policy, and Practice* series highlights current trends and legal issues in the education of students with disabilities. The books in this series link legal requirements with evidence-based instruction and highlight practical applica- tions for working with students with disabilities. The titles in the *Special Education Law, Policy, and Practice* series are designed not only to be required textbooks for general education and special education preservice teacher education programs but are also designed for practicing teachers, education administrators, principals, school counselors, school psychologists, parents, and others interested in improving the lives of students with disabilities. The *Special Education Law, Policy, and Practice* series is committed to research-based practices working to provide appropriate and meaning- ful educational programming for students with disabilities and their families.

Titles in Series

Developing Educationally Meaningful and Legally Sound IEPs by Mitchell L. Yell, David F. Bateman, and James G. Shriner

Sexuality Education for Students with Disabilities by Thomas C. Gibbon, Elizabeth A. Harkins Monaco, and David F. Bateman

Creating Positive Elementary Classrooms: Preventing Behavior Challenges to Promote Learning by Stephen W. Smith and Mitchell L. Yell

Service Animals in Schools: Legal, Educational, Administrative, and Strategic Handling Aspects by Anne O. Papalia, Kathy B. Ewoldt, and David F. Bateman

Evidence-Based Practices for Supporting Individuals with Autism Spectrum Disorder edited by Laura C. Chezan, Katie Wolfe, and Erik Drasgow

Special Education Law Annual Review 2021 by David F. Bateman, Mitchell L. Yell, and Kevin P. Brady

Dispute Resolution Under the IDEA: Understanding, Avoiding, and Managing Special Education Disputes by David F. Bateman, Mitchell L. Yell, and Jonas Dorego

Advocating for the Common Good: People, Politics, Process, and Policy on Capitol Hill by Jane E. West

Related Services in Special Education: Working Together as a Team by Lisa Goran and David F. Bateman

The Essentials of Special Education Advocacy by Andrew M. Markelz, Sarah A. Nagro, Kevin Monnin, and David F. Bateman

Disability and Motor Behavior: A Handbook of Research by Ali S. Brian and Pamela S. Haibach-Beach

Supporting and Accommodating Students with Special Health Care Needs by Azure D. S. Angelov and Mary Jo Rattermann

You're Hired! Practical Strategies for Guiding Individuals with Autism Spectrum Disorder to Competitive Employment by Patricia S. Arter, Tammy B. H. Brown, and Jennifer Barna

Unraveling Dyslexia: A Guide for Teachers and Families by Kristin L. Sayeski

Disability, Intersectionality, and Belonging in Special Education: Socioculturally Sustaining Practices by Elizabeth A. Harkins Monaco, L. Lynn Stansberry Brusnahan, Marcus Charles Fuller, and Martin Odima Jr.

A School Leader's Guide to Action Research: Practical Connections and Uses with Data-Driven Decision-Making by Mary E. Little, Dena D. Slanda, and Elizabeth Cramer

For a full list of books in this series, visit https://rowman.com/Action/SERIES/_/RLSELPP/Special-Education-Law,-Policy,-and-Practice.

Disability, Intersectionality, and Belonging in Special Education

Sociculturally Sustaining Practices

Edited by Elizabeth A. Harkins Monaco,
L. Lynn Stansberry Brusnahan,
Marcus C. Fuller, and Martin Odima Jr.

ROWMAN & LITTLEFIELD
Lanham • Boulder • New York • London

Published by Rowman & Littlefield
An imprint of The Rowman & Littlefield Publishing Group, Inc.
4501 Forbes Boulevard, Suite 200, Lanham, Maryland 20706
www.rowman.com

86-90 Paul Street, London EC2A 4NE

Copyright ©2024 by The Rowman & Littlefield Publishing Group, Inc.

All rights reserved. No part of this book may be reproduced in any form or by any electronic or mechanical means, including information storage and retrieval systems, without written permission from the publisher, except by a reviewer who may quote passages in a review.

British Library Cataloguing in Publication Information Available

Library of Congress Cataloging-in-Publication Data

Names: Monaco, Elizabeth A. Harkins, 1981– editor. | Stansberry Brusnahan, L. Lynn, editor. | Fuller, Marcus C., editor. | Odima, Martin O., Jr., editor.
Title: Disability, intersectionality, and belonging in special education : socioculturally sustaining practices / Elizabeth A. Harkins Monaco, L. Lynn Stansberry Brusnahan, Marcus C. Fuller, and Martin Odima Jr.
Description: Lanham, Maryland : Rowman & Littlefield, 2024. | Series: Special education law, policy, and practice | Includes bibliographical references and index.
Identifiers: LCCN 2023050658 (print) | LCCN 2023050659 (ebook) | ISBN 9781538175811 (cloth) | ISBN 9781538175828 (paperback) | ISBN 9781538175835 (ebook)
Subjects: LCSH: Children with disabilities—Education. | Children with social disabilities—Education. | Culturally relevant pedagogy. | Educational equalization. | Special education.
Classification: LCC LC4015 .M584 2024 (print) | LCC LC4015 (ebook) | DDC 371.9—dc23/eng/20231127
LC record available at https://lccn.loc.gov/2023050658
LC ebook record available at https://lccn.loc.gov/2023050659

Contents

FOREWORD   xi

PART I: From the Culture of Disability to Disability Culture

CHAPTER 1: HISTORICAL AND MODERN CONTEXTS OF CULTURE
AND THE IMPACT ON BELONGING   2
*Elizabeth A. Harkins Monaco, Paul I. McGill, Catherine M. Constable,
Chelda Smith Kondo, Miles Forma, L. Lynn Stansberry Brusnahan*

   Abstract   2
   Guiding Questions   2
   Key Terms   3
   Culture   4
   Reframing Historical Social Construction of Disability   19
   A Modern View of Culture   21
   Cultural Expressions in Schools   24
   Summary   26
   References   26

CHAPTER 2: INTERSECTIONALITY IN THE CONTEXT OF DISABILITY   32
*Sara Wildman, L. Lynn Stansberry Brusnahan, Sharde Theodore,
Meaghan McCollow, James Williams, Erin Fitzgerald Farrell,
Elizabeth A. Harkins Monaco, Marcus C. Fuller*

   Abstract   32
   Guiding Questions   33

Key Terms	33
The Impact of Intersectional Sociocultural Identities	34
Intersectional Competence in Special Education	46
Summary	54
References	56

CHAPTER 3: DISABILITY CULTURE IN THE DEAF AND AUTISTIC COMMUNITIES — 63
Gulnoza Yakubova, John Pirone, Veronica Y. Kang, Dylan Kapit, James Williams, Elizabeth A. Harkins Monaco

Abstract	63
Guiding Questions	63
Key Terms	64
Disability as a Sociocultural Identity	65
Disability Culture in Educational Contexts	72
Inequities in Education	77
Summary	81
References	83

PART II: Critical Theories That Influence Our Views of Disability and Race

CHAPTER 4: CRITICAL RACE THEORY: THE DOS, THE DON'TS, THE ALREADY DONES, AND THE STOP DOINGS — 88
Marcus C. Fuller, Jasmine Fleming, Joseph Cremona, Elizabeth A. Harkins Monaco

Abstract	88
Guiding Questions	88
Key Terms	89
The History of CRT	90
The Dos: What Is CRT?	93
The Don'ts: What CRT Is Not	100
The Already Dones: Critical Race Theory in Education	104
The Stop Doings: Barriers to Teaching through a Critical Race Theory Lens	108
Summary	116
References	117

CHAPTER 5: THE JOURNEY OF DISABILITY STUDIES: CONTEMPLATING DISABILITY CRITICALLY — 120
Kara B. Ayers, Lydia Ocasio-Stoutenburg, David J. Connor, Marcus C. Fuller

| Abstract | 120 |
| Guiding Questions | 121 |

Key Terms	121
Disability Studies	122
Discovering the Need for Critical Disability Studies	127
Seeking Racial Justice	130
Looking Forward	142
Summary	143
References	144

CHAPTER 6: THE HISTORY OF DISABILITY, DISABILITY MODELS, AND A VIEW FOR THE FUTURE: THE PAST IS PROLOGUE   150
Kendra V. Saunders, Michelle Mercado, Liza Citron, Marcus C. Fuller

Abstract	150
Guiding Questions	151
Key Terms	151
Introduction to the History of Disability Rights in the United States	152
Models of Disability	154
The Language of Disability	162
Disability in the Media	166
Models of Disability in Education	169
Summary	173
References	174

PART III: Educational Frameworks That Champion Equity

CHAPTER 7: INTERSECTIONAL SOCIOCULTURAL COMPETENCY AND EDUCATIONAL EQUITY   180
L. Lynn Stansberry Brusnahan, Kenyon Andrews, Rebecca A. Wade, Amy Eelkema Baxter, Martin Odima Jr.

Abstract	180
Guiding Questions	180
Key Terms	181
Equity	181
Summary	214
References	215

CHAPTER 8: SOCIOCULTURALLY SUSTAINING PRACTICES: THE WHAT, THE WHY, AND THE HOW   219
Lindsay M. Griendling, Colin Rose, L. Lynn Stansberry Brusnahan, Sandy Smith, Eric Elmore, Elizabeth Thao, Martin Odima Jr., Elizabeth A. Harkins Monaco

Abstract	219
Guiding Questions	220
Key Terms	220

What and Why Culturally and Linguistically Sustaining Pedagogy?	220
Embedding Practices into Special Education Teaching Frameworks	235
From Culturally and Linguistically Sustaining Practices to Socioculturally Sustaining Practices	236
Special Education Teaching Frameworks	244
Summary	251
References	251

CHAPTER 9: EDUCATIONAL PRACTICES TO ACKNOWLEDGE AND INCORPORATE STUDENTS' SOCIOCULTURAL IDENTITIES AND EXPERIENCES 256

Martin Odima Jr., Sandy Smith, Eric Elmore, Ambra L. Green, Elizabeth Thao, L. Lynn Stansberry Brusnahan, Elizabeth A. Harkins Monaco

Abstract	256
Guiding Questions	256
Key Terms	257
Special Education	257
Now What: REMIXed Education	262
Summary	283
References	284

PART IV: Social and Cultural Rights Movements That Impact Special Education

CHAPTER 10: DISABILITY RIGHTS: THE IMPACT OF SOCIAL AND CULTURAL MOVEMENTS ON SPECIAL EDUCATION 290

Aaron Campbell, Susannah Boyle, Jonte' C. Taylor, Elizabeth A. Harkins Monaco, Dana Patenaude, Cindy Bentley

Abstract	290
Guiding Questions	290
Key Terms	291
Ableism	291
Social and Cultural Rights Movements in the Twentieth Century	293
Disability as a Cultural Phenomenon	301
Effective Interventions for Increasing a Sense of Belonging	305
Summary	307
References	307

CHAPTER 11: THE PUSH AND PULL OF THE LITIGATION-LEGISLATION-LITIGATION CYCLE 312

Jacquelyn Chovanes, David Bateman, Ruth Eyres, Catherine Constable, Bob Eyres, L. Lynn Stansberry Brusnahan

Abstract	312
Guiding Questions	312

Key Terms	313
US Special Education Law	314
Impact of Activism on Language	321
Inclusion and Least Restrictive Environment	322
Disproportionality	325
Educational Frameworks	329
Summary	338
References	338

CHAPTER 12: INTERSECTIONAL BELONGING IN SPECIAL EDUCATION — 344

Michelle Kalos, Elizabeth Finnegan, Shelley Neilsen Gatti, Salita Callicutt, Emily O'Brien Rank, L. Lynn Stansberry Brusnahan, T. Collin Brusnahan, Olivia Parry, Nathaniel Lentz, Yokasta Urena

Abstract	344
Guiding Questions	344
Key Terms	344
Factors That Impact Special Education	345
Special Education's Impact	357
Creating a Sense of Belonging	369
Summary	372
References	373
GLOSSARY	381
INDEX	397
ABOUT THE CONTRIBUTORS	417

Foreword

Oluwatobi Abubakare and Marcus C. Fuller

During my middle school days, there is an event that will always be forever ingrained in my memory:

> *It was presentation day in my English and Language Arts (ELA) class where each student had to present on a particular topic of interest. As such, I chose autism because that was my main interest at the time, and I recently read a TIME issue that was about "The Secrets of Autism." I was motivated to present, but when the teacher called my name to stand in the front of the classroom, reality finally hit me, "I have to speak . . . and I have to speak in front of all these eyes staring back at me." I felt frozen and immovable despite constantly losing my balance ever so slowly as a side effect of my cerebral palsy. I felt like a storm was inside of me, raging all over, trembling my nerves all over. I hear, in the distance, "Tobi . . . Tobi, start to speak now," repeat over and over, with every instance getting firmer. I yelled in my head that I want to speak and desperately tried to move my young mouth muscles, yet nothing was moving. At this point, small canons of laughter emerge and somehow my inability to speak is seen as attention-seeking by the teacher. She firmly describes me as being disruptive and says she will report me to the principal if I do not speak now. I am still silent. An eternity has passed, and I am finally ordered back to my seat, in the corner of class.*

Other students throughout the class had disruptive moments, but none were seen as disruptive by my teacher or called out as disruptive by the teacher. They were ignored. While my class was filled with students of color (including other Black students), I was much darker than everyone. I was also the only disabled student in the class. Although I am autistic, I was not formally diagnosed with autism until late senior year of high school. Rather, my IEP was filled with "emotional disturbance," "selective mutism," and "cerebral palsy" and a 504 plan for asthma, but few to no accommodations were either in place or enforced for anything concerning my selective mutism.

While I attended school where most of my peers looked like me or shared identities similar to mine (low-income, racially marginalized, first-generation immigrant, multilingual, and disabled), rarely did I have practitioners that looked like me or the majority of the other students in my school district. Because of this experience, I had a harder time recognizing the various racial, class, and ableist microaggressions from my teachers since everyone was getting them in some shape or form. However, that day in ELA class, I was treated much differently.

My inability to speak was not seen as an opportunity to provide an alternate, more accessible approach to doing the assignment but a moment to ignore the multiple sociocultural needs of a disabled student in favor of maintaining an educational atmosphere saturated with racial and ableist microaggressions. Unfortunately, that was one of many moments I continued to experience throughout my preK–12 education. White disabled students have different needs than Black disabled students, and even more so a Black autistic student who is also a first-generation immigrant with a physical disability. In my experience, this was lost on so many of the practitioners in my journey. Most of my IEP accommodations in preK–12 focused on my physical disability and neglected my known and unknown nonphysical disabilities. I struggled emotionally and mentally throughout my preK–12 education in a way that impacted my ability to truly thrive in my education, not just due to my disabilities but because my needs as a Black and immigrant student were rarely met by my white practitioners.

It was not until I arrived at college that it became apparent to me that these issues I was experiencing occurred on a broader and more widespread level. Attending college at a top-ranked Predominately White Institution (PWI) as a Black, disabled, low-income student forced me to reconcile with my past experiences in ways that I was not able to before while also providing more circumstances for micro- and macroaggressions in different forms by professors, staff, students, and the overall institution. Practitioners must consider the intersectional needs of their students and implement sociocultural practices that are inclusive of all the identities. Because my story is not unique, resources like this textbook—*Disability, Intersectionality, and Belonging in Special Education: Socioculturally Sustaining Practices*—are crucial to helping practitioners recognize that disabled students not only have intersectional needs because of their disabilities but are students with other sociocultural identities that further impact their needs and their positionality in educational spaces.

There are over fifty contributors to this textbook offering firsthand real-life experiences and the application of research and other scholarly works around disability and diversity. These contributors provide a broad range of sociocultural identities (i.e., race, ethnicity, nationality, religion, sex, age, occupation, and disability) that still only represent a small sample of the diversity of our world. By no means does this textbook show all perspectives, frameworks, theories, or strategies within disability and special education; rather, its purpose is to offer a deeper understanding of disability, culture, and special education; to spotlight voices of those that tend to be silenced; and to provide opportunities for practitioners to continue their journey to intersectional competence.

Each chapter highlights why it is critical for practitioners to understand their disabled students' intersectional needs and to implement strategies—such as socioculturally sustaining practices, intersectionality, and antiracism practices—that support the whole student, because students are rarely *just* disabled (or even disabled in just one way). Each chapter highlights several key terms at the beginning and many of these terms are used throughout the textbook. The terminology used throughout is meant to provide a clear understanding of the way we speak about diversity and disability, and to provide representation for populations that have been historically marginalized or othered. For example, terms like People of the Global Majority (PGM) offer a more-inclusive alternative to terms like BIPOC or People of Color that still center the white American experience, whereas the interchanging of people with disabilities (person-first language; PFL) and disabled people (identity-first language; IFL) are used to respect perspectives and populations on both sides of use-of-language discussions.

Terminology like PGM, PFL, IFL, and other sociocultural identifications help some people feel included and foster a sense of belonging, yet the same terms may be triggering, derogatory, or unwelcoming to others. Furthermore, the traditional understanding and preferences around disability have been constructed by researchers and scholars (mostly influenced by the medical model) who are not a part of the disability community themselves. Great consideration should be taken when choosing how to label someone else's identity; the best rule of thumb is to ask the person how they wish to identify and/or to what identities they ascribe. Additionally, it is important to note that language changes and terms can vary over time, region, and as the dominant narrative shifts.

The textbook is split into four parts.

> Part I: *From the Culture of Disability to Disability Culture.* The first section of the book provides a deep understanding of culture, the culture of disability, and disability cultures.
>
> - Chapter 1: *Historical and Modern Contexts of Culture and the Impact on Belonging* provides a historical context of the social trends that have impacted the experiences of people with disabilities and describes how Intersectionality and Social Identity Theory help to define a modern view of disability as a social identity. This chapter contextualizes how culture and cultural expressions are traditionally approached in schools.

- Chapter 2: *Intersectionality in the Context of Disability* describes how the layering of multiple sociocultural identities and factors impact the education, access, and experience of those in special education. This chapter offers strategies that practitioners can implement to disrupt and enact change to promote an equity-base educational environment.
- Chapter 3: *Disability Culture in the Deaf and Autistic Communities* offers sight on how the Deaf and Autistic communities cultivate their identities and influence cultures of disability. This chapter concludes with strategies that encourage educational equity for these communities.

Part II: *Critical Theories that Influence Our Views of Disability and Race.* The second section of the book focuses on critical theories that influence our views of disability and race, as disability and race are inextricably connected.

- Chapter 4: *Critical Race Theory: The Dos, the Don'ts, the Already Dones, and the Stop Doings* describes the tenets of Critical Race Theory and how it is and isn't being used in today's education system. This chapter concludes with areas in which practitioners can incorporate concepts from Critical Race Theory into their own educational practices.
- Chapter 5: *The Journey of Disability Studies: Contemplating Disability Critically* shows how Disability Studies and Critical Race Theory reconstruct the notion of disability beyond the deficit-based perspective of the traditional medical model. This chapter equips practitioners with strategies that leverage critical disability theory to improve the educational experiences of disabled students.
- Chapter 6: *The History of Disability, Disability Models, and a View for the Future: The Past Is Prologue* gives an overview of the various models that describe disability and the way society thinks about disability. This chapter highlights action steps you can take to promote a more inclusive and respectful environment for all students with disabilities.

Part III: *Educational Frameworks That Champion Equity.* The third section of this book offers school and classroom strategies and frameworks that champion equity.

- Chapter 7: *Intersectional Sociocultural Competency and Educational Equity* presents tools to advance the sociocultural consciousness and reflection of practitioners to best serve disabled students. This chapter provides an assessment to help understand your own personal intersectional sociocultural competence.
- Chapter 8: *Socioculturally Sustaining Practices: The What, the Why, and the How,* defines and aligns culturally and linguistically sustaining practices with intersectionality theory to position socioculturally sustaining practices that provide an equitable educational experience for students. This

chapter expresses ways to embed culturally and linguistically sustaining pedagogy into other educational frameworks like Universal Design for Learning (UDL), Response to Intervention (RTI), Positive Behavioral Interventions and Supports (PBIS), and Social Emotional Learning (SEL).
- Chapter 9: *Educational Practices to Acknowledge and Incorporate Students' Sociocultural Identities and Experiences* introduces a REMIXed approach to special education that continuously revises, modifies, and innovates to support students with diverse sociocultural identities. This chapter provides tools and strategies that provide a plethora of ways to advocate for social justice and provide a continuum of services for all students.

Part IV: *Social and Cultural Rights Movements That Impact Special Education.* The final section of the book wraps up with social and cultural rights movements that influence the field of special education.

- Chapter 10: *Disability Rights: The Impact of Social and Cultural Movements on Special Education* provides additional context for the social phenomenon of disability and the oppressive systems that have historically minoritized disabled persons. The chapter provides information on how disability is traditionally viewed within education and opportunities to infuse disability as a cultural identity in the classroom.
- Chapter 11: *The Push and Pull of the Litigation-Legislation-Litigation Cycle* offers a historical context of the language and legislation around special education. This chapter synthesizes current educational access, discusses unaddressed needs, and incorporates evidence-based practices from a sociocultural perspective.
- Chapter 12: *Intersectional Belonging in Special Education* spotlights influences and the shared values of special education such as free appropriate public education (FAPE) and least restrictive environment (LRE). This chapter emphasizes the continued evolution of special education and disability rights movements that are rooted in the value of belonging and the work of advocacy for and with students, families, and educators.

We hope this book inspires you to integrate concepts of disability, intersectionality, and belonging into your education environments and creates a spark for practitioners everywhere to continue their journey in intersectional sociocultural competence. Practitioners need to move away from the dichotomy of good and bad, right and wrong, normal and abnormal, and to realize that our work doesn't exist in polarity. "Human experiences cannot be accurately understood by prioritizing any one single factor or constellation of factors" (Hankivsky et al., 2014, p. 2).

PART I

From the Culture of Disability to Disability Culture

CHAPTER 1

Historical and Modern Contexts of Culture and the Impact on Belonging

Chapter authors: *Elizabeth A. Harkins Monaco, Paul I. McGill, Catherine M. Constable, and Chelda Smith Kondo*

Vignette authors: *Miles Forma and Elizabeth A. Harkins Monaco*

Editor: *L. Lynn Stansberry Brusnahan*

ABSTRACT

Feeling connected to a larger social community or culture is considered an essential human need, but what happens when you are isolated from these kinds of social connections? The purpose of this chapter is to provide a historical context of culture as a [global] social trend and offer a few examples of how cultural expressions impact the experiences of people with disabilities. Then, we use two frameworks to shape a modern view of culture that includes disability. Finally, we contextualize how culture and cultural expressions are traditionally approached in schools.

GUIDING QUESTIONS

- How has culture historically been defined and expressed across the globe?
- How have traditional expressions of culture historically impacted individuals with disabilities' senses of belonging?
- What is a modern view of culture?
- How is culture typically represented and celebrated in schools?
- What kinds of cultural expressions are demonstrated in schools?

KEY TERMS

Art	Gestalt Phenomena	Social Identity Theory
Belonging	Intersectionality	Sociocultural Construct,
Cognitive Grouping	Language	Social Construct, and
Communicative Competence	Mass Culture	Social Identity
	Ritual	Social Power
Culture	Social Capital	Sociolinguistics

A discussion on culture starts with exploring belonging. **Belonging**, or feeling connected to a larger social community, is considered an essential human need (Rokach, 2020). Having a sense of belonging influences our health and well-being and is bidirectionally connected to social and cultural considerations, norms, and rituals:

- When people feel supported by their social network, they are better equipped to cultivate their emotions and strengths to participate in cultural events (Gable & Reis, 2010; Pressman et al., 2009).
- Social relationships, social environments, and cultural events foster cohesion among groups of people (Begen & Turner-Cobb, 2015; Feeney & Collins, 2015; Lakey & Orehek, 2011) by improving feelings of inclusion (Leary, 2010), increasing trust (Hillebrant et al., 2011), and reducing the impact of exclusion (DeWall et al., 2010).

Social connections are very important, especially during times of stress. They contribute to the development of culture and have a strong hold on the individuals who connect within them. Without these kinds of connections, individuals feel a sense of loss or feel increasingly insignificant (Atabek & Nurnazar, 2021), and their mental and physical health is negatively affected (Rook & Charles, 2017). A holistic physician noted that "humans are highly social, communal animals that are meant to live in families, tribes, and communities, and when they lack those connections they suffer, as was evidence by many during the COVID-19 pandemic and lockdown" (Weil, 1997, as cited in Rokach, 2020, para. 2). It is often considered against the norm to discuss the negative impacts of a lack of connection on individuals, which prevents us from addressing, solving, or processing these problems. This can be increasingly problematic for disabled people.

This chapter provides the historical context of culture as a social trend, traditional expressions of culture, and the impact on people with disabilities. Finally, we offer two frameworks to conceptualize culture today and how it is traditionally approached in schools.

CULTURE

Culture is historically conceptualized as a way to understand the world. In the nineteenth century, it was defined through a cultural-philosophical lens, but in the twentieth century, researchers started defining culture as the global sociocultural phenomenon we are familiar with today. Culture is "adaptive, communicative, recreational, ideological, commercial, consumer, informational-epistemological, value-orientational" (Atabek & Nurnazar, 2021, para. 4), and it is shared among communities of people who connect with each other over these (Rokach, 2020). Much of the modern research regarding culture claims it as "reality, contextuality, ideology, and mythology" (para. 4), something that is complex with its own "genesis, specificity and development trends" (para. 1) and includes types of art and the development and use of technology and media (Atabek & Nurnazar, 2021). Culture is recognized as (a) shared history; (b) expression of identity and meaning; and (c) pride (Boyle et al., 2016). Culture then is broad and encompasses the "artifacts of creative expression, but also the activities, meaning systems, rituals and rhythms of everyday life that define a group or society" (Bennett, 1998; Hawkins, 1993; Williams, 1989, as cited in Stevenson, 2006, p. 354).

Mass culture is a way to define the sociocultural phenomenon that is most influential; otherwise known as **dominant culture**, it pervades all types of culture and is defined as the "orientation towards the tastes and needs of the 'average person'" (Atabek & Nurnazar, 2021, para. 3). Mass culture is built on the (a) ability to influence or convert artifacts created in other cultures as consumer goods; (b) reliance on and influence of mass media as the primary way to consume the value system of the "average person" (Atabek & Nurnazar, 2021); and (c) shared, similar beliefs and expressions.

Expressions of Culture

Cultural expressions, or **rituals**, are "a type of expressive, symbolic activity constructed of multiple behaviors that occur in a fixed, episodic sequence, and that [tend] to be repeated over time" (Rook, 1985, p. 252), and are instrumental when creating culture. When rituals occur among mass culture, they influence how individuals initiate, foster, and terminate relationships with others (Campos & Kim, 2017; Hofstede et al., 1997; Mojaverian & Kim, 2013; Rokach, 2020). In the next sections, we examine the following expressions of culture: (a) communication and language, (b) food, (c) marriage, (d) religion, and (e) art.

Communication and Language

One of the most influential rituals is **communicative competence**, or having linguistic knowledge and a functional means of purposeful communication in one's native or studied language. Communicative competence, or communication, has three main competencies: (a) sociolinguistic, (b) linguistic, and (c) pragmatic (Furkatovna, 2022). While the patterning in linguistics and pragmatics is important and will be briefly explained earlier, we are going to first focus on the social implications of language, or language as a form of "expressive culture."

Sociolinguistics. The theory of **sociolinguistics**, or the scholarship of how language is used in culture (Ember, 2016), outlines how both verbal and nonverbal language play a role in social relationships, one of the "most important tool[s] with which we express ourselves to others, define and designate everything that surrounds us and in which we participate" (Furkatovna, 2022, p. 75). The ethnography of **language** is defined as speaking techniques within individual cultures that center the traditions of oral literature and subsequent social norms (Eastman, 1984; Hymes, 1972). Sociolinguistic competence is quite important then, as it means individuals can purposefully use their knowledge, skills, and abilities to communicate according to a variety of socio-communicative rules and contexts. In other words, individuals usually belong to several different kinds of social groups and play different roles in each group, and so they need a basic understanding of elements of language, social interactions, and intercultural communication considerations within each context (Furkatovna, 2022).

There are cultural elements of communication that determine necessary communicative styles. "The specificity of intercultural communication lies in the fact that the choice of a particular language system does not imply that, together with the language, the communicant, for whom this language is not native, will adhere to the appropriate communicative style" (Furkatovna, 2022, p. 76). For example, verbal communication is very detailed in Arabic, where the speaker is expected to be verbose, use rich and expressive language, and infuse vivid images and comparisons. In the Japanese language however, communication tends to be brief and relies more heavily on nonverbal communication such as looks, poses, or gestures (Furkatovna, 2022).

Linguistics. Linguistic competence is defined by various researchers in different ways. Here, linguistic competence refers to the knowledge of linguistic rules, the ability to perform linguistic operations, and the ability to represent concepts in linguistic terms. Linguistic competence refers to "knowledge, judgment and skill in the linguistic code of the spoken or written language(s) in the individual's family and broader social community..." (Light & McNaughton, 2014, p. 4). Linguistic competence can be lost due to brain injury, or it may develop differently due to sensory impairment (i.e., hearing loss), social deprivation, or specific forms of neurodiversity and intellectual impairment.

Pragmatics. **Pragmatics** involves knowledge of social rules for language use, and pragmatic competence is concerned with language use and the functionality of communication. **Pragmatic competence** is the ability to communicate successfully through the consideration of physical, social, and conversational contexts. For example, learning how to take turns in a conversation, inferring information about the participants, and maintaining topics such that personal contributions to the conversation are relevant. Pragmatic competence involves the use of nonverbal cues, referred to as nonverbal communication codes of attitude and emotion in social interaction. For example, in the American classroom, students are expected to raise their hands prior to speaking, while at a baseball game, screaming a single word (e.g., Popcorn!) is an appropriate performative. On the playground, loud and fast talk can get control. These codes can enhance, diminish, or replace verbal communication and can include bodily contact, eye-gaze, facial and gestural changes, head moves, and paralinguistic cues such as tone, timing, and accent (Harper et al., 1978). These nonverbal behaviors are critical to understand along with verbal communicative norms.

Pragmatic competence also requires learning the rules of discourse. For example, the rules for using language in an elementary classroom are different from rules for using language at home. When a parent asks the question, "What did you do at school?", the child knows that this is a (direct) request for information because their parent doesn't know what happened. When a classroom teacher uses a similar syntactic form, "What did Jack do with the beans?", students understand that this is not a request for information because the teacher knows the answer. This is an indirect request for the child to act by telling the teacher the answer (Dore, 1977).

Linguistic and pragmatic competence are inextricably related, and necessary for successful interpersonal communicative connection. Together these competencies support communication, interpersonal relationships, and social identity. Intervention and educational goals that include interpersonal communications in increasingly different contexts, are necessary to provide persons with complex communication challenges greater access to social opportunity. Children who exhibit echolalia (i.e., repetition of words), or hyperlexia (i.e., innate ability to decode or sound out words), for example, may exhibit well-formed structural features of language, however they may not be successful in communication because their listeners' communication skills are what is upheld as the norm. This kind of context means their language is not related to the listener's social context, or the characteristics of their listeners.

Communication, Language, and Disability

As communication competencies vary immensely in sociolinguistics, pragmatic functions, and nonverbal messaging, so does the relationship between culture, communication and language, and disability. To better understand the relationship, we first must discuss and define how these entities are intertwined with each other. Communication, language, and disability are inextricably connected through culture, impacting one's access to belonging and connection. In nearly all cultures, language use is a primary means of human interaction. Language and communication impairments are found cross-culturally, but they impact communities quite differently. In the United States, communicative competence is measured when classifying disabilities, and the education system prioritizes language and communication development for all students, especially those with disabilities. As listed in table 1.1, there are a number of disabilities that communication and language-related difficulties impact. We also included resources to learn more about these disabilities:

Table 1.1. Common Communication and Language-Related Disabilities

Category	Disability	Resource
Fluency	• Stuttering/Cluttering	*Stuttering and cluttering.* Psychology (Ward, 2017).
Speech Sound Disorders	• Phonological Processing • Structural Disorders (e.g., cleft palate) • Articulation Disorder	*Speech sound disorders.* Plural (Bleile, 2015).
Motor Speech Disorders	• Dysarthria • Apraxia of Speech • Cerebral Palsy	*Motor speech disorders.* Mosby (Duffy, 2020).
Neurogenic/ Cognitive Communication	• Traumatic Brain Injury • Right Hemisphere Disorder • Aphasia • Dementia • Alzheimer's Disease	*Neurogenic communication disorders.* Thieme (Worral & Frattali, 2000).
Swallowing and Feeding	• Dysphagia	*Dysphagia: Treatment in children and adults.* Mosby (Groher & Crary, 2020).
Expressive/ Receptive Language	• Specific Language Impairment • Developmental Language Disorders • Dyslexia • Auditory Processing Disorders • Language Comprehension Disorder	Understanding dyslexia in the context of developmental language disorders. *Language, Speech, and Hearing Services in Schools, 49*(4) (Adloff & Hogan, 2018). Editorial: Auditory processing disorder. *Ear Hear, 39*(6) (Moore, 2018).
Voice and Resonance	• Vocal Fold Paralysis • Spasmodic Dysphonia • Mutational Falsetto • Artificial Larynx • Vocal Nodules	*Voice disorders.* Plural (Sapienza & Hoffman, 2021).
Pragmatic Language	• Autism Spectrum Disorder • Pragmatic Language Disorder • Social Communication Disorder • Selective Mutism	*Handbook of pragmatic language disorders.* Springer Nature (Cummings, 2021).

Communication and Language-Related Disabilities

In the United States, disability affects approximately 25 percent of adults, totaling around 61 million, and is more likely in women, older people, Native cultures and Alaskan Natives, adults with low incomes, and adults living in southern states (Okoro et al., 2018). The presence of disability in the schools varies in severity and type. For example, children with Specific Learning Disability (SLD) represent over 30 percent of students receiving services under an individualized education program (IEP), followed by almost 20 percent of students labeled with speech-language impairments, and students with hearing loss at 1 percent (Hussar et al., 2020).

VIGNETTE 1: MEET MILES

I am a thirty-five-year-old Jewish man. My primary disability is Cerebral Palsy (CP). This disability is primarily a motor disorder caused by a brain injury during pregnancy or during the birth process. Individuals with CP have unique physical characteristics, as well as other neurologically related difficulties. My body can move around independently on the floor at my house. For example, when I have to go to the bathroom, I can get up onto my knees and I can crawl into the bathroom. I can grab with two hands onto one bar that's next to the toilet. I can pull myself onto the toilet seat because my upper body is really strong. I use an augmentative alternative communication (AAC) system to communicate. I live with a housemate and friend as well as two other adults. Since we all have physical disabilities, there is always staff to assist us in our daily routines.

Every impairment manifests differently and affects the three tenets of communicative competence differently. For example, children with language-learning impairments can develop theory of mind, understand the context, and make correct assumptions about their communicative partners, but they may not be able to formulate their messages with clear sentences, adequate vocabulary, or with enough speed (Schwartz Offek & Segal, 2022).

VIGNETTE 2: MILES'S COMMUNICATION FRUSTRATIONS AND SUCCESSES

When I was young, most of my interactions were with my parents and my speech therapist. I did not have much experience in conversation with peers, nor did I know the rules of classroom discourse such as

- *Listen more than talk*
- *Be prepared to answer specific questions*

- *Stay on the teacher's topic*
- *Stay in one place*
- *Change activity only when the teacher says*

There is a difference between being able to communicate with symbols and pictures versus using language to communicate. When I had my first communication boards, they were very limited. There was no way that I could say something in a real emergency... for example, one time my dog ate my socks and I hurried into my parents room to tell them but I could only tell them by pointing to my sock and my foot. So my parents kept trying to guess what I was trying to tell them. They were really frustrated and I was really frustrated as well.

Originally, my communication board only had four pages that I could use. The speech therapist that worked at the elementary school really didn't have the experience of adding to or designing a communication board. The reading teacher didn't know how to modify her strategies to find a method of teaching me to read. Therefore my language and learning development were "stunted."

A huge change came for me when my speech therapist recommended that the school district contact a speech language and literacy specialist who had the experience of using speech perception rather than speech production to teach reading to a nonspeaking student like me. I began by sliding a large block across my tray as I heard a word. The tray had three panels marked. I began by identifying one of three vowels in a word I heard. Soon I could identify the vowel and last and first sounds in words. Then I learned to spell the words that I heard. Thereafter my reading progressed very quickly.

Soon letters and words replaced simple pictures on my manual board. Now I could ask questions and explain rather than point, gesture, and hope. I could read stories and novels with words that I never saw before, and my vocabulary improved. When I was introduced to a high-tech Augmentative Alternative Communication (AAC) system, I preferred to use my manual board because at the time, it was faster. However as I got more adept with written language, I felt more prepared and confident in learning to use a complex AAC device. Importantly, the AAC device gave me a voice! Soon I became very motivated to get better using the AAC device and decided to complete my bar mitzvah. As I prepared for my bar mitzvah, I became totally immersed in becoming efficient with using my AAC device.

It is the responsibility of education practitioners, speech and language pathologists, and those involved in creating an environment where all students can access the curriculum to be mindful of their own bias when it comes to various forms of communication. Honoring students' preferred or alternative means of communication is key. See chapters 10 and 11 for more information about alternative means of communication. Teacher interactions with students can play a vital role in one's language and communication confidence.

VIGNETTE 3: *MILES'S TEACHERS AND THEIR BIASES*

My fourth and fifth grade teachers stereotyped me as intellectually impaired, different, and challenged. My experience in those grades had a huge negative impact on me and was emotionally challenging. In 1996, the vast majority of psychologists had no training or very limited experience in assessing nonspeaking individuals. Further, since I had limited motor skills, performance-based assessments were not feasible. Subsequently, several of the people I encountered assumed that my intellectual abilities were commensurate with my limited motor abilities. This presumption affected my class placements which negatively impacted my self-esteem and mental health for much of my life. I still maintain a defensive posture when the topic of my intellectual competency is implied or discussed.

The kinds of relationships between students and teachers play a significant role in fostering successful communication skills. A longitudinal study found children's receptive vocabulary development in the early years was closely related to quality of teacher-student interactions (Yang et al., 2021). One way educators can increase the generalization of language and/or communication skills learned during academic instruction is by encouraging all students to have relationships outside of the classroom. Extracurricular activities have long been shown to offer opportunities for students to learn the values of teamwork, individual and group responsibility, physical strength and endurance, competition, diversity, and a sense of culture and community (National Center for Education Statistics [NCES], 1995). Studies show there is a general agreement among teachers toward extracurricular activities, however it can be difficult to supervise or organize these efforts without it negatively affecting their already-busy workloads (Yusof & Abdulgalil, 2017). Despite teacher enthusiasm, clubs and extracurricular activities with limited preparation affect the generalization of speaking skills with students, encouraging the planning of more effective strategies to promote communication and language in schools (Yusof & Abdulgalil, 2017).

Communication and Language Disabilities as Culture

In this section, we will offer an example of how sharing the experiences of language or communication disabilities creates a sense of belonging. In the United States, there are an estimated three million individuals with a "fluency disorder" (which we recognize has roots in deficit-based framing) such as stuttering or cluttering (National Institute on Deafness and Other Communication Disorders [NIDCD], 2016). Many people with stuttering (PWS) have experienced employment discrimination, unjust school experiences, conversational partners completing their sentences, and overall negative public opinions (Boyle et al., 2016). In response, PWS began formulating camaraderie, supporting each other, and creating bonds to address the systems of oppression they experience. Some persons with stuttering choose to use techniques to modify or reduce the frequency of stuttering, others choose to embrace their stuttering and not make volitional changes to their speech (Boyle et al., 2016). They developed self-help groups, websites, creative writing, social networking groups, music, podcasts, bracelets, and T-shirts that embrace stuttering (Boyle et al., 2016). In addition to support groups, their advocacy improved interventions such as speech and language therapy or other related services such as mental health supports. This is one example of how disability can be framed as a cultural identity, which in this case can be defined by PWS's relationship with several factors, including: social connection, support, pride, and advocacy efforts to address the systems of oppression they experience due to stuttering, including environmental accessibility and culturally dominant attitudes toward language disorders or communication disabilities.

Other forms of cultural expression intersect with disability as well; in the next sections we will examine rituals that are not as easily associated with disability. How are people with disabilities impacted by traditional cultural expressions? Do disabled people have the same kinds of cultural access to their communities as their nondisabled peers?

Food

One of the oldest rituals on earth is meal sharing, or when groups of people eat together; food rituals go back two million years, when hunters would bring food to their social groups to collect, prepare, and divide it among the group. This custom

> may have encouraged the development of kinship systems, such as who eats with whom, the language which was used to discuss food and how to secure it, and for planning the next day's meal. It has been the process that helped bring people together and helped define their groups, rituals and history. (Visser, 1991, as cited in Rokach, 2020, para. 7)

Food rituals are deeply influenced by culture, history, sociology, and psychology and include kinds of food, where and how food is prepared, plus additional factors such as prayers, stories, or the connection shared before, during, and after food is consumed; "breaking bread and sharing it with friends means friendship itself, and also trust, pleasure, and gratitude in the sharing . . . food in general, becomes, in its sharing, the actual bond which unites us" (Visser, 1991, p. 3). How and what people eat reveal a lot about their cultural identities, rites of passage, family or organizational systems, and various manners of behavior and interaction (Rook, 1985). Food, then, is a symbol of belonging and community rooted in tradition (Humphrey & Humphrey, 1988).

Food as a ritual is impactful, meaningful, and has much influence on societal norms, expectations, and behavior. And as with all rituals, compliance fosters belonging while nonconformity can lead to isolation (Eaude, 2020). Thus, a vegan or a vegetarian at a traditional barbecue or Thanksgiving meal might find themselves socially outcast because of their dietary restrictions. Of course, it is always an option to bring one's own food to align with dietary constraints, however, it is not always practical or desired. In certain communities, food accommodation is normalized—be it for health concerns, allergies, or lifestyle choices. And in other spaces, accommodations or nutritional modifications are rejected.

Just as food sharing is a common ritual in many cultures, so too is body shaming (Visser, 2015). Food is one of the few basic needs of humans that can become an addiction. While American culture embraces an abundance of food, it often shames the consequences of eating in excess. Globally, the United States is known for its overindulgence in unhealthy foods, yet we have not reconciled that culture with much of the US adult population being obese (Gilman, 2008). Culture is neither objective nor solely positive. Using this fragmented example of food, the complex nature of food as ritual, expression, basic need, and as culprit is illuminated.

Food and Disability

There are attitudinal, cultural, and social trends that affect the treatment and condition of disabled people and their access to food. For example, in some cultures, mothers of babies with disabilities may be advised not to breastfeed because of a social assumption that the child will not be able to lead a productive life or have a long life span even with those kinds of nutrients (Groce et al., 2014). The needs of people with disabilities could also impact how much time is dedicated to feeding. For example, a child with low muscle tone and spasticity would require increased feeding time and protocol (Lumos, 2013). When disabled children are either not able to or not encouraged to feed themselves, additional time from caregivers is required (Gannotti et al., 2004). These considerations may result in children with disabilities consuming less nutritious food, eating smaller quantities of food, or not being fed at all (Nogay, 2013). Other issues are when disabled children are on alternative diets (Werner, 2009), which places significant economic burdens on caregivers as specialized diets are typically more expensive.

VIGNETTE 4: *MEET LIZ*

I am a white female who has an autoimmune disease, celiac disease. This is classified as a physical or health disability/chronic illness under the Americans with Disabilities Act (ADA). The only treatment is a medically prescribed, gluten-free diet. If I consume gluten, I experience intestinal symptoms that have long-term effects on a host of my organs and bodily systems. Completely eliminating gluten from my diet is incredibly challenging because gluten is found in many common foods and there are issues of cross-contact. Cross-contact occurs when gluten-free food is exposed to a gluten-containing ingredient. This happens at buffets, in fryers, on pans, cutting boards, sponges, refrigerator doors, shelves, silverware, and when flour is in the air (i.e., flour can stay airborne for twelve to twenty-four hours).

It's hard to avoid gluten in food, too, because it can be found in surprising places like medications, sauces, dressings, soups, alcohol, and candy, for example. It's very easy to accidentally "gluten yourself" if you don't know what's in your food. This is particularly tricky in the United States because the United States doesn't have consistent food-labeling laws; sometimes food is labeled wheat-free, but gluten is also found in barley, rye, and oats. I am constantly learning about different ingredients that contain gluten, which gets complicated because any one of these could: starch, modified food starch, hydrolyzed vegetable or plant protein, textured vegetable protein, dextrin, maltodextrin, glucose syrup, caramel, malt flavoring, malt extract, malt vinegar, brown rice syrup. This is not a comprehensive list, but you can see why it's hard to buy food.

Restaurants and other people's kitchens are challenging to navigate. Many people—including professional chefs—don't know what ingredients are in their food, nor do they follow kitchen protocol that would eliminate cross-contact. This means when others make plans to dine out, I often have to decide whether to (a) advocate going to a different restaurant, (b) eat beforehand, (c) ask about kitchen protocol and hopefully order something plain, or (d) opt out of the experience altogether. This is very challenging in groups, at large events, in professional environments, and while traveling.

I depend on buying foods that I know are safe, so I don't have to face uncertainties with food or restaurants, but this comes at a cost . . . literally. The economic burden of celiac is a lot. Gluten-free products are significantly more expensive than comparable non-gluten-free products (e.g., on average, upward of 183 percent). I work full time with a decent salary, as does my partner, so we balance these costs together. We cannot afford to double buy our food, so everyone eats gluten free in our home.

Disabled people are at increased risk to experience difficult mealtimes due to the very nature of their disabilities; they are more apt to experience higher stress levels, malnutrition, and long-term significant health issues (Adams et al., 2012). "Both [malnutrition and disability] are major global public health problems, both are key human rights concerns, and both are currently prominent within the global health agenda" (Groce et al., 2014, abstract). Malnutrition can even cause or contribute to an individual's disability, at any developmental stage including in utero. Other times, the impairment is the cause of malnutrition. For example, oral motor difficulties for people with cleft palates or cerebral palsy can lead to decreased nutrient intake, poorer health, and sometimes even early death (Adams et al., 2012). Some disabled people need additional nutrients to address health problems associated with their disability while other impairments, like cystic fibrosis or celiac disease, mean that the individual must carefully manage specially adapted diets and run the risk of increased malnutrition which can create long-term health issues like muscle wasting, loss of function, and chronic pain (Groce et al., 2014). Sometimes having disabilities puts individuals at risk for autoimmune disorders, increased food intolerances, or allergies. People with Down syndrome, for example, are more likely to be dually diagnosed with celiac or Crohn's disease, and there is ongoing research linking autism with food intolerances.

> **VIGNETTE 5: *LIZ DISCUSSES THE CHRONIC ILLNESS PART OF CELIAC***
>
> *I am chronically ill. While it is likely my small intestine has healed since my diagnosis, I experience nausea, vomiting, diarrhea, constipation, and stomach discomfort and pain more than what is considered "normal." I get motion sickness, and I have been ill in public many times. And there are always new triggers to look for, e.g., GI issues during COVID-19. I take a LOT of vitamins and pack medication when I travel.*
>
> *Many people with celiac also face infertility, bone weakness, and nerve damage. All of these are irreversible. There is an increased risk for severe malabsorption of nutrients, other autoimmune diseases, and non-gastrointestinal health challenges (e.g., joint pain, osteopenia or osteoporosis, bone fractures, and rashes). I have some of these chronic health issues, and I get screened yearly for others, with an assurance from my doctors that it is "only a matter of time." There are emotional risks, too, like anxiety and depression. I am anxious, which affects all aspects of my life.*
>
> *Many (i.e., likely at least half) who have celiac disease remain undiagnosed due to a lack of access to medical care, a lack of referrals to specialists, and healthcare bias, among other factors. For example, as a white woman, it took me about ten years to get a proper diagnosis. But what about those who face gender and racial disparities in healthcare? Historically, celiac disease is associated and diagnosed in white people, but Singh and colleagues (2018) found that celiac is a global public health issue and underdiagnosed among other racial or ethnic groups; they cited a lack of association, and therefore screenings, for celiac in non-white patients, due to a medical affiliation or bias between celiac and white patients.*
>
> *It is important to have a comprehensive medical team, for example, a gastrointestinal (GI) specialist, a nutritionist, a dietician, a mental health provider, plus regular medical screenings, tests, and follow-up care. I have the privilege of a full-time job with a state insurance plan, but even that is not enough. Certain specialists are not covered by my insurance. I have to advocate for yearly screenings, and I need a referral from my primary care doctor to see specialists. I am a researcher by trade, which means I have the skills and resources to find current research and training, gluten-free exhibitions, and information about policy and activism around celiac and autoimmune diseases. I try to educate myself as much as possible and then approach my medical team to seek clarity and ask specific questions, rather than waiting for their guidance.*

Caregivers and service providers may not know how to feed disabled children or how to teach the child to feed themselves, and this is especially impactful on those who are physically vulnerable, who face heightened risks or unknown health issues that are life-threatening, for example, the impacts of COVID-19. This is especially important for people with cerebral palsy who may need special seating or positioning or for people with Down syndrome who are at increased risk of choking or developing pneumonia. A high-quality diet is needed for prompt healing and to control further health problems, but caregivers may struggle to meet these increased nutritional needs or lack access to necessary dietary supplements (Groce et al., 2014).

Poor nutrition impacts health and weight across genders. While there may be information about how these issues affect those who do not identify on the gender binary (i.e., male/female; for more information see chapter 2), we recognize that research is limited. Therefore, with reservation, we focus on health and weight as reported about the gender binary. Cisgender girls with disabilities are statistically more underweight—and more malnourished—than cisgender boys with disabilities (Tüzün, 2013), which is particularly problematic in disadvantaged communities with limited resources and food shortages. Poor nutrition can lead to suboptimal pelvic growth in girls which increases the risk that their future children will also have issues with pelvic growth. Statistically, more than half of girls with disabilities will have children of their own (WHO/UNFPA, 2009), so the impact is intergenerationally significant. Some people have disabilities that cause them to be less mobile (Olusanya, 2013), genetic impairments (e.g., Sotos syndrome), or intellectual or emotional impairments that place them at greater risk for eating disorders. All of these issues can have serious long-term and generational consequences for health and development.

Impact on Belonging

Disabled people are at increased risk to experience difficulty at mealtimes, which may impact their sense of belonging. They may not be able to participate in communal meals easily or at all.

VIGNETTE 6: *LIZ'S EXPERIENCES WITH ABLEISM*

The combination of my restrictive diet and challenges with cross-contact means that I navigate stressful food situations every time I leave my house. I am not able to make spontaneous food decisions, and I have faced insecurities around food before. I get anxious in social and professional situations. Many times, events or gatherings are centered around food. I also face ableist attitudes and comments regularly; people ask invasive questions about my intentions, my weight, or my health. People forget about, misunderstand, or dismiss my needs; they don't take them seriously; or they may not understand or listen to me when I explain celiac is a disease as opposed to an allergy, restriction, or preference. People assume they know more about celiac than I do; they cite misconceptions, offer me unsolicited advice, assume or minimize my intent or condition, or insist on what I can or should eat. People assume things about me, my health, or my choices when I get sick, and I get asked, told, or scolded to try food that

- *was made in a kitchen that has gluten or hasn't been vetted for protocol*
- *could have hidden gluten or hasn't been vetted for ingredients*
- *is labeled "gluten friendly," "wheat free," or is not labeled at all*
- *isn't bread, pasta, or cake*
- *has no visible gluten, for example, crumbs, or the visible gluten was removed, such as croutons*

Marriage

Marriage is one of the most globally recognized and respected rituals across countless cultures (Levine et al., 1995). In the United States, marriage is state-sanctioned and endorsed through various benefits. Institutions, organizations, as well society afford married people social privileges. In addition to love and security, social status makes marriage appealing to many. It is no wonder lesbian, gay, bisexual, transgender, queer or questioning, intersex, asexual, and more (LGBTQIA+) activists desired and rightfully pursued marriage equality. But for people with disabilities whose income, nutrition, and healthcare are federally subsidized, access to marriage threatens their safety net. The US Social Security Disability Insurance (SSDI) and Supplemental Security Income (SSI) programs provide various benefits and securities to people with disabilities, including healthcare. However, if a person with a disability receiving those benefits marries a person without a disability, their benefits will likely end (Social Security, n.d.). The rationale behind this policy is that the spouse without a disability would be able to provide employer-based health insurance to their spouse—never mind that it is highly unlikely that employer-provided private health insurance has the capacity to sustain the medical expenses of a chronically disabled person. Furthermore, it is forcing those dependent on these benefits from engaging in cultural rituals that bond people together.

The risk of losing public benefits is not limited to a marriage but rather is a part of a comprehensive economic barrier structure (Edin & Reed, 2005). For instance, when a disabled person is able to acquire a job with competitive pay, their federal healthcare benefits are threatened if their employer provides healthcare options. This means people with disabilities often have to choose between a fulfilling career and upward mobility and having their basic healthcare needs met. This is largely because the regular daily and perennial maintenance of a person's healthcare needs when they are disabled often exceeds the coverage of employer-provided health insurance (Social Security, n.d.). For information about how Disability Studies frames this, see chapter 6.

The marriage penalties described here is a form of structural oppression that people with disabilities endure. From a grassroots perspective, people with disabilities need direct actions from the general population as well as aggressive and humanizing interventions from political actors. All experience social pressures as they mature, however, disabled children often need additional support because adults in their schools regularly marginalize them in deficit-based ways (Egard et al., 2022). At the intersection of a marginalized racial, economic, disabled, and gendered identity, people experience unique challenges that impair their academic and social-emotional growth; see chapter 2 for examples. For more information about how to fight these intersectional oppressions, seek out organizations like the Arc, a disability advocacy organization fighting for the civil rights of people with disabilities. Their policy initiatives include educational equity, employment training, wage rights, and housing access (Arc Minnesota, 2022).

Religion

From access issues to belief systems, individuals with disabilities are impacted by the culture of their religion. As with most institutions in Western society, religious institutions are not designed with disability accessibility in mind. The physical structures of religious institutions may comply with the Americans with Disabilities Act (ADA, n.d.; see chapters 10 and 11 for more information about the ADA), but often the compliance and maintenance of those accommodations become the responsibility of people with disabilities (Egard et al., 2022). So, even when structural accommodations such as designated parking spots, ramps, and dropped curbs are in place, access to information shared such as large print, Braille, sign language, color contrast to improve visual documentation, or text-to-speech software is not afforded (Egard et al., 2022).

In addition to access issues, views of disability can be based on cultural religious or spiritual beliefs. Many religions regard disability as a curse, punishment, or disease inflicted upon a person or family due to immorality, which socializes many people into fearing and distancing themselves from those with disabilities (Schumm & Stoltzfus, 2011). For religions that take up charity as part of their work, people with disabilities are often pitied and considered tragedies or victims of misfortune (Schumm & Stoltzfus, 2011)—more on religion in chapters 5 and 6.

In Christianity and Judaism, disability is framed in doctrine as a curse or result of disobedience and promotes healing as the goal (Schumm & Stoltzfus, 2011). In Islam, disability is contextualized as God's will, which is neither positive nor negative. The different approaches to disability affect the socialization of persons without disabilities toward the disabled population and in many instances the degree of respect and humanization that is extended. Disabled people are often denied common social courtesies in religious spaces, which in turn facilitates and perpetuates social isolation. Even in instances where a person with a disability is treated with extreme kindness and charity, the spirit in which those gestures are carried out can be patronizing (Egard et al., 2022). See chapter 6 for more on the Charity Model of Disability. Therefore, the widely accepted benefits of participating in religious communities—such as higher purpose structure, faith, and a community of like-minded people with similar beliefs—are often undermined by mistreatment and social isolation.

Art

Traditionally **art** has been defined as forms of creative and cultural expression through music and theater, while entertainment has referred to more contemporary forms, including festivals and events. Through art, creative expression includes physical, sculptural and pictural art, street art, writing, visual art, music, movement, film, and more recently, television and multimedia. We suggest that the combination of these concepts are central elements of the culture of any society. Art is so influential that it has shaped "economic development and the expression and maintenance of local and regional identities" (Stevenson, 2006, p. 354), but despite that, it is not typically defined by the mass culture; most validated art is provided by the private sector. Even when art is offered to the public through government-supported galleries or theater companies, these are "under considerable pressure to succeed as 'industries' by either finding complementary sources of funding or tailoring their programmes to meet the (popular) preferences of audiences/markets rather than the creative priorities of artists and producers (Stevenson, 2000)" (Stevenson, 2006, p. 354).

When we consider imagery, disability is often limited to that which is visible or observable by simply looking at the person. People with observable disabilities like visual impairments, hearing impairments, muscular dystrophy, locomotor disabilities, cerebral palsy, or dwarfism, become the de facto representation of disability in the arts (Brueggemann, 2012). The media's overrepresentation of physical disabilities perpetuates the marginalization of invisible disabilities (Schatz & George, 2018), as hidden disabilities such as autoimmune diseases, chronic pain, neurological disorders, or mental health conditions tend to be dismissed and invalidated. While for some, having a nonapparent or invisible-to-the-eye disability might support their social inclusion if they are able to mask sufficiently for the communities they're engaging with, the masking comes at the expense of needs being met and often limits authentic relationship-building (Shakespeare, 2015). This is even before we consider multiple disabilities which can coexist in an individual. Furthermore, for some with nonapparent disabilities, the "hidden" nature of that disability may become apparent over time or given a particular circumstance. For instance, a person with Crohn's disease may be able to avoid certain situations for an extended period but their disability may be outed or triggered if they are unable to. The voluntary or involuntary revelation of their disability can be socially ostracizing.

VIGNETTE 7: *LIZ'S SOCIAL ISOLATION*

I often feel very vulnerable and burdensome to those around me. Sometimes I am isolated and left out of social situations. Sometimes I isolate myself because I don't feel safe or included. I am constantly assessing the risks of advocating for my needs, whether it's worth asking for accommodations, if I am able to bring my own food, or if it's better to not attend (my "social risks"). Oftentimes entire events are food based, for example, a celebratory luncheon, a retirement party at a restaurant, weddings, birthday parties, etc. I get anxious when I know food is involved and am apprehensive about the microaggressions that will surely take place.

The hidden nature of my disability usually becomes apparent over time or because of a particular event or circumstance, and the revelation is often socially ostracizing. People are confused; they get defensive when I can't eat food prepared in their kitchens; or they perceive I am being rude and rejecting them, their history, their family, or their culture when I need accommodations to participate in events, like at weddings. Food at weddings is an integral part of the celebration; it honors cultural traditions and promotes a sense of belonging among the invited guests. Usually I have to bring my own food and cake, and people have made faces at me, made rude comments, stared, or whispered and pointed.

Within all spheres of life be it the creation of arts, organizational leadership, knowledge production and dissemination, politics, medicine, or business, there is an underrepresentation of people with disabilities at the helm (Schatz & George, 2018). This is also evident in how we conceive art. There are different forms of art and none have taken on the work of humanizing and amplifying people with disabilities (Schatz & George, 2018). While there are outliers like Frida Kahlo who was both the creator and the subject of her art, by and large representations of people with disabilities in the various art forms are either deficit based or nonexistent (Brueggemann, 2012). For more information about how disability is portrayed in modern film and television, see chapters 6 and 12.

The importance of diversity becomes salient when we consider how much overlooking (whether intentional or unintentional) occurs when the perspectives of affected populations are not present when decisions are being made. Thus, people with disabilities and the communities that care for them often are positioned as responders to said decisions, which takes the form of activism.

VIGNETTE 8: *LIZ'S PLEA*

Usually, if people ask about my needs, it is in response to my condition and comes with the expectation of how I can fit my needs into what they have already planned. Instead of making assumptions or planning on my behalf (particularly dangerous when others are not aware of the nuances of celiac), I appreciate when people ask me up front about how they can support my needs in their planning, and then actually listen to what I have to say.

REFRAMING HISTORICAL SOCIAL CONSTRUCTION OF DISABILITY

In an inclusive society where we view inaccessibility as a burden rather than disabilities, it would be possible for some people with disabilities to work, parent, be happy, express their talents, be sexy, date and marry, be stylish, active, successful, be activists, intimate, involved, helpful to others, high achieving, high earning, and most importantly self-determined. Being part of a vulnerable population should not determine the quality of life of anyone.

Unfortunately, even "allies" can perpetuate the infantilization of people with disabilities when they regard everyday acts as extraordinary or inspirational (Schatz & George, 2018). For instance, when a person with a disability has a fulfilling career, is in a loving and healthy partnership, when they are academically achieving, or even have a positive attitude—it can be undermining and dehumanizing to frame them as heroic or brave, or exceptional. People are more than their disability, gender, race, or any other social location and they often do not appreciate having a singular category be the lens through which their accomplishments and worth are filtered. People with disabilities do not exist as motivation for people without a disability. More information on social perception of disabled people is covered throughout this text.

Reframing the social construction of people who are disabled allows for a humanization that is asset-based (Egard et al., 2022). Even as we consider language and communication, and the ways they are leveraged toward the construction of a disabled social identity—we see that disability is framed in the deficit. This concept is explored through much of this text. The word disability is the combination of the word ability and the prefix dis. Dis- means apart from, not, or non (Lederer et al., 2014). Looking at a few examples of other words that use the prefix dis-: we can look at disown which is to not own, distill which is to extract, disarm means to be unarmed, disagree means to not agree, disorder is a lack of order, or disallow which is the opposite of allowing. The prefix dis has a negative association. For more on how the disability community is reclaiming this label, see chapters 3 and 6. It is incumbent on those with the privilege of being nondisabled to consider what policies, practices, and cultural norms we could adopt and adapt to be more inclusive of people who are disabled. In a culture that normalizes conformity, people with visible disabilities are at a grave social disadvantage (Egard et al., 2022). Not only are their intellectual abilities undermined but their bodies are infantilized. When a person belongs to a social group that is institutionally and socially minoritized, the temptation to mask their differences is understandable. However, doing so limits their capacity to have their basic needs met and certainly hinders prospects for them to be accepted and to belong as they are.

Human beings are in perpetual pursuit of community, therefore when an individual has a stigmatized social identity, such as a disability, there are a few approaches they can take to establish and sustain community (Dirth & Branscombe, 2018). If the disability is visible, it may be impossible to camouflage as a person without a disability. Still, some with visible disabilities might disassociate from others with visible disabilities to minimize the impact and mediation of their impairment. This individualistic strategy is exhausting and often yields the unintended and undesired consequence of enhanced isolation. Alternatively, a person with a disability might intentionally join or create community with others who are also disabled. In so doing, that individual might discover it easier to find commonalities and similarities between them and their community members which fortifies communities. This is how disabled communities and cultures have formed.

Capitalism affects belonging in that it disempowers those without capital through exploitation and exclusion. The exploitation is far-reaching—extending from the aesthetic and the intellectual to assessments of labor aptitude and appraisals of criminality. Similarly, exclusions span the social realm to one's quality of life and well-being. Thus, opportunities for commonly pursued quality-of-life milestones such as marriage, higher education, or employment or promotion are compromised and that hinders overall inclusion into mainstream society. In a capitalist society, disabled people are in a constant struggle to earn or sustain the support they need to exist. Capitalism seeks to force independence on each individual regardless of their legitimate dependence on a system which is self-serving (Russell, 2019). For more information on how these economic perspectives frame or define disability, see chapter 6.

A MODERN VIEW OF CULTURE

Our definition of culture and belonging today is rooted in elements of social psychology combined with our Westernized, evolving view of cultural identity, expression, and belonging. Social psychologist Henri Tajfel (1978) studied the connections between **cognitive grouping**, which is another way to describe when people exaggerate the differences and similarities between groups of people (Islam, 2014), and **gestalt phenomena**, where the whole is greater than the parts (Hogg & Williams, 2000). Tajfel found that groups of people identify themselves into social groups of "us" versus "them" by connecting with others who have similar beliefs, behaviors, and lived experiences. Tajfel used **Social Identity Theory** (SIT) to explain why we feel connected to others based on a combination of (a) emotional connections, (b) feelings of social protection, and (c) increased self-identity (Tajfel, 1978; Tajfel & Turner, 1979). This sense of belonging reinforces individuals' preferences for their own social groups, but it also results in increased exaggerations of how each group is different from others (Islam, 2014), which reinforces inequities between them (Kumashiro, 2000). See chapter 2 for examples of the intersectional nature of sociocultural identities.

Social Identity Theory

To understand how social identity theory fits with cultural belonging today, we need to break down individual **sociocultural constructs** (e.g., **social identities** or **social constructs**). One's sociocultural identity indicates who they are within the groups they belong to and is often characterized by linguistic or behavioral attributes. Examples of sociocultural identities include but are not limited to: disability, race, ethnicity, religion, socioeconomic status, language, gender, and sexual identity (Kumashiro, 2000); people ascribe across different social identities, some more prevalent than others. Those who ascribe more strongly to specific social identities often connect with others based on shared values, rituals, and lived experiences that center those identities. For example, someone whose Christian identity is important to them is likely to connect with other individuals who strongly identify as Christian through Christian rituals and cultural expressions.

Pause and Reflect

- What are your sociocultural identities?
- Which of your sociocultural identities do you think of most often?
- Which of your sociocultural identities do you not think about?
- What kinds of assumptions do you make about others based upon their sociocultural identities?

Implications of Social Capital

Sociocultural identities have **social capital**, due to their influence on social structures and impact. There are dominant and nondominant sociocultural identities; those who ascribe to dominant sociocultural identities often also ascribe to the dominant culture, which in turn controls much of the social power. Those who are oppressed, minoritized, excluded, or isolated from mass culture tend to belong to nondominant sociocultural groups. For example, nondisabled people are typically portrayed by the media as the "norm" and therefore considered part of the dominant social group. Disabled individuals then are part of the nondominant group and are more likely to experience oppression, exclusion, or isolation.

Mass or dominant culture (Causadias & Umana-Taylor, 2018) impacts how most people think, interact, and feel, and define the "norms" of society. For example, dominant culture creates norms that are based on communal identities that are created within group membership (Islam, 2014). When certain sociocultural identities have the majority of the social power, it ultimately affects everyone's access to mainstream societal benefits, such as equal wealth, education, or legal protections.

Social capital is complex because its value shifts depending on the context (Hoyle et al., 2022). For instance, speaking African American Vernacular English (e.g., Ebonics outside of the academy) may not be considered valuable in academic spaces, but that same skill set affords the speaker access and perhaps acceptance into nuanced cultural spaces with other speakers of Ebonics. Social capital comes in the form of network, identity, material skills, and competencies, and then a limitless set of other variables that can work to enhance a person's quality of life and self-determination (Hoyle et al., 2022). In patriarchy, being a cisgender male increases one's social capital just as being cisgender female or female-identifying decreases one's social capital. But contextualizing social capital is not as simple as the input of identity with the output of an advantage or a disadvantage. Human beings are complex and never reduced to an individual identity; therefore, our intersectional identities create unique algorithms to quantify the net worth of our social capital—and that value, much like currency, fluctuates depending on its context (Hoyle et al., 2022).

Intersectionality Theory

Imagine the social impact of belonging to more than one nondominant group. Kimberlé Crenshaw coined the term **intersectionality** in 1989 as a way to understand how multiple social identities overlap to increase oppression, discrimination, prejudice, bias, or stereotyping in the legal system for Black, cisgender women. Crenshaw's work around intersectionality is explored through much of this volume. The combination of disability status with other nondominant sociocultural identities creates a multilayered system of oppression. People with disabilities cross the lines of race, ethnicity, gender, age, religion, sexual orientation, gender identity, gender expression, and socioeconomic status (although this is not a comprehensive list) and make up the largest "minority" group in the United States (Office of Disability Employment Policy, 2022). For example, when an individual identifies as Latine and disabled, they are more likely to experience racism and ableism at the same time. These kinds of examples are found across many kinds of social constructs (see chapter 2); this volume will offer insight on many intersecting, disabled experiences, but by no means do we suggest that we speak toward all intersectional oppressions.

> **Pause and Reflect**
>
> - How do you experience intersecting sociocultural identities?
> - What are ways you ascribe to dominant sociocultural identities?
> - What are ways you ascribe to nondominant identities?

Multidimensionality of Disability

If culture is broadly acknowledged as (a) shared history; (b) expression of identity and meaning; and (c) pride (Boyle et al., 2016), the very concept of disability as a culture is validated and reinforced because the experience of having a disability impacts one's feelings, actions, and experiences, and therefore can be contextualized across various environments, expectations, norms, and experiences.

Just like other sociocultural identities (e.g., race, sexuality, gender), disability is multidimensional:

- Disability is not a monolith.
- Even when disabled people share labels or diagnoses, they may vary in how they relate to, identify with, and treat or address their disability.
- Individuals with disabilities may not culturally connect with their disabled identities, and therefore may not identify with or belong to disability communities.
- Disabled individuals' additional sociocultural identities may better provide a sense of belonging (e.g., a Black disabled person may better connect with other [nondisabled] Black people rather than disabled people of a different race).

This multidimensionality influences (a) how individuals with disabilities perceive themselves; (b) how society perceives them; (c) how perceptions interact to create, reinforce, or violate societal rules and one's sense of belonging; and (d) how individuals function in certain environments (Fuller et al., 2021; Pearson et al., 2018). Sometimes whether someone is considered disabled is dependent upon how other social groups engage with, support, and categorize them. For example, when someone has a specific dietary need due to their disability, others may feel like they are rejecting them, their history, their family, or their culture. They may not accommodate for this individual, or perhaps they judge, isolate, or forget about the individual and their needs. In this case, having a disability violates the cultural experiences of sharing food, ultimately impacting the person's sense of belonging.

CULTURAL EXPRESSIONS IN SCHOOLS

Schools are a microcosm of the larger society and therefore, in theory, should fully reflect the culture and cultural expressions of larger communities. In the United States, schools traditionally celebrate observable cultural expressions through food, fashion, festivals, folklore, famous people, and flags (Shunnarah, 2008). Do these Fs mean schools are preparing students to fully develop an understanding of and respect for the nuances and intersections among various cultures? For example, does eating a burrito create a deeper understanding of Mexican culture? When one considers "flags" as a form of cultural expression, do they consider the disability pride flag? The LGBTQIA+ flag?

Pause and Reflect

- How can practitioners consider sociocultural identities in cultural expressions?
- How can practitioners embrace disability as a sociocultural identity into their classrooms and schools?

One term that is currently used in schools is culturally and linguistically sustaining practices (CLSPs; see chapters 2, 4, 7, 8, and 12), but what about intersectional practices that are inclusive of all sociocultural identities? Consider when food is used as a reward for students with disabilities. This kind of reward system can have consequences on students' health, their relationship with food, and it could even emphasize that [disabled] students need to "earn" the right to eat. Other times, cultural values with food are ignored, for example, when students who need assistance with fine motor skills use chopsticks at home. Are they taught to use or supported in using chopsticks at school?

There is a correlation and arguably causation between those who succeed in schools and those who succeed professionally (Stolp & Smith, 1995). Academic achievement is linked to economic success which supports ideal quality-of-life outcomes (Stolp & Smith, 1995). However, schools are not designed for the success of people with disabilities, and the evidence of that is apparent both in schools and in the workforce. Simply put, disabilities impact nearly every aspect of one's quality of life including participation in school (Kaplan et al., 2022). Children with disabilities rarely experience affirming representation in school curriculums if they are represented at all. Moreover, adults with authority rarely reflect the diversity of existing disabilities. The lack of demographic representation in leadership, authority, knowledge production and dissemination, skills, and/or talents perpetuates the stereotype of people with disabilities as underachieving (Kaplan et al., 2022).

Schools as an Equalizer

The culture of schools places a premium on certain identities and will often accommodate and increase opportunities for members of those demographic groups to have their needs met. In the United States, compulsory schooling was designed simply for white males (Harris & Buckey, 2018). Nearly two hundred years later, white males continue to be the standard by which schooling is conceived and affected (Harris & Buckey, 2018). Then it is no wonder why people with differences find schools to be socially, structurally, curricularly inaccessible, and ostracizing.

If schools were to live up to the ideal of functioning as an equalizer, then equity-based interventions would increase belonging. Schools can exist as places that remove barriers, increase access, and innovate opportunities for inclusion or they can sustain and maintain barriers of exclusion (Wiggan, 2011). Arguably, the effort needed to be inclusive of people with disabilities is no greater than the effort needed to be inclusive of those with other demographic differences such as English learners, girls, Black, queer, under-resourced children, or highly mobile children, those performing below grade level standards, and those performing above grade level standards, those who are Asian, Pacific Islander, or Indigenous. This is why we are suggesting intersectional sociocultural considerations are at the center of your work.

SUMMARY

Inaccessibility for those with disabilities can substantially limit a person's capacity to perform life activities such as hearing, breathing, working, walking, maintaining relationships, having a continuous and sustained positive sense of self, engaging in social interactions, and countless other tasks and life activities that nondisabled people take up (Hoyle et al., 2022). However, so too can major life events and other non-health-related circumstances hinder a person from performing or participating in the previously stated tasks and activities. For instance, a person in mourning, dealing with recent transitions, experiencing a language barrier, or simply being consumed by interest or commitment may be limited in their capacity to perform life activities. The culture of the Western world is such that the onus for overcoming the barriers to such activities is on the individual, even when society sets up specific barriers for those with disabilities (Egard et al., 2022). Disability activist Gregory Mansfield, argues that accessibility is not charity, generosity, amenity, or gratuity but rather it is something we as individuals in a collective society should ensure (Mansfield, 2019). However, culturally and historically, people with disabilities have not been adequately accommodated. In a society that prioritizes productivity through the exploitation of bodies and minds, it is not surprising that disabled people would be undervalued and excluded. Western society has adopted a dogmatic social construction of disability (Russell, 2019). Rather than acknowledging that people with disabilities have different needs, for example, religious beliefs that regard disability as a form of punishment from a higher power exert societal impact. Therefore, being disabled is stigmatized, leading to oppression in and exclusion from community spaces (Schumm & Stoltzfus, 2011).

The varied nuances of culture are complex and continually changing which means that establishing intersectional, multicultural learning communities in schools should also change and evolve. Additionally, the variables mediating one's schooling experience can range from dietary limitations that hinder one's participation in food-based events, to classrooms or entire learning facilities that are not universally designed for independent mobility, learning, or access. Over time as our language around disabilities and culture has shifted, those advances have outpaced the policies, practices, and socializations needed for the inclusion of people with disabilities in a way that is empowering and leads to self-determination. Across institutions, be it faith-based, education, government, or entertainment, communities with disabilities continue to be regarded as unable.

REFERENCES

Adams, M. S., Khan, N. Z., Begum, S. A., Wirz, S. L., Hesketh, T., & Pring, T. R. (2012). Feeding difficulties in children with cerebral palsy: Low-cost caregiver training in Dhaka, Bangladesh. *Child Care Health Development, 38*(6), 878–88.

Adloff, S., & Hogan, T. (2018). Understanding dyslexia in the context of developmental language disorders. *Language, Speech, and Hearing Services in Schools, 49*(4), 762-77.

Americans with Disabilities Act. ADA.gov. (n.d.). Retrieved January 1, 2023, from https://www.ada.gov/

Arc Minnesota. (2022). https://arcminnesota.org/

Atabek, S., & Nurnazar, P. (2021). The phenomenon of mass culture. *Zien Journal of Social Sciences and Humanities, 1*(1), 49-52.

Begen, F. M., & Turner-Cobb, J. M. (2015). Benefits of belonging: Experimental manipulation of social inclusion to enhance psychological and physiological health parameters. *Psychology & Health, 30*(5), 568-82. https://doi.org/10.1080/08870446.2014.991734

Bennett, T. (1998) *Culture: A reformer's science.* Allen & Unwin.

Bleile, K, (2015). *Speech sound disorders.* Plural.

Boyle, M. P., Daniels, D. E., Hughes, C. D., & Buhr, A. P. (2016, March). Considering disability culture for culturally competent interactions with individuals who stutter. *Contemporary Issues in Communication Science and Disorders, 43,* 11-22. https://doi.org/10.1044/cicsd_43_s_11

Brueggemann, B. J. (2012). *Arts and humanities.* Sage.

Campos, B., & Kim, H. S. (2017). Incorporating the cultural diversity of family and close relationships into the study of health. *American Psychologist, 72*(6), 543-54. https://doi.org/10.1037/amp0000122

Causadias, J. M., & Umaña-Taylor, A. J. (2018). Reframing marginalization and youth development: Introduction to the special issue. *American Psychologist, 73*(6), 707.

Crenshaw, K. (1989). Demarginalizing the intersection of race and sex: A Black feminist critique of antidiscrimination doctrine, feminist theory, and antiracist politics. *University of Chicago Legal Forum, 1989*(1), 139-67. https://chicagounbound.uchicago.edu/uclf/vol1989/iss1/8/

Cummings, L. (2021). *Handbook of pragmatic language disorders.* Springer Nature Australia. https://doi.org/10.1007/978-3-030-74985-9

DeWall, C., MacDonald, G., Webster, G. D., Masten, C. L., Baumeister, R. F., Powell, C., . . . Eisenberger, N. I. (2010). Acetaminophen reduces social pain: Behavioral and neural evidence. *Psychological Science, 21*(7), 931-37. https://doi.org/10.1177/0956797610374741

Dirth, T. P., & Branscombe, N. R. (2018). The social identity approach to disability: Bridging disability studies and psychological science. *Psychological Bulletin, 144*(12), 1300.

Dore, J. (1977). Children's illocutionary acts. In R. Freedle (Ed.), *Discourse production and comprehension* (vol. 1, pp. 227-44). Ablex.

Duffy, J. R. (2020). *Motor speech disorders.* Mosby.

Eastman, C. M. (1984). An ethnography of Swahili expressive culture. *Research in African Literatures, 15*(3), 313-40.

Eaude, T. (2020). *Identity, culture and belonging: Educating young children for a changing world.* Bloomsbury.

Edin, K., & Reed, J. M. (2005, Fall). Why don't they just get married? Barriers to marriage among the disadvantaged. *Future Child, 15*(2), 117-37.

Egard, H., Hansson, K., & Wästerfors, D. (2022). *Accessibility denied: Understanding inaccessibility and everyday resistance to inclusion for persons with disabilities.* Taylor & Francis.

Ember, C. R. (2016). Commentary: Considering language as expressive culture. *Journal of Language Evolution, 1*(1), 60-61.

Feeney, B. C., & Collins, N. L. (2015). A new look at social support: A theoretical perspective on thriving through relationships. *Personality and Social Psychology Review, 19*(2), 113–47. https://doi.org/10.1177/1088868314544222

Fuller, M. C, Harkins Monaco, E. A., Stansberry Brusnahan, L. L., & Lindo, E. J. (2021). In E. A. Harkins Monaco, M. C. Fuller, & L. L. Stansberry Brusnahan (Eds.), *Diversity, autism, and developmental disabilities: Guidance for the culturally sustaining educator* (pp. 1–22). Council for Exceptional Children.

Furkatovna, N. M. (2022). Verbal and nonverbal behavior communication in sociolinguistics. *Eurasian Journal of Academic Research, 2*(4), 74–77. https://doi.org/10.5281/zenodo.6468680

Gable, S. L., & Reis, H. T. (2010). Good news! Capitalizing on positive events in an interpersonal context. In M. P. Zanna (Ed.), *Advances in experimental social psychology* (vol. 42, pp. 195–257). Academic. https://doi.org/10.1016/S0065-2601(10)42004-3

Gannotti, M. E., Kaplan, L. C., Handwerker, W. P., & Groce, N. E. (2004). Cultural influences on health care use: Differences in perceived unmet needs and expectations of providers by Latino and Euro-American parents of children with special health care needs. *Journal of Developmental Behavioral Pediatrics, 25*(3), 156–65.

Gilman, S. L. (2008). *Diets and dieting: A cultural encyclopedia*. Routledge.

Groce, N., Challenger, E., Berman-Bieler, R., Farkas, A., Yilmaz, N., Schultink, W., . . . Kerac, M. (2014). Malnutrition and disability: Unexplored opportunities for collaboration. *Pediatric and International Child Health, 34*(4), 308–314. https://doi:10.1179/2046905514Y.0000000156

Groher, M., & Crary, M. (2020). *Dysphagia: Clinical management in children and adults*. Mosby.

Harper, R., Wiens, A., & Matarazzo, J. (Eds.). (1978). *Nonverbal communication: The state of the art*. John Wiley & Co.

Harris, D., & Buckey, A. W. (2018). *Class and education*. Essential Library.

Hawkins, G. (1993). *From Nimbin to Mardi Gras: Constructing community arts*. Allen & Unwin.

Hillebrant, H., Sebastian, C., & Blakemore, S. J. (2011). Experimentally induced social inclusion influences behavior on trust games. *Cognitive Neuroscience, 2*(1), 27–33. https://doi.org/10.1080/17588928.2010.515020

Hofstede, G., Hofstede, G. J., & Minkov, M. (1997). *Cultures and organizations*. McGraw-Hill.

Hogg, M. A., & Williams, K. D. (2000). From *I* to *we*: Social identity and the collective self. *Group Dynamics Theory Research and Practice, 4*(1), 81–97. https://doi.org/10.1037/1089-2699.4.1.81

Hoyle, J. N., Laditka, J. N., & Laditka, S. B. (2022). "Eventually I'm gonna need people": Social capital among college students with developmental disability. *Research in Developmental Disabilities, 127*, 104270.

Humphrey, T. C., & Humphrey, L. T. (1988). *We gather together: Food and festival in American life*. UMI Research Press.

Hussar, B., Zhang, J., Hein, S., Wang, K., Roberts, A., Cui, J., . . . Dilig, R. (2020). The condition of education 2020 (NCES 2020-144). US Department of Education. Washington, DC: National Center for Education Statistics. https://nces.ed.gov/pubsearch/pubsinfo.asp?pubid=2020144

Hymes, D. H. (1972). On communicative competence. In J. Pride & J. Holmes (Eds.), *Sociolinguistics* (pp. 269–85). Penguin.

Islam, G. (2014). Social identity theory. *Journal of Personality and Social Psychology, 67,* 741-63.

Kaplan, A. G., Tobin, C., Dolcetti, T., & McGowan, J. (2022). Representation matters: Board books with children with disabilities. *Children and Libraries, 20*(3), 15-23.

Kumashiro, K. (2000). Toward a theory of anti-oppressive education. *Review of Educational Research, 70*(1), 25-53.

Lakey, B., & Orehek, E. (2011). Relational regulation theory: A new approach to explain the link between perceived social support and mental health. *Psychological Review, 118,* 482-95. https://doi.org/10.1037/a0023477

Leary, M. R. (2010). Affiliation, acceptance, and belonging: The pursuit of interpersonal connection. In S. T. Fiske, D. T. Gilbert, & G. Lindsey (Eds.), *Handbook of social psychology* (pp. 864-97). Wiley. https://doi.org/10.1002/9780470561119.socpsy002024

Lederer, V., Loisel, P., Rivard, M., & Champagne, F. (2014). Exploring the diversity of conceptualizations of work (dis)ability: A scoping review of published definitions. *Journal of Occupational Rehabilitation, 24*(2), 242-67.

Levine, R., Sato, S., Hashimoto, T., & Verma, J. (1995). Love and marriage in eleven cultures. *Journal of Cross Cultural Psychology, 26*(5), 554-71.

Light, J., & McNaughton, D. (2014). Communicative competence for individuals who require Augmentative and Alternative Communication: A new definition for a new era of communication? *Augmentative and Alternative Communication, 30*(1), 1-18.

Lumos. (2013). *Lumos' pioneering training projects.* http://wearelumos.org/stories/lumos-pioneering-training-programmes

Mansfield, Gregory. [@GHMansfield]. (2019, March 10). *Accessibility is not charity. Accessibility is not generosity. Accessibility is not an amenity. Accessibility is not a gratuity. You don't bestow access. You ensure it.* [Tweet]. Twitter. https://twitter.com/ghmansfield/status/1104920369893425153

Mojaverian, T., & Kim, H. S. (2013). Interpreting a helping hand: Cultural variation in the effectiveness of solicited and unsolicited social support. *Personality and Social Psychology Bulletin, 39*(1), 88-99. https://doi.org/10.1177/0146167212465319

National Center for Education Statistics (NCES). (1995). *Extracurricular participation and student engagement.* US Department of Education. https://nces.ed.gov/pubs95/web/95741.asp

National Institute on Deafness and Other Communication Disorders (NIDCD). (2016). *Stuttering: What is stuttering?* National Institutes of Health (NIH). US Department of Health and Human Services. https://www.nidcd.nih.gov/health/stuttering

Nogay, N. H. (2013). Nutritional status in mentally disabled children and adolescents: A study from Western Turkey. *Pakistan Journal of Medical Science, 29*(2), 614-18.

Office of Disability Employment Policy. (2022). *Disability employment statistics.* US Department of Labor. https://www.dol.gov/agencies/odep/research-evaluation/statistics

Okoro, C. A., Hollis, N. D., Cyrus, A. C., & Griffin-Blake, S. (2018). Prevalence of disabilities and health care access by disability status and type among adults—United States, 2016. *Morbidity and Mortality Weekly Report, 67*(32), 882-87. https://doi.org/10.15585/mmwr.mm6732a3

Olusanya, B. O. (2010). Is undernutrition a risk factor for sensorineural hearing loss in early infancy? *British Journal of Nutrition, 103,* 1296-1301.

Pearson, J. N., Hamilton, M-B., & Meadan, H. (2018). "We saw our son blossom": A guide for fostering culturally responsive partnerships to support African American autistic children and their families. *Perspectives of the ASHA Special Interest Groups, 3*(1), 84-97.

Pressman, S. D., Matthews, K. A., Cohen, S., Martire, L. M., Scheier, M., Baum, A., & Schulz, R. (2009). Association of enjoyable leisure activities with psychological and physical well-being. *Psychosomatic Medicine, 71*(7), 725-32. https://doi.org/10.1097/PSY.0b013e3181ad7978

Rokach, A. (2020). Belonging, togetherness and food rituals. *Open Journal of Depression, 9*, 77-85. https://doi.org/10.4236/ojd.2020.94007

Rook, D. W. (1985). The ritual dimension of consumer behavior. *Journal of Consumer Research, 12*, 251-64. https://doi.org/10.1086/208514

Rook, K. S., & Charles, S. T. (2017). Close social ties and health in later life: Strengths and vulnerabilities. *American Psychologist, 72*, 567-77. https://doi.org/10.1037/amp0000104

Russell, M. (2019). *Capitalism and disability: Selected writings by Marta Russell*. Haymarket.

Sapienza, C., & Hoffman, B. (2021). *Voice disorders*. Plural.

Schatz, J. L., & George, A. E. (Eds.). (2018). *The image of disability: Essays on media representations*. McFarland.

Schumm, D., & Stoltzfus, M. J. (2011). *Disability in Judaism, Christianity, and Islam: Sacred texts, historical traditions, and social analysis*. Springer.

Schwartz Offek, E., & Segal, O. (2022). Comparing Theory of Mind development in children with Autism Spectrum Disorder, Developmental Language Disorder, and typical development. *Neuropsychiatric Disease and Treatment, 14*(18), 2349-59.

Shakespeare, T. (2015). *Disability research today*. Routledge.

Shunnarah, C. (2008). The cross-cultural classroom. *New York Times*. https://lessonplans.blogs.nytimes.com/2008/09/25/the-cross-cultural-classroom/

Singh, P., Arora, A., Strand, T. A., Leffler, D. A., Catassi, C., Green, P. H., . . . Makharia, G. K. (2018). Global prevalence of celiac disease: Systematic review and meta-analysis. *Clinical Gastroenterology and Hepatology: The Official Clinical Practice Journal of the American Gastroenterological Association, 16*(6), 823-36. https://doi.org/10.1016/j.cgh.2017.06.037

Social Security. Benefits for people with disabilities. (n.d.). Retrieved January 1, 2023, from https://www.ssa.gov/disability/

Stevenson, D. (2000). *Art and organisation: Making Australian cultural policy*. University of Queensland Press.

———. (2006). The arts and entertainment: Situating leisure in the creative economy. In C. Rojek, S. M. Shaw, & A. J. Veal (Eds.), *A handbook of leisure studies*. Palgrave Macmillan. https://doi.org/10.1057/9780230625181_21

Stolp, S., & Smith, S. C. (1995). *Transforming school culture: Stories, symbols, values & the leader's role*. ERIC Clearinghouse.

Tajfel, H. (1978). The achievement of inter-group differentiation. In H. Tajfel (Ed.), *Differentiation between social groups* (pp. 77-100). Academic.

Tajfel, H., & Turner, J. C. (1979). An integrative theory of intergroup conflict. In W. G. Austin & S. Worchel (Eds.), *The social psychology of inter-group relations* (pp. 33-47). Brooks/Cole.

Tüzün, E. H., Güven, D. K., Eker, L., Elbasan, B., & Bülbül, S. F. (2013). Nutritional status of children with cerebral palsy in Turkey. *Disability Rehabilitation, 35*(5), 413-17.

Visser, M. (1991). *The rituals of dinner*. Grove Weidenfeld.

———. (2015). *The rituals of dinner: The origins, evolution, eccentricities, and meaning of table manners* (Kindle edition). Open Road Media.
Ward, D. (2017). *Stuttering and cluttering*. Psychology.
Weil, A. (1997). *8 weeks to optimum health: A proven program for taking full advantage of your body's natural healing power*. Knopf.
Werner, D. (2009). *Disabled village children*. Hesperian Foundation.
Wiggan, G. A. (2011). *Education for the new frontier: Race, education and triumph in Jim Crow America (1867–1945)*. Nova Science.
Williams, R. (1989). *Keywords: A vocabulary of culture and society*. Fontana.
World Health Organization/United Nations Population Fund (WHO/UNFPA). (2009). Promoting sexual and reproductive health for persons with disabilities. WHO/UNFPA guidance note. https://www.unfpa.org/sites/default/files/pub-pdf/srh_for_disabilities.pdf
Worral, L., & Frattali, C. (Eds). (2000). *Neurogenic communication disorders*. Thieme.
Yang, N., Shi, J., Lu, J., & Huang, Y. (2021). Language development in early childhood: Quality of teacher-child interaction and children's receptive vocabulary competency. *Frontiers in Psychology, 12*. https://doi.org/10.3389/fpsyg.2021.649680
Yusof, N. A., & Abdulgalil, M. (2017). Teachers' attitudes towards the use of extra-curricular activities in enhancing students' speaking skills. *International Journal of Academic Research in Progressive Education and Development, 6*(3), 117–28. https://doi.org/10.6007/IJARPED/v6-i3/3168

CHAPTER 2

Intersectionality in the Context of Disability

Chapter authors: *Sara Wildman, L. Lynn Stansberry Brusnahan, Sharde Theodore, and Meaghan McCollow*

Vignette authors: *James Williams, Erin Fitzgerald Farrell, Sara Wildman, and Sharde Theodore*

Editors: *Elizabeth A. Harkins Monaco and Marcus C. Fuller*

ABSTRACT

A singular identity is frequently the sole focus within special education and its systems, leaving the whole identity of the individuals receiving services and support as a flat, one-dimensional feature. Individuals, however, are multidimensional, with complex sociocultural identities and experiences. This chapter highlights the intersectional sociocultural identities of individuals within the context of special education support and services. The authors explore and provide examples of intersecting sociocultural identities and discuss factors, considerations, and impacts on access to education and services, including bias and disproportionality within special education. They connect critical theories and typical practices within integrated multi-tiered systems of support, specifically focused on special education. Finally, the chapter provides suggestions for ways practitioners and administrators can disrupt and enact changes in special education and its systems to enhance the educational experiences of its students specifically within an equity-based framework.

GUIDING QUESTIONS

- What are some of the factors, considerations, and impacts on access and services related to intersecting sociocultural identities and special education?
- How are students with disabilities impacted by intersecting sociocultural identities (e.g., race, socioeconomic, gender, sexuality)?
- What is the connection between intersectionality and evidence-based practices within integrated multi-tiered systems of support (e.g., RTI and PBIS), specifically focused on special education?
- What are some ways educators might interrupt and enact changes in systems to enhance the quality of education for students specifically within an equity-based framework?

KEY TERMS

Bias
Cisgender
Culturally and Linguistically Sustaining Practices
Disability
Disproportionality
Dysphoria
Gender
Gender Expression
Gender Identity
Gender Variance
Implicit Bias
Integrated Multi-Tiered System of Support
Intercultural Competence
Intersectionality
Intersex
Marginalization
Nonbinary
Positive Behavioral Interventions and Support
Response to Intervention
Sexuality
Sexual Identity
Sociocultural
Socioculturally Sustaining Practices
Socioeconomic Status

Often the special education system only focuses on how a student qualifies for special education based on disability categories as defined by the Individuals with Disabilities Education Act (IDEA) (see chapter 11), however, that takes away from looking at the whole identity of the student receiving support. Education practitioners need to respond to multiple intersecting sociocultural, economic, and political markers of identities and think "intersectionally" because preK–12 students are multidimensional, with complex sociocultural identities and experiences (Boveda, 2016; Boveda & Aronson, 2019; Grant & Zwier, 2011). This multidimensionality complexity includes students identifying across more than one sociocultural identity.

In the United States, students are forced to navigate educational spaces that are established by dominant groups (e.g., white, male, heterosexual, nondisabled) whose societal norms, values, and preferences are asserted as the standard for all (Graff & Vazquez, 2013; Wakelin, 2008). This mindset leads to biased perceptions of sociocultural identities that fall outside of the established norms (O'Connor & Fernandez, 2006; Perouse-Harvey, 2022). For example, students who may learn differently than what historically has been the norm can be referred and identified for special education services with significant evidence of differences in social etiology related to racialized placement in special education (e.g., Cruz & Firestone, 2022; Shifrer 2018; Shifrer & Fish, 2020). This is often attributed to **bias**, which can be conscious or unconscious, or a tendency to prefer one identity over another and prevents objective perceptions (Gatewood et al., 2019).

This chapter illustrates how students with traditionally minoritized sociocultural identities are disproportionately referred for special education services and are often placed in more restrictive settings and suspended at higher rates than their white peers (National Center for Learning Disabilities [NCLD], 2020). Identification problems exist beyond the typical preK–12 educational system as students labeled with disabilities can be significantly impacted in areas such as their socioeconomic status throughout their lives (Maroto et al., 2019). For instance, research shows that 28 percent of disabled Americans live at or below the poverty line, which is one of the highest rates of poverty for a single sociocultural identity in the United States (Erickson et al., 2013).

In this chapter, we expound upon Social Identity Theory and how sociocultural identities intersect and lead to disproportionality in special education. We highlight intersecting sociocultural identities of individuals within the context of special education supports and services by showcasing stories from the field—from educational practitioners, an adult with a disability, and a parent—as they relate to the intersecting sociocultural identities including disability. This chapter goes in depth into four multidimensional identities of disabled individuals; however, we recognize there are many more identities and intersections that impact students. We discuss factors, considerations, and impacts on access to education and services related to intersecting sociocultural identities, including bias and disproportionality, that appear within special education, and we offer guidance to practitioners to reflect on ways they can start to address their biases. Finally, we provide suggestions for ways practitioners and administrators can disrupt and enact changes in special education and its systems to enhance the educational experiences of students specifically within an equity-based integrated multi-tiered systems of support (MTSS) framework.

THE IMPACT OF INTERSECTIONAL SOCIOCULTURAL IDENTITIES

Since the 1970s, Social Identity Theory (SIT) has been based on three ideas (a) social categorization, (b) social identification, and (c) social comparison (Vinney, 2019), but we know that the intersection of social identities and culture and how that impacts the human experience is an ever-evolving topic. The intersectional nature of sociocultural identities is described as a recognition of these assumptions: (a) people are characterized simultaneously by multiple interconnected or intertwined socially constructed categories, (b) each category is embedded with a dimension of inequity or power, and (c) categories and their significance are fluid and dynamic (Else-Quest & Hyde, 2016). See chapter 1 for an introduction to these topics.

Research has demonstrated that students' sociocultural identities impact educators' interpretation of disability, including their expectations for the students' academics and behaviors (Sullivan et al., 2019). These interpretations can impact and lead to inequities in education. For example, there is evidence that students' nondominant sociocultural identities result in disproportionate identification for special education, placement in more restrictive educational settings, and high rates of discipline (NCLD, 2020). **Disproportionality**, or the difference between the proportion of a given demographic group and the proportion of that group in the population (Voulgarides et al., 2013), is critical in special education. Disproportionality is discussed in depth throughout this book.

The disproportionate number of students identified with disabilities based on their sociocultural identities and placed in special education is not a new dilemma (Blanchett, 2006). An extensive body of research documents the educational inequities that have historically affected students with marginalized sociocultural identities in schools in the United States (Artiles, 2011; Shifrer, 2013). For example, researchers have documented the disproportionate representation of Black, Latine, and Indigenous students at the highest risk of receiving a disability label (Blanchett, 2006; Coutinho et al., 2002; National Research Council, 2002; Skiba et al., 2006). Other sociocultural identities, such as socioeconomic status and gender, are also associated with special education identification (Cruz & Firestone, 2022). These intersections will be discussed later in this chapter.

Being inappropriately identified as needing special education, placed in a restrictive setting, and disciplined frequently and harshly based on sociocultural identity can negatively affect student outcomes and lead, for example, to increased dropout rates, lower rates of employment, and higher risk of incarceration (NCLD, 2020). In this chapter, we discuss factors, considerations, and impacts on access to education and services related to individuals with disabilities and four common intersecting sociocultural identities highlighted in figure 2.1, specifically racial identity, socioeconomic identity, gender identity, and sexual identity.

Intersections of Disability, Race, and Ethnicity

In this section, we discuss how students with disabilities are impacted by the sociocultural identity of race and ethnicity including racial and ethnic bias and discrimination issues. Disparities in special education placement have historically perpetuated inequities for racially and ethnically minoritized groups (Artiles, 2011; Dunn 1968; Shifrer 2013; Waitoller et al., 2010). Educators must

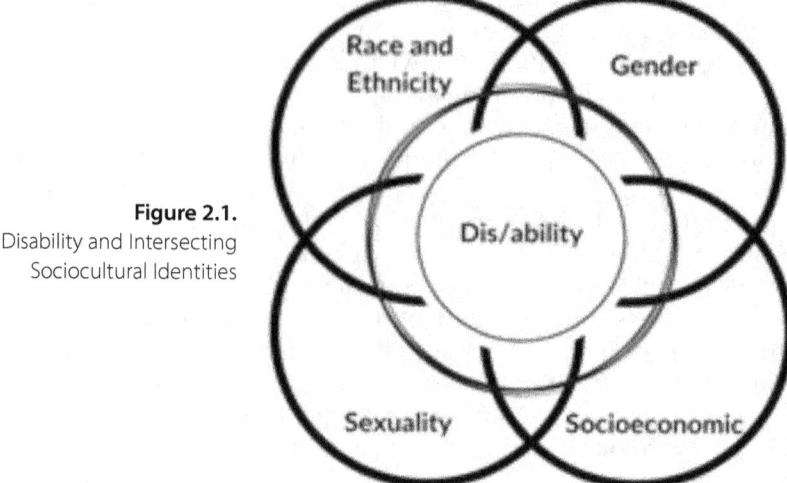

Figure 2.1.
Disability and Intersecting Sociocultural Identities

understand the "layering of student identities," the "power of cultural practices," and the "racialization of disabilities" in working to create justice and equity in schools (Artiles, 2011, pp. 431–32; Cruz & Firestone, 2022). Studies have implicated racism (i.e., prejudice or discrimination against people based on racial or ethnic identity) and xenophobia (i.e., dislike of or prejudice against people from other countries) as embedded in larger contexts that impact schools (see Artiles, 2011; Elder et al., 2021; Ray 2019; Shifrer & Fish, 2020).

The US educational system has a long and deep-rooted history of inequitable policies and procedures fueled by racialized oppression and discrimination affecting racially and ethnically diverse students (Artiles, 2013). Students of the global majority often face the gravest school outcomes, including high rates of exclusionary discipline (e.g., suspension and expulsion) and disproportionate rates of special education placement (Artiles, 2013; Blanchett, 2006). The racial and ethnic identities of students also influence how they are perceived in school and thus impact their school experiences. For example, teachers' biases against racially and ethnically diverse students are correlated to disparities in school discipline. One study found Latine students were underrepresented in office referrals relative to their white peers at the K–6 grade levels, but in grades 6–9 they were overrepresented compared to their white peers (Rueda, 2015). Moreover, this study revealed that when Latine students misbehaved, teachers were less inclined to interpret their behavior as problematic and less inclined to discipline them as compared to their Black peers (Rueda, 2015).

The differences in how students are treated based on their race and ethnicity highlight a significant bias that impacts the treatment and disciplinary actions imparted to traditionally marginalized students across their school matriculation. Additionally, the impact of bias has been found to impact students from the beginning of their educational trajectory. A Yale University study found that preschool teachers of all racial backgrounds were disproportionately monitoring the actions of Black boys when asked to identify adverse behaviors in their classroom overall (Gilliam et al., 2016). These findings call attention to how intertwined racial bias is woven into the systems of education and special education and that there is a critical need to call attention to underlying systems of inequities that have been embedded in our education system.

Racialization of Disability

Researchers posit that disparities within special education placement for racially minoritized students are due to unconscious, stereotyped perceptions that lead to overrepresentation (Skiba et al., 2014). Students of color who are labeled with a disability face a "double jeopardy" that has historically plagued the educational system (Blanchett, 2006). Black students with disabilities receive higher rates of disciplinary referrals for subjective infractions (e.g., defiance and aggression) and are placed in more restrictive educational settings compared to their non-Black peers with and without disabilities (Mendoza et al., 2020).

The prevalence of punitive measures used against students of color has been compared to carceral practices (Annamma et al., 2014; Triplett et al., 2014), as the correlation between disparities within the education system and the criminal justice system is so high that there is a name for it: the [pre]school-to-prison pipeline (Annamma, 2018; Annamma et al., 2014; Skiba et al., 2014). Disabled students are approximately three times more likely to be incarcerated compared to their nondisabled peers and make up approximately 70 percent of individuals in juvenile detention centers (Snydman, 2022).

Pause and Reflect

- How are you considering sociocultural (e.g., racial and ethnic) differences between yourself and a student before referring for a special education evaluation or disciplinary action?
- How are you ensuring you are not pushing your sociocultural (e.g., racial and ethnic) norms on students?
- How are you treating individual students equitably?

Intersection of Disability and Socioeconomic Status

It is important to not only look at how racial identities impact disproportionality within special education but also how the combination of disability with other sociocultural identities impacts educational experiences. In this section, we focus on the current statistics that link disability to socioeconomic status (SES).

When examining disability alongside students' SES, the identification process can have biases and unintended (or intended) consequences, such as diminished life outcomes and an increase in opportunity gaps. Past research shows that there is a positive correlation between poverty and special education (NCLD, 2020), which can be attributed to the experiences or perceived experiences about disability and SES (e.g., lead exposure, low birthweight, and malnutrition). See chapters 4, 6, and 11 for more information about these assumptions, experiences, and intersections.

Within the United States, a study of three states found that although there may be a positive correlation between poverty and special education and that some of that correlation may be appropriate, there is also problematic data (Schifter et al., 2019). As compared to middle- or upper-income households, the study found that students from low-income households are identified more often in subjective disability categories; and, once identified as such, they are more likely to be placed in substantially separate classrooms where there tend to be lower expectations for success, worse education outcomes, and higher stigma associated with special education (Schifter et al., 2019). The National Center for Learning Disabilities notes that "children living at or below the federal poverty level are more than twice as likely to be identified with specific learning disabilities (SLD) as children in households with income four times the poverty level" (2020, p. 3). "Such stereotypes can contribute to over-pathologizing whereby practitioners perceive minority group members as more disturbed or as requiring more treatment . . . depending on the characteristics or status of the student, [it can] contribute to both under- and over-identification of disability" (Sullivan et al., 2019, p. 92). This can be partially attributed to ambiguity and vague eligibility criteria in the IDEA and "the subjective nature of certain evaluation processes coupled with the lack of informed observations can allow for bias . . . and mistakes within the special education eligibility process" (NCLD, 2020, p. 7).

Several disability areas have exclusionary factors that must be considered before determining whether a student is eligible for special education services. For example, school teams may use exclusionary factors when determining eligibility under Specific Learning Disability (SLD) to determine that the learning disability is not primarily due to environmental, cultural, or economic disadvantage. When educators are making these decisions outside of an equity lens, it is extremely difficult to determine whether a student's low academic achievement is primarily the result of one of these factors.

Pause and Reflect

- How are you considering sociocultural (e.g., socioeconomic) differences between yourself and a student before referring for a special education evaluation or disciplinary action?
- How are you ensuring you are not pushing your sociocultural (e.g., socioeconomic) status norms on students?
- How are you treating students equitably?

Intersection of Disability and Gender

We start this section with definitions, but it is important to note that language changes and terms can vary over time and as the dominant narrative shifts. **Gender** is a social construct of what it "typically" means to be female or male, however, it is often conflated with the **sex** assigned at birth, which is what medical professionals decide when looking at a newly born infant's exterior genitals, a vulva or a penis, and declaring the infant to be either female or male. Gender itself may match one's sex assigned at birth or it may not. Variations in exterior and/or interior genitals can result in one being **intersex** or having both male and female sex organs or other sexual characteristics, which is sometimes evident at birth and other times not evident until puberty or later. Being intersex is not the same as being nonbinary or transgender. **Nonbinary** is used by people who do not identify as either female or male but as being somewhere in between, including more than one gender identity, or other altogether (e.g., Two-Spirit). **Cisgender** (i.e., **cis**) is a term describing individuals whose gender identity aligns with the sex they were assigned at birth (i.e., female or male). **Transgender** (e.g., **trans**) is used by people whose gender identity differs from the sex assigned at birth. Individuals might identify as both nonbinary and transgender if their sex assigned at birth (e.g., male, female) does not match their gender identity (e.g., nonbinary, genderqueer). A study at the University of Cambridge Autism Research Center found that transgender and gender-diverse individuals have elevated rates of neurodevelopmental conditions such as autism, attention deficit hyperactivity disorder (ADHD), bipolar disorder, depression, learning disorders, obsessive-compulsive disorder (OCD), and schizophrenia as compared to cisgender individuals (Warrier et al., 2020).

Gender identity is not outwardly visible to others and is people's own internal sense of self and their gender (e.g., man, woman, neither, or both). Gender identity can correlate with people's assigned sex at birth or not. **Gender expression** is outwardly visible to others and how people present gender, through behavior, clothing, haircuts, or other characteristics. Society identifies cues as masculine or feminine, although what is considered masculine or feminine varies. **Gender variance**, which is a difference between the sex a person was assigned at birth and the gender a person identifies with and experiences, exists in all races, ethnicities, cultures, and socioeconomic statuses. Gender does not cease to exist in isolation of disabilities with some studies suggesting high rates of gender variance in people with specific disabilities (Bedard et al., 2010). Having a gender identity that does not conform to the sex assigned at birth is not a mental disorder. When this variance causes discomfort or distress, this is referred to as gender "**dysphoria**" (DSM 5) or "incongruence" (ICD 10), although we recognize this has roots in deficit-based framing.

The Impact of Gender Mismatches

A parallel argument to the ways racial mismatch between students and teachers could undermine educational achievement through implicit bias, some propose the female-dominated teacher workforce imposes norms on students that are developmentally appropriate for females but implicitly disadvantage males. **Implicit bias** is the unconscious bias a teacher may have against a student or group of students based on their sociocultural identities that are dependent on stereotypes and include unconscious reactions and attitudes (Staats, 2016). There is a lack of information about gender mismatches between those who do not identify with the gender binary, and therefore with reservation, this section focuses on the cisgender teaching and student populations. In general, some claim that cis males are not at a systematic disadvantage because of the predominantly cis female teacher workforce for a student body that is evenly split by gender (Hansen & Quintero, 2018). But there are discrepancies. Since the early 1980s, both the number of cis women entering teaching and the proportion of teachers who are female identifying have gone up to over 76 percent. This leaves males underrepresented in the educator workforce (Hansen & Quintero, 2018; Ingersoll et al., 2021). The Equality of Opportunity Project conducted research on gender and found there are Black-white intergenerational gaps for cis males but not females—meaning Black boys lag behind white boys on a number of dimensions, while almost no gap exists between Black and white girls (Chetty et al., 2018).

As previously discussed, the educational system wrestles with issues of disproportionality in the identification of disabilities and behavior-based discipline which leads to over- and underrepresentation among specific sociocultural identities, including gender, relative to the overall student population (Marsh & Walker, 2022; Schifrer et al., 2011; US Department of Education, 2006). Depending on the state, data reveals cis males are more likely to be identified for special education services than cis females (Coutinho & Oswald, 2005; US Department of Education, 2006), even though the identified cisgender populations of males and females in US schools are roughly equivalent (US Census Bureau, 2021). Students who identify as cisgender male not only face overidentification due to race but also tend to be overrepresented in high-incidence disability categories. The challenge with this is that when cis males are disproportionately placed in special education classes, they experience low expectations and labels which can lead to exclusion (Losen et al., 2014; Kirk & Okazawa-Rey, 2010; Marsh & Walker, 2022).

Under the disability label of autism, more males are identified than females, even with equal symptomatology (Parish-Morris et al., 2017). Research suggests that girls with autism may "camouflage" or mask struggles with social communication by behaving in ways that are superficially typical, thus complicating identification (Atwood, 2006; Lai et al., 2011). Another example of gender mismatch is that autistic girls tend to use nonverbal gestures in ways that are more noticeable than autistic boys, despite similar struggles with nonverbal social communication (Rynkiewicz, 2011).

There is yet another gender mismatch when cisgender teachers have nonbinary students. This is currently playing out in schools as evidenced by the attack on gender-neutral bathrooms. Examination of special education literature indicates that very few studies have focused on determining the confluence of gender and disability in their educational experience from students' perspectives (Connor, 2008; Petersen, 2006, 2009; West-Olatunji & Baker, 2006).

VIGNETTE 1: *JAMES'S PERSPECTIVE ON GENDER*

My name is James Williams and I am a non-Hispanic white, autistic, cisgender male who goes by he/him/his pronouns. At the public high school I attended, the vast majority of students in special education were male. The majority of my friends in high school, whether they were from special education or general education, were female—the only notable exceptions were other males with disabilities and a few males that did not conform to the social norms of my high school. It was difficult for me to relate to many of my male peers because of the social expectations for students to expect their same gender classmates to know their gender's unspoken social expectations. Since one primary deficit of autism is the inability to pick up unspoken social expectations or "hidden curriculum" without being directly instructed, it was common for autistic people at my high school to be socially shunned by their same gender peers because they could not pick up unspoken social cues, while different gender peers would sit them down and teach them the unspoken social expectations of their gender's social culture. As a result, many of my male peers would shun me (and sometimes bully me) after I failed to properly display appropriate behavior toward them.

On the other hand, my female peers would sit me down and give me extensive social lessons regarding the social expectations and rules regarding how to interact with them. One girl in particular, alongside some of her girlfriends, ended up actively mentoring me regarding the social rules I would be expected to follow. I routinely referred to her as my "social coach." In my high school, male students with disabilities had mostly female friends, and female friends with disabilities had mostly male friends. Having mostly female friends, I observed how my autistic female friends often were given very different social expectations compared to myself as an autistic male, and how people treated us differently because of our gender differences. I saw how many autistic behaviors that I grew up being reprimanded for displaying because they were "inappropriate" were perceived as inappropriate because of my male gender, and that many of my female friends routinely engaged in those behaviors but were not disciplined for them because they were female, and as a result, many of those behaviors may have equally been due to their autism but were seen as appropriate based on gender. I also observed behaviors that I was not getting disciplined for because of my male gender that my female friends were routinely getting disciplined for as well.

Observing the double standards in which we were being treated because of our gender differences, and how our gender often determined which behaviors were being perceived by others as being autistic (while other equally autistic behaviors were not being perceived as such because they were considered "appropriate" behavior for teenagers of our gender) helped us conclude that there was clearly an observable bias regarding how people viewed our autistic traits.

The rule of thumb was that many people only tended to view something as an "autistic" trait if it deviated from societal rules of appropriateness for the gender of the person displaying the behavior or trait, while other autistic traits would not be seen as autistic if the behaviors were not perceived as inappropriate when they were displayed.

(continued)

VIGNETTE 1: *Continued*

My friends and I also concluded that unfair gender double standards apply to all gender identities—not just females as so many commonly assume—and that both males and females are treated unfairly at times due to their gender when they have autism or another disability. Indeed, one thing the "social coach" pointed out to me, her guy friends with disabilities were far more likely to be sent to detention and receive suspensions compared to her for behaviors that teachers never sent her to detention for. She concluded that she was not going to detention as often because she was female, and told me that she concluded that the detentions and suspensions so many of her guy friends were going through weren't just about behavior problems, they were due to them being male which led to their behaviors being seen as more of a problem and less tolerated by teachers and other professionals.

It is important that we acknowledge and respond to the needs of those with a disability who also experience gender variance in regard to identity and expression. We lack specific outcome data for these groups, however, we reference the aforementioned study at the University of Cambridge Autism Research Center that found increased rates of transgender and gender-diverse individuals in neurodiverse communities (Warrier et al., 2020). As practitioners, we can prepare individuals with disabilities to advocate for all of their sociocultural identities to reduce discrimination, stigma, rejection, and abuse and improve outcomes in areas such as social communication. We should remain open-minded about how gender identity and expression may present and listen to our students, without making quick assumptions or judgments due to our own anxiety or knowledge base about the topic. We must also be careful not to create further barriers to accessing help, but listen, learn, and better understand to help students be their full and authentic selves.

VIGNETTE 2: *PARENT PERSPECTIVE ON GENDER IDENTITY*

My husband and I are on a journey of self-discovery supporting three children, who experience intersecting marginalized social identities that include not only disabilities, to become their best selves. My teenager is navigating the world with depression and anxiety along with their gender identity. My teenager has challenges navigating the world that their peers without disabilities or who do not identify as LGBTQIA+ do not have. When you add in changes to pronouns and a name change, this becomes difficult to maintain. We typically accept nicknames or names that a student prefers to be called to shorten their name, but as soon as a gender identity is associated with it, people have judgments and or difficulty navigating this change.

As a family we have supported our oldest child through three name and pronoun changes (she/they/he). As soon as he helped us to understand that this was important to him that we support him in this change, we were on board every time. It can be difficult to make these changes (especially when you have a sibling with autism who does not adjust to change well), but we asked him for time to adjust and we all came with him on this journey. The more recent name change and pronoun change came over the summer before entering high school. We talked through the changes as a family, we adjusted, even prepared him with a one-page intro-

duction of himself and his needs to give to his teachers on day one. This way he didn't need to use his deadname at all and he could explain to teachers without experiencing his debilitating anxiety in a one-pager. Things were going great; this really helped the transition into high school go smoothly for him and his teachers were very supportive.

The day came when he had a substitute teacher in a class. His typical teacher left all of the instructions, correct names to use for students, but something got lost in the shuffle. The substitute teacher called his deadname. He wanted so badly to leave that identity behind him and not have that name come up in high school. So, he didn't answer, he curled up in a ball of anxiety and did not respond to the teacher calling his deadname. We got calls and texts that our child was missing from school, so we texted our child, he was in school, it must have been a mistake. When he came home from school, he was upset so it took a while for him to share the devastating experience. After conversations with his school about what happened, they suggested that he fill out the official paperwork to have his name changed on school documents. He was very excited about this, because it would mean that his deadname would no longer appear on any school records, therefore this could not happen again. When he brought the paperwork home, we gladly signed it, and this is no longer a problem he or we have to worry about.

It's been a hard couple of years with the victories few and far between. Navigating the appropriate mental health support for my child with depression and anxiety, who is also LGBTQIA+, has been challenging. But when I saw him light up when we signed the papers to officially change his name, I cried tears of joy. I feel my job as an adult is to support my kids. By making it their burden to tell us why it's important that we use certain pronouns or call them a preferred name, we make it harder for them to exist in the world as their authentic selves. It's not about us. In some cases it is a matter of life and death.

> **Pause and Reflect**
>
> - How are you considering gender differences between yourself and a student before referring for a special education evaluation or disciplinary action?
> - How are you ensuring you are not pushing your gender-based norms on students?
> - How are you treating students equitably?

Intersection of Disability and Sexual Identity

Human sexuality is complex and shows up in varied ways across individuals. **Sexuality** can be defined as being "experienced and expressed in thoughts, fantasies, desires, beliefs, attitudes, values, behaviors, practices, roles and relationships. . . . influenced by the interaction of biological, physiological, social, economic, political, cultural, legal, historical, religious, and spiritual factors" (WHO, 2006). When moving down from the overall construct of sexuality, which is inherent in all human beings, a discussion of sexual identity might follow. **Sexual identity** is how one thinks about their own sexuality and how one expresses that sexuality. Terms associated with sexual identity can include heterosexuality (e.g., "straight") and homosexuality (e.g., lesbian, bisexual, gay, queer, asexual, pansexual), which are sexual orientation terms, and can include how one identifies, doesn't identify, or chooses not to identify with these orientations. However, sexual identity includes more than sexual orientation and also comprises behaviors, values, desires, and practices (e.g., kinks, fetishes, abstinence) and beyond. Like disability, sexual identities cross all genders, races, ethnicities, disabilities, nationalities, body types, and socioeconomic statuses.

There are several models of sexuality that account for a variety of factors and influences on one's sexuality. One such model is the biophysical model (Lindau et al., 2003), which provides a comprehensive approach that includes psychological influences (e.g., body image, experience, emotions, motivation, self-concept), biological influences (e.g., physical appearance, dis/ability, sexual arousal and response), and sociocultural influences (e.g., ethical, media, religious, socioeconomic, gender, disability). It is beyond the scope of this chapter to dive deeply into cultural and biological underpinnings of sexuality, however, what should be apparent is that sexuality is complex and involves a wide range of variations, all of which surpass while also including gender, gender identity, dis/ability, and orientation, and interact with one's culture, race, ethnicity, values, and beliefs.

Sexually healthy development can be described as the following (Haffner, 2022).

- An adult who understands that one can have sexual feelings without acting on them.
- An adult who engages only in sexual behaviors that are life affirming and enhancing and not harmful to self or others.

As stated earlier, sexuality is part of being human and all human beings have a right to information and resources about their sexuality (Weeks, 1998). As educators and administrators, we might find discomfort in being positioned to acknowledge, address, and/or educate our learners about sexuality. However, we must consider the whole being of the individuals we are educating, recognizing that the development of healthy relationships, knowledge and understanding of our bodies, and self-advocacy skills are all a part of healthy sexuality. A consideration that must be made is how information is accessed.

Many adults who grew up pre-2000s, learned about sexuality by asking questions and either received a well-grounded response, got an unclear response, or were denied information altogether. These adults may have then accessed information from books and/or from peers. After the early 2000s, youth and adolescents were more likely to access the internet to find information and answer their questions. It is worth noting this difference and being aware of how information is accessed and what may be the benefits versus problems these sources of information provide. It may also be clear from this that information may be much more available, even if that information is inaccurate or a misrepresentation of reality.

Disability and sexuality have a complicated history, which has frequently involved harm in the form of institutionalization and forced sterilization (Servais, 2006; Wehmeyer, 2013). Eugenics has had a significant impact on the intersection of disability and sexuality, with long-standing impact. See chapters 10 and 11 for more information on the Eugenics movement. Still today, there are attitudes toward sexuality for individuals with disabilities that continue these harmful ideas, particularly for individuals with intellectual disabilities in regard to sexual orientation (Abbott & Howarth, 2007), gender identity and expression (Wilson, 2006), and the ability to manage sexual thoughts and behaviors (Gilmore & Chambers, 2010). Frequently more attention is paid to the physical, cognitive, and other adaptive living skills of individuals with disabilities (Murphy & Elias, 2006). Educators, then, should acknowledge the whole person and include acknowledgment of sexuality and access to sexuality education. The perpetuation of attitudes and perceptions that ignore or fail to recognize the sexuality of all humans, including those with both low and high incidence disabilities, oppresses this population in regard to sexuality (McCollow et al., 2021).

Developing sexuality and coming into an identity around sexuality is an important and expected part of becoming an adult, however, this part of development is often denied, treated as an inconvenience, or suppressed altogether for individuals with intellectual disabilities (Wilkinson et al., 2015). While not every educator or administrator feels comfortable talking about sexuality, there is a significant difference between being uncomfortable and denying the existence of sexuality. While not every educator will be called upon to provide sexuality education, every educator can reflect on their own views, attitudes, beliefs, and biases related to sexuality and how they might adjust these views and/or put these views aside in order to support the students they are preparing to live full adult lives. Full adult lives include sexuality and recognition of how sexuality fits into adult living.

The oppression that individuals with disabilities experience can be viewed in multifaceted ways. Not only does disability itself contribute but every intersecting identity has the potential to contribute to marginalization. Think about what was discussed in chapter 1 regarding the disability community's access to the right to marry as compared to the LGBTQIA+ community's access to the right to marry. Now think about the impact of being disabled in the LGBTQIA+ community. For sexuality, the impact of disability has the effect of being an overriding identity, suppressing societal acknowledgment of their sexuality to near nonexistence (Wilkinson et al., 2015). This also connects with the gender spectrum. For example, cisgender women with disabilities identify concerns with sexual well-being and experiences (Vaughn et al., 2015), sexual activity of cisgender men with disabilities (Hellemans et al., 2010), ability to marry, live with partners, and raise children (Ailey et al., 2003). When it comes to oppressed sexual identities (e.g., lesbian, bisexual, gay), individuals with disabilities experience increased bullying, harassment, and discrimination (Leonard & Mann, 2018; Toft & Franklin, 2020), with some even referring to LGBTQIA+ individuals with intellectual disabilities as being "invisible" (Löfgren-Mårtenson, 2008).

Pause and Reflect

- Reflect on your thoughts and ideas related to disability and sexuality. What comes to mind as you consider the intersections of disability and sexuality?
- Reflect on your thoughts and ideas when considering the intersection of intellectual disability and sexuality. Do those thoughts change?
- How might you ensure that sexual identity is considered across the spectrum of disability?
- How might you check your own bias and values related to sexual identity to support students who may have different values and hold sexual identities different from your own?
- How are you treating your students equitably?

INTERSECTIONAL COMPETENCE IN SPECIAL EDUCATION

It is important for educators to enhance their intersectional competence in order to examine and counteract multifaceted biases. Intersectional competence prepares practitioners to identify how sociocultural identity markers impact students within the educational system in complex ways, such as teacher bias, educational access, and federal policies. Practitioners must recognize and address how intersections of sociocultural identities provide privileges and barriers that correlate to opportunity gaps. In order to do this, educators must recognize their role in perpetuating educational barriers and actively collaborate with members of the school and community to create equitable opportunities for students (Boveda & Aronson, 2019).

Research has identified **culturally and linguistically sustaining practices** or **socioculturally sustaining practices** to enact equity in schools. These practices emphasize the need for school-based practices that aim to empower students from marginalized backgrounds (Paris & Alim, 2017), and they foster academic success, sociocultural competence, sociocultural consciousness, and linguistic preservation as essential strategies for creating equitable learning opportunities in a multicultural classroom (Ladson-Billings, 1995; Paris & Alim, 2017; Rose & Frederick-Clarke, 2016). Socioculturally sustaining practices decenter dominating Eurocentric ideology in the educational system and reject the notion that students need to demonstrate success based on white, middle-class standards (Paris & Alim, 2017). We suggest using an intersectional lens to develop socioculturally sustaining practices that promote student success (Gay, 2002). This is discussed in depth throughout the book.

VIGNETTE 3: *EDUCATOR PERSPECTIVE ON RACE AND CULTURE*

Using Writing to Embed Cross-Cultural and Racially Affirming Practices

As a Black female novice special education teacher, writing class always seemed to be one of the trickiest areas of my instructional schedule. It was the only content area where I could pretty much do what I wanted, as long as I was addressing students' individualized education program (IEP) goals and grade-level skills. While the other core content areas (i.e., reading and math) consisted of a more-dictated curriculum, I was allowed to have autonomy over how I delivered the writing curriculum. However, I only had twenty minutes allotted for writing instruction and I had to support a group of first and second grade students with a range of needs including handwriting, grammar, and narrative writing.

The curriculum provided objectives for the writing components, but I was allowed to decide how to deliver them. Therefore, I utilized that time to implement sustaining practices. My class consisted of a majority of Black students (i.e., twelve Black students and two Latine students). Thus, it was important for me to expose students to the diverse and rich culture of their native land. Historically, Western media has depicted Africa and African people as impoverished and primitive. It was crucial for me to eradicate these tropes and allow students to gain a scope of the African diaspora. It also provided a level of affirmation and self-confidence for my Black students that builds resilience when faced with racism as they get older. Additionally, it was beneficial to provide non-Black students a positive and authentic experience when learning about other cultures in order to build respect and appreciation across different racial groups.

At the time, my cousin was teaching in Sierra Leone through AmeriCorps. Therefore, I used this opportunity to facilitate a cross-cultural activity between my students in the United States and her students in Sierra Leone. The focus of my writing unit was letter construction, so my students were able to use the skills they were learning about writing letters to ask my cousin's students about their culture and school experiences. I also incorporated opportunities for students to learn about Sierra Leone and other countries in Africa via videos and stories about the languages, holidays, and history.

At the conclusion of the writing unit, which was during the winter season, I had students create holiday cards for their Salone pen pals and we conducted a service project by sending toiletries to Sierra Leone along with our letters. Once the Salone students received their cards and items, my cousin sent us back pictures and videos, which I shared with my students during our class holiday party. I found that my students engaged in the project and I found it to be a valuable and intentional way to build multicultural awareness and have students use the product of their learning to conduct an act of service.

> **Pause and Reflect**
> - How can practitioners ensure racial bias does not impact special education referral and identification and contribute to disproportionality?
> - In what ways can practitioners enhance their intersectional sociocultural competence to support historically marginalized students with disabilities?
> - How can practitioners ensure that placement in more restrictive settings for students of color is based on identified needs and not bias?

Barriers in Special Education

There are benefits for students enrolled in special education, such as access to services, accommodations, and other rights under the law, although this can sometimes complicate the objective nature of the qualification decisions of individualized education program (IEP) teams. Some educators can see those benefits as a way of ensuring students from low-income families get the extra support they may need to meet grade-level requirements, especially when the schools are located in low-income areas and do not have the funding to access extra services. This inequity among schools can mean that students in lower-funded schools do not have access to the same resources which then leads to an even further gap for "not only are these children not receiving equal resources but [they] are also not receiving the extra supports they need in order to succeed" (Carter & Welner, 2016, p. 15).

Research has shown that "identification for special education can also result in lowered expectations, stigma, and segregation from general education classrooms" (Schifter et al., 2019). Students with disabilities often face lower status value and are viewed as less competent. This not only impacts these students while in preK–12 education but later in life as well. Current research shows that "the negative effects of disability resulted in hierarchies of disadvantage" where those with multiple intersecting identities reported the lowest total income and "had a greater reliance on income sources outside the labor market for economic security" (Maroto et al., 2019, p. 66).

Research has also found that intersecting sociocultural identities influence social interactions while "simultaneously accounting for particular experiences unique to the overlap of multiple social categories" (Maroto et al., 2019, p. 68). When students experience multiple nondominant sociocultural identities, the outcomes of not only their educational experiences but also their life experiences are impacted. It is imperative that, as practitioners, we are aware of the decisions we make to qualify students for special education and actively engage in strategies to combat our biases and assumptions and, therefore, inequities. We all have biases and blind spots. These are "products of our surroundings, cultures, experiences, and our upbringings" (Sullivan, 2021). It is important for educators to put in the work (e.g., attend training) so we can recognize our blind spots and watch out for them (Sullivan, 2021, p. 7).

VIGNETTE 4: SCHOOL ADMINISTRATOR PERSPECTIVE ON SOCIOECONOMIC STATUS

As a white middle-class female principal at a Special Education Academy in a large county in California, I did not share the same social identities as the majority of my high school students. My school included students who had emotional and behavioral challenges and each student came from low socioeconomic status with over 90 percent identifying as students of color. Although I did not match their sociocultural identities, I believed students were much more than their special education label and wanted to put my pedagogical theories into practice.

I went into the school with the foundational belief that I wanted this school to be a different experience for my students. There was one thing that was a glaring truth that I couldn't hide. I was a white cisgender woman. A majority of my students came either from a single-parent household, were living in a local group home, or were living with extended family. I had students coming in and out of juvenile court schools and institutions who were on probation for a myriad of reasons. I knew nothing of their lived experiences, and I needed to stay away from saying, "I understand how you feel." I didn't understand what they felt or where they lived or what environment they went home to.

It was only a couple of months into my leadership when I first went to a training on culturally responsive teaching. I sat back and listened to this amazing woman of color talk about checking our biases and really listening to the students we serve. I had to dig deep to think of what sociocultural identities I felt I belonged to. I just knew what I was not. I was not poor. I was not multilingual. I was not queer. I was a white woman. But thinking of my own identity made me check my biases toward what people appear to be or what we read them to be. As much as I didn't want to, I still put my students in a box: Bilingual ✓. Not white ✓. From a broken home ✓. Having an IEP and a disability ✓. If I really wanted to start to shift the system, I needed to see each of them as a whole person and not just the separate social identities they fell into.

Things that year were very difficult, but about to get much more difficult than I could have imagined. Not only were we about to experience a global pandemic, but we were also experiencing a racial awakening in light of the national spotlight on the murder of George Floyd, a Black man, at the hands of police and caught on video for the world to see. I knew that my students were struggling at home without access to the food they would get at school, the safe place to rest and get away from the difficulties their lives entailed, and I felt pretty helpless at first.

The school district I was working in set up food pickup options two times a day, but there were families we served that did not have personal transportation or money to get to a high school site more than five miles away from their home, so we delivered to their homes. We saw the inequity of internet services for our students so we got hotspots and then learned how to set it up for the families that didn't know how to connect a device to the hotspot. When we started holding IEP meetings for our students and their families, we set up a computer in a separate room at school to maintain safe distance, while providing them a secure place to conduct the IEP meeting.

I took this time to dive even deeper into how to not make assumptions that I knew what was best or always have the answers. I listened to students and families. I knew our students had multiple sociocultural identities, each with a unique set of needs, and it was up to us to see the whole student and make a decision to support the families however we could. We helped with food, gas, or rides to meet basic needs. We advocated for support when our school could not provide the support the student and family needed.

(continued)

VIGNETTE 4: *Continued*

I know my situation was very different from other administrators at that time. Due to the size of the school, I had the privilege to really get to know my students and their families. We created relationships that led to trusting us to support their needs. As students started making their way back onto campus that next school year, our staff really tried to understand the multifaceted needs of our students. I did empathy interviews with each of the students and asked them their opinion on their current school experiences and their past ones too. I asked them to share whether they felt safe and felt like they belonged. They gave me feedback on ways to improve the school culture.

One student in particular gave me really good feedback. I asked him what he thought of his high school experience so far. He told me that when he was in 4th grade, his teachers didn't understand him or his behaviors. His teacher at that time recommended that he be assessed for special education and his parents didn't really understand what that all meant. They were Spanish-only speakers and didn't have any experience with special education. The school qualified him under the category of emotional disturbance. His parents did not understand what that meant. Because comprehensive school sites do not always have the personnel or resources to serve students in the least restrictive environment (LRE), the school had him attend a separate school site. He was now an 11th grader and had not been given the opportunity to be on a comprehensive school site for most of his educational experience. His parents did not have a very trusting relationship with schools since the schools had consistently called the parents to complain and discipline him. The school personnel did not take the time to learn the sociocultural factors that may have been contributing to his behavior. He went on to share how he felt his behavior kept spiraling out of control because there were no positive peer models. "Everyone at my school was bad, so I had to one-up them to stay safe." The pandemic increased his feelings of isolation and being out of control. A year prior to this conversation, he overdosed and was hospitalized. We held multiple IEPs after his hospitalization to really ask ourselves if we were a high enough level of service or if he truly needed a residential treatment center (RTC). But we listened to the family, we listened to the student. We listened to the sociocultural and socioeconomic state of the family (because of not being required to attend school daily, he had started going to work with his dad and contributing to the family income). We made home visits, increased his mental health support, and agreed to allow him to stay enrolled in our school. A year later, he shared that including him, his family, and their sociocultural identities into consideration had helped his parents start to trust the school system again. We were able to partner with the family and eventually see him graduate high school with a diploma. I am not sure that would have been the case if we didn't take his whole identity into consideration.

I learned a lot about being an educator at that school. Sure, it was extremely difficult at times, but what made the experience even more special was how I was able to truly listen to many different perspectives from students and families that have typically been marginalized because of their social identities. I was far from perfect and I am sure I made many mistakes, but seeing the families' and students' appreciation made a lot of the difficulties worth it.

Pause and Reflect

- When determining special education qualification, how are you addressing implicit biases (i.e., educator, referral team, structural system) during the referral and identification process?
- How do you utilize tiers of interventions and prevention to ensure students are receiving support?
- How do you maintain high expectations for your students when they come from sociocultural identities that differ from your own (e.g., race and ethnicity, gender, socioeconomic status, disability)?

Integrated Multi-Tiered Systems of Support

One purpose of a **Multi-Tiered Systems of Support** (MTSS) educational model of assessment and instructional service delivery is to prevent identified challenges with traditional and biased approaches to special education identification that lead to disproportionality (Hoover & Soltero-González, 2018). The word "integrated" added to MTSS (I-MTSS) stresses the importance of interconnecting academic and social emotional and behavioral supports. For example, academic access can be impacted by behavior. I-MTSS combines academic and social emotional and behavioral supports into a three-tiered system of evidence-based universal screening and graduated levels of interventions matched to learner's needs with progress monitored frequently to make important educational decisions about changes in instruction or goals (NCLD, 2020).

I-MTSS includes Tier 1 universal screening for all students, and Tiers 2 and 3 include targeted support, data-based progress monitoring, and interventions that increase in intensity based on learner need. Data-based decision-making (a) provides high-quality instruction to students, (b) uses frequent data collection to monitor students' progress based on instruction, and (c) makes subsequent instructional and special education eligibility decisions based upon collected data (Fuchs & Fuchs, 2006). I-MTSS can be thought of as an umbrella framework that includes both Response to Intervention (RTI), which is a multitiered framework primarily for academic supports, and Positive Behavioral Interventions and Supports (PBIS), which is a multitiered framework for social-emotional and behavioral supports. More specifically, **Response to Intervention** (RTI) is a three-tiered prevention model of instruction and assessment to determine the need for academic instructional support created because research identified biased tests can contribute to the overrepresentation of socioculturally diverse students in special education (Proctor et al., 2012). RTI supports the individualized academic needs of all students using data-based decision making based on universal screening and progress monitoring of evidence-based interventions (Cavendish et al., 2016). Similar to RTI, **Positive Behavioral Interventions and Supports** (PBIS) is an evidence-based multitiered system to teach and support all students focused on positive social emotional and behavioral support for behavioral, academic, social, emotional, and mental health. RTI and PBIS both focus on providing support and prevention strategies at different levels of intensity based on what the student needs—at the schoolwide (Tier 1), targeted (Tier 2), and individual (Tier 3) levels of support. See chapters 7, 8, and 9 for more information on these systems.

I-MTSS Tier 1 Universal Supports

Tier 1 universal support for all students ensures students receive high-quality evidenced-based instruction. The purpose of Tier 1 interventions and supports is to especially take into account not only students' academic and instructional needs but their cultural and social emotional and behavioral needs as well (Montalvo et al., 2014). To truly plan for all students, educators embed practices that take into account multiple, intersecting, and diverse sociocultural identities into Tier 1 prevention supports. Tier 1 includes socioculturally sustaining practices and reflects the values of the local community. See figure 2.2 for examples of how to provide Tier 1 universal support with an equity-based focus in academics and social emotional and behavioral domains.

I-MTSS Tier 2 Secondary Supports

At Tier 2, schools move students who have been identified as requiring additional academic or social emotional and behavioral support to the next tier of support. The purpose of Tier 2 is to ensure that students who need additional support receive evidence-based interventions and more frequent monitoring on progress of core academic and social emotional and behavioral areas. Educators use appropriate measures in order to monitor student growth on a weekly or biweekly basis during Tier 2. Figure 2.2 includes examples of how to provide Tier 2 interventions with an equity-based focus.

I-MTSS Tier 3 Individual Supports

At Tier 3, schools provide students who do not show "adequate growth" with Tiers 1 and 2 support with more-intensive interventions. The purpose of Tier 3 support is to provide interventions based on the individualized needs of students. If these Tier 3 interventions do not result in adequate progress, schools will refer the student for a special education evaluation. Figure 2.2 includes examples of how to provide Tier 3 interventions with an equity-based focus.

Intersectionality in the Context of Disability

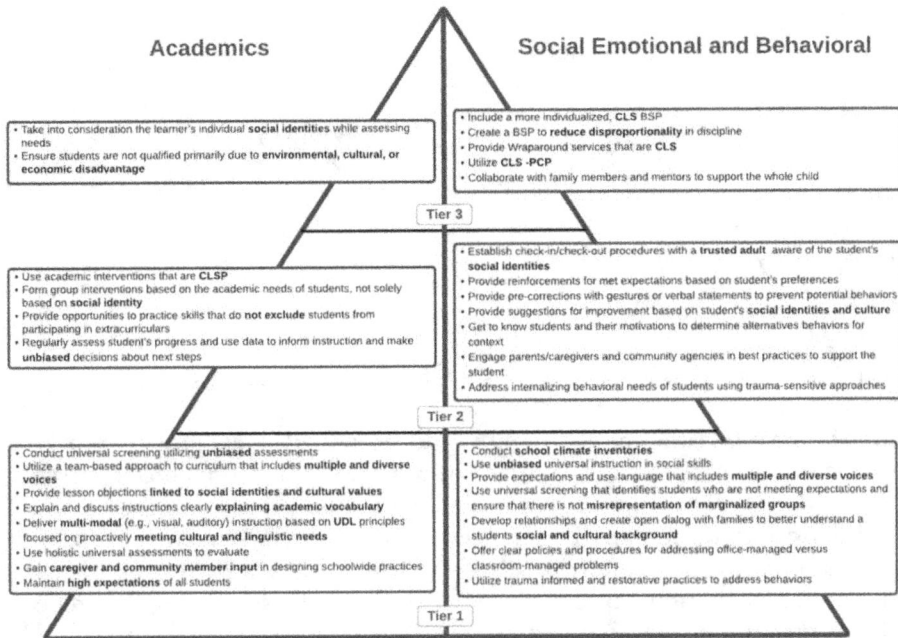

Figure 2.2. Examples of Integrated Multi-Tiered Systems of Support (I-MTSS)

Socioculturally Sustaining Person-Centered Planning

If Tier 1 and Tier 2 support has not been significant enough, schools should utilize a socioculturally sustaining person-centered planning (PCP) approach to plan to meet an individual's Tier 3 needs. There are numerous PCP approaches (e.g., "Making Action Plans," "Planning Alternative Tomorrows with Hope," "Whose future is it anyway?," "It's my future! Planning for what I want in my life") available to provide the structure and guidelines for how to specifically engage in this individualized planning process (Bolding et al., 2010; New Jersey Coalition for Inclusive Education, 2013; Pearpoint et al., 1993; Wehmeyer et al., 2004). An essential element of the PCP process is to provide a voice to the student so they can help choose supports that can lead to a fulfilling life where they have equitable opportunities for success and a sense of belonging. Figure 2.3 includes some basic common components of a socioculturally sustaining PCP approach.

When engaging in socioculturally sustaining PCP, the goal is to listen to, support, and empower the student to pursue their vision (e.g., desired outcomes, hopes, dreams, aspirations, goals, and priorities) and plan for the life that they want. Sociocultural self-determination considerations are discussed many times in this book. To start the planning process, the student with the disability and individuals in the student's life beyond just educational profes-

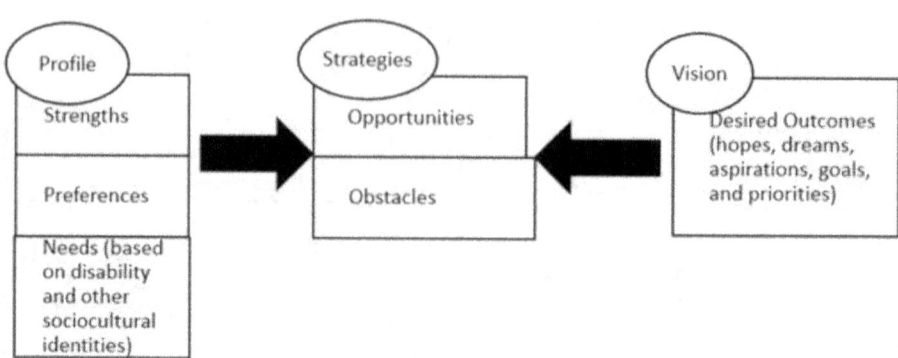

Figure 2.3. Socioculturally Sustaining Person-Centered Planning Components

sionals, including the family, friends, and potentially neighbors, coworkers, or others they know from their communities, create a personal profile describing the student for whom the plan is being developed based on the individual's intersectional strengths, preferences, and needs. While creating the profile, this team discusses the individual's story from a historical (from birth) to a contemporary (current) perspective. A socioculturally sustaining PCP reflects what is most important to the individual. The team considers the individual's disability alongside other sociocultural identities to help guide planning. In some cultures, the family and community norms will have a direct impact on the vision. The team utilizes the personal profile and the vision as the base upon which to plan, moving toward the articulation of educational goals that include identified skills the student needs to develop to achieve their desired outcomes. With student input, the team considers opportunities and identifies strategies to help the individual gain the needed skills to achieve their vision. The team must ensure support strategies that are socioculturally sustaining. Equally important, the team identifies how to lessen or work around obstacles and challenges that might be encountered in the achievement of desired outcomes. Teams can utilize questions, like the examples in table 2.1, to guide the socioculturally sustaining PCP process. Lastly, the team must include the specific support strategies that will assist the student in moving toward their dream in a written action plan, which outlines what needs to be done, who will do it, and by when.

SUMMARY

While disability might be the backbone of a student's individualized education program, it is imperative to consider intersectional sociocultural identities in order to provide equitable education opportunities. Historically minoritized students are at a higher risk of being inappropriately placed in special education programs and receiving services in more restrictive settings, which

Table 2.1. Socioculturally Sustaining Person-Centered Planning

Profile	Your Story	<ul><li>Who are you?</li><li>What name would you like to be addressed by?</li><li>What are your pronouns (e.g., he/him, she/her, they/them, ze/zir, fae/faer)?</li><li>What parts of your life and/or sociocultural identities are important to consider in planning for your future (e.g., disability, race, gender, sexuality, socioeconomic status, ethnicity, religion)?</li></ul>
	Strengths	<ul><li>What are your positive qualities and strengths?</li><li>What are things you would not change about yourself?</li><li>What are things you are most proud of?</li><li>What are things you are good at and/or find easy?</li></ul>
	Preferences	<ul><li>What are your likes, interests, hobbies, essential routines, preferences, and other important elements, such as favorite activities, places, and people that make you happy and you want to be part of your adult life?</li></ul>
	Needs	<ul><li>What parts of your life do you need support with or to acquire additional skills to be successful (e.g., budgeting, transportation, cooking, interview skills)?</li><li>What are your disability-related needs? What are your other needs?</li></ul>
Vision	Dream or Desired Outcomes	<ul><li>What is your vision for where you would like to see yourself in the future? Are there familial or cultural expectations that will influence your future dreams?</li><li>What is your dream career? Are there any familial or cultural influences to the type of employment you seek?</li><li>What is your preferred living arrangement and where do you want to live as an adult? Are there any familial or cultural influences on the type of living arrangements you seek (e.g., do you want to live on your own or with family or a roommate or a partner)?</li><li>Who are the most important people in your life that you want to maintain relationships with as an adult (e.g., friendships)?</li><li>How involved will your family and/or cultural community be in your adult life?</li><li>Do you want to go to postsecondary school or seek other forms of education after high school (e.g., technical school, community college, university)?</li><li>What kinds of relationships do you want to have (e.g., romantic partner, friends, common-interest groups)?</li></ul>
Strategies	What Works and Doesn't Work	<ul><li>What would a "perfect day" look like for you as an adult?</li><li>What support or help do you need to achieve your dream? To avoid obstacles?</li><li>What are supports that work for you when learning new skills (e.g., frequent breaks, adaptations, visual supports, preferred time of day to start or end)?</li><li>What are supports that have not worked in the past for you when learning new skills (e.g., waiting, multistep instructions, verbal instructions, standing or sitting too long, unclear expectations)?</li><li>What are your "dislikes," things that are possible sensitivities, or triggers that you prefer to avoid (bright lights, loud noises)?</li></ul>

leads to short- and long-term consequences, such as receiving a less-rigorous curriculum and developing a low self-concept (NCLD, 2020). Thus, it is the responsibility of educators to be aware of the potential to misidentify students who need universal support through a more socioculturally sustaining education. Moving beyond approaching special education services through a singular lens means practitioners must focus on meeting students' multiple intersecting sociocultural identities and experiences. Additionally, it is imperative that educators understand the magnitude of disproportionality for students of different sociocultural identities and take action to correct it and prevent it from happening (NCLD, 2020).

Using four examples of disability across the intersections, this chapter provided some integrated multi-tiered systems of support strategies, including a socioculturally sustaining person-centered approach. For more ideas on this, see chapter 7. As more research is completed on the impacts of understanding the whole child and their multifaceted sociocultural identities in education, the key takeaway from this chapter is to approach teaching beyond a one-dimensional understanding of how sociocultural identities impact learning.

REFERENCES

Abbott, D., & Howarth, J. (2007). Still off limits? Staff views on supporting gay, lesbian and bisexual people with intellectual disabilities to develop sexual and intimate relationships? *Journal of Applied Research in Intellectual Disabilities, 20*(2), 116–26.

Ailey, S. H., Marks, B. A., Crisp, C., & Hahn, J. E. (2003). Promoting sexuality across the life span for individuals with intellectual and developmental disabilities. *Nursing Clinics, 38*(2), 229–52.

Annamma, S. A. (2018). Mapping consequential geographies in the carceral state: Education journey mapping as a qualitative method with girls of color with dis/abilities. *Qualitative Inquiry, 24*(1), 20–34.

Annamma, S. A., Connor D., & Ferri B. (2013). Dis/ability critical race studies (DisCrit): Theorizing at the intersections of race and dis/ability. *Race Ethnicity and Education, 16*(1), 1–31.

———. (2016). A truncated genealogy of DisCrit. In *DisCrit: Disability Studies and Critical Race Theory in education* (pp. 1–8). Teachers College Press.

Annamma, S., Morrison, D., & Jackson, D. (2014). Disproportionality fills in the gaps: Connections between achievement, discipline and special education in the school-to-prison pipeline. *Berkeley Review of Education, 5*(1), 53–87.

Artiles, A. J. (2011). Toward an interdisciplinary understanding of educational equity and difference: The case of the racialization of ability. *Educational Researcher, 40*(9), 431–45. https://doi.org/10.3102/0013189X11429391

———. (2013). Untangling the racialization of disabilities: An intersectionality critique across disability models. *Du Bois Review: Social Science Research on Race, 10*(2), 329–47. https://doi.org/10.1017/S1742058X13000271

Atwood, K. D. (2006). *Recognition of facial expressions of six emotions by children with specific language impairment*. Theses and Dissertations. 738. https://scholarsarchive.byu.edu/cgi/viewcontent.cgi?article=1737&context=etd

Bedard, C., Zhang, H. L., & Zucker, K .J. (2010). Gender identity and sexual orientation in people with developmental disabilities. *Sexuality and Disability, 28*(3), 165-75. https://doi.org/10.1007/s11195-010-9155-7

Blanchett, W. (2006). Disproportionate representation of African American students in special education: Acknowledging the role of white privilege and racism. *Educational Researcher, 35*(6), 24-28. https://doi.org/10.3102/0013189X035006024

Bolding, N., Wehmeyer, M. L., & Lawrence, M. (2010). *It's my future! Planning for what I want in my life: A self-directed planning process*. US Department of Health and Human Services, Administration on Developmental Disabilities. https://beachcenter.lsi.ku.edu/sites/default/files/inline-files/Beach/Its%20My%20Future.pdf

Boveda, M. (2016). *Beyond special and general education as identity markers: The development and validation of an instrument to measure preservice teachers' understanding of the effects of intersecting sociocultural identities*. FIU Electronic Theses and Dissertations. http://digitalcommons.fiu.edu/etd/2998

Boveda, M., & Aronson, B. (2019). Special education preservice teachers, intersectional diversity, and the privileging of emerging professional identities. *Remedial and Special Education, 40*(4) 248-60. https://doi.org/10.1177/0741932519838621

Carter, P. L., & Welner, K. G. (2016). *Closing the opportunity gap: What America must do to give all children an even chance*. Oxford University Press.

Cavendish, W., Harry, B., Menda, A. M., Espinosa, A., & Mahotiere, M. (2016). Implementing response to intervention: Challenges of diversity and system change in a high-stakes environment. *Teachers College Record, 118*(5), 1-36. https://doi.org/10.1177/016146811611800505

Chetty, R., Friedman, J. N., Hendren, N., Jones, M. R., & Porter, S. R. (2018). *The opportunity atlas: Mapping the childhood roots of social mobility* (Working Paper 25147). National Bureau of Economic Research.

Connor, D. J. (2008). *Urban narratives: Portraits in progress. Life at the intersections of learning disabilities, race, and social class*. Peter Lang.

Coutinho, M. J., & Oswald, D. P. (2005). State variation in gender disproportionality in special education findings and recommendations. *Remedial and Special Education, 26*, 7-15.

Coutinho, M. J., Oswald, D. P., & Best, A. M. (2002). The influence of sociodemographics and gender on the disproportionate identification of minority students as having learning disabilities. *Remedial and Special Education, 23*, 49-59. https://doi.org/10.1177/074193250202300107

Crenshaw, K. (1989). Demarginalizing the intersection of race and sex: A Black feminist critique of antidiscrimination doctrine, feminist theory, and antiracist politics. *University of Chicago Legal Forum, 1989*(1), 139-67.

Cruz, R. A., & Firestone, A. R. (2022). Understanding the empty backpack: The role of timing in disproportionate special education identification. *Sociology of Race and Ethnicity, 8*(1), 95-113. https://doi.org/10.1177/23326492211034890

Druery, J. E. (2018). *Fostering sense of belonging: A multi-case study of Black male retention initiatives*. Electronic Theses and Dissertations. Paper 2934. https://doi.org/10.18297/etd/2934

Dunn, L. M. (1968). Special education for the mildly retarded—Is much of it justifiable? *Exceptional Children, 35*(1), 5–22.

Elder, T. E., Figlio, D., Imberman, S., & Persico, C. (2021). Segregation and racial gaps in special education. *Education Next, 21*(2), 62–66.

Else-Quest, N. M., & Hyde, J. S. (2016). Intersectionality in quantitative psychological research: Theoretical and epistemological issues. *Psychology of Women Quarterly, 40*(2), 155–70. https://doi.org/10.1177/0361684316629797

Erickson, W. A., von Schrader, S., Bruyère, S. M., & VanLooy, S. A. (2013). The employment environment: Employer perspectives, policies, and practices regarding the employment of persons with disabilities. *Rehabilitation Counseling Bulletin, 57*(4), 195–208. https://doi.org/10.1177/0034355213509841

Fuchs, D., & Fuchs, L. S. (2006). Introduction to response to intervention: What, why, and how valid is it? *Reading Research Quarterly, 41*(1), 93–99.

Gatewood, E., Broholm, C., Herman, J., & Yingling, C. (2019). Making the invisible visible: Implementing an implicit bias activity in nursing education. *Journal of Professional Nursing, 35*(6), 447–51.

Gilliam, W. S., Maupin, A. N., Reyes, C. R., Accavitti, M., & Shic, F. (2016). Do early educators' implicit biases regarding sex and race relate to behavior expectations and recommendations of preschool expulsions and suspensions? *Yale University Child Study Center, 9*(28), 1–16.

Gilmore, L., & Chambers, B. (2010). Intellectual disability and sexuality: Attitudes of disability support staff and leisure industry employees. *Journal of Intellectual and Developmental Disability, 35*(1), 22–28.

Graff, C. S., & Vazquez, S. L. (2013). Family resistance as a tool in urban school reform. In E. B. Kozleski & K. K. Thorus (Eds.). *Ability, equity, and culture: Sustaining inclusive urban education reform* (pp. 80–106). Teachers College Press.

Grant, C. A., & Zwier, E. (2011). Intersectionality and student outcomes: Sharpening the struggle against racism, sexism, classism, ableism, heterosexism, nationalism, and linguistic, religious, and geographical discrimination in teaching and learning. *Multicultural Perspectives, 13*(4), 181–88.

Haffner, D. W. (2022). *Reflections from a lifetime advocating for sexual justice* [keynote presentation]. Sexual Health Program 2022 Plenary, University of Michigan.

Hansen, M., & Quintero, D. (2018). How gender diversity among the teacher workforce affects student learning. *Brown Center Chalkboard*. Brookings. https://www.brookings.edu/blog/brown-center-chalkboard/2018/07/10/how-gender-diversity-among-the-teacher-workforce-affects-student-learning/

Hellemans, H., Roeyers, H., Leplae, W., Dewaele, T., & Deboutte, D. (2010). Sexual behavior in male adolescents and young adults with autism spectrum disorder and borderline/mild mental retardation. *Sexuality and Disability, 28*(2), 93–104.

Hoover, J. J., & Soltero-González, L. (2018). Educator preparation for developing culturally and linguistically responsive MTSS in rural community elementary schools. *Teacher Education and Special Education, 41*(3), 188–202.

Ingersoll, R., Merrill, E., Stuckey, D., Collins, G., & Harrison, B. (2021). Seven trends: The transformation of the teaching force. *Research Report*. Consortium for Policy Research in Education, University of Pennsylvania.

Integrated Multi-Tiered System of Support. (2021). I-MTSS Research Network. https://mtss.org/overview/

Kirk, G., & Okazawa-Rey, M. (2010). Identities and social locations: Who am I? Who are my people? In M. Adams, W. J. Blumenfeld, R. Castañeda, H. W. Hackman, M. L. Peters, & X. Zúñiga (Eds.), *Readings for diversity and social justice* (chapter 2, pp. 8–14).

Ladson-Billings, G. (1995). Toward a theory of culturally relevant pedagogy. *American Educational Research Journal, 32*(3), 465–91.

Lai, M. C., Lombardo, M. V., Pasco, G., Ruigrok, A. N., Wheelwright, S. J., Sadek, S. A., . . . Baron-Cohen, S. (2011). A behavioral comparison of male and female adults with high functioning autism spectrum conditions. *PloS ONE, 6*(6), e20835.

Leonard, W., & Mann, R. (2018). *The everyday experiences of lesbian, gay, bisexual, transgender and intersex (LGBTI) people living with disability.* No. 111 GLHV@ARCSHS, La Trobe University.

Lindau, S. T., Laumann E. O., Levinson W., & Waite, L. J. (2003). Synthesis of scientific disciplines in pursuit of health: The Interactive Biopsychosocial Model. *Perspectives in Biology and Medicine, 46*(3), S74–86. https://doi.org/10.1353/pbm.2003.0055

Löfgren-Mårtenson, L. (2009). The invisibility of young homosexual women and men with intellectual disabilities. *Sexuality and Disability, 27*(1), 21–26.

Losen, D., Hodson, C., Ee, J., & Martinez, T. (2014). Disturbing inequities: Exploring the relationship between racial disparities in special education identification and discipline. *Journal of Applied Research on Children, 5*(2), 15.

Maroto, M., Pettinicchio, D., & Patterson, A. C. (2019). Hierarchies of categorical disadvantage: Economic insecurity at the intersection of disability, gender, and race. *Gender & Society, 33*(1), 64–93. https://doi.org/10.1177/0891243218794648

Marsh, L. T. S., & Walker, L. J. (2022). Deficit-oriented beliefs, anti-Black policies, punitive practices, and labeling: Exploring the mechanisms of disproportionality and its impact on Black boys in one urban "No-Excuses" charter school. *Teachers College Record, 124*(2), 85–116.

McCollow, M. M., Heroux, J. R., & Kemper, T. (2021). Supporting the right to gender and sexuality diversity and disability. In E. H. Harkins Monaco, M. C. Fuller, & L. L. Stansberry Brusnahan (Eds.), *Diversity, autism and developmental disabilities: Guidance for the culturally sustaining educator.* CEC DADD Prism Series.

Mendoza, M., Blake, J. J., Marchbanks, M. P., & Ragan, K. (2020). Race, gender, and disability and the risk for juvenile justice contact. *Journal of Special Education, 53*(4), 226–35. https://doi.org/10.1177/0022466919845113

Montalvo, R., Combes, B. H., & Kea, C. D. (2014). Perspectives on culturally and linguistically responsive RTI pedagogics through a cultural and linguistic lens. *Interdisciplinary Journal of Teaching and Learning, 4*(3), 203–19.

Murphy, N. A., & Elias, E. R. (Council on Children With Disabilities). (2006). Sexuality of children and adolescents with developmental disabilities. *Pediatrics, 118*(1), 398–403.

National Center for Learning Disabilities (NCLD). (2020). *Significant disproportionality in special education: Current trends and actions for impact.* 1–14. Washington, DC. https://www.ncld.org/wp-content/uploads/2020/10/2020-NCLD-Disproportionality_Trends-and-Actions-for-Impact_FINAL-1.pdf

National Research Council. (2002). *Minority students in special and gifted education.* Committee on Minority Representation in Special Education. Division of Behavior and Social Sciences and Education. National Academy Press.

New Jersey Coalition for Inclusive Education. (2013). *Plotting your course: A guide to using the maps process for planning inclusive opportunities and facilitating transitions.* https://

static1.squarespace.com/static/5b0edb3f266c07458c681630/t/5b730a1121c67c6a5339e474/1534265887736/MAPS+Manual+.pdf

O'Connor, C., & Fernandez, S. D. (2006). Race, class, and disproportionality: Reevaluating the relationship between poverty and special education placement. *Educational Researcher, 35*(6), 6–11.

Paris, D., & Alim, H. S. (Eds.). (2017). *Culturally sustaining pedagogies: Teaching and learning for justice in a changing world.* Teachers College Press.

Parish-Morris, J., Liberman, M. Y., Cieri, C., Herrington, J. D., Yerys, B. E., Bateman, L. . . . & Schultz, R. T. (2017). Linguistic camouflage in girls with autism spectrum disorder. *Molecular Autism, 8*(1), 48. https://doi.org/10.1186/s13229-017-0164-6

Pearpoint, J., O'Brien, J., & Forest, M. (1993). *Planning possible positive futures (PATH): Planning Alternative Tomorrows with Hope (PATH) for schools organizations, businesses, and families.* Inclusion.

Perouse-Harvey, E. (2022). Seeing the unseen: Applying intersectionality and disability critical race theory (DisCrit) frameworks in preservice teacher education. *Teachers College Record, 124*(7), 51–81. https://journals.sagepub.com/doi/abs/10.1177/01614681221111429

Petersen, A. (2006). An African-American woman with disabilities: The intersection of gender, race, and disability. *Disability & Society, 21*(7), 721–34. https://doi.org/10.1080/09687590600995345

———. (2009). "Ain't nobody gonna get me down": An examination of the educational experiences of four African American women labeled with disabilities. *Equity & Excellence in Education, 42*(4), 428–42. https://doi.org/10.1080/10665680903245284

Proctor, S. L., Graves Jr., S. L., & Esch, R. C. (2012). Assessing African American students for Specific Learning Disabilities: The promises and perils of response to intervention. *Journal of Negro Education, 81*(3), 268. https://doi.org/10.7709/jnegroeducation.81.3.0268

Ray, V. (2019). A theory of racialized organizations. *American Sociological Review, 84*(1), 26–53. https://doi.org/10.1177/0003122418822335

Rose, C., & Frederick-Clarke, H. (2016). *Culturally and linguistically sustaining practices (C.L.S.P) continuum.* Boston Public Schools Office of Opportunity Gaps. https://www.bostonpublicschools.org/cms/lib/MA01906464/Centricity/Domain/2218/OG%20CLSP%20Continuum.pdf

Rueda, E. (2015). The benefits of being Latino: Differential interpretations of student behavior and the social construction of being well behaved. *Journal of Latinos and Education, 14*(4), 275–90. https://doi.org/10.1080/15348431.2015.1025955

Rynkiewicz, A. (2011). The use of computer technology and the internet in teaching and therapy of individuals with autism spectrum disorders (ASD). *Annales Universitatis Paedagogicae Cracoviensis. Studia Psychologica, 4*(1), 161–73.

Schifter, L., Grindal, T., Schwartz, G., & Hehir, T. (2019, January). *Students from low-income families and special education.* Century Foundation. https://tcf.org/content/report/students-low-income-families-special-education/

Servais, L. (2006). Sexual health care in persons with intellectual disabilities. *Mental Retardation and Developmental Disabilities Research Reviews, 12*(1), 48–56.

Shifrer, D. (2013). Stigma of a label: Educational expectations for high school students labeled with learning disabilities. *Journal of Health and Social Behavior, 54*(4), 462–80.

———. (2018). Clarifying the social roots of the disproportionate classification of racial minorities and males with learning disabilities. *Sociological Quarterly, 59*(3), 384–406.

Shifrer, D., & Fish, R. (2020). A multilevel investigation into contextual reliability in the designation of cognitive health conditions among US children. *Society and Mental Health, 10*(2), 180–97.

Skiba, R. J., Arredondo, M. I., & Williams, N. T. (2014). More than a metaphor: The contribution of exclusionary discipline to a school-to-prison pipeline. *Equity & Excellence in Education, 47*(4), 546–64. https://doi.org/10.1080/10665684.2014.958965

Skiba, R. J., Poloni-Staudinder, L., Gallini, S., Simmons, A. B., & Feggins-Azzis, R. (2006). Disparate access: The disproportionality of African American students with disabilities across educational environments. *Exceptional Children, 72*(4), 411–24.

Snydman, J. (2022). *Unlocking futures: Youth with learning disabilities and the juvenile justice system*. National Center for Learning Disabilities.

Staats, C. (2016). Understanding implicit bias: What educators should know. *American Educator, 39*(4), 29.

Studocu. (2012). What are social identities? List the big 8 identities. https://www.studocu.com/en-gb/document/university-of-oxford/sociology/sociology-social-identities-what-are-social-identities-list-the-big-8-identities/26008773

Sullivan, A. L., Sadeh, S., & Houri, A. K. (2019). Are school psychologists' special education eligibility decisions reliable and unbiased?: A multi-study experimental investigation. *Journal of School Psychology, 77*, 90–109. https://doi.org/10.1016/j.jsp.2019.10.006

Sullivan, E. T. (2021). School counselors have implicit bias. Some are ready to address it. EdSurge News. https://www.edsurge.com/news/2021-04-06-school-counselors-have-implicit-bias-some-are-ready-to-address-it

Toft, A., & Franklin, A. (2020). Sexuality and gender identity in the lives of young, disabled LGBT+ persons: Initiating a dialogue. In *Young, Disabled and LGBT+* (pp. 3–12). Routledge.

Triplett, N. P., Allen, A., & Lewis, C. W. (2014). Zero tolerance, school shootings, and the post-Brown quest for equity in discipline policy: An examination of how urban minorities are punished for white suburban violence. *Journal of Negro Education, 83*(3), 352–70.

US Census Bureau. (2021). *2019 National and state population estimates*. https://www.census.gov/newsroom/press-kits/2019/national-state-estimates.html

US Department of Education NCES 2006-071. (2006). *The condition of education 2006*. http://www.nces.ed.gov/pubs2006/2006071.pdf

Vaughn, M., Silver, K., Murphy, S., Ashbaugh, R., & Hoffman, A. (2015). Women with disabilities discuss sexuality in San Francisco focus groups. *Sexuality and Disability, 33*(1), 19–46.

Vinney, C. (2019). Understanding Social Identity Theory and its impact on behavior. ThoughtCo. https://www.thoughtco.com/social-identity-theory-4174315

Voulgarides, C. K., Zwerger, N., & Noguera, P. (2013). *Identifying the root causes of disproportionality*. New York University Technical Assistance Center on Disproportionality.

Waitoller, F. R., Artiles, A. J., & Cheney, D. A. (2010). The miner's canary: A review of overrepresentation research and explanations. *Journal of Special Education, 44*(1), 29–49.

Wakelin, M. M. (2008). Challenging disparities in special education: Moving parents from disempowered team members to ardent advocates. *Northeastern Journal of Law and Social Policy, 3*(2), 263.

Warrier, V., Greenberg, D. M., Weir, E., Buckingham, C., Smith, P., Lai, M. C., . . . Baron-Cohen, S. (2020). Elevated rates of autism, other neurodevelopmental and psychiatric diagnoses, and autistic traits in transgender and gender-diverse individuals. *Nature Communications, 11*(1), 3959. https://doi.org/10.1038/s41467-020-17794-1

Weeks, J. (1998). The sexual citizen. *Theory, Culture & Society, 15*(3–4), 35–52.

Wehmeyer, M. L. (2013). *The story of intellectual disability*. Brookes.

Wehmeyer, M., Lawrence, M., Garner, N., Soukup, J., & Palmer, S. (2004). *Whose future is it anyway? A student-directed transition planning process*. 2nd ed. Beach Center on Disability.

West-Olatunji, C. A., & Baker, J. C. (2006). African American adolescent males: Giving voice to their educational experiences. *Multicultural Perspective, 8*(4), 3–9.

Wilkinson, V. J., Theodore, K., & Raczka, R. (2015). "As normal as possible": Sexual identity development in people with intellectual disabilities transitioning to adulthood. *Sexuality and Disability, 33*(1), 93–105.

Wilson, D. (2006). Gender identity, cross-dressing and gender reassignment and people with learning disabilities. *Tizard Learning Disability Review, 11*(2), 4–11. https://doi.org/10.1108/13595474200600012

World Health Organization (WHO). (2006). Defining sexual health. *Sexual and reproductive health (SRH)*. https://www.who.int/teams/sexual-and-reproductive-health-and-research/key-areas-of-work/sexual-health/defining-sexual-health

CHAPTER 3

Disability Culture in the Deaf and Autistic Communities

Chapter authors: *Gulnoza Yakubova, John Pirone, and Veronica Y. Kang*

Vignette authors: *John Pirone, Dylan Kapit, and James Williams*

Editor: *Elizabeth A. Harkins Monaco*

ABSTRACT

Through self-determination, self-advocacy, and shared space, language, and experience, different disability communities have fostered a sense of belonging. The purpose of this chapter is to discuss how Deaf and Autistic communities cultivated their Deaf and Autistic identities and the impact of disability culture on education. We provide a framework of equity to help understand what conditions render equity and inequity for the signing Deaf and Autistic communities.

GUIDING QUESTIONS

- What are examples of sociocultural disabled identities?
- How is disability culture reflected globally?
- What is the impact of disability culture on education?
- What implications does disability culture hold for practitioners in educational contexts?

KEY TERMS

American Sign Language
Audism
Autism
Autistic Identity
Autistic Self-Advocacy Network
Deaf-Centric and ASL-Centric Spaces
Deaf Culture
Deaf Gain
Deaf Space
DEAF-WORLD
Deafhood
Deafness
Dysconscious Audism
Equity Literacy
Formulated Experiences
Independence
Linguicism
Medical Model of Disability
Neurodiversity
Self-Determination
Strength-Based Approach

Throughout history, people with disabilities have fought to create their own culturally disabled senses of identity, shared understanding, and mutual connection in relation to language, cultural expressions, and a sense of pride in their disabled identities. For instance, Deaf people have a culture of their own, a language of their own, and a community of their own. **Deaf culture** refers to a group of deaf people who share similar experiences of being deaf, signed languages, beliefs, values, norms, histories, and arts (Holcomb, 2012; Leigh et al., 2020). Culturally Deaf people embrace and celebrate their Deaf identity. This may be no surprise to some, but many nondeaf people find it intriguing, perplexing, or shocking. It may be even more shocking to learn that Deaf culture is not a contemporary phenomenon as it has been around since the 1700s.

Similarly, **neurodiversity**, or neurological diversity, offers a frame to (a) increase acceptance and inclusion of neurological differences; (b) form a shared identity; and (c) defy oppression (Singer, 2017). Coined by Judy Singer in 1998, the origin of the term neurodiversity goes back to the autism rights movement but different disability communities have adopted the term (Kapp, 2020) to promote equity and inclusion. Neurodiversity incorporates the fundamental identity of neurologically diverse (i.e., neurodivergent) people and calls for efforts to improve the accessibility of society toward people (Botha & Gillespie-Lynch, 2022; Fletcher-Watson et al., 2018). Figure 3.1 gives examples of some neurodiversity, but we are not suggesting this is an exhaustive list.

Though currently neurodiversity encompasses other disabilities, this chapter focuses specifically on Autistic identity. The **Autistic identity** embraces a sense of identity and sees autism as a different way of thinking and functioning rather than an illness or deficit to be cured (Singer, 2017).

The purpose of this chapter is to give readers a broad overview of how certain disability groups have connected with their disabled identity as a sociocultural construct, particularly within the context of the Deaf and Autistic communities. The chapter discusses the impact of disability as a sociocultural

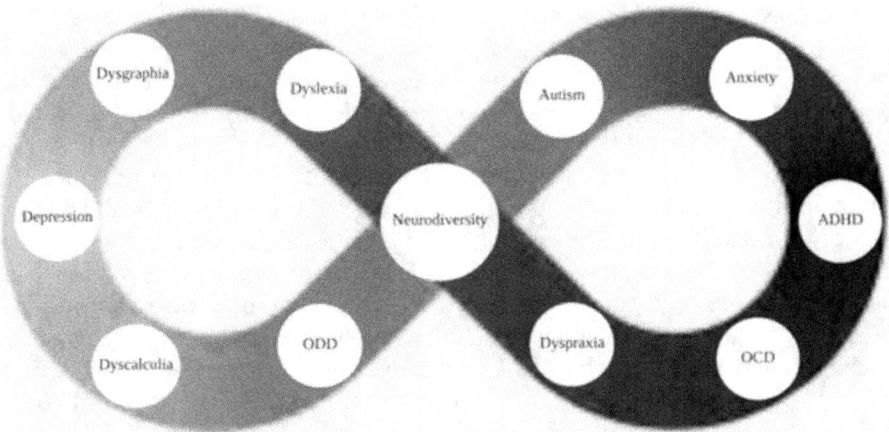

Figure 3.1. Neurodiversity

identity on education and offers a framework to understand the conditions which render equity and inequity for individuals from the signing Deaf and Autistic communities.

DISABILITY AS A SOCIOCULTURAL IDENTITY

This chapter discusses how the Autistic and Deaf communities express their Autistic and Deaf identities through art, language, humor, shared history, lived experiences, values, and beliefs (Gill, 1995, p. 18). These communities embrace **disability culture**. Disability culture is nuanced: (a) there are many kinds of disability cultures; (b) disability intersects with other sociocultural identities, experiences, and relationships; and (c) disability is not a monolith in that one group or community can differ from another (Peters, 2000). More details can be found in chapter 1.

Deaf Identity and Culture

Before we discuss Deaf culture further, it is important to understand the meaning of **deafness** given that there are two completely different perspectives. One is the biomedical perspective that being deaf is biologically defective and needs to be corrected (Reagan et al., 2020). This perspective is rooted in the notion of normalcy that disability is abnormal (Annamma et al., 2013). The other perspective is sociocultural and biocultural that being Deaf is a gain and that being Deaf offers a rich language, culture, and community (Bauman & Murray, 2009). Culturally, Deaf people reject the biomedical perspective because it denies their own existence and does not embrace Deaf culture. For this chapter, the term "deaf" refers to those who are biologically and corporally deaf without any specific reference to whether or not they use sign language or identify with Deaf culture (Kusters et al., 2017). If a particular group of deaf people use sign language or practice Deaf culture, then the appropriate terms to describe them are "signing Deaf" or "culturally Deaf," but with an important understanding that the terms are not mutually exclusive (Kusters et al., 2017).

The current literature shows that Deaf culture has been around since the eighteenth century when the first deaf school in the world was established in France (Holcomb, 2012; Lane et al., 1996; Leigh et al., 2020; Padden & Humphries, 1988). The establishment of the first school created a space for Deaf people to come together, interact in their own ways, develop ways of communication, and connect their shared experiences of being deaf. This space is called **Deaf space** or what deaf people would sign **DEAF-WORLD**, which refers to Deaf people getting together in certain places such as social clubs, political associations, and deaf schools, not to a specific geographic location (Lane et al., 1996). The deaf space or DEAF-WORLD is what created Deaf culture and Deaf community (Holcomb, 2012; Lane et al., 1996; Leigh et al., 2020; Padden & Humphries, 1988).

American Sign Language (ASL) is one of the signed languages that is commonly used among deaf people in the United States. ASL is a full and natural language with its own structure and does not represent spoken language. Tapping on the shoulder to get one's attention, maintaining eye contact, and giving detailed information are several instances of cultural norms. ASL is one important element of Deaf culture; other cultural elements include communal beliefs, values, history, art, and literature. Signing Deaf people have a range of beliefs and values such as being Deaf is a gift and having Deaf children is important for the existence of signed languages, Deaf culture, and communities. Signing Deaf people have produced a great variety of artistic works such as ASL poetry, folklores, storytelling, and humor. There are many well-known names and literary works that signify Deaf culture. Structural racism, sexism, and other oppressive systems exist within Deaf communities including Deaf schools where white people are the majority, and, as a result, Deaf artists of the global majority are often denied opportunities to showcase their expression of art. This is why we are highlighting them here: Dr. Nathie Marbury, Manny Hernandez, Mark Morales, Rosa Lee Timm, and Justin Perez.

Not all deaf people are members of Deaf culture for various reasons. One is that the term "deaf" also includes those with a range of hearing levels and those who lose hearing due to illness or age. Most people with mild hearing loss or who lose hearing over time often have little or no interest in becoming a member of Deaf culture because they are experiencing a completely different phenomenon where they do not rely on visual and manual modality for their everyday lives and rarely access deaf space. The second reason is the presence of **audism**, which is the notion that being able to hear is superior (Humphries, 1977). Ninety-six percent of all deaf children have nondeaf parents and nondeaf parents often receive advice from medical teams, educational professionals, and several organizations discouraging the use of sign languages and participation in Deaf culture (Hall, 2017; Humphries et al., 2017; Murray et al., 2019). As a result, those deaf individuals may internalize a form of audism or **dysconscious audism** (Gentz, 2003), which means that they accept dominant hearing privileges and norms. Those individuals with dysconscious audism struggle to see themselves as a part of Deaf culture until they overcome audist barriers to gain access to Deaf spaces and receive more exposure to Deaf culture.

VIGNETTE 1: *MEET JOHN*

I am a signing Deaf, white, straight, cisgender male. I am only deaf in the hearing family. My parents did not accept it when they learned that I was deaf until they received similar opinions from different doctors. My mother did a lot of research, which is a rarity for most nondeaf parents, and visited several different schools. She and my father decided to place me in one deaf school whose approach was to teach both signed English and oralism (spoken English).

Globally, there is no universal Deaf culture or signed language. Most countries have their own Deaf culture and signed language. According to the World Federation of the Deaf (2023), 193 countries each have their own signed language(s) and 74 of them officially recognize a signed language(s) (World Federation of the Deaf, 2023). While there are no official statistics on the number of countries that have a Deaf culture, it is highly likely that those countries with the presence of signed language also have a Deaf culture. Many studies share a similar argument that language and culture are interrelated and inseparate. As those 193 countries have signed languages and cultures, they do not share the same language or culture due to different geographical boundaries and varying legal, social, and economic conditions.

In terms of deaf experiences, Deaf people from all over the world may share similar experiences. For example, two American scholars created a concept called **Deaf Gain** that challenges the ideology of normalcy and argues that being deaf has intrinsic and extrinsic values (Bauman & Murray, 2014). Deaf people in India found the concept to be true and created a video promoting Deaf Gain with examples of their own experiences (Sign Library, 2022). Another example is that deaf people in the United States strongly promote the concept of **Deafhood** that was first introduced in the United Kingdom in 2003. Deafhood is a journey that each deaf individual has to find their Deaf identity (Ladd, 2003). Not all deaf individuals have the same journey or process toward the actualization of their Deaf identity because they do not share similar external conditions such as familial support, availability and usage of language and communication, education (i.e., deaf school and public school), and the presence of deaf role models and peers. Deaf Americans and deaf Britons share similar experiences when it comes to their Deaf identity processes.

VIGNETTE 2: *JOHN'S HOME ENVIRONMENT*

Before I discuss in detail my educational experience, I want to share my home environment that played a role in my journey. My parents and siblings took a few sign language classes so they could communicate with me. My mother was the most fluent in my family and other members used a mix of communication—home signs, fingerspelling, and some signs. During breakfast and dinner time, long trips, and bedtime, my parents and siblings rarely engaged me in a meaningful conversation or a story. My communication with them was often superficial. There was never a moment where they talked about Deaf culture. I recall several moments where my parents mentioned the possibility of a cure for deafness (cochlear implants and reported miracles in Yugoslavia) and, at that time, I was surprisingly excited. Even though my family is literally wonderful and loving, the home environment did not nurture my Deaf identity and misled me into thinking that being deaf is not normal. Having the thought of deaf not being normal is what prevented me from embracing my own Deaf identity and what made me want to be like hearing people.

Autistic Identity and Culture

Autism was previously identified as a rare clinical disorder with childhood onset (Kanner, 1943) and people with an autism diagnosis were thought to require institutionalization. Yet over the decades, understanding of autism has expanded to include autistic people without what was classified as significant language, cognitive, and adaptive behavior challenges (American Psychiatric Association [APA], 1994). While initially considered a disease or a debilitating childhood condition that inhibited prospects for independent living, education, and employment, **autism** is now a widely recognized neurodevelopmental disability described as a spectrum of conditions (APA, 2013). Autism is a lifelong disability with heterogeneous characteristics (Happé & Frith, 2020), where each person can display diverse characteristics which led Autistic people to coin the slogan "If you met one autistic person, you met one autistic person" (Shore, 2003).

Similarly to the disability rights movement described in chapters 10 and 11, in recent years Autistic people started to form their own social justice movement in which they recognize and advocate for identity as a form of neurological diversity, hence, the neurodiversity movement was born (Singer, 2017). In 2004, the **Autistic Self Advocacy Network** (ASAN) in the United States was formed with the goal to advocate for the rights of Autistic people so that Autistic people have equal access, rights, and opportunities and make their voices heard in the conversations that affect them, with the slogan "Nothing about us without us" (Charlton, 2000). The humanness of an Autistic identity challenges the notion that difficulties in social interaction, one of the core diagnostic features of autism, are relational. The neurodiversity movement resists efforts to camouflage autistic behaviors in order to fit the "normal" way of functioning expected in mainstream society (Singer, 2017).

One of the core features of the neurodiversity framework is embracing **Autistic identity** rather than seeing it as something to cure. The majority of Autistic people identify themselves as "Actually Autistic" and use identity-first language, however, many still feel that their voices are not heard and that people without disabilities utilize deficit-focused perspectives in research and practice (Jones et al., 2020). For more on identity-first language, see chapters 6 and 11.

> **VIGNETTE 3: *HOW JAMES LEARNED ABOUT AUTISTIC CULTURE***
>
> *My name is James Williams and I am a non-Hispanic white, autistic, cisgender male who goes by he/him/his pronouns. One element that has become a defining part of "autistic culture" is the preference among many autistic adults to be referred to via "identity-first language" (as an autistic person) versus "person-first language" (as a person with autism), which is the preferred form of language among people with most other disabilities. Although this preference may seem odd as it deviates from the preferences of many people with other disabilities, it actually has a logical explanation, one that is rooted in the origins of autistic culture.*
>
> *I started attending an all-inclusive disability conference annually that was mostly comprised of attendees of all disabilities and their families. While at that conference, I myself dealt with many social challenges while attempting to meet people with other disabilities, and also learned about some of the origins of the "identity-first language" preferences among many autistic people. It was explained to me that, historically, due to those social challenges, many autistic people have never been fully accepted into the disability community at large. This community, in turn, is the community that has encouraged and promoted "person-first language" for disabled people.*
>
> *The end result is that many autistic people, unable to find acceptance in either the disability community or the neurotypical world, created their own "autistic culture" independently of the disability community. In the process, "autistic culture" has attempted to establish that "identity-first language" is the preferred language for autistic people. One of the reasons why this choice was made is based on the experiences that many autistic people have had wherein they are inherently unable to separate their identity from being autistic; because autistic people routinely engage in behaviors revealing with autism on a daily basis, many autistic people cannot separate their personhood from their autism—thus, they prefer to be called "autistic people," because to them, that is technically what they are.*

Another example of constructing identity rather than using a diagnostic label is evident among people diagnosed with Asperger's syndrome. We acknowledge the sordid history of Hans Asperger (see chapter 10), but studies have shown that people with Asperger's have actively identified themselves as part of the specific affinity group Aspie identity and community, thus, framing their diagnosis and disability as a cultural identity (Parsloe, 2015). Similarly, Autistic people—including those who were diagnosed as adults—describe the process of constructing their identity following their diagnosis of autism. The diagnosis served as a pathway to finding their identity and affinity groups, and creating positive self-perceptions by moving away from "an abnormal neurotypical" to "a normal autistic person" (Tan, 2018). Yet, Autistic identity can look different for each person based on other identities intersecting with the person and their experiences with the environments around them (Cohen et al., 2022). Examining Autistic identity development through an intersectional lens is an emerging area of work in understanding the diversity of Autistic people's identities and how these shape their lived experiences throughout each person's lifespan (Botha & Gillespie-Lynch, 2022; Cohen et al., 2022).

VIGNETTE 4: *MEET DYLAN*

I am a white, queer, transmasculine, nonbinary, Jewish, mentally ill, autistic individual who also has Attention Deficit Hyperactivity Disorder (ADHD). Aside from my social identities, I also strongly identify as an educator. My background is in elementary special education, and now I am almost finished with a PhD in Special Education, where my focus is on creating a queer- and trans-inclusive, autistic-focused sex education curriculum. Like many people who were assigned female at birth, I was not formally diagnosed with autism as a kid, and have self-diagnosed as an adult. However, despite not being diagnosed and not being in any sort of specialized setting, being autistic deeply informed my K–12 experience. I was diagnosed with ADHD in elementary school, and have been on stimulants ever since. I do not think I would have graduated from high school, college, or graduate school without the help of medication. Now frequently referred to as twice exceptional, the label that I was given in elementary school was gifted and talented learning disabled (GTLD). I did not struggle academically and in fact excelled, but my neurodivergence impacted me in many other ways.

Cohen et al. (2022) explored the identity development of Autistic adolescents and adults (ages 15–35) in the United States found that receiving stigmatizing messages about autism from teachers and peers was common, especially following the disclosure of an autism diagnosis. Both peers and teachers had narrow and negative views of these students, viewing them through a deficit lens rather than seeing strengths and other parts of identities. Furthermore, when examining the intersection of autism with other sociocultural identities (e.g., gender, sexual orientation, racial or ethnic diversities), Autistic women and non-white Autistic people reported experiencing more negative attitudes and biases from teachers than Autistic men and white Autistics. Yet these Autistic people constructed their Autistic identities, and other identities intersecting with their Autistic identities, while resisting negative and ableist comments and stigma from their peers and teachers (Cohen et al., 2022).

VIGNETTE 5: *DYLAN'S SCHOOL EXPERIENCES*

The main way that my undiagnosed autism impacted my K–12 experience was mostly through my social life. I was a very "quirky" or "weird" kid, and so I got bullied a lot. I did not really know how to make friends or how to be a good friend, and as a result I did not really have good friends until I got to college. In elementary school, the bullying got so bad that I frequently elected to spend recess indoors. There was not someone inside to watch me, so I would usually spend recess in the special education classroom with the students who could not go outside for recess, which is where I fell in love with disability work. I attribute my love of the disability world to these experiences as a child. I came out as queer in middle school, which increased the bullying tenfold in middle and high school.

I do not think I got what I needed in most ways at all throughout my K–12 education, and it wasn't until I went off to college that I got to explore all the ways that my various marginalized identities all intersected with my educational experiences. I think I felt incredibly stuck during my formative K–12 education years, and it wasn't until I moved to New York City for college that I got to explore the freedom that came with claiming my identities. In fact, the day after I graduated high school, I came out as trans and changed my name, and I have never once looked back!

Growing up undiagnosed autistic and then coming out as queer as a kid was definitely not easy, and a lot of that is because those identities were not being openly discussed while I was growing up, and therefore I don't think any of the adults in my life really knew how to meet my needs.

My elementary school teachers were definitely not all the way sure what to do with me, or how to teach in ways that would help me succeed. I was very successful academically, but I was struggling in many other ways and I do not think my teachers knew enough about autism or neurodivergence at the time to support me in ways that would have set me up to be successful in other ways. The stereotypes about autistic folks who were assigned female at birth definitely all applied to me, as I was definitely pretending that I knew what was going on socially and masking in order to fit in, when in reality I was always absolutely clueless as to what I was "supposed" to be doing. By the time I got to middle and high school, I was masking my autism all of the time in order to avoid being bullied for being "weird," but by that time I had come out as queer and was being bullied for that instead.

The fact that I was very successful academically definitely got in the way of me getting other types of services that I needed, because I was "too smart to be autistic." As someone who now does autism research, it has been really interesting to discover how rapidly our understanding of autism has changed since I was growing up, and even more over the past few years. I grew up with significant financial privilege which meant that I had access to some of the best doctors, but even the world-renowned psychologist who did my neuropsychological evaluations missed that I had autism, so I think I am a great example of how the narrative that autism is a boys' disorder directly harms people assigned female at birth.

Since no one was discussing this with me as a child, all my exploration of all my identities, both the marginalized ones and the privileged ones, has had to happen as an adult.

DISABILITY CULTURE IN EDUCATIONAL CONTEXTS

What implications does disability culture hold for practitioners in educational contexts? In the United States, two concepts—**independence** and **self-determination**—come to mind when talking about ways disabled people create cultures. In a participatory action research study of thirty disabled university students in the Midwest region of the United States, one of the values that defined their disability culture was **independence** (Forber-Pratt, 2019). Independence was valuable as it involved centering their voices and capacity, for instance, by using equipment and devices (i.e., wheelchairs, prosthetic) and taking care of personal hygiene independently (Forber-Pratt, 2019).

Self-Determination

In the disability literature, the term **self-determination** has been used to refer to the state of being autonomous, to make choices, develop goals, and advocate for oneself (Wehmeyer & Palmer, 2000). Self-determination is defined in countries of the Western hemisphere, and tends to value individualistic pursuits over collective pursuits. In fact, it is one of the predictors of success in adult life in the Western hemisphere (Shogren & Ward, 2018). For instance, autistic college students in the United Kingdom who acted in a self-determined manner were able to positively influence their academic, socialization, daily living, and other aspects of their university experiences (Lei & Russell, 2021).

While independence and self-determination are important concepts in some communities (e.g., Western hemisphere), there are geographical differences in what communities value and how different disability groups create their disability identity and affinity groups. Furthermore, the majority of self-determination research has been spearheaded by scholars in the Western hemisphere and tested with the participant samples in certain geographic regions. Yet when scholars explored the concept of self-determination with individuals from other geographic locations, participants expressed different viewpoints on their values and notions of independence and self-determination. Kim et al. (2022) interviewed five Korean American mothers of 7- to 13-year-old autistic youth and found that the Korean American autistic youth valued disabled individuals collectively, alongside their family members, with particular relevance toward older individuals (e.g., caregivers) or individuals of higher authority (e.g., service providers). They valued working together to make decisions and set goals for the future that aligned with the desires, needs, and values of the family as a whole rather than each individual member of the family (Kim et al., 2022). Another study conducted with parents of young autistic children in Taiwan found that parents highly valued the need to promote self-determination skills in their children from young ages but struggled promoting self-determination (Chu, 2018) pending on what was considered the severity of the child's condition and other cultural factors, such as environment and family systems. Another study examined the perceptions of preservice special education teachers in Saudi Arabia about the alignment of self-determination theory as used in Western countries and the cultural assumptions (Alansari, 2021). These preservice practitioners (PSP) perceived the need to use collectivist approaches rather than the individualistic approach as recommended in self-determination theory. For more examples of how collectivism could be considered in special education, see chapters 9 and 12.

These findings provide implications for practitioners such as childcare providers, general and special educators, or other related service providers who collaborate with diverse children within the larger disability communities, cultures, and diverse geographic regions. For practitioners who collaborate with older individuals (i.e., adolescents and adults), these findings provide insights to what disabled individuals and their family members value and prefer with regard to decision-making and goal-setting processes, and to what degree collective, family-centered approaches should be valued. See chapter 9 for examples of how this contributes to disproportionality in disciplinary action. Practitioners should use caution in generalizing these findings and learn individual student and family priorities, needs, and preferences to inform their selection of research-based practices and guide their work accordingly.

Disability Culture in Schools

This section will focus on the differences between mainstream schools and deaf schools. Mainstream schools are where most teachers and students are nondeaf and English speakers and English is the only medium of instruction. Deaf students attending mainstream schools will need accommodations to access English-centered instruction and communication. Deaf schools are completely different, especially those promoting bilingual-bicultural policies and practices, in that all students are deaf and the medium of instruction is sign language. The key difference between the types of school is equitable space. Deaf schools with bilingual-bicultural approaches provide language space where deaf students build their own language and receive instruction in their own language, cultural space where deaf students develop their cultural identity, and social space where deaf students interact with their own peers, freely engage in extracurricular activities and leadership opportunities, and access their own communities. Mainstream schools do not provide similar spaces as deaf schools but accommodations for deaf students to access their hearing- and English-centered space.

The current educational policies and practices have a profound impact on Deaf culture and signed languages in numerous ways. The federal law, Individuals with Disabilities Education Act (IDEA), is one prime example. This law, enacted in 1990, protects disabled students' rights to public education. The two key principles of IDEA are inclusion and least restrictive environment

(LRE). Public schools are required to provide disabled students with access to the general education curriculum at no cost and to ensure that disabled students receive support and access services. For more information about IDEA, see chapters 10 and 11. Since the enactment of IDEA, the number of deaf students being placed in public schools increased significantly while fewer deaf students went to deaf schools. According to the National Center for Education Statistics (NCES, 2019), 88 percent of all deaf students attended public schools as opposed to almost 8 percent in deaf schools. IDEA has also affected the choice of language and communication methods for deaf students. From 2000 to 2012, the Gallaudet Research Institute (2013) shows that the number of deaf students using sign language decreased from 55 percent to 39 percent. IDEA is responsible for those placement and language shifts because it requires schools to create a team of professionals whose task is to develop an individualized education program (IEP) for each disabled student. IDEA affords the IEP team with the authority to determine placement options (i.e., mainstream school and deaf school) and language or communication methods for disabled students. Most IEP teams are nondeaf and English-speaking and have little or no knowledge of ASL and Deaf culture (Hall, 2017; Pirone, in press). In addition, IDEA has a particular stipulation that IEP teams need to consider the placement of disabled students in the least restrictive environment (e.g., public schools) as the first option (IDEA, 2004). These conditions are what contributed to the significant shift in the usage of sign language and the number of deaf students in deaf schools.

To nondeaf professionals, it may seem inclusive that 88 percent of all deaf students are now in public schools with nondeaf peers and that they are in the least restrictive environment with accommodations. However, deaf students' lived experiences show more exclusion than inclusion, even with accommodations. According to numerous studies, deaf students experienced a wide range of issues such as isolation, no or limited access to sign language, poor-quality interpreting and other services, and lack of deaf peers and teachers (Foster, 1989; Oliva, 2004; Oliva & Lytle, 2014; Pirone et al., 2018; Stinson & Liu, 1999). One common misconception nondeaf educators hold is that accommodations would make the environment less restrictive and more inclusive. For example, research has found that some ASL interpreters render barriers when they performed poorly due to their language proficiency, intercultural competence, and/or lack of professionalism (Pirone et al., 2018). Even with excellent services, deaf students still experience barriers and it's largely due to the centeredness of English and hearing ability in social, linguistic, and cultural spaces within public schools (Pirone & Mayo, 2022). This centeredness creates a key barrier to deaf students' ability to build their own language, cultural identity, and social connections with other peers with shared experiences and biocultural identity (being deaf). Accommodations such as interpreting services do not alter that centeredness but only facilitate deaf students' access to the majority's space. The deaf centeredness found in deaf schools is that they communicate and deliver instruction in sign language, impart their deaf epistemologies (knowledge and experiences) to deaf students, and, more importantly, provide spaces where deaf students can flourish socially, linguistically, and culturally.

> **Pause and Reflect**
>
> - Do schools acknowledge, incorporate or center disability culture? Why or why not?
> - What are the effects of not acknowledging disability as an identity to be proud of?
> - What are the possibilities of agency for disabled students, if they are educated in spaces that honor their disabled identities?
> - What are the possibilities of agency for nondisabled students, if they are educated in spaces that honor disabled identities?

VIGNETTE 6: *JOHN'S SCHOOL EXPERIENCES*

When I was 4 or 5 years old, I went to a deaf school. Everyone signed, but, at that time, it was not American Sign Language (ASL). The school used Signed Exact English (SEE), which is not a language but a sign system that tries to duplicate English. When I was in elementary school, I wore hearing aids and took classes to learn how to speak. All teachers were hearing. I recall three key moments that influenced my journey. One is that my parents sometimes asked me to show my speaking ability to their friends or relatives and were so joyous after I spoke certain words such as "happy birthday" and "apple pie." This moment gave me a sense that being able to speak was important and superior to sign language. The second moment was that I threw away my hearing aids in the forest near my school because I hated the feeling of vibration in my ears and I couldn't make sense of what each vibration meant. My parents were so upset about it and asked me to find the hearing aids, which were never found (intentionally). However, my parents eventually accepted the fact that hearing aids didn't work for me. The third moment, the memorable one, is a deaf storyteller, who came to my school once a week or so to share stories about her deaf experience. She used ASL and was culturally Deaf. I recall that I was mesmerized by her and her stories but did not take a moment to think about or make a connection between her stories and my identity. My school did not create time or space to discuss the stories and what they meant for me as a deaf student, and that they might make a difference in my journey.

As I moved to middle school and high school, the school made a huge change and they abandoned SEE and used ASL as the medium of instruction. The school also employed a bilingual and bicultural approach, but it was gradually incorporated into institutional policies and practices. I finally had a few deaf instructors who taught English, biology, and physical education. I recall that I was always excited when I was in classes with deaf instructors because

(continued)

VIGNETTE 6: *Continued*

it was so easy to learn and interact with them. All of my peers were deaf and used ASL. I played sports such as basketball and everyone signed. The strange thing is that I did not think about my identity and it was probably because it was the norm just like hearing people do not think about their hearing identity when they were in their own space. What was stranger is when I was in my sophomore year, I wanted to transfer to a public school because I did not feel like I had good academic skills. I remember clearly that I looked at my brother and how many books he had to carry to his school and looked at how many books I had to carry, which was none. This comparison gave me an idea that I was not smart and I wanted to be like my brother so I made a request to go to a public school. I ended up going to a public school for two years and I was the only signing deaf student there. I had one and the same interpreter for all classes and a private tutor, who was hearing and knew ASL, helped me with my English skills. I remember that I did not have any thought about my own identity or Deaf culture because I was so preoccupied on elevating my academic skills. I recall vividly that I felt good being in a public school because, based on my ill perception, I was finally normal just like everyone else.

The whole journey I had from elementary school to high school and home environment did not lead me to discover and embrace my Deaf identity until I went to college. I was able to actualize my Deaf identity when I met and interacted with deaf instructors and deaf peers who also happened to be community leaders and advocates when I was in college. I also took two college courses on Deaf culture and history and that made a huge difference.

Disability and Oppression in Schools

Through the macro lens, most barriers deaf students have experienced are a result of institutional policies, practices, and ideologies that are rooted in two forms of oppression—**audism** and **linguicism** (Bauman, 2004; Lane, 1992; Eckert & Rowley, 2013; Pirone, in press; Pirone & Mayo, 2022; Skutnabb-Kangas, 1988). Audism occurs when "one is superior based on one's ability to hear or behave in the manner of one who hears" (Humphries, 1977, p. 12). Linguicism differs from audism in that it is language-based. Linguicism is "ideologies, structures, and practices which are used to legitimate, effectuate, regulate and reproduce an unequal division of power and resources (both material and immaterial) between groups which are defined on the basis of language" (Skutnabb-Kangas, 1988, p. 13). One example is that, even though there are ample deaf and ASL-signing professionals, most English-speaking and nondeaf professionals are given the power to decide what, how, and where deaf students should learn, communicate, and interact. The second example is the space where English and the use of sound dominate and that has a strong effect on deaf students. The third example is the ideology that educators have about deafness and that influences their perception of ASL and Deaf culture. The prevailing notion of normalcy is that being deaf is not normal and that signing (e.g., American Sign Language) other than speaking English is considered inferior. This ideology is powerful because it can shape nondeaf professionals' decisions and practices.

Pause and Reflect

- What other types of disability oppression are found in schools?
- What does ableism look like in schools?

VIGNETTE 7: *JOHN'S DEAF IDENTITY AND CULTURE*

There were challenges and conflicts that were not a result of my identity and culture, rather, external conditions around me. In my home environment, all members were nondeaf and spoken English was the center of all conversations. In school, the majority were nondeaf and there were practices that made me learn how to speak and use a sign system. These conditions created a challenge for me to develop my Deaf identity because they gave me an idea that being deaf or ASL is not a norm. There was another condition that my school did not create any time or space for me to learn and discuss Deaf culture. Having a space like that would've helped me make sense of my own experiences, but it didn't happen.

I recognize that my other identities—white, male, cis, straight, and middle-class status—play a role in my journey. For instance, my parents lived in a wealthy town that was able to support the placement of me in a deaf school in a different town. Many deaf children and their parents did not have that privilege due to their subjugated identities. Also, given that my parents are white, abled, and financially comfortable, they had the privilege to access resources and advice from professionals. They received advice that I should wear hearing aids and learn to speak. As a result, that negatively affected my identity development. Interestingly, my privileged identities prolonged my progress toward my self-actualization of Deaf identity. For instance, I valued academic skills so much that that distracted me from exploring my own Deaf identity. This value may reflect whiteness, masculinity, and economic status.

INEQUITIES IN EDUCATION

To address inequities in education, practitioners need to consider several changes that they need to make. One is **equity literacy**. The framework of equity literacy is centered on one's understanding of equity and inequity and justice and injustice (Gorski & Swalwell, 2015). Equity literacy is completely different from cultural literacy and it has been argued that an understanding of a particular culture does not necessarily mean one will understand equity (Gorksi, 2016). Equity literacy helps educational practitioners build "the knowledge and skills necessary to become a threat to the existence of inequity in their spheres of influence" (Gorski, 2016, p. 225). Those with a high level of equity literacy will be able to recognize, respond, and redress inequity and then cultivate and sustain equity. Equity literacy helps educators and administrators recognize and use their sphere of influence to combat audism and linguicism that reside in institutional ideologies, policies, and practices (Pirone, in press). We suggest this will also combat ableism.

> **Pause and Reflect**
> - How can practitioners consider combat ableism?
> - How can practitioners engage with equity literacy to better understand equity and justice for disabled students, including those who also identify with other minoritized sociocultural identities?

The second change for practitioners to consider is to create **Deaf-centric** and **ASL-centric spaces** within public schools. Such spaces make it possible for signing deaf students to learn and build their signed language skills, Deaf cultural identity, and deaf epistemologies by interacting with signing deaf instructors and peers in their signed language on a daily basis (Pirone & Mayo, 2022). This can also be extended to **disability-centric spaces**, where all students can learn about disabled culture and identities. The third change to consider is **formulated experiences**. "To formulate requires getting outside of it, seeing it as another would see it, considering what points of contact it has with the life of another so that it may be got into such form that he can appreciate its meaning" (Dewey, 1916). In other words, practitioners need to formulate an experience not by observing but by engaging in an environment where aural/oral is not the primary orientation. Practitioners will gain a rich experience when they see what it is like to learn and interact using visual and manual modes. This, too, can be extended across disability.

> **Pause and Reflect**
> - How can practitioners consider and create disability-centric spaces in their work?
> - How can practitioners use formulated experiences to engage in other environments? How can they use that experience to inform their practices?

VIGNETTE 8: *JOHN'S BARRIERS IN SCHOOL*

When I was in my deaf school, what worked for me is direct and full access to communication and instruction. Also, the school created a space that invited deaf students to learn together and interact. Having a signing and culturally deaf storyteller was a huge impact and could increase the magnitude of impact if there was a room for discussion.

I experienced many barriers when educational professionals had a limited or no understanding of Deaf culture and lived experiences of being deaf, were not fluent in ASL, and did not actively seek resources to help support deaf students' identity development. The best way to support deaf students is that public schools hire deaf professionals to work with deaf students. Signing and culturally deaf professionals are ideal role models when deaf students seek support to build ASL skills and develop their cultural identity. Also, nondeaf professionals need to take a series of trainings on diversity, equity, inclusion, and justice to build a deeper understanding of what conditions render inequity affecting signing deaf students.

One significant factor that affected my journey from K–12 is a lack of ASL and Deaf culture curriculum. I did not learn ASL formally but only English (reading/writing) and was not provided access to ASL literature. I also did not take any class to learn more about Deaf culture, history, experiences, and arts. It is so crucial that deaf students have a space to learn and discuss all aspects of ASL, Deaf culture, and Deaf Studies. This kind of space will help facilitate deaf students' identity development.

Addressing Intersectional Inequities

Earlier parts of this chapter discussed how there are different types of disability culture (Peters, 2000), as well as the fact that different signs are used to refer to the same word in American Sign Language versus Spanish or any other non-English sign languages. These examples show that when the materials—the verbal, nonverbal, and written communication, the format or mode, environment, and activities—within an educational opportunity mirror the culture which the students and families come from, their educational experience can be more socially valid (Wolf, 1978) and culturally meaningful.

Studies have shown benefits to asset-based and culturally relevant approaches. In one study, a bilingual interventionist who shared the same cultural background as the families taught new vocabularies to four Asian immigrant children with Down syndrome in families' homes. The interventionist implemented a naturalistic, play-based intervention in which any forms of communication—including the use of gesture, eye contact, reaching, and vocalization—were acknowledged, expanded, and reinforced to teach (Kim & Kang, 2020). As a result, the caregiver and the student identified the student's preferred play materials and activities that mirrored their everyday routines (e.g., Asian doll figures making noodles with the kitchen toy set). Because the intervention was delivered in the children's preferred language (i.e., Korean), they were actively engaged to learn new vocabularies through play during a short duration of time (i.e., about two months) and caregivers reported the intervention process and outcome as beneficial, meaningful, and enjoyable for their children. Socioculturally sustaining practices were also successfully used in order to enhance transition planning and outcomes of autistic youth. For instance, in an adapted transition program for Spanish-speaking families and autistic youth, researchers considered several factors when developing a culturally responsive practice. They developed an iterative process that included a needs assessment as well as relationship-building with the community and stakeholders—reviewing the literature on best practices, creating/adapting the strategies, obtaining feedback from the community/stakeholders and updating the practices, and implementing and revising/updating the practice as necessary to meet the needs of the target participants (Kuhn et al., 2020).

Utilize a Strengths-Based Approach

Furthermore, when developing culturally responsive practices, it is important to consider using strength-based approaches. Historically, interventions were designed from a medical model of disability and focused on a deficit-based approach in teaching new skills (Anderson, 2022; Shuck et al., 2021). As a result, many disabled people have expressed the harmful and traumatic effects of practices used with a **medical model of disability**; the Autistic community has specifically spoken against trying to fix the innate traits of Autistic people (Anderson, 2022). Thus, designing interventions using a **strengths-based approach** can help improve the social validity and acceptability of practice among neurodiverse people. For instance, listening to and centering Autistic voices, supporting an Autistic person's identity and allowing them to be themselves rather than trying to make them camouflage their autistic traits, and constantly examining perspectives of Autistic people on the perceived ethicality and benefits of practices on enhancing their quality of life are some ways to design strength-based interventions (Shuck et al., 2022).

Pause and Reflect

- How can practitioners address intersectional oppressions in their classrooms and schools?
- How can practitioners incorporate a strengths-based approach in their work with students with disabilities?

VIGNETTE 9: *WHAT DOES (AND COULD HAVE) WORK(ED) FOR DYLAN*

Since my journey to understanding all of my identities has taken place in adulthood, I have been much better about self-advocacy and asking for necessary accommodations in college and graduate school than I ever was during my K–12 education. In college, I was able to get time and a half on tests, take my tests in a private room, and wear noise-canceling headphones, all of which made a huge difference in my academic success. I can only imagine how much more academically successful I might have been in my K–12 years if I had been taught self-advocacy skills or knew how to ask for what I needed, or even what my options for accommodations were.

I am currently in a doctoral (PhD) graduate program where I am experiencing a combination of academic burnout and autistic burnout, so I am once again having to get comfortable asking for what I need. I have been struggling to write lengthy academic text, so as I head toward my dissertation, I am trying to figure out alternative ways of demonstrating knowledge in order to be assessed in ways that make sense for me as an autistic individual. Academia is not set up to make space for alternative assessments, but I am taking what we know about the importance of alternative assessments for K–12 students and explaining that that cannot stop when someone graduates high school. It is a continued journey of self-advocacy and standing up for what I know I need!

Center Disability Culture

When considering the importance of asset-based and culturally and linguistically sustaining approaches in education, it is essential to preserve, honor, and center disability cultures. Disability culture can be woven into instruction when the educators seek, build, and maintain genuine relationships with the students and their family members to understand their everyday experiences, values, and strengths (NAEYC, 2019). Early intervention supports a wide range of developmental domains including language, communication, social emotional, physical, and cognitive skills of children of ages birth to three, and is designed to be family-centered and inclusive and representative of all cultural backgrounds (DEC, 2014). Practitioners should engage in ongoing and regular communication and interaction with the families to understand and incorporate the ecological systems (Bronfenbrenner, 1992) of each student including their individual preferences; the family dynamic and interactions; the student's and the family's engagement, lived experiences, and positions in their communities (i.e., neighborhoods); and finally, the student's cultural identity and background (Chiarello, 2017; Meadan et al., 2016).

In addition to considering family collaboration, practitioners can consider several other factors when working with students across different age groups and the life span. For example, when working with individuals with disabilities, practitioners could consider materials such as books and toys that reflect disability to help students understand, communicate, and develop a sense of pride and ownership of their disabilities. Integrating visual and physical representation of disability cultures beginning in early childhood educational and play materials and content could be critical in not only increasing disabled learners' sense of belonging, confidence, and socialization with their peers but also nondisabled learners' understanding, awareness, and acceptance of people with different types of disabilities (Meyer, 2021). When working with older children transitioning to postschool life, using person-centered approaches and conducting needs and strengths-based assessments, and being equal partners with students and their families is critical to ensuring the use of personalized and culturally and linguistically appropriate and sustaining practices (Kuhn et al., 2020). Together, when family collaboration and the representation of the disability culture are taken into consideration in educational contexts, practitioners could create a welcoming, inclusive, and equitable space for all.

SUMMARY

This chapter discussed how disability communities have created their own cultural identities in the context of Deaf and Autistic identities. Both Deaf and Autistic people have rejected the medical model of disability and embraced the sociocultural, biocultural, and neurodiversity models to form sociocultural identities. Similarities between both of these communities lie in taking pride in one's own identity and seeing the disability not as a medical condition that needs to be cured but rather as an innate difference in how people function in the society. While Deaf and Autistic people have formed communities around these identities, it is important to note not all people with deafness may associate themselves with the Deaf identity and not all Autistic people may associate themselves with the Autistic identity. The findings in this chapter should not be generalized to all disabled communities or to all deaf and Autistic people across cultures and geographic regions. Furthermore, language and cultural differences both within the same country and across countries may present differences between one community and another.

VIGNETTE 10: *JAMES'S ADVICE*

In contrast, although people with other disabilities have many unique challenges and deficits, many of them sense that they are a person with a unique self and that their disability does not necessarily impact them all of the time—thus, many of them prefer to use "person-first language," which is also what professionals are trained to use while working with disabled people in educational settings. However, in an attempt to try to argue that "identity-first language" is the sole preference for autistic people, "autistic culture" has ignored that there are many unique ways in which autistic people have preferred to address themselves, that not all autistic people prefer "identity-first language," and that some autistic people do prefer "person-first language," or a wide variety of other forms of identity languages.

Personally, I do not care one way or the other what language is used to identify me. I grew up using "person-first language" and being addressed as an autistic person with "person-first language." When I was a child, this term was not offensive, even though it is now considered to be. As an adult, I have had no problem switching to addressing autistic people with "identity-first language" to show respect to other autistic people with that preference. I myself, however, do not feel offended either way, whether or not I am called an "autistic person" or a "person with autism." However, although I am not perfect, I always try my best to call my friends with whatever language they identify with.

These kinds of cultural considerations have implications for practitioners when designing culturally inclusive and appropriate teaching techniques. Partnering with the individual and family members as equal partners to understand intersectional strengths and needs as well as sociocultural values—and developing an individualized intervention for each individual, obtaining feedback from the student and family throughout the process, refining and implementing the intervention—can be useful in creating an inclusive learning environment that is respectful of learner differences.

REFERENCES

Alansari, R. (2021). An inquiry into the alignment between the theoretical assumptions of self-determination theory and the cultural assumptions of Saudi Arabian educators [ProQuest Information & Learning]. In *Dissertation Abstracts International Section A: Humanities and Social Sciences, 83*(3-A).

American Psychiatric Association (APA). (1994). *Diagnostic and statistical manual of mental disorders.* 4th ed. American Psychiatric Publishing.

———. (2013). *Diagnostic and statistical manual of mental disorders.* 5th ed. American Psychiatric Publishing.

Anderson, L. K. (2022). Autistic experiences of applied behavior analysis. *Autism, 27*(3), 737–50. https://doi.org/10.1177/13623613221118216

Annamma, S. A., Boelé, A. L., Moore, B. A., & Klingner, J. (2013). Challenging the ideology of normal in schools. *International Journal of Inclusive Education, 17*(12), 1278–94.

Bauman, H. D. L. (2004). Audism: Exploring the metaphysics of oppression. *Journal of Deaf Studies and Deaf Education, 9*(2), 239–46.

Bauman, H. D., & Murray, J. (2009). Reframing: From hearing loss to deaf gain. *Deaf Studies Digital Journal, 1*(1), 1–10.

———. (2014). *Deaf gain: Raising the stakes for human diversity.* University of Minnesota Press.

Botha, M., & Gillespie-Lynch, K. (2022). Come as you are: Examining autistic identity development and the neurodiversity movement through an intersectional lens. *Human Development, 66*(2), 93–112. https://doi.org/10.1159/000524123

Bronfenbrenner, U. (1992). *Ecological systems theory.* Jessica Kingsley.

Charlton, J. I. (2000). *Nothing about us without us: Disability oppression and empowerment.* University of California Press.

Chiarello, L. A. (2017). Excellence in promoting participation: Striving for the 10 Cs—Client-centered care, consideration of complexity, collaboration, coaching, capacity building, contextualization, creativity, community, curricular changes, and curiosity. *Pediatric Physical Therapy, 29,* 16–22. https://doi.org/10.1097/PEP.0000000000000382

Chu, S.-Y. (2018). Family voices: Promoting foundation skills of self-determination for young children with disabilities in Taiwan. *Asia Pacific Education Review, 19*(1), 91–101.

Cohen, S. R., Joseph, K., Levinson, S., Blacher, J., & Eisenhower, A. (2022). "My autism is my own": Autistic identity and intersectionality in the school context. *Autism in Adulthood, 4*(4), 315–27. https://doi.org/10.1089/aut.2021.0087

Dewey, J. (1916). *Democracy and education: An introduction to the philosophy of education.* Macmillan.

Division for Early Childhood (DEC). (2014). *DEC recommended practices in early intervention/early childhood special education.* https://www.dec-sped.org/dec-recommended-practices

Eckert, R. C., & Rowley, A. J. (2013). Audism: A theory and practice of audiocentric privilege. *Humanity & Society, 37*(2), 101–30. https://doi.org/10.1177/0160597613481731

Fletcher-Watson, S., Adams, J., Brook, K., Charman, T., Crane, L., Cusack, J., . . . Pellicano, E. (2018). Making the future together: Shaping autism research through meaningful participation. *Autism, 23*(4), 943–53. https://doi.org/10.1177/1362361318786721

Forber-Pratt, A. J. (2019). (Re)defining disability culture: Perspectives from the Americans with Disabilities Act generation. *Culture & Psychology, 25*(2), 241–56.

Foster, S. (1989). Reflections of a group of deaf adults on their experiences in mainstream and residential school programs in the United States. *Disability, Handicap & Society, 4*(1), 37–56.

Gallaudet Research Institute. (2013). *Regional and national summary report of data from the 2011–12 annual survey of deaf and hard of hearing children and youth.* Washington, DC: GRI, Gallaudet University. Retrieved from https://www.gallaudet.edu/documents/Research-Support-and-International-Affairs/Intl%20Affairs/Demographics/AS12_RegNat.pdf

Gentz, E. N. (2003). *Dysconcious Audism and Critical Deaf Studies: Deaf Crit's analysis of unconscious internalization of hegemony within the Deaf community.* University of California.

Gill, C. J. (1995). A psychological view of disability culture. *Disability Studies Quarterly, 15*, 16–19. http://www.independentliving.org/docs3/gill1995.html

Gorski, P. (2016). Rethinking the role of "culture" in educational equity: From cultural competence to equity literacy. *Multicultural Perspectives, 18*(4), 221–26.

Gorski, P. C., & Swalwell, K. (2015). Equity literacy for all. *Educational Leadership, 72*(6), 34–40.

Hall, W. C. (2017). What you don't know can hurt you: The risk of language deprivation by impairing sign language development in deaf children. *Maternal and Child Health Journal, 21*(5), 961–65.

Happé, F., & Frith, U. (2020). Annual Research Review: Looking back to look forward—Changes in the concept of autism and implications for future research. *Journal of Child Psychology and Psychiatry, 61*(3), 218–32. https://doi.org/10.1111/jcpp.13176

Holcomb, T. K. (2012). *Introduction to American Deaf culture.* Oxford University Press.

Humphries, T. (1977). *Communicating across cultures (deaf-hearing) and language learning.* Union Institute and University.

Humphries, T., Kushalnagar, P., Mathur, G., Napoli, D. J., Padden, C., Rathmann, C., & Smith, S. (2017). Discourses of prejudice in the professions: The case of sign languages. *Journal of Medical Ethics, 43*(9), 648–52.

Individuals With Disabilities Education Act (IDEA), 20 U.S.C. § 46588 (2004).

Jones, D. R., Nicolaidis, C., Ellwood, L. J., Garcia, A., Johnson, K. R., Lopez, K., & Waisman, T. C. (2020). An expert discussion on structural racism in autism research and practice. *Autism in Adulthood, 2*(4), 273–81. https://doi.org/10.1089/aut.2020.29015.drj

Kanner, L. (1943). Autistic disturbances of affective contact. *Nervous Child, 2*, 217–50.

Kapp, S. K. (Ed.). (2020). *Autistic community and the neurodiversity movement.* https://doi.org/10.1007/978-981-13-8437-0

Kim, S., & Kang, V. Y. (2020). The effect of enhanced milieu teaching on vocabulary acquisition for Korean American children with Down Syndrome. *Journal of Special Education, 55*(2), 113–26.

Kim, S., Kim, J., Yan, M. C., & Kang, V. Y. (2022). Korean-American mothers' perceptions of self-determination of primary school children with Autism Spectrum Disorder. *International Journal of Disability, Development and Education, 69*(5), 1601–16.

Kuhn, J. L., Vanagas, S. B., Salgado, R., Borjas, S. K., Magaña, S., & DaWalt, L. S. (2020). The cultural adaptation of a transition program for Latino families of youth with Autism Spectrum Disorder. *Family Process, 59*(2), 477–91. https://doi.org/10.1111/famp.12439

Kusters, A., De Meulder, M., & O'Brien, D. (Eds.). (2017). *Innovations in Deaf Studies: The role of Deaf scholars*. Oxford University Press.

Ladd, P. (2003). *Understanding Deaf culture: In search of Deafhood*. Multilingual Matters.

Lane, H. L. (1992). *The mask of benevolence: Disabling the Deaf community* (p. 104). New York: Knopf.

Lane, H. L., Hoffmeister, R., & Bahan, B. J. (1996). *A journey into the Deaf-World*. Dawn Sign Press.

Lei, J., & Russell, A. (2021). Understanding the role of self-determination in shaping university experiences for autistic and typically developing students in the United Kingdom. *Autism*, 25(5). https://doi.org/10.1177/1362361320984897

Leigh, I. W., Andrews, J. F., Harris, R. L., & Ávila, T. G. (2020). *Deaf culture: Exploring Deaf communities in the United States*. Plural Publishing.

Meadan, H., Snodgrass, M. R., Meyer, L. E., Fisher, K. W., Chung, M. Y., & Halle, J. W. (2016). Internet-based parent-implemented intervention for young children with autism: A pilot study. *Journal of Early Intervention*, 38(1), 3–23. https://doi.org/10.1177/1053815116630327

Meyer, L. E. (2021). Including disability in early childhood curricula: Evaluating and using children's books. *YC Young Children*, 76(4), 29–36.

Murray, J. J., Hall, W. C., & Snoddon, K. (2019). Education and health of children with hearing loss: The necessity of signed languages. *Bulletin of the World Health Organization*, 97(10), 711.

NAEYC. (2019). Defining and recognizing high-quality early learning programs: NAEYC's 10 accreditation standards. *Teaching Young Children*, 13(1). https://www.naeyc.org/defining-recognizing-high-quality-early-learning-programs

Oliva, G. A. (2004). *Alone in the mainstream: A Deaf woman remembers public school* (vol. 1). Gallaudet University Press.

Oliva, G. A., & Lytle, L. R. (2014). *Turning the tide: Making life better for Deaf and hard of hearing school children*. Gallaudet University Press.

Padden, C. A., & Humphries, T. L. (1988). *Deaf in America: Voices from a culture*. Harvard University Press.

Parsloe, S. M. (2015). Discourses of disability, narratives of community: Reclaiming an Autistic identity online. *Journal of Applied Communication Research*, 43(3), 336–56. https://doi.org/10.1080/00909882.2015.1052829

Peters, S. (2000). Is there a disability culture? A syncretisation of three possible world views. *Disability & Society*, 15(4), 583–601.

Pirone, J. (in press). Equity literacy offers a way to reduce language deprivation by combating audism and linguicism. *Deaf Studies Digital Journal*.

Pirone, J. & Mayo, C. (2022). Deaf culture, associational inclusion, and ending waste in education. *Journal of School and Society*, 7(2), 19–30.

Pirone, J. S., Henner, J., & Hall, W. (2018). American Sign Language interpreting in a mainstreamed college setting: Performance quality and its impact on classroom participation equity. In *Deaf eyes on interpreting* (pp. 45–57). Gallaudet University Press.

Reagan, T., Matlins, P. E., & Pielick, C. D. (2020). Teaching Deaf culture in American Sign Language courses: Toward a critical pedagogy. *Foreign Language Annals*, 53(2), 270–91.

Schuck, R. K., Tagavi, D. M., Baiden, K. M. P., Dwyer, P., Williams, Z. J., Osuna, A., . . . Vernon, T. W. (2021). Neurodiversity and autism intervention: Reconciling perspectives through a naturalistic developmental behavioral intervention framework. *Journal of*

Autism and Developmental Disorders, 52(10), 4625–45. https://doi.org/10.1007/s10803-021-05316-x

Shogren, K. A., & Ward, M. J. (2018). Promoting and enhancing self-determination to improve the post-school outcomes of people with disabilities. *Journal of Vocational Rehabilitation, 48*(2), 187–96. https://doi.org/10.3233/JVR-180935

Shore, S. M. (2003). *Beyond the wall: Personal experiences with Autism and Asperger Syndrome.* 2nd ed. Autism Asperger Publishing.

Sign Library. (2022, September 28). *Deaf Gain—Indian Sign Language—ISL* [Video]. YouTube. https://www.youtube.com/watch?v=2r223gx6EME

Singer, J. (2017). *NeuroDiversity: The birth of an idea.* Self-published.

Skutnabb-Kangas, Tove. (1988). Multilingualism and the education of minority children. In T. Skutnabb-Kangas & J. Cummins (Eds.), *Minority education: From shame to struggle* (pp. 9–44). Multilingual Matters.

Stinson, M., & Liu, Y. (1999). Participation of deaf and hard-of-hearing students in classes with hearing students. *Journal of Deaf Studies and Deaf Education, 4*(3), 191–202.

Tan, C. D. (2018). "I'm a normal autistic person, not an abnormal neurotypical": Autism Spectrum Disorder diagnosis as biographical illumination. *Social Science & Medicine, 197,* 161–67. https://doi.org/10.1016/j.socscimed.2017.12.008

US Department of Education, National Center for Education Statistics (NCES). (2019). *Digest of education statistics, 2018* (NCES 2020-009).

Wehmeyer, M. L., & Palmer, S. B. (2000). Promoting the acquisition and development of self-determination in young children with disabilities. *Early Education and Development, 11*(4), 465–81.

Wolf, M. M. (1978). Social validity: The case for subjective measurement or how applied behavior analysis is finding its heart. *Journal of Applied Behavior Analysis, 11*(2), 203–14.

World Federation of the Deaf. (2023, August 18). *The legal recognition of National Sign Languages.* http://wfdeaf.org/news/the-legal-recognition-of-national-sign-languages/

PART II
Critical Theories That Influence Our Views of Disability and Race

CHAPTER 4

Critical Race Theory: The Dos, the Don'ts, the Already Dones, and the Stop Doings

Chapter authors: *Marcus C. Fuller, Jasmine Fleming, and Joseph Cremona*

Vignette authors: *Joseph Cremona and Jasmine Fleming*

Editor: *Elizabeth A. Harkins Monaco*

ABSTRACT

Critical Race Theory (CRT) is a controversial topic in education, the media, and society, sparking a lot of confusion about what this theory entails, how it is used in the preK–12 education system, and its intent as a critical theory. The purpose of this chapter is to explore the chronological development of CRT and understand the tenets and purpose of CRT. This chapter discusses what embedding a CRT philosophy of teaching looks like in the classroom versus what CRT philosophy doesn't teach. Finally, the chapter provides resources, activities, and classroom management strategies that support a CRT framework that can be implemented right now.

GUIDING QUESTIONS

- What are the core tenets of Critical Race Theory?
- How has Critical Race Theory historically impacted educational practices?
- What are common misbeliefs about Critical Race Theory and how can we dispel them?
- How can practitioners use Critical Race Theory to identify and enact change to current educational practices?

KEY TERMS

Colorblindness
Critical Race Theory
Critical Theory
Culturally and Linguistically Sustaining Practices
De Facto Segregation
Interest Convergence
Intersectionality
Material Determinism
Multiculturalism
People of the Global Majority
Privilege (White Privilege)
Race
Race-Evasiveness
Racism
Whiteness

Critical Race Theory (CRT) is a cross-disciplinary framework to explore how laws, social and political movements, and media shape and are shaped by social conceptions of race and ethnicity (Delgado & Stefancic, 1993; Dixson & Rousseau, 2005; Lynn & Dixson, 2013). CRT has become a center of discourse in the field of education. Social media, activist groups, and other societal entities have perverted and distorted CRT into something that is thought to indoctrinate or terrorize students (Sawchuk, 2021). The widespread misunderstanding of CRT and how it intersects with the prekindergarten to grade 12 (preK–12) classrooms in the United States has many districts questioning what CRT is and if it should be taught to our students. As of 2023, seven states, Arkansas, Florida, Idaho, Iowa, New Hampshire, Oklahoma, and Tennessee, have banned CRT from the classroom environment, while the following sixteen states have bans in progress: Georgia, Alabama, Kentucky, Louisiana, Michigan, Missouri, Montana, Ohio, Pennsylvania, Rhode Island, South Carolina, Texas, Utah, Washington, West Virginia, and Wisconsin (World Population Review, 2023). CRT is a theory, a framework, a practice—not a curriculum; it is a way of looking at an issue through the lens of race and realizing that racism is woven into the fabric of our laws and institutions, including education. This framework looks at similar issues to those examined in the fields of civil rights legal scholarship or ethnic studies but broadens these perspectives by threading other important variables such as history, context, economics, self-interest, bias, and unconsciousness into the theory (Delgado & Stefancic, 2001).

Since its conception in the early 1970s, CRT's goal has been to connect both the cause and the context for disparities and inequalities in social and academic outcomes within marginalized groups (Lynn & Dixson, 2013). Since then scholars, researchers, and practitioners have continued to use CRT to analyze educational norms and policies that govern our classrooms to identify practices that perpetuate whiteness through expectations regarding student behavior, assessment, and academic achievement (Lynn & Dixson, 2013). Scholars, like Kimberlé Crenshaw (2016), speak about how intersectionality among sociocultural identities creates compounding layers of oppression that people who only share one of these identities may not understand. Derrick Bell (1980) discussed the topic of interest convergences, and how social progress only happens if it benefits whiteness. For decades, concepts of CRT have been used to help analyze educational practices to promote justice, equity, diversity, and inclusion (JEDI; Jenks et al., 2001) in the classroom and create a sense of belonging for students. So how and why are districts banning CRT in the classroom? Before we answer that, let's first understand what CRT entails.

This chapter outlines the history of CRT from legal studies to educational practices. It provides a clear delineation of the tenets of CRT, how CRT is currently used in education, and what CRT does not entail. Lastly, the chapter provides further implications to incorporate concepts of CRT into your schools.

THE HISTORY OF CRT

Critical Race Theory spans back to the late 1900s, starting with its work in Critical Legal Studies (Lynn & Dixson, 2013) along with civil rights activists of the 1970s, 1980s, and1990s (Hartlep, 2009). The overturned "separate but equal" policy in *Brown v. Board of Education* created many years of legal, economic, and educational measures in an effort to dismantle racism and oppression. However, during the presidency of Richard Nixon (1969–1974), many of those gains were halted or again overturned as he began to influence a more conservative Supreme Court through his second term (Lynn & Dixson, 2013). In response to the laws made by the more conservative court, the culmination of Critical Legal Studies (CLS) came about during the later 1970s (Lynn & Dixson, 2013).

CRT was born from the need to examine and critically analyze the laws of the land and the ways in which these laws disenfranchised certain populations in our society. One of the earliest contributions to this can be found in Oliver Holmes's *The Common Law* (1881), which states

> The life of the law has not been logic: it has been experience. The felt necessities of the time, the prevalent moral and political theories, intuitions of public policy, . . . have had a good deal more to do than the syllogism in determining the rules by which men should be governed. (p. 147)

Furthermore, a statement by Supreme Court Chief Justice Charles Hughes in 1907 proclaimed that the Constitution was not designed to be an impartial or blind document to protect the rights of all its citizens but rather the Constitution is what the judges say it is. This notion that the law can and should be interpreted based on an individual basis is also seen in a 1920 Supreme Court statement that described the "sociological jurisprudence" (White, 1972) on the impact society has on creating and maintaining laws. All of these court statements express the concept of legal realism or the realization that the legal system is not as blind as Lady Justice appears.

Critical Race Theory and Critical Legal Theory became more prominent in the 1970s with publications from two pivotal scholars from the field. In 1975, Derrick Bell published "Serving Two Masters: Integration Ideals and Client Interests in School Desegregation Litigation" and theorized about **interest convergence** (IC), which ultimately became an important tenet of CRT. He described interest convergence as how every civil rights movement forward was only allowed when aligned with economic or political advantages for those in power, namely white, upper-class males. In 1977, Alan Freeman wrote another crucial piece that helped promote the importance and the need for CRT titled "Legitimizing Racial Discrimination through Antidiscrimination Law: A Critical Review of Supreme Court Doctrine." This seminal piece shed light on the false belief that a colorblind justice system treats all as equal. Freeman explained how the law has never been blind and illustrated multiple occasions in which the Supreme Court explicitly upheld the use of racial classifications. These two pieces shifted the field of legal studies and provided the mechanism for more scholars to shed light on the issues that were being raised through CRT.

In 1988, *Harvard Law Review* published Kimberlé Crenshaw's "Race, Reform, and Retrenchment: Transformation and Legitimation in Antidiscrimination Law," where she explained the importance of dismantling notions of colorblindness or any other neoconservative ideology and recognized the impact race has on the legal system. Crenshaw, a prominent scholar within CRT, explained how colorblindness is still "othering" and only through antidiscrimination laws can we eliminate racial oppression (Crenshaw, 1988).

In 1989, the first CRT conference was held in Madison, Wisconsin, in a convent (Delgado & Stefancic, 2001). The conference was orchestrated by Crenshaw and another of Dr. Bell's graduate students. This continuing conference provides yet another spark for theorists and researchers to understand and identify the impact race has on societal norms and our legal system. In 2020, the conference featured *Intersectionality and Critical Race Theory*, which brought the issues of intersectionality, race, feminism, and legal studies all under one roof.

Many other scholars have also contributed to the development of CRT, including acclaimed founder Richard Delgado. In 1989, Delgado's "Storytelling for Oppositionists and Others: A Plea for Narrative" appeared in the *Michigan Law Review*. The article expressed the importance of storytelling within the American legal system. Delgado, along with Stefancic, also published "Why Do We Tell the Same Stories?: Law Reform, Critical Librarianship, and the Triple Helix Dilemma" in 1989. Storytelling and the use of counter-storytelling are a big part of Delgado's work and show the importance of leveraging the stories of oppressed people along with the jurisprudence of the nation. Delgado (1989) stated

> it is the prevailing mindset by means of which members of the dominant group justify the world as it is, that is, with whites on top and browns and blacks at the bottom. Stories, parables, chronicles, and narratives are powerful means

for destroying mindset—the bundle of presuppositions, received wisdoms, and shared understandings against a background of which legal and political discourse takes place. (p. 2413)

Delgado, along with Stefancic, wrote a bibliography titled "Critical Race Theory: An Annotated Bibliography" in which they outlined ten themes that encompass the body of work for CRT that scholars and practitioners should consider. See table 4.1 for themes within CRT scholarship.

Table 4.1. Themes within Critical Race Theory Scholarship

- critique of liberalism
- storytelling/counter-storytelling and "naming one's own reality"
- revisionist interpretation of American civil rights law and progress
- a greater understanding of the underpinnings of race and racism
- structural determinism
- race, sex, class, and their intersections
- essentialism and anti-essentialism
- cultural nationalism and separatism
- legal institutions, critical pedagogy, and the minorities in the bar
- criticism and self-criticism

(Delgado & Stefancic, 1993)

A pioneer in bringing CRT into the field of education is Gloria Ladson-Billings. In her article "Toward a Critical Race Theory of Education" (1995), she and Tate stated three central positions:

- Race continues to be a significant factor in determining inequity in the United States.
- US society is based on property rights, rather than human rights.
- The intersection of race and property creates an analytic tool through which we can understand social (and, consequently, school) inequity.

Ladson-Billings's research focused primarily on K–12 grade classrooms and used CRT to examine the impact race and racism have in education. She continued to shed light on the importance of incorporating a CRT framework into educational curriculum planning, classroom design, and educational policy. In "The Evolving Role of Critical Race Theory in Educational Scholarship" (2005), she reflected on research and practice within this intersection of CRT and education since it was first introduced in 1994. The article empowered future scholarship in the field and encouraged upcoming scholars to use CRT "as a valuable tool for making sense of persistent racial inequities in US schools" (Ladson-Billings, 2005, p. 115).

CRT continues to be analyzed by many scholars across multiple disciplines including, but not limited to, education, ethnic studies, sociology, law and policies, and medicine (Ledesma & Calderón, 2015). As CRT scholars continue to collaborate across the United States, they welcome knowledge from nonlegal disciplines such as European philosophers Antonio Gramsci and Jacques Derrida. CRT scholars also collaborate with and have informed various political activist figures like Dr. Martin Luther King Jr., Malcolm X, Sojourner Truth, W. E. B. Du Bois, and many others (Crenshaw, 2016; Delgado & Stefancic, 2001; Lynn & Dixson, 2013). It is essential to know the concepts and history of CRT to be able to discern scholarship centered on theory and efforts to create confusion about CRT.

THE DOS: WHAT IS CRT?

To understand how CRT is being infused into education, you first must understand the tenets of CRT. Delgado and Stefancic (2001, 2017) identified several tenets that outline the common threads of CRT as (a) the notion that racism is "normal," and not an aberration; (b) the idea of white interest convergence for social progress; (c) race is a socially constructed concept; (d) intersectionality; and (e) use of storytelling and counter-storytelling to promote unique voices and unknown historical perspectives. Figure 4.1 visually presents these tenets together.

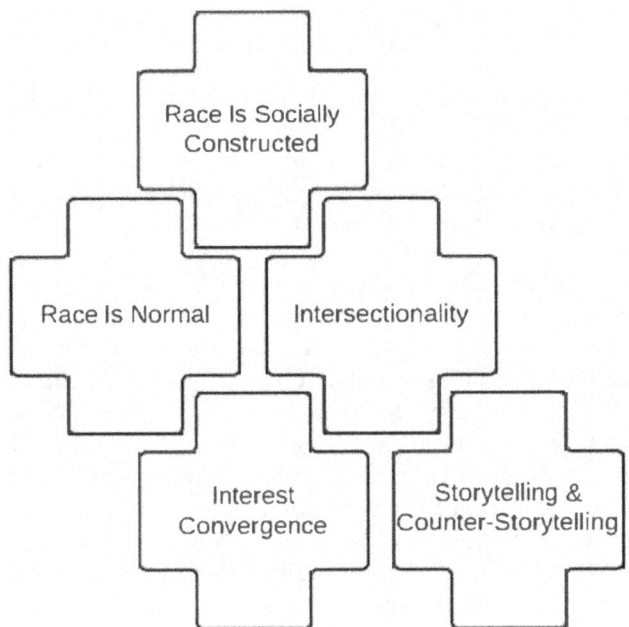

Figure 4.1. Tenets of Critical Race Theory
Source: Adapted from Delgado and Stefancic, 2001, 2017.

Racism Is "Normal"

One fundamental concept, or tenet, of CRT is that racism is "normal" or ordinary and not aberrational (Delgado & Stefancic, 2017). Racism is a common concept experienced by people of the global majority (Lim, 2020), every day in the United States and around the world. **People of the global majority** (PGM) is an alternative term for BIPOC (Black, Indigenous and People of Color) or BAME (Black Asian and Minority Ethnic) that affirms and encourages nonwhite persons as belonging to the majority population of the globe (Immigration Law Practitioners' Association [ILPA], 2022). The term PGM focuses the conversation on the ethnically diverse who make up about 85 percent of the world population (Hawthorne, 2023). This term is inclusive of all non-white people around the world and does not center the American or white experience against the rest of the world (Lim, 2020).

Because racism is at the core of our nation, many racist policies and practices can go unnoticed unless called out. Even when originally marketed as a way of inclusion, concepts like colorblindness are rooted in racism and discriminatory ideologies. Many practitioners have heard the phrase "I don't see color," usually when referring to disciplinary action or accommodations. This is a common example of **colorblindness**, a racial ideology that aims to treat all students equally, regardless of their race (Williams, 2011).

Pause and Reflect

Think of the last time you or someone else claimed to be colorblind.

- Did the phrase "I don't see color" acknowledge and include the marginalized sociocultural identity or force the individual with those identities to conform to the white majority?

On the surface, colorblindness seems like a move toward accepting diversity; but by not seeing color or stating, "I treat all my students the same," we deny the racial experiences of that student, and there is an implication that we hold students to the same mainstream white, Christian, cisgender, ideology that we believe all students should have, regardless of their sociocultural identities. This type of ideology overlooks the racial heritage of people from the global majority and silences their unique perspectives. Policies that support colorblindness or race-neutrality force people from the global majority to assimilate to unknown norms and then punish them at an overrepresented rate when they do not conform (Harper & Hurtado, 2007). Such examples include a Black student being labeled as disruptive when talking loudly while a white student is called energetic. Another example is how Black teenage boys in the judicial system are often tried as adults while their white counterparts are treated as children with their lives ahead of them. Through a colorblind lens, one would rationalize these issues—everyone must follow the rules or the law is the law—without considering how racism impacted these actions. Suppressing a sociocultural identity by requiring an individual to conform in order to be accepted into a group is a form of discrimination; if that identity is based on race, then such suppression is racism. In his book *Racism without Racists*, Bonilla-Silva (2006) explained how colorblind ideology has become its own form of racism (colorblind racism) as it hides inequity behind the guise that there is already equality. Colorblindness holds that since we are all equal, we are all treated equally and every person has equal chances to live and thrive in society if they try. This ideology negates any factors of race that have historically determined and still continue to determine who has power and privilege in the United States. A colorblindness ideology is not part of the solution but yet another part of the problem. A better alternative to colorblindness is a multiculturalism ideology that acknowledges, identifies, and promotes racial and ethnic differences (Williams, 2011).

Practitioners tend to believe and often are taught that it is wrong to see their students through a racial lens. Goldstein (2001), in her discussion of colorblindness in white preservice practitioners (PSP), stated "We have been taught that colorblindness—not seeing color or racial difference at all—is the best way to work in a racially diverse classroom" (p. 4). She added that many of her white PSP would say that "there is only one race, the human race" and that by holding such views the PSP felt they were "not participating in racism if they ignore color" (p. 4).

Colorblindness for whites also extends inward to themselves in that many do not see themselves racially (DiAngelo, 2018). According to DiAngelo (2018), white people (like herself) tend not to see white as a race or to have a racial identity at all. Many whites even choose to see themselves through their ethnic identity instead. DiAngelo noted that white people are socialized to believe that race and culture were something "other people" have and that they are "just normal" (p. 7). Goldstein (2001) echoed this point, noticing that her PSP struggled to recognize their racial identity when asked to group themselves by race. This positions white people as the standard (typical or dominant) and everyone else outside of them has a race—for example, racism without racists (Bonilla-Silva, 2006). Because white people don't see themselves racially, they see (physically) the race of "others" but don't see race as a determining factor of life chances or opportunity. Nor can they see or accept how their race has allotted them privileges not afforded to Black and other marginalized sociocultural identities. White privilege is so entrenched in our racially structured society that it can be invisible to white people.

Another concept that showcases how racism is ingrained into our society is through white meritocracy (Hartlep, 2009). In many cases, white wealth, whether it be politicians, celebrities, or royalty, is praised for the charity it gives to diverse sociocultural communities, despite being the cause of these disparities. For instance, someone may be praised for building a multicultural center on part of the land their family "acquired" in the past, without actually giving it back or making amends to the people from which the land was taken. This do-good notion society credits them while simultaneously helping to maintain white privilege and power and allows whiteness to feel absolved of responsibility for how this privilege and power impact people of the global majority (Hartlep, 2009). This concept of meritocracy creates an illusion of support for justice, equity, diversity, and inclusivity while allowing white wealth to maintain power, or only give some away if they too can benefit.

Interest Convergence

Similar to meritocracy, is **interest convergence** (IC), or the extent to which white people will support change or racial progress as long as they too can benefit (Bell, 1980; Delgado & Stefancic, 2017; Hartlep, 2009). This can also be described as **material determinism**, or how one's choice is influenced by power and materialistic factors. Bell, a founding figure of CRT, first wrote about IC as he argued that the landmark case *Brown v. Board of Education* was to benefit whiteness and lessen the pushback from people of the global majority after World War II and the Korean War who served as "somewhat" equals on the battlefield (Bell, 1980). For more about *Brown v. Board of Education*, see chapters 5, 10, and 11. Since then, scholars of CRT have used the theory of interest convergence to identify historical accounts, as well as accounts in current society, that promote social justice only to the extent that it also benefits whiteness. In other words, interest convergence states that social and civil advancements for PGM will only triumph when their interests "converge" with white America (Milner IV, 2008).

CRT scholars use several examples throughout the history of civil rights legislation to help describe interest convergence. Continuing with *Brown v. Board of Education*, Tate, Ladson-Billings, and Grant (1993) illustrated how the ruling failed to substantially improve the educational experience of PGM due to its restrictive view of equity. Instead of a vision of education that challenged the fundamental structure of schools that reproduced the same inequitable social hierarchies that existed in society, the *Brown* decision created a mechanism for covert racism where segregation can be deemed legally acceptable if it's a secondary outcome and not the intent of the policy. This leads to another example of interest convergence, de facto segregation. **De facto segregation** describes instances where segregation in fact (de facto) exists, but it's not from legislation overtly segregating students by race (William, 2017). Thus, many de facto segregated schools were not unconstitutionally segregated. In addition, the existence of this "accidental racism" created more barriers for civil rights activists and Black plaintiffs who attempted to prove that the segregated schools resulted from discriminatory motives (William, 2017). De facto segregation is still seen in society today. Many districts' geographic characteristics determine the type of students you will see in your classroom and possibly the type of education the students will receive. Another example of the harm from de facto segregation is redlining. Housing redlining is the practice of denying an otherwise eligible, creditworthy applicant a loan for a house in a particular neighborhood. Lending institutions have a grim history of "redlining" people of the global majority out of successful, up-and-coming [white] neighborhoods, thus limiting their assets and ability to acquire and maintain property and wealth, despite having the means to secure them.

A prominent illustration of interest convergence is the parable of the space traders within Bell's (1992) *Faces at the Bottom of the Well: The Persistence of Racism*. The story tells of alien space traders that visit and wish to give the United States (a) enough gold to balance the federal, state, and local government debts; (b) a special chemical capable of unpolluting the American environment; and (c) a safe nuclear engine and fuel to replace the depleting fossil fuel supplies to trade for all of the nation's African Americans. The American government (i.e., majority of white politicians) deliberated the issue and by the time the space traders returned on Martin Luther King Day, America passed the referendum to trade the African Americans to the space traders.

> The last Martin Luther King holiday the nation would ever observe dawned on an extraordinary sight. In the night, the Space Traders had drawn their strange ships right up to the beaches and discharged their cargoes of gold, minerals, and machinery, leaving vast empty holds. Crowded on the beaches were the inductees, some twenty million silent black men, women, and children, including babes in arms. . . . There was no escape, no alternative. Heads bowed, arms now linked by slender chains, black people left the New World as their forebears had arrived. (Bell, 1992, p. 173)

This parable helps to identify two concepts within interest convergence—that whiteness has power and privilege to have such a political debate without fear or subjugation, and how society will attempt to portray segregation and hardships as sacrifice, patriotism, and courage for Black people due to the resources that America gains in the return (Hartlep, 2009).

Race Is Socially Constructed

Another concept under CRT is the notion that race is a social construct. See chapters 1 and 2 for more information about social constructs. The phenomenon that race is socially constructed is not to deny race as a "real" thing; rather the term is used to describe that society, or groups within a society, agree to attribute certain meanings or assumptions based on one's race (Harry et al., 2007). This is evident when we look at how the definition of race has changed throughout US history. To start, consider the *Dred Scott v. Sandford* case, whereby the Supreme Court declared that "Negroes," whether free or enslaved, were not citizens. This case reached the Supreme Court after

Dred Scott declared that residence in a free territory secured his freedom from slavery. The Supreme Court decided that no matter whether enslaved or freed, African Americans were not considered citizens. The definition of race continues to become cloudy when looking at the "one drop rule" during the Jim Crow era. This concept contradicted the traditional practice of inheriting your biological father's status and race. However, this rule set the standard that if either of your biological parents, grandparents, or any traceable ancestor was African American (i.e., one drop) then you were considered African American. This limited many freed African Americans from acquiring rights and access to wealth during this time.

Intersectionality

The social construct of race is also evident when considering how race impacts and intersects with other sociocultural identities. This framework, one of the core themes of this text, was first introduced by Kimberlé Crenshaw (1991). **Intersectionality** describes the compounding impact of discrimination due to multiple nondominant identities. Intersectionality is one of the core themes of this text. These layers of identity oppression can both be experienced within and across sociocultural groups such as socioeconomic class, race, sexuality, gender, disability, ethnicity, nationality, and religion (Ledesma & Calderón, 2015). One common example is how Black women are often asked to take a stance on one issue while having to neglect another. For example, when Black women fight for racial equity, they are told this is not a place for feminism, or while fighting for gender equity, they are told it's not a race issue. This "either-or" thinking systemically restricts Black women from effectively advocating for all their intersecting needs.

A more relevant example in special education is when we look at the intersection of disability and race. One commonality among the Black community is the lack of trust in law enforcement; however, a common outlet of support for disabled persons is to seek help from authority figures (i.e., law enforcement). A special education practitioner colleague recently described her revelation of the danger in which she inadvertently placed some of her Black, disabled students by suggesting that if they are ever lost, in distress, or in need of support, they should seek a police officer for help. This revelation has become more widespread after seeing the laundry list of Black bodies being gunned down by police including Freddie Gray, Sandra Bland, Tamir Rice, Eric Garner, Stephon Watts, Laquan MacDonald, Charleena Lyles, Kevin Matthews, Quintonio LeGrier, Korryn Gaines, Natasha McKenna, Eric Smith, Anthony Lowe, Daniel Prude, and George Floyd. These persons, along with many others killed by police, gave fuel to the "Say Their Names" campaign to ensure that these names would not go unnoticed or grouped into another statistic (visit https://sayevery.name/ for a more comprehensive list). According to the Center for American Progress, more than 50 percent of victims of police violence identify as disabled (Thompson, 2021). In this case, the intersection between race and disability is deadly.

In recent years, the concept of intersectionality is seen through examples such as changes in Muslim discrimination in the United States, current immigration policies, and societal understanding of Black as a monolith. There have been previous misconceptions in the United States about Muslim people, but after the 9/11 attacks, Muslims were viewed as terrorists and subjected to heightened discrimination and violence (Subedi, 2013). This illustrates how societal assumptions and stereotypes can shift after national events or among generations. A similar example can be found in the current discrimination in the US migration policy. The tendency to overgeneralize all people of Latine descent as undocumented or illegal immigrants creates misinformation and restricts societal views of Latine American citizens to that of criminals based solely on their race. Another example of the social construct of race is apparent in the concept of essentialism (Ladson-Billings, 2021), which is the belief that all of a certain culture or society think, act, and believe in the same manner. This is also commonly explained as a culture not being a monolith or all acting the same; see chapters 1 and 2 for more information. While there are several aspects shared by many persons of the same culture, the assumption that all people of that culture should act and feel the same is a dangerous overgeneralization that grossly impacts US policies and societal ideologies. Seeing race as a social construct allows us to critically reflect on our understanding of racial constructs that might create policies and practices that are barriers to the educational success of students.

Pause and Reflect

Consider the different sociocultural identities that you subscribe to or that are ascribed to you.

- How do your sociocultural identities overlap, intersect, and show up in how you navigate your current environment?
- How do your sociocultural identities affect the way you learned in school?

Storytelling and Counter-Storytelling

The final component of CRT discussed in this chapter is the importance of storytelling and counter-storytelling. Storytelling provides a platform for diverse communities that offers an unbiased opinion and gives voice to experiences that usually aren't highlighted at the proverbial table. Counter-storytelling can be used to provide alternative perspectives to the misbeliefs that have been perpetuated through historical accounts. Counter-storytelling and storytelling can be used to disprove the misguided notion of neutrality of history. This belief tries to state that the history presented in school curriculum and perpetuated by media and mainstream society is a history fit for all citizens and accurately depicts the lives and accomplishments of all Americans. However, through storytelling, first-person accounts of these events are able to shed additional light on some of the dark spots in our history.

Another concept that can be combated with the use of storytelling is the notion of race neutrality (i.e., not targeting or impacted by race) in systemic institutions (Chambers, 2002). This is a common stance for people who oppose seeing the impact race has on many US institutions such as healthcare, education, housing, incarceration, and employment. People who see these systems as racially neutral may say phrases like "Why do you always have to bring race into it?" or "Does everything have to be about race?" As described in the first tenet of CRT, race is ingrained in our everyday lives and affects many of the processes in which society participates. Through storytelling, we are granted the opportunity to hear from a different perspective and begin to understand the impact race has on people's lives. By eliminating race, we overgeneralize the stories of the American people and threaten diversity by assimilating all experiences into that of the mainstream understanding.

With storytelling and counter-storytelling, students can receive additional information about monumental events in US history that most often are not acknowledged in curriculum textbooks. The accurate and detailed depiction of the genocide, brutalization, and slaughtering of certain populations throughout US history is often removed from the academic curriculum. Currently, mainstream education still favors the historical understanding of white, cisgender males, which in most cases erases any contradicting perspectives of a different culture. In fact, as this chapter is being written, there are various state legislatures imposing bans on textbooks and teaching like this that focus on diversity, race, and/or racism. Mainstream education contributes to the oppression of the most at-risk populations by not showcasing their stories and by alienating them from society without any knowledge of their culture's contributions (Hackman & Rauscher, 2004). Without the use of storytelling, an accurate understanding of US history will be foreign to the nation's next generation of citizens.

THE DON'TS: WHAT CRT IS NOT

The beginning of this chapter noted that some media outlets and politicians have vilified CRT, espousing false beliefs and claiming that CRT is "un-American" or "racially divisive," or that it pits socioculturally diverse students against white students—as "oppressed" and "oppressor" (George, 2021). Our hope is, through better understanding, practitioners will be able to disestablish such falsities and accurately demonstrate how to incorporate CRT into the educational environment, which is beneficial for the whole classroom and the school at large. We have identified several major misconceptions about CRT; while some of these statements may be prevalent in the media, we find little to no value in replicating this rhetoric outside of this educational dialogue. Instead, we have provided statements that are factual and evidence-based to equip and inform practitioners for future discussions.

CRT Is Being Taught in the K–12 Curriculum

As of 2023, close to a majority of all states have bans or working legislation against CRT in the classroom (World Population Review, 2023), and many of those laws only vaguely define what is being banned. That is because CRT is a framework or a way to organize the critical analysis of how racism molded the legal system and other American institutions such as education (Delgado & Stefancic, 2001); it is not a curriculum that is being taught in school, such as mathematics, reading, or sciences. Furthermore, most CRT work is written in academic and legal language and published in scholarly journals, which practitioners in the preK–12 environment don't usually access. Classroom practitioners are not preparing lesson plans to teach their third graders that racism is ordinary, to discuss interest convergence, or to examine the social construction of race. However, practitioners do have the option to take the ideas from CRT to create a more socioculturally competent and sustaining environment.

For example, as practitioners begin to understand CRT's emphasis on storytelling and counter-storytelling, they can critically reflect on the stories shared in their classrooms. By being mindful of the limited perspectives available to students, educators can begin to diversify these perspectives by adding books to classroom libraries from diverse authors and illustrators or broadening the books read during read-aloud. Practitioners can also bring in cultural informants to tell their own stories and share their perspectives. Going beyond this, older students could even discuss the similarities and differences from their sociocultural knowledge and historical understanding compared to what they learned from the cultural informants.

CRT Demoralizes White People and Calls Them Racist

CRT helps us realize that racism is woven into the fabric of our society, impacting the way we think and the laws we make. The focus of CRT is systemic societal issues of race and racism. CRT emphasizes the outcomes of these issues, not the actions of any individual (Sawchuk, 2021). For example, understanding how redlining has negatively impacted people of the global majority doesn't attack any individual bank manager but examines the loan banking system as a whole and how its practices reinforce racism. The same can be true as we look at our district's educational policies on zero-tolerance, dress codes, and appearance restrictions, special education identification and referral, communication with parents, as well as our assumptions and biases, and help us to critically analyze how they impact traditionally marginalized students and support racism. History has provided a sometimes-inaccurate account of many things we were taught throughout our education. Through CRT, practitioners can begin to deconstruct those inaccuracies and gain new knowledge from diverse perspectives. CRT is not demoralizing white people but rather insisting that white people, along with the rest of the world's population, examine the role each one of us plays in the continuation of systemic racism (George, 2021; Sawchuk, 2021).

If there is a fear of demoralizing white students, practitioners can use CRT and intersectionality to highlight shared identities in the classroom, as discussed throughout this volume. As students begin to understand their own sociocultural identities and how their culture fits into the puzzle of our world, they start to see these differences as alternate perspectives and not "abnormal" or "wrong" (Fuller et al., 2021b). Students who apply the tenets of CRT can deconstruct their prior schema about historical events and analyze the privileges and roles played in support of racism, without feeling demoralized. Students learning under this framework move past the notion of who's at fault and move toward finding solutions and advocating. A common quote by Will Smith (rapper, actor, and influencer) explains the difference between fault and responsibility as he states, "It doesn't matter whose fault it is, if it's your responsibility to fix it" (YouTube, 2018). He illustrates several scenarios describing parents from battered homes not cycling those traumas to their children, or people from broken marriages healing from that baggage as they move on. He goes on to say that as long as we are worried about fault, we are in victim mode. This concept of fault is one CRT cares little about, focusing rather on those with power and privilege taking on the responsibility for change, whether it be at the federal level or in the classroom.

CRT Pits White People against People of the Global Majority

CRT does not pit white people against individuals from traditionally oppressed sociocultural identities. This misconception parallels those that depict CRT as being about oppressors versus oppressed, blaming white people, or claiming all white people are racist. As described previously, CRT focuses on systems of racism and how their outcomes impact PGM. CRT scholars do not agree that all white people are racists or create these categories to label each individual as oppressor or oppressed. Instead, CRT scholars argue that institutions favor whiteness by creating norms from the "ideal" of whiteness. This favor gives privilege to white people over other racial or ethnic identities. This privilege also creates power and leverage to keep this hierarchy in place, supporting the dominant culture of whiteness. This means that people can intend not to be racist but still make choices to perpetuate racism. CRT does not care if you, as an individual, are racist, but seeks to highlight how one is contributing to racism and to find ways of dismantling biases and barriers.

Instead of labeling individuals as oppressed or oppressor, practitioners can use CRT to identify school practices that force all stakeholders to conform to white, Westernized ideology. School leaders can use intersectionality to help identify the most vulnerable students who face increased risk factors. After understanding that racism is common and ordinary, it is easier to spot educational practices that drive racism. Practitioners who look at patterns and practices through a CRT lens are more likely to listen and seek advice from diverse perspectives (*storytelling*) and see how whiteness benefits from these policies (*interest convergence*). Practitioners, knowledgeable of CRT, can resist contributing to racial issues like colorblindness and are able to reflect on their own understanding of diversity and belonging.

CRT, Culturally and Linguistically Sustaining Practices, Anti-Racism, and Social Justice Work

Critical Race Theory is not synonymous with culturally and linguistically sustaining practices (CLSP) or, as termed in this text, socioculturally sustaining practices. Utilizing CRT does not signify that a practitioner is anti-racist or participating in social justice work. These other frameworks and teaching ideologies may share similarities with or even pay homage to CRT when conceptualized, but that does not make them the same. Take culturally relevant teaching, a predecessor to CLSP that emerged in the 1990s. This approach attempts to embed ethnicity and racial background into the instruction to spark intellectual curiosity which, while important, tends to fall short of overtly addressing systemic racism (Rhodes et al., 2022). On the other hand, an anti-racist practitioner would address systemic racism as a social construct as well as the concept of intersectionality in a manner similar to CRT scholars. Yet an anti-racist practitioner would not have the time to examine laws, policies, and practices to be able to properly pinpoint those systemic areas nor is it likely they would offer their expertise toward solutions. Even educational institutions that focus on social justice work centered around diversity, equity, and inclusivity most likely are not conducting CRT research nor explicitly teaching the tenets of CRT to their students. Just because a program has a focus on race does not make it synonymous with the critical framework and other analytical attributes of CRT.

As described throughout this chapter, it can be easy to misconstrue CRT and mistake it for other educational theories that focus on race and diversity. It is important to keep this distinction in mind to combat misconceptions about CRT and be able to accurately describe the pedagogical frameworks from which your district plans and implements instruction. Holding "all things race" under the umbrella of CRT does a disservice to the legal scholar conducting CRT research and analysis, and confuses educational practitioners and caregivers who are unsure of the education their children are receiving. Using proper terminology to describe the strategies applied in the classroom environment and being able to accurately communicate those practices with parents are key characteristics of a successful parent and school partnership. Be careful of scholars claiming to work with CRT who do not work within the tenets of ideology (Ledesma & Calderón, 2015). We must be critics of CRT by helping to ensure that researchers, practitioners, and others in the field of education are not simply adding CRT to their conference presentations, academic journal submissions, and other works while not actually doing true justice to the concept of CRT (Lynn & Dixson, 2013). We must be able to properly identify these major issues and not cause more harm by adding to the confusion.

> It's because they're nervous about broad social things, but they're talking in the language of school and school curriculum. That's the vocabulary, but the actual grammar is anxiety about shifting social power relations. (Day, 2021, para. 9)

THE ALREADY DONES: CRITICAL RACE THEORY IN EDUCATION

Similar to the birth of CRT, special education reform was born of a need to address inequity in educational outcomes by altering the education meant to accommodate the differing needs of students. Chapters 11 and 12 offer more information on special education reform. Both CRT and special education address educational inequity at the root, locating the "problem" needing to be changed within the institution itself, not within the students. Both movements are designed to allow practitioners to "see" students more holistically and adapt our teaching to their needs to make high educational standards and equitable quality of life attainable. Socioculturally diverse students with disabilities experience intersectional discrimination in schools; see chapter 2 for examples. CRT allows us to see the ways in which a student's disability alongside their race, ethnicity, gender, socioeconomic status, and other sociocultural identities impact schooling, presenting specific needs that must be met in order to reduce inequitable educational outcomes.

Implementing a CRT Framework into the PreK–12 Classroom

Historically, CRT has been used to review current laws and policies and to provide a lens to assess and identify practical tools and strategies. CRT can also show us how race and racism manifest themselves within the preK–12 classroom and help us to combat these issues within the context of policy and community engagement (Ledesma & Calderón, 2015). A review of the CRT literature offers suggestions for the field to move forward, outlining several themes that branch from CRT into education in both the preK–12 classroom and higher education (Ledesma & Calderón, 2015). The themes within the grade school literature use CRT to analyze certain aspects of the educational system, such as (a) curriculum and pedagogy, (b) teaching and learning, (c) schooling, (d) policy and finance, and (e) community engagement (Ledesma & Calderón, 2015). One common way that practitioners can use the guidance of CRT to help increase engagement and a sense of student belonging is to consider the cultural representation in the literature and signage available. Aligned with the CRT concept of storytelling and counter-storytelling, providing diverse sociocultural representation in literature gives students the opportunity to see themselves, gain a sense of belonging, and take pride in the contributions of people who are like them. Table 4.2 provides a checklist that aligns with the CRT tenets for the reflective practice of practitioners and activities within the preK–12 and higher education setting.

Table 4.2. Checklist of CRT Framework and Student Activities

Tenets	Practitioners	Students	
		K–12 Classroom	Higher Education
Race is "normal"	• Identify patterns of racism in school policies and regulations. • Reflect on your personal understanding of racism and its impact on your students.	• Teach advocacy skills for a student's race the same as you would for a disability. • Discuss how students' race and background create or remove opportunities for academic success.	• Identify ways that institutions support and perpetuate racism. • Facilitate dialogue that orients solutions to ending everyday systemic racism.
Interest convergence	• Investigate how policies can portray the betterment of people who experience oppression, while ultimately advancing the cisgender, white, male standard. • Create classroom rules and expectations based on the needs of your students and not societal norms.	• Discuss the notion of fairness, equity, and equality. • Play the change rule game (where the rule keeps changing to ensure that a target player wins no matter what). Discuss how students felt being the target player or the others.	• Identify policies and educational practices that show interest convergence. • Discuss "good practice" strategies to create a welcoming classroom environment.

(continued)

Table 4.2. *Continued*

Tenets	Practitioners	Students K–12 Classroom	Students Higher Education
Race is socially constructed	• Understand the concept of race and racial groups held by your school district. • Identify policies and educational practices that force students to assimilate and lessen their connection to their culture.	• Discuss different social scenarios to showcase how events impact people differently (intersectionality). • Highlight common sociocultural stereotypes represented in your class and provide accurate narratives.	• Identify ways to advocate for the intersecting needs of race, disability, and other social constructs. • Investigate the impact mainstream media has had on the definition of race throughout history.
Intersectionality	• Understand your sociocultural identities and how the intersections impact the way you show up in society. • Identify and observe the sociocultural identities of your students.	• Have students complete and share a sociocultural identity activity. • Discuss the sociocultural identities of the classroom that differ from the community or school district.	• Evaluate the ways in which laws and policy align with a typical sociocultural identity and how intersectionality affects each student. • Discuss current educational policies and make amendments that support a more inclusive environment.
Storytelling and Counter-storytelling	• Invite guest speakers from different races and use cultural informants to gain diverse perspectives. • Incorporate diverse authors in text and classroom libraries.	• Promote storytelling through prompts during journal writing and show-and-tells that focus on their sociocultural uniqueness. • Investigate how different communities share and tell stories (i.e., different versions of Cinderella or God).	• Create spaces that highlight stories of the most vulnerable populations. • Advocate for policies that consider first-person accounts as valid and factual sources of information.

Pause and Reflect

Consider the tenets of Critical Race Theory and the examples provided earlier.

- What are some ways you can incorporate CRT concepts into your classroom? Your instruction? Your daily practices?

VIGNETTE 1: *EDUCATOR'S STORY OF THE TRUE COST OF A NICKNAME*

At the start of the school year, as a first-year high school math practitioner in a middle-class suburban school district, I was reviewing my class rosters for any 504 Plans, medical alerts, Individualized Education Program (IEP) plans, and English Language Learner (ELL) documentation that needed to be reviewed and signed. My student population is predominantly Caribbean and African, with students from Trinidad and Tobago, Nigeria, and Haiti. As I run through the lists, I notice some names that are relatively difficult to pronounce. I try to sound them out but think, "I'm sure they have a nickname. That will make my life so much easier when trying to conduct class. I do not want to embarrass myself or butcher students' names in front of the whole group!"

At the start of my first-period Honors Geometry class, I assigned all students to their respective seats. I stated their first and last name as it is printed on the roster. When I came across one of my students, Chukwudumaga, a sophomore of Nigerian descent, I was definitely struggling with his pronunciation. Before saying his name, I looked at it and accidently made a face, as if something was wrong. As I stood in front of the class, I attempted the young man's name and said it incorrectly. I could see the embarrassment on the student, by this time the snickering from the students had ensued. I tried to take the attention off of the situation by asking Chukwudumaga if he had any nicknames, like Chuck or Chuckie. Chukwudumaga shakes his head, indicating "no," and sinks back into his chair uncomfortably.

What I failed to realize at that moment was the gravity of Chukwudumaga's name. To me, it's just a name—to Chukwudumaga, my student, it's a part of his identity. After building rapport with him I realized he was named after his great-grandfather, who bravely immigrated to the United States to get his family out of Nigeria during the Civil War in 1967. His name, translated, means "God leads me," symbolic of his family's strong religious background, a core value that has shaped him into a once-confident young man who now sits slouched over and embarrassed. Lastly, his name brings memories of family vacations in Nigeria, reminiscent of the beautiful blue waters of Lagos, and the smell of egusi (goat stew), foofoo, and jollof rice.

As a practitioner, this scenario keeps me mindful that something seemingly minute, like a name, has much more meaning than it presents at face value. Changing one's name can create an erasure of one's identity, which for some, is the only thing connecting a student to their culture or family. I no longer ask students to provide a nickname just to make it easier for me, and really, how hard is it? If we can pronounce Bronfenbrenner Ecological Model, the Pythagorean theorem, and Galileo Galilei, then surely my class can spend a few minutes accurately pronouncing our students' names. In doing so, we foster a sense of belonging and cultural acceptance in the classroom and demonstrate respect and appreciation for that culture and, furthermore, the student.

THE STOP DOINGS: BARRIERS TO TEACHING THROUGH A CRITICAL RACE THEORY LENS

Much of the controversy surrounding CRT neglects that its intention is to provide practitioners with a means to analyze the glaring and evident disparities between diverse sociocultural youth and their white peers. As these disparities occur across racial lines, socioeconomic statuses, and levels of ability, the need to examine the specific role race plays in students' learning experiences is prevalent. Preservice practitioners (PSP) can learn the knowledge and skills necessary to address these needs in their preparation training courses. However, research shows that practitioners largely enter the profession unprepared to serve students from diverse backgrounds (Ramsay-Jordan, 2020). Figure 4.2 highlights the primary barriers to a CRT-prepared practitioner workforce and strategies to effectively break through these barriers.

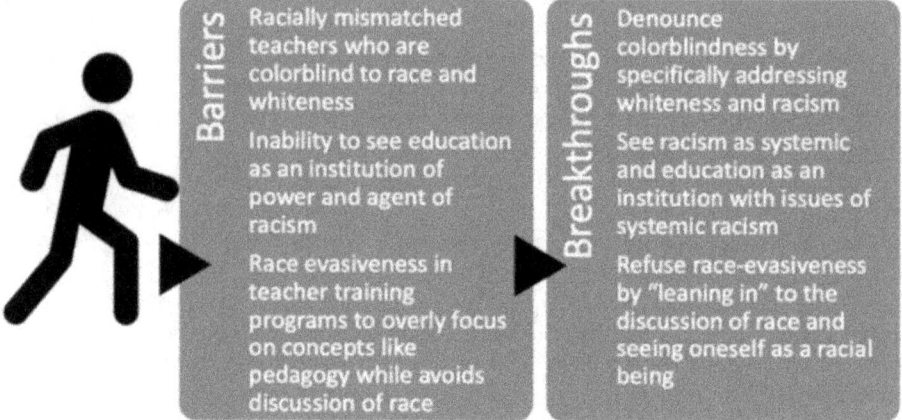

Figure 4.2. Barriers and Breakthroughs to a CRT-Prepared Practitioner Workforce

Implementing a Critical Race Theory Framework into Higher Education

A literature review of laws, policies, and equitable access to high-quality education identified three main barriers for higher education institutions to use CRT: (a) colorblindness, (b) selective admissions policy, and (c) campus racial climate (Ledesma & Calderón, 2015). These themes systemically create barriers for students from traditionally oppressed sociocultural identities to access quality education, and for faculty to become successful role models in positions of prestige. Only through the collaboration and synthesis of CRT scholarship and educational practices can institutions properly combat racism and lessen the burden of oppression.

One concept reviewed through a CRT lens is the lack of continuity among white cisgender women practitioners and their diverse students. Schools are becoming increasingly multicultural with many districts having school student populations that are 90 percent or more socioculturally diverse (Ramsay-Jordan, 2020, p. 2). The issue is not that the practitioners are white women or that the students are diverse but that many practitioners are unprepared to deal with the disconnect that a racial and sociocultural mismatch presents (Howard, 2019). No one can leave their race or other sociocultural identities outside of the classroom. Further, while Black and brown youth grow up with knowledge of racial differences and racism early in life, white people are not likely to see themselves as white or have any understanding of race at all (Howard, 2019). Thus, the racial and cultural mismatch between the education workforce and student body renders many white practitioners unable to understand or interpret, let alone integrate and appreciate, the distinct racial, sociocultural, and linguistic differences of diverse student populations. Research shows that white practitioners who are adept at understanding and interrogating race are more effective practitioners and students feel able to develop more trusting relationships (Howard, 2019). As race (and other sociocultural) identities are central parts of students' and practitioners' ways of being, thinking, behaving, and communicating, the ability to not only analyze but embrace racial, sociocultural, and linguistic differences is a necessary skill for effective practitioners (Ladson-Billings, 2005).

Being an Agent of Race

One of the themes in the CRT education literature is colorblindness. Colorblindness enables practitioners to maintain racist, deficit views that blame the students, their families, and their culture when they underperform in school. While research clearly displays the existence of racism in many facets of society (Crenshaw, 1988; Delgado & Stefancic, 1993; DiAngelo, 2018; Fuller et al., 2021a; Harkins Monaco et al., 2022), colorblindness leads practitioners to blame diverse student outcomes on race while simultaneously claiming not to see racial differences (Bonilla-Silva, 2006).

Contrarily, Black youth are raised by their families and communities to recognize race and racism in adolescence (DeCuir-Gunby, 2009). For instance, a study found that Black students were likely to be socialized toward positive racial identity development as early as seven years old (Harper, 2007). This study found that Black families taught their children about race and the existence of structural racism early in life. Black youth who were taught about racial discrimination early were better able to conceptualize inequity and embraced their Black racial identity as a central tenet of their academic achievement (Harper, 2007). Another study found practitioners, schools, and curricula are powerful factors in diverse students' racial identity development (Wright, 2009). When students had practitioners and curricula that embraced, uplifted, and accurately represented their race and culture, students felt fueled toward higher academic achievement. Results support that historically oppressed socioculturally and linguistically diverse students (Ramsay-Jordan, 2020) achieve better academically when their race and culture is embraced, not ignored. Conversely, another researcher found that practitioners who lacked racial competency had more negative teaching experiences and developed distrusting relationships between students, school personnel, and the community (Milner IV, 2008). Thus, colorblindness not only harms the students but creates negative, mistrustful, and contentious relationships that make teaching difficult.

It is essential to renounce, remove, and counteract colorblind ideology to learn to teach through a CRT lens. It is impossible to learn to properly grapple with race and not interrogate whiteness. White practitioners must learn to see how their race, culture, and privilege shape how they view and interact in society and how their race impacts how they see students and behave in the classroom. Only once practitioners can learn to place themselves in the racial hierarchy of society can they learn to effectively teach socioculturally diverse students.

Education as a Racist Institution

One reason colorblindness is so harmful is that it inhibits the ability to examine the persistence of structural racism. As practitioners confront their blind spots, they must also move beyond individual behaviors and realize racism is systemic. Following the tenet of CRT that racism is ordinary, racism is woven into the fabric of many of our nation's institutions and societal norms (Delgado & Stefancic, 2001). The institution of education is no different. While the desire to teach is often born of great ideals like the love of children and a service mindset, it is very important to know that education does not live in a bubble shielded from racism by practitioners' good intentions—quite the contrary, in fact. Education is the main battleground in which racism thrives. Thus, while the removal of colorblindness reveals that racism exists in us, CRT reveals that racism exists in the institutions in which we work, including our classrooms.

Practitioners, school district policymakers, and curricula enforce decisions that privilege students who align with the dominant white culture and discriminate against those least assimilated to its norms (Howard, 2019; Ladson-Billings, 2005). It is well documented that traditionally oppressed students display different educational outcomes than their white peers (Howard, 2019). In almost every measure from grades, standardized test scores, behavior, grades, dropout rates, and college completion rates, results for socioculturally diverse students diverged from their white peers (Harper & Hurtado, 2007). These discrepancies are widely known as the "achievement gap," although new research supports use of the term "opportunity gap" to acknowledge that these discrepancies are due to the opportunities students have access to and not their ability to achieve (Ladson-Billings, 2007). Many researchers have attempted to explain the opportunity gap, blaming the outcomes on poverty (Harper &

Hurtado, 2007). However, it has been proven that the opportunity gap persists across socioeconomic status. This means that even where diverse youth and white youth are equally poor or equally wealthy, the white youth still show better scores (Ladson-Billings, 2007). This demonstrates that the significant divider is the students' race. See chapter 2 for more examples. Through a CRT lens, practitioners move past racially based thinking like students don't care, students aren't motivated, students are too disinterested, or students don't want to succeed, and cease to believe that the problem lies in the students themselves as they begin to acknowledge the systemic racial factors that impact the students' performance and classroom environment.

Race-Evasiveness in Professional Development

CRT allows practitioners to shine much-needed light on the racially motivated practices that cause the opportunity gaps to persist. Seeing the problem through a CRT lens enables practitioners to ameliorate the classroom environment to eliminate the racism that is within their control. However, the final barrier to a well-prepared CRT workforce is race-evasiveness. **Race-evasiveness** is the refusal to discuss or examine race or racism or its impact on institutions (Chang-Bacon, 2002). A race-evasive environment (whether it be an individual or policy) will avoid, evade, deter, and even disrupt any attempt to discuss or examine race or racism. Race-evasiveness is as sinister as colorblindness in that it can cause the evasion of discussion of racism even when the person sees racial differences (Chang-Bacon, 2002). A person can see race and know racism exists and still refuse to examine or address it under race-evasiveness. As with any problem, the key to solving it is to examine and address it. Race-evasiveness has kept practitioners from addressing racism in classrooms, school districts, and in practitioner training and professional development as a final stronghold in keeping racism alive and protected.

In Robin DiAngelo's book *White Fragility* (2018), she detailed the persistent avoidance, resistance, and deflection she's faced leading professional development on racism with fellow white people. DiAngelo noted that the extreme levels of anger deflection displayed demonstrated intense emotional discomfort discussing racism. While they were ignorant of and unprepared to examine racism, DiAngelo found that participants were socialized to see racism as individual acts of mean-spirited discrimination. Attempting to explain institutional racism, she found many were determined to maintain the individual view of racism so they could continue to feel distanced or disconnected from racism.

Race-evasiveness happens everywhere; education is not without its impact. The educational spaces where race-evasiveness is most impactful are in classrooms, school policies, professional development, and practitioner training. In the classroom, race-evasiveness takes the form of avoiding conversations about race between practitioners and students. The concept may arise from a text, from course content, or even as a question from students. Students, particularly those with sharp critical thinking skills, have a knack for pointing out racism. Several canonical texts used in English Language Arts and history blocks imply or directly explore racism—it's unavoidable. It is absolutely essential for practitioners, of all races, to lean into these conversations rather than try to ignore, downplay, or deflect them. Any such attempts will feel disingenuous to students and can cause them to doubt your ability to interrogate racial issues in the future (Jenks et al., 2001; Williams, 2011).

Race-evasiveness also pervades school districts' policies. School officials, such as principals, superintendents, and school policy creators, have the power to dictate the curricula, texts, rules, and policies practitioners will implement. This power allows racial policies to be implemented with little pushback; for example, policymakers create and maintain policies that ban or penalize traditionally Black forms of hair and dress under the guise of neutral dress codes. School districts use their power to evade interrogation of racism in their curricula or policies. One common way school districts evade discussion of race and racism is through blocking and/or banning texts that discuss race or forms of racial oppression like slavery. Practitioners and educational leaders have lost their jobs trying to share the racial backstory behind historical US events like the Civil War (Bergner, 2022), and some school districts have voted to ban texts that tell counter-stories that challenge whitewashed histories (World Population Review, 2023). School district conduct and appearance policies have also been weaponized in the perpetuation of racism.

In-service practitioners are subject to race-evasiveness during professional development. Often mandated by the school district, professional development meetings seek to address common issues faced in educational practice. As racism and other forms of discrimination grow, social justice, diversity, equity, and inclusivity initiatives are of top importance in professional development. Practitioners can use race-evasiveness to hinder the progress of social justice, diversity, equity, and inclusivity initiatives when they try to resist or avoid race-based professional development by calling them "irrelevant" or a "waste of time." While every minute of instructional time is precious, every opportunity provided to make one's teaching practice better and more equitable is valuable. Seeing such professional development as worthless demonstrates a lack of care and understanding of issues of great importance to students and families. Similarly, believing that race or social justice, diversity, equity, and inclusivity professional development are only for Black or diverse colleagues is race-evasive.

Another example of race-evasiveness is when white practitioners communicate with individuals from different sociocultural identities. When diverse practitioners call out instances of racism, white practitioners will employ race-evasiveness by accusing them of "playing the race card," rather than taking the problem seriously and reflecting. A race-evasive practitioner might call the socioculturally diverse practitioners complainers who "make everything about race." Another similar form of deflection is casting down accounts of racism with personal anecdotes of one's own experiences of discrimination to trivialize a colleague's racial experience. This is a bad teaching practice as it creates discordant and distrustful relationships between practitioners and their teaching teams (Chang-Bacon, 2002) and hinders collaboration between practitioners by continuing to allow racism to flourish.

The final area where race-evasiveness hinders racial progress is in practitioner training. Colleges and universities are typically the first places PSP are exposed to the truth of racism. Thus, there is often a likelihood that race-evasiveness will be implemented to eliminate the discomfort white students may feel about the topics centered around social justice, diversity, equity, and inclusivity. In 2023, Eastern Florida State College was required to cancel a civil rights course under Florida's "Stop WOKE Act" that bans any discussion of race or racism if it makes any student uncomfortable (Wagner, 2023). The colorblindness and race-evasiveness of practitioners, curricula, and school policies blocks students from learning about racism earlier on. This harms white students especially because, unlike racially and ethnically diverse youth who grow up with racial awareness, white youth are raised to either not see or not understand racism (DiAngelo, 2018). To prepare practitioners to teach using a CRT lens, practitioner education must confront systemic racism in their institutions and resist race-evasiveness.

Practitioner education institutions, like colleges and universities, can be complicit with race-evasiveness on a programmatic level. Too many practitioner education programs avoid discussion of race by focusing too heavily on pedagogical methods. Obviously, practitioner training is needed to teach pedagogy. But to do so at the expense of integrating the social forces (like race and socioeconomic class) that impact teaching just as much as methodology is race-evasive. For example, Christine Sleeter (2001) showed how most practitioner education consists of methods courses, content courses (i.e., reading, writing, math), and child psychological development courses. Many have added a singular vague "diversity" course to superficially glance over identity issues. Furthermore, such courses are rarely mandated in the education core curriculum or held to the same grade point average (GPA) standards as education or psychology courses (Sleeter, 2001). This lack of focus on diversity creates thousands of certified practitioner graduates with no training in issues like race that dramatically impact teaching and are a major factor in their classrooms.

As discussed throughout this text, students are deeply tied to each of their sociocultural identity categories like their race, socioeconomic class, ethnicity, language, ability, and religion. Practitioner training that only teaches pedagogy misses the opportunity to teach PSP to truly teach the "whole child."

Education programs should include and mandate courses that specifically teach PSP to conceptualize how racism, sociology, and even geographical issues like segregation and gentrification change the context of classrooms. Race dictates how students are seen, treated, and allotted opportunities in society (Howard, 2019). Sociology shows how factors like income and socioeconomic status organize society. The geography of the place where one teaches—like the population, whether it is urban or rural, and the level of housing segregation—dictates the race and socioeconomic status makeup of the student body. Including and requiring these courses for certification provides space for PSP to explore how race, socioeconomic status, and location shape who students are, where they are from, and how to best teach them.

PSP themselves can also resist and evade race talks from professors during their college career. In practitioner education programs that integrate social justice, diversity, equity, and inclusivity into their coursework, PSP may use race-evasiveness to avoid or even combat anti-racist training (Chang-Bacon, 2022). For example, professors who have PSP reflect on how their race alters their teaching are met with visual disapproval and even outright refusal (Sleeter, 2017). Race-evasive PSP refute such integration as irrelevant to learning good teaching. A research study found that white PSP who were race-evasive toward training attempted to discredit professors who centered race coursework (Hambacher & Ginn, 2021). The practitioners challenged the professors' authority and even questioned the professors' teaching acumen to department heads, all in attempts to evade and foil race-reflective tasks. The study also found that these practitioners' angry and deflective actions were particularly harmful and disruptive to socioculturally diverse professors and practitioners, and even white practitioners who were culturally competent. PSP use race-evasiveness to weaponize their course evaluations against the professors in further attempts to punish and discredit them for speaking up on race matters in education (Hambacher & Ginn, 2021). Professors who work under race-evasive department heads sometimes lose their jobs or become alienated from their colleagues, being called divisive troublemakers. Race-evasive PSP also attempt to avoid student-teaching placements with predominantly diverse student populations or in diverse neighborhoods. All these actions reveal the effort and great lengths race-evasive PSP will go to to avoid simply reflecting on how race impacts the education offered to socioculturally diverse students.

Rather than avoiding the self-reflection and interrogation necessary to understand racism, it is essential for PSP to openly embrace the journey. Race-evasiveness is harmful because it prevents the conversations needed to reveal and keep racism from happening. As DiAngelo (2018) points out, the first forays into the facts of racism can unearth some seriously uncomfortable feelings and truths. Feelings of guilt, shame, or anger are common and understandable when confronting one's contribution or benefit from discrimination and racism. However, practitioners must "lean in" and work through emotions alongside people of the global majority to rectify the effects of systemic racism and promote social justice, diversity, equity, and inclusivity. As described in the tenets of CRT earlier, listen to the voices and stories of the people of the global majority and your students. Be slow to be defensive and have empathy (not pity) for those who have dealt with the effects of racism. Seek understanding about diverse feelings of fear and assimilation over white feelings of guilt and discomfort. Recognize that individuals from traditionally marginalized identities have more expertise with racism having lived the experience.

To become more culturally competent and move away from race-evasiveness, one must become anti-racist. Anti-racism is not a stance that simply says, "I am not racist!" An anti-racist is someone who sees that racism exists and harms their students. Anti-racists acknowledge their complicity in it and actively work every day to undo and overturn racism.

Pause and Reflect

This text offers a lot of strategies to build your intersectionality competence. As you read, ask yourself:

- What are the ways I can explore and develop my own anti-racism?
- How can I incorporate this evidence-based practice in an anti-racist way?

A truly effective practitioner of diverse student bodies must desire a fair and equitable education for their most vulnerable students. Leaning in and confronting racial biases shows students we can be trusted. It shows that we will strive for the best for them even if it means more work or discomfort for us. In this way, we show students we are advocating both with them and for them in the quest for equity.

VIGNETTE 2: *THE TALE OF TWO PRACTITIONERS*

It is a rainy spring day. Ironically, rainy days somehow always make the students more lively. Folding up my dripping umbrella, I walk through the school's octagonal halls to find my students' 7th-grade English class for their student teaching observation. I step in just as their lesson is about to begin and find a seat in the back of the class. The twenty-seven Black and Brown preteens come in and find their seats. The classroom is cluttered but in a warm way; the desks are grouped in four, surrounding a well-worn carpet, conducive to all the talking the students were doing as they come in from lunch. My preservice teachers that I'm here to observe teach in pairs. Tia and Meghan. Tia, junior secondary English education major, has a bright and energetic demeanor, showing excitement to teach their first lesson. Meghan, also a junior English Education major, wore her usual warm and kind presence. Her small stature contrasted with the big smile she wore as she walked in.

(continued)

> ### VIGNETTE 2: *Continued*
>
> *Their lesson begins. Having previewed their well-crafted lesson plan I was excited to see how they executed it. The objective was to get students to put themselves in a character's shoes and argue what they would do differently and better in that situation. During a turn and talk, a table of four male students gets particularly noisy. Meghan stands rooted in a spot near the front of the class, oddly close to the front door. Tia flows about the classroom, moving from table to table listening to and adding to students' conversations. She squats to join the noisy group's conversation. They're deep into a debate on what they would do if they were the story's protagonist. Meghan stood nervously at the board. Reconvening the groups, Tia gathers common answers as Meghan records them on the smartboard.*
>
> *Closing the lesson, the class is dismissed to science. I invite both student practitioners to a table to reflect on how the lesson went and give feedback. To Tia, the lesson went great. She saw the noisy group of boys as a sign that they were engaged in the content. Meghan interjects that she was disappointed. She feels their talking was disruptive and misbehavior. Perplexed Tia asks how that could be when they were on task discussing the text. Meghan didn't know. All she heard was noise. I ask Meghan why she didn't come to the table rather than staying at the front. If they were off task, then why not redirect them? Meghan pauses and looks down. After a deep breath, she says, "Because I was afraid. They're so much bigger than me! What if they get mad at me? They could overpower me and I'd never be able to defend myself!" Eyes wide, Tia exclaims, "We are the same size! You think I could?" Concerned, I wonder why Meghan would fear for her safety at all. Dejectedly, she said she didn't know but silently, we all know. Tears in both practitioners' eyes now, Meghan says, "because Tia, you're Black. I knew they would respect you. You are safe."*
>
> *Meghan had absorbed those classic racist stereotypes of Black folks; that they're loud, violent, and to be feared. The kids didn't get to just be kids. Had Meghan learned to recognize and confront such racist tropes, she'd be able to see that what she saw as a threat of violence was actually a major teaching win! She'd see that Tia wasn't better because she was Black and safe but because she listened and she tried.*

SUMMARY

This chapter highlighted the tenets of Critical Race Theory and explored the chronological development of CRT in education. The goal of CRT is to shine a light on the disparities racism causes, enabling us to diagnose the root of inequity. CRT focuses on actions and systems, not individuals, and moves the focus from intent to effect, as we look at educational practices and policies. This is not alarmist rhetoric, because racism continues to thrive in institutions like education every time the stakeholders and policymakers choose to deny or ignore its existence. Using a CRT lens to examine injustice in education empowers practitioners to attack racism head-on. Colorblindness, denial of institutional racism, and race-evasiveness prevent practitioners from learning to effectively use Critical Race Theory. Simple mindset changes in practitioner education can remove these barriers. By revitalizing practitioner training, preservice and in-service practitioners can learn to confront racism—first in themselves and then in the institutions where they serve.

REFERENCES

Bergner, D. (2022, October 14). Daring to speak up about race in a divided school district. *New York Times*. https://www.nytimes.com/2022/09/06/magazine/leland-michigan-race-school.html

Bell Jr., D. A. (1975). Serving two masters: Integration ideals and client interests in school desegregation litigation. *Yale Law Journal*, 85(4), 470.

———. (1980). Brown v. Board of Education and the interest-convergence dilemma. *Harvard Law Review*, 93(3), 518–33.

———. (1992). *Faces at the bottom of the well: The permanence of racism*. Hachette UK.

Bonilla-Silva, E. (2006). *Racism without racists: Color-blind racism and the persistence of racial inequality in the United States*. Rowman & Littlefield.

Brown, K. D. (2013). Teaching in color: A critical race theory in education analysis of the literature on preservice teachers of color and teacher education in the US. *Race, Ethnicity and Education*, 17(3), 326–45. http://doi.org/10.1080/13613324.2013.32921

Chambers Jr., H. L. (2002). Colorblindness, race neutrality, and voting rights. *Emory Law Journal*, 51, 1397.

Chang-Bacon, C. K. (2022). "We sort of dance around the race thing": Race-evasiveness in teacher education. *Journal of Teacher Education*, 73(1), 8–22.

Crenshaw, K. W. (1988). Race, reform, and retrenchment: Transformation and legitimation in antidiscrimination law. *Harvard Law Review*, 101, 1331–87.

———. (1991). Mapping the margins: Identity politics, intersectionality, and violence against women of color. *Stanford Law Review*, 43(6), 1241–99.

———. (2016). *Intersectionality* [keynote presentation]. Women of the World 2016.

Day, T. L. (2021, October 21). His view: Claims of CRT being taught in public schools are false. *Moscow-Pullman Daily News*. https://dnews.com/opinion/his-view-claims-of-crt-being-taught-in-public-schools-are-false/article_d094eb77-6358-5fc5-9579-8c80149da672.html

DeCuir-Gunby, J. T. (2009). A review of the racial identity development of African American adolescents: The role of education. *Review of Educational Research*, 79(1), 103–24.

Delgado, R. (1989). Storytelling for oppositionists and others: A plea for narrative. *Michigan Law Review*, 87(8), 2411–41.

Delgado, R., & Stefancic, J. (1989). Why do we tell the same stories?: Law reform, critical librarianship, and the triple helix dilemma. *Stanford Law Review*, 42, 207–25.

———. (1993). Critical Race Theory: An annotated bibliography. *Virginia Law Review*, 79(2), 461–516.

———. (2001). An introduction to Critical Race Theory. *Critical Race Theory: The cutting edge* (pp. 1–167). Temple University Press.

———. (2017). Chapter II. Hallmark Critical Race Theory themes. In *Critical Race Theory (third edition): An introduction* (pp. 19–43). New York University Press.

DiAngelo, R. (2018). *White fragility: Why it's so hard for white people to talk about racism*. Beacon.

Dixson, A. D., & Rousseau, C. K. (2005). And we are still not saved: Critical Race Theory in education ten years later. *Race Ethnicity and Education*, 8(1), 7–27.

Freeman, A. D. (1978). Legitimizing racial discrimination through antidiscrimination law: A critical review of Supreme Court doctrine. *Minnesota Law Review*, 62, 1049. https://scholarship.law.umn.edu/mlr/804

Fuller, M. C., Stansberry-Brusnahan, L. L., & Harkins Monaco, E. A. (2021a). Infusing intersectional pedagogy into the cultural sustaining classroom. *Division of Autism and Developmental Disorders Online Journal, 27*–41.

Fuller, M. C., Carrero, K. M., & Hunter, W. (2021b). Preparing educators and coaching cultural competence and disability awareness. In E. A. Harkins, M. C. Fuller, & L. L. Stansberry-Brusnahan (Eds.), *Diversity, autism, and developmental disabilities: Guidance for the culturally responsive educator*. Prism Series, 13. Council for Exceptional Children.

George, J. (2021, May 26). Critical Race Theory isn't a curriculum. It's a practice (opinion). *Education Week.*

Goldstein, T. (2001). "I'm not white": Anti-racist teacher education for white early childhood educators. *Contemporary Issues in Early Childhood, 2*(1), 3–13.

Hambacher, E., & Ginn, K. (2021). Race-visible teacher education: A review of the literature from 2002–2018. *Journal of Teacher Education, 72*(3), 329–41. https://doi.org/10.1177/0022487120948045

Harkins Monaco, E. A., Stansberry-Brusnahan, L. L., & Fuller, M. C. (2022). Guidance for the antiracist educator: Culturally sustaining pedagogies for disability and diversity. *TEACHING Exceptional Children.* https://www.sciencegate.app/document/10.1177/00400599211046281

Harper, B. E. (2007). The relationship between Black racial identity and academic achievement in urban settings. *Theory into Practice, 46*(3), 230–38. https://www.jstor.org/stable/40071494

Harper, S. R., & Hurtado, S. (2007). Nine themes in campus racial climates and implications for institutional transformation. *New Directions for Student Services, 120,* 7–24.

Hartlep, N. D. (2009). Critical Race Theory an examination of its past, present, and future implications. Online Submission. https://eric.ed.gov/?id=ED506735

Hawthorne, B. (2023). Who are People of the Global Majority and why it matters. Britt Hawthorne [blog]. https://britthawthorne.com/blog/people-global-majority/

Howard, T. C. (2019). *Why race and culture matter in schools: Closing the achievement gap in America's classrooms.* Teachers College Press.

Immigration Law Practitioners' Association (ILPA). (2022). People of the global majority. https://ilpa.org.uk/people-of-the-global-majority/

Jenks, C., Lee, J. O., & Kanpol, B. (2001). Approaches to multicultural education in preservice teacher education: Philosophical frameworks and models for teaching. *Urban Review, 33,* 87–105.

Ladson-Billings, G. (2005). The evolving role of Critical Race Theory in educational scholarship. *Race, Ethnicity and Education, 8*(1), 115–19.

———. (2007). Pushing past the achievement gap: An essay on the language of deficit. *Journal of Negro Education, 76*(3), 316–23.

———. (2021). Critical Race Theory—What it is not! In M. Lynn & A. D. Dixon (Eds.), *Handbook of Critical Race Theory in education* (pp. 32–43). Routledge.

Ladson-Billings, G., & Tate, W. F. (1995). Toward a critical race theory of education. *Teachers College Record, 97*(1), 47–68.

Ledesma, M. C., & Calderón, D. (2015). Critical Race Theory in education: A review of past literature and a look to the future. *Qualitative Inquiry, 21*(3), 206–22.

Lim, D. (2020). I'm embracing the term "people of the global majority." Medium. https://regenerative.medium.com/im-embracing-the-term-people-of-the-global-majority-abd1c1251241

Lynn, M., & Dixson, A. D. (Eds.). (2013). *Handbook of Critical Race Theory in education* (pp. 181–94). Routledge.

Milner IV, H. R. (2008). Critical Race Theory and interest convergence as analytic tools in teacher education policies and practices. *Journal of Teacher Education, 59*(4), 332–46. https://doi.org/10.1177/0022487108321884

Ramsay-Jordan, N. (2020). Using tenets of critical race pedagogy to examine white pre-service teachers' perceptions of their Black students' race and culture. *Multicultural Education, 27*(2), 2–17. https://files.eric.ed.gov/fulltext/EJ1280883.pdf

Rhoads, M., Fecich, S., Jakubowski, C. T., & Leichtman, K. (2022). Critical conversation two: Critical Race Theory vs. culturally responsive teaching. In *Crush it from the start: 50 tips for new teachers* (pp. 84–85). School Rubric.

Sawchuk, S. (2021, May 18). What is Critical Race Theory, and why is it under attack? *Education Week*.

Sleeter, C. E. (2001). Preparing teachers for culturally diverse schools: Research and the overwhelming presence of whiteness. *Journal of Teacher Education, 52*(2), 94–106. https://www.researchgate.net/publication/249704298_Preparing_Teachers_for_Culturally_Diverse_Schools

———. (2017). Critical Race Theory and the whiteness of teacher education. *Urban Education, 52*(2), 155–169. https://doi.org/10.1177/0042085916668957

Subedi, B. (2013). The racialization of South Asian Americans in a post-9/11 era. In M. Lynn & A. D. Dixson (Eds.), *Handbook of Critical Race Theory in education* (pp. 187–200). Routledge.

Tate, W. F., Ladson-Billings, G., & Grant, C. A. (1993). The *Brown* decision revisited: Mathematizing social problems. *Educational Policy, 7*(3), 255–75.

Thompson, V. (2021, February 10). Understanding the policing of black, disabled bodies. Center for American Progress. https://www.americanprogress.org/article/understanding-policing-black-disabled-bodies/

Wagner, A. (2023). A civil rights class has been canceled due to one student's "Discomfort." MSNBC/TikTok. https://www.tiktok.com/@msnbc?lang=en

White, G. E. (1972). From sociological jurisprudence to realism: Jurisprudence and social change in early twentieth-century America. *Virginia Law Review, 58*, 999–1028.

Williams, M. T. (2011, December 27). Colorblind ideology is a form of racism: A colorblind approach allows us to deny uncomfortable cultural differences. *Psychology Today, 27*.

World Population Review. (2023). Critical Race Theory ban states: States with bans against Critical Race Theory. https://worldpopulationreview.com/state-rankings/states-that-have-banned-critical-race-theory

Wright, B. L. (2009). Racial-ethnic identity, academic achievement, and African American males: A review of literature. *Journal of Negro Education, 78*(2), 123–34.

YouTube. (2018, January 31). Fault vs, responsibility by Will Smith full speech (w/subtitles). WhateverItTakesMotivation. YouTube. https://www.youtube.com/watch?v=Ln21-WhJyec

CHAPTER 5

The Journey of Disability Studies: Contemplating Disability Critically

Chapter authors: *Kara B. Ayers, Lydia Ocasio-Stoutenburg, and David J. Connor*

Vignette author: *Lydia Ocasio-Stoutenburg*

Editor: *Marcus C. Fuller*

ABSTRACT

Critical Disability Theory (CDT) integrates disability studies and Critical Race Theory scholarship to reconceptualize disability beyond the confines of deficits-based definitions and medical model perspectives. This reconceptualization is an important strategy to oppose the invisible and insidious impacts of ableism. Through a lens informed by CDT, disability is viewed as a natural—and even valued—component of human variation. Rather than seeking to overcome or eliminate disability, the eradication of ableism is prioritized as a goal to improve our society. The purpose of this chapter is to define CDT for practitioners by discussing the historical implications of ableism, paternalism, and the maintenance of systems of poverty and isolation. This chapter explores the intersection of disability and other socially constructed, marginalized identities, like race, gender, and sexual orientation. Binary divisions between disabled and nondisabled, between normal and abnormal, and between able to learn and not able to learn will be dismantled. The purpose of this chapter is to equip readers with strategies to leverage CDT to improve their educational practices within the classroom and beyond.

GUIDING QUESTIONS

- How does Critical Disability Theory view disability?
- How has Critical Disability Theory impacted education practices historically and what future implications are predicted?
- How does Critical Disability Theory describe the intersection of multiple marginalized sociocultural identities?
- How can we leverage Critical Disability Theory to enact improved educational practices?

KEY TERMS

Ableism
Access
Black Disability Studies
Critical Disability Studies in Education
Critical Disability Theory
Disability Critical Race Theory
Disability Justice Movement
Disability Studies
Medical Model
Models of Disability
Neurodiversity and Neurodivergence
Normality
Social Model
Universal Design
Universal Design for Learning

The civil rights movement in the United States had been growing for decades but became prominent during the 1950s when Black Americans sought social justice within a society that had historically oppressed them in all aspects of life, including: freedom of speech, freedom of movement, housing, employment, and education. Having captured the attention of the nation and the world by demonstrations of courage that brought unprecedented success in creating social change, other groups were inspired to mobilize and call attention to injustices they were subjected to, based upon one or more aspects of their identity. For example, the women's movement in the 1960s rapidly evolved to claim justice for females in all realms of society, creating a new sense of liberation filled with possibilities ("women's lib" becoming part of everyday conversation). Yet initially this movement only benefited white middle-class women—who were most vocal and used for campaigning; later attempts began to encompass a fuller spectrum of womanhood. Likewise, at the close of the decade, the LGBTQIA+ (lesbian, gay, bisexual, transgender, queer or questioning, intersex, asexual, and more) community revolted, demanding a stop to the violence, harassment, and intimidation against them, claiming the need for equal rights and protection within the law. See chapter 2 for examples of the LGBTQIA+ and disability intersections. Similarly, people with disabilities saw the opportunity to forge their own civil rights movement, demanding they be fully included, provided accommodations if needed, and given access to all aspects of society that nondisabled people took for granted, including: public and commercial buildings, transportation systems, employment, education, restaurants, entertainment, community activities, and so on. More information on these movements can be found in chapters 10 and 11.

What characteristics do these civil rights movements have in common? Briefly stated, they all are grassroots movements of people united by an aspect of their identity that confront a history of oppression and violence, actual and symbolic; illustrate interlocking aspects of oppression within societal, structural, cultural, and personal realms; challenge widespread misinformation and stereotyping; assert lived "truths" that run contrary to many mainstream (mis) understandings; claim the right for equality under the law and protection from discrimination; and seek full participation in society. In sum, all these things occur when an aspect of sociocultural identity necessarily becomes politicized in the pursuit of social change.

In this chapter we cover the historical impact Critical Disability Theory has had on society and educational practices as well as provide a clear understanding of how Critical Disability Theory views disability. This chapter continues to uncover the vast depth of intersectionality while offering strategies and intervention that are grounded in Critical Disability Theory to improve educational practices.

DISABILITY STUDIES

As part of social change, academic movements developed and grew, with fields such as Black Studies, Women's Studies, Gay and Lesbian Studies becoming established in universities. Similarly, **Disability Studies** (DS) as an academic field developed in the 1970s, in part because of shifts in society that recognized people with disabilities as now having greater rights under the law. For example, the Education for All Handicapped Children Act (1975) passed by the US Congress, marked the end of an era in which public education was denied to generations of students with disabilities. Over four decades later, the ruling is now known as the Individuals with Disabilities Education Improvement Act (IDEIA, 2004) and continues to provide students with disabilities many guarantees including a "free appropriate public education" (FAPE), an appropriate evaluation, an Individualized Education Program (IEP), placement in the least restrictive environment (LRE), parent involvement, and procedural safeguards in the form of due process. Part of the shift in thinking about disability that prompted Disability Studies to emerge was the need to explore, rethink, reframe, and better understand what being disabled in society actually meant.

From its inception, scholars of Disability Studies have been critical about how society predominantly thinks about disability, exploring such questions as: Who is generating the disability knowledge and how many of these individuals identify with a disability? How is the knowledge used? Who benefits from its generation, circulation, and use? What is its relationship to the everyday lives of people with disabilities? To what degree does knowledge help people with disabilities (Davis, 2021)? By exploring these and other questions, it became clear there existed multiple and significantly different ways to think about disability.

What researchers, activists, and artists within Disability Studies revealed was that fields of study such as science, medicine, psychology, and special education overwhelmingly viewed disabled people as sick, damaged, dysfunctional, disordered, and primarily in need of a cure. This approach is mostly known as the **Medical Model of Disability** and tends to pervade many fields of study and most aspects of society. The medical industry defines disability as a deficit or sickness in need of cure and forms the basis of how most professionals are taught to view disability (Shyman, 2016). See chapter 6 for more models. In analyzing the power dynamics of what counts as knowledge, and according to whom and in what context, these fields of study came under critique by those in DS for their unquestioned adherence to the medical model. Their default position, intentional or not, casts disabled people in medical terms that overwhelmingly portray them in a negative light, as "less than" or inferior to nondisabled people. Defining disability in more favorable terms, therefore, became a primary goal of DS. Furthermore, the mantra of "Nothing about us without us" (Charlton, 1998) conveyed the desire of disabled people to always be present when disability-related issues were being discussed in relation to theory, practice, policy, and research, thereby empowering them to speak to the potential impact (or lack thereof) on their lives.

With their critical stance, scholars and activists in DS articulated a radically different framework for thinking about disability called the **Social Model**. This model presented people with disabilities as part of natural human variation, and illustrated how human attitudes and physical barriers that pervade society are what truly disable people (Linton, 1998). Through this model, DS scholars do not deny that bodily differences exist, whether physical, sensory, emotional, cognitive; however, they assert that it's not these differences that count so much but rather our reactions and biases toward them. In other words, while people may have impairments, there's nothing intrinsically wrong with them. It is therefore incumbent on us all to ask why this line of thinking or evaluation according to different models of understanding disability is important for practitioners. Practitioners have more than one framework through which to think about important disability-related questions. Consider table 5.1 to view critical reflection questions on your own ideas and beliefs about disability. Taken together, these questions reveal some of the complexities involved in understanding disability and best ways to work with disabled students in educational settings.

Table 5.1. Critical Reflection Questions for Disability Studies

- What does the concept of disability mean?
- What is the relationship between disability and social justice?
- What is the relationship of disability, social justice, and education?
- What is the practitioner's role in educating students with disabilities?
- What is the most effective way(s) to plan for, instruct, and assess students with disabilities?
- What is the right placement for students with disabilities?
- What are the best ways to support families?
- What is the relationship between disability and the purpose of education? Special education?

VIGNETTE 1: *MOVING ISAIAH*

Upon enrolling in a new district, we were invited for a tour of the school and its facilities. Everyone showed up, teachers, therapists, administrators, even some representatives from the school district. We brought Isaiah with us. People stared at us.

Who were we? And more specifically who was I, who was Isaiah, and what did that represent? I was a new parent, but not just any parent. I was also a newly hired faculty at the university in a college town. I had a child who was going to be enrolled at the school, and not just any child. He was a child who they didn't know yet, but who had this diagnostic label of Down syndrome and did not have expressive language. And we were Black.

And we were Black.

I am adding "we were Black" not as an additive fact but as a consequential fact that made meaning of almost every interaction before, during, and after. I was Black, a woman, and faculty and in special education, teaching some of their future teachers. I was also the mother of a child who needed academic and communication support, with the eligibility label of intellectual disability. The options for him at the school were limited and they knew that, acknowledged that. In many ways they had made considerable effort to do a delicate dance with us and I understood why. For one, there was some glimmer, some illusion of power I had as faculty, a disruption to the typical power-down structure of school personnel-parent engagements. Secondly, this was overlaying history. In recent years, most of the Black faculty who had disabled children in the school district did not stay, citing the numerous problems in the school district as one of their primary reasons for leaving. I did not know this, of course, until after I had uprooted my entire family. So, within me was this worry, fear that I had taken him from where he was happy to a place where he would not be understood, both because of the presentation of his disability and because we were Black. More importantly, he was alone, as one of only a handful of Black boys in the school and the only Black disabled boy in his class.

Shortly after this initial encounter, the school psychologist invited us in to get some parental input. She was a white woman who shared that she graduated from her school psychology program in recent years, and spoke in a soft and gentle tone. I say this because she picked up on nuance, she was familiar with some terminology based on the questions she asked. Similarly, one of Isaiah's teachers was in her first year as a new teacher, a young white woman with a kind smile, who always had something positive to offer.

We can begin to contemplate the issues raised by these questions through engaging with the field of DS which is, in essence, multidisciplinary in nature, encompassing sociology, the humanities, law, science, and so on. Within DS, the subfield of **Disability Studies in Education** (DSE) has grown significantly over the last twenty years, largely challenging the dominance of the medical model used within the academic field of special education that is encoded in laws and embedded throughout everyday practices in schools such as inclusive education. The medical and social models conceptualize and present inclusive education quite differently. Researchers and practitioners who view inclusion of students with disabilities via the medical model see inclusive education primarily as a technical endeavor that is often erroneously reduced to placement, in other words, the movement of segregated special education settings to general education. Conversely, researchers and practitioners who view inclusive education from a social model perspective see the provision of equitable educational opportunity within general education as a right, and an endeavor worthy of struggle.

Critical special education practitioners and DSE scholars have frequently been derided by traditionalists in the field of special education, accused of being highly impractical and out of touch with reality:

> "Alternatives" to science or "alternative narratives" (now a fashionable idea in postmodernist education) include social determinism, cognitive relativism, and disability studies. If special education as a field of study and practice wants to survive for the sake of the educational needs of students [with] disabilities, it needs to claim unabashedly its commitment to science-based evidence and practices while rejecting forcefully claims based on social determinism and cognitive relativism. (Kauffman et al., 2017, p. 8)

Decades of research on inclusive education support the work of critical special education practitioners, affirming that all students have the right to belong, without needing to earn it through achieving specific standards (Baglieri, 2017). Furthermore, successful inclusive classrooms have evolved through grassroots thinking and efforts by practitioners, students, and parents, all working together toward finding out "what works" for a specific child within a learning community (e.g., Berman & Connor, 2017). There are various approaches and strategies to support students with disabilities in inclusive classrooms, but in acknowledging the diversity of disability, there is no set blueprint or one-size-fits-all template. Such strategies are based on ongoing observations, evidence-based practices, holistic approaches, and problem-solving techniques as needed. Think about equity literacy (EL) as discussed in chapter 3. In brief, the support of disabled students in inclusive classrooms can best be described not as a predictable "scientifically controlled" trajectory but more akin to the meanderings of jazz music, always moving forward with riffs and improvisations based upon dynamic interchanges. In other words, successful inclusive classrooms are based on a flexible approach to instruction in an environment that can be modified at any given moment to accommodate a variety of student needs, rather than that which is typically seen in traditional classrooms. In inclusive classrooms, DSE provides instruction that goes beyond a technical response to empower teachers to broaden their pedagogy to reach a more diverse body of students. For example, consider the framework of **Universal Design for Learning** (UDL; Novak & Couros, 2022), an approach that helps teachers proactively design lessons and curricula for all students in their classes. Teachers strive to make all lessons accessible, having taken time to get to know their students' strengths, likes, and areas of need. UDL is covered in many chapters of this book.

Valuing a Critical Theoretical Perspective on Disability

Many preservice practitioners (PSP) go through their teacher certification programs without critically analyzing the medical model framework they are being educated through. It is important to emphasize the value of more critical approaches to conceptualizing disability that challenge oppressive understandings. Critical approaches reject deficit-based understandings of disability and, instead, emphasize assets-based lenses that "presume competence" (Biklen & Burke, 2006) of disabled students. Critical special education practitioners also emphasize the value of being grounded in an ethic of caring rather than an ethic of curing. A critical approach to disability is rooted in the disability rights movement's desire to have access to all aspects of society, including inclusive classrooms (Danforth, 2021).

For many practitioners, the word "critical" can initially seem harsh, even off-putting, perhaps having associations with what we've all felt at some point, being "unfairly criticized by others." Therefore, it is important to emphasize the use of critical theory in education in a constructive way. **Critical theory** is a method of analyzing how power is constructed in social, cultural, and historical ways, including examining the cultural assumptions of our society (Abdi & Misiaszek, 2022). Critical theory analyzes these power structures that impact people's lives and determines more liberating ways of educating students. Critical practitioners must cultivate self-reflectivity as they constantly evaluate contexts, situations, and values (their own and those of others) to counter oppression embedded within everyday practices.

Pause and Reflect

- How are you engaging in self-reflectivity?
- Do you regularly evaluate your own contexts, situations, and values to counter oppression?
- Do you regularly evaluate other contexts, situations, and values to counter oppression?

When analyzing how power operates, consideration must be given to prioritizing the lived experiences of people with disabilities and their views, including ideas such as the legitimacy of interdependence, as independence is not possible, nor even desirable, for everybody (Oliver, 2009). Additionally, practitioners who value a critical disability studies perspective value cross-cultural intersectionality, as disability is recognized as an intersectional experience that crosses multiple aspects of identity (Erevelles, 2011). Thinking critically around the topic of disability is complex, often uneasy, but also imperative. Theories we use inform our decisions, actions, and words, shape our everyday practices, and have the potential to reinvigorate conversations about what we do and why. While it can be challenging to achieve a balance between how theory informs practice and how practice informs theory (Ferri & Connor, 2021), we acknowledge that this process is a form of activism and an integral part of the field of education.

Pause and Reflect

Consider the major concepts that you as an educator incorporate into your teaching philosophy.

- How do these concepts affect your interactions with students with disabilities?
- How do these concepts affect your interactions with students of the global majority?

DISCOVERING THE NEED FOR CRITICAL DISABILITY STUDIES

Within the last forty to fifty years, a branch of disability studies has evolved called **Critical Disability Studies** (CDS) which includes the transdisciplinary analyses of other theoretical fields such as queer, feminist, and critical race theory. As Goodley (2013) notes, CDS explains "the centrality of disability when we consider the politics of life itself" (p. 631). Infusing the idea of balancing theory with professional development practices through activism, we can see the value of CDS in forging change. Yet in current society, the support and advocacy for people with disabilities has ironically fostered oppressive beliefs and practices that benefit the feelings and ideologies of the nondisabled more than the population they are intended to serve. Therefore, a CDS approach becomes desirable to integrate into education programs for teachers (Connor, 2022), social workers (Meekosha & Dowse, 2007), and rehabilitation counselors (Magasi, 2008), providing the framework to illustrate how certain beliefs and educational practices can enable or further disable people. This line of inquiry has led many scholars and researchers to use CDS as a lens to evaluate the education system, forming a branch of studies called **Critical Disabilities Studies in Education** (CDSE).

Becoming grounded in CDSE means professionals view education through a critical eye that rejects deficit-understandings of disability in favor of valuing natural human diversity. Moreover, the value of CDSE encompasses an ability to span, and unite, connections among theory, research, practice, and policy through education. For example, CDSE encourages engagement with other fields that can potentially offer a different insight into understanding disability and lived experiences. A CDSE disposition provides a consistent alternative to limited and medicalized notions of disability by accessing political, social, cultural, historical, and individual understandings of disability, while seeking to redefine how disability is understood by the mainstream media and dominant society (for more information, see chapters 1 and 6). Using a CDSE framework in educational planning and curriculum also diversifies research through culturally and linguistically sustaining practices (CLSP; also discussed in chapters 2, 4, 7, 8, and 12), centering disabled people as participants and collaborators rather than subjects (Gonzalez et al., 2017).

The identification of patterns across countries is useful in studying international trends, which can highlight similar problems such as overrepresentation of marginalized, indigenous, and immigrant youth through a CDSE lens (Cooc & Kiru, 2018). The engagement between different countries has highlighted the importance of considering customs, beliefs, and practices when constructing educational policies and school norms. In terms of practice, CDSE continues to emphasize the moral and ethical dimensions of inclusive education, while still maintaining that legal and technical aspects are present. Practitioners can move toward more inclusive education by incorporating disability directly into the curriculum. Understanding and learning about disability helps students (and frankly school faculty and staff, as well) see disability as one of many formative markers of identity—like race, gender, and sexual orientation—that must be included and explored as part of human experience (McKinney, 2016).

Critical Disability Theory and Intersectionality

Bronfenbrenner's (1977) Ecological Systems Theory conceptualizes the structural arrangement of our society and how we are nested within layers of systems that are complex and dynamic. For example, inequities identified at a policy level will have substantial impact on (a) what is being researched and how it is being researched; (b) the allocations and distributions of funds and resources; (c) multiple systems, such as health and education; and (d) practices, all of which impact people's daily lives. The interactions of these entities must be examined to understand their collective impact on disabled people, their caregivers, and systems of support, especially for people who are holding multiple nondominant identities.

The first step is to acknowledge that there are inequities at the broader systems level that impact disabled people in magnified ways, and most especially disabled people of color, or disabled People of the Global Majority (PGM). Understanding these "interlocking oppressions" at the broader levels, as contributed by scholar Patricia Hill Collins (1990), is central to understanding the inequities experienced on the everyday microlevel, where we encounter intersectionality. Intersectionality is a concept that has been used, co-opted, rescripted, and often diluted when applied to situations, uprooted out of its historical context in Black feminism and critical legal scholarship. Intersectionality is not the same as multiculturalism, although the latter has contributed to significant understandings of how to value and incorporate the richness and diversity of students and their families into the classroom (Banks & McGee Banks, 1993; Moll & Arnot-Hopffer, 2005). All of us hold multiple identities; a person might have one identity or no identity that has been historically oppressed. Additionally, people may share multiple identities but may not have had the experience of intersectionality, that is, both the subtle and obvious forms of oppression, discrimination, othering, maltreatment, or the denial of opportunity and advancement based on these identities (Crenshaw, 1989). Intersectionality reflects the confluences of racism, ableism, classism, homophobia, sexism, and other discriminatory ideologies that impact people's lived experiences. Voices such as Angela Davis, bell hooks, Audre Lorde, Fannie Lou Hamer, Toni Morrison, Kimberlé Crenshaw, and Patricia Hill Collins set the groundwork for grasping a critical understanding of this phenomenon which Crenshaw would later coin as "intersectionality." Intersectionality, while being a phenomenon where inequity is amplified, can also be a source of great change.

Pause and Reflect

As Kimberlé Crenshaw (1989) noted, the most powerful and transformative work occurs at the margins.

- Identify the minoritized identities that are represented in your classroom.
- How might you better accommodate these identities and better program curricular offerings to increase your students' sense of belonging?

Going back to Bronfenbrenner's model of ecological systems, the dynamic changes are not only unidirectional, simply moving from the broader systems to the personal level; but perhaps one of the greatest exercises of our democratic system is the power of people to challenge structural inequities and promote social change. Grassroots social movements (i.e., driven by people) have a tremendous impact on policies that shape research, systems, and practices to improve people's lives. Many of the social movements and the civil rights movement have purposely and, at times, indirectly pushed for policies that shape the educational systems of today. See chapters 4, 10, and 11 for more information about social movements as related to disability. However, people often look at the outcomes of civil rights litigation in the educational context without examining the necessity to assert education as a civil right, and one to which all children are entitled. For example, even though we know that "free appropriate publication education" protections under IDEA have not always existed as a value, we may gloss over the root causes that manifest at the systemic and policy level.

SEEKING RACIAL JUSTICE

The historic landmark Supreme Court case *Brown v. Board of Education* (1954) (see chapters 4, 10, and 11) resulted from grassroots activism, a movement of people to enact and address policy change in the name of educational justice. The decades of legal segregation and exclusion of children of color from public schools called for Black civil rights activists and their allies to mobilize to address these inequities. At the source of these inequities lies racism, seen by the effort to conceptualize Black people as inferior (Omi & Winant, 2015). While many use the argument of race as a construct to deny or minimize the existence of racism, it is a clear example of the power that social perceptions must translate into material realities for people.

Considering how the medical model contributes to a pathological, deficit-view of disability, this model has not only helped to construct race but also has contributed to a pathological and deficit-view of people racialized as Black. The contribution of the role of research in racism is an often-overlooked phenomenon, as craniometry, phrenology, and other pseudoscientific experimentations supported the racist agenda of eugenics. The conceptualization of Black people as less-than-human property thus has political, economic, and systemic consequences across several domains. Medical experimentation on the Black body translated into perceptions about pain, healthcare, and its delivery (Roberts, 2014). Racism served the economic agenda of the transatlantic enslavement of African people, while also justifying the denial of their rights to access and obtain property and knowledge, such as education. Education became an elite property for the white middle class, with intelligence testing used as a tool to restrict access to education in the United States and in Europe for Black students.

The grassroots efforts of the civil rights movement were imperative for securing successful legislation and rendering the exclusion of children of color from the public education classroom unconstitutional. The legislation, however, was not enough to disrupt the ideological underpinnings. Social media and other information outlets provide us with numerous historical accounts of the disturbing imagery of white parents shouting at children of color as they approached school steps during integration. Critical race scholars have examined the experiences of students of color post-*Brown*, which have evidenced structural, overt, and nuanced inequities in resources, teaching, and enrichment for students of color. Derrick Bell (1980) described the persistent disparate outcomes in advocating for children of color and their families, despite the legal protections in public school post-integration. Gloria Ladson-Billings (2007) disrupted the "achievement gap" narrative, which perpetuated the myth of innate biological differences between Black and white students, supplanting it with the "opportunity gap" to emphasize the disparities in educational support and resources, while underscoring the "moral and educational debt" owed to children of color by the educational system. Racial stereotypes have manifested in the realities for Black parents as well, such as assuming these parents are uninvolved or irresponsible with regard to their child's learning without considering other factors like transportation and time off work (Brantlinger, 2001; Howard & Reynolds, 2008; McGee & Spencer, 2015).

CDS explains historical and present oppression of disabled students in educational settings, but its application is further called upon to demonstrate practical utility in its application (Hosking, 2008). CDS offers educators a framework to identify (a) what needs improvement; (b) who can drive transformative change; and (c) how previous definitions of normality or neutrality included their own biases and what we can do to lead social change (Bohman, 2005).

What Needs Improvement?

In an attempt to eradicate bias, many practitioners have inadvertently dismissed their students' identities by embracing approaches that actively overlook or reject direct consideration of disability, race, gender identity, sexual orientation, and other identities. The historical, systemic, and structural dimensions of these identities remain even if they are not openly discussed or considered in the classroom setting (Gay, 2010). Failing to reject the ideology that doesn't see aspects of identity can also result in missing important cues for change, including an overrepresentation of students of the global majority and students with disabilities referred to the office for disciplinary action, and an underrepresentation of students of color, students with disabilities, and students of marginalized groups in school-sponsored activities and organizations (Milner, 2012).

To facilitate important relationships between knowledge, experience, and expertise, practitioners must see, not overlook, diversity and reflect on their privileges and marginalized experiences. Reflecting upon your position(s) in society fosters awareness in the ways students navigate their world. This awareness elicits opportunities to amplify students' perspectives in curricula and the classroom as we come to realize that, regardless of intent, a deliberately dismissive approach to identity has silenced our students who need the most practice in using their voices. Many of the stories and resources, like children's literature, aimed to teach children about race, gender, and disability may inadvertently reinforce stereotypes (Dunn, 2013). Practitioners must be critically aware of assumptions in assigned texts that message people as pitiable or successful only if they overcome disability. Texts and other classroom media that disrupt these misconceptions are especially important tools (Donovan & Weber, 2021). Due to the perseverance of ableist messages, it may be necessary to help students see disabling aspects of society (i.e., the girl can't enter the building because it's not accessible) in contrast to characteristics of disability (i.e., the girl can't enter the building because she's in a wheelchair).

Who Drives Transformative Change?

Policymakers and school administrators make key decisions that impact students with disabilities, yet inclusive education that recognizes the strength of diversity within our students is rarely in existence. Linda Ware (2018) proposed three interdependent components to advance the reality of inclusion: practice, policy, and research. Common across these components is a need for inventiveness rather than adoption of generalized curricula or practice. This presents another aspect of CDS which is human agency, evident in disrupting the hierarchy that has stifled transformative change initiated from a grassroots or teacher-led approach.

Addressing power dynamics in who drives change is a critical task for every district and every school. In addition to empowering teachers, the voices and perspectives of people with disabilities must be elevated within our schools. Learning about disability is important but it is far more essential to learn with disabled people and from the direct experiences of people with disabilities from our students' communities.

Redefining Normality

The concept of normality, and how it has been constructed throughout history has had a tremendous impact on school climate, educational delivery, and whether classrooms are welcoming spaces for students. **Normality** or what is defined as normal is socially constructed, depending on norms that change and shift through history (Freud, 1999). However, assessing normality—in intelligence, behavior, presentation, and expression—impacts the expectations and experiences of disabled students (Annamma et al., 2013). Some argue how normality in any of these dimensions is assumed to exist along a standard, statistical curve. Not only does this fail to account for the range and variation across human beings, it also fails to account for the range and variation within each human being. Researchers have highlighted the faulty scientific standards in accordance with which these were created (Dudley-Marling & Gurn, 2010) that have manifested into theories about children's intelligence, abilities, and behaviors (Artiles, 2011; Gould, 1996). For example, from Freudian psychology models to Skinner's behaviorism, we have labeled student behaviors as "deviant" when socialization, emotional, and behavioral presentations do not fit into the established norms (Wills-Jackson, 2019).

Faults in the ideology of normality lie in the idea of a normal standard, which creates hierarchies of academic, social, and physical presentation and performances. History has demonstrated how intelligence testing has been used to designate some disabled children as less worthy of a high-quality education, especially disabled children of color (see *PARC v. The Commonwealth of Pennsylvania* in chapters 11 and 12). Second, despite efforts from politicians and some researchers, normality can't, and shouldn't be, measured (e.g., via intelligence testing or standardized assessments). While these measures may seem objective and unbiased, they result in disproportionate labeling and eligibility. This is the "dilemma of difference," which several critical scholars have emphasized (Artiles, 2011; Losen & Orfield, 2002; Minow, 1990). While it qualifies children to receive additional support and services in school settings, it can also result in placements that are not inclusive or in lowered expectations and opportunities, and stigmatization. Practitioners conducting assessments must assess their own stereotypes and biases about children with disabilities, children of the global majority, and disabled children of the global majority. Without examining this lens, children of the global majority with disabilities will continue to be disproportionately referred to special education and overrepresented in the categories of intellectual and developmental disabilities (IDD) and emotional and behavioral disorders (EBD) (Harry & Klingner, 2022; Kalyanpur & Harry, 2012). These can have long-term consequences, as students labeled with IDD and EBD have among the lowest rates of employment (Wagner & Cameto, 2004).

Seeking Disability Justice: The Educational Context

Mirroring the grassroots efforts of the civil rights movement, the parent advocacy movement used similar arguments in seeking educational justice for their children with disabilities in the decade after *Brown*. In response to the very deficit-based, static views of disabilities, parents organized and formed disability organizations to present the counternarrative that their children could learn and had the right to do so (Turnbull & Turnbull, 2015). Early history's public perceptions attributed disability to supernatural causes, generating fear and stigma (Carey, 2009). During the era of Enlightenment in Europe and the United States, these views were replaced by a medical model, or "disability-as-deviance," as children with disabilities were perceived as inferior and less than their peers without disabilities (Artiles, 2011). Many parents, practitioners, and administrators alike supported myths that inclusion of disabled students in classrooms would perhaps "rub off" on their nondisabled peers. Such ideologies have real consequences, as parents found themselves unable to work and support their families due to their children being excluded from public schooling. Concerted efforts among prominent white and middle-class parents resulted in the creation of the field of special education which not only legalized the supports and services that children should receive, it also carved out a position for parents to be a part of the educational decision-making processes, as discussed in chapters 11 and 12. Much like *Brown*, the Education for All Handicapped Children Act (EAHCA, 1975), which later became IDEA, was considered a victory. This was vital for the inclusion of, protection, and support for children with disabilities in classrooms. Critical disability scholars, however, have emphasized how the outcomes were not beneficial for "ALL" children (Artiles, 2011; Blanchett, 2010), as with, for example, the erasure of Deaf culture in schools, as discussed in chapter 3. Just as social perceptions and racism continued to manifest in inequities for children of the global majority, disabled children of the global majority began to experience what some scholars referred to as a "double jeopardy"—the reality of experiencing multiple forms of oppression at once, or intersectionality (Fierros & Conroy, 2002).

Indeed, the reality of disabled children of the global majority was that segregation and exclusion occurred within the school walls, post-*Brown*, post-IDEA, despite the legal protections (e.g., de facto segregation as discussed in chapter 4). CDS centers intersectionality by exploring the decades of scholarship that have documented the disproportionate referrals of students of color into special education, particularly in the more stigmatized disability categories of IDD and EBD. During the integration of public schools—as white and middle-class parents removed their children from public schools to prevent them from being educated alongside children of the global majority in a phenomenon known as "white flight"—researchers have documented how Black, Latine, and Indigenous children have been placed into specialized academic tracks and segregated classrooms, disproportionately labeled with IDD and EBD, all while being underserved educationally (Donovan & Cross, 2002; Eitle, 2002; Harry & Klingner, 2022; Mercer, 1973). Data from the Office for Civil Rights continues to show disproportionate suspensions and expulsions among Black boys and girls with disabilities, as well as Indigenous and multiracial boys with disabilities (OCR, 2021).

Seeking Disability Justice: The Everyday Lived Experience

As the children with disabilities transitioned into adulthood, they began advocating for their own autonomy and independence in the United States through the Disability Rights Movement in the 1970s. Disabled advocates and their allies were responsible for key changes in reimagining the lives of people with disabilities that countered prescriptive, clinical, and practitioner-driven ways. This transcended the school context, going beyond to consider housing, employment, continuing education, recreation, and community integration. The aforementioned "nothing about us without us" was not just a mantra but a manifesto; disabled people had had enough of the decisions made for them, including the well-intentioned decisions of their caregivers and providers (Charlton, 1998). A similar movement occurred in the United Kingdom, with the Union of the Physically Impaired Against Segregation (UPIAS) in 1976 (NDACA, n.d.). Although it was not until the year 1990 that the Americans with Disabilities Act (ADA) was enacted in the United States to ensure that all public spaces were accessible for people with disabilities, the legislation was again a victory. See more on this and related legislation in chapters 10 and 11.

Pause and Reflect

Review the current executive board of your institution and the most recent policies that have been enacted.

- Does the executive board represent diverse sociocultural identities that are present in the classroom (e.g., race, gender, disability status, SES)? If not, why?
- Does the executive board represent sociocultural identities that are homogenous? If so, why?
- Do the recent policies adequately represent the population that they intend to serve?
- What personnel or objectives could you put into place to increase your executive board's diversity?

As with the parent advocacy movement, a similar argument about representation is applied when considering disability rights and under-recognition of Black disability activists, who often led and organized the charge. Many advocates have critiqued the disability rights movement for diminishing the experience of intersectionality as part and parcel of the call for justice. The hashtag #DisabilityTooWhite, created by Black disability activist Vilissa Thompson in 2016, expressed sentiments similar to Derrick Bell's interest convergence (more in chapter 4), noting how the solidarity between white and Black and brown disability advocates in addressing oppression seems to exist, so long as disability was centered, without considering the confluence of racism (Mulderink, 2020). Black disabled advocates expressed their disappointment in white disability advocates' silence over systemic racism when it came to the murders of George Floyd, Armaud Arbery, and Breonna Taylor in 2020, yet there was vocality in systemic ableism in the ways in which life-saving treatments were being disseminated during the COVID-19 pandemic.

Arguably, some white disabled advocates have felt that taking the focus off disability may stall the forward momentum that has been so difficult to come by for disabled people, potentially taking attention from the efforts to dismantle ableism. However, this is problematic for several reasons. First, scholars have emphasized that while many white disability activists who share a single oppressed identity can partake in solidarity based on disability, they may also minimize their own privilege and proximity to white norms (Mulderink, 2020). In addition, the neutral, race-evasive view of disability is dangerous as it fails to account for the experiences of racism and ableism acting in tandem, which have a profound impact on people's lived experiences. For a deeper look at race-evasiveness, see chapter 4. A lens that incorporates intersectionality considers how racism, ableism, sexism, classism, and other forms of discrimination and social inequities are inextricably linked. Hankivsky and colleagues, in their emphasis on intersectionality as a transformative tool for analyzing policy, noted one critical tenet, "Human experiences cannot be accurately understood by prioritizing any one single factor or constellation of factors" (2012, p. 35).

Reframing Research: Shifting the Paradigm

Through our discussion of history, it is clear how policy and people's lived experiences are closely connected, yet research is also a part of this interaction. During the deinstitutionalization movement in the 1980s, questions emerged across several fields about the rights of disabled people and the history and future of research. Documented histories of experimentation and abuse in research and institutions of care have led to feelings of mistrust among disabled people and their families (Carey, 2009). A social view of disability began to lead many researchers invested in disabled peoples' lives to question if they should continue to investigate causality or social determinants of the disability experience (e.g., physiological, genetic, phenotypic, cognitive, emotional, social, and behavioral profiles), or to shift their efforts toward the ecologies and systems which create barriers for well-being. Throughout history many psychologists and researchers have pathologized and blamed families for their children's disabilities (Caplan & Hall-McCorquodale, 1985; Olshansky, 1962; Solnit & Stark, 1959). Explorations were even more pathologizing for disabled PGM and their families, whose homes and communities were considered "environmental" contributors to their being "at-risk" for disability, disregarding the systemic oppressions impacting their lives over generations (Carey, 2009; Artiles 2011). Researchers began to look at intangible constructs that have material consequences, such as stigmatization and their impact on service delivery (e.g., Goffman, 1963); labeling and the impact on student's self-perceptions and internalized disablism (e.g., Hernández-Saca, 2019; Hudak, 2014); the exclusion of disabled people as collaborators in research teams and as valid producers of knowledge (e.g., Taylor, 2018); as well as the ways in which research collaborations have not been meaningful for families or children's outcomes (e.g., Stoep et al., 1999).

Applying what is theoretical into what is practical in the school context should incorporate the same shift in paradigm that is required for research. Fundamental to this understanding is the role of the medical model in the educational system. The static and deficit conceptualization of disability as only a chronic illness, something negative, and necessary to be "fixed" is still deeply entrenched. De Valck and colleagues (2001) described the medical community's overreliance on a cure-oriented practice rather than a care-oriented practice, which they noted, "loses the context" and "neglects the functional, social, and emotional aspects of [clients'] health" (p. 119). These embedded perceptions about disability continue to have a stronghold on the entire gamut of the educational system, from educational policy, to program offerings, to practitioner decisions and behaviors. Assessments of students in schools, for example, presumed to be objective, result in labeling and services, opportunities offered, and the expectations of students. Quite often these are low, failing to respond to student needs, identities, presentations, and cultures (Paris & Alim, 2017; Pickard, 2019). Waitoller and King Thorius (2022) critiqued how even the most asset-based pedagogies fail to consider disability as a culture and build strong disability identities. How do we prepare young people with disabilities for autonomy and decision making as adults when these experiences often devalue them? As disability scholar Mike Oliver noted, supporting the needs and concerns among disabled people and their families requires appropriate responses, which extend beyond interventions, toward "policy developments, or political action, as sometimes radical alternatives" (1998, p. 1447).

DisCrit and Its Impact on Practice

Disability Critical Race Theory (DisCrit) emerged as a framework by Annamma, Connor, and Ferri (2013) to capture the overt and nuanced ways in which race and disability have been historically viewed as "collusive" in their impact on the education and other systems of care that affect children with disabilities and their families (p. 6). DisCrit drew from Disability Studies and Critical Race Theory and expands on the conceptualization of intersectionality by Crenshaw (1993; see figure 5.1 for tenets of DisCrit). This framework acknowledges the tensions and conflicts inherent to the field of special education, whose traditions have upheld deficit-framed views and norms toward a cure-oriented rather than care-oriented ethic. Current special education programs are often steeped in ableism, seeking to fix children or at the very least reward them for being able to mask their disability, their identity, and their culture, while upholding white and ableist norms. Second, this framework was

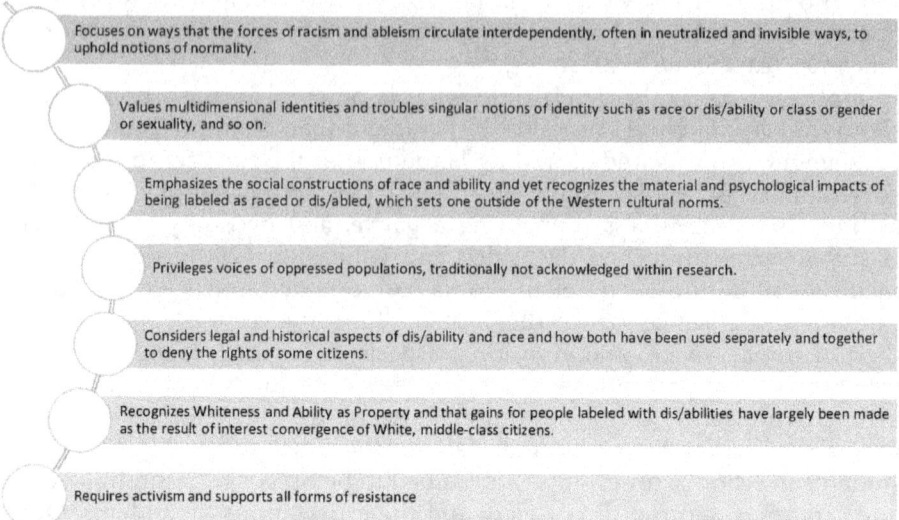

Figure 5.1. Tenets of Disability Critical Race Theory (DisCrit)
Source: Adapted from Connor et al., 2016.

a redress to disability studies which had been largely underrepresented and erased, excluding the experiences of Black disabled people and their families. As noted in previous sections, an alternative perspective was offered by the emerging subfield of DSE, which was to understand that there are both intrinsic and extrinsic challenges that exist for disabled people but that negative social perceptions about people are what create substantial barriers. Yet even subfields such as DSE have been critiqued for their overrepresentation and focus on white disability perspectives, without consideration of the impact of intersectionality as well as Black and brown disabled student identities and perspectives (Bell, 2011).

For further reading, research and practice informed by DisCrit, see Connor et al., 2016; Annamma et al., 2022; Ferri et al., 2023.

Critical Race Theory (CRT; see chapter 4) has long analyzed and addressed the historical and pervasive discriminatory experiences among Black children in schools. However, this fell short of including or acknowledging the disability experience among Black and brown disabled students, who had been experiencing myriad injustices in schools. This has raised questions among critical scholars about why studies addressing the needs of disabled students of color seem to be separate from studies focused on addressing the needs of students of color overall. One narrative that has been popularized to explain this phenomenon is understanding the complexity and construction of race, intelligence, and disability (Zuberi & Bonilla-Silva, 2008). Scholars have described how disability, through the construction of intelligence and illness, has been used to render Black individuals as inferior throughout history. While it has been theorized that this is a reason for an apparent "distancing from disability" that seems to occur in addressing the needs of Black communities, Black disabled feminist scholar Sami Schalk (2022) describes this as both reductive and misplaced. Emphasizing how the disability movement has excluded Black voices and perspectives, Schalk explains how it has also failed to acknowledge the activism among Black disabled advocates, noting the "multiple complex and nuanced ways that Black people, historically and contemporarily, have engaged with disability beyond simple distancing or denial" (p. 6). This perspective considers the disenfranchisement of disabled people of color from disability advocacy rather than implying a lack of engagement on their part.

DisCrit's seven tenets have contributed several key perspectives regarding the lives of disabled students of color and, particularly, the ways in which disabled students of color and their families have experienced special education and its processes. Tenet 4, for example, underscores the value of voice in both research and in practice, promoting how centering voices that have been traditionally and historically underrepresented expands ways of knowing. Stoep and colleagues (1999) implemented a novel collaborative, community-based participatory model for supporting children with mental illness. They described how this not only challenged traditional researcher/family-as-subjects design, it also noted that the "more people were invested . . . the science was strengthened" (p. 339). In a similar way, inclusion of disabled researchers of color as well as families of children with disabilities is vital to better inform school approaches and interventions (Johnson et al., 2021). Many color- and disability-evasive methods in the classroom are often decontextualized and do not account for the ways in which school structure, curricula, and climate contribute to the othering and harm inflicted upon disabled children of color (Klingner & Edwards, 2006).

Several scholars have used DisCrit to explore the overt and nuanced experiences of intersectionality among disabled students of color in schools. A study by Gillborn and colleagues (2016) exemplified the hegemony of racism and power in describing how Black middle-class families in the United Kingdom were unable receive the eligibility of autism and learning disabilities (LD) for their children, despite their expressed concerns to providers. Several studies have documented the experiences among Black families reporting practitioners not acknowledging their suspicions about their children and autism, leading to a delay in supports and services (e.g., Gourdine et al., 2011). Yet this study underscored the critical role of social perceptions and power in outcomes, as these parents' middle-class socioeconomic experiences were not able to overturn the racist and valued-disability perceptions held by practitioners. Hernández-Saca (2019) highlighted the testimony of a young Latine girl with a

LD, whose experiences of microaggressions and internalized (dis)ableism were attributed to the ways in which the school setting both constructed and valued intelligence and LD. Applying the DisCrit framework in a critical autoethnography, Black scholar and mother of a disabled child, Ocasio-Stoutenburg (2021) described the lived experience of intersectionality in her account of her child's clinical and schooling experiences. She recalled how paraprofessionals, subscribing to racist, adultifying, and stereotypical perceptions about Black children, mistreated one of her son's peers, a Black boy with Down syndrome, who they presumed to be bigger and fearless. Uncovering the ways in which undocumented disabled students and their families experience the special education process, Padia and Traxler (2021) used DisCrit to expand on the connections and interference of immigration, fear of deportation, and engagement with law enforcement among two Latine disabled students. This study used intersectionality to detail their experiences, from struggles regarding the eligibility process to the lack of ethics of care and the inadequate support that these students deserved but did not receive.

VIGNETTE 2: *WHEN PARENTS TELL THE STORY*

I began to unfold our story, starting with the story of Isaiah's entrance into the world and the not-so-warm welcome by the obstetrician. I start here because it is perhaps the clearest case for people to understand that parents of children with Down syndrome, and in my case, a Black mother of a child with Down syndrome, have encounters with professionals and systems very early on where there is clear ableism (as in the recommendation for me to terminate, and then to have no more children), the racial and misogynistic microaggressions (in the doctor's repeating of facts to me slowly, documenting my racialized identity in every visit, or ignoring me during our visit), to the blatant violence and intersectionality (walking out on me mid-labor, forcefully pulling on my placenta, referring to my baby as "it," and telling me I better not have more children). This was an undercurrent which was, praise God, followed by a period of bliss, where we were able to experience joy of a beautiful Black son who was developing, laughing, and trying to speak. We had wonderful practitioners in early intervention and providers in those early days until the transition into preschool. Here we were slapped in the face by the segregation within the inclusive classroom as we witnessed Isaiah and his classmate, a brown Indian boy, separated from the rest of their class. We began to shift our trust in the educational system to a case-by-case basis, just as we had done with the healthcare system and its practitioners. We could easily be failed by systems by virtue of our identity, whether we had money, or some claim of social status, or not.

As we began to document the school experiences, we moved school districts, from the schools with lower resources that did not understand children, to try perhaps schools with higher resources, assuming they understood children? They did not. Not knowing my rights back then, I accepted the placement decisions based on what was available versus what was appropriate for my child. It was not until I had enrolled in my doctoral program that we left the public school system and enrolled him in a private Catholic school where we were able to capture what meant the most to us as his parents: that he was safe, he was learning, he was valued, he was treated as a human being, and he had a sense of belonging. Above all, he had community, he had friends. We remained there for several years.

Then in the meeting, my husband took over the story:

> During COVID, we lost something. Everyone was at home, you know, she was writing her dissertation. So I was doing school with Isaiah on Zoom. It was fine. It was us parents that had to show the teacher that the kids needed breaks. And we would break and come back. It became a routine. But then the COVID [infection] rates were so high and remember there was no vaccine for his age at first. We had to keep him home because we couldn't risk it.

He then described when we sent him back.

> Then we were able to send him back. And I remember the first day back at school, you know, he was excited. But his friends were waiting for him at the door. Now remember, this is a school where most of the kids had Down syndrome, a few kids with autism. Most of the kids were Black or Latino. And his boys, they were Black boys his age and a little older, they called his name, ISAIAH! They hugged him, and they were laughing, and they were all happy. And that's when it hit me. He had friends. And I took that for granted. And I wonder sometimes, did we make a mistake, coming here.

And my husband's voice broke.

And I looked around, and everyone was sobbing. I was sobbing, because he had never told me this and the feelings of guilt and regret hit me with a force so strong that I could not breathe.

Community was a highly valued part of our well-being as a family, of his well-being at school. He wasn't othered, he wasn't chastised or misunderstood. It was not perfect. But he had moments to shine, to get out his energy, to learn, to be encouraged, to be believed in, to be welcomed. Welcomed and loved. Not in spite of his Down syndrome, not in spite of being Black, but because of it all.

A few weeks later, we received a report. It began,

> Due to Isaiah and his family's intersectionality . . .

I corrected it.

> Due to Isaiah and his family's experiences of intersectionality . . .

The rest of the report contained a well-summarized account of everything we shared, in its correct context. I cried reading it as if it were someone else's story and not our own. Throughout the report she never dropped the Dr. title before my name, ever referring to me as "mom"—there was something she understood about documenting who I was for the team. The story was not in retrospect, the words on the document were not flat. They were a charge for the reader. Make it better. Welcome this family. Listen.

And for the first time in a long time, I felt like we were heard by public school personnel, though they did not look like us.

While DisCrit has been used to examine problems, it has also offered ways to develop solutions that are useful for practitioners, as well as other school personnel. Through a systematic, collective, and equity-focused process, practitioners can use DisCrit, along with other key conceptual frameworks (e.g., Geneva Gay's work in *Culturally Responsive Teaching*, 2010; Gorski's *Equity Literacy*, 2019) to gather interdisciplinary and community collaborators into reflective dialogues. The goal of this work was to use collective thought to inform what preservice special education practitioners should know to best serve a range of students in their classrooms. Kulkarni and colleagues (2021) utilized DisCrit's tenets to address the scarcity of research studies exploring intersectionality within science teacher education. This analysis raised some important tensions that occur among research, education, and practice, which are particularly evident around science education and the preparation of preservice practitioners to teach this discipline. These researchers noted the overreliance on resources and accommodations, while the expectations for students to learn in the same ways that students without disability labels learn (e.g., science literacy) remain.

DisCrit has also been used with pedagogical approaches to support preservice practitioners' learning across multiple contexts. **Universal Design for Learning** (UDL), for example, is an approach that emerged from the social model of disability, focusing on adjustments to promote access for all people (more on UDL can be found throughout this text). UDL is a framework which promotes accessibility in the classroom through multiple means of representation, multiple means of engagement, and multiple means of action and expression (CAST, 2018).

Through DisCrit, addressing the perceptions of preservice practitioners provides support for some of the critiques of UDL. For example, critics argue that UDL fails to address racism and other forms of discrimination, while also reinforcing troubling concepts of normativity that have been so prevalent throughout the history of education (Fornauf & Mascio, 2021). The authors concluded that their students had persisting internalized expectations for normalcy, evidenced in their surprise at the number of students requiring accommodations and supports. This study not only reflected the ways in which DisCrit can be implemented to understand communities' magnified experiences of multiple oppressions but also to unpack some of the ways in which practitioners, through actions and/or expectations, may contribute to these oppressions.

LOOKING FORWARD

The field of special education is troubled and, in many ways, stifled by a eugenic history of education and the ways that messages about disability are conveyed. Stigmatization and devaluing not only have an impact on community integration but most certainly are manifested in whose voices are included as policymakers, changemakers, interventionists, researchers, and practitioners. Patterns of discrimination and deeply entrenched systemic and structural inequities have disenfranchised disabled people, caregivers of disabled people, and especially children of color with disabilities. Collins described the pervasive problems of schooling in its expectation for children of color to assimilate as "part of the larger social effort to socialize racial ethnic children into their proper subordinate places in systems of racial and class oppression" (2016, p. 382).

For this reason, we can use tools and frameworks such as DisCrit to reimagine schools as places of learning and support, places which support from a nurturing, care-based ethic. We cannot take actions against or redesign the structures and systems without addressing those who enact policy and deliver services. DisCrit allows the embrace of the full identity of an individual, engaging within the great dilemma of taking on a social view of disability while also needing to partake in the labeling system to receive needed supports (Minow, 1990).

We can draw from both understanding the constructed nature of things while also recognizing the activism and criticality that is needed to advance the field. Building upon the legacy left behind by disability scholar Mike Oliver (1998), we can acknowledge both the "crucial importance of learning from disabled people's experience to understand meanings of disability" and "[tying them to] the solutions to social action and change" (p. 1448). Deepening this work to include intersectionality, we also see the purpose and promise of creating new legacies, as Black disability scholar Sami Schalk (2022) expressed, "May we avenge the suffering of our ancestors, earn the respect of future generations, and be willing to be transformed by the work again and again and again. Let's begin" (p. 22).

SUMMARY

DisCrit, because of its focus on intersectionality, can be used by both educational researchers and higher educational faculty alike. Its tenets can be used to uncover, challenge, question, and explore existing practices, methods, and pedagogical tools. Scholars have also demonstrated how to use DisCrit as a means of self-evaluation and reflective practice, particularly useful for preservice practitioners in examining their own potential biases, ableism, or culturally discriminatory views of students with disabilities and their families. It should be noted that using intersectionality analytical tools is not without its challenges. Hankivsky and colleagues (2012)—using a similar framework to analyze how intersectionality is operationalized in healthcare, known as Intersectionality-Based Policy Analysis (IBPA)—noted the likelihood of encountering personal and institutional rejection of intersectional frameworks because of the aims of addressing social justice. Such frameworks may not be aligned with social or political beliefs and pressures. However, DisCrit and

Table 5.2. DisCrit Resources and Information about Normalcy

Assessments
• Cultural Reciprocity (Kalyanpur & Harry, 2012). A four-step process, involving the practitioners' examination of their own biases and stereotypical perceptions of the child and family. Similar to implicit bias assessments. • Multidisciplinary Teaming with Culturally and Linguistically Competent Personnel. (Georgetown National Center for Cultural Competence [NCCC]). Members in the assessment process who respond to the presentation and needs of students.
Planning and Decision Making
• Equitable Partnerships in Planning (Turnbull & Turnbull, 2015). Family members, teachers/practitioners, and student teams with power-sharing vs. power-over structures for decision making. • Co-advocacy (Ocasio-Stoutenburg, 2021). • Authentic Partnerships in Pre-IEP and Transition Meetings (Cavendish & Connor, 2018). • Culturally Responsive Transition Planning (Thoma et al., 2016).
Supports and Curricular Design
• Assistive Technology with wraparound, holistic family support. • Intersectionally Conscious Collaborations (Boveda, 2019; Boveda & Weinberg, 2020). • Culturally Responsive Emotional and Behavioral Support (Bal et al., 2012). • Sustaining Disability (Waitoller & King Thorius, 2022). • Developing a Disability Identity (Baglieri & Lalvani, 2020). • Meaningful Community Connections for Black Mothers of Children with ASD (Morgan et al., 2023).

other frameworks that consider intersectionality can be perceived in the same way as the major disability advocacy movements that have impacted education—as a means for contesting, reframing, and disrupting from the margins, itself one of the many "expressions of resistance" (Annamma et al., 2013, p. 18). To learn more about DisCrit and ways to disrupt the perceptions about normalcy, please consider the following resources in table 5.2.

REFERENCES

Abdi, A., & Misiaszek, G. W. (2022). *The Palgrave handbook on critical theories of education.* Palgrave MacMillan.

Annamma, S. A., Connor, D., & Ferri, B. (2013). Dis/ability critical race studies (DisCrit): Theorizing at the intersections of race and dis/ability. *Race Ethnicity and Education, 16*(1), 1–31.

Annamma, S., Ferri, B., & Connor, D. J. (Eds). (2022). *DisCrit expanded: Inquiries, reverberations & ruptures.* Teachers College Press.

Artiles, A. J. (2011). Toward an interdisciplinary understanding of educational equity and difference: The case of the racialization of ability. *Educational Researcher, 40*(9), 431–45.

Baglieri, S. (2017). *Disability Studies and the inclusive classroom.* Routledge.

Baglieri, S., & Lalvani, P. (2020). *Undoing ableism: Teaching about disability in K–12 classrooms*. Routledge.

Bal, A., King Thorius, K., & Kozleski, E. (2012). *Culturally responsive positive behavioral support matters*. Equity Alliance.

Banks, J., & McGee Banks, C. (1993). *Multicultural education: Issues and perspectives*. Wiley.

Bell, C. M. (Ed.). (2011). *Blackness and disability: Critical examinations and cultural interventions* (vol. 21). LIT Verlag

Bell Jr., D. A. (1980). Brown v. Board of Education and the interest-convergence dilemma. *Harvard Law Review, 93*(3), 518–33.

Berman, D. L., & Connor, D. J. (2017). *A child, a family, a school, a community: A tale of inclusive education*. Peter Lang.

Biklen, D., & Burke, J. (2006). Presuming competence. *Equity & Excellence in Education, 39*(2), 166–75.

Blanchett, W. (2010). Telling it like it is: The role of race, class, and culture in the perpetuation of learning disability as a privileged category for the white middle class. *Disability Studies Quarterly, 30*(2). https://dsq-sds.org/article/view/1233

Bohman, J. (2005). Critical Theory. *Stanford encyclopedia of philosophy*. http://plato.stanford.edu/archives/spr2005/entries/critical-theory/

Brantlinger, E. (2001). Poverty, class, and disability: A historical, social, and political perspective. *Focus on Exceptional Children, 33*(7), 1–19.

Bronfenbrenner, U. (1977). Toward an experimental ecology of human development. *American Psychologist, 32*(7), 513.

Brown v. Board of Education, 347 U.S. 483 (1954).

Caplan, P. J., & Hall-McCorquodale, I. (1985). Mother-blaming in major clinical journals. *American Journal of Orthopsychiatry, 55*(3), 345–53.

Carey, A. C. (2009). The feebleminded versus the nation: 1900–1930s. In *On the margins of citizenship: Intellectual disability and civil rights in twentieth-century America* (pp. 52–82). Temple University Press. http://www.jstor.org/stable/j.ctt14bs8th.7

CAST. (2018). Universal Design for Learning guidelines version 2.2. Retrieved from http://udlguidelines.cast.org

Cavendish, W., & Connor, D. (2018). Toward authentic IEPs and transition plans: Student, parent, and teacher perspectives. *Learning Disability Quarterly, 41*(1), 32–43.

Charlton, J. I. (1998). *Nothing about us without us: Disability, oppression, and empowerment*. University of California Press.

Collins, P. H. (1990). Black feminist thought in the matrix of domination. In P. H. Collins (Ed.), *Black feminist thought: Knowledge, consciousness, and the politics of empowerment* (pp. 221–38). Unwin Hyman.

Connor, D. J. (2022). Revamping a graduate course to (in)fuse Disability Studies: The politics of representation in "The Study of Learning Disabilities in Children and Adolescents." *Journal of Teaching Disability Studies, 3*. https://jtds.commons.gc.cuny.edu/issues/table-of-contents-issue-3/

Connor, D. J., Ferri, B. A., & Annamma, S. (Eds.). (2016). *DisCrit: Disability Studies and Critical Race Theory in education*. Teachers College Press.

Cooc, N., & Kiru, W. E. (2018). Disproportionality in special education: A synthesis in research and trends. *Journal of Special Education, 52*(3), 163–73.

Crenshaw, K. (1993). Mapping the margins: Intersectionality, identity politics, and violence against women of color. *Stanford Law Review, 43*(6), 1241–99.

Danforth, S. (2021). From harmful to helpful. In B. Ferri & D. Connor (Eds.), *How teaching shapes our thinking about dis/abilities* (pp. 63–76). Peter Lang.

Davis, L. (Ed.). (2021). *The disability studies reader*. 6th ed. Taylor and Francis.

De Valck, C., Bensing, J., Bruynooghe, R., & Batenburg, V. (2001). Cure-oriented versus care-oriented attitudes in medicine. *Patient Education and Counseling, 45*(2), 119–26.

Donovan, M. S., & Cross, C. T. (Eds.). (2002). *Minority students in special and gifted education*. Washington, DC: National Academy Press, National Research Council Committee on Minority Representation in Special Education.

Donovan, S. J., & Weber, R. (2021). Navigating characters, coursework, and curriculum: Preservice teachers reading young adult literature featuring disability. *English Education, 53*(3), 204–23.

Dunn, P. A. (2013). Challenging stereotypes about disability for a more democratic society. *English Journal, 103*(2), 94–96.

Education for All Handicapped Children Act (EAHCA), Public Law 94-142 (1975).

Ellis-Robinson, T. (2020). Bringing DisCrit theory to practice in the development of an action for equity collaborative network: Passion projects. *Ethnicity and Education, 24*(5), 703–18.

Eitle, T. M. (2002). Special education or racial segregation: Understanding variation in the representation of Black students in educable mentally handicapped programs. *Sociological Quarterly, 43*(4), 575–605.

Erevelles, N. (2011). *Disability and difference in global contexts: Enabling a transformative body politic*. Palgrave MacMillan.

Ferri, B. A., & Connor, D. J. (2021). Bridging theory and practice through story. In D. J. Connor and B. A. Ferri (Eds.)., *How teaching shapes our thinking about dis/abilities: Stories from the field* (pp. 305–15). Peter Lang.

Ferri, B. A., Connor, D. J., & Annamma, S. A. (Eds.). (2023). *Enacting Disability Critical Race Theory: From the personal to the global*. Routledge.

Fierros, E. G., & Conroy, J. W. (2002). Double jeopardy: An exploration of restrictiveness and race in special education. In D. J. Losen & G. Orfield (Eds.), *Racial inequity in special education* (pp. 39–70). Harvard Education.

Fornauf, B. S., & Mascio, B. (2021). Extending DisCrit: A case of Universal Design for Learning and equity in a rural teacher residency. *Race, Ethnicity and Education, 24*(5), 671–86.

Freud, S. (1999). The social construction of normality. *Families in Society, 80*(4), 333–39.

Gay, G. (2010). *Culturally responsive teaching: Theory, research, and practice*. 2nd ed. Teachers College Press.

Gillborn, D., Rollock, N., Vincent, C., & Ball, S. (2016). The black middle classes, education, racism, and dis/ability: An intersectional analysis. In D. Connor, B. Ferri, & S. Annamma (Eds), *DisCrit: Disability Studies and Critical Race Theory in education* (pp. 35–54). Teachers College Press.

Goffman, E. (1963). *Stigma: Notes on the management of a spoiled identity*. Simon & Schuster.

Gonzalez, T. E., Hernández-Saca, D., & Artiles, A. J. (2017). In search of voice: Theory and methods in K–12 student voice research in the US, 1990–2010. *Educational Review, 69*(4), 451–73.

Goodley, D. (2013). Dis/entangling critical disability studies. *Disability & Society, 28*(5), 631–44.

Gorski, P. (2019). Avoiding racial equity detours. *Educational Leadership, 76*(6), 56–51.
Gourdine, R. M., Baffour, T. D., & Teasley, M. (2011). Autism and the African American community. *Social Work in Public Health, 26*(4), 454–70.
Hankivsky, O., Grace, D., Hunting, G., Ferlatte, O., Clark, N., Fridkin, A., . . . & Laviolette, T. (2014). Intersectionality-based policy analysis. In O. Hankivsky (Ed.), *Policy Analysis Framework* (pp. 33–46). Institute for Intersectionality Research and Policy.
Harry, B., & Klingner, J. (2022). *Why are there so many students of color in special education? Understanding race and disability in schools.* 3rd ed. Teachers College Press.
Hernández-Saca, D. I. (2019). Re-framing master narratives of dis/ability through an affective lens: Sophia Cruz's LD story at her intersections. *Anthropology & Education Quarterly, 50*(4), 424–47.
Hosking, D. L. (2008). Critical Disability Theory. A paper presented at the 4th Biennial Disability Studies Conference at Lancaster University, UK, Sept. 2–4, 2008. https://www.lancaster.ac.uk/fass/events/disabilityconference_archive/2008/papers/hosking2008.pdf
Howard, T. C., & Reynolds, R. (2008). Examining parent involvement in reversing the underachievement of African American students in middle-class schools. *Educational Foundations, 22*, 79–98.
Hudak, G. (2014). *Labeling: Pedagogy and politics.* Routledge.
Individuals with Disabilities Education Improvement Act (IDEIA) of 2004. (2004). Pub. L. No. 108–446, 118 Stat. 2647.
Johnson, K. R., Bogenschutz, M., & Peak, K. (2021). Propositions for race-based research in intellectual and developmental disabilities. *Inclusion, 9*(3), 156–69.
Kalyanpur, M., & Harry, B. (2012). Cultural reciprocity in special education: Building family–professional relationships. *Child & Family Behavior Therapy, 34*(4), 357–63.
Kauffman, J. M., Anastasiou, D., & Maag, J. W. (2017). Special education at the crossroad: An identity crisis and the need for a scientific reconstruction. *Exceptionality, 25*(2), 139–55.
Klingner, J. K., & Edwards, P. A. (2006). Cultural considerations with Response to Intervention models. *Reading Research Quarterly, 41*(1), 108–17.
Kulkarni, S., Nusbaum, E., & Boda, P. (2021). DisCrit at the margins of teacher education: Informing curriculum, visibilization, and disciplinary integration. *Race, Ethnicity and Education, 24*(5), 654–70.
Ladson-Billings, G. (2007). Pushing past the achievement gap: An essay on the language of deficit. *Journal of Negro Education, 76*(5), 316–23.
Linton, S. (1998). *Claiming disability: Knowledge and identity.* New York University Press.
Losen, D., & Orfield, G. (2002). *Racial inequity in special education.* Civil Rights Project at Harvard University, Harvard Education Press.
Magasi, S. (2008). Infusing disability studies into the rehabilitation sciences. *Topics in Stroke Rehabilitation, 15*(3), 283–87.
McGee, E., & Spencer, M. B. (2015). Black parents as advocates, motivators, and teachers of mathematics. *Journal of Negro Education, 84*(3), 473–90.
McKinney, C. (2016). Cripping the classroom: Disability as a teaching method in the humanities. *Transformations: The Journal of Inclusive Scholarship and Pedagogy, 25*(2), 114–27.
Meekosha, H., & Dowse, L. (2007). Integrating critical disability studies into social work education and practice: An Australian perspective. *Practice, 19*(3), 169–83.
Mercer J. (1973). *Labeling the mentally retarded.* University of California Press.

Milner, H. R. (2012). Losing the color-blind mind in the urban classroom. *Urban Education, 47*(5), 868–75. https://doi.org/10.1177/0042085912458709

Minow, M. (1990). *Making all the difference: Inclusion, exclusion, and American law.* Cornell University Press.

Moll, L. C., & Arnot-Hopffer, E. (2005). Sociocultural competence in teacher education. *Journal of Teacher Education, 56*(3), 242–47.

Morgan, E. H., Shaw, B. D., Winters, I., King, C., Burns, J., Stahmer, A., & Chodron, G. (2023). Paths to Equity: Parents in partnership with UCEDDs fostering Black family advocacy for children on the autism spectrum. *Developmental Disabilities Network Journal, 3*(1). https://digitalcommons.usu.edu/ddnj/vol3/iss1/5

Mulderink, C. E. (2020). The emergence, importance of #DisabilityTooWhite hashtag. *Disability Studies Quarterly, 40*(2).

National Disability Arts Collection & Archive (NDACA). (n.d.). https://the-ndaca.org/

Novak, K., & Couros, G. (2022). *UDL now! A teachers' guide to applying Universal Design for Learning.* 3rd ed. CAST.

Ocasio-Stoutenburg, L. (2021). Becoming, belonging, and the fear of everything Black: Autoethnography of a minority-mother-scholar-advocate and the movement toward justice. *Race, Ethnicity and Education, 24*(5), 607–22.

Oliver, M. (1998). Theories in health care and research: Theories of disability in health practice and research. *BMJ (Clinical research ed.), 317*(7170), 1446–49.

———. (2009). *Understanding disability: From theory to practice.* 2nd ed. Red Globe.

Olshansky, S. (1962). Chronic sorrow: A response to having a mentally defective child. *Families in Society, 43*(4), 190–93.

Omi, M., & Winant, H. (2015). *Racial formation in the United States.* 3rd ed. Routledge.

Padia, L. B., & Traxler, E. (2021). "Traerás tus Documentos" ("You will bring your documents"): Navigating the intersections of disability and citizenship status in special education. *Race Ethnicity and Education, 42*(5), 687–702.

Paris, D., & Alim, H. S. (Eds.). (2017). *Culturally sustaining pedagogies: Teaching and learning for justice in a changing world.* Teachers College Press.

Pickard, B. (2019). A framework for mediating medical and social models of disability in instrumental teaching for children with Down syndrome. *Research Studies in Music Education, 43*(2), 110–28.

Retief, M., & Rantoa, L. (2018). Models of disability: A brief overview. *Theological Studies, 74*(1). https://hts.org.za/index.php/hts/article/view/4738/10993

Roberts, D. (2014). *Killing the Black body: Race, reproduction, and the meaning of liberty.* Vintage.

Schalk, S. (2022). *Black disability politics.* Duke University Press.

Shyman, E. (2016). The reinforcement of ableism: Normality and the medical model of disability, and humanism in Applied Behavioral Analysis and ASD. *Intellectual and Development Disabilities, 54*(5), 366–76.

Solnit, A. J., & Stark, M. H. (1959). Pediatric management of school learning problems of underachievement. *New England Journal of Medicine, 261*, 988–93.

Stoep, A. V., Williams, M., Jones, R., Green, L., & Trupin, E. (1999). Families as full research partners: What's in it for us? *Journal of Behavioral Health Services & Research, 26*(3), 329–44.

Taylor, A. (2018). Knowledge citizens? Intellectual disability and the production of social meanings within educational research. *Harvard Educational Review, 88*(1), 1–25.

Thoma, C. A., Agran, M., & Scott, L. A. (2016). Transition to adult life for students who are Black and have disabilities: What do we know and what do we need to know? *Journal of Vocational Rehabilitation, 45*(2), 149–58.

Turnbull, R., & Turnbull, A. (2015). Looking backward and framing the future for parents' aspirations for their children with disabilities. *Remedial and Special Education, 36*(1), 52–57.

US Department of Education, Office for Civil Rights (OCR). (2021). *Civil rights data collection (CRDC) for the 2017–18 school year.* Released October 2020, updated May 2021, available at https://www2.ed.gov/about/offices/list/ocr/docs/crdc-2017-18.html

Wagner, M., & Cameto, R. (2004). *The characteristics, experiences, and outcomes of youth with emotional disturbances. A report from the National Longitudinal Transition Study-2.* 3(2)National Center on Secondary Education and Transition, University of Minnesota (NCSET).

Waitoller, F., & King Thorius, K. (Eds). (2022). *Sustaining disabled youth: Centering disability in asset pedagogies.* Teachers College Press.

Ware, L. (2018). The aftermath of the articulate debate: The invention of inclusive education. In C. Clark, A. Dyson, & A. Millward (Eds.), *Towards inclusive schools?* (pp. 127–46). Routledge.

Wills-Jackson, C. (2019). A historical perspective of the field of emotional and behavioral disorders: A review of literature. *International Journal of Psychology and Counselling, 11*(8), 81–85.

Zuberi, T., & Bonilla-Silva, E. (Eds.). (2008). *White logic, white methods: Racism and methodology.* Rowman & Littlefield.

CHAPTER 6

The History of Disability, Disability Models, and a View for the Future: The Past Is Prologue

Chapter authors: *Kendra V. Saunders, Michelle Mercado, Liza Citron, and Marcus C. Fuller*

Vignette authors: *Michelle Mercado and Liza Citron*

Editor: *Marcus C. Fuller*

ABSTRACT

The language used and viewpoints held in society are crucial to the acceptance and success of disabled people, and, indeed, society as a whole. These viewpoints and language have changed greatly over time; thus, it is vital to develop an understanding of how and why these changes occurred, and how to keep this momentum of improvement in the future. The purpose of this chapter is to review these social, historical, and linguistic elements, and discuss how they have and can contribute to negative viewpoints (such as othering and segregation) or positive ones (such as inclusion and acceptance of human reciprocity). The chapter begins with a history and definitions of disability and disability rights. Next, we highlight the models of disability that are used in society to understand and shape both societal opinion and public policy. The chapter then discusses the language used around disability, why semantics is vital to acceptance, and societal/cultural representations of disability (such as in television, literature, and art). Finally, this chapter introduces action steps that we, as a society, can take to shape a more inclusive and respectful future for all people, not just those in positions of status, power, or ability.

GUIDING QUESTIONS

After reading this chapter you will be able to answer the following questions:

- What is the history of disability?
- What are the major models we use to understand disability?
- What is the language we use to discuss disability?
- How can you help improve societal perspectives and inclusion of disability?

KEY TERMS

Charity Model of Disability
Cultural Model of Disability
Disability
Economic Model of Disability
Emic Perspective
Etic Perspective
Handicap
Human Rights Model of Disability
Identity-First Language
Identity Model of Disability
Impairment
Medical Model of Disability
Models
Person-First Language
Semantics
Social Model of Disability
Universal Design for Learning

According to the World Health Organization (2022), people with disabilities make up the world's largest minoritized group, with over one billion members and this figure continues to grow. In essence, it is a group that experiences oppression and that anyone can unexpectedly join at any given time, and most likely will join as they age. A change in ability status can occur at birth or throughout one's life. There is a long and varied history related to disability and what it means to be considered "disabled" in the Western world. As explained in chapter 5, the history of treatment for disabled people is mostly seen through a deficit model that explains disability as something inherently inferior or wrong about disabled people that requires medication or intervention. These attitudes have persisted through time and shape today's society's views around disability.

Some of the earliest understanding of disability comes from the Ancient Greek Empire (around fourth or fifth century BCE), in which disabled people were viewed as inferior and cursed because they did not meet the standard of perfection (Garland, 2020). During this time, disability was viewed negatively by society and children who were born with disabilities were often abandoned; adults with disabilities often took on jobs that used their disabilities as a source of entertainment for nondisabled people (Garland, 2020). However, Greek people also sought to understand disability through logic and reasoning (Shreve, 1982). For example, the Greeks believed that epilepsy was related to "mind disturbance," and that deaf people would struggle to learn due to their perceived inability to communicate (Shreve, 1982). There is also evidence that the Ancient Greek people were pragmatic. For example, there is evidence of welfare programs for certain groups, including disabled people, as well as ramps to healing sanctuaries in regional areas (although the ramps may have had multiple purposes such as bringing animals in for sacrifice—possibly an early idea related to universal design, described later in this chapter), and model prosthetics (such as an ear made of ceramic, a stand-in for the area the person would want to be healed; Sneed, 2020). After the fall of the Roman and Greek Empires (146 BCE), a brief period of a more sympathetic outlook toward those with disability can be found with the early Christian church (beginning around 27–33 CE), although the deficit-model persisted. Churches began to organize structured services for daily activities for people with disabilities through the homes of their parishioners, which in turn led to the loss of autonomy regarding their own destiny for those people under the care of the church (Shreve, 1982). Similar to the Greeks before them, the early Christians sought to understand why disabilities existed. Their belief centered on disability as imperfection or immorality, which led early Christians during the Middle Ages to become fearful of those with disabilities and see them as sinful. Moving into the Renaissance period, there was a push toward treating those with disabilities with better medical care and providing them with an education (Shreve, 1982). For the first time in Western history, there seemed to be a shift in social norms and increased inclusion of disabled people in society. For more information about the intersections of religion and disability, see chapters 1, 2, and 12.

This chapter highlights how various models of disability influence and are reinforced by the way society understands disability, the language we use to discuss disability, the intersection of race and disability, and the role played by media and culture. In addition, the chapter illustrates the connection to educational frameworks like Universal Design for Learning (UDL) and Integrated Multi-Tiered Systems of Support (IMTSS).

INTRODUCTION TO THE HISTORY OF DISABILITY RIGHTS IN THE UNITED STATES

Social norms and increased inclusion for people with disabilities played a large role in the fight for disability rights in the United States. In 1935, Public Law 74-271 or the Social Security Act was signed into law by the first disabled president, Franklin Delano Roosevelt (although his disability status was not truly known by the public) established the first program of permanent support for people with disabilities, along with support for other groups. Over the course of the next few decades, additional laws providing rights, protections, and support to disabled people were passed. The impact of racial desegregation in schools from *Brown v. Board of Education* in 1954 also provided opportunities for children with intellectual disabilities (ID) to be educated in public schools (Institute on Disabilities, 2019). This case changed the practices of institutionalizing students with ID and moved to education and support.

In the 1970s, two additional milestones were achieved with the passage of Public Law 93-112 or the Rehabilitation Act of 1973 and Public Law 94-142 or the Education for All Handicapped Children Act of 1975. Both laws provided new protections for people with disabilities across disability types, ages, and industries. The Rehabilitation Act of 1973 provided protections related to affirmative action and nondiscrimination in federal employment within the executive branch and government contractors/subcontractors; opportunities for access to support for education, employment, and in other settings; and funding to make more aspects of the government accessible through technology for disabled people (United States Government [USGOV], 1973). Additionally, this law provided a framework as well as defining a disabled person as "any person who (a) has a physical or mental impairment which substantially limits one or more of such person's major life activities, (b) has a record of such an impairment, or (c) is regarded as having such an impairment" (USGOV, 1973). Two years later, the Education for All Handicapped Children Act of 1975 was the first to guarantee a free, appropriate, public education (FAPE) for all children with disabilities in the least restrictive environment (LRE).

Industries that received public funds were the target of the Rehabilitation Act of 1973. However, people with disabilities interact, work, and live in many areas that do not have contact with public funding. Consequently, there was a groundswell of support to get a new law enacted to specifically include private industries, although when the bill was first introduced in 1988, various business and religious groups objected to the inclusion of private industries in nondiscrimination clauses due to the perceived higher cost of employing disabled people while not seeing any added value (Milden, 2022). Disability rights activists sought to end the stalling of the legislation and participated in the "Capitol Crawl Protest" on March 12, 1990, to demand the passing of the American with Disabilities Act (ADA). Coming from over thirty states, more than one thousand protesters participated in the event to demand an end to the delay (Institute on Disabilities, 2019). In the mold of the previous civil rights protests, participants chanted statements such as "What do we want? ADA! When do we want it? Now!" (Institute on Disabilities, 2019). At the end of the day of protesting, many protesters discarded their assistive devices (e.g., wheelchairs, walkers, canes) to start crawling up the steps of the Capitol Building, which gave the protest its name (Heumann & Joiner, 2020). The protest proved successful in ending the stalling of the legislation, and the ADA was finally signed into law on July 26, 1990. This day continues to be celebrated as a monumental moment within the disability rights movement.

The ADA prohibits the discrimination of disabled people in all areas of life such as schools, jobs, communication, and transportation regardless of public or private setting. Its passage provided civil rights protections similar to those granted to other already-recognized marginalized groups. The Individuals with Disabilities Education Act (IDEA) further recognized disabled students as members of society with additional safeguards like LRE and FAPE that promote inclusion, individualized learning, and planning for after graduation. For more information about this and other relevant legislation, see chapters 4, 10, 11, and 12. Furthermore, Rosa's Law officially made the term "mental retardation" obsolete in federal legislation and policy and replaced it with "intellectual disability." The law is named after Rosa Marcellino, a nine-year-old with Down syndrome, who worked with her family to have the old term removed from the laws in Maryland (Institute on Disabilities, 2019). These changes in society, along with many others, led to the creation of Disability Studies (see chapter 5), the multidisciplinary approach to the specific study of disability in society. This movement, born out of the Disability Rights Movement in the United States and the United Kingdom during the 1960s and 1970s, has disabled scholars and advocates at the helm seeking to reconceptualize the understanding of disability (Finkelstein, 2001).

MODELS OF DISABILITY

To better understand the different Models of Disability, first let's delineate the difference between disability, impairment, and handicap or handicapped. A **disability** is defined as "any condition of the body or mind (impairment) that makes it more difficult for the person with the condition to do certain activities (activity limitation) and interact with the world around them (participation restrictions)" (Centers for Disease Control and Prevention [CDC], 2020a, para. 4). This can include areas that may immediately come to mind such as movement, vision, and hearing, as well as others that may not connect as quickly such as remembering, learning, thinking, or difficulty in social relationships. Under the previous definition, another word appears: impairment. The World Health Organization (WHO) defines **impairment** as something that occurs "in a person's body structure or function, or mental functioning" (CDC, 2020a). This may include memory loss, loss of a limb, vision loss, or hearing loss. The term **handicapped** has a more varied history, and shows how much language about disabled people has changed over time. "Handicap" has a connection to another word that was previously used to address disabled people, "affliction" (Bayton, 1998). An affliction or burden was thought to be thrust upon a disabled person by God for specific reasons, such as building patience or teaching nondisabled people how to have pity on others (Bayton, 1998). **Handicap** comes from a game called "hand in cap," which then found a connection to racing and considered certain aspects that could slow the

Table 6.1. Differences in Disability Terms

Disability	Impairment	Handicap
Any restriction or lack of ability to perform an activity in the manner or within the range considered "normal" for a human being.	Any loss or abnormality of psychological, physiological, or anatomical structure or function.	A disadvantage for a given individual that limits or prevents the fulfillment of a role that is "normal." Currently, this is not viewed as a positive term.

horses down. Thereafter, the term began to be used in the context of being "handicapped in the race of life" (Bayton, 1998). Frequently used throughout history, "handicapped" has fallen out of favor in recent years as "disabled" became the preferred term among disability activists. Table 6.1 provides a better understanding of the differences between these terms.

Models of disability have long been a focus of disability rights because they instruct society how to interpret and interact with people with disabilities (Smart, 2004). **Models** are defined as the perceptions or ideas that define disabled people and the reactions of nondisabled people toward disabled people (Smart, 2004). Models carry an important task because they provide a framework for how we interact with, understand, and address disabled people. Models help to provide definitions of the construct, explain the causes/effects of the construct, and inform policy decisions; they may also help to shape an individual's understanding of the construct to which they belong and may inadvertently augment (or reduce) the perceived social value of the people who belong to that construct (Smart, 2004). Given their importance, it is imperative to clearly understand a delineation of the multiple models that impact the way the world processes the framework of disability in general and within the disabled community.

The definition of disability provided by the CDC (2020a) focuses specifically on the body and how the differences in the body can impact the interactions of the disabled individual. It is a broad definition that includes both physical issues (visible) and mind-related issues (nonapparent or invisible; more on the implications of nonapparent disabilities can be found in chapter 1). On the other hand, the World Health Organization (2022) defines disability as the relationship between individuals with a health condition (e.g., cerebral palsy, Down syndrome, dementia, blindness, or depression) and personal and/or environmental factors (e.g., negative attitudes, inaccessible transportation and public buildings, and limited social support). This is most closely related to the Social Model of Disability. There are similarities between both definitions as they both take into account nonapparent and visible disabilities. However, the definition given by the WHO puts more of an onus on the world surrounding disabled people to make changes.

One way to make sense of these different approaches to understanding disability is to review the various models of disability. According to the **Medical**

Model of Disability, which first was adopted around the mid-1800s, disabled people need to be changed, "cured," or treated through medical intervention before they can be fully included in society (Olkin, 1999). Within the Medical Model, the focus is solely on the body and its limitations—closely related to the CDC definition of disability. This is a deficit-based model, in which any "defected" body is not acceptable and must be changed to the greatest extent possible to allow for success in society. Some terms connected to the Medical Model are: retarded, invalid, cripple, handicapped, spastic (Creamer, 2009). Many of these terms have been deemed derogatory but continue to be used in everyday language to refer to people with disabilities, oftentimes without any understanding of the harm these words can have in society. While named the Medical Model, this framework is used in many fields, including politics, education, and commerce, to describe and dictate how society views and interacts with disability. In education, the Medical Model is used in a common practice of "Refer, Test, Place"—applied when a practitioner determines that a student is not doing well in class and refers them for testing by the school psychologist to be placed in special education. This frequently occurs in the absence of any interventions. The suspected disability is assessed only as it relates to observations of the child, without consideration of environmental factors.

Given the rather negative nature of the Medical Model, there was a push to gain a better understanding of the interactions of disabled people in the context of the world around them through a social justice lens. Thus, the Social Model was created. This model seeks to display the issues that disabled people face as members of an ableist society. The **Social Model of Disability** rejects the basic tenets of the Medical Model and sees disability as a socially constructed issue (Oliver, 1981). The Social Model of Disability was created by Michael Oliver (1981), a disability rights self-advocate and professor of Disability Studies. Within the Social Model, as barriers are removed disability becomes less and less of an issue. For example, if a wheelchair-user is unable to enter an inaccessible building, is that due to the user's impairment (i.e., the person uses a wheelchair for mobilization) or to society's lack of motivation to accommodate better accessibility (i.e., elevators, wheelchair lifts, and ramps)? If the ramp is available for all to use, is the disability still an issue? These are core questions that the Social Model seeks to answer, and it establishes a new line of inquiry about society's understanding of what really constitutes a "disability." According to the Social Model, instead of focusing on the wheelchair-user as the problem, we should focus on what we can do to make the world accessible, regardless of ability status.

In 1976, the Union of the Physically Impaired Against Segregation (UPIAS), a UK-based group, produced a document to address the underpinnings of its model called the *Fundamental Principles of Disability*, explaining:

> [D]isability is a situation, caused by social conditions, which requires for its elimination, (a) that no one aspect such as incomes, mobility or institutions is treated in isolation, (b) that disabled people should, with the advice and help of others, assume control over their own lives, and (c) that professionals, experts and oth-

ers who seek to help must be committed to promoting such control by disabled people. (UPIAS, 1976, p. 3)

As exemplified in this quote, a major goal of this model is to acknowledge that disabled people face oppression due to their status as disabled people. Furthermore, society needs to become aware of this oppression and stop this cycle from occurring to allow for the full participation of disabled people in society.

The disability models that have come after the Social Model tend to still have some connections back to this model. For example, the **Identity Model of Disability** (Brewer et al., 2012), which holds many of the same beliefs as the Social Model, seeks to also affirm disability. This model posits that disability should be treated and affirmed as an identity in the same way that racial, gender, or sexuality identity is affirmed. As a result, the use of person-first language is discouraged, and identity-based language is encouraged—so instead of using "person with a disability," the encouraged terminology would be "disabled person." Understanding the framing of this model makes this push toward identity-based language appropriate. For example, people in society do not typically say an Asian person is a "person with an ancestry connected to the continent of Asia," thus separating the person from their identity. If disability is to truly be viewed as an identity to be affirmed, it is imperative to use identity-based language. More about person-first language and identity-based language is discussed later in this chapter and in chapter 11. Similarly, the **Cultural Model of Disability**, which is also connected to the Social Model, seeks to have society see the value of disabled people as a connection to diversity as a cultural group (Junior & Schipper, 2013). This can be seen with Deaf community, where deafness is not seen as a "problem" to be solved but rather as an identity or cultural community that functions as any other community with its own customs and communication styles (see chapter 3). The goal is to change the perspective of disability as being negative and instead to view it as a beautiful and important part of one's culture.

The previous models (medical, social, cultural) are among the most cited and applied models when addressing disability. However, the following are a few other influential yet less frequently cited models. The first, which still has some connection to the Social Model, is the **Human Rights Model of Disability**. This model is based on the concept that disabled people have basic human rights that must be respected and recognized by the government and society at large (Degener, 2017). The guiding principle is that society should take an active role in ensuring that these rights are properly delivered. Degener (2017) highlights important factors with this model. This model has several goals that differ from the Social Model, while still carrying some similarities. For example, this model seeks to emphasize the humanity of the disabled community (like the Identity Model) and uses that as a theoretical framework to support policies that give disabled people their rights. Another difference is that this model (unlike the Social Model) truly embraces the concept that disabled people do have specific bodily challenges that may make their lives difficult. Furthermore, the Human Rights Model believes that these factors should be considered, especially from a social justice perspective. Based on these differences alone, it can be concluded that while the Social Model can provide an explanation for certain societal ills that can be included in the overall disabled experience, the Human Rights Model attempts to provide constructive proposals to improve the lives of disabled people through policy and practice.

The **Charity Model of Disability** has the closest connection to the Medical Model because disability is considered an issue within the individual. There is some evidence that it actually predates the Medical Model (Henderson & Bryan, 2011). In this model, disabled people are viewed as victims worthy of "pity." The concept is that they are unable to be independent thinkers or to live on their own or without people who do not have a disability unless those people are their caretakers (Henderson & Bryan, 2011). Disability, because it is connected to the individual, makes the person worthy of pity (Henderson & Bryan, 2011). It may be difficult to understand how this model still makes sense in the current day. However, if you notice the consistent reactions to interabled couples—a couple in which one member has a disability while the other does not—it becomes more apparent that some aspects of the Charity Model inform the biases present in today's society. The idea that an interabled couple could be together because they are in a romantic relationship, and not because the nondisabled partner is a caretaker, can seem like a foreign concept for some people in society. Another common supposition is that the nondisabled partner is taking advantage of the disabled partner because they are unable to make independent decisions. This model is still active in many religions that align sainthood and grace to charity and caretaking of the "less fortunate" (i.e., people who are poor and people who are disabled). For more information about the nuanced legalities of interabled relationships, see chapter 1.

Finally, the **Economic Model of Disability** focuses on the economic contribution (or lack thereof) of disabled members (Armstrong et al., 2006). The degree of impairment experienced by the disabled person is directly related to the financial outcomes for the disabled person (loss of earnings), the businesses (lower productivity and profit margins), and the government (welfare to support the disabled person, as needed). Looking back to the history of disability rights, it is clear that this model has played a relatively large role in the disability-related legislation in the United States and is often utilized by governments to formulate disability policy (Smart, 2004). Much of the concern has been related to increasing participation in education and workplaces to lead to higher societal contributions. Think back to the definition of disability as outlined in the Rehabilitation Act of 1973, "any person who (a) has a physical or mental impairment which substantially limits one or more of such person's major life activities; (b) has a record of such an impairment; or (c) is regarded as having such an impairment" (USGOV, 1973). This shows that the disability is directly connected back to the ability to participate in society (substantially limits a major life activity). Table 6.2 offers descriptions and relationships to each of the models discussed in this chapter.

Table 6.2. Models of Disability

Models of Disability	Etic/Emic Perspective	Tenets	Examples in Society	Examples in Education
Medical Model	Etic	Disability is within the person, and needs to be "cured" or "fixed"	Use of cochlear implants to "correct" a hearing loss	"Refer, test, place" protocol Completely separate special education services, without consideration of inclusion
Social Model	Emic	Disability only occurs because society has failed to remove barriers	Building codes that require the use of ramps, curb cuts, tactile paving, and elevators to increase accessibility	An inclusive classroom where students with and without disabilities learn together to increase access to quality education Use of Universal Design for Learning (UDL)
Identity Model	Emic	Disability is an identity, just like race or gender, and should be affirmed	Disability pride organizations or groups especially targeted toward connecting disabled people with fellow disabled people, often within the same classification of disabilities (i.e., blind, wheelchair user, autistic)	An inclusive classroom where students with and without disabilities learn together, and all students are expected to be capable learners Students are encouraged to take pride in their disabled identity; likely also includes a UDL framework
Cultural Model	Emic	Disability is a beautiful and impactful culture unto itself	Affinity groups and organizations based on disability culture (Deaf culture, Blind culture, Autistic culture)	An inclusive classroom where students with and without disabilities learn together, and all students are expected to be capable learners Students are encouraged to create and/or join affinity groups based on their disabled identification

(continued)

Table 6.2. Continued

Models of Disability	Etic/Emic Perspective	Tenets	Examples in Society	Examples in Education
Human Rights Model	Emic	Disability rights are a social justice concern, and should be viewed as human rights	Americans with Disabilities Act (ADA) Any laws that ensure *all* people, both disabled and nondisabled, have their rights guaranteed	Use of Universal Design for Learning (UDL) Specific legal rights for disabled students through Section 504 plans and Individualized Education Programs (IEPs)
Charity Model	Etic	Disabled people are victims of tragedy, and should be subject to pity and help from nondisabled people	Basis or inspiration for charity fundraising, meant to "pull at the heartstrings" or instill pity for those who are comparatively "worse off" to compel nondisabled people to help financially	Completely separate special education services, without consideration of inclusion Separated students may only be seen by their nondisabled peers on special occasions, which may lead to feelings of pity or inspiration
Economic Model	Etic	Disabled people are mostly connected to their economic contributions, or their inability to contribute	The basis/definition of the Rehabilitation Act of 1973 Laws in various nations related to preparing people with disabilities for the workforce so that they can be "productive"	Section 504 plans with a focus on accommodations to help the student become competitive in the economy Individualized Education Programs (IEPs) with a focus on modifications to help the student become competitive in the economy

How We View Disability

Models of disability have fueled and perpetuated many assumptions about disabled people and their life prospects, reinforcing the beliefs and biases that society inaccurately holds. These biases can form from a simple ignorance or lack of experience with disabled people. Many have not met someone they know to be disabled, especially with the prevalence of invisible or nonapparent disabilities. These attitudes are present in the pathologization and denigration of disability—the assumption that disability must always be problematic and must always be negative. This pathologization and external view of disability is referenced as the **etic perspective**, where viewpoints tend to be "objective," analytical, and external to the situation or individual (Goode, 1992). Etic perspectives are considered more scientific and more objective, although when applied this doesn't hold true (Leong, 2008). Clinical and diagnostic paperwork, school records, and psychological studies are all created and viewed through the etic perspective, which often serves to problematize, devalue, and find fault with the student or population being observed (Goode, 1992). Put simply, etic perspectives tend to dehumanize their subject(s) and only look at the "problems" derived from disability.

Emic perspectives are considered "native viewpoints," in that they are internal to the person or group in question, and often are seen as more subjective and less valid (Goode, 1992). Emic perspectives, however, can take into account the external circumstances acting on the subject, as well as personal testimony and more in-depth analysis and observation of the subject. These perspectives, especially in the fields of education and psychology, may result in better outcomes for the subject by recognizing intersectionality and acknowledging the underlying traits of disability (Goode, 1992; Leong, 2008). In other words, etic perspectives look through the eyes of the observer and how society perceives disability; emic perspectives see through the lens of the person with disability and how they navigate and interact with society. By using an emic approach to instruction and planning, educators can focus on students' strengths and respect them as people and not subjects.

One example of the contrast and effects of etic and emic perspectives comes through David Goode's (a lifelong disability researcher) interaction with Bobby (a man diagnosed with Down syndrome). Goode (1992) shares that he first learns about Bobby from his clinical records, which were seemingly written from a medical model perspective. As such, these records were hyper-focused on Bobby's inadequacies and deficits and outlined the attempts to "correct" these issues (etic perspective). Goode notes that Bobby was never assessed through the lens of his strengths, competence, and his inherent value as a human being (emic perspective). The etic perspective of the medical records, serving to find fault in him, provided a grim portrait of an inept, incompetent, and hopeless individual who did not have a bright future ahead of him. This was in comparison with the more positive, helpful, and hopeful outlook that could be provided by an emic perspective.

The files also included very little that was positive about Bobby; everything they contained served to categorize Bobby as "incompetent" and "low functioning." Utilizing an emic perspective, Goode was able to observe Bobby's level of competence, his understanding of daily situations and how to manipulate them, and his complex mental ability in weighing different situations and outcomes (Goode, 1992). The etic perspective served as a barrier to true communication between Bobby and the staff/researchers as well as depicting a gross oversimplification of who Bobby was as a person; the emic perspective allowed a greater window into Bobby's life and facilitated genuine communication between him and others.

Research literature often focuses on what disabled people cannot do, bypassing what they have to say and what they can do. Interventions focus on what caregivers or neurotypical outsiders decide are "problems," often leaving aside insight from autistic adults who speak from the experience of having endured sometimes traumatizing interventions. Research and perspectives are rooted in an etic approach and limit the understanding of the disability, silencing the voices of those with the disability. While an etic perspective may have its merit in certain situations, it tends to not recognize a student's strengths, capabilities, and personality. Emic perspectives take external influences into account, and also recognize a student's strengths. An emic approach encourages the student and positions them for success more than is typical with a traditional etic approach. Examining table 6.2 offers you a way to connect the Models of Disability across perspectives.

THE LANGUAGE OF DISABILITY

Sociology and social psychology both play major roles in the way we interact with and interpret disability, especially the way people, disabled and abled alike, view disabilities and talk about them. A shared understanding of the meaning of words is important to communicate and interact successfully within today's society. Language has long been understood to be an important factor in addressing disability. Beth Haller (2010), scholar of disability in the media, explains the importance of language to disability rights activists:

> Language has always had the power to define cultural groups. The words used to refer to a group of people are important: they have ramifications for self-perception, but they also play a large role in shaping what the general public believes about the group. Activists and scholars in the US disability rights movement have for the last several decades been calling for what they term "appropriate language" because, like other social groups before them, they contend that what they are called is intrinsic to their identity as people with disabilities. They insist that they, not others, should define these terms. The language used in stories about disability, they say, helps shape what the public understands about the disability condition. (p. 49)

Haller (2010) goes on to state that language is also important to the way that the media covers disability; the choice of words used by journalists to discuss disability further shapes how society frames disability as a construct. This becomes vital when considering that, for some in society, the first time they encounter many types of disabilities might be through media representation. The use of language also delves into the field of **semantics**, the branch of linguistics and logic concerned with meaning. For more information on sociolinguistics, see chapter 1. Disability Studies uses semantics to help understand the true meanings of words that refer to disability, both on the surface and running deep below. One of the most common discussions of disability involves how we refer to those associated with disability.

Stop and think. Do you say "disabled people" or "people with disabilities"? This is an issue of **identity-first language** (IFL) or **person-first language** (PFL). PFL quite literally puts the person first! An individual's personhood comes before their disability or other identity, such as a person with ADHD or a person with a learning disability. In contrast, IFL puts the person's identity before their personhood, focusing on the disability and/or identity. Examples of IFL include: an Autistic student, a Blind man, or a Deaf person. Proponents of PFL argue that focusing on a person's personhood above their disability advocates for them to not be defined by their disability (Collier, 2012). However, when you look at this language more closely and notice how it is used with other types of identities, this becomes less clear (e.g., the Deaf and Autistic communities as described in chapter 3).

Other identities such as gender, religion, and sexuality are usually identified through IFL. You would most likely say "a gay man" or "a gay person," "a Jew" or "a Jewish person," or simply "a woman." These identities appear to be important and intrinsic to the person, and they come before the word "person." In fact, some of them don't even include the word "person" at all! You wouldn't call a gay man a "man who experiences gayness" or a Black woman "a woman who is Black." Black people, women, or gay people are not exclusively defined by their identity, and yet IFL is still commonly used to refer to these groups. We must question the assumption that someone's disability defines them, any more than a gay man being gay defines him, or a Black woman being Black and female defines her. Not only is PFL clunky (e.g., a person with a learning disability), but if you must be reminded of one's personhood by putting it before their identity, there exists a bigger problem than just the language being used. Calling someone a woman does not make them any less of a person, even though the word "person" doesn't appear in there at all!

Pause and Reflect

- Do you tend to default to IFL or PFL? Why? Where did you learn this association?
- Have you asked someone with a disability how they prefer to be addressed? Why or why not?

As you may have noticed, the authors specifically chose to use a mixture of IFL and PFL throughout this chapter. Opinions related to this topic vary greatly, and oftentimes the best option is to speak with someone with direct experience. Here are some thoughts, coming directly from a disabled person, to help you decide what language to use.

> **VIGNETTE 1: *A CONVERSATION WITH MELISSA, A LIFELONG WHEELCHAIR USER***

Melissa has used a wheelchair since a young age, due to an incident which happened at birth. She is an independent, thirty-something, professional woman. When prompted about the language she prefers to use (either IFL or PFL), she said:

> It depends on the day. Some days I will refer to myself as "disabled," "wheelchair user," or as a "person with a disability." I think what's important is that people ask me how I would like to be referred to instead of assuming that they know. I can't speak for everyone within the disabled community about this issue because it is not a hard and fast rule, but I do feel comfortable saying that asking the person their preference is the best option.
>
> I do not like the term "handicapped" because of the negative connotation connected to it. Once I found out the history of that word, I knew that I would no longer be using it. The other terms that I don't care for are "wheelchair bound" and "confined to a wheelchair." I don't like those terms because they are simply not true. My wheelchair provides me with the freedom to live my life as an independent person, so I am not bound or confined to it. It is actually the opposite!

Toward the end of the conversation, Melissa mentioned that language is important to her because it typically sets the tone for how people will treat her in their interactions:

> From the time I was a young girl, I noticed that when people took time to use language that was respectful toward me, it impacted the entire interaction. This extends to all settings starting back to when I was a student in K–12, through college, graduate school, and now in the workplace. It shows that people care and that they fully understand my value as a human being who happens to also have a disability.

The Etymology of "Disability"

As discussed in chapter 1, generally disability is considered as negative because of the Latin prefix/root "dis-", meaning apart or having a negative force (Collins English Dictionary, 2012). Disability simply means that one is not (dis-) able to do (ability) a particular thing. Calling someone disabled acknowledges their disability and makes it clear that they do struggle with societal barriers like gatekeeping, ableism, and myriad other social issues. It acknowledges that disabled people's lives are different from those of nondisabled people in numerous ways because of their disability, as well as because of how society treats them. It does not imply that they can't achieve anything but recognizes that there are barriers that disabled people have to overcome to succeed.

One potential reason for the IFL preference is that it tries to take back the identity of disability by shifting the social connotation of the word "disability" from negative to positive, or at the very least, to something that is just there and exists similar to other sociocultural categories (e.g., race, gender, nationality, religion). One example is in the fostering of a sense of community for disabled people (see chapters 1 and 3), whether it be in-person or through the internet and social media. Social media allows disabled people to congregate and form a space they call their own, to share experiences, and to get their ideas out into the world that has historically silenced their voices. This creates a shared culture of disability and allows disabled people to be proud of their disability identity and share their experiences with others.

The use of language is also important in the way we label individuals within the disabled community. Some diagnoses have overlapping symptom profiles that can cause medical professionals (i.e., doctors, psychologists) in clinical settings to have difficulty choosing between disability diagnoses, despite students exhibiting similar symptoms. For example, childhood lead poisoning (CLP) and autism present similar symptom profiles which, in rare cases, can lead to children being misdiagnosed or in the clinician choosing one diagnosis over another (Hauptman et al., 2019). The difference in labeling may be due in part to the more negative connotation CLP has in comparison to autism. CLP is thought of as an issue related to lower socioeconomic status (SES; poverty), which is further degraded when compounded by the intersection of disability, race, sex, and ethnicity (i.e., other groups that experience intersectional oppression). See chapter 2 for more on the intersections of disability and socioeconomic status. Societal understanding that lead-based materials are found in inexpensive, usually subsidized, housing creates a bias of the "type of people" with this disability. Along with associating CLP with poverty, some also have the misguided notion that the parents should have known or that they somehow caused their child's disability, while autism is generally regarded as having unknown causes. Labeling a person as autistic provides them with greater access to services and more attention in research. This also means that society doesn't have to consider the uncomfortable intersections of socioeconomic status, race, and disability.

Similarly, functionality and severity labels have linguistically been in debate (Chawla, 2019). These terms follow more of a Medical Model of Disability, as a system perpetuated by many nondisabled people to categorize and validate disabled people by their functionality or responsibility to contribute in a way that is favored by society (Gillespie-Lynch et al., 2017). A "low-functioning" label is often used to lower expectations and, by expecting less of a person, enforces the idea that they "can't possibly go anywhere." Conversely, a "high-functioning" label is generally used to deny accommodations one may need, and even to deny recognition of someone's disability, while keeping unrealistic expectations. This often results in overexertion and burnout as students attempt to meet these high standards without the tools that would help them to succeed. Such labels often function more as self-fulfilling prophecies rather than accurate assessments of an individual's capabilities or presumed competence. This is parallel to other considerations in education, for example, the opportunity gap in lieu of the achievement gap (see chapters 4 and 5).

DISABILITY IN THE MEDIA

In today's society, there are numerous representations of disability in the media, and a myriad of subconscious norms communicated through these representations. Often these subtexts either support societal assumptions about disabled people or consciously seek to refute them. Many assumptions or stereotypes surround the disabled community: a lack of maturity, a lack of humanity, a lack of a moral center, and more. Perhaps the most insidious assumption is the assumed lack of capability or potential success for people with disabilities and the removal of their accommodations and supports (Tuke, 2023).

This assumption is widespread, and it affects real people in various ways, such as in their progress in school if it is used to deny accommodations or suppress the success of disabled students. It also affects expectations of individuals in their workplaces. If they are assumed to be incapable, disabled people are more likely to be denied employment or not even considered for an interview. Furthermore, it perpetuates the false notion that disabled people cannot advocate for themselves or offer valid ideas and opinions.

This societal belief that disabled people are inferior, incompetent, or incapable of success is certainly reflected in the popular television show, *The Good Doctor*, which centers around an autistic surgical resident hired by his mentor, the president of the hospital. His coworkers all think that he shouldn't be there, purely because he's autistic (Shore et al., 2017–present). Many of the characters hold the belief that he couldn't be capable of being a decent doctor because he is autistic. *(It is worth noting that the actor himself is not Autistic.)* The same is true of Tyrion Lannister from *Game of Thrones*—he couldn't possibly be a good king, prince, or advisor because he is disabled, despite his disability being a physical one that does not impact his cognition or functioning. Another *Game of Thrones* character, Brandon Stark, is seen this way as well after he becomes paralyzed; even when later he gains the powers of a seer, as though transcending his physical boundaries (Benioff et al., 2011–2019).

Perhaps the most disingenuous example of this devaluing of disabled people can be seen in Ryan Hayes *(Special)*, a gay man diagnosed with cerebral palsy (CP) working at a social media startup (Dokoza et al., 2019–2021). He is already singled out because of his awkward gait and his sexuality, and when an opportunity comes up to attribute his visible disability manifestations to a car accident rather than CP, he takes it. Storylines like this indicate that having people assume one is injured in a car accident is preferable to being diagnosed with CP.

Yet some shows seek to shatter this ideology, such as *Reasonable Doubts*. The show focuses on Deaf Assistant District Attorney for Chicago, Tess Kaufman. Kaufman, while Deaf (made obvious in the show), is successful and presumed to be capable by many who work with her. Her Deafness isn't a barrier to her capability but something that perhaps allows her to find commonality with her partner, Detective Dickie Cobb, a hearing child of a Deaf father. The show portrays Tess as disabled, while also being successful and capable. The same should be expected and validated for Ryan, Tyrion, Brandon, and perhaps all the characters in the media—and real people—who are disabled (more on the media in chapter 12).

Pause and Reflect

- How do you see disabled people in TV shows or movies? Do the characters have agency? Are they highlighted only because of their disabilities? Are the actors disabled? Did the studio hire disabled consultants or writers?
- How have these examples shaped your conscious or unconscious perspectives about disability?

VIGNETTE 2: *PARENTING*

It's difficult for others to know and understand the beauty, challenges, and successes of parenting a child with a disability. You fiercely love your child and will move mountains in one moment and in the next, you'll be frustrated with how unjust and unfairly your child is treated. There seems to be a constant push-pull relationship with navigating school services, accessing medical and therapy services, and ensuring that your child has the support and modifications they need to be successful in school, in order to reach their fullest potential.

Learning about the disabilities of each of my sons happened at different times in their lives. My oldest son, Antonio, was in 10th grade when he received his diagnosis of dysgraphia and ADHD–Inattentive Type, after years of inconsistent struggles in school. For my youngest son, Alejandro, my husband and I knew right away when he was born that things were different. My labor was quick with Alejandro and after one push, he came out. He initially struggled with breathing on his own, had high blood sugars, and looked "different" from our other children when they were born. Several doctors were quick to point out that Alejandro's right ear was misshapen, his jaw was small and pointy, he had a sacral dimple, and he was long and skinny.

(continued)

VIGNETTE 2: *Continued*

He was the largest baby in the neonatal intensive care unit (NICU), as he was twenty-three inches long and weighed eight pounds, seven ounces. Fifteen months later, Alejandro was diagnosed with Sotos syndrome, a rare genetic condition causing rapid physical growth in the early years of life, along with motor, speech, and cognitive delays. In middle school, he was diagnosed with Autism, ADHD, and Epilepsy. Despite learning about each of my sons' disabilities at different times in their lives, my response to parenting and supporting them has always been the same: fierce advocacy and maintaining high expectations, especially when others expect less from them.

Growing up, Antonio was always a happy, funny, and honest kid. During his early elementary school years, learning came easy for him and he excelled with his academics. Teachers commented on his love of learning and love of science. He dreamed of working for NASA one day. As the years progressed and the academics became more challenging in middle school, he had to spend more time completing assignments than his peers did. He always seemed to understand the material, but it just took much longer and he needed more help from adults to complete the work. As time passed and he had different teachers, many underestimated his abilities or assumed he wasn't putting forth his best effort. In 10th grade, Antonio had a neuropsychological evaluation, in order to find a profile of his strengths and weaknesses. This would help us (and him) find out about how he best learned and to find the right supports and strategies to maximize his potential. It was at that time he was diagnosed with dysgraphia and ADHD–Inattentive Type. We worked with the school to develop a 504 plan that would provide protection, modifications, and accommodations at school. When teachers followed the plan, Antonio was successful and confident. When teachers inconsistently provided modifications and accommodations, it was frustrating for Antonio and us (as his parents) because the challenges showed up in his poor grades or his dejected mood. It felt like a constant battle with the teachers who did not follow the 504 plan, because Antonio always needed to fail in order to "prove" he needed the modifications and accommodations.

Alejandro's educational path was much different, as he had several health needs and medical diagnoses. His main diagnosis of Sotos syndrome stumped teachers, since they'd never heard of it, nor had they ever had another student with the same condition. I spent a lot of time educating teachers and staff about Sotos syndrome and what that meant for Alejandro. He was twice the size for his age, grew rapidly, and was developmentally delayed. For example, when Alejandro was four, he looked like an eight-year-old, but talked like a two-year-old. Academic and behavioral expectations always had to be adjusted. I reminded Alejandro's teachers to set realistic expectations, but also to challenge him. Over the years, Alejandro benefited from specialized instruction, modifications, accommodations, and parents who encouraged the IEP team to maximize his academic and functional potential. As a result of the support Alejandro received from his family and IEP teams over the years, he plans to attend a transition program while taking computer classes at the local community college after high school.

When I think of all of the specialized instruction, services, and accommodations that both of my sons received at school over the years, I am humbled and grateful for the time period we live in. We live during a time where the parents of a student with a disability and a student with a disability are both legally protected and have access to an education and opportunities that were essentially nonexistent almost fifty years ago. Prior to legislation requiring public education for children with cognitive or emotional disabilities, deafness, blindness, or motor impairments, there were few educational opportunities for disabled children. Parents either had to educate their disabled child at home or pay for an expensive private education and I am grateful for the free education and services both my sons received at school.

MODELS OF DISABILITY IN EDUCATION

Table 6.2 showcases how the different models of disabilities are embedded within our society, further emphasized by the previous section on disability in the media. This section will discuss the impacts in educational practices. In the early 1990s, a new approach to designing learning activities for all students was developed—**Universal Design for Learning** (UDL). As introduced in chapters 2 and 5, UDL is an evidenced-based framework to improve teaching and learning for all students, giving them an opportunity to succeed alongside their peers (Mosen, 2022). UDL was designed to provide *all* individuals with an equal opportunity to learn based on three principles: representation, action and expression, and engagement. Each principle includes guidelines that provide a framework, tools, and resources that practitioners can use to improve learning (Mayer et al., 2014). The benefits of UDL include developing a flexible approach for curriculum design and instruction that focuses on ways students access material and assignments, approach learning, and show what they know (Waisman et al., 2023). Mosen (2022) noted that:

> UDL applies to teaching in a similar way that universal design for the built environment ensures access features such as ramps, lifts and ground surface tactile indicators are considered from the point of design and available for all to use. (p. 1)

From a disability perspective, UDL aligns well with the Social Model of Disability, since the focus is on removing social and environmental barriers, not the disability itself. The effort to identify and eliminate social and environmental barriers, while applying UDL principles and strategies, results in a more accessible and inclusive classroom for all students (Mosen, 2022).

Incorporating integrated multi-tiered levels of support (I-MTSS) into the classroom enhances the educational equity for all students despite any oppressions due to their race, disability, or SES (Rose et al., 2020). Emic perspectives can be included to promote inclusion through frameworks such as Response to Intervention (RTI) and Positive Behavioral Interventions and Supports (PBIS). These frameworks look at the students' current abilities and offer support based on their needs. Through RTI, practitioners provide all students with access to effective instruction and adequate support and resources for learning (Robinson, 2010). Through PBIS, students are met with high expectations, incorporating the students' culture and experiences to enhance their learning and sense of belonging (Klingner et al., 2005). I-MTSS and RTI are discussed several times in this text.

When practitioners use emic perspectives and hold high expectations, they promote an inclusive and conducive learning environment where their disabled students can show their true potential. Scot Danforth, a scholar in disability studies in education, defines inclusion as "educating . . . students with disabilities in general education classrooms" (2014, p. 4). He describes "highly included" students as those with disabilities who spend more than 80 percent of their time in the general education environment. This percentage continues to rise from 39 percent in 1992, to 61 percent in 2011, to 66 percent in 2020. (Danforth, 2014; National Center for Education Statistics, 2022). "The variability of students' abilities is no longer good [sic] reason to create segregated classrooms and schools . . . [but instead] a rationale for more creative and effective teaching in the general classroom" (Danforth, 2014, p. 5).

Yet many practitioners face barriers to full inclusion in the classroom, whether from social issues, lack of resources, or actions of their schools' administrations (Villegas, 2021). General education practitioners tend to have little experience or training with disabled students or in how to differentiate curriculum. This is a systemic issue that shares fault across the spectrum from the school administration to the institutions of higher education the practitioners attended. Another major issue lies in the resources and support practitioners have at their disposal (Mokaleng & Möwes, 2020). This is yet another issue that falls on the school to resolve, which can often mean appealing or protesting to the local authorities who frequently are the ones responsible for the lack of resources. The stigmas regarding disability also make full inclusion difficult (Anega et al., 2021). Those who are not disabled may feel as though segregated schooling is what they have known, and resist change, despite the fact that inclusion benefits everyone in the classroom or school (Connor & Ferri, 2007).

Cosier and Ashby (2016) listed a number of strategies practitioners may use to promote inclusion, specifically focusing on such applications of disability studies in education. They explain the effects of strategies such as: confronting judgments made about students solely based upon their disability (i.e., bias, see chapter 2), advocating for disabled students' rights to access course materials and curricula (i.e., self-determination), and facilitating connection with the students' peers by discussing and lessening assumptions made about them based primarily on their disability (i.e., the culture of disability, see chapters 1 and 3). These often indicate intentional and directed effort from the educators themselves (Cosier & Ashby, 2016).

Race and Disability in Schools

Gloria Ladson-Billings focuses on community in the classroom as an effort toward inclusion. Although she studied inclusion along racial lines, her strategies along with many of her colleagues focus on race, disability, and diversity to promote inclusion within education (Cruz & Firestone, 2022; Ladson-Billings, 1995; and Maroto et al., 2019). Race and disability intertwine in a way that often disadvantages people of the global majority (PGM; for an introduction to PGM, see chapter 4). For example, children of foreign-born mothers in the United States tend to have a higher occurrence of high support needed for autism phenotypes (Becerra et al., 2014). The same holds for US-born African Americans and Hispanics compared to US-born whites. Unanswered is whether these differences point to medical differences, social differences, or a combination of both that lead to a difference in symptom presentation, interpretation, and diagnosis in these children.

In school settings, the related status of race influences how a child's disability is classified and the type and quality of services they receive (Howard et al., 2021). Although disabilities occur regardless of race, ethnicity, or SES, researchers continue to see these factors influencing the age of diagnoses, classification of symptoms, and the quality of services and supports offered to children and families (Golson et al., 2022; Mandell et al., 2005). The persistent intersection of race and disability alongside other sociocultural identities makes it imperative for educators to consider across factors as they interact with students in educational settings.

In her efforts to build community, Ladson-Billings (1994) emphasizes a sense of familiarity, ease, and comfort with the students. One of the most important methods to facilitate this sense of community is the use of "deliberate pedagogical strategies"—such as class trips or the way(s) in which the students are referred to (as family, for example)—both of which promoted familiarity and community-building. The teachers also created systems of collective responsibility and rewards, once again fostering a sense of fellowship between the students, as well as between the students and the teacher (Ladson-Billings, 2009). Ladson-Billings also highlights that the recognition of cultural views, independence of study/ideas, and connecting education to experience are especially vital to the creation of a successful classroom community, and, as we can see, a successful level of inclusion in the classroom. This sense of community, she emphasizes, comes down to providing a stable environment, embracing personal differences, and promoting a sense of camaraderie and collective responsibility, all of which can be implemented in special education inclusion efforts (Ladson-Billings, 1994, 1995).

Pause and Reflect

- How can practitioners connect education to experience in the classroom?
- How can practitioners embrace personal differences and promote a sense of camaraderie and collective responsibility?

VIGNETTE 3: *MEET LIZA*

I am a disabled, autistic, Ashkenazi, queer woman who deals with mobility limitations, chronic pain, migraines, and dysautonomia, all of which affect my functioning day-to-day. When I was nine years old, my family and I moved to Central New York. Up until this point, I was homeschooled, and doing well with the curriculum and expectations. This all changed when I was thrown into the world of the public school system. At first, many of my difficulties there were social, as an autistic Jewish girl, I stood out—to say the least. Soon after came the analysis of my grades, the repeated IQ tests, the assessments when called down to the school psychologist's office, etc. The school considered it to be an eligibility evaluation for academic accommodations. To get these accommodations, I had to fit into the small limitations of the "box" they had set out for me. My struggles were manifested in lower grades and lower IQ scores. I had to show my deficits in a way they considered deserving or suitable for accommodation. They (as special education generally does), viewed me through the fault-finding, outsider, etic perspective, and viewed my disability through the medical model.

This view and method of evaluation, however, failed to account for my true struggles—the effort needed to keep my grade where I deemed it "should" be. I was doing extra work to process the information that I was learning, as to keep my grades to a decent standard. Yet it was this same work, and these same grades, that kept my processing difficulties and my disability as a whole from being recognized and accommodated. The school could have helped me to complete work at the same level and with the same amount of effort as my peers, but since I, to them, appeared to be doing "well enough" without these accommodations, I was thought to not need them. I quickly learned that, while it might cost me accommodations, masking would allow me to make my way through these systems more easily.

Many of the professionals I encountered were not used to accommodating disabled people who advocated for themselves, they had a very narrow view of what was disability, who dealt with it, and who was "disabled enough" for their services. My ability to advocate for myself in a higher education setting, and my emphasis on achieving high grades (often spending the last bits of energy I had to attain them, to the point where I was then incapable of doing other, necessary tasks) showed that, in their eyes, I was not "disabled enough." These ideas show a fundamental misunderstanding of the purpose of accommodations. Accommodations don't make completing work and showing one's potential easier, they effectively make it possible.

These assumptions of competence, accommodations, and societal views of disability affect every aspect of my life, from driving and police encounters, to mental healthcare, to disciplinary methods I will refuse to take as a teacher. For example, I keep a clear passport case in my car with a card in it stating that I'm autistic and I might respond in a way a police officer doesn't expect, or that I might not be able to talk at all. As an autistic person, I know I have a higher likelihood of being seen as threatening or having an interaction with police turn violent or fatal, because I'm "different," and that difference is often seen as wrong just like Judson Albahm, George Floyd, and many others. Prone restraint has also been used in schools and has ended up killing students like Max Benson. I was restrained numerous times in my childhood, against my will. I tend to think, could that have been me and could it have turned fatal?

It's worth thinking about these situations, and the questions they conjure. How do these societal views, these lack of accommodations, and these threats to our ability to work, or even to live, affect our participation in society, and in an inaccessible world? How do they affect our ability to learn, to contribute, to thrive?

One of the things that helps me the most to this day is when people presume that I am competent, regardless of how I may look or seem one day to the next. I am just as competent on a day when I am put together as I am on days I am not. Yet, on both occasions, I need my accommodations in order to make these achievements and demonstrate my competence. Second, acknowledge my disability and don't use euphemisms like "differently abled." By acknowledging my disability, one acknowledges that I have different experiences in society, and may have barriers to access them. Third, whether someone is a professional, an educator, a parent, etc., do not assume that their experience is above the lived experiences of a disabled individual (like me) discussing their needs, their experiences in an inaccessible world. Do not assume that you "know best" what I need, or violate my space in order to try to "help" (i.e., grabbing the handles of my wheelchair to get up a hill or over a bump, without asking and without my direct and express consent).

As disabled people, we are valid, we are competent, we are capable, we are diverse, and we are worth accommodating and accepting. We are worth being listened to, and worthy of participation in society, and of acceptance into the society. We are worthy of respect. We are human!

SUMMARY

Disabled people know the stories shared earlier all too well. Researchers, practitioners, advocates, parents, and disabled people themselves will continue to support the notion that every person, disabled or otherwise, is deserving of basic respect and faith in their success simply on the basis that they are human, just like anyone else (Kliewer, 1988). Danforth (2014) states that inclusion and reduction of stigma is necessary in disability education. Different societies see disability in different ways, as is evidenced by the lower rates of diagnosis among different countries (e.g., with non-Western countries and/or ethnicities often appearing to have underrepresentation of disability; CDC, 2020b; United Nations Statistics Division, 2017). Yet disability has become something that often forms a bond or an understanding between those who identify with or have lived a similar experience. A disability affects someone's life and the way in which the world views and interacts with them (i.e., Social Model of Disability), and we as society must recognize this.

The language we use to describe and identify disability is one step on the way to recognizing just that. The way we, as a society, view and discuss disabled people has a direct impact on the way we treat them and the way we encounter them when we meet. Semantics, social psychology, and many other disciplines all express the importance of understanding disability through multiple perspectives and models that acknowledge the impact disability has on society, as well as the conditions and expectations we assume for disabled people. As practitioners, it is vital to consider these different perspectives and approaches when reflecting on your biases and instruction for students with disabilities.

REFERENCES

Anega, J., Boecker, G., & Churchill, H. (2021). The effects of stigma on students with learning disabilities and inclusive classroom practices. *Community Psychologist, 54*(3). https://www.communitypsychology.com/effects-of-stigma-on-students-with-learning-disabilities/

Armstrong, S., Noble, M., & Rosenbaum, P. (2006). Deconstructing barriers: The promise of socioeconomic rights for people with disabilities in Canada. In R. E. Howard-Hassmann & C. E. Welch Jr., *Economic rights in Canada and the United States* (pp. 149–68). University of Pennsylvania Press. https://doi.org/10.9783/9780812204780.149

Azad, G. F., Gormley, S., Marcus, S., & Mandell, D. S. (2019). Parent–teacher problem solving about concerns in children with autism spectrum disorder: The role of income and race. *Psychology in the Schools, 56*(2), 276–90. https://doi.org/10.1002/pits.22205

Bayton, D. (1998). Language matters: Handicapping an affliction. Disability History Museum. https://www.disabilitymuseum.org/dhm/edu/essay.html?id=30

Becerra, T. A., von Ehrenstein, O. S., Heck, J. E., Olsen, J., Arah, O. A., Jeste, S. S., Rodriguez, M., & Ritz, B. (2014). Autism Spectrum Disorders and race, ethnicity, and nativity: A population-based study. *Pediatrics, 134*(1), e63–e71. https://doi.org/10.1542/peds.2013-3928

Benioff, D., Weiss, D., Martin, G., Strauss, C., Doelger, F., Caulfield, B., . . . Nutter, D. (Executive Producers). (2011–2019). *Game of Thrones* [TV series]. HBO Entertainment; Television 360; Grok! Television; Generator Entertainment; Startling Television; Bighead Littlehead.

Brewer, E., Brueggemann, B., Hetrick, N. & Yergeau, M. (2012). Introduction, background, and history. In B. Brueggemann (Ed.), *Arts and humanities* (pp. 1–62). Sage.

Centers for Disease Control and Prevention (CDC). (2020a). Disability and health overview: Impairments, activity limitations, and participation restrictions. *Disability and Health Promotion.* https://www.cdc.gov/ncbddd/disabilityandhealth/disability.html

———. (2020b, September 16). Infographic: Adults with disabilities: Ethnicity and race. *Disability and Health Promotion.* https://www.cdc.gov/ncbddd/disabilityandhealth/materials/infographic-disabilities-ethnicity-race.html

Chawla, D. S. (2019, July 2). Large study supports discarding the term "high-functioning autism." *Spectrum.* https://www.spectrumnews.org/news/large-study-supports-discarding-term-high-functioning-autism/

Collier, R. (2012). Person-first language: What it means to be a "person." *CMAJ: Canadian Medical Association Journal (Journal de l'Association médicale canadienne), 184*(18), E935–E936. https://doi.org/10.1503/cmaj.109-4322

Collins English Dictionary. (2012). dis-. https://www.dictionary.com/browse/dis#:~:text=a%20Latin%20prefix%20meaning%20%E2%80%9Capart,Also%20di%2D

Collins, K. M. (2013). *Ability profiling and school failure: One child's struggle to be seen as competent.* Lawrence Erlbaum.

Connor, D., & Ferri, B. (2007). The conflict within: Resistance to inclusion and other paradoxes in special education. *Disability & Society, 22*(1), 63–77. 10.1080/09687590601056717. https://www.researchgate.net/publication/248912608_The_conflict_within_Resistance_to_inclusion_and_other_paradoxes_in_special_education

Cosier, M., & Ashby, C. (2016). Disability studies and the work of educators. In M. Cosier and C. Ashby (Eds.), *Enacting change from within: Disability studies meets teaching and teacher education* (pp. 1–19). Peter Lang.

Creamer, D. B. (2009). *Disability and Christian theology: Embodied limits and constructive possibilities*. Oxford University Press.

Cruz, R. A., & Firestone, A. R. (2022). Understanding the empty backpack: The role of timing in disproportionate special education identification. *Sociology of Race and Ethnicity, 8*(1), 95–113. https://doi.org/10.1177/23326492211034890

Danforth, S. (2014). *Becoming a great inclusive educator*. Peter Lang.

Degener, T. (2017). A new human rights model of disability. In V. Della Fina, R. Cera, & G. Palmisano (Eds.), *The United Nations Convention on the rights of persons with disabilities: A commentary* (pp. 41–60). Springer.

den Houting, J. (2019). Neurodiversity: An insider's perspective. *Autism, 23*(2), 271–73. https://doi.org/10.1177/1362361318820762

Dokoza, A., Norsoph, E., O'Connell, R., Spiewak, T., & Parsons, J. (Executive Producers). (2019–2021). *Special* [TV series]. Warner Bros. Television; That's Wonderful Productions; Campfire; Stage 13.

Finkelstein, V. (2001, December 1). The social model of disability repossessed. *Manchester Coalition of Disabled People*. https://disability-studies.leeds.ac.uk/wp-content/uploads/sites/40/library/finkelstein-soc-mod-repossessed.pdf

Fuchs, D., Mock, D., Morgan, P. L., & Young, C. L. (2003). Responsiveness-to-Intervention: Definitions, evidence, and implications for the Learning Disabilities Construct. *Learning Disabilities Research & Practice, 18*(3), 157–71. https://doi.org/10.1111/1540-5826.00072

Garland, R. (2020, October). How was a disabled Greek person treated in society? In *The other side of history: Daily life in the ancient world* [lecture series]. Wondrium. https://www.wondriumdaily.com/how-was-a-disabled-greek-person-treated-in-society/

Gillespie-Lynch, K., Kapp, S. K., Brooks, P. J., Pickens, J., & Schwartzman, B. (2017). Whose expertise is it? Evidence for autistic adults as critical autism experts. *Frontiers in Psychology, 8*, 438. https://doi.org/10.3389/fpsyg.2017.00438

Golson, M. E., Haverkamp, C. R., McClain, M. B., Schwartz, S. E., Ha, J., Harris, B., & Benallie, K. J. (2022). Influences of student race/ethnicity and gender on autism special education classification considerations. *Autism, 26*(6), 1423–35. https://doi.org/10.1177/13623613211050440

Goode, D. A. (1992). Who is Bobby? Ideology and method in the discovery of a Down Syndrome person's competence. In P. M. Ferguson, D. L. Ferguson, & S. J. Taylor (Eds.), *Interpreting disability: A qualitative reader* (pp. 197–212). Teachers College Press.

Granshaw, S. I. (Ed.). (2021, September). Neural networks and neurodiversity. *Photogrammetric Record, 36*(175), 192–96. https://doi.org/10.1111/phor.12376

Haller, B. A. (2010). *Representing disability in an ableist world: Essays on mass media*. Advocado.

Hauptman, M., Stierman, B., & Woolf, A. D. (2019). Children with Autism Spectrum Disorder and lead poisoning: Diagnostic challenges and management complexities. *Clinical Pediatrics, 58*(6), 605–12. https://doi.org/10.1177/0009922819839237

Henderson, G., & Bryan, W. (2011). *Psychosocial aspects of disability*. Charles C. Thomas.

Heumann, J., & Joiner, K. (2020). *Being Heumann: An unrepentant memoir of a disability rights activist*. Beacon.

Horovitz, M., Matson, J. L., Hattier, M. A., Tureck, K., & Bamburg, J. W. (2013). Challenging behaviors in adults with Intellectual Disability: The effects of race and Autism Spectrum Disorders. *Journal of Mental Health Research in Intellectual Disabilities*, 6(1), 1–13. https://doi.org/10.1080/19315864.2011.605989

Howard, J., Copeland, J. N., Gifford, E. J., Lawson, J., Bai, Y., Heilbron, N., & Maslow, G. (2021). Brief report: Classifying rates of students with Autism and Intellectual Disability in North Carolina: Roles of race and economic disadvantage. *Journal of Autism and Developmental Disorders*, 51(1), 307–15. https://doi.org/10.1007/s10803-020-04527-y

Institute on Disabilities. (2019). *Disability rights timeline*. Temple University. https://disabilities.temple.edu/resources/disability-rights-timeline

Iudici, A., Favaretto, G., & Turchi, G. P. (2019). Community perspective: How volunteers, professionals, families and the general population construct disability: Social, clinical and health implications. *Disability and Health Journal*, 12(2), 171–79. https://doi.org/10.1016/j.dhjo.2018.11.014

Jo, H., Schieve, L. A., Rice, C. E., Yeargin-Allsopp, M., Tian, L. H., Blumberg, S. J., . . . Boyle, C. A. (2015). Age at Autism Spectrum Disorder (ASD) diagnosis by race, ethnicity, and primary household language among children with special health care needs, United States, 2009–2010. *Maternal and Child Health Journal*, 19(8), 1687–97. https://doi.org/10.1007/s10995-015-1683-4

Junior, N., & Schipper, J. (2013). Disability studies and the Bible. In S. McKenzie & J. Kaltner (Eds.), *New meanings for ancient texts: Recent approaches to biblical criticisms and their applications* (pp. 21–37). Westminster John Knox.

Jurecic, A. (2007). Neurodiversity. *College English*, 69(5), 421–42. http://www.jstor.org/stable/25472229

Kapp, S. K. (Ed.). (2020). *Autistic community and the neurodiversity movement: Stories from the frontline*. Springer Nature. https://doi.org/10.1007/978-981-13-8437-0

Kapp, S. K., Gillespie-Lynch, K., Sherman, L. E., & Hutman, T. (2013). Deficit, difference, or both? Autism and neurodiversity. *Developmental Psychology*, 49(1), 59–71. https://doi.org/10.1037/a0028353

Kliewer, C. (1988). *Schooling children with Down syndrome* (pp. 1–10). Teachers College Press.

Ladson-Billings, G. (1994). What we can learn from multicultural education research. *Educational Leadership*, 51(8), 22–26.

———. (1995). Toward a theory of culturally relevant pedagogy. *American Educational Research Journal*, 32(3), 465–91.

———. (2009). *The Dreamkeepers: Successful teachers of African American children*. Jossey-Bass.

Leong, F. T. L. (2008, June 25). *Etic-emic distinction*. Sage Knowledge. https://sk.sagepub.com/reference/counseling/n376.xml

Logeswaran, S., Hollett, M., Zala, S., Richardson, L., & Scior, K. (2019). How do people with intellectual disabilities construct their social identity? A review. *Journal of Applied Research in Intellectual Disabilities*, 32(3), 533–42. https://doi.org/10.1111/jar.12566

Mandell, D. S., Novak, M. M., & Zubritsky, C. D. (2005). Factors associated with age of diagnosis among children with autism spectrum disorders. *Pediatrics*, 116(6), 1480–87. http://go.gale.com/ps/i.do?p=AONE&sw=w&issn=00314005&v=2.1&it=r&id=GALE%7CA140304285&sid=googleScholar&linkaccess=abs

Maroto, M., Pettinicchio, D., & Patterson, A. C. (2019). Hierarchies of categorical disadvantage: Economic insecurity at the intersection of disability, gender, and race. *Gender & Society, 33*(1), 64–93. https://doi.org/10.1177/0891243218794648

Mayer, A., Rose, D. H., & Gordon, D. (2014). *Universal Design for Learning: Theory and practice*. CAST Professional.

Milden, I. (2022). Examining the opposition to the Americans with Disabilities Act of 1990: "Nothing more than bad quality hogwash." *Journal of Policy History, 34*(4), 505–28. doi:10.1017/S0898030622000185

Mokaleng, M., & Möwes, A. D. (2020, May 20). Issues affecting the implementation of inclusive education practices in selected secondary schools in the Omaheke Region of Namibia. *Journal of Curriculum and Teaching, 9*(2). https://files.eric.ed.gov/fulltext/EJ1255869.pdf

Mosen, J. (2022, March 23). Exploring the intersection between Universal Design for Learning and the human rights model of disability. Cognition Education: New Zealand [blog]. https://www.cognitioneducation.co.nz/udl-disability/

National Center for Education Statistics. (2022). Students with disabilities. *Condition of Education* [annual report]. US Department of Education, Institute of Education Sciences. https://nces.ed.gov/programs/coe/indicator/cgg

O'Connell, R. (Writer). (2019–). *Special* [TV series]. Netflix.

Oliver, M. (1981). A new model of the social work role in relation to disability. In J. Campling (Ed.), *The handicapped person: A new perspective for social workers* (pp. 19–32). RADAR.

Olkin, R. (1999). *What psychotherapists should know about disability*. Guilford.

Pellicano, E., & den Houting, J. (2022). Annual research review: Shifting from "normal science" to neurodiversity in autism science. *Journal of Child Psychology and Psychiatry, 63*(4), 381–96. https://doi.org/10.1111/jcpp.13534

Robinson, G. G. (2010). *Culturally responsive beliefs and practices of general and special education teachers implementing response to intervention (RTI) in diverse elementary schools*. University of North Carolina at Greensboro.

Rose, J., Leverson, M., & Smith, K. (2020, April). *Embedding culturally responsive practices in Tier I—Delaware PBS*. Center on PBIS. http://www.delawarepbs.org/wp-content/uploads/2020/07/Rose-Leverson-_-Smith-2020-Embedding-Culturally-Responsive-Practices-in-Tier-I.pdf

Schalock, R. L., Luckasson, R., & Tassé, M. J. (2019). The contemporary view of intellectual and developmental disabilities: Implications for psychologists. *Psicothema, 31*(3), 223–29. https://doi.org/10.7334/psicothema2019.119

Shore, D. Gordon, S., Kim, D. D., Gunn, E., Kim, D., Lee, S., . . . Grasi, J. (Executive Producers). (2017–present). *The Good Doctor* [TV series]. Sony Pictures Television Studios; ABC Signature; Shore Z Productions; 3AD; EnterMedia.

Shreve, M. (1982). *The movement for independent living: A brief history*. For the Council of Independent Living. https://mwcil.org/wp-content/uploads/2017/08/Movement-for-IL-by-Shreve.pdf

Singer, R. (Writer). (1991–1993). *Reasonable Doubts* [TV series]. National Broadcasting Company.

Smart, J. (2004). Models of disability: The juxtaposition of biology and social construction. In T. F. Riggar & D. R. Maki (Eds.), *Handbook of rehabilitation counseling* (pp. 25–49). Springer.

Sneed, D. (2020). Live chat: While the ADA turns 30, the Greeks were protecting disabled rights nearly 3000 years ago. S. Lowry (Ed.), Long Beach Post. https://www.youtube.com/watch?v=uEcg-F54cZM&list=PLmyeRr4fPAS2lzaabDTATfS59IucPr2Rs&index=5

Tincani, M., Travers, J., & Boutot, A. (2009). Race, culture, and Autism Spectrum Disorder: Understanding the role of diversity in successful educational interventions. *Research & Practice for Persons with Severe Disabilities, 34*(3–4), 81–90. https://doi.org/10.2511/rpsd.34.3-4.81

Tuke, H. (2023, February 6). *My life as a 20 year old living with a visual impairment.* Victa Parents Portal. https://www.victaparents.org.uk/my-life-as-a-20-year-old-living-with-a-visual-impairment/

Union of the Physically Impaired Against Segregation (UPIAS). (1976). *Fundamental principles of disability.* https://disability-studies.leeds.ac.uk/wp-content/uploads/sites/40/library/UPIAS-fundamental-principles.pdf

United Nations Statistics Division. (2017). *Disability statistics.* https://unstats.un.org/unsd/demographic-social/sconcerns/disability/statistics/#!/countries

United States Government (USGOV). (1973). Rehabilitation Act of 1973, Public Law 93-112. https://www.govinfo.gov/content/pkg/COMPS-799/pdf/COMPS-799.pdf

Villegas, T. (2021, July 7). The biggest barriers to inclusive education. Think Inclusive [blog]. MCIE (Maryland Coalition for Inclusive Education). https://www.thinkinclusive.us/post/barriers-to-inclusive-education

Waisman, T. C., Williams, Z. J., Cage, E., Santhanam, S. P., Magiati, I., Dwyer, P., . . . Gillespie-Lynch, K. (2023). Learning from the experts: Evaluating a participatory autism and universal design training for university educators. *Autism, 27*(2), 356–70. https://doi.org/10.1177/13623613221097207

Weiss, L., & Brunstetter, B. (Writers). (2013, February 11). Human/Need/Desire [season 2, episode 6]. *Switched at Birth* [TV series]. ABC Family/Freeform.

World Health Organization (WHO). (2022, March 7). Disability. World Health Organization: Newsroom. https://www.who.int/en/news-room/fact-sheets/detail/disability-and-health#

Zhao, J., Chhetri, J. K., Chang, Y., Zheng, Z., Ma, L., & Chan, P. (2021). Intrinsic capacity vs. multimorbidity: A function-centered construct predicts disability better than a disease-based approach in a community-dwelling older population cohort. *Frontiers in Medicine, 8,* 753295. https://doi.org/10.3389/fmed.2021.753295

PART III

Educational Frameworks That Champion Equity

CHAPTER 7

Intersectional Sociocultural Competency and Educational Equity

Chapter authors: *L. Lynn Stansberry Brusnahan, Kenyon Andrews, Rebecca A. Wade, and Amy Eelkema Baxter*

Vignette author: *Amy Eelkema Baxter*

Editor: *Martin Odima Jr.*

ABSTRACT

As educators, we need tools that will support our ongoing journey to educational equity and sociocultural consciousness, which is an awareness and desire to act against societal inequities that disadvantage individuals. This consciousness includes acknowledging sociocultural identity differences between educators and the students in classrooms to better serve and support ALL students. The purpose of this chapter is to provide educators tools for critically conscious internal self-examinations and reflections on personal sociocultural identities and biases to further growth and contribute to our ability to guide students in a similar process. This chapter introduces an assessment to help educators examine personal intersectional sociocultural competence.

GUIDING QUESTIONS

- What is educational equity and how is equity different from equality?
- How can I, as an educator, engage in critical self-examination and guide my students in an exploration of their sociocultural identities?
- How can I, as an educator, engage in deep critical self-reflection of personal biases with action-planning steps?
- How can I, as an educator, examine my intersectional sociocultural competency so I am better able to meet the needs of my students with diverse identities?

KEY TERMS

Bias	Intersectional	Racism
Critical Consciousness	Competence	Sociocultural
Culture	Intersectionality	Consciousness
Disability	Marginalization	Sociocultural Identity
Discrimination	Oppression	Socioculturally
Equity	Prejudice	Sustaining Practices
	Race	

We are on an ongoing journey to educational equity, through anti-ableist and anti-racist intersectional sociocultural competence. **Sociocultural** is a term that represents our diverse social and cultural identities and sociocultural consciousness is an awareness and desire to act against societal inequities that disadvantage people of the global majority based on their identities (Ladson-Billings, 2006). **Intersectional competence** captures educators' awareness of how sociocultural identity differences simultaneously intersect within the context of school environments (Boveda & Aronson, 2019). This chapter provides tools for us, as practitioners, to identify and examine personal sociocultural identities, biases, and intercultural competence to more equitably serve and support ALL students. This chapter begins with an in-depth discussion of equity and then offers tools to engage in critical consciousness to further educator growth and strengthen our ability to guide students in a similar process. Additionally, the chapter introduces an assessment to help educators examine their intersectional sociocultural competency within the school setting.

EQUITY

Educators have a professional obligation to advance equity just as all students have the right to learning opportunities that help them achieve their full potential as engaged learners (NAEYC, 2019). To eliminate predictable and persistent opportunity gaps for historically oppressed populations of students, we must shift away from "equality" where all students receive the same to "equity" where individual students receive what they need. Table 7.1 includes an explanation of the terms equity and equality, along with justice, diversity, and inclusivity:

Table 7.1. Book Analogy

Justice is providing all students access to books.
Diversity is recognizing that students are different so they might need or prefer different books.
Equity is making sure every student gets a book that is right for them and meets their needs.
Equality is making sure all students get the same book regardless of their needs or preferences.
Inclusivity is providing a "sense of belonging" through an environment that allows students to read the book they want without judgment.

Some educators believe they engage in social justice by treating all students equally. Treating everyone the same may ensure that all students receive the same condition (e.g., same type of instruction, identical environment, access to matching materials), yet because of the complexity of needs, these conditions may not impact students in the same way or lead to the same outcomes. You may have heard an educator say, "I don't think of my students in terms of their race or ethnicity" or "I don't see color." When educators declare they are colorblind, they are generally communicating that they don't favor any one student and believe that they treat all their students in a fair manner. See more about the effects of colorblindness in chapter 4. Because this mindset does not acknowledge or see the student's complex and multifaceted identities, it renders these identities invisible. Ignoring any aspect of a student's identity can hinder a practitioner's ability to truly understand their own and their student's behaviors and can cause students to lose confidence in a school environment that is unfamiliar to them. We must take into consideration that the complexities of students' sociocultural identities affect their access, engagement, expectations, and agency.

Equity focuses on varying the conditions (e.g., different types of instruction, variety of environments, access to multiple materials) in an effort to ensure the same outcome for all students. Our ongoing educational journey to provide equity to our students requires us to identify and overcome obstacles (i.e., factors that hinder, block, or stop) and barriers (i.e., factors that prevent movement or access) arising from personal perspectives and systemic structures (Polusny et al., 2008). Educators need to uphold principles of justice, work to eliminate structural inequities that limit learning opportunities for students who have been historically oppressed, embrace diversity as strengths, and ensure inclusive opportunities for all learners (NAEYC, 2019).

Inclusivity means that "we are in this together." It's about creating a sense of belonging for all and making sure that everyone has access to opportunities and resources. For more on belonging, see chapter 1. Inclusion refers to the act of including or being included within a group or community. As introduced in chapter 1, this implies there is a dominant group allowing someone to participate with them. Inclusivity is the quality of being inclusive and actively seeking out and embracing diversity while making sure that all individuals feel valued and respected. Inclusivity is about creating a sense of belonging in an environment where everyone's unique perspectives and experiences are recognized and celebrated. Inclusivity is not about assimilation as it involves recognizing and respecting differences and ensuring that everyone has a voice and is able to participate fully in all settings.

Typically, in society, a dominant group, through power and positionality, establishes its norms, values, and preferences as the standard against which everything is measured. In the United States, dominant standards are typically viewed from identities such as Westernized, European American or Anglo-European (e.g., non-Latine), white, male, cisgender, affluent, English-speaking, and nondisabled. Dominant standards can be imposed on those with disabilities who experience them as **ableism** (i.e., discrimination based on ability identity). People also encounter them as **bias** (i.e., the favoring of one identity over another); **discrimination** (i.e., unjust treatment based on identity); **exclusion** (i.e., being prevented from taking part in something or not being included based on identity); **oppression** (i.e., being treated unjustly based on identity); **prejudice** (i.e., being judged according to preconceived opinions about identity that are not based on reason or experience); **racism** (i.e., negative treatment based on racial or ethnic identity); and **stereotyping** (i.e., being evaluated based on widely held but fixed and oversimplified ideas about a particular identity) because of unequal power relationships (Merriam-Webster.com, 2023).

Practitioners who think they are developing "equal" opportunities may actually be contributing to inequity without realizing it. Everyone comes to the table with varying depths of support, so it's essential to recognize these variations and tailor approaches to suit students' preferences and needs. To ensure success and fairness, teachers must create an ecosystem within the classroom that provides *equitable* opportunities. Think about a tree: the more opportunities a tree has to get to the resources it needs to grow (e.g., water, air, nutrients, sunlight), the more it grows. However, even if the amount of these resources were the same, the trees still would not grow in the same way; each type of tree has unique needs and the soils they are planted in differ. Soil helps anchor a tree's roots and soil structure influences tree growth by affecting the movement of water, air, and nutrients. Trees may need more or less water because soil structure influences the amount that makes its way to the tree's roots; trees in good-quality soils already have the opportunity to grow to their fullest potential and experience fewer problems.

From the outset, factors such as discrimination make the foundation on which some learners stand unequitable. **Disability** is any condition of the body or mind (e.g., impairment) that makes it more difficult for the person with the condition to do certain activities (e.g., activity limitations) and interact with the world around them (Centers for Disease Control and Prevention [CDC], n.d.). Discrimination due to disability, and the double or triple layer of discrimination due to the intersections of students' sociocultural identities, can impede access to opportunities. Despite this, some students will have greater access to success through advantage, opportunity, or privilege, while many times inherent inequity prohibits this. Some students will not have access to the same opportunities. It is not special treatment to help all students reach their highest potential; it is about giving them what they need to reach their maximum potential. Thinking about our tree analogy—would you question having to provide more water to some trees? Would you think, "This is unfair to the other trees"?

When considering this in an educational setting, for some students, access to help with homework may be limited due to factors they do not control, such

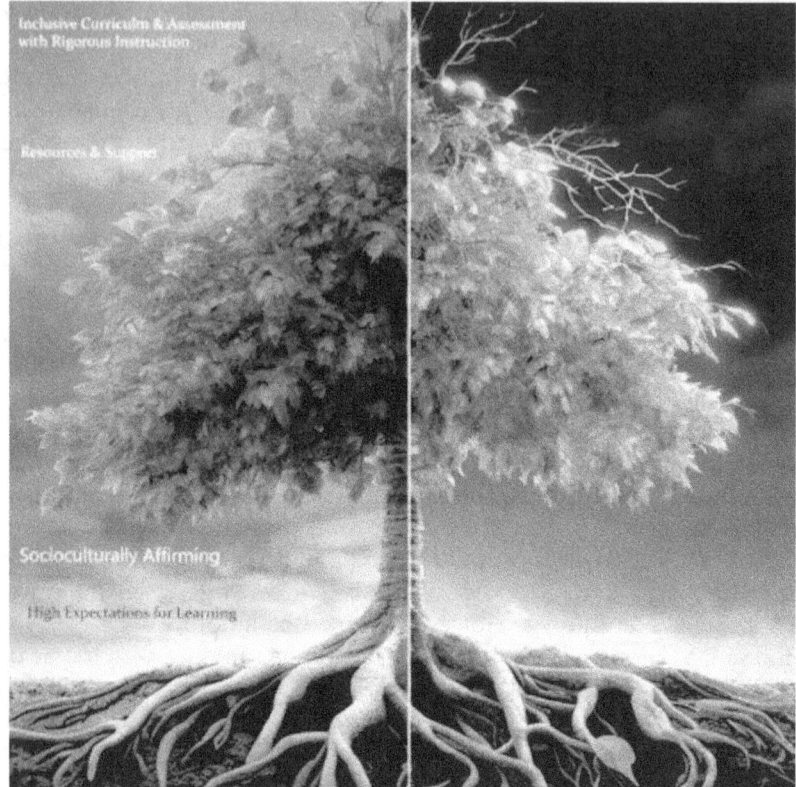

Figure 7.1. Equitable Foundation for Growth and Success

as housing insecurities, paid job requirements, limited parental education, or English-language proficiency. These students may need additional resources—not because they are deficient but because societal structures place them at a disadvantage. Students deserve support—not because they can't succeed on their own but because they may need a different foundation than their peers. At a minimum, to provide an equitable education, educators must ensure that all students have (a) a socioculturally affirming learning environment, (b) high expectations for learning, (c) inclusive curriculum and assessment with rigorous instruction, and (d) resources and needed support.

Pause and Reflect

- How are foundational roots—(a) access to a socioculturally affirming learning environment, (b) high expectations for learning, (c) inclusive curriculum and assessment, and (d) resources and areas of support—connected to equity and student success in school?

When striving for equity, we must acknowledge bias and adjust imbalances, which contribute to opportunity gaps. Achieving success in the classroom starts with equity and respect for each and every student. Teachers must engage students through an intersectional lens, with socioculturally sustaining course materials in which students can see multiple layers of themselves reflected. Embracing the fact that every student brings a unique sociocultural background to the learning community can empower practitioners to be more understanding and responsive to individual learning styles. Practitioners need to make learning more meaningful by centering students' sociocultural identities in every aspect of the classroom.

Intersectional Consciousness

Embedding and building capacity for sociocultural consciousness in our teaching is important as students in special education experience the construct of disability and additional intersecting sociocultural identities, which can further marginalize them. The concept of **intersectionality**, conceived by Crenshaw (1991) and expanded by other researchers (e.g., Collins, 2019), explains how power and oppression occur at the intersection of multiple and intersecting sociocultural identities. **Sociocultural identities** are social, cultural, economic, and political constructs created in society based on, but not limited to, disability, ethnicity, gender, nationality, race, sexuality, socioeconomic status, religious or spiritual affiliation, and others. **Culture** is our shared understanding and meaning within which we live and includes the ever-changing customs, interactions, traditions, and values of the socioculturally constructed groups with which we identify (Nieto, 2004; Rogoff, 2003; Yep, 2002). See previous chapters for more details on these concepts.

Educators play a pivotal role in the success or failure of socioculturally diverse learners in the field of special education (Salas & López, 2008). Educators who are aware of their own sociocultural identities are better prepared to work with students from diverse backgrounds (Salas & López, 2008). Educators who strive for educational equity provide students access to opportunities based on their needs and work to eliminate disproportionality (Singleton & Linton, 2006). They understand that every student embarks on their educational journey from a different foundation and starting point. Some students have access to welcoming, affirming, and robust learning infrastructures, while others may not have the same resources. Having insight into students' unique sociocultural identities offers educators the opportunity to attempt to make equitable learning conditions for all.

Sociocultural Identities

As noted in chapters 2 and 9, it is important to note the documented disparity between practitioners and students. Many students will never have an educational experience with a teacher who mirrors their identities during their years of schooling (Duarete, 2000). This disparity problem is forecast to get worse, due to national teacher shortages, especially in special education (Salas & López, 2008). Thus, it is important that we prepare educators to be socioculturally competent across the life span (Tyler & Smith, 2000). Researchers call for special education practitioners to explore how their own intersectional experiences impact their teaching pedagogy and their beliefs regarding students (Salas & López, 2008).

The use of critical consciousness and reflection is an instrumental strategy when delving into professional development and personal growth. This is true whether the tools are being used by educators for their own growth or as a strategy for their students in the classroom. **Critical consciousness** is the "process of continuously reflecting upon and examining how our own biases, assumptions, and cultural worldviews affect the ways we perceive difference and power dynamics" (Pitner & Sakamoto, 2005, p. 2). When educators take time for critical self-reflection of sociocultural identities and personal biases, it can have a positive impact on students (Fievre, 2021). With purpose and intent, **sociocultural consciousness**, which includes critical self-reflection and inquiry, allows educators to examine their beliefs and values, which inform how they show up each day and how they craft instruction (Larrivee, 2000).

Without critical sociocultural consciousness and self-reflection, educators remain in a "reflexive loop" (Argyris, 1990), which determines how they select data, add personal meaning, make assumptions informed by the interpretation of selected data, draw conclusions, adopt beliefs, and determine actions (Larrivee, 2000). This loop must be interrupted by action.

Pause and Reflect

Engage in critical self-reflection and inquiry.

- Consider your sociocultural awareness. Where are your blind spots?
- Now think about intersectionality. How do layers of oppression impact sociocultural identities and experiences?
- How can this reflection fuel future action in your classroom? In your school?

In order to shift the outcome for students to one focused on equity—and to create a learning environment where all are valued, embraced, and celebrated—as educators, we must actively work toward anti-ableist and anti-racist pedagogy to achieve intersectional sociocultural competency. This work is essential to connect with our students and the resources available to them. To provide equitable learning environments, we must examine our own personal sociocultural identities and beliefs, including biases, that have shaped us and become part of our identity. We must also be cognizant of our students' identities and experiences in order to understand how these are the same, different, and blend in an educational setting.

Engage in Critical Consciousness: Self-Examination of Sociocultural Identities

Practitioners must strive to attain educational equity and raise the success rate of all to eliminate disproportionality and narrow opportunity gaps between students (Singleton & Linton, 2006). Because educators engage with students from multiple and intersecting socioculturally diverse backgrounds, it is important to explore how personal sociocultural identities come together and influence beliefs, planning, teaching, and learning daily in classrooms (Azmitia & Mansfield, 2021; Rosaldo, 1998; Salas & López, 2008). The literature presents many visuals and analogies to utilize to identify personal sociocultural identities. For example, there are identity wheels, identity webs, culture trees, and icebergs. See the Professional Development Guide for examples. In this chapter, we utilize the analogy of an onion.

Researchers have explored the social significance of DreamWork's hit 3D-animation movie *Shrek* from a variety of theoretical perspectives focusing on social issues such as identity (Lacassagne et al., 2011). In the movie, Shrek said that ogres are like onions because they have layers. For humans, this analogy provides a way to understand the different layers of sociocultural identities that make up who we are. Just like an onion, it can take some peeling away from outer appearances to understand the core of who we are. Like an onion, our identities in our outer layer are visible to the eye, while there are many other sociocultural identities that are hidden deep down that others do not see.

Some of our identities are privileged while others may be oppressed. For example, a white male student with a disability may be privileged because of his skin color and gender yet oppressed because of his disability status. Some of our sociocultural identities are more visible and/or have more status. Our defining of "master status" sociocultural identities are the ones we most relate to (Crossman, 2019). Master status can be ascribed to us by ourselves or by others; it refers to the tendency to place more emphasis on one sociocultural identity, such as disability, race, or sexual orientation, as being more significant than any other aspect of an individual (Hughes, 1963). Master status can impact how one self-identifies or how others speak about a person. For example, a teacher may refer to an individual with a disability utilizing person-first language (PFL), while an autistic individual may refer to themselves utilizing identity-first language (IFL) because they place more emphasis on this identity (Stansberry Brusnahan et al., 2023). For more information on person-first and identity-first language, see chapters 5 and 11.

Some of our visible sociocultural identities cause us to unconsciously develop expectations for ourselves and others, based on these identities (Berger et al., 2017). For example, some practitioners may have lower expectations for a student receiving special education services.

When striving to implement more equitable practices, it is important to peel back and uncover our personal and our students' layers of sociocultural identities, created by ourselves or by society. By uncovering our sociocultural identities, we can better understand ourselves and our students. Our outward layers of identity include the identities and behaviors we embrace, assign, or expect of ourselves or others. This is our core notion of ourselves. We present these outer layers as our identities or appearances to the world, such as the color of our skin. People often judge others based on these external factors.

Cultivating an understanding of ourselves and others beyond our core or visible surfaces can help us all learn to appreciate each other. Engaging with students on a deeper level requires educators to explore the depth and layers of personal sociocultural identities. Educators can model how to examine our sociocultural identities beyond our core or visible layer for our students. This journey will nourish and engage the teacher and student relationship. By learning to appreciate our complex identities, we can develop an understanding of how to make more equitable learning environments for all students. When we and our students understand ourselves and others better, we can relate to each other better and engage in relationship development.

By engaging in this process, we educators can better understand ourselves and those around us. Understanding ourselves is the first step in understanding others. Yielding an awareness of our attitudes, beliefs, morals, and values can often be hard to do, especially those that we usually keep to ourselves. We need to engage with ourselves to discover the hidden aspects of who we are. Our identities can influence our outlooks and form the basis of our biases, influencing how we act and how others interact with us. Cultivating an awareness of these influences can help us make better decisions and form deeper connections. Figure 7.2 highlights this concept.

Identify Personal Sociocultural Identities

The first step in intersectional competence for practitioners is to explore our own personal sociocultural identities. As we grow up and mature, we move beyond interests-based definitions of ourselves—"I am a gymnast"—to begin to recognize and understand how a mosaic of sociocultural identifiers constitutes our identity (Nelson, 2021). Some sociocultural identifiers are often unexamined and unspoken within schools and homes. For example, in the areas where a person is a member of the dominant or advantaged social group, the category is usually not mentioned (Tatum, 2003). That element of their sociocultural identity is so taken for granted—by both the individual and the group

Intersectional Sociocultural Competency and Educational Equity 189

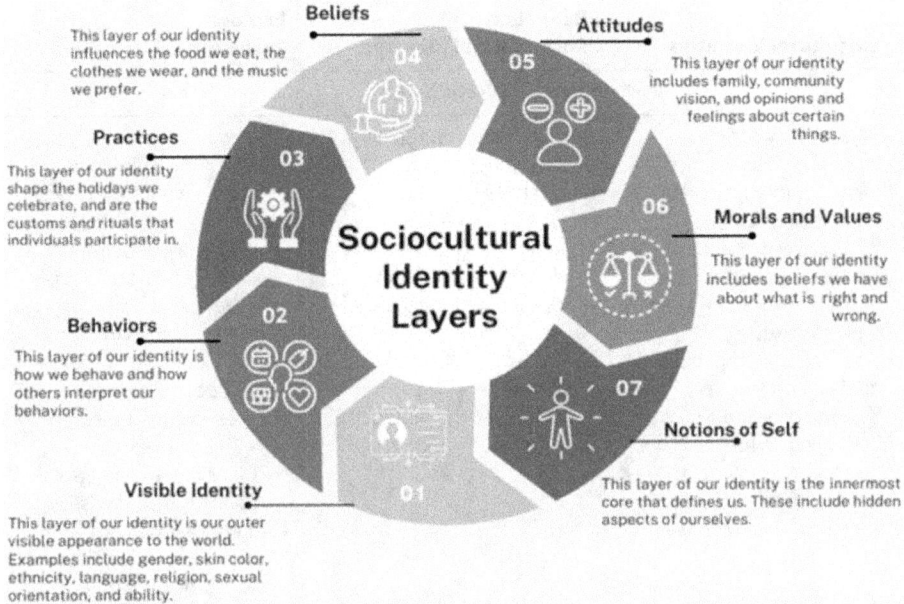

Figure 7.2. Sociocultural Identity Layers

to which they belong—that it goes without comment (Tatum, 2009). Table 7.2 includes a list of sociocultural identities in column 1, but we acknowledge that this list is not comprehensive. Columns 2 and 3 provide ways to reflect and activities to explore with students.

It is important to contextualize your sociocultural identities so you can engage learners in ways that are socioculturally sustaining. Here are some examples of how educators might explain their sociocultural identity:

- I am a cisgender college-educated middle-class educator who was born in the United States.
- I am a gay, middle-aged, white cis male teacher.
- I am a Muslim, first-generation American originally from Somalia, female, school professional for whom English is my second language.
- I am nonbinary, white, school educator.
- I am a Black cisgender female and a special education teacher.

It is important for practitioners to take a deep dive into personal identity and identify how educators and students' sociocultural identities manifest themselves in everyday life. As referenced throughout this text, note that culture is much more than holidays, types of food, religious traditions, or language—it encompasses an individual's unique and collective lived experiences that offer them a sense of belonging. See chapter 1 for more details. Recog-

Table 7.2. Sociocultural Identity Exploration

Sociocultural Identities	Reflect on Sociocultural Identities	Explore Sociocultural Identities
Disability		
• What are my cognitive, emotional, developmental, mental, and physical abilities or disabilities? • What are ways being disabled or nondisabled shapes my experiences with other people? • What are ways that having a disability provides or creates barriers to feeling a sense of belonging? What are ways being nondisabled provides a sense of belonging?	• How do my cultural communities view disability? • How is my disability defined (e.g., impairment, distinct culture, Deaf culture, Autistic culture)? • How is my disability represented in mass culture? Positive? Negative? Not at all?	• Read books that include people with disabilities and are written by disabled individuals. Point out how people talk about their disability while reading. • Invite guests and visit individuals in the community and have them talk about their disabilities. • Use strengths-based language to explain disabilities and articulate disability characteristics. • Identify school and community resources that would meet the needs of individuals with disabilities as adults. • Practice explaining the disability and disability characteristics.
Ethnicity		
• What social groups do I share a sense of belonging with based on ethnic heritage? • What are my indigenous affiliations? • What are ways my ethnicity shapes my experiences? • What are ways my ethnicity changes how others interact or view me? • In what ways do I interact with others outside of my ethnic identity?	• How are my ethnic identities defined in my culture? • How is my ethnicity represented in mass culture? Positive? Negative? Not at all?	• Explore diverse ethnic people, communities, and culture. • Inventory the environment and determine what ethnicities are represented and who is missing. • Prioritize and implement strategies to expand the range of diverse ethnicities in the environment.

Sociocultural Identities	Reflect on Sociocultural Identities	Explore Sociocultural Identities
Gender		
• What is my innermost concept of gender in which I see myself (e.g., masculine, feminine, nonbinary), which may/may not conform to my biological sex assigned at birth? • What are ways my gender, gender identity, or gender expression changes how others interact, treat, or view me?	• How are concepts such as gender, gender identity, and gender expression represented in my culture? • How do my assumptions about gender affect my sense of belonging? • How is my gender represented in mass culture? Is gender only portrayed in the traditional (binary, e.g., male and female) sense? Are a variety of gender identities and expressions positively represented? Negatively? Not at all?	• Watch the documentaries *Two Spirits* and *Kumu Hina* and discuss how these two cultures recognize, revere, and integrate gender. • Read books and discuss gender, gender identity, and gender expression. • Identify challenges individuals may face as adults based on identities such as gender, gender expression, and gender identity.
Race		
• What are my physical characteristics that are a result of genetic ancestry and attributes such as skin pigmentation and hair texture? • What are ways my race changes how others interact or view me? • In what ways do I interact with others outside of my racial identity?	• How are racial identities defined in my culture? • How does race lend itself to developing belonging? • How do I experience systemic barriers because of my race? • How is my race represented in mass culture? Positive? Negative? Not at all?	• Discuss race and racism and the impact it has on individuals. • Read about being an anti-racist. • Identify racial barriers and discuss what anti-racism looks like in schools, the classroom, job sites, and the community.

Source: Stansberry Brusnahan et al., 2023; University of Michigan, n.d.; University of Wisconsin–Madison, n.d.; Vanderbilt University, n.d.

nizing sociocultural identities helps us examine any biases and stereotypes we bring into the classroom that may hinder learning equity. Here are examples of how an educator might contextualize their own culture.

- My culture is based on my Southern roots. I speak English with a Southern accent, am Southern Baptist, and eat okra and collard greens.
- I live in the city and a lot of my culture is based on my urban roots. I love to participate in the arts, including attending the symphony orchestra, ballet, and art museums. I enjoy fine dining and French cuisine as my family roots include a French heritage.

- I am originally from a small farming community up north. My culture is steeped in Scandinavian traditions including celebrating winter activities and eating foods like Swedish meatballs, gravlax, and cinnamon rolls.
- I grew up on the West Coast and my culture is based on surfing and sunshine. I enjoy activities that keep me on the beach or in the water. Wearing T-shirts, shorts, and sandals makes me feel at home.

Pause and Reflect

After identifying your sociocultural identities, respond to the following reflection questions.

- Who do you share your sociocultural identities with?
- How do you interact with the individuals you share sociocultural identities with?
- Are there certain sociocultural communities or individuals with whom you feel more comfortable expressing your true self?
- Which aspects of your sociocultural identity do you think about the least and why?
- Why do we tend to think more about certain aspects of our sociocultural identities than others?
- What are your most poignant and unforgettable moments, both positive and negative, that have arisen from your sociocultural identities?
- What was a time you felt conflicted, isolated, or misunderstood based on your sociocultural identities?
- What was a time you experienced a sense of belonging and pride that filled you with strength and confidence based on your sociocultural identities?
- What level of comfort do you have with revealing aspects of your sociocultural identities to the world?
- Are there particular aspects of your sociocultural identities that you feel more comfortable sharing than others?
- What aspects of your sociocultural identities bring you the most joy and pride?
- What aspects of your sociocultural identities give you a sense of purpose and fulfillment?
- What aspects of your sociocultural identities have been a source of struggle, acceptance, and self-love, either in the past or present?
- Which aspects of your sociocultural identities play a major role in your life and which do you think play a minor role?
- How do the various components of your sociocultural identities shape the lens through which you see yourself and the world around you?

- What aspects of your sociocultural identities do you find the most fascinating?
- Which parts of your sociocultural identities do you feel are most impacted by oppression, and which do you believe grant you the most privilege?
- In what ways do you feel disconnected from your sociocultural identities?
- Which aspects of your sociocultural identities would you like to explore more deeply?
- Have you ever stopped to think about how your sociocultural identities shape your interactions with others?
- Have you ever considered which aspects of your sociocultural identities have the most significant impact on how others perceive or label you?
- What are the positive and negative effects of your sociocultural perceptions and how do they shape your experiences in the world?
- How do your different contexts—whether it be at school, home, work, or in your wider communities—impact your sociocultural identities, which can shift depending on the environment or the people you are around?

Examine Bias

After identifying our personal sociocultural identities, practitioners want to acknowledge similarities and differences between ourselves and our students and analyze and monitor personal biases based on diversity. **Bias** is a preference for or against something or someone (Harry et al., 1999). Biases can be conscious or unconscious. Unconscious, hidden, or **implicit bias** can work in the background without us even knowing it—but understanding this phenomenon can help educators create more inclusivity in environments (Romero et al., 2020; Staats et al., 2017). These biases can be stereotypes held by an individual without their awareness (Staats et al., 2017).

Biases occur unconsciously based on stereotypes and attitudes that may or may not be indicative of or reflect our conscious beliefs (Gullo, 2020; Hinton, 2107). Unconscious or implicit bias can take over our thoughts and actions in high-intensity situations. For example, demanding classrooms that require multitasking and making quick decisions force educators to rely on reactions with little time to devote to cognitive resources that reduce the force of unconscious bias (Cameron et al., 2012; Olson & Fazio, 2009). It is important to understand the impact of our biases because they can influence the treatment of a student and create conditions that impact learning. They have the potential to create long-term, inequitable academic and behavioral outcomes (Chin et al., 2020; Chugh et al., 2005; Dhaliwal et al., 2020; Gullo et al., 2019; McKown & Weinstein, 2008; Okonofua et al., 2016; Romero et al., 2020; Rubie-Davies et al., 2006; Tenbrunsel & Messick, 2004; Tenenbaum & Ruck, 2007; Warikoo et al., 2016).

Educators step into the classroom as full and whole human beings, with the expanse of their lived experiences shaping their beliefs and values intricately connected to each of their actions (Brookfield, 2017). Recognizing these biases and critically reflecting on their origin is a critical consciousness strategy that all educators must engage in. When educators allow these biases to remain unchecked, the lens through which we teach will mirror our own sociocultural identities and lived experiences (e.g., centering whiteness and Eurocentric beliefs and values)—allowing the counternarratives and perspectives to remain missing.

Critically conscious self-reflection is "the sustained and intentional process of identifying and checking the accuracy and validity of our teaching assumptions" (Brookfield, 2017, p. 3) and allows educators to dig deep into the origins of our own story, identifying how our biases influence and impact life outcomes for learners. Here are examples of what bias could look like in practitioners:

- A practitioner sends a Black student out of the room for specific behavior but does not send out a white student who engages in similar behavior.
- A practitioner operates under the belief that a student who does not engage in debates in class does not have knowledge of the content and stops seeking out this student's points of view.
- A practitioner operates under the belief that a student whose first language is not English and who remains silent in class does not understand the curriculum and therefore will not be able to learn the content in the classroom.
- A practitioner does little to consider what narratives are absent from the curriculum and utilizes a curriculum that explores only a Eurocentric lens (i.e., focused on white, Westernized [European] history).
- A practitioner perceives noninterest in learning from students from communities that do not connect with the Eurocentric content, which impacts these students' grades.
- A practitioner focuses on teaching a student to live independently after high school, but the family's culture does not view this as a preferred living arrangement.

If we do not acknowledge biases, we create conditions and perpetuate beliefs that impact learning and have long-term, negative effects on students, including systemic discrimination (i.e., prejudicial treatment based on identity), oppression, and inequitable outcomes (Chugh et al., 2005; Tenbrunsel & Messick, 2004). Cultivating awareness and critically and consciously reflecting will help uncover any biases you have and how they are shaped

Intersectional Sociocultural Competency and Educational Equity 195

by your identities and experiences in a systemically social-conferred world (Zoino-Jeannetti & Pearrow, 2020).

When we examine systemic and personal biases and how they can affect our beliefs about a student's successes and impact their ability to perform educationally (McKinney & Schaefer Whitby, 2020), we are better able to authentically connect with students, deepen our understanding of internalized and unconscious biases, and challenge our perspectives by questioning our understanding and beliefs (Hahn & Gawronski, 2019). Use the tool in figure 7.3 to engage in critical self-examination and reflection of personal biases:

BIAS SELF-REFLECTION
Embrace Bias-Challenging and Be Optimistic: Our Biases & Brains Can Evolve.

B — Become Grounded in Who You Are and Willing to be Vulnerable Through a Critical Self-Study Where You Examine and Reflect on Your Own Social Identity Lens.
- What are my personal social identities? I am aware of my social identity and cultural personal biases.
- How are my social identities similar and different from my students?
- What are my acquired assumptions and stereotypes about social identities? How did I learn or acquire any racist or ableist attitudes I possess?
- How do my assumptions and stereotypes about social identities infiltrate their way into my practices?
- How can I presume competence and create opportunities, contexts, and conditions that provide equitable experiences for students?
- How can I harness my positionality and privilege in my role as an educator to expand access and ensure equitable experiences for students?
- Does my curriculum and teaching materials demonstrate representation of diverse perspectives, voices, and social identities?

I — Interrogate and Acknowledge Personal and School-Wide / System Bias.
- How does examining my own social identity help me identify and acknowledge my personal bias and its influence on education?
- What are my assumptions and stereotypes about different social identities, and how did I learn these beliefs?
- How do my thoughts or beliefs differ from my students and impact their success in the classroom?
- What role have my biases played in perpetuating inequities within the classroom, and how can I disrupt my autopilot-biased judgments about others?
- How does my school reproduce disparities in student outcomes based on social identity biases?

A — Acquire Social Identity Knowledge and Open Yourself to the Experiences of Others.
- What knowledge and experiences have I encountered that have significantly impacted my life?
- What are some of the hopes, aspirations, losses, and disappointments that my students may encounter?
- How can I focus on commonalities that we all share to remind me that there is more that unites me and my students than divides us?
- I take a step back and consider how differences in my and my students' social identities and cultures may influence future actions and students' learning.
- I am mindful of the diverse social identities and cultures of students I interact with, understanding the impact of their histories and current realities on my teaching and behavior.

S — Strategize the Acquired Knowledge to Apply Empathy, Take Action, Build Trust, Create Change, and Combat Bias.
- How can I be an ally to individuals who experience bias in schools and create a classroom based on respect that disrupts current inequities?
- How can I Implement, model, and advocate for culturally sustaining practices within my classroom and school environment?
- How can I work with cultural informants and create partnerships with others (e.g., colleagues, students, parents) to help me grow culturally and ensure equitable practices?

Figure 7.3. B.I.A.S.

> **Pause and Reflect**
> - How have my sociocultural identities helped inform my beliefs and values about myself? About others?
> - What are the experiences I have had based on my sociocultural identities that have supported or disrupted my beliefs, values, and biases?

A practice that can be used during the critical self-reflection practice and action planning is a "journey map," which is a graphic organizer that provides a reflective space for an educator to examine a belief or an interaction. Table 7.3 includes reflection questions that can be used during the journey map process. Answer these questions, which are intentional, purposeful, and perhaps a bit vague, to truly reflect and deepen the reflective practice process, specifically around sociocultural identity, impact (e.g., oppression), and bias (e.g., conscious, unconscious), and lean into the unexamined parts of personal sociocultural identity. This reflective practice is most beneficial and effective when it is used in an ongoing manner to gauge growth (e.g., weekly, monthly).

Table 7.3. Journey Map

Journey Map
Directions
Reflect on one of the following prompts about an event in a specific context (e.g., school setting). Support answers with examples from your experience.
• *A step toward understanding and adjusting for one's bias is to recognize intersectional oppression.* Reflect on an experience where you felt ableism, discrimination, disrespect, inequity, oppression, prejudice, privilege, stereotyping, or racism. • *A step toward understanding and adjusting for one's bias is to recognize implicit biases.* Reflect on an experience where you either experienced, engaged in, or witnessed unconscious bias based on sociocultural identities.
What was the event? (Name the event/interaction that occurred that you are reflecting on.) What happened? (Describe how language and actions played a role in the situation or not.) What were you thinking during the event? Who was impacted? What were you thinking about after the event? What did you learn and what is your plan for the future during a similar event? For example, what action will you take to shift your educational practice?

Navigating Intersectional Sociocultural Competence: Proficiency Scale for Educators

After gaining a basic understanding of personal identities and bias, explore intersectional sociocultural competence. Intersectional sociocultural competence prepares educators to identify how sociocultural identity markers impact students within the educational system in complex ways, such as the layering of teacher bias, educational access, and federal policies (Boveda & Aronson, 2019). Stages for building intersectional sociocultural competence look and sound different for each person and different cultural assessments utilize different terms along a continuum of growing, building skills, and gaining competency. There are some essential elements to becoming more competent (Cross et al., 1989).

- Value diversity.
- Engage in sociocultural self-assessment.
- Be conscious of the dynamics inherent when sociocultural identities interact.
- Acquire institutionalized sociocultural knowledge.
- Develop adaptations to service delivery reflecting an understanding of diversity between and within sociocultural identities.

Pause and Reflect

Consider what these elements look like from an intersectional lens.

- How do you value diversity?
- How do you develop the capacity for self-assessment?
- How are you aware of the dynamics inherent in social interaction?
- How do you develop service delivery that reflects an understanding of diversity between and within identities?

As educators gain intersectional sociocultural competence, they are better able to implement **socioculturally sustaining practices**; in addition to implementing culturally responsive and linguistically sustaining practices, they are able to move beyond respecting and valuing diverse languages, cultures, and ways of being and thinking to consider how all of these elements interact. An explicitly anti-colonialist and anti-deficit stance, culturally sustaining practices seek to center and nurture the diverse linguistic, literate, and cultural lives of our learners (Paris & Alim, 2017). Intercultural competence is defined as "a set of congruent behaviors, attitudes, and policies that come together in a system, agency, or among professionals and enable that system, agency, or those professionals to work effectively in cross-cultural situations" (Cross et al., 1989, p. 28).

In an intersectional sociocultural competence assessment, educators identify areas to improve proficiency and build an equitable classroom space that celebrates diverse learning styles and focuses on the whole child. As illustrated in figure 7.4, the *5As of Intersectional Sociocultural Competence* focuses

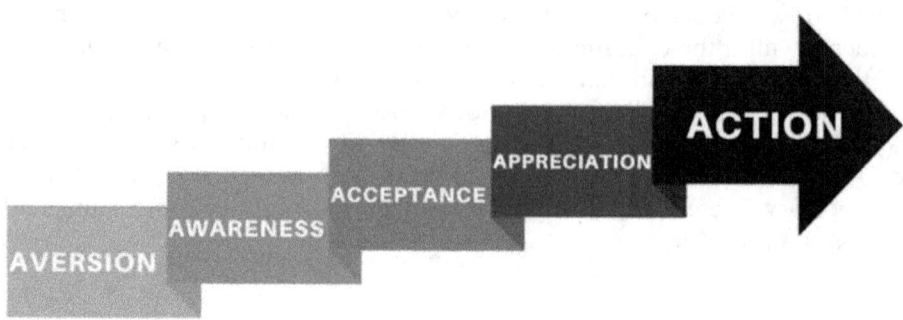

Figure 7.4. 5As of Intersectional Sociocultural Competence

on five factors: (a) aversion, (b) awareness, (c) acceptance, (d) appreciation, and (e) action. This assessment provides educators a means to critically and consciously reflect and self-evaluate their actions, behaviors, beliefs, and values and is based on adaptations to a variety of sources including Broadwell's (1969) *Multicultural Reflective Behavior Analytic Practice*, Mayfield's (2020) intercultural competence exercises, and Cross and colleagues' (1989) continuum. The 5As assessment helps identify current proficiency and provides suggestions to move forward in the development of intersectional sociocultural competence to cultivate a school environment where all students feel valued and can thrive, learn, and express themselves freely.

Assessments are a great way for educators to gain insights into their own sociocultural awareness and biases, as well as their capacity to embrace diversity. As practitioners, we can use this information to move forward in our professional development and growth and to take action to create equitable classroom environments. We may not see ourselves in each statement within the assessment but where we see the most attributes are where we typically fall in the continuum. The purpose of engaging in this activity is to provide a tool for self-reflection, but we cannot stop there. After completing the assessment in figures 7.5 through 7.11, use the scoring guide in figures 7.12 through 7.16 to determine a primary sociocultural competency stage, which is the starting point for the ongoing journey to intersectional sociocultural competence. As educators, we need to consistently engage in intentional activities and practices that push us toward the action stage of the continuum where we work to create a learning environment where all students feel valued and supported.

Directions

1. Read the numbered attributes for each of the 5As. For further clarification, read the "look and sounds like . . ." examples.
2. Place a checkmark next to any of the attributes that resonate or describe your actions, beliefs, feelings, or values.
3. Total the number of checkmarks in each of the 5A areas at the bottom of each section.
4. Refer to the scoring sheet to interpret your results.

AVERSION

ATTRIBUTES OF AVERSION (10)

1. I approach my instruction and teaching methods the same every time I teach, not considering sociocultural identities. I believe students should assimilate.
2. I am indifferent, do not think about, give little significance to, or ignore my and my students' sociocultural identities, including our similarities and differences, within the classroom.
3. I avoid discussing sociocultural identity with my students due to discomfort or because I don't want some students to think they are being singled out and don't fit in because they are not part of the majority.
4. I view and treat all the students in my classroom the same, without considering the impact of sociocultural identities, which might be an outdated mindset, but I have the best intentions.
5. I place little value in and/or do not attend training and development that addresses the improvement of sociocultural and linguistic competence, as I see no benefit to my classroom practices.
6. I don't give special consideration to students based on their sociocultural identities. I believe too much emphasis is placed on non-dominant sociocultural identities, with dominant groups neglected.
7. I lack the knowledge and/or capacity to respond effectively to diverse interests, needs, and preferences based on my student's sociocultural identities and may inadvertently engage in practices that result in discrimination.
8. I view sociocultural identity as a negative or positive aspect of a student. I may have a preference for some identities over others, which could result in the disproportionate allocation of resources and different (higher or lower) expectations for students based on their identities.
9. I avoid or do not immerse myself in my students' diverse backgrounds and may be intolerant of different sociocultural identities that comprise my own ethics, morals, and values. For example, I believe some students lack success because they and/or their families place little value on education.
10. I inadvertently or purposefully engage in attitudes, policies, structures, and practices within a system or organization that may be destructive to particular sociocultural identities.

_ Total Checkmarks

LOOKS AND SOUNDS LIKE:
- SILENCE!
- "I DON'T LIKE FEELING UNCOMFORTABLE."
- "ALL LIVES MATTER."

LOOKS AND SOUNDS LIKE:
- "I AM WHITE AND MY LIFE HASN'T BEEN EASY. I HAVE WORKED HARD FOR EVERYTHING I HAVE."
- "THIS IS AMERICA SO STUDENTS SHOULD SPEAK ENGLISH."
- "I HAVE BLACK FRIENDS OR RELATIVES."
- "I DON'T SEE COLOR."

LOOKS AND SOUNDS LIKE:
- DON'T DO ANYTHING OR FOLLOW THROUGH WHEN A STUDENT USES A RACIAL SLUR
- "HOW IS WHAT I AM DOING AS AN EDUCATOR GOING TO MATTER WHEN STUDENTS' PARENTS DON'T SHOW UP AT SCHOOL OR VALUE EDUCATION?"

LOOKS AND SOUNDS LIKE:
- "MY STUDENTS MIGHT FEEL LIKE THEY DON'T FIT IN, SO I DON'T TALK ABOUT THAT."
- "STUDENTS WITH DISABILITIES WON'T LEARN ANYTHING OR FIT IN (MISFIT) WITH PEERS IN A GENERAL EDUCATION CLASSROOM."

Figure 7.5. 5As of Intersectional Sociocultural Competence Assessment: Aversion

AWARENESS

ATTRIBUTES OF AWARENESS (10)

○ 11. I'm open to understanding and respecting different sociocultural identities through the practice of self-reflection on how my own background and the backgrounds of others have an impact on teaching and learning in the classroom.

○ 12. I understand the importance of developing sociocultural competency and recognize the similarities and differences between my and my students' backgrounds and lived experiences.

○ 13. I identify and reflect on my and my students' sociocultural identities and am trying to figure out how to use this knowledge to create an equitable classroom environment.

○ 14. I try to recognize and address my personal bias and educational systemic bias in order to provide students with diverse sociocultural identities with the best possible education in my classroom.

○ 15. I am willing to engage in conversations about different sociocultural identities in my classroom.

○ 16. I embrace diverse perspectives and highlight multiple viewpoints in my classroom (e.g., class discussions, materials within the classroom, bulletin boards, textbooks).

○ 17. I inspire students to develop a multifaceted perspective through examples of positive sociocultural identity differences within the classroom.

○ 18. I pause to reflect on my attitudes related to sociocultural identity and consider my beliefs and emotions towards students with diverse backgrounds before engaging in teaching and interactions with students.

○ 19. I am aware of my strengths and areas for growth to teach and respond effectively to sociocultural diverse students within the classroom.

○ 20. I recognize privilege and understand how different social and systemic factors can impact certain groups with advantages or disadvantages within the classroom.

_ Total Checkmarks

LOOKS AND SOUNDS LIKE:
- "I KNOW WE'RE DIFFERENT BUT LET'S TRY TO UNDERSTAND EACH OTHER"

LOOKS AND SOUNDS LIKE:
- "BASED ON MY EXPERIENCES, THIS IS MY ASSUMPTION."

LOOKS AND SOUNDS LIKE:
- SHOW AWARENESS AND APPRECIATION FOR CULTURAL DIVERSITY.

LOOKS AND SOUNDS LIKE:
- "I UNDERSTAND BECAUSE I AM WHITE, I HAVE PRIVILEGE."

Figure 7.6. 5As of Intersectional Sociocultural Competence Assessment: Awareness

ACCEPTANCE

ATTRIBUTES OF ACCEPTANCE (20)

○ 21. I demonstrate acceptance and respect for diverse sociocultural identities through the use and/or adaption of evidence-based and culturally and linguistically sustaining practices within my classroom.
○ 22. I articulate principles, rationale, and values for sociocultural and linguistic competence in all aspects of my teaching.
○ 23. I implement specific policies and procedures that integrate sociocultural and linguistic competence into each core function of the classroom.
○ 24. I develop structures and strategies to ensure students, families, and community participation in the planning, delivery, and evaluation of my classroom practices.
○ 25. I engage in and support professional development to equip myself with knowledge and tools to foster and improve sociocultural and linguistic competency and tackle implicit bias.
○ 26. I collect and analyze data using variables that have a meaningful impact on socioculturally and linguistically diverse student groups.
○ 27. I allow for some time in my classroom to assess sociocultural and linguistic competence and practice principles of community engagement that result in the reciprocal transfer of knowledge and skills between myself and my students.
○ 28. I acknowledge diversity and strive to create a learning environment that supports different ways of thinking and consciousness of the diverse backgrounds and experiences of other people.
○ 29. I am comfortable with ambiguity and diverse environments and can navigate some complex and challenging situations in the classroom when working with students and families from diverse sociocultural identities.
○ 30. I recognize the necessity to push the boundaries of my comfort zone and am beginning to identify ways to collaborate with people with different perspectives, backgrounds, and life stories.

LOOKS AND SOUNDS LIKE
- Commit to providing culturally and linguistically responsive services that respect the diversity of the community served.
- Integrating cultural and linguistic competence into each core function of the organization through a systematic approach that involves all levels of the organization.

LOOKS AND SOUNDS LIKE
- Conduct focus groups with diverse community members to gather insights on specific issues or topics.

LOOKS AND SOUNDS LIKE
- Conduct periodic assessments of its cultural and linguistic competence at the organizational level, using established tools and benchmarks.

LOOKS AND SOUNDS LIKE
- Use appropriate methods to analyze the data collected, such as disaggregating data by race, ethnicity, and language proficiency and using statistical methods to identify disparities or trends.

___ Total Checkmarks

Figure 7.7. 5As of Intersectional Sociocultural Competence Assessment: Acceptance

ACCEPTANCE

ATTRIBUTES OF ACCEPTANCE (20)

○ 31. I approach each child and family without judgment, which allows me to embrace ambiguity while adapting to diverse perspectives and gracefully guiding sensitive classroom discussions.

○ 32. I engage and interact with students and families from different sociocultural identities and strive to build strong relationships through interactive activities like reading, home visits, discussions, and learner inventories.

○ 33. I am knowledgeable about different cultures and can communicate and collaborate effectively with people from diverse backgrounds.

○ 34. I use different teaching methods for learners with varying learning styles or adapt materials to be culturally and linguistically appropriate and maintain high standards for students from all sociocultural identities and cultures to strive for excellence.

○ 35. I engage with students from diverse backgrounds, actively listen to what students have to say, and ask questions to clarify their points of view.

○ 36. I approach collaborations with an open mind, recognizing that there may be different ways of thinking and working, and I am willing to consider new ideas and approaches.

○ 37. I am willing to take risks and try new things, even if they are outside of one's usual comfort zone.

○ 38. I am flexible in my thinking and approach and can adapt to different perspectives and working methods.

○ 39. I value diversity and believe everyone has something unique and valuable to contribute.

○ 40. I am attuned to the needs and experiences of others and strive to create a supportive and welcoming environment for all.

LOOKS AND SOUNDS LIKE:
- INTERPRET INFORMATION IN A WAY THAT CONFIRMS THEIR EXISTING BIASES ABOUT A PARTICULAR CULTURE, EVEN IF THE INFORMATION CAN BE INTERPRETED IN A DIFFERENT WAY

LOOKS AND SOUNDS LIKE:
- IDENTIFY, USE, AND/OR ADAPT ACCESSIBILITY AND PROMISING PRACTICES THAT ARE CULTURALLY AND LINGUISTICALLY COMPETENT

LOOKS AND SOUNDS LIKE:
- USE APPROPRIATE METHODS TO ANALYZE THE DATA COLLECTED, SUCH AS DISAGGREGATING DATA BY RACE, ETHNICITY, AND LANGUAGE PROFICIENCY, AND USING STATISTICAL METHODS TO IDENTIFY DISPARITIES OR TRENDS

LOOKS AND SOUNDS LIKE:
- PROVIDE OPPORTUNITIES FOR CAPACITY BUILDING AND SKILL DEVELOPMENT FOR ALL PARTNERS, INCLUDING COMMUNITY MEMBERS, STAFF, AND VOLUNTEERS, IN ORDER TO FOSTER A CULTURE OF LEARNING AND COLLABORATION

_ Total Checkmarks

Figure 7.7 (*continued*). 5As of Intersectional Sociocultural Competence Assessment: Acceptance

APPRECIATION

ATTRIBUTES OF APPRECIATION (10)

○ 41. I am passionate about sociocultural sensitivity and am committed to learning about and respecting another person's beliefs and values rooted in their ethnic or racial background.

○ 42. I am seeking opportunities to shift my mindset and learn more about different sociocultural identities, and I am committed to attending sensitivity training to appreciate sociocultural diversity better.

○ 43. I acknowledge that my values and beliefs (i.e., my attitudes) about equality may be inconsistent with my behaviors, and ironically, I may be unaware of it.

○ 44. I am comfortable with sociocultural differences and their impact on behavior while continually seeking new sociocultural immersion opportunities.

○ 45. I embrace diversity, showing respect for individuals and their sociocultural backgrounds, allowing me to make meaningful connections with people of all backgrounds.

○ 46. I seek unique and extraordinary talents in students from all sociocultural identities.

○ 47. I genuinely appreciate sociocultural identity diversity and why it matters.

○ 48. I explore languages through a critical lens to shed light on words and terms that reflect power dynamics and shape my perception of reality.

○ 49. I understand the importance of building resilience, empowering students to make their own decisions, and cultivating an inner sense of control.

○ 50. I understand the impact of the environment (i.e., poverty, home life, community) on behavior and learning.

LOOKS AND SOUNDS LIKE:
- IDENTIFYING AND ACKNOWLEDGING THE UNIQUE STRENGTHS AND SKILLS THAT INDIVIDUALS OR TEAMS BRING TO THE TABLE.

LOOKS AND SOUNDS LIKE:
- ESTABLISHING MECHANISMS OR PROGRAMS THAT ALLOW INDIVIDUALS OR TEAMS TO BE RECOGNIZED AND APPRECIATED BY THEIR PEERS OR SUPERIORS.

LOOKS AND SOUNDS LIKE:
- TAKING THE TIME TO LISTEN TO INDIVIDUALS OR TEAMS, ENGAGING IN MEANINGFUL CONVERSATIONS, AND SHOWING INTEREST IN THEIR IDEAS AND PERSPECTIVES.

LOOKS AND SOUNDS LIKE:
- VALIDATING DIFFERENT CULTURAL TRADITIONS AND CLEARLY COMMUNICATING RESPECT
- ADVOCATING FOR FAIR REPRESENTATION AND AMPLIFYING UNHEARD VOICES

_ Total Checkmarks

Figure 7.8. 5As of Intersectional Sociocultural Competence Assessment: Appreciation

ACTION

ATTRIBUTES OF ACTION (10)

- 51. I almost always strive to create a learning environment that is engaging and relevant to my learners' sociocultural identities, including disabilities.
- 52. I routinely and actively strive to build meaningful connections with learners by engaging in activities such as reading, home visits, interviews, and learner inventories.
- 53. I usually actively engage in conversations with colleagues to better understand diverse and marginalized learners' needs, experiences, and concerns.
- 54. I habitually and actively strive to be an accomplice (e.g., ally, collaborator, partner) in my teaching, and I am committed to promoting racial justice and equity in my classroom.
- 55. I typically show genuine and authentic kindness and build positive connections and relationships based on trust and respect with students and their families from all sociocultural identities.
- 56. I generally offer a supportive and welcoming environment for students from all sociocultural identities and connect with students and their families thoughtfully and consistently.
- 57. I explicitly create engaging learning activities that reflect the sociocultural identities and experiences of my students, their families, and the community and that are relevant to the students' lives and the world outside of the classroom.
- 58. I identify and support students' sociocultural consciousness.
- 59. I am passionate and engaging in group discussions with people from diverse sociocultural identities and backgrounds.
- 60. I empower students to analyze and question their beliefs, values, and experiences and how these shape their perceptions of themselves and others, as well as their behaviors - while modeling this critical self-reflection.

LOOKS AND SOUNDS LIKE:
- SEEK TO UNDERSTAND HOW FACTORS IN STUDENTS' ENVIRONMENTS INFLUENCE THEIR LIVES AND LEARNING
- USE EXAMPLES IN CLASS THAT CONNECT TO STUDENTS' LIVES, EXPERIENCES, PRIOR KNOWLEDGE
- ENCOURAGE STUDENTS TO DRAW FROM THEIR KNOWLEDGE OF MULTIPLE LANGUAGES

LOOKS AND SOUNDS LIKE:
- FOSTER STUDENT IDENTITY DEVELOPMENT (WHO AM I?) THROUGH VARIOUS CLASSROOM ACTIVITIES/ DISCUSSIONS
- CREATE A PHYSICAL ENVIRONMENT OF THE CLASSROOM (WALL DECORATIONS, ETC.) THAT REFLECTS THE STUDENTS' LIVES, CULTURES, INTERESTS IN A WAY THAT DOES NOT AFFIRM STEREOTYPES

LOOKS AND SOUNDS LIKE:
- MAKE INTENTIONAL EFFORTS TO KNOW AND UNDERSTAND STUDENTS' PARENTS, FAMILIES, AND COMMUNITIES
- CRAFT AND DEVELOP LESSONS THAT ARE ENRICHED WITH EXAMPLES FROM THE UNIQUE EXPERIENCES OF STUDENTS

LOOKS AND SOUNDS LIKE:
- SEEK TO INTENTIONALLY UNDERSTAND AND CONNECT ASPECTS OF STUDENTS' CULTURE, HISTORY, INTERESTS, PRIOR KNOWLEDGE, AND BACKGROUNDS TO THE CURRICULUM
- CRAFT AND DEVELOP LESSONS THAT ALLOW STUDENTS TO SEE THEMSELVES REPRESENTED

_ Total Checkmarks

Figure 7.9. 5As of Intersectional Sociocultural Competence Assessment: Action

Intersectional Sociocultural Competency and Educational Equity

Directions

1. Once you have completed the self-examination, add up your checkmarks in each of the 5A categories.
2. To gauge your current level of intersectional sociocultural competence, take a look at the descriptions.
3. Then, look over the reflective practice ideas to move forward on the journey to sociocultural competency as an educator.
4. Complete an action plan that includes goals that push you to consistently engage in intentional activities and practices toward the action stage of the continuum.

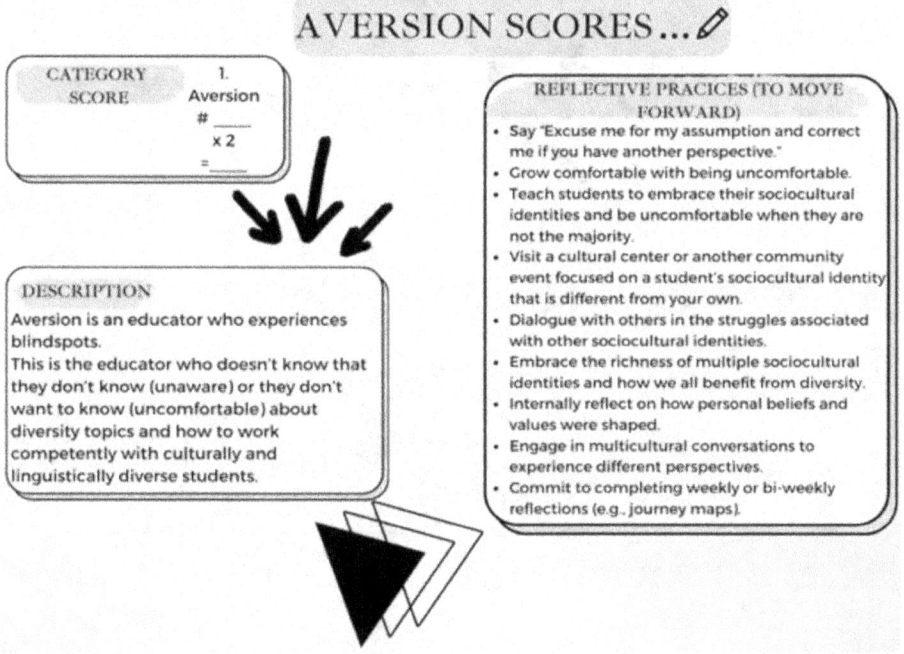

Figure 7.10. 5As Scoring Guide: Aversion

AWARENESS SCORES...

CATEGORY SCORE
2.
Awareness
#___
x 2
=___

DESCRIPTION
Awareness is when cultural and linguistic topics are new skills that are emerging. This is the educator who knows that they don't know or want to learn. This educator is discovering the power of unlearning and learning.

REFLECTIVE PRACICES (TO MOVE FORWARD)
- Engage in learning activities that focus on sociocultural identities.
- Seek out cultural informants to identify areas you lack knowledge or are uncomfortable.
- Be willing to walk away from cultural destructiveness.
- Challenge the norm.
- Dare to question the established curriculum, policies, beliefs, assumptions, and practices.
- Be willing to feel discomfort (cognitive dissonance) when embedded biases are being challenged.
- Embrace the journey of understanding culture and its significant role in the personal identities, life ways, and even mental and physical health of individuals and communities.
- Engage in diverse conversations.
- Challenge biased statements from colleagues.
- Take into account the dynamic perspectives of learners and parents as valuable in the school and classroom atmosphere.
- Stimulate student cooperation within the classroom.
- Complete bi-weekly reflective journey maps.
- Identify a journey partner you can process and reflect on experiences and interactions with others.

Figure 7.11. 5As Scoring Guide: Awareness

ACCEPTANCE SCORES...

CATEGORY SCORE
3.
Acceptance
#___
=___

DESCRIPTION
Acceptance is conscious competency.
This is the educator who knows they need to practice and takes control of skills.

- Use culturally and linguistically appropriate methods to collect data from diverse communities, such as using bilingual staff, interpreters, or translated materials.
- Be willing to invest time and resources in building strong partnerships and engaging stakeholders in meaningful ways.
- Engage in regular self-reflection and seek feedback from learners and colleagues to continuously improve one's teaching approach and effectiveness.
- Seek out opportunities to learn about different cultures and experiences or engage in respectful dialogue with those who hold different viewpoints.
- Seek out collaborations with individuals from diverse backgrounds.
- Broaden individual perspectives.
- Build stronger and more inclusive relationships with others.
- Collaborate with colleagues to develop new teaching strategies or partner with community organizations to provide additional resources and support.
- Build relationships with students from diverse backgrounds and actively seek out opportunities to learn about their experiences and perspectives.
- Participate in professional development opportunities focused on sociocultural competence and diversity.
- Collaborate with colleagues from diverse backgrounds and be open to new ideas and approaches.
- Incorporate diverse perspectives into lesson plans and classroom activities.
- Be aware of personal cultural biases and actively work to overcome them.
- Provide opportunities for students to engage with mentors and role models from a variety of backgrounds.
- Help students develop distinct skills and networks they need to succeed.
- Engage in continued reflective practices.

REFLECTIVE PRACICES (TO MOVE FORWARD)
- Delve into self-reflection and assessment, and break down the skills into manageable chunks with lots of practice and conscious effort to master these skills and demonstrate this knowledge.
- Demonstrate a commitment to ongoing improvement and learning, with a focus on continuous assessment and evaluation of the organization's cultural and linguistic competence.
- Use inclusive language that acknowledges the diversity of cultures and languages represented in the organization and in the community it serves.
- Engage in focus groups with diverse community members to gather insights on specific issues or topics.
- Establish diversity and inclusion committees to promote diversity and inclusion within the organization and ensure that diversity and inclusion are integrated into all aspects of the organization.
- Provide incentives to students and fellow staff who demonstrate a commitment to cultural and linguistic competence and contribute to diversity and inclusion efforts.
- Establish feedback mechanisms for individuals and teams to provide feedback on their own cultural and linguistic competence and on the school's overall cultural competence.

Figure 7.12. 5As Scoring Guide: Acceptance

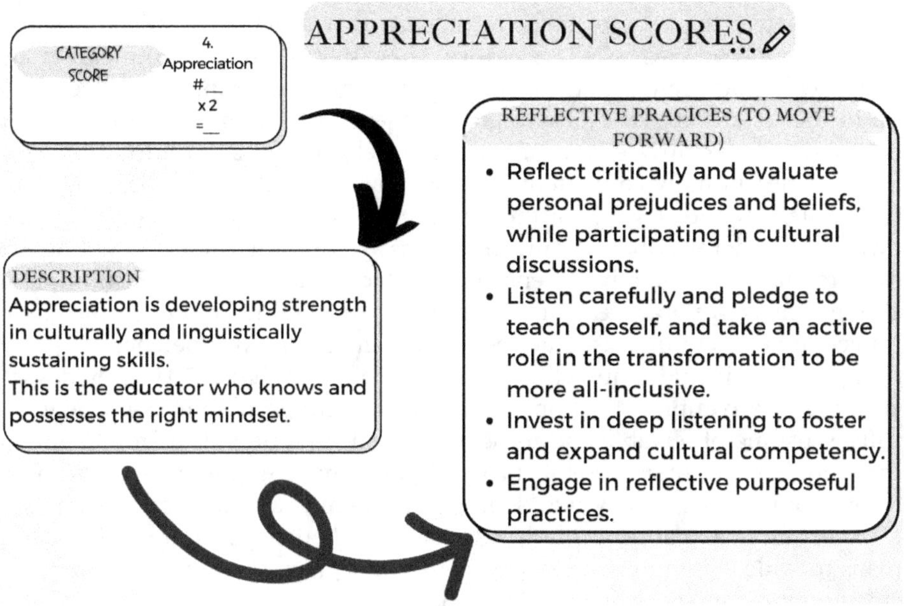

APPRECIATION SCORES

CATEGORY SCORE
4. Appreciation
#___
x 2
=___

DESCRIPTION
Appreciation is developing strength in culturally and linguistically sustaining skills.
This is the educator who knows and possesses the right mindset.

REFLECTIVE PRACICES (TO MOVE FORWARD)
- Reflect critically and evaluate personal prejudices and beliefs, while participating in cultural discussions.
- Listen carefully and pledge to teach oneself, and take an active role in the transformation to be more all-inclusive.
- Invest in deep listening to foster and expand cultural competency.
- Engage in reflective purposeful practices.

Figure 7.13. 5As Scoring Guide: Appreciation

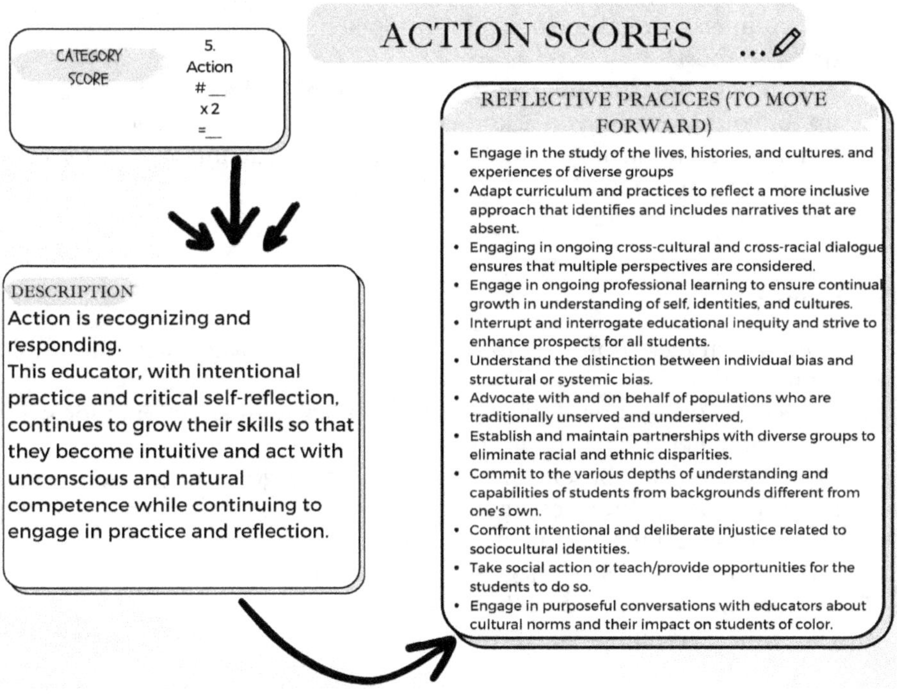

ACTION SCORES

CATEGORY SCORE
5. Action
#___
x 2
=___

DESCRIPTION
Action is recognizing and responding.
This educator, with intentional practice and critical self-reflection, continues to grow their skills so that they become intuitive and act with unconscious and natural competence while continuing to engage in practice and reflection.

REFLECTIVE PRACICES (TO MOVE FORWARD)
- Engage in the study of the lives, histories, and cultures. and experiences of diverse groups
- Adapt curriculum and practices to reflect a more inclusive approach that identifies and includes narratives that are absent.
- Engaging in ongoing cross-cultural and cross-racial dialogue ensures that multiple perspectives are considered.
- Engage in ongoing professional learning to ensure continual growth in understanding of self, identities, and cultures.
- Interrupt and interrogate educational inequity and strive to enhance prospects for all students.
- Understand the distinction between individual bias and structural or systemic bias.
- Advocate with and on behalf of populations who are traditionally unserved and underserved.
- Establish and maintain partnerships with diverse groups to eliminate racial and ethnic disparities.
- Commit to the various depths of understanding and capabilities of students from backgrounds different from one's own.
- Confront intentional and deliberate injustice related to sociocultural identities.
- Take social action or teach/provide opportunities for the students to do so.
- Engage in purposeful conversations with educators about cultural norms and their impact on students of color.

Figure 7.14. 5As Scoring Guide: Action

As we strive for a more inclusive educational system, it's essential to be aware of our scores across all categories. These scores can reveal our conscious and unconscious beliefs and values, which in turn can impact how we show up in the classroom. By examining our beliefs and actions, we can interrupt our biases and cultivate more supportive behaviors that promote intersectional socioculturally competent learning environments. This candid look at the challenges and rewards of the job is the gateway to understanding one's own unique identity and ongoing journey as an educator. After completing the assessment, it is imperative to engage in reflection and create an action plan. Use the "reflective practices to move forward" suggestions in the scoring guide for activity ideas to increase intersectional sociocultural competence.

Figure 7.15 includes an action plan template and figure 7.16 provides an example of a completed action plan. After reflecting on your assessment results, set some observable and measurable goals that provide a "roadmap" to move forward in intersectional sociocultural competence. Use an action plan throughout the year as a way to define goals, identify and determine strategies for meeting goals, and decide how to assess whether goals are met. Action plans provide a comprehensive way to monitor progress on intersectional sociocultural competence and meeting goals.

Pause and Reflect

- Which intersectional sociocultural competence category did you identify with most?
- As you reflect on the statements in that category, what emotions came up for you? How did you acknowledge your emotions/reactions?
- What are some actions you could engage in that might move you along the continuum?

Directions

1. Complete intersectional sociocultural competence assessment and fill in scores.
2. Reflect on how to move forward on the journey to intersectional sociocultural competency as an educator.
3. Write one or two observable and measurable goals to grow in intersectional sociocultural competence and create a learning environment where all students feel valued and supported.
4. Determine actionable strategies to meet the goals.
5. Decide how to assess goals that have been met.
6. Fill in the start and targeted completion dates.

GOALS ACTION PLAN

ASSESSMENT SCORES:
AVERSION
AWARENESS
ACCEPTANCE
APPRECIATION
ACTION

ASSESSMENT SCORES:
AVERSION
AWARENESS
ACCEPTANCE
APPRECIATION
ACTION

ASSESSMENT SCORES:
AVERSION
AWARENESS
ACCEPTANCE
APPRECIATION
ACTION

GOAL #1

GOAL #2

GOAL #3

START DATE

START DATE

START DATE

TARGET DATE

TARGET DATE

TARGET DATE

STRATEGIES
☐ _____
☐ _____
☐ _____
☐ _____

STRATEGIES
☐ _____
☐ _____
☐ _____
☐ _____

STRATEGIES
☐ _____
☐ _____
☐ _____
☐ _____

ASSESSMENT
☐ _____
☐ _____
☐ _____
☐ _____

ASSESSMENT
☐ _____
☐ _____
☐ _____
☐ _____

ASSESSMENT
☐ _____
☐ _____
☐ _____
☐ _____

Figure 7.15. 5As Action Plan

GOALS ACTION PLAN EXAMPLE

NAME: TEACHER GOALS

ASSESSMENT SCORES:
AVERSION [8]
AWARENESS [14]
ACCEPTANCE [10]
APPRECIATION [4]
ACTION [2]

ASSESSMENT SCORES:
AVERSION [8]
AWARENESS [14]
ACCEPTANCE [10]
APPRECIATION [4]
ACTION [2]

ASSESSMENT SCORES:
AVERSION
AWARENESS
ACCEPTANCE
APPRECIATION
ACTION

GOAL #1
Participate in a professional development opportunity to increase awareness of bias during the assessment process.

GOAL #2
Collaborate with a colleague from a different sociocultural background to gain a minimum of two new ideas and approaches to teaching and instruction using socioculturally sustaining practices.

GOAL #3

START DATE
09/01/20xx

START DATE
09/01/20xx

START DATE

TARGET DATE
11/01/20xx

TARGET DATE
11/01/20xx

TARGET DATE

STRATEGIES
- Attend district workshop on examining educator bias during the assessment process on 10/11/20XX.

STRATEGIES
- Observe XXXX in their classroom and identify 2 socioculturally sustaining practices that the educator utilizes that can be incorporated into my classroom.

STRATEGIES

ASSESSMENT
- Pass post-test assessment in district workshop.

ASSESSMENT
- Have XXXX observe me in the classroom and ensure I have incorporated the two socioculturally sustaining practices with fidelity.

ASSESSMENT

Figure 7.16. 5As Action Plan Example

In the following vignette, an educator opens up about her journey to understanding her intersectional sociocultural competence and shares her personal sociocultural identities, including impacts of power, privilege, defensiveness, and blind spots when working to meet the needs of students with disabilities.

VIGNETTE 1: *AMY'S EDUCATION PERSPECTIVE*

I thought I had a good grasp of what it meant to not be part of the majority due to the color of my skin after living and teaching in the Republic of the Marshall Islands for three years. I had experienced not being waited on while standing in line at the bank and the grocery store, and also being pulled over by the police while driving even though I hadn't broken any laws. These everyday experiences gave me a culture shock and made me realize how different my life was back home. I had never stopped to consider how many advantages I had in life and took for granted because I was white. Even though I was in the minority on the island, most of the people in positions of authority on the island looked like me; they were white. "Remember what this feels like" I kept thinking, so that I can understand and empathize with people who don't have the same privileges. When I came home, I decided the only school district I wanted to work for was the one that educated me. I wanted to give back, so I ended up being hired as a special education teacher and went back to school to get my license in special education. I was confident in my ability to build relationships and connect with my students. I was also willing and interested in learning new strategies and interventions for working with my special education students. I believed that my background and lived experience would be sufficient for me to be an effective educator in an educational setting that over-identifies Black males. My thinking and attitude was steeped in white privilege.

Personal Biases—Action Planning Steps
Reading The Dreamkeepers *by Gloria Ladson-Billings (1994) changed the way I think about teaching. In it, Ladson-Billings writes about the importance of teaching to learners' abilities, creating a productive learning environment, and more. I was challenged by the significance of teaching to learners' abilities instead of their disabilities. Ladson-Billings stresses the importance of making students the producers of their learning, not just the receivers, to create an engaging and productive classroom culture. Students feel more comfortable and are more likely to participate when they feel like they are a part of the classroom community. It was time to give up my iron-fisted, authoritative control in my teaching practice and invite my students to orchestrate their own learning process.*

Around this same time, I participated in diversity training that was life-changing for me as a white female educator. I never realized how much my personal biases could affect my relationships with my learners and their families until I was challenged to examine them. It was eye-opening to learn about the different ways that I could be more inclusive in my classroom and my daily interactions. For the first time in my life, I was encouraged to have open conversations about race. These conversations allowed me to reflect on my personal biases and how they have shaped my interactions with others. Additionally, during a diversity workshop exercise, people were asked questions based on dominant culture values and then asked to line up according to the score they got. I still remember the activity vividly. The activity segregated us

(continued)

VIGNETTE 1: *Continued*

based on the color of our skin. This kind of segregating activity may be triggering for some. For me, participating in this exercise was a profound turning point, a paradigm shift, as I continued down my path of inner reflection.

As a white person, the first thing I needed to learn was how to start talking about race. It can be difficult and uncomfortable, but it's so important. I was raised like many white people of my generation to think we don't see skin color, to be colorblind, and that it's not polite to talk about race. But if we don't talk about it, we'll never move forward. I used to think that avoiding discussions about skin color and race was the polite thing to do. But I've since realized that those messages were really about avoiding discomfort. Fortunately, I was working in a building where many of us were learning to have conversations about diversity through professional development training. This training taught us how to have these types of conversations in a way that is respectful and engaging. This training gave me the framework and foundation for being an ally and participating in conversations about race. It was like finding a muscle that I thought I had, and now I needed to exercise and strengthen that muscle. This continues to be the analogy that I use when I talk with white educators about the importance of talking about race.

I learned I needed to check my biases about the families of my learners. I had listened to and participated in conversations with white educators who blamed learner behavior on the parents. Where did these assumptions come from? How were they affecting my work with learners and their families? I was quick to judge my learners' families and assign blame without any evidence. But the more I thought about my assumptions, the more I realized I needed to change my thinking. I also needed to actively challenge the assumptions of my white colleagues. As I spoke with more parents and learned about their goals for their children, I realized that we all want the same thing: for our kids to be successful. Once I stopped looking outward and assigning blame, and instead looked inward, I was able to make another positive change in my life. My persistent question to myself became "What do **I** need to do and change so that all of my students feel embraced, appreciated, affirmed, and encouraged?"

I started talking about race with my students organically. When behavioral incidents happened in the building or outside during recess, my students would bring it up in class and want to discuss the fairness of the discipline that was handed out by teachers—mostly white. We would have some really great discussions about race and equity, and it was clear that my students were really engaged in the conversations. I started my teaching career with the mindset that adults should back each other up when disciplining. However, as I listened to and questioned my learners about their perceptions and what they had witnessed, it was often quite clear that they witnessed a double standard in discipline. I no longer automatically support discipline consequences. Instead, I take my findings to the teacher(s) in question, and sometimes administration, for difficult conversations. This also means that conversations around race and equity are occurring more frequently in the classroom with my students. They knew that by bringing up concerns around any issue, they would get my time and attention. I would not shy away from conversations that included and centered around race. I saw this as an opportunity to have difficult conversations with my students and colleagues, especially my white colleagues. It's easy for white people and educators to step back and stay quiet, but I wanted to engage in this conversation.

Sociocultural Competency

I often talk about the importance of building trust with our learners. Trust is earned and is never given in any relationship. This means that when I say I'm going to do something, I absolutely have to follow through and be as consistent as is humanly possible. The day I knew I was on the right track with my own growth as an ally was when I overheard a conversation between a staff member and a student. The student of color had been sent to a calming room to de-escalate and was very upset and was looking for an ally to discuss what they saw as a racial inequity in how discipline was being handled. My colleague saw me and asked if I would be willing to join their conversation. He turned to the student and said I could be trusted. We were able to have a supportive conversation where the student felt heard and validated.

I'm always learning and growing—I make mistakes all the time. When I look back at my assumptions that I knew it all and didn't really need to learn anything new, I am amazed at the amount of white privilege flowing from my words and attitude. I have come to realize how crucial it is to participate in conversations about race and privilege, especially as a white person. I know that I have the privilege of being able to step into and out of these conversations as I please. Staying engaged in courageous and brave conversations is like building muscle—it takes perseverance and stamina, as well as a personal commitment to myself that I continually reflect, admit when I am wrong, and reengage again.

Pause and Reflect

From your perspective:

- What does it mean to have a disability intersect with other oppressed sociocultural identities?
- What role do sociocultural identities play in education?
- How do your students' intersecting sociocultural identities cause tension and strife, such as power dynamics, unfairness, bigotry, and unfair labeling?
- How will you uncover how bias, defensiveness, and lack of awareness shape your experiences?
- Describe the challenges/conflicts/vulnerabilities based on your students' sociocultural identities in school environments.
- Describe your power, privilege, discrimination, prejudice, bias, stereotyping, oppression, racism, defensiveness, and blind spots.

SUMMARY

This chapter provided tools for educators to engage in critical consciousness and self-examination of their personal sociocultural identities. After identifying sociocultural identities, practitioners can use the questions in this chapter to engage in deep, critical self-reflection of personal biases. An examination of bias is important as it can impact learning outcomes. Practitioners can also utilize the provided tools to guide students in an exploration of their sociocultural identities and intersectional experiences. Lastly, this chapter provided the *5As of Intersectional Sociocultural Competence Assessment* tool so educators can examine their sociocultural competency. Gaining intersectional sociocultural competence can help practitioners better meet the needs of all students, including those who possess diverse sociocultural identities, and contribute to educational equity. Practitioners should reject any blanket universal educational approaches indifferent to the reality that sociocultural identity groups are situated differently relative to societal practices and resources in our school systems. They should center justice, equity, diversity, and inclusivity in planning and teaching so as to avoid creating environments that disable and categorize students into sociocultural constructed groups through labeling, discrimination, and exclusion from the mainstream (Powell, 2009; Waldschmidt, 2018). See table 7.4 for an example of a commitment to equity statement. In closing, the authors of this book challenge practitioners to draft a commitment to equity statement to post in work areas, schools, and classrooms.

Table 7.4. Example Commitment to Equity Statement

Commitment to Equity Statement
I am committed to creating an environment that is inclusive, equitable, and free from bias in my educational practice. I recognize that biases can have a profound impact on student learning and success, and I believe that it is my responsibility to address these biases head-on. I am committed to:
• Engaging in ongoing self-reflection to identify and address my own biases. • Creating an affirming learning environment that is inclusive and welcoming for all students. • Incorporating socioculturally sustaining and reflective practices into my instructional methods and materials. • Actively seeking out and incorporating diverse perspectives and experiences into my instructional methods and materials. • Providing resources and support for students who have experienced the effects of bias. • Holding myself accountable for creating and maintaining an equitable and inclusive learning environment, and regularly assessing my progress toward this goal.
I understand that this work is ongoing and requires continuous reflection, dialogue, and action. I am committed to this process and look forward to working with my students, colleagues, and community to create a more equitable future for all.
[Your Name]

REFERENCES

Argyris, C. (1990). *Overcoming organizational defenses. Facilitating organizational learning.* Allyn and Bacon.

Azmitia, M., & Mansfield, K. C. (2021). Editorial: Intersectionality and identity development: How do we conceptualize and research identity intersectionalities in youth meaningfully? *Frontiers in Psychology, 12.* https://doi.org/10.3389/fpsyg.2021.625765

Berger, R., Quiros, L., & Benavidez-Hatzis, J. (2017). The intersection of identities in supervision for trauma-informed practice: Challenges and strategies. *Clinical Supervisor, 37*(2), 1–20.

Boveda, M., & Aronson, B. (2019). Special education preservice teachers, intersectional diversity, and the privileging of emerging professional identities. *Remedial and Special Education, 40*(4), 248–60. https://doi.org/10.1177/0741932519838621

Broadwell, M. M. (1969). Teaching for learning (XVI). *Gospel Guardian, 20*(41). https://www.wordsfitlyspoken.org/gospel_guardian/v20/v20n41p1-3a.html

Brookfield, S. D. (2017). *Becoming a critically reflective teacher.* 2nd ed. Jossey-Bass.

Cameron, C. D., Brown-Iannuzzi, J. L., & Payne, B. K. (2012). Sequential priming measures of implicit social cognition: A meta-analysis of associations with behavior and explicit attitudes. *Personality and Social Psychology Review, 16*(4), 330–50. https://doi.org/10.1177/1088868312440047

Centers for Disease Control and Prevention (CDC). (n.d.). Disability and health overview. https://www.cdc.gov/ncbddd/disabilityandhealth/disability.html

Chin, M. J., Quinn, D. M., Dhaliwal, T. K., & Lovison, V. S. (2020). Bias in the air: A nationwide exploration of teachers' implicit racial attitudes, aggregate bias, and learner outcomes. *Educational Researcher, 49*(8), 566–78. https://doi.org/10.3102/0013189X20937240

Chugh, D., Bazerman M. H., & Banaji, M. R. (2005). Bounded ethicality as a psychological barrier to recognizing conflicts of interest. In D. Moore, D. Cain, G. Loewenstein, & M. Bazerman (Eds.), *Conflict of interest: Challenges and solutions in business, law, medicine, and public policy.* Cambridge University Press.

Collins, P. H. (2019). *Intersectionality as critical social theory.* Duke University Press.

Crenshaw, K. (1989). Demarginalizing the intersection of race and sex: A Black feminist critique of antidiscrimination doctrine, feminist theory and antiracist politics. *University of Chicago Legal Forum, 1989*(1), 139–67. http://chicagounbound.uchicago.edu/uclf/vol1989/iss1/8

———. (1991). Mapping the margins: Intersectionality, identity politics, and violence against women of color. *Stanford Law Review, 43*(6), 1241–99.

Cross, T., Bazron, B., Dennis, K., & Isaacs, M. (1989). *Towards a culturally competent system of care, volume 1.* CASSP Technical Assistance Center, Center for Child Health and Mental Health Policy, Georgetown University Child Development Center.

Crossman, A. (2019). What is a master status? The defining social position a person occupies. ThoughtCo. https://www.thoughtco.com/master-status-3026399

Dhaliwal, T. K., Chin, M. J., Lovison, V. S. & Quinn, D. M. (2020). Educator bias is associated with racial disparities in learner achievement and discipline. Brookings: Brown Center Chalkboard. https://www.brookings.edu/articles/educator-bias-is-associated-with-racial-disparities-in-student-achievement-and-discipline/

Duarete, A. (2000). Wanted: 2 million teachers, especially minorities. *Education Digest, 66*(4), 19–23.

Fievre, M. J. (2021). Culturally responsive teaching: Teaching strategies that support students' individuality. Edutopia. https://www.edutopia.org/article/teaching-strategies-support-students-individuality/

Gullo, G. (2020). Equity endeavors through the justice for bias framework: Principals addressing implicit bias in schools. In P. Youngs, J. Kim, & M. Mavrogordato (Eds.), *Exploring principal development and teacher outcomes: How principals can strengthen instruction, teacher retention, and learner achievement*. Routledge.

Gullo, G. L., Capatosto, K., & Staats, C. (2019). *Implicit bias in schools: A practitioner's guide*. Routledge.

Hahn, A., & Gawronski, B. (2019). Facing one's implicit biases: From awareness to acknowledgment. *Journal of Personality and Social Psychology, 116*(5), 769–94. https://doi: 10.1037/pspi0000155

Harry, B., Rueda, R., & Kalyanpur, M. (1999). Cultural reciprocity in sociocultural perspective: Adapting the normalization principle for family collaboration. *Exceptional Children, 66*(1), 123–36. https://doi.org/10.1177/001440299906600108

Hinton, P. (2017). Implicit stereotypes and the predictive brain: Cognition and culture in "biased" person perception. *Palgrave Communications, 3*(17086). https://doi.org/10.1057/palcomms.2017.86

Hughes, E. C. (1963). Race relations and the sociological imagination. *American Sociological Review, 28*(6), 879–90.

Lacassagne, A., Nieguth, T., & Dépelteau, F. (2011). *Investigating* Shrek: *Power, identity, and ideology*. Springer.

Ladson-Billings, G. (2006). Yes, but how do we do it? In J. Landsman & C. W. Lewis (Eds.), *White teachers/diverse classrooms: A guide to building inclusive schools, promoting high expectations and eliminating racism* (pp. 29–42). Stylus.

———. (2009). *The dreamkeepers: Successful teachers of African American children*. Jossey-Bass.

Larrivee, B. (2000). Transforming teaching practice: Becoming the critically reflective teacher. *Reflective Practice, 1*(3), 293–307. https://doi.org/10.1080/713693162

Learning for Justice. (2007). Teaching tolerance: Culture worksheet. Southern Poverty Law Center. https://www.learningforjustice.org/sites/default/files/general/181.%20TT_Handout_POE_Culture%20Worksheet.pdf

Mayfield, V. (2020). *Cultural competence now: 56 exercises to help educators understand and challenge bias, racism, and privilege*. ASCD.

McKinney, T., & Schaefer Whitby, P. J. (2020, Fall). Intersectional pedagogy. *DADD Express*. Teachers' Corner. Council for Exceptional Children.

McKown, C, & Weinstein, R. S. (2008). Teacher expectations, classroom context, and the achievement gap. *Journal of School Psychology, 46*(3), 235–61. https://doi.org/10.1016/j.jsp.2007.05.001

Merriam-Webster.com. (2023). Definitions: ableism; bias; discrimination; exclusion; oppression; prejudice; racism; stereotyping. https://www.merriam-webster.com/

National Association for the Education of Young Children (NAEYC). (2019). https://www.naeyc.org/our-work/initiatives/equity

Nelson, S. M. (2021). Teaching social identity. *Middle Grades Review, 7*(3). https://scholarworks.uvm.edu/mgreview/vol7/iss3/8

Nieto, S. (2004). *Affirming diversity: The sociocultural context of multicultural education*. 4th ed. Allyn & Bacon.

Olson, M. A., & Fazio, R. H. (2009). Implicit and explicit measures of attitudes: The perspective of the MODE model. In R. E. Petty, R. H. Fazio, & P. Briñol (Eds.), *Attitudes: Insights from the new implicit measures* (pp. 19–63). Psychology Press.

Okonofua, J. A., Walton, G. M., & Eberhardt, J. L. (2016). A vicious cycle: A social-psychological account of extreme racial disparities in school discipline. *Perspectives on Psychological Science, 11*(3), 381–98.

Okunola, A., & Sanusi, T. (2022). Racial equity: 12 key words & phrases to know and understand in this moment. *Global Citizen.* https://www.globalcitizen.org/en/content/racial-equity-equality-key-words-phrases/

Paris, P., & Alim, H. S. (2017). *Culturally sustaining pedagogies: Teaching and learning for justice in a changing world.* Teachers College Press.

Pitner, R., & Sakamoto, I. (2005). Cultural competence and critical consciousness in social work pedagogy. In *Encyclopedia of social work* [online]. Oxford University Press. https://doi.org/10.1093/acrefore/9780199975839.013.888

Polusny, M. A., Dickinson, K. A., Murdoch, M., & Thuras, P. (2008). The role of cumulative sexual trauma and difficulties identifying feelings in understanding female veterans' physical health outcomes. *General Hospital Psychiatry, 30*(2), 162–70. https://doi.org/10.1016/j.genhosppsych.2007.11.006

Powell, J. (2009). Post-racialism or targeted universalism? *Denver University Law Review, 86*(3).

Rogoff, B. (2003). *The cultural nature of human development.* Oxford University Press.

Romero, L. S., Scahill, V., & Charles, S. R. (2020). Restorative approaches to discipline and implicit bias: Looking for ways forward. *Contemporary School Psychology, 24*(3), 309–17.

Rosaldo, R. (1998). *Culture and truth: The remaking of social analysis.* Beacon.

Rubie-Davies, C., Hattie, J., & Hamilton, R. (2006). Expecting the best for students: Teacher expectations and academic outcomes. *British Journal of Educational Psychology, 76*(3), 429–44.

Salas, L., & López, E. J. (2008, Summer). Cultural identity and special education teachers: Have we slept away our ethical responsibilities? *Journal of the American Academy of Special Education Professionals (AASEP),* 47–53.

Singleton, G. E., & Linton, C. (2006). *Courageous conversations about race: A field guide for achieving equity in schools.* Corwin.

Staats, C., Capatosto, K., Tenney, L., & Mamo, S. (2017). *State of the science: Implicit bias review.* 2017 edition. Kirwan Institute for the Study of Race and Ethnicity.

Stansberry Brusnahan, L., Harkins, E., Fuller, M., & Dixon, K. (2023). Diversity, equity, and inclusion: Teaching intersectional self-determination skills with a focus on disability, social identity, and culture. *TEACHING Exceptional Children, 55*(5). https://journals.sagepub.com/doi/abs/10.1177/00400599231155587

Tatum, A. W. (2009). *Reading for their life: (Re)building the textual lineages of African American adolescent males.* Heinemann.

Tatum, B. D. (2003). *"Why are all the Black kids sitting together in the cafeteria?": And other conversations about race.* Basic.

Tenbrunsel, A. E., & Messick, D. M. (2004, June). Ethical fading: The role of self-deception in unethical behavior. *Social Justice Research, 17,* 223–36. https://doi.org/10.1023/B:SORE.0000027411.35832.53

Tenenbaum, H. R., & Ruck, M. D. (2007). Are teachers' expectations different for racial minority than for European American students? A meta-analysis. *Journal of Educational Psychology, 99*(2), 253–73. https://doi.org/10.1037/0022-0663.99.2.253

Tyler, N., & Smith, D. (2000). Welcome to the TESE special issues: Preparation of culturally and linguistically diverse special educators. *Teacher Education and Special Education, 23*(4), 261–63.

University of Michigan. (n.d.). Social identity wheel. LSA Inclusive Teaching. https://sites.lsa.umich.edu/inclusive-teaching/social-identity-wheel/

University of Wisconsin–Madison. (n.d.). Lesson 1: Social identity. Libraries: Teaching & Learning. https://lo.library.wisc.edu/DEI_foundations/lesson_1.html

US Department of Health and Human Services. (2000). Amendments to P.L. 106-402: The Developmental Disabilities Assistance and Bill of Rights Act of 2000. Administration for Children and Families, Administration on Development Disabilities.

Vanderbilt University. (n.d.). Social identity. https://cdn.vanderbilt.edu/vu-wp0/wp-content/uploads/sites/140/2016/04/27192427/Social-Identity.pdf).

Waldschmidt, A. (2018). Disability–Culture–Society: Strengths and weaknesses of a cultural model of dis/ability / Handicap–Culture–Société: forces et faiblesse d'un modèle culturel des dis/abilities. *Alter, 12*(2), 65–78. https://doi.org/10.1016/j.alter.2018.04.003

Warikoo, N., Sinclair, S., Fei, J., & Jacoby-Senghor, D. (2016). Examining racial bias in education: A new approach. *Educational Researcher, 45*(9), 508–14. https://doi.org/10.3102/0013189X16683408

Yep, G. A. (2002). My three cultures: Navigating the multicultural identity landscape. In J. N. Martin, L. A. Flores, & T. K. Nakayama (Eds.), *Intercultural communication: Experiences and contexts* (p. 61). McGraw-Hill.

Zoino-Jeannetti, J., & Pearrow, M. (2020). Exploring power: An examination of social privilege and social capital of future educators. *Educational Studies, 56*(5), 506–18. https://doi:10.1080/00131946.2020.1799218

CHAPTER 8

Socioculturally Sustaining Practices: The What, the Why, and the How

Chapter authors: *Lindsay M. Griendling, Colin Rose, L. Lynn Stansberry Brusnahan, Sandy Smith, and Eric Elmore*

Vignette author: *Elizabeth Thao*

Editors: *Martin Odima Jr. and Elizabeth A. Harkins Monaco*

ABSTRACT

The purpose of this chapter is to define culturally and linguistically sustaining practices, provide an overview of their genesis, and describe how socioculturally sustaining practices can transform students' and families' educational experiences. This chapter uses intersectionality theory as the lens for exploring how this approach supports students who identify with various or multiple historically disenfranchised groups. Then, we explain how this more nuanced understanding of students' sociocultural ways of being transforms education from a process that is intended *for* students and families into a process of co-navigation *with* students and families. This chapter includes a description of how different interpretations across institutions and organizations impact the implementation of this approach. Finally, this chapter highlights what socioculturally sustaining practices look like when implemented in schools and discusses embedding these practices in education frameworks, such as Universal Design for Learning (UDL), Integrated Multi-Tiered Systems of Support (I-MTSS) (i.e., Response to Intervention [RTI] and Positive Behavioral Interventions and Supports [PBIS]), and Social Emotional Learning (SEL).

GUIDING QUESTIONS

- What is culturally and linguistically sustaining pedagogy and why should educators adopt this pedagogy?
- How can culturally and linguistically sustaining pedagogy transform traditional assumptions about family involvement?
- What does socioculturally sustaining pedagogy look like in implementation/practice in educational frameworks, such as Universal Design for Learning (UDL), Integrated Multi-Tiered Systems of Support (I-MTSS) (e.g., Response to Intervention [RTI] and Positive Behavioral Interventions and Supports [PBIS]), and Social Emotional Learning (SEL)?

KEY TERMS

Co-navigation
Culturally and Linguistically Sustaining Pedagogy
Demystification
Domains of School Engagement: Attendance,
Attachment, and Achievement
Intersectionality
Multi-Tiered Systems of Support
Norming
Positive Behavioral Interventions and Supports
Response to Intervention
Social Emotional Learning
Socioculturally Sustaining Practices
Universal Design for Learning

With significant growth in diverse populations within our schools, it is imperative that we examine socioculturally sustaining practices that can contribute to more equitable practices and positive outcomes for our students. This concept is rooted in culturally and linguistically sustaining pedagogy, which we will define in this chapter.

WHAT AND WHY CULTURALLY AND LINGUISTICALLY SUSTAINING PEDAGOGY?

As introduced in previous chapters, culturally and linguistically sustaining pedagogy is an approach to teaching that educators can adopt to perpetuate and foster students' sociocultural identities, incorporating it into practices as part of schooling in order to promote positive social transformation (Paris, 2012; Paris & Alim, 2017). It comprises "collaborative, collective, critical, and loving environments that support young people's cultural identities, academic investments, and critiques of white middle-class values" (Paris & Alim, 2017, p.

29). Additionally, this pedagogy examines and honors students' sociocultural and communal practices and preferences for engagement; provides access to opportunity and power; and seeks to eradicate educational policies that minimize or ignore the cultural and linguistic assets and skills of communities of color (Paris & Alim, 2017).

The Genesis of Culturally and Linguistically Sustaining Pedagogy

The genesis of culturally and linguistically sustaining pedagogy dates back to the early 1970s, as researchers sought to understand more about the dominant culture. They correlated academic performances across students' racial and ethnic identities and then identified how various educational structures and practices could be transformed. These scholars recognized cross-cultural discontinuity between (a) the communicative and instructional practices implemented in schools across socioeconomic status and (b) the ways students traditionally communicate and learn. Finally, they explored the purposeful inclusion of cultural and linguistic practices within instruction to improve learning outcomes (Cazden & Leggett, 1981; Erickson & Mohatt, 1982; Hymes, 1971; Jordan, 1985; Mohatt & Erickson, 1981; Philips, 1972, 1976; Vogt et al., 1987). These early works employed a plethora of names for this, including communicative *competence* (Hymes, 1971; Philips, 1972, 1976), as well as culturally *appropriate* (Au & Jordan, 1981), *congruent* (Mohatt & Erickson, 1981), *compatible* (Jordan, 1985; Vogt et al., 1987), and *responsive* (Cazden & Leggett, 1981; Erickson & Mohatt, 1982) education.

Culturally Relevant Pedagogy

Ladson-Billings (1995, 2022) calls attention to the common focus on student achievement in studies as a function of predominantly microsocial structures (i.e., cultural mismatch between teachers' and students' interpersonal or communicative interactions). Ladson-Billings acknowledges that studies employing the term culturally *responsive* teaching start pointing to structural changes that are needed beyond teacher-student interactions, such as the way that students are expected to participate in or engage with curriculum content. However, these studies all neglect to account for larger, sociopolitical structures that reproduce social inequalities within schools. Instead, Ladson-Billings (1995) offers the term culturally *relevant* pedagogy as a model that "not only addresses student achievement but also helps students accept and affirm their cultural identity while developing critical perspectives that challenge inequities that schools (and other institutions) perpetuate" (p. 469). Defining this further, Ladson-Billings (1995) explains that culturally relevant pedagogy is based on three principles, which are highlighted in table 8.1.

Table 8.1. Culturally Relevant Pedagogy

Students need to . . .
- Experience academic success
- Develop and maintain cultural competence
- Explore and develop critical perspectives (i.e., critical consciousness) that aid them in challenging inequities that they may currently experience in school and other institutions

Source: Adapted from Ladson-Billings, 1995.

Culturally Responsive Teaching

Synthesizing and further making sense of the existent literature, Gay (2000/2018) reintroduces the phrase culturally *responsive* teaching as she argues that, regardless of the name, "the ideas about why it is important to make classroom instruction more consistent with the cultural orientations of ethnically diverse students, and how this can be done, are virtually identical" (p. 36). She proceeds by describing eight distinguishing characteristics of this approach, which are highlighted in table 8.2.

Gay (2000/2018) does not reject any aspect of culturally *relevant* teaching that was previously conceived by Ladson-Billings (1995) and earlier scholars within this text. Rather, she explicitly states that culturally *responsive* is her preferred term for this approach, and she draws upon the findings of those earlier related works, and then synthesizes the literature base to offer more expansive descriptions of how it is practiced in schools.

Culturally Sustaining Pedagogy

Paris (2012) later questions whether the terms *relevant* and *responsive* actually support the goals of maintaining students' cultural ways of being, valuing, and sharing across cultural and linguistic differences, and developing their critical consciousness, as Ladson-Billings (1995, 2022) and Gay (2000/2018) intended. Instead, Paris (2012) offers the term culturally *sustaining* pedagogy, arguing that this phrasing makes supporting cultural and linguistic pluralism among students and teachers a more explicit, central goal of this pedagogical approach. Ladson-Billings (2014) later welcomes this shift in terminology, recognizing a previous tendency toward very static, limited, and superficial notions of culture and culturally sustaining pedagogy when translating this approach to practice.

Table 8.2. Culturally Responsive Teaching

Culturally *Responsive* Teaching is...	because it...
Validating and Affirming	• acknowledges the legitimacy of students' cultural heritages • meaningfully bridges students' home and school experiences • uses students' learning styles to tailor instruction • teaches students to understand and celebrate their own and others' sociocultural heritages • integrates various sociocultural backgrounds in all subjects and skills that are taught
Comprehensive and Inclusive	• allows students to maintain their identity and connection with their sociocultural groups and communities • develops students' sense of shared responsibility • helps students acquire an ethic of success while developing intellectually, socially, emotionally, and politically
Multidimensional	• permeates all aspects of learning, including curriculum content, instructional strategies, and assessment, as well as the classroom context and climate
Empowering	• promotes students' academic competence • promotes students' personal confidence • gives students the courage and will to challenge the status quo and relentlessly pursue success
Transformative	• confronts and transcends the cultural hegemony of traditional curriculum content and classroom instruction • develops students' critical consciousness
Emancipatory	• centers cooperation, community, and connectedness • encourages and enables students to find their own voices • helps students become active participants in their learning • engages students in multiple ways of knowing and thinking
Humanistic	• helps students become more open, receptive, and respectful toward their own and others' viewpoints and perspectives • helps students acquire deeper and more accurate knowledge of the identities, cultures, lives, experiences, and accomplishments of diverse peoples
Normative and Ethical	• elucidates how traditional schooling in the United States is Eurocentric culturally responsive education in actuality • calls attention to the ways that traditional policies and practices are shaped by and reflective of this dominant group's sociocultural identities, perspectives, and experiences

Source: Adapted from Gay, 2000/2018.

Culturally and Linguistically Sustaining Practices

Re-centering the intended focus on both cultural *and* linguistic pluralism, Rose and Frederick-Clarke (2016) introduced a framework called **Culturally and Linguistically Sustaining Practices** (CLSP), which relies upon the scholarship and research of the three preceding models (i.e., culturally relevant, responsive, and sustaining pedagogies; Gay, 2000/2018; Ladson-Billings, 1995; Paris, 2012; Paris & Alim, 2017). These practices draw upon, infuse, and evoke students' existing schema, experiences, funds of knowledge, and perspectives to optimally facilitate learning. In addition, culturally and linguistically sustaining practices intentionally seek racial and cultural equity and pluralism by deliberately tailoring district-wide norms, policies, and practices to affirm the identities of and expand opportunities for historically oppressed students. Table 8.3 provides an overview of the three basic competencies of culturally and linguistically sustaining practices.

Table 8.3. Culturally and Linguistically Sustaining Practices Competencies

Competencies include . . .
• Bringing awareness to the biases that inform our systems and personal sociocultural views
• Participating in authentic relationship-building with students, parents, and communities to learn about their sociocultural backgrounds
• Using the prior two competencies to adapt current practices in ways that match students' needs and build on their assets

Source: Adapted from Rose & Frederick-Clarke, 2016.

Socioculturally Sustaining Practices

Students have complex identities that are uniquely composed of the values, norms, traditions, histories, and languages of the various sociocultural groups and individuals whom they identify and interact with at home, school, and their broader community context. When a student identifies with a sociocultural group that has been historically minoritized (i.e., treated as insignificant or peripheral and relegated to a powerless position within society based on their sociocultural group) or oppressed (i.e., subjected to unjust treatment based on sociocultural group), they may also have similar experiences if the systems, structures, or processes that acted to oppress that community are left unnoticed and unchanged. Individuals who identify with two or more historically minoritized groups may experience compounding forms of oppression—a concept referred to as *intersectionality*.

We want to focus on intersectional practices that are inclusive of supporting students from all sociocultural identities, not just those defined as culturally and linguistically diverse. Families who are culturally and linguistically diverse are often defined as those whose primary language is not English or who are not of European American descent (Rossetti et al., 2017). In this book, we expand on this with the term **socioculturally sustaining practices**, to be inclusive and to value intersecting sociocultural identities and experiences. Sociocultural (social identity + culture) includes linguistic diversity as well as race, gender, ethnicity, socioeconomic class, and other identities.

As discussed in previous chapters, intersectionality is a theoretical framework that seeks to examine the experiences of individuals who identify with multiple nondominant sociocultural groups, as well as the organizational structures and responses that uphold systems of oppression (Crenshaw, 1989). For example, racist structures or procedures present within schools may act to minoritize a student of the global majority; however, if that student also has autism and comes from a lower socioeconomic status, racism, ableism, and classism may work in tandem to negatively impact their educational experience. See chapter 2 for more about these intersections.

Researchers assert that students with intersectional experiences face an increased likelihood of experiencing psychological distress, including symptoms of anger, depression, and anxiety. Psychological distress negatively impacts students' relationships with peers and adults which, in turn, decreases their perceptions of school connectedness and the extent to which students feel cared for, actively involved with, and supported by individuals with whom they interact in school (Lohmeier & Lee, 2011). Research further indicates that a lack of school connectedness negatively impacts students' motivation and engagement in school, as well as their overall academic performance (Cholewa & West-Olatunji, 2008). To mitigate the aforementioned and improve outcomes for multiply minoritized students, scholars contend that educators must understand and adopt socioculturally sustaining practices into their teaching repertoire (Cholewa & West-Olatunji, 2008; Delpit, 2006; Gay, 2000/2018; Ladson-Billings, 1995; Paris, 2012).

How Do Socioculturally Sustaining Practices Transform Relationships?

In this section, we examine how to transform the relationships between families and practitioners. Family involvement in schools has traditionally been viewed through a deficit lens. That is, if families are not actively involved in their child's education in ways that their child's school approves of or values—such as by attending Back-to-School Night or parent-teacher conferences—then it is often assumed they don't care or that their child's education will suffer (Calabrese Barton et al., 2004). This deficit lens also extends to families' involvement in special education. Despite federal policy requiring collaboration with families in the development of a child's individualized education program (IEP), schools tend to implement practices that prioritize efficiency (e.g., electronic IEP systems with pre-scripted, drop-down menus and tightly scheduled meetings) and delegitimize families' knowledge of their child and voice in their child's education (Bacon & Causton-Theoharis, 2013). Additional, specific ways that families are affected by this deficit are discussed in other chapters; but, ultimately, the deficit model of family involvement neglects the invaluable personal and relational experiences that families can offer as a guide toward more equitable school systems, structures, and practices.

When socioculturally sustaining practices are effectively implemented, however, deficit-based assumptions of family involvement are transformed, and all members of the school community (i.e., school professionals, families, and students) co-navigate educational decision-making processes. When **co-navigation** occurs, school professionals consider, discuss, and establish the purposes, norms, and functions of schooling *with* rather than *for* students and families. In other words, school professionals are actively engaging in ongoing, meaningful conversations with students and families about what they desire and wish to sustain through education. The idea of schools being accountable to the students and families comprising the broader school community is a central component of socioculturally sustaining practices (Paris & Alim, 2017; Rose & Frederick-Clarke, 2016). Table 8.4 presents a framework of teacher-family solidarity that examines common values of socioculturally sustaining pedagogy and critical family engagement (Hong et al., 2022).

Table 8.4. Framework of Teacher-Family Solidarity

Component	Definition
Humanizing Families	• Practitioners build relational trust through one-on-one positive relationships with students and families. • Families are invited into the classroom community and the learning that takes place there. • Practitioners demonstrate vulnerability by seeking guidance from families about how to best support their child.
Respecting Family Autonomy	• Families' experiences are at the forefront of practitioners' efforts to support their child. • Families feel free to share their concerns about schooling, giving them agency and decision-making power in schools.

Source: Adapted from Hong et al., 2022.

Implementation of Socioculturally Sustaining Practices

There are systemic issues related to implementation of socioculturally sustaining practices in organizations, including spaces of educational hegemony and the practicality of putting them into action. There are ways to address these, however, through a shared understanding of socioculturally sustaining practices, including how to follow cultural and linguistic competencies to develop professional standards.

Spaces of educational hegemony. Schools across the United States do not serve a monolithic population. The diversity in our society puts an emphasis on the importance of districts, schools, and classrooms to support students of all backgrounds, as well as to prepare students for a democratic, pluralistic society. For many reasons (e.g., social, economic, political), not doing so may be an existential threat to the survival of society. Pressures working against such support in the educational landscape include a history of hegemony (i.e., dominance, especially by one social group over others) as well as the significant and growing sociocultural differences between educators and students, as empirical evidence illustrates the importance of a student/practitioner cultural match (Gershenson et al., 2016; Gershenson et al., 2018).

Historical and current mainstream discourse about what knowledge is relevant, what values and behaviors are necessary or typical, and who can achieve in school affects the beliefs and practices of professionals working in education. Ingrained beliefs often affect actions and decision-making at all levels of educational and other social systems, leading to a deficit paradigm in which marginalized groups need to be fixed or converted in order to do well in school (Apple, 2004; Foucault, 1980; Hammond, 2015; Paris, 2012; Valenzuela, 1999). The clash between traditionally minoritized cultures and cultural capital expected in schools often results in a mindset that students are incapable or challenged learners, thus reinforcing hegemonic discourse for both the educational professional and the student (Steele, 2010). Structurally, these issues are reinforced by district policies, programs, and systems that, for whatever intention, often add more impediments. In addition, reform efforts that are applied universally often have disparate outcomes that continue to perpetuate and, in some cases, may exacerbate gaps in opportunities afforded to students who experience oppression.

Practicality. Focusing on socioculturally sustaining practices helps to mitigate what was discussed previously and other realities confronted in the education ecology. Theory and research support this notion but there are even further practical implications for why socioculturally sustaining practices may be a superior approach. In order to be positioned to sustain student's sociocultural identities, educational systems and their staff need to have deep knowledge and respect for students and their communities. Although that may seem like a monumental feat to achieve broadly in the current climate and structures of American schooling, the necessary journey toward that end promotes progress for equitable change.

For those who currently subscribe, consciously or unconsciously, to practices guided by hegemony, socioculturally sustaining practices directly confront assumptions, norms, definitions of, and conditions for excellence (Gay, 2000/2018; Ladson-Billings, 1995; Paris, 2012). This is true no matter the political or social orientation of the actors. It may also have more utility than other progressive educational frames when considering implementation. While using terms such as liberatory (i.e., to set free) and abolitionist (i.e., a person who wants to stop a harmful practice) to define educational reform models might have merit, they may lead to problematic historical entanglements in practice. Framing the work as liberatory, for instance, may lead to damaging paternalism, as this phrasing may insinuate that school staff (i.e., people in positions of power) are doing something *for* students and families who are subordinate to them, thereby restricting students' and families' freedoms and responsibilities in their own educational experience. Historical and modern examples—from residential Indigenous schools to "no excuses" charter schools—demonstrate how reform models claiming to be liberatory can have culturally destructive results (Spring, 2010; Valenzuela, 1999). Think about the conflicts in school placements for the Deaf community as discussed in chapter 3.

Without a strong and explicit focus on reflection, even those who claim to act for progressive ends often contribute to the oppression of nondominant populations (Sibley & Barlow, 2018). In addition, defining the work for a purpose not directly connected to student success lends itself to students being regarded as symbols versus actors with agency. In contrast, socioculturally sustaining practices by definition actively emphasize the need for continual learning and reflection by practitioners as a prerequisite to action, making them less susceptible to the consequences of hegemonic and paternalistic practice.

Shared understanding. In order for socioculturally sustaining practices to take root in districts and schools, a shared understanding of what they look like in practice is needed, as well as an awareness of why they are considered best practices. Without a clear definition and framework of core practices across organizational domains, it is impossible to operationalize socioculturally sustaining practices in a way that allows for the creation of aligned professional development, support, and eventually accountability (TNTP, 2015).

A broad conceptual definition allows for **norming** and **demystification** of the terms and language used to describe practices. Culturally and linguistically sustaining practices, as well as socioculturally sustaining practices, are undergirded by three essential elements: (a) high academic achievement; (b) student cultural competence; and (c) sociopolitical consciousness (Ladson-Billings, 1995; Paris, 2012). Definitions can be useful for gaining consensus from those inside and outside of the organization, as they create a starting point for stakeholders to come to a shared understanding and agreement around how an organization should enact socioculturally sustaining practices. Developing a shared understanding and mutual agreement among all stakeholders, in turn, ensures buy-in as well as aligned focus. It is also useful for coherence when aligning other wide-ranging definitions such as a vision statement.

An accompanying operational framework gives the broad conceptual definition necessary structure within the different domains and workstreams in a district or school. It allows everyone in the community to see themselves in the work and will point to core practices and expectations. Although there will and should be differences in implementation across different contexts, strategic processes and clear input are needed to create a sustainable structure that supports individual and organizational learning, development, and accountability aligned with socioculturally sustaining practices.

Competencies. In accordance with the core practices in the operational framework, there are competencies practitioners need to continually develop in order to implement socioculturally sustaining practices with fidelity. It is one thing to know what needs to get done and another to bring it to fruition. Beyond the knowledge of what culturally and linguistically sustaining or socioculturally sustaining practices are, practitioners must continually develop skills to deliver them (Lindsey et al., 2009). An example that includes that developmental approach is the CLSP Continuum which identifies three core staff competencies (Rose & Frederick-Clarke, 2016). Table 8.5 provides a brief description of the competencies, moving from competence to proficiency. The table includes a brief description of each of the three competencies, attributes, and observable behaviors both at the individual and organizational level. Additional descriptions of each competency follow the table.

Table 8.5. Culturally and Linguistically Sustaining Practices (C.L.S.P.) Continuum

Cultural Competence ⟶ Cultural Proficiency

Competency 1: Awareness Understanding Bias and Developing One's Lens	**Competency 2: Learning Cultural Learning/ Relationship Building**	**Competency 3: Action Implementing Culturally and Linguistically Sustaining Practices**
Sufficient analysis of one's own culture to understand the lens that one brings to their role; familiarity with one's biases along with knowledge of where to find compensatory resources; ability to recognize and disrupt the effects of their personal bias(es).	Ability to build authentic relationships with students, families, and communities to create a learning partnership. Rigorous inquiry and investigation into students' backgrounds.	Utilizes the cultural knowledge of students, families, and communities to adapt practices, materials, and environments to engage, innovate, and facilitate deep learning. Is culturally and linguistically sustaining, in that it is both validating and connected to cultural schema to maximize learning opportunities through rigorous instruction and the use of data to reflect and adjust practices.

(continued)

Table 8.5. *Continued*

Cultural Competence ⟶ Cultural Proficiency

Competency 1: **Awareness** Understanding Bias and Developing One's Lens	Competency 2: **Learning** Cultural Learning/ Relationship Building	Competency 3: **Action** Implementing Culturally and Linguistically Sustaining Practices
Attributes		
• Recognizes and considers one's own surface, shallow, and deep cultural influences and social location and how these impact their personal communication style, performance expectations, pedagogy, etc. • Acknowledges and values culture as fundamental to relationships and learning. • Understands that culture can be used to empower or enervate, especially in contacts with marginalized cultures. • Understands the power dynamics between dominant and nondominant cultures and/or persons from different social locations as well as the historical and sociological contexts of these dynamics. • Is willing and able to recognize and intentionally disrupts personal biases by reflecting on their cultural frame and/or social location, widening interpretations, and recognizing triggers.	• Proactively examines cultures in order to build relationships with students, families, and communities through communication that refrains from making assumptions about class, race, ethnicity, disability, age, home life, language, etc. • Builds strong, working relationships with students and families employing a two-way communication style that proactively engages them beyond problem issues or concerns and acknowledges differing degrees of comfort with traditional schooling from different families/subgroups. • Uses rapport and alliance-building techniques to create the trust needed for deep learning in the classroom.	• Empowers students by setting high academic goals and expectations for all students. Refrains from deficit-based thinking and provides students with appropriate academic and social emotional support and encouragement. • Provides learning opportunities and experiences that prepare students to persevere and become independent and critical learners. • Prepares students for standardized assessment but most importantly gives opportunities to learn through authentic assessments. • Uses quantitative and qualitative data to inform practices and necessary adjustments. • Challenges traditional curricula that excludes the contributions and perspectives of traditionally underrepresented racial and ethnic groups; allows students to "see" themselves reflected in the curricula in positive and substantial ways.

Cultural Competence → Cultural Proficiency

Competency 1: **Awareness** Understanding Bias and Developing One's Lens	Competency 2: **Learning** Cultural Learning/ Relationship Building	Competency 3: **Action** Implementing Culturally and Linguistically Sustaining Practices
Observable Behaviors Individuals		
<ul><li>Evidence of reflective behavior (e.g., journaling, regular meetings).</li><li>Evidence of positive offsets for cultural safety, informed by self-reflection (e.g., positive proximity and visibility techniques, trigger control).</li><li>Evidence of closing disparities such as those regularly found in disciplinary/punitive tools.</li><li>Evidence of reading texts and other professional development relevant to race, class, gender, and culturally proficient instruction.</li></ul>	<ul><li>Evidence of proactive and positive contact with students and parents/caregivers with regular and timely communication.</li><li>Evidence of soliciting feedback/suggestions from students, parents/caregivers, and community when possible.</li><li>Evidence of rapport and alliance-building techniques (e.g., knowledge of students' interests, affirming language) especially for triggering students/that trigger the instructor.</li><li>Ensures that instruction is void of destructive actions such as microaggressions.</li><li>Provides timely asset-based feedback that holds high standards and specific actionable steps that convey assurance of capability.</li><li>Evidence that students are involved in setting learning goals.</li></ul>	<ul><li>Evidence that social emotional needs of students are responded to appropriately.</li><li>Curriculum and instruction is culturally relevant, responsive, and rigorous for all.</li><li>Teacher provides appropriate scaffolds for students to progress and become independent learners on grade-level tasks.</li><li>Employs cooperative groups and co-construction of knowledge, representing different modalities.</li><li>Explicitly teaches norms of school.</li></ul>

(continued)

Table 8.5. *Continued*

```
     Cultural Competence              Cultural Proficiency
  ═══════════════════════════════════════════════════════════▶
```

Competency 1: **Awareness** Understanding Bias and Developing One's Lens	Competency 2: **Learning** Cultural Learning/ Relationship Building	Competency 3: **Action** Implementing Culturally and Linguistically Sustaining Practices
Observable Behaviors Organizations		
• Scheduling and/or administration of professional development sessions focused on race, class, gender, and culturally proficient instruction. • Intentional scheduled time for reflective exercises for staff. • Evidence of collective assessment of organizational structure, policies, and schoolwide practices for bias(es). • Evidence of text-based discussion with staff.	• Parents/caregivers and community members are on decision-making bodies. • Structures for feedback from students, families, and communities are in place. • Events and structures are available and accessible at school and in communal locations to increase the engagement of all families, with flexibility for those who cannot meet at traditional times.	• Welcoming school/classroom environments that celebrate diversity and the accomplishments of students. • Ongoing professional learning that develops staff's instructional and relational abilities and allows for collaboration and reflection. • Provides opportunities for students, parents/caregivers, and community members to learn/construct curriculum. • Schoolwide disaggregation of data including educational and social measures (e.g., discipline measures) to monitor for gaps. • Systemizes culturally and linguistically sustaining practices (e.g., monitoring for CLSP for all staff and structures for the work to be ongoing).

Source: Adapted from Rose & Frederick-Clarke, 2016.

Pause and Reflect

- What are ways to shift the continuum's focus from cultural and linguistic sustainability to intersectional sociocultural sustainability?

Competency 1: Awareness: Understanding Bias and Developing One's Lens. In order for practitioners to be able to effectively connect with students, they must continuously reflect on their views and understandings of culture. Practitioners need a broad understanding of the historical foundations of race and culture within their locality, the country, and across the world, as well as a broad understanding of their effects on policies, structures, attitudes, and practices within their society. With that broad understanding, one needs to constantly interrogate how these factors impact the context in which they work, and their own personal beliefs and behaviors. This ongoing awareness-building safeguards against the perpetuation of hegemonic thought and behavior as staff interact and attempt to build relationships with the populations whom they serve, especially when those populations have been historically oppressed (Sibley & Barlow, 2018).

Competency 2: Learning: Cultural Learning/Relationship Building. In order for practitioners to be able to operationalize culturally and linguistically or socioculturally sustaining practices, they must have a strong understanding of those they serve in order to build authentic relationships with students and families comprising the broader school community. This requires that staff have respect for sociocultural identities that might differ from their own, as well as the humility to learn from those they serve. Competency 1 will help folks develop this lens, but intentional spaces both inside and outside of classrooms need to be created for relationships to be built. These relationships are key to positioning practitioners to access the sociocultural wealth of communities and, in turn, to support the aspirations, needs, and success of students (Paris & Alim, 2017; Valenzuela, 1999; Yosso, 2005).

Competency 3: Action: Implementing Culturally and Linguistically Sustaining Practices. In order for practitioners to implement culturally and linguistically or socioculturally sustaining practices, they must move away from an educational model that forces students—especially those outside of the dominant group—to fit into a box, divesting themselves of who they are in order to fit the traditional, Eurocentric mold of what it means to be "successful" in school. Instead, they need to shift toward practices that would center and embed students' sociocultural identities into the instructional core and general practices of an educational organization. The ability to create and ameliorate these conditions within the organization relies heavily on the strength of the prior two competencies, both in the individual's development and the organization's ability to support it. The development of the third competency requires that practitioners be given the support and space to create culturally and linguistically or socioculturally sustaining practices regardless of subject matter or position in the organization.

Developing Competency. There are multiple organizational elements that leaders must examine when trying to develop culturally linguistically or sociocultural competencies. Although there are some differing views, general consensus around the components comprising effective professional learning experiences include that: (a) they are connected tightly to the curriculum and pedagogy; (b) they are supported by tools and protocols; (c) they are situated within a larger community of learning within and between schools; (d) they are sustained in duration; and (e) there are clear expectations and accountability tied to the learning experience (Coggshall et al., 2012; Jensen et al., 2016). While there is much variability among organizations and the individuals who inhabit them, this research has implications for the structures of professional learning in an organization developing socioculturally sustaining practices.

Along with effective components of professional learning, leaders must consider different types of strategies that will support the proliferation of socioculturally sustaining practices on the ground. Many researchers call for professional learning to be voluntary in order to foster optimal results, especially when dealing with issues of equity (Tatum, 2007). Much of this can be attributed to volunteers' willingness to engage, as well as their ability to focus on specific skills that an individual practitioner considers meaningful to their work. While that might be preferred, it does seem to be at odds with the strategic goal of having systemwide socioculturally sustaining practices—that is, if professional development is optional, how do you ensure all practitioners acquire the necessary skills for implementing these practices? Leaders might take a balanced approach with some baseline subject matter being mandatory, while others incorporate elements of choice within their learning experiences. Table 8.6 outlines some policy and practice recommendations for supporting a strong professional learning system.

Table 8.6. Policy and Practice Recommendations

Recommendations for Supporting Professional Learning

- Adopt professional learning standards
- Evaluate and redesign the use of time and school schedules to increase opportunities for professional learning and collaboration
- Regularly conduct staff needs assessments
- Identify and develop expert teachers as mentors and coaches
- Integrate professional learning into school improvement initiatives
- Provide technology-facilitated opportunities for professional learning and coaching
- Provide flexible funding and continuing education units

Source: Adapted from Darling-Hammond et al., 2017.

Pause and Reflect

- Reflect on how intersectional sociocultural considerations could support professional learning. How can you assess intersectional professional needs?
- Can you create professional partnerships across sociocultural identities (i.e., cultural informants)?
- How does intersectionality impact school improvement initiatives?
- How can intersectionality inform flexible funding and continuing education units?

In addition to these structures and strategies, leaders should focus on complementary areas, such as hiring and retention practices, to ensure those with strong levels of sociocultural competency are added and retained in the system. This can help alleviate the strain on the professional development mechanism by limiting the gap between practitioners' skill and will with implementing socioculturally sustaining practices and improving staff quality within the organization long term, which may be the greatest school-based factor in student achievement (Darling-Hammond, 2000; Wei et al., 2009; Hattie, 2008). Whatever strategies or levers for change an organization enacts, development and accountability must align to ensure students' lived experience in schools reflects the principles of socioculturally sustaining practices.

EMBEDDING PRACTICES INTO SPECIAL EDUCATION TEACHING FRAMEWORKS

Practitioners and educational leaders who adopt socioculturally sustaining practices and culturally and linguistically sustaining pedagogy can positively impact the outcome for all students, including those who have identified disabilities. As mentioned in previous chapters, when practitioners engage and interact with their students, they must be cognizant of any biases that impact their practices and relationships with the students and families they serve. Socioculturally sustaining practices improve the educational program, policies, climate, and curriculum that impact students who receive special education services. Even in special education, oppressive practices and systems need to be disrupted, and we can start by using socioculturally sustaining practices.

Culturally and linguistically sustaining practices prioritize students' identities, but we suggest that socioculturally sustaining practices prioritize the intersections of students' experiences. This approach allows practitioners to adapt instruction to reflect students' identities and improve educational outcomes (Paris & Alim, 2017). Learning is enhanced when practitioners and students recognize each other's identities and lived experiences as a valuable source of knowledge (Caldera, 2018). The key components of both culturally and linguistically and socioculturally sustaining practices are responsive, relevant, and sustaining pedagogy, which are often used interchangeably in both general education and special education environments.

VIGNETTE 1: *MEET ELIZABETH*

I identify as a female, Asian, Hmong American special educator, therefore I consider myself an educator of color. When I build trust with my socioculturally and linguistically diverse students, I honor who they are. I try to figure out what they like and what they don't like. I figure out what activities they enjoy and use that to motivate them to get through their work. I print out the special coloring sheet. I help them put together a puzzle or play with Play-Doh. I feed them and plan special events. I talk about video games and social media and movies and music with them, and I use language that is real and relevant. I encourage them to be free to be themselves while teaching the importance of respect and kindness. I ask them how they are and show genuine interest and/or concern. I also let them know that it's okay to have feelings and guide them in expressing them in socioculturally appropriate ways. I let them know that in my classroom and my space, they will not be judged for who they are, but they will be "checked" for what they do. And I shower them with praise—as many comments as humanly possible for any positive behavior I see (even when preceded by a not-so-positive behavior). I address students as scholars and leaders, and I root for them.

And at the same time, I let them know who I am—someone who wholeheartedly believes that they have amazing and unique gifts to share. What I don't do is judge students' capabilities or limit their opportunities based on the medical model. I review and repeat rules and expectations continuously to reinforce them and set expectations because I am committed to letting them be their best selves. Most of all, I strive to be honest and real about who I am and how I feel, why I show up to my job, and why getting an education is important. I think the time has long passed where the teacher is the person who knows it all—I learn just as much from my students as they do from me, and I let them know that. When students can see that we're all in it together and that as an adult, my job is to bring the love, support, and encouragement they need to get through the hardest parts of their day, they will put their trust in me. This trust leads to the understanding that should I push, redirect, raise my voice, or intervene, I am doing so from a place of sincere love, not control. I am not just another adult trying to control them, I want them to be free to be their whole true selves and have everyone recognize how amazing that is.

FROM CULTURALLY AND LINGUISTICALLY SUSTAINING PRACTICES TO SOCIOCULTURALLY SUSTAINING PRACTICES

The following sections provide examples of how culturally and linguistically sustaining practices are rooted in socioculturally sustaining practices. With culturally and linguistically sustaining practices, schools need to adopt professional behaviors and instructional strategies that sustain or maintain students' cultural and linguistic assets (Gay & Kirkland, 2003) to "validate and connect to the cultural schema to maximize learning opportunities through rigorous instruction and the use of data to reflect and adjust practices" (Rose & Frederick-Clarke, 2016, competency 3). Here, we suggest specific ways practitioners can *communicate, understand, learn, teach, utilize, reflect,* and *empower* to move from cultural and linguistic considerations to sociocultural considerations.

Table 8.7. C.U.L.T.U.R.E.

Communicate and engage in courageous conversations about diverse sociocultural identities in brave school spaces.

Understand the lens one brings to their role and engage in rigorous inquiry, investigation, and analysis of personal and students' sociocultural identities (including disability) and how these impact planning, teaching, learning, and overall experiences to disrupt the effects of bias(es).

Learn to set up a welcoming and affirming environment that provides a sense of belonging in a community with learning opportunities and experiences that prepare students to persevere and become independent and critical learners.

Teach students sociocultural consciousness and how to challenge traditional curricula and sociopolitical structures that exclude the contributions and perspectives of traditionally underrepresented sociocultural identity groups.

Utilize the sociocultural identities and knowledge of students, families, and communities to adapt practices, materials, and environments to engage, motivate, and facilitate deep learning where individuals see themselves represented.

Reflect and build authentic positive relationships with students, families, and communities to create a learning partnership by being responsive, addressing relevance, and being respectful.

Empower students by setting high academic goals and expectations for all students. Utilize asset-based thinking and provide students with appropriate academic and social/emotional support and encouragement.

Communicate

Socioculturally sustaining practices prioritize communicating. The following is a list of activities to help engage in these kinds of "courageous" or brave conversations (Singleton & Linton, 2006).

- Grow comfortable with being uncomfortable during conversations around sociocultural identities and diversity.
- Teach students to embrace their sociocultural identities and acknowledge discomfort when not in the majority.
- Engage in conversations to explore different perspectives.
- Engage in, sustain, and deepen dialogue (e.g., interracial, intracultural, cross-racial, cross-cultural) about ableism and racism.
- Provide, amplify, and value diverse voices to be heard, side-by-side with students and their families.
- Address persistent disparities in school settings intentionally, explicitly, and comprehensively in conversations.
- Call ourselves and others to more truth and growth and examine what we think we know, understanding that we will not be perfect and we will make mistakes.
- Communicate with language that refrains from making assumptions about class, race, ethnicity, ability, age, home life, and other sociocultural identities (Rose & Frederick-Clarke, 2016, competency 2 attribute).

- Identify communication styles that are the same or different between the teacher and the students (e.g., Standard English, African American Vernacular English, Spanglish).
- Recognize and consider personal sociocultural influences and sociopolitical location and how these impact communication style (Rose & Frederick-Clarke, 2016, competency 1 attribute).
- Listen, observe, and learn from learners and their families.
- Use interpreters and translate communications.
- Embrace the richness of multiple sociocultural identities and note how we all benefit from diversity.
- Seek out sociocultural informants to identify areas where you lack knowledge or are uncomfortable so you can process and reflect on experiences and interactions with others.
- Use inclusive language that acknowledges the diversity of sociocultural identities and languages represented in the schools and in the communities they serve.

Pause and Reflect

- Describe how you engage in courageous conversations and create brave spaces where individuals feel affirmed, nurtured, and safe, both physically and emotionally, to freely convey emotions and share experiences, especially after adverse events, without fear of prejudice, negative judgment, or punitive consequences from others.

Understand

Socioculturally sustaining practices include understanding the lens one brings to their role. The following is a list of activities focused on engaging in rigorous inquiry, investigation, and analysis of personal and students' sociocultural identities and how these impact planning, teaching, learning, and overall experiences to disrupt the effects of bias(es) (Rose & Frederick-Clarke, 2016, competencies 1 and 2; Schaefer Whitby et al., 2021).

- Check yourself at the door and anticipate sociocultural identity differences.
- Identify personal sociocultural identities.
- Internally reflect on how personal beliefs and values were and are shaped based on sociocultural identities.
- Recognize and consider personal sociocultural influences and sociopolitical location and how these impact behaviors, expectations, pedagogy, and other areas (Rose & Frederick-Clarke, 2016, competency 1 attribute).
- Guide students to explore and understand their sociocultural identities.

- Identify similarities and differences between practitioners' and students' sociocultural identities.
- Identify behaviors, expectations, and other areas that are the same or different between the practitioners' and the students' sociocultural constructs and then embed into lessons so they are meaningful for learners.
- Engage in critical, ongoing self-reflection to address biases and impact on students and families.
- Be willing to experience cognitive dissonance when embedded biases are being challenged.
- Question, challenge, and reframe biased statements from others.

Pause and Reflect

- Describe how you engage in critical, ongoing self-reflection to address biases and the impact of biases on students and their families.

Learn

Socioculturally sustaining practices include setting up welcoming and affirming environments that provide a sense of belonging in communities with learning opportunities that prepare students to persevere and become independent and critical learners (Rose & Frederick-Clarke, 2016, competency 3).

- Create a welcoming and affirming classroom environment for all students to optimize learning.
- Create an environment that includes clear and high expectations for all students' learning.
- Provide content that reflects students' backgrounds, where there are opportunities for students to "see" themselves and others reflected in the curricula and their academic experiences positively and substantially in the environment (Hammond, 2015; Rose & Frederick-Clarke, 2016, competency 3).
- Embed sociocultural identities including disabilities in class with representations in the textbooks, instructional materials, and symbolic communication (e.g., images, public displays) (Gay, 2000/2018; Ladson-Billings, 2002).
- Create respectful learning environments in which students' sociocultural identities are valued and contribute to successful academic outcomes.
- Embed learners' first language(s) in instruction and utilize pictures and graphics to support comprehension in the environment (Baker, 2021).
- Correctly pronounce students' names.
- Provide visuals and supports to make content linguistically comprehensible.

- Display students' works on the walls.
- Integrate socioculturally sustaining teaching to increase a sense of belonging for all students and sustain innovation in the classroom.
- Acknowledge and value sociocultural constructs as fundamental to relationships with students in the learning environment (Rose & Frederick-Clarke, 2016, competency 1 attribute).

Pause and Reflect

- Describe how you create a welcoming and inclusive environment where students' sociocultural backgrounds and native languages are welcomed, affirmed, and celebrated.

Teach

Socioculturally sustaining practices include teaching students critical consciousness as well as challenging traditional curricula and sociopolitical structures that exclude the contributions and perspectives of traditionally underrepresented sociocultural identity groups (Ladson-Billings, 1995). The following is a list of activities focused on teaching sociocultural consciousness.

- Teach students to understand current inequities and patterns of injustice within the local context and how they are reproduced by established systems and structures.
- Provide students opportunities to gain an understanding of social injustices in their own and in other communities (Ladson-Billings, 2002).
- Understand that sociocultural constructs can be used to empower or enervate (Rose & Frederick-Clarke, 2016, competency 1 attribute).
- Understand power dynamics between dominant and minoritized sociocultural communities, as well as the historical and sociological contexts of these dynamics (Rose & Frederick-Clarke, 2016, competency 1 attribute).
- Invite family and community members to speak in the classroom and discuss social justice inequities they have experienced.
- Identify silos and roadblocks caused by policies, specifically looking for opportunity gaps.
- Provide students opportunities to positively connect similarities and differences across sociocultural communities in class (Tatum, 2007; Wood & Jucius, 2013).
- Make students aware of intersectional access and equity realities.
- Incorporate societal curriculum in the classroom and teach students how to critically analyze and counteract sociocultural groups' representation (Ladson-Billings, 2002).

- Equip students with strategies to navigate, subvert, and/or counter the dominant cultures that they encounter in the multiple contexts in which they live (Jackson & Knight-Manuel, 2019).
- Brainstorm and help students implement strategies to address social injustices that impact their sense of belonging.
- Recognize and intentionally disrupt personal biases by reflecting on personal sociocultural identities and frame (Rose & Frederick-Clarke, 2016, competency 1 attribute).
- Provide opportunities where students can practice strategies to overcome obstacles they face now and may encounter in the future after graduation (Jackson & Knight-Manuel, 2019).
- Discuss resiliency and the ability to make choices.
- Emphasize why representation is important.
- Point out and discuss omissions of diverse sociocultural identities in identified fields (Ladson-Billings, 2002; Schaefer Whitby et al., 2021).

Pause and Reflect

- Describe how you prepare students to address current inequities and patterns of injustice within the local context that are reproduced by established systems and structures, and how these patterns of injustice impact students.

Utilize

Socioculturally sustaining practices include utilizing the sociocultural knowledge of students, families, and communities to adapt practices, materials, and environments to engage, motivate, and facilitate deep learning where individuals see themselves represented (Rose & Frederick-Clarke, 2016, competency 3). The following is a list of activities focused on utilizing sociocultural identities and knowledge.

- Assess sociocultural attitudes, values, strengths, and needs of the student population and integrate those multilayered perspectives into curricula and programs to build inclusion and equity.
- Design and implement a curriculum that is a mirror of the classroom, school, and surrounding community.
- Use "bridges" and scaffolding to increase learner interest and link to sociocultural background knowledge.
- Incorporate real-world learning scenarios in activities that present problems that students can relate to in order to increase interest and allow them the opportunity to use their own sociocultural awareness to solve the problems.

- Tap into students' families for learning opportunities, such as inviting guests to speak to learners and share their knowledge, to engage and motivate learners.
- Incorporate knowledge of learners' language(s), learning strengths, and needs in lessons.
- Allow for the use of bilingual resources.
- Include multidimensional materials in lessons.
- Address relevant and real experiences and link what is being learned to the students' sociocultural experiences.
- Provide opportunities for learners to connect their multifaceted sociocultural identities and experiences to new content during lessons.
- Connect students into the greater community with scholars, authors, and leaders from a variety of sociocultural backgrounds.
- Provide knowledge about the contributions of diverse sociocultural identities to culture, education, and a variety of disciplines (Ladson-Billings, 2002; Schaefer Whitby et al., 2021).

Pause and Reflect

- Describe how you use the sociocultural identities and knowledge of students, families, and communities to adapt practices, materials, and environments to engage, motivate, and facilitate deep learning.

Reflect

Socioculturally sustaining practices include reflecting and building authentic positive partnerships with students, families, and communities. The following is a list of activities focused on being responsive, addressing relevance, and being respectful (Rose & Frederick-Clarke, 2016, competency 2).

- Examine sociocultural constructs in order to build, nurture, and facilitate caring, humanizing relationships with students and families (Rose & Frederick-Clarke, 2016, competency 2 attribute).
- Engage in ongoing efforts to get to know your students and their families beyond the surface level.
- Ask questions, build rapport, and value the full humanity of all students and families.
- Build strong, working relationships with students and families employing a two-way communication style that proactively engages them beyond problem issues or concerns and acknowledges differing degrees of comfort with traditional school from different sociocultural identities (Rose & Frederick-Clarke, 2016, competency 2 attribute).

- Use support and alliance-building techniques to create the trust needed for relationship development and deep learning in the classroom (Rose & Frederick-Clarke, 2016, competency 2 attribute).
- Value and respect students' and families' native languages.

Pause and Reflect

- Describe how you cultivate positive and respectful relationships with students and their families, where they feel free to express and share their reflective thoughts and ideas.

Empower

Socioculturally sustaining practices include empowering students by setting high academic goals and expectations for all students. Utilize asset-based thinking and provide students with appropriate academic and social/emotional support and encouragement (Rose & Frederick-Clarke, 2016, competency 3). The following is a list of activities focused on empowering students.

- Identify students' and families' strengths, needs, expectations, routines, values, beliefs, experiences, and priorities.
- When required to conduct assessments, utilize socioculturally sustaining assessments.
- Examine intersections of opportunity gaps. For example, be intentional about disaggregating data by race and ethnicity and disability.
- Measure progress with formal and informal socioculturally sustaining assessment tools to gather more accurate information about students.
- Build inclusion with multitiered learning opportunities and whole-school initiatives.
- Use grade-level curriculum and scaffold to support language.
- Conduct ongoing and regular socioculturally sustaining assessments of students' responses and attitudes toward curriculum.
- Teach challenging material in a way that is learner-centered.
- Encourage students to reflect on and share their goals and achievements.
- Integrate teaching and learning strategies that value different learning needs and experiences.
- Monitor student engagement and adjust the pacing of instruction accordingly.
- Provide opportunities for students to work in socioculturally diverse cooperative groups.
- Include games into learning.
- Use learning stations with a variety of materials that are differentiated.
- Support technology literacy among all students.

- Provide positive and ongoing feedback to facilitate students' growth.
- Include multiple and varied opportunities for learners to demonstrate their knowledge.
- Encourage learners to share ideas through personal narratives and storytelling (Nguyen, 2021).
- Build equity in extracurricular engagement to increase professional and personal development in career paths.
- Examine inclusion and belonging patterns across classes, programs, and other aspects of school.
- Encourage students to make choices in their learning based on their experiences, values, needs, and strengths.

Pause and Reflect

- Describe how you set high academic goals and expectations for all students and utilize asset-based thinking to provide students with appropriate academic and social-emotional support and encouragement.

Now that you have learned ways to "operationalize" practices, we will examine educational frameworks currently in place and assess their connection to socioculturally sustaining practices.

SPECIAL EDUCATION TEACHING FRAMEWORKS

When schools embed socioculturally sustaining practices into evidence-based educational frameworks, they can implement interventions and gather data to better meet students' complex needs. In this section, we will challenge you to think about how to embed socioculturally sustaining practices in Universal Design for Learning (UDL), Integrated Multi-Tiered Systems of Support (I-MTSS) (e.g., Response to Intervention [RTI] and Positive Behavioral Interventions and Supports [PBIS]), and Social Emotional Learning (SEL).

Universal Design for Learning (UDL)

As discussed throughout this volume, Universal Design for Learning (UDL) is a framework that designs curriculum and instruction proactively rather than retrofitting it later to meet a student's needs. UDL requires teachers to understand their students' backgrounds and sociocultural identities to plan effective lessons, create a nurturing environment, and provide the curriculum in ways that all students have access (Kieran & Anderson, 2019). When universal design practices are implemented, students have more opportunities to access the instruction, impacting them academically, physically, socially, and emotionally (Kieran &

Anderson, 2019). UDL is not a "one-size-fits-all approach"—rather, it provides students with what they need individually to learn effectively.

A substantial amount of research shows that using UDL methods on a classroom and schoolwide level helps create access for students from all different backgrounds (Kieran & Anderson, 2019). If educators adopt socioculturally sustaining practices within UDL, they have the ability to remove many barriers that traditionally oppressed students face (Kieran & Anderson, 2019). This is so important because "UDL principles without explicitly considering how sociocultural differences and perspectives affect learning may increase the disparity in student achievement for students of color" (Kieran & Anderson, 2019, p. 1).

One way to do this is to participate in "crosswalks" that identify UDL practices explicitly connected to socioculturally sustaining practices. For example, perhaps there is a lesson that incorporates the UDL principle *Multiple Means of Engagement*. This lesson might ask students to create affirmations and express their sociocultural values and beliefs about themselves (Steele, 2010). Or it may ask students to create digital podcast book reviews on texts that have main characters with backgrounds and experiences similar to their own. Students can share their podcasts with their peers and the school community.

Once the crosswalk is complete, practitioners should convene to discuss the tools, strategies, practices, and activities that already combine UDL with socioculturally sustaining practices and identify areas that require more modification. This kind of conversation allows the school community to acknowledge and praise positive practices while pinpointing areas that need more focus. Activities like the one discussed earlier can help recruit the interests of students and promote sustained effort and persistence by allowing them to understand their sociocultural identities and community connections.

Integrated Multi-Tiered Systems of Support (I-MTSS)

Integrated Multi-Tiered Systems of Support (I-MTSS) is defined in this book as a comprehensive and equitable framework for integrated academic and behavioral support. MTSS has three tiers:

- Tier 1 utilizes evidence-based practices and instruction to meet the needs of 80 percent or more of the students.
- Tier 2 supplements core instruction and provides additional support for the approximately 10 to 15 percent of students who require supports such as additional time, exposure, and opportunities to learn and practice specific skills.
- Tier 3 provides the most intensive supports to between 1 to 5 percent of the student population by specialized personnel (Wexler, 2018).

Tier 3 is where schools complete assessments to determine eligibility for special education. To effectively implement the I-MTSS model, it is crucial that the continuum consider diverse sociocultural identities and embed socioculturally sustaining practices. In other words, I-MTSS must take into account and support the unique backgrounds and needs of every student to be truly effective.

Embedding socioculturally sustaining practices into I-MTSS helps create a more inclusive and equitable learning environment, thus setting the stage for improved performance by all students. Research demonstrates that the implementation of culturally and linguistically sustaining practices within I-MTSS leads to improved academic outcomes for English Language Learners (ELLs) (Freeman-Green et al., 2021; Hoover & Soltero-González, 2018), and so we suggest that by incorporating socioculturally sustaining practices within I-MTSS, educators can provide targeted interventions that are culturally responsive, sustaining, and intersectional. The crosswalk strategy could be used again to review all I-MTSS interventions and assess the extent to which they include socioculturally sustaining practices. Schools that adopt I-MTSS utilize both Response to Intervention (RTI) and Positive Behavioral Interventions and Supports (PBIS).

Response to Intervention

Response to Intervention (RTI) is the three-tiered process used to identify and support students by using a problem-solving model to determine the type and intensity of support needed and to evaluate its effectiveness over time (Collaborative for Academic, Social, and Emotional Learning [CASEL], 2023). Within I-MTSS, which is broad in scope and encompasses multiple aspects of school functioning including academics and behaviors, RTI focuses specifically on the academic aspects of assessment and intervention processes. "RTI calls for general and special education teachers to collaboratively offer students systematic, research-based, and data-driven interventions" (Gomez-Najarro, 2023, p. 649). Incorporating RTI in this way provides a foundation for academic success.

Criticisms of RTI question whether the design adequately addresses the intersectional needs of socioculturally diverse students. The extent to which RTI considers any kind of sociocultural need depends on the preparedness of teachers at each tier. Gomez-Najarro (2023) states that "unequal access to high-quality, socioculturally competent practitioners significantly impacts the disparate academic outcomes experienced by students from historically marginalized groups" (p. 649).

Pause and Reflect

Reflect and ask yourself:

- How does the current system of Response to Intervention contribute to the intersectionality of racism and ableism?

There are ways in which RTI can be effectively applied to consider complex sociocultural identities in the development of assessment and intervention strategies (Gomez-Najarro, 2023). Researchers caution against overlooking cultural and linguistic variability by relying solely on standardized instructional protocols and assessments (Gomez-Najarro, 2023). Avoid an "identity-blind, one-size-fits-all approach to RTI implementation" where school professionals fail to consider the students' identities "as a complex dance with one's sense of agency and position within the social world" (Gomez-Najarro, 2023, p. 58). To effectively implement RTI, provide opportunities for educators to create interventions that embrace and value students' multiple and intersecting sociocultural identities. Additionally, incorporate intervention materials that feature socioculturally diverse characters or figures. Sometimes, academic interventions don't portray students who are of the global majority. Moreover, as discussed in chapter 4, schools must reject adopting a "colorblind approach" to RTI implementation by reframing the discussion around race and ethnicity in relation to academic data. Similar to the strategies mentioned earlier, practitioners need to create opportunities to discuss how racism and other systems of oppression impact academic needs, while simultaneously analyzing classroom and schoolwide data for important decision making.

Positive Behavioral Interventions and Supports

Incorporating frameworks such as **Positive Behavioral Interventions and Supports (PBIS)** provides a foundation for developing strong relationships between students and adults in schools. This book defines PBIS as a framework for promoting positive behaviors in schools (Center on PBIS, n.d.). More specifically, it is a preventative approach through positive reinforcement, clear expectations, and a continuum of three tiers of support and interventions. PBIS follows the I-MTSS format in that there are three tiers that become more individualized as the rate of necessary support increases. Tier 1 universal strategies create a positive learning environment for all students. These expectations are then defined and explicitly taught to all students for each area of the school, including classrooms. For instance, safe behavior in the hallway may include traveling on the right side of the hall and keeping objects to oneself. Teachers then reinforce the desired behavior by providing positive feedback when students exhibit it. PBIS is designed to drive interventions and ensure students remain engaged in learning, yet provide a short-term solution to implement appropriate interventions and move students out of Tiers 2 and 3.

An important aspect of PBIS is establishing schoolwide expectations for all students, such as "be safe, be responsible, and be respectful." There are critiques that question whether schools are actually focusing on compliance rather than increasing engagement and academic opportunity. Research shows that when PBIS is implemented with fidelity and the school has consistent norms, language, and expectations, practitioners interact more positively with students (Chaves, 2020), and all school staff are more likely to acknowledge and praise positive behaviors (Clayton et al., 2020). This means it is critical that when creating expectations around the PBIS framework, school leaders are centering sociocultural identities.

Chapter 3 introduced us to the concept of *individualistic* versus *collectivist* practices in US special education. The US dominant values favor individualistic perspectives that emphasize the well-being and contributions of individuals within the group. See chapter 11 for how these views impact legislative policy. Individualistic instructional practices and school policies that originate from that mindset are intended to foster *independence* and *individual* success. However, many cultures adhere to a collectivist value system, which focuses on the well-being of the family or group. Collectivism emphasizes *interdependence* and *group* success. For example, a study found that Chinese students, who were generally culturally oriented toward collectivism, reported higher behavioral control (i.e., self-regulation and impulse control) than their counterparts in the United States, who were generally culturally oriented toward individualism (Li et al., 2018). See chapter 3 for more examples.

One of the ways this may manifest in the classroom is that a child from a collectivist culture may be inclined to work with others, and to help others, even when the task is individually assigned. A practitioner from an individualistic culture may consider that child's actions to be cheating and may respond with disciplinary action by sending the student to the principal's office (Trumbull et al., 2020). This type of response contributes to the disproportionate number of students of the global majority who are excluded in school (i.e., in-school and out-of-school suspension and expulsion).

Utilizing PBIS creates a common behavioral language and code for the campus. As such, it is imperative to collect input from all sociocultural backgrounds—practitioners, students, families, and staff members—when defining behavioral expectations across settings. Research also demonstrates that when culturally and linguistically sustaining practices are embedded in PBIS, there are more positive ratings of observed student behavior, particularly when practitioners report higher self-efficacy in behavior management practices (Larson et al., 2018). Therefore, it is incumbent upon practitioner preparation programs and school administrators to prepare future and current practitioners to design the PBIS framework incorporating these kinds of approaches. When students understand what is expected of them, they can find a sense of security in the educational environment, develop feelings of connectedness, and build relationships with the people within. The following Classroom Snapshot 1 provides an example of how to incorporate socioculturally sustaining practices into PBIS.

CLASSROOM SNAPSHOT 1: *MR. BAPTISTE'S CLASSROOM*

Incorporating Socioculturally Sustaining Practices into Positive Behavioral Interventions and Supports (PBIS)

Mr. Baptiste is a 7th grade social studies teacher. Many of the students in his class are immigrants or first-generation Americans. Mr. Baptiste tells the class that his classwide expectations match the schoolwide expectations of "be safe, responsible, and respectful." To ensure that he is incorporating the likely mix of collectivist and individualistic cultures of the students, Mr. Baptiste creates small groups, randomly assigns members to the groups, and asks that each group provide examples and non-examples of each of the expectations in "be safe, responsible, and respectful." Mr. Baptiste incorporates the examples and non-examples into the expectations and uses those examples throughout the year to reinforce and redirect behavior. For example, if an agreed upon example of "be respectful" is to give attention to the person who is speaking in class, Mr. Baptiste can precorrect students by saying, "Julio is going to answer the next question. Remember to give Julio your attention so he knows you are listening." Mr. Baptiste can also redirect behavior by saying, "In this class, we agreed to show respect by giving our attention to the person who is speaking. Please give Julio your attention by facing him."

Social and Emotional Learning

Social Emotional Learning (SEL) is a framework designed to help students acquire the knowledge and skills to establish healthy identities, manage emotions, foster empathy, and develop and maintain positive relationships (CASEL, 2023). By prioritizing the establishment of meaningful connections among students, families, and staff through sociocultural awareness, mutually defined expectations, and a nurturing school environment, it is reasonable to expect that there will be a positive impact on attendance, attachment, and achievement. The National Center for School Engagement (NCSE) identifies three domains to bolster engagement in schools: (a) attendance, (b) attachment, and (c) achievement (NCSE, n.d.).

The evidence base for implementing SEL programs into existing curricula is strong. Results from a meta-analysis that examined over two hundred studies involving more than 270,000 students found those who participated in SEL programs showed improved behavior in the classroom, increased ability to manage stress and negative emotions, and heightened positive attitudes about themselves, others, and school (CASEL, 2023). Furthermore, the inclusion of SEL was consistently successful with all demographic groups inside and outside the United States. This reinforces the notion that SEL can support students from diverse sociocultural backgrounds and geographic contexts (Taylor et al., 2017). In addition, because SEL emphasizes the promotion and instruction of skills rather than the delayed response and treatment of skill deficits, SEL programs are effective for students with learning disabilities (Hagarty & Morgan, 2020).

One example of SEL is restorative practices. **Restorative practices** refer to a holistic approach that emphasizes building relationships and repairing harm in schools (International Institute for Restorative Practices, n.d.). These practices are proactive and use preventative methods to (a) promote positive behavior and (b) address conflicts in a way that promotes healing and restoration for all parties involved and can be blended into the MTSS framework (Vincent et al., 2021). Restorative practices can involve a variety of socioculturally sustaining practices, strategies, and activities, such as circles, mediations, and reparations, all intended to build relationships and address harm in an inclusive and supportive environment. These practices promote the development of empathy, compassion, and effective communication skills among students, teachers, and other school staff members. For example, school professionals can implement intergroup dialogue (IGD) techniques, which involve planned, sustained encounters between members of two or more social identity groups who have a history of conflict (IUPUI, 2023). A restorative circle is a facilitated group process in which participants share their experiences and perspectives in nonjudgmental environments. Mediation is a process where trained individuals help disputing parties identify the conflict and harm caused and work together to find a mutually agreed-upon solution. Each of these examples incorporates listening without judgment.

A student may come from a different set of sociocultural experiences than others in the class, and it is up to practitioners to ensure that no one assumes that another's way of doing things is wrong simply because it does not match what they experience in their own cultures. The application of restorative practices offers significant potential for addressing these kinds of discipline discrepancies; several other chapters discuss why this is especially critical for disabled students of the global majority (Kervick et al., 2019).

All of these frameworks rely on the entirety of the school community to be critical of their practices and beliefs. When all work together, it is possible for classrooms and schools that utilize UDL, MTSS, RTI, PBIS, and SEL to provide opportunities for intersectional experiences to be repositioned to the center of instruction. In order for this to be possible, a few critical questions should be addressed:

- Are the basic needs, based on students' sociocultural identities, being met?
- What other needs do students have academically, functionally, and socially, based on their sociocultural identities?
- What evidence-based and schoolwide practices can be leveraged to give students from all sociocultural identities the most optimal environment to learn and grow?

Schools must work creatively to provide a continuum of service on a schoolwide level that meets the needs of socioculturally diverse students. If we are not actively using these frameworks with a sociocultural focus, we may continue to spin toward injustice and inequity for our students.

SUMMARY

This chapter provided an overview of the genesis of culturally sustaining pedagogy, as well as a description of how it can transform students' and families' educational experiences. This chapter discussed intersectionality theory and the utilization of this theory as the lens for exploring how culturally and linguistically sustaining pedagogy can inform socioculturally sustaining practices. Next, the chapter explained how a more nuanced understanding of socioculturally sustaining practices could transform education from a process that is intended *for* students and families into a process of co-navigation *with* students and families. We provided a description of how different interpretations across institutions and organizations impact the implementation of socioculturally sustaining practices. Finally, we concluded with an overview of what socioculturally sustaining practices look like in special education teaching frameworks, and how to move toward socioculturally sustaining practices in intersectional school contexts and educational practices.

REFERENCES

Alim, H. S., Baglieri, S., Ladson-Billings, G., Paris, D., Rose, D. H., & Valente, J. M. (2017). Responding to "cross-pollinating culturally sustaining pedagogy and universal design for learning: Toward an inclusive pedagogy that accounts for dis/ability." *Harvard Educational Review, 87*(1), 4–25.

Apple, M. (2004). *Ideology and curriculum.* Routledge.

Aspen Institute. (2018). *Pursuing social and emotional development through a racial equity lens.* https://www.aspeninstitute.org/wp-content/uploads/2018/05/Aspen-Institute_Framing-Doc_Call-to-Action.pdf

Au, K. H., & Jordan, C. (1981). Teaching reading to Hawaiian children: Finding a culturally appropriate solution. In H. Trueba, G. Guthrie, & K. Au (Eds.), *Culture and the bilingual classroom: Studies in classroom ethnography* (pp. 139–52). Newbury House.

Bacon, J. K., & Causton-Theoharis, J. (2013). "It should be teamwork": A critical investigation of school practices and parent advocacy in special education. *International Journal of Inclusive Education, 17*(7), 682–99. https://doi.org/10.1080/13603116.2012.708060

Baker, W. (2021). English as a lingua franca, translanguaging, and EMI in Asian higher education: Implications for pedagogy. In W. Tsou & W. Baker (Eds.), *English-medium instruction translanguaging practices in Asia.* Springer. https://doi.org/10.1007/978-981-16-3001-9_2

Barton, A. C., Drake, C., Perez, J. G., St. Louis, K., & George, M. (2004). Ecologies of parental engagement in urban education. *Educational Researcher, 33*(4), 3–12. https://doi.org/10.3102/0013189X033004003

Caldera, A. (2018). Woke pedagogy: A framework for teaching and learning. *Diversity, Social Justice, and the Educational Leader, 2*(3), 1.

Cazden, C., & Leggett, E. (1981). Culturally responsive education: Recommendations for achieving Lau remedies. In H. Trueba, G. Guthrie, & K. Au (Eds.), *Culture and the bilingual classroom: Studies in classroom ethnography* (pp. 69–86). Newbury House.

Center on PBIS. (n.d.). *What is PBIS?* https://www.pbis.org/pbis/what-is-pbis

Chaves, L. (2020). *Secondary school administrators' perceptions and opinions regarding the implementation of positive behavioral interventions and supports (PBIS)* [Master's thesis, California State University, Stanislaus]. ScholarWorks. http://hdl.handle.net/20.500.12680/p5547w90v

Cholewa, B., & West-Olatunji, C. (2008). Exploring the relationship among cultural discontinuity, psychological distress, and academic outcomes with low-income, culturally diverse students. *Professional School Counseling, 12*(1), 54–61.

Clayton, J., Robertson, D., & Sotomayor, T. (2020). Opportunities and access: Exploring how school district leaders make meaning of equity in practice through positive behavioral interventions and supports. *International Journal of Education Policy and Leadership, 16*(4).

Coggshall, J. G., Rasmussen, C., Colton, A., Milton, J., & Jacques, C. (2012). *Generating teaching effectiveness: The role of job-embedded professional learning in teacher evaluation.* National Comprehensive Center for Teacher Quality.

Collaborative for Academic, Social, and Emotional Learning (CASEL). (2023). *Fundamentals of SEL.* https://casel.org/fundamentals-of-sel/

Crenshaw, K. (1989). Demarginalizing the intersection of race and sex: A Black feminist critique of antidiscrimination doctrine, feminist theory, and antiracist politics. *University of Chicago Legal Forum, 1989*(1), 139–67. https://chicagounbound.uchicago.edu/uclf/vol1989/iss1/8/

Darling-Hammond, L. (2000). Teacher quality and students' achievement. *Education Policy Analysis Archives, 8*(1).

Darling-Hammond, L., Hyler, M. E., & Gardner, M. (2017). *Effective teacher professional development.* Learning Policy Institute. https://learningpolicyinstitute.org/product/teacher-prof-dev

Erickson, F., & Mohatt, C. (1982). Cultural organization and participation structures in two classrooms of Indian students. In G. Spindler (Ed.), *Doing the Ethnography of Schooling* (pp. 131–74). Holt, Rineholt & Winston.

Foucault, M. (1980). *Power/knowledge.* Pantheon.

Freeman-Green, S., Driver, M. K., Wang, P., Kanuru, J., & Jackson, D. (2021). Culturally sustaining practices in content area instruction for CLD students with learning disabilities. *Learning Disabilities Research & Practice, 36*(1), 12–25. https://doi.org/10.1111/ldrp.12240

Gay, G. (2000/2018). *Culturally responsive teaching theory, research, and practice.* Teachers College Press.

Gay, G., & Kirkland, K. (2003). Developing cultural critical consciousness and self-reflection in preservice teacher education. *Theory into Practice, 42*(3), 181–87. https://doi.org/10.1207/s15430421tip4203_3

Gershenson, S., Hart, C. M. D., Hyman, J., Lindsay, C. A., & Papageorge, N. W. (2018). *The long-run impacts of same-race teachers.* NBER Working Paper No. 25254, revised February 2021.

Gershenson, S., Holt, S. B., & Papageorge, N. W. (2016). Who believes in me? The effect of student-teacher demographic match on teacher expectations. *Economics of Education Review, 52*(1), 209–24.

Gomez-Najarro, J. (2023). Identity-blind intervention: Examining teachers' attention to social identity in the context of response to intervention. *Urban Education, 58*(4), 645–74. https://doi.org/10.1177/0042085919860561

Hagarty, I., & Morgan, G. (2020). Social-emotional learning for children with learning disabilities: A systematic review. *Educational Psychology in Practice, 36*(2), 208–22. https://doi.org/10.1080/02667363.2020.1742096

Hammond, Z. (2015). *Culturally responsive teaching and the brain: Promoting authentic engagement and rigor among culturally and linguistically diverse students.* Corwin/Sage.

Hattie, J. (2008). *Visible learning.* Routledge.

Hong, S., Baloch, M. H., Conklin, K. H., & Warren, H. W. (2022). Teacher-family solidarity as culturally sustaining pedagogy and practice. *Urban Education,* [OnlineFirst]. https://doi.org/10.1177/00420859221131809

Hoover, J. J., & Soltero-González, L. (2018). Educator preparation for developing culturally and linguistically responsive MTSS in rural community elementary schools. *Teacher Education and Special Education, 41*(3), 188–202. https://doi.org/10.1177/0888406417753689

Hymes, D. (1971). *On communicative competence.* University of Pennsylvania Press.

Indiana University–Purdue University Indianapolis (IUPUI). (2023). *Intergroup dialogue: Work together for social change.* Indiana University–Purdue University Indianapolis, Division of Diversity, Equity, & Inclusion. https://diversity.iupui.edu/offices/crdp/intergroup-dialogue/index.html

International Institute for Restorative Practices (IIRP). (n.d.). *Restorative practices for educators.* https://www.iirp.edu/professional-development/restorative-practices-for-educators

Jackson, I., & Knight-Manuel, M. (2019). "Color does not equal consciousness": Educators of color learning to enact a sociopolitical consciousness. *Journal of Teacher Education, 70*(1), 65–78. https://doi.org/10.1177/0022487118783189

Jensen, B., Sonnemann, J., Roberts-Hull, K., & Hunter, A. (2016). *Beyond PD: Teacher professional learning in high-performing systems.* National Center on Education and the Economy.

Jordan, C. (1985). Translating culture: From ethnographic information to educational program. *Anthropology & Education Quarterly, 16*(2), 105–23. https://doi.org/10.1525/aeq.1985.16.2.04x0631g

Kervick, C. T., Moore, M., Ballysingh, T. A., Garnett, B. R., & Smith, L. C. (2019). The emerging promise of restorative practices to reduce discipline disparities affecting youth with disabilities and youth of color: Addressing access and equity. *Harvard Educational Review, 89*(4), 588–610. https://doi.org/10.17763/1943-5045-89.4.588

Kieran, L., & Anderson, C. (2019). Connecting Universal Design for Learning with Culturally Responsive Teaching. *Education and Urban Society, 51*(9), 1202–16. https://doi.org/10.1177/0013124518785012

Ladson-Billings, G. (1995). Toward a theory of culturally relevant pedagogy. *American Educational Research Journal, 32*(3), 465–91.

———. (2002). But that's just good teaching! The case for culturally relevant pedagogy. In S. J. Denbo & L. M. Beaulieu (Eds.), *Improving schools for African American students: A reader for educational leaders* (pp. 95–102). Charles C Thomas Publisher, Ltd.

———. (2014). Culturally relevant pedagogy 2.0: A. K. A. the remix. *Harvard Educational Review, 84*(1), 74–84.

———. (2022). *The dreamkeepers: Successful teachers of African American children.* Wiley.

Larson, K. E., Pas, E. T., Bradshaw, C. P., Rosenberg, M. S., & Day-Vines, N. L. (2018). Examining how proactive management and culturally responsive teaching relate to student behavior: Implications for measurement and practice. *School Psychology Review, 47*(2), 153–66.

Li, J-B, Vazsonyi, A. T., & Dou, K. (2018). Is individualism-collectivism associated with self-control? Evidence from Chinese and U.S. samples. *PloS ONE, 13*(12), e0208541. https://doi.org/10.1371/journal.pone.0208541

Lindsey, R., Robins, K., & Terrell, R. (2009). *Cultural proficiency: A manual for school leaders.* Corwin/Sage.

Lohmeier, J. H., & Lee, S. W. (2011). A school connectedness scale for use with adolescents. *Educational Research and Evaluation, 17*(2), 85–95. https://doi.org/10.1080/13803611.2011.597108

Mohatt, G., & Erickson, F. (1981). Cultural differences in teaching styles in an Odawa school: A sociolinguistic approach. In H. Trueba, G. Guthrie, & K. Au (Eds.), *Culture and the bilingual classroom: Studies in classroom ethnography* (pp. 105–19). Newbury House.

National Center for School Engagement (NCSE). (n.d.). About us. https://schoolengagement.org/about/

Nguyen, H. P. (2021). Class reflection activities to close out a tough year. Edutopia. https://www.edutopia.org/article/class-reflection-activities-close-out-tough-year/

Ok, M. W., Rao, K., Bryant, B. R., & McDougall, D. (2017). Universal Design for Learning in pre-K to grade 12 classrooms: A systematic review of research. *Exceptionality, 25*(2), 116–38.

Paris, D. 2012. Culturally sustaining pedagogy: A needed change in stance, terminology, and practice. *Educational Researcher, 41*(3), 93–97.

Paris, D., & Alim, H. (Eds.). (2017). *Culturally Sustaining Pedagogies: Teaching and learning for justice in a changing world.* Teachers College Press.

Philips, S. U. (1972). Participant structures and communicative competence: Warm Springs children in community and classroom. In C. B. Cazden, V. P. John, & D. Hymes (Eds.), *Functions of language in the classroom* (pp. 370–94). Teachers College Press.

———. (1976). Some sources of cultural variability in the regulation of talk. *Language in Society, 5*(1), 81–95. https://doi.org/10.1017/S0047404500006862

Rose, C., & Frederick-Clarke, H. (2016). *Culturally and linguistically sustaining practices (C.L.S.P.) continuum.* Boston Public Schools Office of Opportunity Gaps. https://www.bostonpublicschools.org/cms/lib/MA01906464/Centricity/Domain/2218/OG%20CLSP%20Continuum.pdf

Roski, M., Walkowiak, M., & Nehring A. (2021). Universal Design for Learning: The more, the better? *Education Sciences, 11*(4), 164. https://doi.org/10.3390/educsci11040164

Rossetti, Z., Sauer, J. S., Bui, O., & Ou, S. (2017). Developing collaborative partnerships with culturally and linguistically diverse families during the IEP process. *TEACHING Exceptional Children, 49*(5), 328–38.

Schaefer Whitby, P. J., Harkins Monaco, E. A., Hill, D., & McNeal, K. M. (2021). Teaching diverse students with disabilities socio-political consciousness and self-advocacy. In E. A. Harkins Monaco, M. C. Fuller, & L. L. Stansberry Brusnahan (Eds.), *Diversity, autism, and developmental disabilities: Guidance for the culturally sustaining educator.* Council for Exceptional Children.

Sibley, C., & Barlow, F. (Eds.). (2018). *The Cambridge handbook of the psychology of prejudice: Concise student edition.* Cambridge University Press.

Singleton, G. E., & Linton, C. (2006). *Courageous conversations about race: A field guide for achieving equity in schools.* Corwin.

Spring, J. (2010). *Deculturalization and the struggle for equality: A brief history of the education of dominated cultures in the United States.* McGraw-Hill Education.

Steele, C. (2010). *Whistling Vivaldi: How stereotypes affect us and what we can do.* W. W. Norton.

Tatum, B. D. (2007). *Can we talk about race?: And other conversations in an era of school resegregation.* Beacon.

Taylor, R. D., Oberle, E., Durlak, J. A., & Weissberg, R. P. (2017). Promoting positive youth development through school-based social and emotional learning interventions: A meta-analysis of follow-up effects. *Child Development, 88*(4), 1156–71.

TNTP (The New Teacher Project). (2015). *The mirage: Confronting the hard truth about our quest for teacher development.* https://tntp.org/publications/view/the-mirage-confronting-the-truth-about-our-quest-for-teacher-development

Trumbull, E., Greenfield, P. M., Rothstein-Fisch, C., Maynard, A. E., Quiroz, B., & Yuan, Q. (2020). From altered perceptions to altered practice: Teachers bridge cultures in the classroom. *School Community Journal, 30*(1), 243–66.

Valenzuela, A. (1999). *Subtractive schooling: U.S.–Mexican youth and the politics of caring.* State University of New York Press.

Vincent, C., Inglish, J., Girvan, E., Van Ryzin, M., Svanks, R., Springer, S., & Ivey, A. (2021). Introducing restorative practices into high schools' multi-tiered systems of support: Successes and challenges. *Contemporary Justice Review, 24*(4), 409–35.

Vogt, L. A., Jordan, C., & Tharp, R. G. (1987). Explaining school failure, producing school success: Two cases. *Anthropology & Education Quarterly, 18*(4), 276–86. https://doi.org/10.1525/aeq.1987.18.4.04x0019s

Wei, R. C., Darling-Hammond, L., Andree, A., Richardson, N., & Orphanos, S. (2009). *Professional learning in the learning profession: A status report on teacher development in the US and abroad.* School Redesign Network at Stanford University.

Wexler, D. (2018). School-based multi-tiered systems of support (MTSS): An introduction to MTSS for neuropsychologists. *Applied Neuropsychology: Child, 7*(4), 306–16. https://doi.org/10.1080/21622965.2017.1331848

Wood, S., & Jucius, R. (2013). Combating "I hate this stupid book!": Black males and critical literacy. *Reading Teacher, 66*(8), 661–69.

Yosso, T. (2005). Whose culture has capital? A critical race theory discussion of community cultural wealth. *Race Ethnicity and Education, 8*(1), 69–91.

CHAPTER 9

Educational Practices to Acknowledge and Incorporate Students' Sociocultural Identities and Experiences

Chapter authors: *Martin Odima Jr., Sandy Smith, Eric Elmore, and Ambra L. Green*

Vignette author: *Elizabeth Thao*

Editors: *L. Lynn Stansberry Brusnahan and Elizabeth A. Harkins Monaco*

ABSTRACT

What experiences and backgrounds do our students bring to school that could be acknowledged and incorporated into their school day? What are the contributing factors that interfere with providing academic opportunities for students in special education? The purpose of this chapter is to introduce a REMIXed approach to special education that continuously revises, modifies, and innovates to support students with diverse sociocultural identities. The tools and strategies presented here provide a plethora of ways to advocate for social justice and provide a continuum of services for all students. This chapter will help educators imagine a school environment that considers and supports socioculturally sustaining practices.

GUIDING QUESTIONS

- What are the contributing factors that interfere with providing academic opportunities for students in special education?
- In what ways can special education be delivered through a socioculturally sustaining lens in various parts of the educational experience (such as literacy, math, writing, IEPs, and evaluation process)?

KEY TERMS

Active Listening
Artificial Intelligence
Assistive Technology
Behavior-Specific Praise
Cultural Adaptation
Cultural Discontinuity
Cultural Mismatch
Culturally and Linguistically Sustaining Practices
Culturally Sustaining Pedagogy
Direct Instruction
Extended Attachment Theory
Free Appropriate Public Education
Individualized Education Programs
Learning Partnerships
Least Restrictive Environment
Opportunities to Respond
Philosophical Chairs
Positive Behavioral Interventions and Supports
PreCorrection
Progress Monitoring
Restorative Practices
Social Emotional Learning
Socratic Seminar
Special Education
Textured Teaching
Transdisciplinary Teams

Educators make thousands of decisions each school day which trigger thoughts and actions rooted in unconscious bias and influence whether students' sociocultural identities and background experiences are considered or dismissed in their classrooms and schools; these decisions impact students' academic and social success. For example, note the effects of racial bias, as discussed throughout this text. This chapter provides practical strategies to challenge your thinking, grow as an anti-racist and anti-ableist educator, and create discretionary spaces for students so they can bring their authentic selves to school. We will explore how practitioners can implement schoolwide and classroom-focused evidence-based practices that are socioculturally sustaining. This chapter aims to (a) highlight challenges that students with intersecting sociocultural identities face on a schoolwide and classroom level; (b) explore evidence-based strategies that have been known to support all students; and (c) provide practical tools that integrate socioculturally sustaining practices into schoolwide frameworks. Effective implementation of these approaches depends on teachers building strong relationships with and maintaining high academic expectations for all students.

SPECIAL EDUCATION

Special education in the United States aims to ensure that students with disabilities can access the general education curriculum in an environment that imposes minimal limitations on their learning and social experiences. This concept is known as the **least restrictive environment** (LRE). Federal regulations emphasize the significance of educating disabled children alongside their nondisabled peers to the greatest extent feasible, promoting inclusivity and equal opportunities for all students (Office of Special Education and Rehabilitative Services, 1997). If found eligible for special education services, a student is provided with an **Individualized Education Program** (IEP). The main purpose of the student's IEP is to provide a detailed plan and accountability system on the support the student must receive to ensure they are provided with a **free appropriate public education** (FAPE; Kauffman et al., 2018). No matter the student's disability, FAPE ensures that they will receive a free educational program, and their IEP will be tailored to support their programming in accordance with their needs. This includes using state standards to drive instructional practices. As such, strong systems of support must be in place so students can thrive and realize their full potential.

Challenges in Special Education

Attending school for some may not always be simple, but disabled students face challenges that are more substantial compared to their nondisabled peers. This section focuses on understanding which contributing factors create systemic issues in education, such as (a) a lack of strong relationships; (b) underrepresentation of teachers of color; (c) stigmas and beliefs about disability; and (d) the intersection of sociocultural identities.

Lack of Strong Relationships

Today, it is widely accepted that educators must be able to forge enduring and authentic relationships with their students, especially students with disabilities (Crouch et al., 2014). According to a review of literature related to this topic, **Extended Attachment Theory** may have an impact on the student-teacher relationship when a student has a disability (Geddes, 2003). Extended attachment theory applies to a child's sense of emotional stability, fostered by a warm and caring connection between them and their teacher (Gross et al., 2017; Zee et al., 2020). In a learning environment, a practitioner is often viewed as a child's second caregiver because they play a critical role in helping students feel safe and comfortable when stress builds up in the classroom (Hamre & Pianta, 2001; Zee et al., 2020). When strong bonds are not developed between the practitioner and the student, the student may feel dysregulated in the classroom environment (Geddes, 2003). This often plays out in the classroom through what practitioners define as undesired or maladaptive behavior or inappropriate social-emotional competencies (Zee et al., 2020).

Lack of Representation

As our understanding of culture evolves, so too does our understanding of the unique needs of students in special education. Therefore, it is important to integrate strategies that recognize and acknowledge the experiences of all students. Many students who belong to the global majority face increased obstacles to education. In the United States, special education has long been seen as a program to serve students with disabilities, but practitioners are not often known to be disabled. In fact, a lack of practitioners represent the students they serve, which is a serious concern, especially for students of the global majority. Research indicates white special educators are of the dominant culture and do not share their students' sociocultural identities (Fish, 2019), and that policy reforms should be implemented to increase teacher diversity to better reflect the student population (Fish, 2019; King & Darling-Hammond, 2018; Villegas & Irvine, 2010). Research shows that all students feel affirmed and represented when they have teachers of color (Villegas & Irvine, 2010). Families also thrive when their children have teachers who share a similar racial or ethnic background, as they are more apt to feel a greater sense of trust and understanding (Vilson, 2016). All students, including white students, benefit from having an educator of color at least once in their academic careers. Researchers have found that students with a teacher of color demonstrate improved self-efficacy, or the perception that they can successfully complete tasks (Blazar, 2021), and are more likely to graduate high school and enroll in a postsecondary institution (Merisotis & McCarthy, 2005). These findings are attributed to the fact that teachers of color are more likely to engage in socioculturally sustaining practices (Will, 2022).

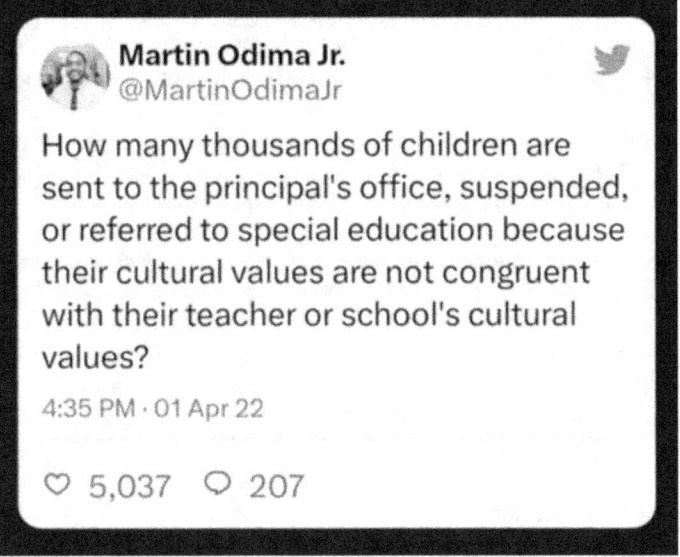

Figure 9.1. A former special education teacher's tweet about the unintended consequences of discipline in schools.
Source: Adapted from Odima, 2022.

Students of the global majority experience barriers to success when there is a perceived difference in sociocultural values between students and teachers (Taggart, 2017). This belief and value gap is called **cultural discontinuity**, a phenomenon where "cultural value-based learning preferences and practices of many ethnic minority students—those typically originating from home or parental socialization activities—are discontinued at school" (Tyler et al., 2008, p. 281). Further, students who feel their sociocultural values and beliefs align with those of the school are more likely to be motivated and do better academically (Taggart, 2017). Conversely, when there is a mismatch between the student and the school's culture, this can lead to poor academic performance and negative psychological outcomes. Sociocultural differences may result in a **cultural mismatch**, which is the "unawareness of the tactics, rules, nuances, and idiosyncrasies" (Johnson et al., 2017, p. 3), between teachers and their students. Cultural discontinuity and mismatch could lead to the consequences mentioned in the tweet in figure 9.1.

VIGNETTE 1: *MEET MS. LIZZ THAO*

I identify as a female, Asian, Hmong American educator, therefore I consider myself an educator of color. Educators of color are scarce, and educators who are in special education are even more so. However, because of this fact, I am and continue to be inspired by this profession. I have always wanted to help people and work well with youth, but as any educator will tell you, it is so much more than just that. I am able to have a perspective from a unique view—I am a person of color who can advocate for her students of color in an educational system embedded with the perspective of the dominant white culture. As an "academic," I am able to navigate the system, learn it, and bring valuable information back to benefit the students and families who need the most support. Therefore, one of the most valuable gifts I have brought to the table is my ability to understand and respect the rights of parents and families. Growing up Hmong fostered a natural ability to work with families, translating to several skills that serve me well as an educator. I am never daunted by the prospect of calling a parent or holding a meeting in person. I create strong relationships with the parents and guardians of students to reinforce expectations but also set the precedence that no matter what environment they are in, there are always expectations the child will be held to. I strive to reassure families that special education is not a judgment on the quality of their care but a system to support their child's success in school. I understand how important a cultural community is, and I am able to educate other colleagues about these considerations as well.

Stigma of Special Education

Students who access special education services may feel stigmatized by their teachers, peers, families, and communities; this feeling can vary depending on their disability.

> **Pause and Reflect**
>
> Reflect on the Social and Human Rights Models of Disability and ask yourself:
>
> - How do the attitudes of practitioners and school leaders contribute to [disabled] students' sense of belonging?
> - How do school environments contribute to [disabled] students' sense of belonging?
> - How can the Social and Human Rights Models combat the stigma of special education?

"Stigmatization often produces a strong sense of shame" (Heflinger & Hinshaw, 2010, p. 61). A review of the literature suggests that often when disabled students experience this type of shame, they will try to conform to the societal norms of their nondisabled peers. Neurotypical behavior is defined as actions that, according to societal norms, are deemed "typical" (Sasson et al., 2017). This kind of conformation can diminish students' self-perception and lead them to adopt a personality in which they feel they are accepted, a "mask." If students do not fully understand who they are, it is harder for them to recognize their own worth and value, thus continuing to perpetuate the stigma of how their peers and teachers view them.

VIGNETTE 2: *THE STIGMA OF SPECIAL EDUCATION*

As a career special education teacher, I primarily work with students who have educational disabilities and, in particular, students with autism, developmental and cognitive disorders (DCD), or emotional and behavioral disorders (EBD), and mostly with elementary and middle school scholars. As an Asian educator, I have seen my fair share of Asian students fly below the radar of even starting the special education process simply due to the fact that their struggles and behaviors are not as visible. I have seen students of color who are either overlooked—or overidentified.

Even though I identify as Asian and Hmong, I have found that my skills in considering culture and community bridge over to being able to help students and families from many other races and cultures. Growing up Hmong, I was inherently taught to have a healthy respect for teachers. I also learned how my community viewed people with disabilities. In fact, the most commonly used term I remember hearing to refer to someone with a disability was the word "ruam" which literally translates into the word "stupid." This knowledge alone gives so much insight into the Hmong perception of disability. Pieces of information like this gave me a deeper understanding of the cultural considerations for how different racial and cultural communities viewed education, special education, and disability, which allowed me to make intentional and considerate choices when making decisions for a child's IEP. I also have the ability to discern how behaviors might present themselves differently according to race and culture. I aim to use this cultural wealth of knowledge to continue involving and educating families in the special education process.

Intersection of Identities That Impact Students

As mentioned throughout in this book, student experiences are shaped by intersecting sociocultural identities; see chapter 2 for examples with race, gender, sexuality, disability, and socioeconomic status. When students do not identify with dominant sociocultural identities, they may face oppressive structures that hinder their success, which impacts their self-belief and connection to schools (Crenshaw, 1989). Therefore, understanding intersectionality in special education is crucial because it sheds light on the compounded layers of oppression for students.

NOW WHAT: REMIXED EDUCATION

In chapter 8, we proposed taking a multidimensional approach to incorporate socioculturally sustaining practices into Universal Design for Learning (UDL), Integrated Multi-Tiered Systems of Support (I-MTSS), Response to Intervention (RTI), Positive Behavioral Interventions and Supports (PBIS), and Social Emotional Learning (SEL). In this chapter, we dive deeper into socioculturally sustaining practices which (a) provide positive perspectives for caregivers and families; (b) communicate high expectations; (c) push learning to include the context of culture; (d) center students when developing instruction; and (e) position the teacher as a facilitator (Ralabate & Nelson, 2017). A model that builds on these ideas is **textured teaching**, which encourages educational spaces that are student and family-centered, flexible, and experiential, and that integrate interdisciplinary practices that "engage all learners to work toward social justice" (Germán & Paris, 2021, p. 5). This model is dynamic in that it embraces socioculturally sustaining practices and aims to engage all learners to work toward social justice. This model utilizes interwoven, multilayered, and complex approaches and strategies that recognize and value learners' unique identities and create inclusive learning environments that welcome students in their entirety. We propose taking a "REMIXed" approach to socioculturally sustaining practices that incorporates the work of textured teaching (Germán & Paris, 2021; Ralabate & Nelson, 2017). This includes (a) collaborating with families, community members, administrators, and related service providers; and (b) continually improving lesson plans, curriculum, and methods. In that regard, we present asset-based lesson plans, techniques, tools, and ideas to move forward in addressing intersectional inequities for disabled students.

Remixing, layering, and combining educational practices is not new and such practices have been in use for a long time, influenced by the multifaceted nature of students' sociocultural identities and the repertoires in which they participate (Chambers Cantrell et al., 2022). The fundamental principle of socioculturally sustaining pedagogies is built on "many cultural, every day, and academic literacy practices of people of myriad races, ethnicities, cultures, and backgrounds" (Chambers Cantrell et al., 2022, p. 59). With that said, practitioners can enhance their students' learning experiences by combining different strategies and tools, much like a music artist creates a hit song by layering sounds and lyrics. This requires constant revision, modification, and innovation, akin to the work of a disc jockey (DJ) or composer. However, involving the audience in the process is just as important. The classroom environment is also shaped by various practices, strategies, and teacher moves, but no exact formula exists for delivering the perfect lesson. Allowing room for mistakes and giving students control and power in their learning is essential. The following are some practical examples of how to implement socioculturally sustaining practices in school communities, including how to collaborate with families, community advocates, and other individuals who support students with disabilities. We offer lesson plan templates that may be helpful, or practitioners can feel free to take some of the ideas presented and "remix" them based on what works best for students. Figure 9.2 provides an overview of a "REMIXed" educational framework:

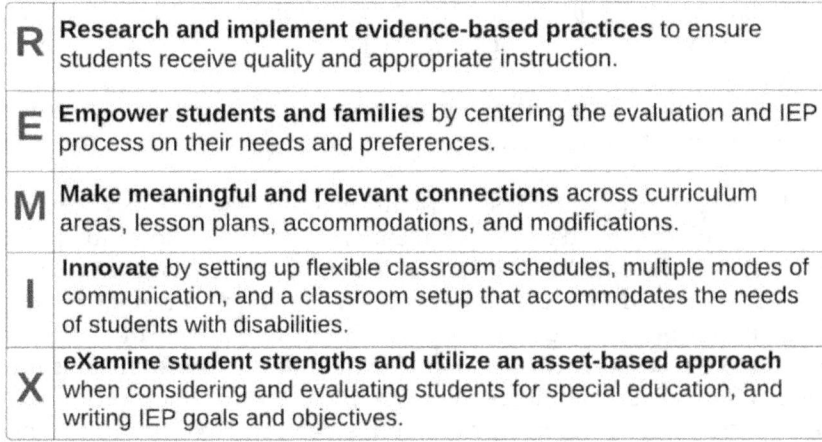

Figure 9.2. REMIXed Educational Framework
Source: Adapted from Germán & Paris, 2021.

REMIXed: Research and Implement Evidence-Based Practices

Teachers must exercise caution when selecting evidence-based practices (EBPs) for socioculturally diverse students. EBPs are often assumed to be universally effective (Wang & Lam, 2017). However, in most cases there is only documented evidence of effectiveness within certain populations in research studies, such as white students of suburban middle-class families. To date, "there is a lack of evidence in the literature supporting the efficacy of EBPs for communities of color" (Wang & Lam, 2017, p. 54). One reason for this lack of efficacy of EBPs is understanding the nuances and depth of sociocultural identities students hold. Students' sociocultural identities "involve complex intersecting social group identity markers, including—but not limited to—race, class, gender, sexual orientation, language, religion, and ability, each of which may shape how persons see themselves as individuals, as well as members of a collective (Gomez-Najarro, 2023, p. 647). Hence, it is crucial that we seek ways for EBPs to be relevant and effective in the context of our students' sociocultural identities. The process when a teacher seeks out robust information about the student's background and sociocultural values, and experience is called **cultural adaptation**. This is a purposeful and collaborative process that involves modifying materials to ensure their relevance for specific populations. By considering sociocultural identity and context, we can align EBPs with the cultural patterns, languages, meanings, and values of students (Wang & Lam, 2017). When implementing EBPs, ask three "wh" types of questions (Ogden & Fixsen, 2014).

- First, ask the *what* question to gain clear and specific descriptions of the EBP, including information about the empirical nature, content, and procedures of the intervention.
- Second, ask the *who* question about the individuals who carry out the interventions and the students for whom the practice was shown to be effective.
- Third, ask the *how* question to identify potential facilitators or barriers in the implementation procedures.

As this chapter explores EBPs, you will see how they have been modified through sociocultural adaptation to enhance their applicability and relevance for the student. In addition, it is important to consider fidelity of implementation and how the teacher uses an intervention or strategy from a multicultural perspective. "This includes both how much of an intervention or strategy someone uses as well as how well the intervention is implemented" (Green & Stormont, 2018, p. 139). For example, a practitioner can increase the fidelity of a lesson by keeping track of how often EBPs occur. They can use a tablet device to record their lesson and tally how many times they used an EBP within their lesson.

This chapter provides several frameworks that have been discussed in this text, but we also suggest that EBPs draw from a "wide range of cultural experiences, knowledge, and perspectives" (Nandakumar et al., 2022, p. 86). The following section provides some evidence-based strategies to utilize with students and families who are socioculturally diverse.

Evidence-Based Strategy #1: Provide Opportunities to Respond

Opportunities to respond (OTR) is an evidence-based practice that provides a set of circumstances in which students must actively respond to academic material or a request (e.g., asking questions, reading aloud, writing answers to a problem). "When implemented at high rates (i.e., a minimum of three OTRs per minute), OTRs have positive results on both the academic and behavioral outcomes for students, especially students with challenging behaviors [or undesired behaviors]" (Green & Stormont, 2018, p. 141). This strategy is effective with students who display what is considered undesired or maladaptive behaviors or who are labeled with an emotional behavior disorder (EBD) because it leads to "increased task engagement and decreases disruptive behaviors" (Green & Stormont, 2018, p. 143). Educators can modify the lesson's pace, demands, and content based on student feedback. See how Ms. Khan utilized this strategy in Classroom Snapshot 1.

CLASSROOM SNAPSHOT 1: *MS. KHAN'S CLASSROOM*

Readers' Workshop—Progress Monitoring Using SMART Goals

Ms. Khan is an elementary school teacher who read the book Esperanza Rising *by Pam Muñoz Ryan to her class. Many of her students are interested in learning about the experiences of immigrants, particularly in light of recent changes to state law that have affected undocumented individuals. Ms. Khan uses various strategies to engage her students during the lesson, including helping them identify key events in the story, build vocabulary, and summarize the chapter's text. One of her students, Rashaun is autistic and has an IEP goal in reading. To help Rashaun participate fully in the lesson, Ms. Khan employs a high questioning rate and provides sentence prompts, which she has practiced with him beforehand. The class engages in a group activity to recall the story's events. At the same time, Rashaun uses a "five-finger retell" graphic organizer to identify parts of the story and predict what happens in the next chapter (a UDL strategy). Ms. Khan provides Rashaun with a SMART goal sheet that aligns with his IEP goals, which helps him self-select strategies to attain his goal and measure his progress over time. Ms. Khan also meets with Rashaun and two other peers for a reading intervention to improve their proficiency in decoding words. Finally, at the end of the lesson, Ms. Khan asks her students to submit an "Exit Ticket" by recording a video or audio or writing down five details they learned from the text they read.*

Pause and Reflect

- What ways can you provide students with an opportunity to select learning strategies that work best for them, track their progress over time, and celebrate their growth?

The teacher in the case study included OTR at the beginning, middle, and end of the lesson. The educator also incorporated direct instruction within the lesson, which is helpful for students who are not considered proficient in reading. **Direct instruction** (DI) is a teacher-led strategy that "provides clear and explicit instruction and has been proven to increase academic achievement and reduce problem behaviors [undesired behaviors]" (Green & Stormont,

2018, p. 143). This means instructing in a systematic and structured manner. Students are successful with direct instruction because they receive sufficient scaffolding in the early stages of acquiring new skills, high rates of OTR, and repeated practice of new skills (Green & Stormont, 2018).

Evidence-Based Strategy #2: Offer Behavior-Specific Praise

Behavior-specific praise (BSP) is an evidence-based practice where educators provide specific positive feedback that "explicitly tells a student what malleable factor within the student's locus of control is being praised" (Royer et al., 2019, p. 113), or "acknowledges a desired behavior in specific, observable, and measurable terms" (IRIS Center, 2012, 2021). This is effective because "BSP provides students specific performance feedback (academic, behavioral, or social), helps students realize what they have specifically done well, reinforces schoolwide expectations, and can make the future occurrence of socially acceptable behavior more likely" (Royer et al., 2019, p. 113). It is suggested that practitioners provide at least four behavior-specific praise statements to one corrective or negative feedback statement (Green & Stormont, 2018). An example is when students come to class prepared with all their materials, the practitioner would then provide a statement like, "Table 3, thank you for remembering to bring your journals to class today!" A non-example would be saying "good job" or "thank you" to the students because it does not identify the specific behavior you want them to display.

BSP can be measured in several different ways. See how Mx. Martin utilized this strategy in Classroom Snapshot 2.

CLASSROOM SNAPSHOT 2: *MX. MARTIN'S CLASSROOM*

Writers' Workshop—Using Podcasts to Support Writing

Mx. Martin is an elementary educator. During a writing lesson for 4th-grade elementary students, Mx. Martin focused on identifying "tone" and "mood" within mentor texts and guided the students in practicing those concepts in their own writing samples. One student in the class, Jakela, has an emotional behavioral disorder, and Mx. Martin kept a log of positive to negative feedback provided in class (BSP). Mx. Martin adopts a flexible approach to the lesson and encourages students to cocreate the lesson plan. In addition, self-regulation strategy prompts are available on all student desks to support their emotional regulation during the lesson. As part of the lesson, the students created podcasts to complement their stories. Although Jakela was the only student in the class with an emotional behavioral disorder, the whole class benefited from Mx. Martin's focus on maintaining a 5:1 ratio of praise statements to reprimands. Mx. Martin's teaching approach fostered a positive and inclusive learning environment for all students in the class.

Pause and Reflect

- What ways can you make the evidence-based practices you incorporate in your lesson plans socioculturally diverse?

Evidence-Based Strategy #3: Utilize PreCorrection Strategies

PreCorrection (PC) is an evidence-based practice designed to eliminate predictable "undesired or maladaptive behaviors" before they occur (Green & Stormont, 2018). The goal of PC is that teachers will "spend less time redirecting students and more time creating positive climates and opportunities to use praise to reinforce appropriate behaviors. Additionally, the use of PC prevents students from repeating undesired behaviors" (Green & Stormont, 2018, p. 141). PC can be particularly effective when used as often as possible, especially when explicitly teaching academic material. PC has been proven effective in increasing positive behavior across age groups (i.e., preschool to high school), in classroom and non-classroom settings, and has been implemented by a variety of educators (e.g., teachers, school staff; IRIS Center, 2012, 2021). See how Mr. Sheyba utilized this strategy in Classroom Snapshot 3.

CLASSROOM SNAPSHOT 3: *MR. SHEYBA'S CLASSROOM*

Math Lesson—Marathon Running and Math

Mr. Sheyba, a 4th-grade teacher, used distance running to teach his students about multiplying and dividing multidigit numbers. He had his students analyze runners' race times from a nearby marathon, identifying the hometowns of each runner from different states and countries. One of Mr. Sheyba's students, Derrick, who has an emotional behavioral disorder, often struggles with transitioning outside for academic activities. To prepare Derrick for the lesson, Mr. Sheyba used the PreCorrection strategy, having a private conversation with him to set rules and expectations for walking outside the school and brainstorm respectful behavior with peers. In addition, Mr. Sheyba aligned the lesson with Derrick's IEP math goal and incorporated a running activity where students could time themselves and calculate their average speed. The lesson was a success! The math activity was engaging for all students and provided a positive and inclusive experience for Derrick.

Pause and Reflect

- What ways can you use the strengths of your students, resources or events in the community, and different learning environments to increase student engagement?

REMIXed: Empower Students and Families

Building and maintaining strong relationships with our students and families means practitioners must be open and acknowledge every kind of family system, which could include "fathers, mothers, grandparents, aunts, uncles, siblings, foster parents, legal guardians, and others who serve in primary care roles for a child with a disability" (Pearson et al., 2021, p. 131). No matter what kind of family and support network exists, it is critical to uplift families, especially for those who identify with multiple minoritized sociocultural identities. As you have learned throughout this text, these groups have historically less positionality within the American public school system and educators should be given the time and resources to learn more about the families of their students and collaborate with them to center their voices. That way they feel empowered to make suggestions and contribute to the learning environment.

Families, especially those with children with complex needs, need to understand the tiers of support that exist in their child's school and the process of special education (e.g., IEPs and evaluations). One way to help families navigate through this process is to assist them with understanding the terminology within special education. Hundreds of acronyms are used within the sphere of special education. It is important that special education teachers, including other school staff, convey the language within IEPs and evaluations so families understand the special education process. Families can then make decisions that best support the beliefs, values, and hopes they have for their child. This section provides some strategies to empower socioculturally diverse students and their families.

Empower Strategy #1: Consider the Language Used in the IEP

The purpose of the IEP is to provide a platform for empowerment and collaboration among teachers, parents, administrators, and related service providers to enhance educational outcomes for all students receiving special education services. When students are identified by how many suspensions they've received, how many days of school they've missed, or how many times they've been sent to the principal's office, we have to think about how language and attitude are playing a role in shaping our beliefs about students, especially those who are of the global majority and have disabilities. Our students' most important identity is who they are as human beings. Changing deficit mindsets into asset-based thinking begins with changing the language used to identify our students and create their narratives.

IEPs are extremely important documents for communicating the services a school needs to provide the student. The individuals involved in developing IEPs need to pool knowledge, experience, and commitment to design an educational program to help the student be involved in and progress in the general curriculum (IDEA, 2004). How a student is conveyed in their IEPs can influence attitudes and beliefs about the student.

Though IEPs should be strengths-driven, too often the language used within IEPs portrays students in negative ways. For example, consider a student classified with an emotional behavioral disorder (EBD). Their IEP describes them according to these behaviors: refusal to follow directions, lack of cooperation skills with peers, and challenges with completing assigned academic work. What if the classroom teacher positioned this student as a leader in the classroom and gave them a classroom job or provided opportunities for voice and choice of how to show their understanding of assignments? "Flipping the script" of how students show up can make their perceived weaknesses into areas of strength. In a student's IEP, a present-level statement could include how this student has used their qualities—taking the lead and a desire for autonomy with learning—by channeling them into assets that benefit the classroom.

Pause and Reflect

- Reflect about how language can contribute to deficit mindsets. How has language played a role in shaping some of your beliefs?
- Reflect on how the way in which a student is conveyed in their IEP can influence attitudes and beliefs about the student. How do you ensure you write IEPs focused on students' positives and strengths?

Empower Strategy #2: Provide Opportunities for Student-Led IEP Meetings

Student-led IEP meetings are when students lead their IEP meetings and advocate for themselves by providing input and sharing options for what helps them learn. See chapter 2 for examples of socioculturally sustaining person-centered planning and see table 9.1 for examples of questions for high school IEP meetings.

Table 9.1. Examples of Questions for Student-Led IEP Meetings

- How is your IEP and special education support helping you succeed in school?
- How is your IEP and special education support inhibiting your progress at school?
- What are your strengths?
- What classes are you interested in taking?
- What classes/school tasks do you like or dislike?
- What type of education or vocational training would you like to consider for your future after graduation?
- Would you like options for assistive technology (AT) to be more independent?
- Describe how you view yourself as a student.
- What are you good at?
- What is challenging for you?
- Describe what kind of assistance you need to be successful at school, home, and/or in the community.

Empower Strategy #3: Build Relationships, Collaborate, and Communicate

Sometimes empowering families does not come easily because of the historical treatment of certain communities. It may be hard for a family to trust a system that has caused them trauma in the past. In order to build strong relationships with families, it is essential to create spaces for healing. **Active listening** is one strategy that can help individuals feel valued and heard. "Deeply listening helps create relationships and moves us closer . . . not listening creates fragmentation, and fragmentation always causes more suffering" (Aguilar, 2013, p. 156). One way to integrate active listening is through a "dyad," where two people participate in a structured conversation geared toward sharing thoughts, experiences, and beliefs about education and personal identity (Aguilar, 2013).

Another way to build strong relationships and communication is to choose "themes" to connect with families "for their potential resonance with the lived experiences of families, many of whom were first-generation immigrants with multicultural backgrounds and multilingual practices, such as names, dreams, and journeys" (Chambers Cantrell et al., 2022, p. 37). Table 9.2 includes questions for families.

Table 9.2. Examples of Theme Questions

Describe any traditional practices, routines, and rituals that you'd like your child to participate in at school.
How does your child best learn?
What kind of skills does your child have that would be helpful to recognize at school?

Some school districts have special education advisory committees or affinity groups that help build connections between families and give families opportunities to voice concerns, celebrate the schools' successes and programming, and create a community for support outside of the school setting.

The US Department of Education, Office for Civil Rights (2022), issued a fact sheet to remind districts that schools must continue to provide free appropriate public education (FAPE) despite the COVID-19 pandemic. Although the guidance emphasized the importance of following this requirement, it also provided flexibility for schools to provide services virtually or through a hybrid learning model. Virtual meetings are now seen as an effective tool for providing specialized instruction and related services, as well as for conducting IEP meetings (Nieves, 2020). This shift to virtual meetings has been embraced by many families who find them more accessible, but the benefits of virtual meetings are not limited to families. They have also prompted practitioners to rethink how they provide student services and support. As a result, online schools that deliver special education services can now reach students who were previously unable to access these resources.

REMIXed Strategy: Make Meaningful and Relevant Learning Environments

When focusing on socioculturally sustaining practices, it is important to create meaningful and relevant learning environments by first establishing strong relationships between practitioners, students, and families. When practitioners establish positive relationships with students, they convey, "I see you, I hear you, I like you, and I believe in you" (Schaefer Whitby et al., 2021, p. 161). However, academic rigor and maintaining high student expectations go beyond building strong relationships (Hammond, 2015).

Once these relationships are in place, we can move on to the next step: creating learning partnerships. Learning partnerships provide the foundation for a dynamic and relevant learning environment that emphasizes student ownership of their learning and a sense of efficacy in the process (Hammond, 2015). This approach emphasizes a balance between student responsibility for learning and the level of support provided by the practitioner (Kieran & Anderson, 2019). Ultimately, practitioners can use this foundation to create a student-centered learning environment where the teacher "provide[s] feedback in ways that affirm the student's capacity to learn yet is honest in pinpointing where he is in relation to his goal and offers concrete steps for improving" (Hammond, 2015, p. 106). In addition, the practitioner can select curriculum, provide effective instruction, and develop learning activities relevant to students' sociocultural identities and experiences with high rigor.

When utilizing lesson plans that include evidence-based learning strategies, technology, and higher-order thinking, practitioners need to consider how sociocultural diversity affects the classroom environment. If the environment and curriculum are not socioculturally sustaining, we can assume that barriers will continue to perpetuate low academic performance for students from diverse backgrounds (Harkins Monaco et al., 2021). This section provides some strategies to ensure that your lesson plans and strategies are meaningful and relevant for students who are socioculturally diverse.

Meaningful and Relevant Strategy #1: Utilize Student Media and Content

Practitioners can create a more meaningful learning environment by incorporating their students' created media, artwork, visuals, and academic exemplars into classroom spaces. While featuring students' artwork has been a traditional practice in classrooms for generations, it is particularly beneficial for students from traditionally marginalized backgrounds and sociocultural identities who may not have had the opportunity. In chapter 1, we discussed the limitations of disabled representation in art, and in chapter 3 we talked about the importance of highlighting the work of Deaf artists of the global majority. The classroom is one space to combat those kinds of intersectional limitations. Although not all classrooms have students who have disabilities, teachers can still use their space as a "canvas" that allows students to express who they are, providing the artists with the opportunity to share their multilayered identities.

Figure 9.3. Canvas Example: Self-Identity
Source: Adapted from Odima, 2023a.

Consider having students participate in a unique project centered on self-identity inspired by the photographic artistry of Wing Young Huie, a well-known photographer based in Minnesota, as illustrated in figure 9.3. Huie has been actively involved in several outreach programs that teach photography to students. He has also collaborated "with students around the country using photography to challenge cultural preconceptions to get beyond the surface and help people connect more deeply. . . . Wing has been photographing the everyday realities of our complex and changing cultural landscape" (Asian American Press, 2016, para 2). By capturing the everyday realities of our constantly evolving cultural landscape, Huie's work provides a platform for students to express their true identities and dispel misconceptions others may have of them (Espeland, 2018). The photograph in figure 9.3 depicts students who participated in this project.

Meaningful and Relevant Strategy #2: Utilize Critical Thinking Activities

Practitioners can create a more meaningful and relevant learning environment by using strategies that require students to develop critical thinking skills. For students with disabilities and for those who are multilingual learners, heterogeneous groups may be the best way to learn these concepts (Artzi et al., 2022). Heterogeneous groups are small groups of students with a wide range of abilities, competencies, and diverse backgrounds with the academic content or skill being taught.

A great way to incorporate heterogeneous groups is by using **Socratic Seminars**. "The purpose of a Socratic Seminar is to achieve a deeper understanding of the ideas and values in a text. In the seminar, participants systematically question and examine issues and principles related to particular content and articulate different points-of-view" (Northwest Association for Biomedical Research, n.d., p. 105). By participating in the conversation, students can express their own meaning through active listening, interpretation, and analysis (Northwest Association for Biomedical Research, n.d.). Socratic Seminars can include students of all abilities if the appropriate accommodations and scaffolding are in place. Moreover, this activity also promotes inclusivity since students are asked to work together to support their claims. "In a Socratic Seminar, the participants carry the burden of responsibility for the quality of the discussion. . . . Students are encouraged to think out loud and to exchange ideas openly while examining ideas in a rigorous, thoughtful manner" (Northwest Association for Biomedical Research, n.d., p. 106).

Another strategy that positions the teacher as a facilitator in learning is having students in Philosophical Chairs. **Philosophical Chairs** is an activity that proposes a controversial idea or topic to students. Students gather in groups according to their topic and perspective and present arguments supporting their viewpoints. After presenting, students have the option to switch groups. This activity encourages students to practice active listening, share their opinions, and experience "visual representation of the ideologies in the room" (Germán & Paris, 2021, p. 100). This exercise is "a versatile way to get students speaking and listening to one another. It is a student-centered strategy that can be used in any content area around many topics. It is set up like a debate—and one explicit objective is for students to be open to 'changing their minds'" (Fletcher, 2022, para 1). Activities like these can promote belonging because everyone is involved in the discussion, and students work together to convey their perspectives.

Meaningful and Relevant Strategy #3: Support Higher-Order Thinking

Practitioners can create more meaningful and relevant learning environments by positioning themselves as facilitators and incorporating various higher-level thinking activities with their students. Too many disabled students are left out of activities that utilize metacognitive skills because it is assumed they do not have the ability to perform the tasks. As discussed throughout this text, Universal Design for Learning (UDL) is a great example of how students can perform complex tasks because various tools and strategies are being utilized to represent the information. UDL allows for engagement in analyzing and synthesizing the information and providing different ways for students to share their understanding. Interweaving these kinds of strategies gives students more control over their learning. For example, when introducing a philosophical topic like "Who is responsible for combating climate change?" practitioners in a co-taught lesson could show their class two visually engaging videos on climate change, with one incorporating sociocultural perspectives about sustainable ways to combat climate change (Peni, 2023). Through these discussions, students can share their experiences, strategize about innovative practices, and advocate for human rights and social justice.

Co-teaching and collaboration between practitioners create classroom environments that are more accessible for students. Using different models for co-teaching can help facilitate different modes of learning and give students various ways to engage with the academic content at their ability level. If you plan to use a co-teaching strategy, with the appropriate amount of planning time and professional development around co-teaching strategies, you may have an opportunity to better focus your strengths in the classroom and provide opportunities for learning from your co-teacher.

REMIXed Strategy: Innovate

It is important to innovate for students. Innovation in education can be defined as "desirable and doable changes in school teaching and learning that mediate individual, collective and organizational development, whether triggered by new pedagogical ideas, new technologies, or new collaborative relations between the school and the world outside" (Sannino & Nocon, 2008, p. 325). In terms of ways to support students, innovative practices can involve a range of improvements, such as using an alternative space for small group instruction or integrating UDL within your lesson plans, or it can include trying out a new technology that engages students in math, reading, or writing. Innovation can be applied to any part of a student's school day, and it does not always have to be completely original or successful the first time you use it. For example, innovating a student's experience at school could be facilitating student-centered programs where students feel seen and valued, like creating a Black Student Union or Girls on the Run Chapter (Davis, 2023; Girls on the Run, 2022). Another example is to ask students to use social media (e.g., Instagram, TikTok, YouTube) to search for potential job pathways or life skills they're interested in learning about, instead of conducting traditional research. The most important thing is that innovation allows for a flexible classroom environment that meets socioculturally diverse needs of students. This section provides some strategies to empower and create flexible classroom environments.

Innovative Strategy #1: Create a Flexible Classroom Environment

One innovative strategy educators can utilize is creating a flexible classroom environment. The traditional setup of student desks is lined up in rows,

U-shaped, or clustered configurations (Bluteau et al., 2022). The problem is that these arrangements are rarely changed or adjusted based on the lesson's learning goals or the student's learning preference (Bluteau et al., 2022). By implementing a flexible classroom layout, educators can provide a range of work surfaces and seating options of varying sizes, heights, and body positions. This allows students to choose their preferred learning environments according to their needs or wants, and to work at their own pace. As a result, students become more independent and take control of their own learning, and they gain valuable skills that can be applied in other settings. Moreover, easily movable furniture in the classroom enables educators to reconfigure the environment to suit different individual or group activities, further promoting a dynamic and adaptable learning space. Overall, a flexible classroom layout creates an environment that fosters independence and decision-making skills while also allowing for adjustments that accommodate a variety of learning needs. Even better, different configurations can facilitate different learning activities and higher-level thinking in the classroom (Bluteau et al., 2022, p. 2).

Flexible seating may be a great strategy to help students with improving learning, broadening well-being, and increasing engagement in the classroom. Sometimes students already require flexible seating as accommodation. Options for seating could include sitting at tables that are lowered closer to the ground, on pillows on the floor at desks, or on wobble chairs rather than chairs with four legs. There are also standing desks. These options are conducive to learning because students can determine what works best for their learning stamina. Although there could be challenges with this kind of flexibility, it has been found that "this type of classroom arrangement allows for implementing teaching practices that can be described as 'flexible,' that is, student-centered, differentiated, and collaborative" (Bluteau et al., 2022, p. 1).

Moreover, it is essential to provide students an opportunity to move, explore, and interact with their physical environment because research positively affects their physical, cognitive, emotional, and social development (Bluteau et al., 2022). Redefining expectations for body movement can be beneficial for students with disabilities, particularly for neurodivergent students, who may benefit from infusing movement within instruction, increasing peer interaction and classroom engagement. The positive impact of movement also extends beyond the activity itself, as individuals in one study were able to generalize positive social behavior outside the classroom (Bhattacharya et al., 2015).

Not only is the classroom environment important, how the student interacts and communicates with their teacher and other peers is as well. As discussed in chapter 3, Deaf students cannot share their culture if they are not given the means to communicate their thoughts and feelings, or if there isn't a space to foster Deaf culture and community in their schools. Other examples include students who need a visual schedule to learn the routines, rituals, and transitions during the day or those who use visuals to communicate their needs, identify their feelings, or select self-regulation strategies.

Table 9.3. Lesson Plan Example

Lesson Plan Template through a "REMIXed Approach" (EBP, UDL, and Socioculturally Sustaining Practices)	
Title of Lesson: Analyzing marathon racing data to practice multidigit multiplication and division	**Teacher:** General Education Teacher **Grade Level:** 4th grade
Lesson Objective: Students will calculate time, speed, and distance using results from a local running race and their racing results. **Language Objective:** Students will learn and apply vocabulary words such as "measure," "estimate," and "average."	**Standard Assessed:** Students can divide multi-digit whole numbers by one- or two-digit numbers using different strategies (e.g., repeated subtraction, mental strategies, partial quotients, commutative, associative, and distributive properties).
Pre-requisite Skills: Students have strategies to do basic fact calculations.	
Student Profile	**IEP Information**
Student Name: Derrick **Disability:** Emotional or Behavioral Disorder **Strengths and Interests (Social and Human Rights Model):** • Loves to read and use technology • Exhibits strong creativity and imagination • Actively engages in classroom discussion with enthusiasm • Proficient in verbal communication, able to articulate thoughts and ideas effectively • Demonstrates critical-thinking skills by asking insightful questions • Highly motivated and willing to put in hard work **Background Information:** • Seeks and desires adult approval and conversations with adults **Sociocultural Information:** • Parents are from Venezuela • English is not first language • Born in America • Values religion • Family focused (collectivism)	**Social Emotional Goal #1:** Derrick will increase structured group participation from 50–80 percent participation in cooperation strategies, such as communicating and collaborating with peers as measured by teacher observational data collection by next IEP. **Math Goal #1:** Derrick will increase accuracy in completing multidigit multiplication and division math problems using concrete, representational, and abstract strategies from 40–70 percent as measured by math exams by the next IEP. **How the Intersectionality of Derrick's Sociocultural Identities Affects Access to General Education Curriculum:** The intersection of Derrick's collectivism and his impairment increases his sensitivity to environmental stimuli. Derrick prefers to work directly with his teachers which means he is not motivated to complete work independently or with his peers. This looks like blurting out answers or interrupting, difficulty with turn-taking, and adhering to others' personal space/boundaries. Derrick actively and enthusiastically engages in classroom discussions. He is proficient in both English and Spanish and has strengths in critical-thinking skills. He is motivated to work closely with adults and thrives on their positive feedback.

Pause and Reflect

- What are ways Derrick's teacher can teach toward the intersectionality of all of Derrick's sociocultural identities and needs?
- How could this kind of teaching help all students in Derrick's class?
- How can Derrick's IEP be written to use asset-based language that centers the intersectionality of Derrick's sociocultural identities?

Socioculturally Sustaining Practice of Focus (REMIXed Education Approach)

- **Research Evidence-Based Strategies**
  Opportunities to Respond (OTR)
  Behavior Specific Praise (BSP)
  PreCorrection (PC)
  Other _____
- **Empower**
  Identify strengths
  Collaboration
  Communication
  Other _____
- **Make Meaningful and Relevant Connections**
  Utilize student created content
  Critical thinking
  UDL strategies
  Other _____
- **Innovate**
  Classroom environment
  Graphic organizers
  Flexible assessments
  Self-monitoring
  Other _____
- **eXamine**
  Cultural differences
  Backgrounds and experiences
  Nonbiased assessment(s) methods
  Other _____

Systematic and Explicit Instruction

Introduction/Anticipatory Set: At the beginning of the lesson, students will watch a video of a paralympic marathon race that took place last year. This will help them understand what a marathon is and identify the characteristics of professional athletes. They will also acknowledge how individuals compete, including wheelchair racers, blind runners, and individuals with other physical disabilities.

I Do:	We Do:	You Do:
In this part of the lesson, the teacher will explain that the lesson will focus on learning algorithms for multidigit division and subtraction using the skills students practiced last week. The teacher will explain the rationale of why it is important to learn these algorithms by providing real examples.	In this part of the lesson, the teacher will display the finish times of previous running races in various ways. This will help students see the diversity of runners who compete in racing competitions, including those who have disabilities and those who travel from different regions and countries to compete.	In this part of the lesson, students will analyze the data of runners from a local race and record their own racing data. Students can record their own results or results from a peer in class. The teacher will use **Behavior Specific Praise** to reinforce desired behaviors shown while peers are partnering and sharing their results.

(continued)

Table 9.3. *Continued*

I Do:	We Do:	You Do:
To ensure students stay on task, the teacher will use **precorrection** to provide prompts and reinforcement for expected social and academic behaviors. While the teacher displays the data, they will use **Opportunity to Respond** strategy to increase engagement.	Students will be provided access to a digital stopwatch app and graphic organizers to calculate their race times.	**Closing:** At the end of the lesson, each student will share the results of their running data with a digital annotation app. They can record their voice, a video, or write their answers.
Universal Design for Learning Examples		
UDL-Representation	**UDL-Action and Expression**	**UDL-Engagement**
Display finish times of previous running races in a variety of ways. Students will see the sociocultural diversity of runners who compete in racing competitions.	Provide students access to a digital stopwatch app and graphic organizers to calculate their race times. Students will create a rubric to assess their understanding using strategies to compute multi-digit division and multiplication problems.	Students will analyze the data of runners from a local race and record their own racing data. Students can record their own results or results from a peer in class
Materials Students will need tablet devices to access the lesson, record time, and submit their independent assignment		
Literary References: MATH Life Curriculum: Multi-Digit Multiplication and Division Strategies		

Source: Adapted from Nandakumar et al., 2022, and Artzi et al., 2022.

Special education practitioners need to think about the tasks students are required to do during the school day and the barriers they face. **Assistive technology** (AT) can give students the capability to access instructional content, but this also means practitioners need to believe that AT is a helpful way for students to exhibit self-determination. Text-to-speech tools will provide students with AT support in writing. AT tools such as a standing desk, table stand, or fitness tracker can be helpful for students who have active bodies and need to move to learn and can also provide helpful feedback to students (Odima, 2023b). Students can also choose what AT works best for them. To be fully inclusive, the classroom environment needs to contain avenues of communication through apps, devices, visuals, gestures, and visual schedules. In addition, seating, positioning, and mobility accommodations should always be present in classrooms. It is also important to lead with an asset-based mindset, giving students opportunities to be independent.

Innovative Strategy #2: Utilize Graphic Organizers

Instructional supports such as graphic organizers can lead to positive outcomes for socioculturally diverse students, especially if students are explicitly taught how to use them for particular skills (Artzi et al., 2022). "Alongside explanations, visual prompts (e.g., gestures, color coding, images) can provide additional support" (Artzi et al., 2022, p. 1) and help students organize information by creating mental models. This strategy is even more effective when combined with innovative technology tools such as annotation apps that allow students to use visuals, words, and other symbols to express thoughts and understanding of the content and practice higher-order thinking skills.

*Innovative Strategy #3: Be Flexible with Assessments
and Integrate Student Self-Monitoring*

Another innovative strategy educators can utilize is flexibility in assessments and self-monitoring. One form of assessment is called **progress monitoring**. Students have more academic success when their teachers use progress monitoring data to inform their instruction (Roehrig et al., 2008). Using progress monitoring methods, like curriculum-based measurement (CBM), to make decisions helps identify potential challenges students are encountering with learning and when to implement support. The result of gathering weekly or biweekly data on students' progress can help identify students who need intervention and determine the efficacy of instructional programs and techniques being applied (Roehrig et al., 2008). For example, teachers can use student CBM data, including achievement tests, informal assessments, academic observations, and baseline data; they can make instructional decisions based on whether or not the student is responding to an intervention (Roehrig et al., 2008). Keep in mind that not every assessment is responsive to sociocultural diversity, nor do the examples on assessments represent all intersections or all identities of students.

Self-monitoring (Bruhn et al., 2015) is a helpful tool for students and gets them excited about their work. A practitioner could share the student's CBM data with the student, show how much progress they've made, celebrate successes, and identify areas for improvement. Sharing this information can be impactful for the student because it can help create autonomy in their learning, especially if there are discussions about what strategies help. A student can create a tailored plan of tools that may help them improve their progress. For example, a student can use video-sharing technology to share their individualized plan with their families. They can use SMART goals (e.g., Specific, Measurable, Achievable, Relevant, and Time-bound) to define parameters that ensure their goals are attainable within a reasonable time frame (Day & Tosey, 2011). See figure 9.4 for an example of a student who wrote a SMART goal using their CBM reading data to create their own success plan for increasing their literacy skills.

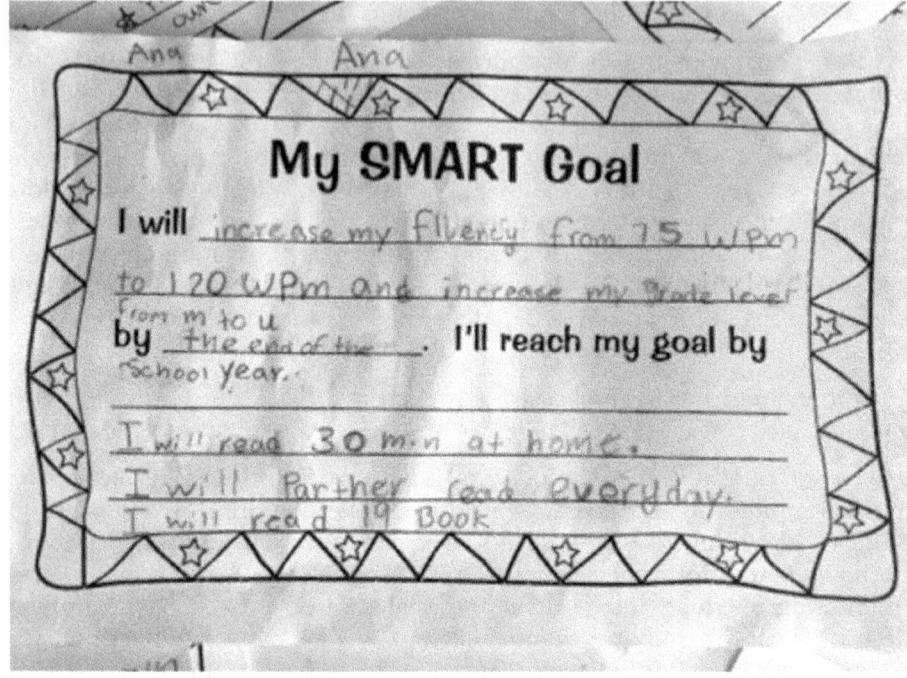

Figure 9.4. SMART Goal Example

Innovative Strategy #4: Utilize Disruptive Technology

Another innovative strategy educators can utilize is disruptive technology. Disruptive technology refers to groundbreaking technological advancements that challenge traditional methods and significantly transform industries, markets, firms, societal norms, and institutions (Schuelke-Leech, 2018). In the context of education, disruptive technology entails the adoption of cutting-edge tools and resources that revolutionize instructional approaches, creating new opportunities for teaching and learning (Crittenden et al., 2019). Disruptive technologies deeply "ingrain the conceptual, inquiry, critical thinking, creativity, and integrative learning skills" needed to enhance learning (Crittenden et al., 2019, p. 5). One tool that will revolutionize education is **artificial intelligence** (AI). AI is an advanced technology that utilizes algorithms to enable machines to make predictions, diagnoses, recommendations, and decisions (Chen et al., 2022). With the increasing use of AI in education, the number of published studies in the field has also increased. While there have been few large-scale reviews conducted to investigate the various aspects of AI in special education comprehensively, Chen et al. (2022) reviewed 4,519 publications from 2000 to 2019 related to AI topics in education. They found that there is growing interest in using AI for educational purposes. Emerging areas include "intelligent tutoring systems for special education; natural language processing for language education; educational robots for AI education; educational data mining for performance prediction" (p. 28).

AI programs are increasingly being used to support students with disabilities by generating lesson plans tailored to their individual needs. AI can (a) analyze the needs of the student and create materials that are accessible, engaging, and adapted to their learning objectives; and (b) provide teachers with automated assessments to monitor the progress of the student and ensure their lessons are meeting the student's needs. Not only does this make it easier to track the student's progress, it also increases student engagement.

Moreover, AI technology can be used to create individualized lesson plans, but the process can be complex and difficult for teachers to understand. There is also the possibility of not adequately addressing the individual student's needs, leading to a lack of accessibility. Additionally, a lack of resources may also limit the ability of teachers to utilize AI-generated lesson plans. While the incorporation of AI into the development of lesson plans and activities for disabled students holds promise, there is still a need on the part of the educator to understand AI's limitations and to use critical thinking and analysis to ensure that the material meets the needs of each student. Furthermore, we need to be mindful of whether the data and algorithms derived by AI are biased (Utecht & Friedman, 2023). This is particularly important when thinking from a racial equity lens. It's important for educators, school leadership, and community members to ask questions like, "Where are the data being used by the AI coming from? Are individuals who are socioculturally diverse represented?"

REMIXed Strategy: Examine

When focusing on socioculturally sustaining practices, it is important to examine students' sociocultural backgrounds and strengths and have an asset-based mindset. Disability identification and interventions primarily focus on what students cannot do rather than what might be possible, often undermining "the competence, mental health, and functioning of both the children and their families" (Mahmic et al., 2021, p. 1). This section provides some strategies to encourage educators to closely examine the "assets and strengths from students' backgrounds, values, beliefs, and experiences, and apply them to instruction and intervention" (Artzi et al., 2022, p. 190).

Examine Strategy #1: Examine, Review,
and Implement Nondiscriminatory Assessment

The first socioculturally sustaining strategy is to examine, review, and implement nondiscriminatory assessment procedures for special education evaluations. IDEA states that students referred for special education services cannot be identified based on their sociocultural identities. However, traditional, published, norm-referenced tests may lack diversity in the norm sample and contain sociocultural bias in test format and items (International Test Commission, 2019). We suggest special education evaluations are done best when completed by **transdisciplinary teams**. Transdisciplinary teams are the most collaborative, cooperative, coordinated, and integrative model (Gargiulo & Bouck, 2021). In a transdisciplinary team, the roles are shared beyond the boundaries of the professionals, so as to maximize communication and reciprocity among team members. The group's job is to consider the student's specific needs and what the student requires. For example, members of the team should be conducting comprehensive interviews with the student's family to help determine their approach to an evaluation.

Transdisciplinary teams can also help schools recognize the value of multilingualism by conducting native language evaluations of linguistically diverse learners. These evaluations assess students' communication skills in all languages, including English, to identify strengths and weaknesses. By comparing these results to those of other students with similar age and language backgrounds, it is considered less biased because more factors that may influence language acquisition are taken into account, including the length of time a student has been learning a language and whether the language was learned sequentially or simultaneously.

Examine Strategy #2: Examine Sociocultural Differences with Assessment

Another socioculturally sustaining strategy is to examine and consider sociocultural aspects with the student's academic, behavioral, social, and functional performance. Transdisciplinary teams can use several strategies during the evaluation process. For example, districts can hire interpreters who are proficient in both the family's language and special education terminology (Soto & Yu, 2014). Interpreters and practitioners should receive frequent and ongoing training for best practices for working with multilingual families (Cheatham & Ostrosky, 2011). If districts don't have language-specific interpreters, check your state's parent advocacy coalition for educational rights or your state's Disability Law Center. They may have resources for interpreters to attend IEP meetings.

Examine Strategy #3: Examine Sociocultural Factors during IEP Process

The current education system often approaches disability from a deficit mindset. This mentality reinforces false narratives that limit opportunities for students. It's important to consider that socioculturally sustaining practices are asset-based and anti-racist because "despite the emergence of socio-ecological, strength-based, and capacity-building approaches, care for children with a disability remains primarily grounded in a deficit-based perspective" (Mahmic et al., 2021, p. 1). An IEP is preserved through a document, or comprehensive roadmap, for delivering services to address identified needs mentioned in the evaluation. According to IDEA (2004), the IEP provides an opportunity for families, teachers, related service providers, administration, and the student to work together for the benefit of the student and evolves over time. The idea of an IEP is that it is a "cornerstone of a quality education for each child with a disability" (IDEA, 2004). Since the IEP is a truly individualized document, it is critical that IEPs include strength-based and asset-based statements to provide a game plan of what considerations should be made about the student to foster the most growth.

SUMMARY

Students with disabilities face many challenges in the educational system, but these challenges can be disrupted by using effective frameworks that include socioculturally sustaining practices implemented with fidelity. Practitioners must work to identify the challenges students face while examining their roles and personal biases that can impact the educational outcomes for traditionally marginalized students. These tools should be used to drive instruction and intervention. To build strong relationships with our students and eliminate the opportunity gaps in our schools, it is not enough to eliminate ineffective practices and use the "good ones."

Educators can fall victim to binary bias, seeking clarity and closure by simplifying complex ideas and situations into two categories (Grant, 2021). While this type of perspective can help educators understand the overwhelming complexity of our school system and the forces that perpetuate inequities, it does very little to address the root causes of the problem. Therefore, we must acknowledge that the inequities in our schools are multidimensional, and our methodologies must be as well. We must continually challenge our implicit biases, acknowledge our sociocultural positionality compared to our students, and implement multiple models shown to support our students on a schoolwide scale.

"The practices we use not only characterize our students' community, but they also improvise and redefine them, sometimes slightly and sometimes drastically" (Chambers Cantrell et al., 2022, p. 59). Building on this idea, the REMIXed approach proposed in this chapter aims to continuously revise, modify, and innovate to support students with diverse sociocultural identities. The tools and strategies presented here provide a plethora of ways to advocate for social justice and provide a continuum of services for all students.

REFERENCES

Aguilar, E. (2013). *The art of coaching: Effective strategies for school transformation.* Jossey-Bass.

Artzi, L., Hsin, L. B., Sanford, A. K., Brown, J. E., & Guin, S. (2022). Meeting the language needs of emergent multilingual students at risk for learning disabilities through multitiered systems of support. *Learning Disabilities Research and Practice, 37*(3), 189–203. https://doi.org/10.1111/ldrp.12288

Asian America Press. (2016). Photographer Wing Young Huie working with high school students and teachers. https://aapress.com/2016/07/photographer-wing-young-huie-working-with-high-school-students-and-teachers/

Bhattacharya, A., Gelsomini, M., Pérez-Fuster, P., Abowd, G., & Rozga, A. (2015). Designing motion-based activities to engage students with autism in classroom settings. *Proceedings of IDC 2015: The 14th International Conference on Interaction Design and Children,* 69–78. https://doi.org/10.1145/2771839.2771847

Blazar, D. (2021). *Teachers of color, culturally responsive teaching, and student outcomes: Experimental evidence from the random assignment of teachers to classes.* EdWorkingPaper No. 21-501.

Bluteau, J., Aubenas, S., & Dufour, F. (2022). Influence of flexible classroom seating on the wellbeing and mental health of upper elementary school students: A gender analysis. *Frontiers in Psychology, 13,* 821227. https://doi.org/10.3389/fpsyg.2022.821227

Bruhn, A., Mcdaniel, S., & Kreigh, C. (2015). Self-monitoring interventions for students with behavior problems: A systematic review of current research. *Behavioral Disorders, 40*(2), 102–21. https://doi.org/10.17988/BD-13-45.1

Chambers Cantrell, S., Walker-Dalhouse, D., & Lazar, A. M. (2022). *Culturally sustaining literacy pedagogies: Honoring students' heritages, literacies, and languages.* Teachers College Press.

Cheatham, G. A., & Ostrosky, M. M. (2011). Whose expertise?: An analysis of advice giving in early childhood parent-teacher conferences. *Journal of Research in Childhood Education, 25*(1), 24–44.

Chen, X., Zou, D., Xie, H., Cheng, G., & Liu, C. (2022). Two decades of Artificial Intelligence in education: Contributors, collaborations, research topics, challenges, and future directions. *Educational Technology & Society, 25*(1), 28–47. https://doi.org/10.30191/ETS.202201_25(1).0003

Crenshaw, K. (1989). Demarginalizing the intersection of race and sex: A black feminist critique of antidiscrimination doctrine, feminist theory and antiracist politics. *University of Chicago Legal Forum, 1989*(1), 139–67.

Crittenden, W. F., Biel, I. K., & Lovely III, W. A. (2019). Embracing digitalization: Student learning and new technologies. *Journal of Marketing Education, 41*(1), 5–14.

Crouch, R., Keys, C. B., & McMahon, S. D. (2014). Student-teacher relationships matter for school inclusion: School belonging, disability, and school transitions. *Journal of Prevention & Intervention in the Community, 42*(1), 20–30.

Davis, A. (Host). (2023, April 13). Reimagining education: How leaders are upping equity and support. [Audio podcast episode]. In MPR News with Angela Davis. https://www.mprnews.org/episode/2023/04/12/reimagining-education

Day, T., & Tosey, P. (2011). Beyond SMART? A new framework for goal setting. *Curriculum Journal, 22*(4), 515–34. https://doi.org/10.1080/09585176.2011.627213

Espeland, P. (2018, August 21). Street photographer Wing Young Huie on his life, his work, and his new McKnight Distinguished Artist Award. MinnPost: Arts and Culture: Artscape. https://www.minnpost.com/artscape/2018/08/street-photographer-wing-young-huie-his-life-his-work-and-his-new-mcknight-distingu/

Fish, R. E. (2019). Teacher race and racial disparities in special education. *Remedial and Special Education, 40*(4), 213–24. https://doi.org/10.1177/0741932518810434

Fletcher, J. (2022). A framework for whole-class discussions. Edutopia. https://www.edutopia.org/article/framework-whole-class-discussions/

Gargiulo, R. M., & Bouck, E. C. (2021). *Special education in contemporary society: An introduction to exceptionality.* 7th ed. Sage.

Gay, G. (2002). Preparing for culturally responsive teaching. *Journal of Teacher Education, 53*(2), 106–16.

Geddes, H. (2003). Attachment and the child in school. Part I: Attachment theory and the "dependent" child. *Emotional and Behavioural Difficulties, 8*(3), 231–42. https://doi.org/10.1177/13632752030083006

Germán, L. E., & Paris, D. (2021). *Textured teaching: A framework for culturally sustaining practices.* Heinemann.

Girls on the Run. (2022). Our impact. Girls on the Run. https://www.girlsontherun.org/what-we-do/our-impact/

Gomez-Najarro, J. (2023). Identity-blind intervention: Examining teachers' attention to social identity in the context of response to intervention. *Urban Education, 58*(4), 645–74. https://doi.org/10.1177/0042085919860561

Grant, A. (2021). *Think again: The power of knowing what you don't know.* Penguin.

Green, A. L., & Stormont, M. (2018). Creating culturally responsive and evidence-based lessons for diverse learners with disabilities. *Intervention in School and Clinic, 53*(3), 138–45. https://doi.org/10.1177/1053451217702114

Gross, J. T., Stern, J. A., Brett, B. E., & Cassidy, J. (2017). The multifaceted nature of prosocial behavior in children: Links with attachment theory and research. *Social Development, 26*(4), 661–78.

Hammond, Z. L. (2015). *Culturally Responsive Teaching and the brain: Promoting authentic engagement and rigor among culturally and linguistically diverse students.* Corwin.

Hamre, B. K., & Pianta, R. C. (2001). Early teacher-child relationships and the trajectory of children's school outcomes through eighth grade. *Child Development, 72*(2), 625–38. https://doi.org/10.1111/1467-8624.00301

Harkins Monaco, E. A., Fuller, M., & Stansberry Brusnahan, L. L. (2021). *Diversity, autism and developmental disabilities: Guidance for the culturally responsive educator.* Prism Series, 13. Council for Exceptional Children.

Heflinger, C., & Hinshaw, S. (2010). Stigma in child and adolescent mental health services research: Understanding professional and institutional stigmatization of youth with mental health problems and their families. *Administrative Policy Mental Health, 37*(1–2), 61–70.

Individuals with Disabilities Education Act (IDEA), 20 U.S.C. § 1400 (2004) and IDEA 34 U.S.C. § 300.39 (2004), Special Education.

International Test Commission (ITC). (2019). ITC guidelines for the large-scale assessment of linguistically and culturally diverse populations. *International Journal of Testing, 19*(4), 301–36. https://doi.org/10.1080/15305058.2019.1631024

IRIS Center. (2012, 2021). *Classroom behavior management (part 1): Key concepts and foundational practices.* https://iris.peabody.vanderbilt.edu/module/beh1/

Johnson, A. D., Anhalt, K., & Cowan, R. J. (2017). Culturally responsive school-wide positive behavior interventions and supports: A practical approach to addressing disciplinary disproportionality with African-American students. *Multicultural Learning and Teaching, 13*(2). https://doi.org/10.1515/mlt-2017-0013

Kauffman, J. M., Hallahan, D. P., Pullen, P. C., & Badar, J. (2018). *Special education: What it is and why we need it.* Routledge.

Kieran, L., & Anderson, C. (2019). Connecting Universal Design for Learning with Culturally Responsive Teaching. *Education and Urban Society, 51*(9), 1202–16. https://doi.org/10.1177/0013124518785012

King, J., & Darling-Hammond, L. (2018). Opinion: We're not doing enough to support teachers of color. *Hechinger Report.*

Mahmic, S., Kern, M. L., & Janson, A. (2021). Identifying and shifting disempowering paradigms for families of children with disability through a system informed positive psychology approach. *Frontiers in Psychology, 12,* 663640. https://doi.org/10.3389/fpsyg.2021.663640

Merisotis, J. P., & McCarthy, K. (2005). Retention and student success at minority-serving institutions. *New Directions for Institutional Research, 2005*(125), 45–58.

Nandakumar, V., McCree, N., & Green, A. L. (2022). Evidence-based and culturally sustaining practices for diverse students with emotional and behavioral disorders. *Intervention in School and Clinic, 58*(2), 84–91. https://doi-org.ezproxy.stthomas.edu/10.1177/10534512211051073

Nieves, K. (2020). 8 tips for conducting virtual IEP meetings. Edutopia. https://www.edutopia.org/article/8-tips-conducting-virtual-iep-meetings/

Northwest Association For Biomedical Research. (n.d.). *Teaching background: Socratic seminar.* https://www.nwabr.org/sites/default/files/SocSem.pdf

Odima, M. [@martinodimajr]. (2022, April 1). How many thousands of children are sent to the principal's office, suspended, or referred to special education because their cultural . . . (Tweet). X (formerly Twitter.com). https://twitter.com/MartinOdimaJr/status/1510007956703752198

———. (2023a, January 23). Incorporating the intersectional needs of students: Disability, culture and inclusivity in schools (series) [PowerPoint slides]. First Educational Resources.

———. (2023b, February 15). The assistive technology SETT process [PowerPoint slides]. University of St. Thomas.

Office of Special Education and Rehabilitative Services, US Department of Education. (1997). 34 CFR 300.550, 20 U.S.C. § 1412(a)(5).

Ogden, T., & Fixsen, D. L. (2014). Implementation science: A brief overview and a look ahead. *Zeitschrift für Psychologie, 222*(1), 4–11. https://doi:10.1027/2151-2604/a000160

Pearson, J. N., Hamilton, M., & Stansberry Brusnahan, L. L., Hussein D. (2021). Empowering families by utilizing culturally sustaining strategies in the education of children with multi-layered identities. In E. A. Harkins Monaco, L. L. Stansberry Brusnahan, and M. C. Fuller (Eds.), *Diversity, autism, and developmental disabilities: Guidance for the culturally responsive educator.* Prism Series, 13. Council for Exceptional Children.

Peni, M. (2023, January). *The sustainable brilliance of Indigenous design*. [Video]. TED Conferences. https://www.ted.com/talks/manu_peni_the_sustainable_brilliance_of_indigenous_design/c

Ralabate, P., & Nelson, L. L. (2017). *Culturally responsive design for English learners: The UDL approach*. CAST Professional.

Roehrig, A. D., Duggar, S. W., Moats, L., Glover, M., & Mincey, B. (2008). When teachers work to use progress monitoring data to inform literacy instruction: Identifying potential supports and challenges. *Remedial and Special Education, 29*(6), 364–82.

Royer, D. J., Lane, K. L., Dunlap, K. D., & Ennis, R. P. (2019). A systematic review of teacher-delivered behavior-specific praise on K–12 student performance. *Remedial and Special Education, 40*(2), 112–28. https://doi.org/10.1177/0741932517751054

Sannino, A., & Nocon, H. (2008). Special issue editors' introduction: Activity theory and school innovation. *Journal of Educational Change, 9*(4), 325–28.

Sasson, N. J., Faso, D. J., Nugent, J., Lovell, S., Kennedy, D. P., & Grossman, R. B. (2017). Neurotypical peers are less willing to interact with those with autism based on thin slice judgments. *Scientific Reports, 7*, 40700. https://doi.org/10.1038/srep40700

Schaefer Whitby, P. J., Harkins Monaco, E. A., Hill, D., & McNeal, K. (2021). Teaching diverse students with disabilities socio-political consciousness and self-advocacy. In E. A. Harkins Monaco, L. L. Stansberry Brusnahan, & M. C. Fuller (Eds.). *Diversity, autism, and developmental disabilities: Guidance for the culturally responsive educator*. Prism Series, 13. Council for Exceptional Children.

Schuelke-Leech, B.-A. (2018). A model for understanding the orders of magnitude of disruptive technologies. *Technological Forecasting and Social Change, 129*(C), 261–74. https://doi.org/10.1016/j.techfore.2017.09.033y

Soto, G., & Yu, B. (2014). Considerations for the provision of services to bilingual children who use augmentative and alternative communication. *Augmentative and Alternative Communication, 30*(1), 83–92.

Steele, C. (2010). *Whistling Vivaldi: How stereotypes affect us and what we can do*. W. W. Norton.

Taggart, A. (2017). The role of cultural discontinuity in the academic outcomes of Latina/o high school students. *Education and Urban Society, 49*(8), 731–61. https://doi.org/10.1177/0013124516658522

Tyler, K. M., Uqdah, A. L., Dillihunt, M. L., Beatty-Hazelbaker, R., Conner, T., Gadson, N., . . . Stevens, R. (2008). Cultural discontinuity: Toward a quantitative investigation of a major hypothesis in education. *Educational Researcher, 37*(5), 280–97. https://doi:10.3102/0013189X08321459

US Department of Education, Office for Civil Rights. (2022, February). *Providing students with disabilities a free appropriate public education during the COVID-19 pandemic*. https://www2.ed.gov/about/offices/list/ocr/docs/fape-in-covid-19.pdf

Utecht, J., & Friedman, T. (Host). (2023, April 13). Is equity getting the spotlight it deserves in our conversations about AI? [Audio podcast episode no. 269]. Shifting Schools: Conversations for K12 Educators. https://sospodcast.org/269-is-equity-getting-the-spotlight-it-deserves-in-our-conversations-about-ai/

Villegas, A. M., & Irvine, J. J. (2010). Diversifying the teaching force: An examination of major arguments. *Urban Review, 42*, 175–92.

Vilson, J. L. (2016). The need for more teachers of color. *Education Digest, 81*(5), 17.

Wang, M., & Lam, Y. (2017). Evidence-based practice in special education and cultural adaptations: Challenges and implications for research. *Research and Practice for Persons with Severe Disabilities, 42*(1), 53–61.

Will, M. (2022, February 8). Teachers of color are linked to social-emotional, academic gains for all students. *Education Week.* https://www.edweek.org/teaching-learning/teachers-of-color-are-linked-to-social-emotional-academic-gains-for-all-students/2022/02

Zee, M., de Bree, E., Hakvoort, B., & Koomen, H. M. Y. (2020). Exploring relationships between teachers and students with diagnosed disabilities: A multi-informant approach. *Journal of Applied Developmental Psychology, 66,* 101101–101112. https://doi.org/10.1016/j.appdev.2019.101101

PART IV

Social and Cultural Rights Movements That Impact Special Education

CHAPTER 10

Disability Rights: The Impact of Social and Cultural Movements on Special Education

Chapter authors: *Aaron Campbell, Susannah Boyle, Jonte' C. Taylor, Elizabeth A. Harkins Monaco, and Dana Patenaude*

Vignette author: *Cindy Bentley*

Editor: *Elizabeth A. Harkins Monaco*

ABSTRACT

Disabled communities have historically faced oppressive systems that prevent them from fostering a sense of belonging. The purpose of this chapter is to discuss these kinds of oppressive systems across the globe and define disability as a social phenomenon and culture, specifically how it is contextualized through shared [disabled] experiences and cultural expressions (language considerations [ASL, AAC, etc.], using art as activism, etc.). Finally, we will provide an overview of how disability is traditionally approached in schools and special education systems and introduce ways to view disability as a cultural identity in the classroom.

GUIDING QUESTIONS

- What are the systems of oppression that have historically prevented disabled communities from fostering a sense of belonging?
- How can disability be viewed as a social and cultural (global) phenomena?
- How can disability be contextualized through shared experiences and cultural expressions?
- How is disability typically viewed and treated in schools?
- How can disability be viewed as a cultural identity in schools?

KEY TERMS

American National Standards Institute
Americans with Disabilities Act
Architectural Barriers Act
Augmentative and Alternative Communication
Barrier-Free Access Movement
Civil Rights Act of 1964
Civil Rights Movement
Complex Communication Needs
Convention on the Rights of Persons with Disabilities
Cultural Identity
Culture
Disability
Education for All Handicapped Children Act
Eugenics
Human-Rights Approach
Individuals with Disabilities Education Act
Joint Committee on Human Rights
Section 504 of the Rehabilitation Act
Universal Design for Learning

Disabled communities have historically faced oppressive systems that prevent them from fostering a sense of belonging. They continue to experience negative attitudes and exclusion from many areas of society which, in turn, influence their social interactions, emotional well-being, and economic potential, all crucial to fostering a sense of belonging. The social, emotional, and economic ties that accompany a sense of belonging serve as protective factors for managing behavior and provide feelings of security that make an individual more resilient (Theisen-Womersley, 2021). This chapter examines how persons with disabilities are constantly in environments (i.e., home, schools, workplaces, and community) that remind them that they are different and at times unwelcome (University of Waikato, 2019), and how oppression of disabled persons influences their sense of belonging. We discuss the need to feel welcome, appreciated, respected, and valued, and why it is crucial that disabled persons feel they are connected to others who support them in reaching their full potential.

ABLEISM

Systems of oppression of disabled persons have been predicated on **ableism**, which is discrimination based on disabled status (Dunn, 2021). For more about ableism, see chapter 5. According to the World Health Organization (WHO), prejudice, stigma, and discrimination threaten the well-being of persons with disabilities. In healthcare systems, disabled persons face attitude, physical, financial, and communication barriers (WHO, n.d.). These barriers also exist in education systems. Historically, persons with disabilities have been placed in special schools and sometimes separated from their families to be educated in residential facilities isolated from the greater society, if they received education at all (Ravassard, 2022). Disabled persons were seen as having limited functioning (impairment) or limited ability to perform functional activities (deficits) (Disabled World, 2022). UNICEF (2021) reported that while progress has been made in educating the world's children with disabilities, there remain hindrances in many countries across all education levels. These hindrances include a lack of understanding of their needs and of trained teachers, the absence of adequate classroom support and accessible facilities. UNICEF (2021) reported that worldwide children with disabilities are most likely to be out of school due to the failure of policymakers to incorporate disability into school services. Advocates push for inclusive schooling for disabled persons noting that it allows these children to integrate socially with their peers and interacting with nondisabled students can support a feeling of belonging and help them develop skills for maintaining relationships later in life (Bright Hub Education, 2022). One study found the perspectives of students with and without disabilities in an inclusive school environment indicated that all students' sense of belonging increased in a positive school culture and students with disabilities were motivated academically by interacting with their peers (Shogren et al., 2015).

Many persons with disabilities are excluded from the workforce. Data collected by the United Nations (2007) estimated that 80 to 90 percent of working-age disabled persons are unemployed in developing countries and the range is from 50 to 70 percent in industrialized nations. Disabled people face multiple barriers that make it more difficult for them to find and keep a job (Sweet, 2021). These barriers include employer misconception of hiring and accommodating a disabled person and lack of access to workspaces or equipment, transportation to get to work, and personal assistance services (National Rehabilitation Information Center, 2017). These barriers influence the economic potential of persons with disabilities and their sense of belonging and well-being.

These beliefs about disabilities continue to contribute to the oppression of persons with disabilities. More recently in Victorian England, common societal views of disabled persons were rooted in pity, discomfort, fear, and a sense of divine judgment (Historic England, 2022). Divine judgment—or how in some cultures, disabilities were and still are thought to be related to sin and considered a form of punishment from God—is not a new concept. In some regions of Africa, disability was/is considered a curse from the ancestors (Makamure, 2017). See chapters 1, 6, and 12 for more about the intersection of religion and disability. In England and America, many persons with disabilities had to fend for themselves, living in poverty on the streets, which became a social issue. Poor/workhouses and asylums became the place of residence for them, but their institutionalization was not voluntary and they lived in overcrowded and unregulated facilities (National Park Service, n.d.).

SOCIAL AND CULTURAL RIGHTS MOVEMENTS IN THE TWENTIETH CENTURY

In the late 1800s and early 1900s, institutions and doctors began to conceptualize disability as a condition a person has and they focused on the prevention, treatment, or curing of the disabling condition (Disabled World, 2022). Figure 10.1 shows a historical timeline of disability rights as described in this section.

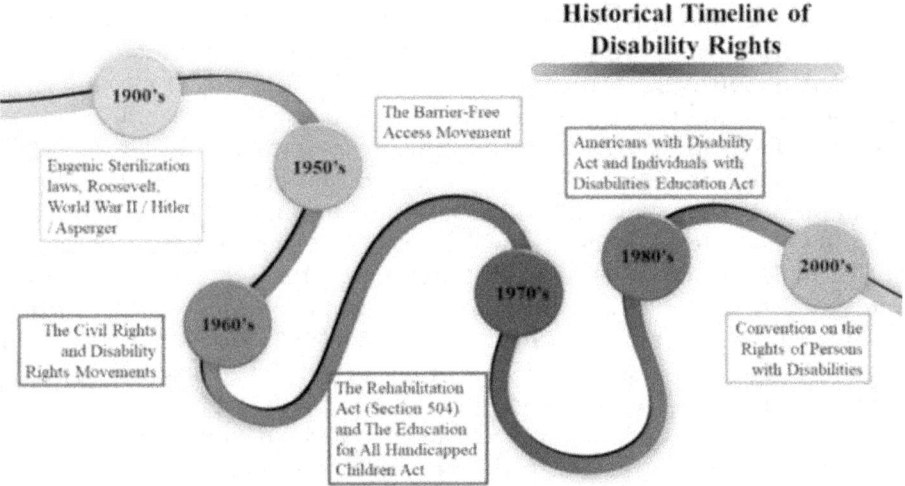

Figure 10.1. Historical Timeline of Disability Rights

1900s through 1940s

During the time period from the 1900s through the 1940s, cruelty toward disabled persons was a part of America's policies and Hitler's movement to create a master race by eliminating disabled persons from the European soil he sought to conquer. In America, the early 1900s ushered in a movement that began with some states passing laws that banned marriages involving individuals with mental and cognitive disabilities (History.com, 2019). In the 1940s to 1950s, some physicians performed thousands of lobotomies that severed connections between parts of the brain, believing lobotomies could significantly reduce what was considered highly disturbing behavior (Meldon, 2017). These repressive acts were part of the overall oppression of disabled persons in an ongoing effort to control their lives.

Later, doctors deemed a person with disability unfit to procreate and performed involuntary sterilization of these patients, otherwise known as **eugenics**, which is the belief that (a) humanity could be improved by controlling genetics (National Park Service, 2017) and (b) managing reproduction to increase the occurrence of heritable characteristics is desirable (Onion et al., 2019). For more information on eugenics, see chapter 5. The Eugenics

Movement meant that individuals with disabilities who doctors deemed unfit received forced sterilization procedures. Thirty-three states passed laws that allowed involuntary sterilization of persons with disabilities. In California, the law was based on protecting the public from the offspring of mentally ill persons (Ko, 2016). The tracing of the tragic period notes that in 1927 the US Supreme Court upheld these laws with one justice writing, "three generations of imbeciles are enough" (History.com, 2019). In 1942, the ruling was overturned, but by that time, thousands of such sterilizations had occurred.

President Franklin Roosevelt was president from 1933 to 1945. During the early twentieth century through World War II, negative attitudes toward disabled persons were tempered in the United States by the election of a president with polio, who used a wheelchair. Although his disability was not widely known, Roosevelt brought an enlightened view toward persons with disabilities to our country. Roosevelt believed that persons with disabilities could pursue optimal health just like anyone else, but they needed a psychologically healthy environment in which to do it (American Psychological Association, 2005). Roosevelt's establishment of a rehabilitation center to treat individuals with polio (i.e., Warm Springs) was the precursor to the concept of independent living for disabled persons. In 1935, Roosevelt's success in getting Congress to pass the Social Security Act led to benefits that not only provided support for those unemployed due to industrial accidents and the elderly, but also for persons with disabilities. Perhaps President Roosevelt's own experiences contributed to the inclusion of support for persons with disability in the Social Security Act.

During the 1935–1941 World War II, Adolf Hitler's objective was to maintain the purity of the German race and the Nazis created the "Law for the Prevention of Hereditarily Diseased Offspring" (History.com, 2019). Hitler's zeal to create the master race led to the sterilization (i.e., eugenics) of thousands of disabled persons, and euthanizing persons with mental and physical disabilities, as well as others deemed "unfit." This resulted in millions of deaths of people not fitting Hitler's view of the superior race. It is posited that Hans Asperger aided Hitler in his efforts to create a superior race (Herman, 2019). Asperger was an Austrian physician and while he was not a known member of the Nazi Party, it was known that he referred children to a Vienna clinic under the control of Germany's Third Reich where between 1940 and 1945, more than eight hundred children were killed as part of Hitler's euthanasia program. It is an open question for some as to whether Asperger was aware of the actions taken by the clinic. Near the end of World War II, he collaborated with others to develop customized therapies for children with what was called autism psychopathy (i.e., Asperger's syndrome). His work with these children with the disorder named after him was reported to be far ahead of his time and he was portrayed as a champion of neurodiversity (Herman, 2019). It has been noted that Asperger's experience growing up with similar characteristics to those he described as autism psychopathy could have contributed to his interest and recognition of them in others (Herman, 2019). Asperger's studies and discovery of autism psychopathy led to the development of therapies and methods of educating individuals who were considered "gifted" in areas and who displayed "challenges" in others.

Pause and Reflect

- Did you know about Asperger's relationship to Germany's Third Reich? If not, why was this not included in your education about disability history? About world history?

1950s and 1960s

As the United States entered the middle of the twentieth century, the collective voices of people who experience oppression (e.g., African American communities; disability rights communities) were starting to be heard. These voices demanded equal and equitable rights and protections that were afforded to other communities as was held in the promise of the US Constitution. As with all movements, the power for change was found in the individuals, the families, and the allied supporters who demanded better conditions and treatment. Along with movements affecting legislative action in the creation of laws, mandates, and acts, many significant points of interest occurred in the courts and through legal verdicts on the side of activists. Movements around "barrier-free" access, civil rights, and disability rights and legal decisions such as *Brown v. Board of Education* were the catalysts of effective change in rights and protections to be afforded to multiple intersectional groups that were traditionally oppressed. For more information on *Brown v. Board of Education*, see chapters 4, 5, and 11.

The Barrier-Free Access Movement

Current wisdom regarding access is largely focused on the concepts of **universal design** (UD). The roots of UD can be found in the **barrier-free access movement** as this movement precedes the UD terminology and implementation by decades. Built around similar needs, the importance of barrier-free environments is clear, as "a barrier-free environment means total independence to many disabled or elderly people who would otherwise need to be dependent upon an institution, a family or an aide" (Steinfeld, 1975, p. 5). This notion of self-sufficiency and independence was the foundation of the barrier-free movement. The 1950s saw the movement ramp up significantly due to the work of disabled veterans and the general disability community.

The current movement for barrier-free access to buildings and architectural structures can be traced back to the end of World War II. Many veterans from that war returned to America with disabilities or developed them after their return. They demanded access to participate fully in the same educational and employment opportunities that were denied to them due to architectural barriers. Along with millions of nonveteran Americans who had disabilities, both groups advocated for the same opportunities afforded to individuals without disabilities. The increased numbers of individuals advocating for barrier-free access, including a growing segment of the population living longer due to life-extending medical advances, provided the strength to push for increased attention at the local, state, and national levels (National Museum of American History, 2017). This movement progressed and pushed for a set of national standards as well as significant legislation on barrier-free accessibility.

After a decade of work by barrier-free advocates, in 1961 the **American National Standards Institute** (ANSI, 1961) published standards on building accessibility for individuals with disabilities. These standards "became the private sector model for a technical standard for accessible features" (Whole Building Design Guide, 2022). The ANSI standards outlined accessibility considerations for buildings and facilities with sections focused on (a) scope and purpose, (b) definitions, (c) general principles and considerations, (d) site development, and (e) buildings. In addition to the ANSI standards, in 1968 Congress passed the **Architectural Barriers Act**. This act required facilities receiving federal funds be accessible to individuals with disabilities in design, construction, and alteration as needed. The combination of the ANSI standards and the Architectural Barriers Act significantly impacted the accessibility of buildings through both social and governmental actions which were possible through the advocacy efforts of the citizenry starting in the 1950s, with impacts reverberating for decades into the future.

The Civil Rights and Disability Rights Movements

While marked by the Civil Rights Act of 1964, the social and cultural progress achieved with this landmark legislation known as the **civil rights movement** had begun decades before. The push for basic human rights for African American citizens of the United States can be traced back to the days of slavery and abolitionist movements. Decades after the Civil War, African Americans were still being discriminated against across age and gender identities in all facets of life including society, employment, and education. The collective voices of advocates regarding equal rights continued to crescendo after the Supreme Court decision in *Brown v. Board of Education of Topeka* (1954). The *Brown v. Board* justices unanimously repealed and repudiated the practices of the "separate but equal" doctrine of educational treatment of children based on race which had been established by the Supreme Court decision in *Plessy v. Ferguson* (1896) over half a century prior. By declaring "separate but equal" unconstitutional, the civil rights movement won a significant battle that led to later social, legal, and legislative victories.

One of the most substantial wins in the civil rights movement was the passage of the **Civil Rights Act of 1964**. As signed by president Lyndon B. Johnson, the act made it illegal to discriminate against any person in the United States based on race, color, religion, sex, or national origin. Additionally, the Civil Rights Act prohibited the (a) unequal requirements for voter registration and (b) discrimination in schools, public services and access, and employment opportunities. This landmark act in civil and labor rights reverberated exponentially not only for African American citizens but for other groups hoping to secure basic human rights.

VIGNETTE 1: *MEET CINDY*

My name is Cindy Bentley. I am an African American woman with an intellectual disability. I was born with fetal alcohol syndrome, seizures, and cocaine in my system. After my mother gave me third-degree burns, I was placed in the foster care system. Back in the 1950s, they didn't know what to do with intellectual disabilities like me so I ended up being placed in an institution. First I went to the school in the institution. After lots of public advocacy and laws were changed, I was sent out to regular elementary, middle, and high schools. I was in mainstream classes, except for math. I was teased and bullied in school, all kinds of things. I think high school was the worst for me. People don't accept you and they know you are different especially when you walk into the special education system. They didn't have IEPs but I wish they did when I was in middle and high school. IEPs help and give you a voice. I taught myself to learn and read because the school didn't have someone to help me. I read between 8th and 10th grade and I'm not ashamed of it. Some of my friends can't read at all. I fit in as best I could. It was very lonely going to school in the 1950s, 1960s, and 1970s. Looking back, I remember the (white) students never sat with us. The Black students sat together. The African Americans were nice, but they weren't my friends. When people look at me, they first look at the color of my skin before anything but I have two things—I also have a disability—one girl said "I won't sit with you, you are R– and stupid." I was in the institution until age twenty-six. I got a guardian, who advocated and she got me out of the institution.

Disability rights was a gradual and steady movement as more Americans were affected by the lack of rights and equal treatment. A significant uptick occurred in advocates for disability rights after the Second World War. Disabled veterans added their voices to the millions of American citizens who had been pushing for fair treatment and access. Although disability rights had been a rallying cry prior to the 1950s, the barrier-free access movement found success for individuals with disabilities in the development of national standards for buildings and facilities (ANSI, 1961) and legal mandates for building accessibility (Architectural Barriers Act of 1968). These progressive steps were aided in their impact by the gains made in the civil rights movement. The passage of the Civil Rights of 1964 provided a blueprint for disability rights advocates to push for similar legislative progress. The notion of equal treatment moved significantly beyond access to buildings and facilities. While still years in the future, the need for fair treatment in education, employment, and society in general was a now-attainable goal with a roadmap for achievement.

1970s

In the 1970s, disability rights activists continued the fight for civil rights for people with disabilities, citing two major victories. In 1973, the **Section 504 of the Rehabilitation Act** was passed, marking the first time in history that disabled people were legally protected. Section 504 offered three main protections: (a) banned discriminatory practices for disabled people in federal agencies and other public institutions receiving federal funds; (b) mandated equal access to public services (e.g., public housing and public transportation services); and (c) allocated funding for vocational training.

Prior to 1961, the United States did not provide public education for any child with a disability (Arkansas State University, 2016). Their education was left solely to parents at their cost. In 1975, the government passed the **Education for All Handicapped Children Act** (EAHCA), which guaranteed equal access to public education for children with disabilities. See chapter 11 for a more in-depth look at these various legislative milestones. The Education for All Handicapped Children Act (predecessor to the ADA) required all schools that receive federal funds to create special education programs for children with disabilities. Prior to 1975, less than half of children with disabilities received education of any kind. The act created opportunities for these children and provided a better education for those already in the system (Encyclopedia.com, 2019). The EAHCA provided funding to states that met the stated criteria (Congress.gov, 1975). The EAHCA ensured children with disabilities the right to a free appropriate public education. In the period following passage of the law, children with disabilities were educated primarily in segregated special education learning environments (Wang, 2009). At that time, the segregated classroom approach was utilized based on benefits such as (a) segregated classrooms are specifically designed to cater to the students' certain "incapacities"; (b) educators in segregated classrooms are able to use a curriculum that is specific to the children's needs; (c) attending classes in segregated classrooms with other children with the same/similar disabilities enhances students' self-confidence; and (d) segregated environments assure the security and sufficient support disabled children need (Jenkinson, 1997). Since that time, views on inclusion have evolved to providing as much access to the general education classroom (the least restrictive environment) as possible.

1990s

Due to the actions of activists, parents of children with disabilities, and lobbying by the Disability Rights Education and Defense Fund, the first

Table 10.1. Americans with Disabilities Act Titles

---

1. Title I protects the rights of employees and jobseekers requiring employers with fifteen or more employees to provide the opportunity for individuals with disabilities to benefit from employment that is available to people who are not disabled.
2. Title II provides access to state and local government services and programs, such as public education, transportation, courts, recreation, voting, and emergency services for individuals with disabilities.
3. Title III applies to businesses including nonprofits including private schools, restaurants, hotels, retail stores, movie theaters, gyms, doctor offices, and hospitals.
4. Title IV requires telecommunications companies to provide services that allow persons with hearing and speech disabilities to communicate.
5. Title V includes other requirements on how to implement the law including prohibiting retaliation against a person who has asserted their rights under the ADA, and directing certain federal agencies to issue guidance explaining the law.

Source: US Department of Justice, 2022.

comprehensive US law was enacted to protect persons with disability from discrimination. The **Americans with Disabilities Act** (ADA) was signed by President H. W. Bush in 1990 (History.com, 2020). The ADA is a civil rights law that guarantees that disabled persons have the same opportunities as everyone else to enjoy employment opportunities, purchase goods and services, and to participate in state and local government programs (US Department of Justice, 2022). As illustrated in table 10.1, the ADA is broken up into sections called titles. It covers a range of physical and mental disabilities and it provides protection in a number of areas (US Department of Justice, 2022).

The enactment of the ADA resulted in a number of lawsuits, some ended up on the docket of the Supreme Court. Issues arose around states' rights, the meaning of disabilities, and a myriad of other concerns (Parrott-Sheffer, 2023). The Americans with Disabilities Act Amendments Act (ADAAA) signed in 2008 by President G. W. Bush clarified and expanded several measures of the original ADA. This included clarifying the law's stance on what it means for a disability to limit a "major life activity." The ADA and its amendments brought about the most sweeping change to how persons with disabilities were to be treated in America and provided remedies for individuals filing complaints against those who fail to comply (Meldon, 2019).

In 1990, the Education for All Handicapped Children's Act was renamed to the **Individuals with Disabilities Education Act** (IDEA; University of Washington, 2022), which further elaborated on the rights of disabled students and their parents (Anti-Defamation League, 2017). Research at the University of Kansas, however, has shown that all students, not just students with disabilities, perform better academically when integrated with general education (Krings, 2015). Yet special education in schools in many states remains a place for segregated education rather than ensuring educational support in general education classrooms.

In 1997 and 2004, additional amendments to the act were made to ensure equal access to education for disabled children. The IDEA federal law supports special education and related services programming for children with disabilities—birth to twenty-one years old. IDEA is designed to ensure that children with disabilities receive a free appropriate public education in the least restrictive environment. In 2006, additional changes to the regulations were passed in 2006 for school-age children and in 2011 for infants and toddlers (Center for Parent Information and Resources, 2017). As illustrated in table 10.2, there are four parts to the IDEA statute (US Department of Education, 2022).

Table 10.2. IDEA Statute

A. Part A includes general provisions such as definitions, Office of Special Education programs, and prescribing regulations.
B. Part B includes provisions to states for educating all children with disabilities ages three to twenty-one.
C. Part C includes provisions for states to provide early intervention services for infants and toddlers (birth through two years) and their families.
D. Part D includes national activities to improve the education of children with disabilities, such as discretionary grants to support state personnel development, technical assistance and dissemination, technology, and parent training and information centers.

The passage of IDEA marked a major milestone in early intervention services and education of children with disabilities. This law also protects the rights of these children and their families. Like ADA, it was also a major civil rights gain for persons with disability. During 2020–2021, the most recent school year reported, 7.2 million children ages three to thirty-one were served under IDEA (National Center for Education Statistics, 2022). While this may seem like an achievement, has it also come with a cost? There are reported conflicts regarding how or if disability culture is honored in public education systems, as described in chapter 3, and questions raised as to whether that has hurt the very communities IDEA is trying to help.

Pause and Reflect

Think about both sides of the fight for inclusion.

- How has IDEA and the push for inclusion helped students with disabilities?
- How has it hurt disabled communities?

2000 to Now

The enactment of amended ADA and IDEA provided support for many persons with disabilities to make choices about how they want to live their lives including living independently (GT Independence, 2020). These laws protect persons with disabilities against discrimination and provide support for early intervention to receive diagnosis and accommodations for a disability. These changes have led to improvement in the lives of many disabled people and increased acceptance by society.

Physicians, caregivers, and activists have increased their efforts to work together to improve the lives of persons with disability (Meldon, 2019). The charity-oriented medical-based approach to disability rights is being replaced by a **human-rights approach**, which seeks ways to respect, support, and celebrate human diversity by creating the conditions that allow meaningful participation (Anderson & Philips, 2012). For more about the models of disability, see chapter 6. The United Nations General Assembly in 2006 adopted the **Convention on the Rights of Persons with Disabilities** (Gordon et al., 2017). In 2008, this convention treaty was put into force to promote, protect, respect, support, and celebrate human diversity by creating the conditions that allow meaningful participation of all persons with disability. It is predicated on the belief that a physical or mental impairment should not diminish human dignity or access to opportunity. This convention treaty is important because for most of history and throughout the world, persons with disabilities have been systematically mistreated by laws and society (Gordon et al., 2017). The convention treaty does not create any new rights or entitlement. It consolidates and expands on existing international laws on the rights of persons with disability. The treaty imposes new legal obligations and supersedes any prior nonbinding international, regional, or domestic standards. Rights covered under the treaty include healthcare, education, work and employment, freedom from violence, abuse, and exploitation, and freedom to live independently and to be included in the community.

There is a treaty in place that is legally binding for United Nations members that promotes and protects the rights of persons with disabilities. What is next for all member nations is to work to put in place national laws and programs to comply with the requirement of the treaty as ratified. In many countries, persons with disabilities continue to be institutionalized. The European Union has sought to promote social inclusion; however, some member countries have done little to address this issue and these countries continue to build such institutions (FXB Center for Health and Human Rights, 2014). Therefore, monitoring of compliance with the treaty is important. In 2012 the **Joint Committee on Human Rights** was established to do so.

DISABILITY AS A CULTURAL PHENOMENON

In chapter 1, **culture** was defined as patterns of collective practices (a) shaped by social environments; (b) adapted, transformed, and specific to communities of people; and (c) linked to periods of time (Waldschmidt, 2018). Traditionally, culture includes narratives and histories, traditions and artifacts, and rituals and customs, but modern culture also includes social behavior, attitudes, and identities (Vester, 2009) and is intricately linked to social inequality (Waldschmidt, 2018). "Knowledge and discourse, identities and institutions, symbolic practices and life styles all are embedded and permeated by power relations, at the same time cultural practices serve to stabilize hegemonic orders" (Waldschmidt, 2018, p. 71). The relationship between and combination of these cultural elements affect one's social positions, relationships, and personal identities (Waldschmidt, 2018).

In the 1980s, sociologists in the United States and United Kingdom started to contextualize **disability** as a combination of these four domains: (a) health, (b) functioning, (c) achievement, and (d) physical appearance. Then in 1994, disability was connected to sociocultural perspectives through a call to end the objectivization of disabled people in theater, literature, paintings, movies, and the media (Shakespeare, 1994). By 2002, advocacy began to frame disability as a cultural trope and as a community with shared history (Garland-Thomson, 2020). It was suggested that it was a disservice for societal focus to be on disabled people's presumed "heavy burdens," and that it would more appropriate to focus on the environmental, attitudinal, and societal barriers that directly impact the perception and treatment of disability (Waldschmidt, 2018)—for example, within the educational or medical systems where the appropriate response to a disability is to treat the impairments through therapeutic, educational, or medical interventions and to guide the individual into accepting and adapting to their conditions. The educational and medical systems are the source of many barriers, however, as discussed throughout this book. Table 10.3 highlights four pillars of the Cultural Model of Disability.

Disability as a Sociocultural Identity

As introduced in chapter 1, **sociocultural identities** form when we subconsciously interpret and incorporate signals from the world around us into our own identity so we can belong (Tajfel, 1978; Tajfel & Turner, 1979). Schools and classroom educators can promote positive cultural identities for all children. In specialized segregated schools and classrooms, the cues sent regarding persons with disabilities can be negative and give disabled children a sense of not belonging, rejection, and isolation from their nondisabled peers. Although it is also noted in the literature and in chapter 3, specialized schools designed and controlled by or classes taught by disabled persons could become sites that promote a positive disability cultural identity (Lawson, 2011).

Sociocultural identities influence how we interpret the world around us and it is important that children with disabilities are included in the world in which they live and that they are made to feel welcomed, accepted, and valued.

Table 10.3. The Four Pillars of the Cultural Model of Disability

Pillar	Definition	Example
Disability is an empty signifier.	Disability and social reactions to disability have a conditional relationship because experiences change across social interactions and settings.	The intersections of disability, health, and food impact one's ability to access and participate in cultural traditions. If health needs for food-related disabilities are accounted for, accommodated for, or included in the planning of the event, there would not be a cultural difference. See chapter 1.
Disability is a category of human differentiation, not an individual feature; disability is naturalized and embodied.	Disability exists only as certain differences that are distinguished as "relevant for health within a given cultural and historical order of knowledge" (Waldschmidt, 2018, p. 75).	Deafness is typically defined as a biological deficiency, and the medical response is to suggest treatment such as cochlear implants. The Deaf community regards Deafness as a cultural difference and adopts types of linguistic competence, e.g., ASL (ScienceDirect, 2017), therefore rejecting the need for a treatment. See chapter 3.
Disability is a result of "prevailing symbolic orders, bodily practices and social institutions, all of which produce normality and deviance, the self and the other, familiarity and alterity" (Waldschmidt, 2018, p. 75).	Disability is defined through historical and cultural contexts, with a particular focus on elements of inclusion, exclusion and power differentials, stigmatization, and sociocultural meanings of [intersectional] experiences and identities (ScienceDirect, 2019; Waldschmidt, 2018).	A common trope in sports is to highlight the performance of Paralympic athletes "despite" their impairments, but Paralympic athletes are remarkable due to their athleticism.
Disability is problematized in society and culture.	Disability is affected by the dominant ways of defining what an issue of health, normality, and functioning are, alongside (a) the institutional design of daily practices and structures and (b) how identities are created and shaped.	People tend to "stare" at disabled people and focus on the challenges the person experiences rather than questioning how to combat barriers to best support them.

Source: Adapted from Waldschmidt, 2018.

Educating this student population in an inclusive environment can promote disability under the concept of diversity. It has been argued that inclusive education should not be assimilation but is meant to celebrate diversity by creating shared experiences of disabled and nondisabled students (Slee, 2018).

Disability as a Culture

As discussed in chapter 3, disability culture provides persons with disabilities with a sense of identity and a sense of belonging. It is a positive concept (Brown, 2002) with people who self-identify based on the Social Model of Disability, defining themselves as individuals who have challenges because of the barriers that society puts in place that limit their accessibility to physical structures, education, and economic opportunities, as well as barriers due to attitudes of decision makers about what disabled persons can do (Gill, 2009). For more information on this model, see chapter 6. The focus should not be on how to fix disabled persons but instead on how to fix the environment around them (Gill, 2009). This is where schools can make a difference.

Schools can advance positive disability cultural identity by eliminating barriers within learning environments. As with other cultural groups, school visuals and classroom materials should reflect the diversity of the students they serve, for example, posters, library books, historical achievements, and contributions. Educators need to increase their sociocultural competence regarding persons with disabilities and work to eliminate their attitudinal biases, which is one of the biggest barriers for disabled persons (Frieden, 2004).

VIGNETTE 2: *CINDY ON FIGHTING ATTITUDINAL BIASES*

Don't assume people with ID cannot learn because they CAN learn. Maybe they aren't going to learn the same as their classmates, but they can learn. Someone I know doesn't have language, but is smart as a whip—she just can't talk. Some people think we can't do anything. We can do a lot. I've been in my own apartment for almost forty years. I have a very good life and a good circle of friends. Don't underestimate what someone can do and listen to people with disabilities. "Nothing about us without us."

People underestimate me. As an adult, I'm the executive director for a statewide People-First advocacy group. People-First is an organization run by people with disabilities for people with disabilities to learn to speak up for themselves, share ideas, friendships, and information. My job coach helps me because I have challenges processing things and keeping things on track and organizing papers. When writing, I dictate and my coach writes my words. There is so much more to me than my job. I am also an athlete. I participate in Special Olympics in lots of different sports. I do bocci, basketball, tennis, soccer, and bowling. I've been to international and world games. I am a global messenger for Special Olympics (see my book, Spirit of a Champion*). I've met two presidents—President Clinton in 2000, President Bush in 2001—in the White House. I met Eunice Shriver and was in her house and I consider myself a friend of Tim Shriver, the president/CEO of Special Olympics.*

As previously noted, persons with disabilities face attitudinal, communications, and physical barriers that limit their access to education, entertainment, healthcare, and other services, but technologies, facial expressions, and gestures can be employed that improve communications and allow persons with disabilities to participate in activities and organizations (University of Technology Sydney, 2018). Physical barriers that limit persons' access to buildings, classrooms, and playgrounds can be removed by improving accessibility, which also includes easier access with the proper door hardware, ramps, access to bathrooms, and other school facilities (US Government Accountability Office, 2020).

EFFECTIVE INTERVENTIONS FOR INCREASING A SENSE OF BELONGING

This section highlights three kinds of evidence-based interventions educators can use to support social interactions and increase a sense of belonging for children with disabilities: (a) providing inclusive practices to foster community; (b) ensuring access to communicative opportunities; and (c) offering cross-age peer mentoring.

Inclusive Practices

As discussed throughout this volume, the framework to promote more inclusive education for all is **Universal Design for Learning** (UDL). In particular, the UDL guidelines offer a way of thinking about multiple options to promote engagement for all learners (CAST, 2018), including how to foster community by designing clear expectations for group learning, providing prompts that guide students in when and how to ask peers and teachers for help, and supporting opportunities for peer interactions (CAST, 2018). For children with disabilities in general education classrooms, models such as co-teaching—where a special educator and general educator work together to provide instruction (Friend et al., 2010)—and push-in service delivery by related service providers, such as speech-language pathologists, can provide support for children with and without disabilities to interact effectively with each other.

Children with disabilities who have extensive support needs (ESN) in a wide variety of areas could benefit from deliberate activities designed to encourage interactions with peers as well as specific practices designed to support those interactions (Carter et al., 2014). All children can benefit from general information about disability and diversity incorporated into relevant activities in school (Lindsay & Edwards, 2013). However, providing general disability information is only the start. Educators can use peer-mediated instruction and supports starting with (a) identifying peers interested in interacting with their disabled peers; (b) providing guidance to such peers (e.g., how to initiate and sustain interactions with specific children with ESN); and (c) helping to facilitate such interactions during an activity (e.g., adapting the activity to provide a clear role for the child with ESN, redirecting conversation away from adults and toward other group members).

Access to Effective Communicative Opportunities

Children with ESN often also have **complex communication needs** (CCN) which can include having limited or no oral speech, having speech not adequate for daily use, having speech only intelligible for familiar partners, or having communication breakdowns when in distress. Such children can benefit from **augmentative and alternative communication** (AAC), which is any method to share thoughts, ideas, feelings, and needs that does not depend on AAC. AAC systems range from unaided (e.g., body language, facial expressions, use of sign language) to low-tech (e.g., communication boards, picture exchange communication systems) to high-tech (e.g., speech-generating devices, communication applications on tablets). There is much to consider when working with children who use AAC, including the recognition that children will likely use multiple modes of communication (e.g., unaided, low-tech, high-tech AAC as well as speech as they are able) (Beukelman & Light, 2020). For more information about origins and evolution of AAC, see chapters 1 and 11.

When looking to increase the sense of belonging, educators should focus on two key practices: (a) making sure the child has access to their AAC system at all times and (b) teaching peers to be effective communication partners with children who use AAC. Too often, children with complex communication needs have their access to their AAC system restricted to certain activities or the vocabulary present in the system is restricted to a small range of vocabulary (McNaughton et al., 2019). See Miles's vignettes in chapter 1 for an example.

Educators should (a) ensure children have access to communicative opportunities throughout the day; (b) model conversational turns on the AAC system; and (c) respond to any communicative attempt. It should also not be assumed that peers will automatically know how to interact with children who use AAC. Since each AAC system should be individualized, peers may need modeling, practice, and feedback to be an effective communication partner with a specific child who uses AAC. Educators should teach peers targeted interaction strategies such as (a) offering choices, (b) asking open-ended questions, (c) providing sincere comments, and (d) waiting after making a comment or asking a question for the child using AAC to respond (Beukelman & Light, 2020). The use of such strategies by peers have been found to improve communication outcomes for children who use AAC (Therrien et al., 2016) and could thus increase a sense of belonging in the school community.

Cross-Age Peer Mentoring

Disabled children can benefit from interactive activities that include other children with disabilities. This can include children with the same or similar disabilities, who could find common ground in their experiences of living with those disabilities, as well as children with different disabilities who share the experience of living in an ableist society. These shared experiences help form their beliefs, values, and customs—that is, they help them to develop their cultural identities. Educators can use the inclusive practices and peer interaction strategies from earlier in the section to foster connection among children with disabilities in classrooms. Educators can also match disabled children with older children with similar disabilities in mentee/mentor relationships. This is known as cross-age peer mentoring and supports children participating in a social activity with an older peer with a similar disability or other background (Karcher, 2014). For children with disabilities, cross-age peer mentoring has been found to (a) improve confidence, (b) increase communication, and (c) decrease loneliness (e.g., Stewart et al., 2013). Cross-age peer mentoring can be conducted in-person or online and may help children with disabilities navigate social media (Raghavendra et al., 2018).

SUMMARY

While the history of these movements is often told as a series of timelines as chronological events with milestones, the fact is that the civil rights and disability rights movements were occurring simultaneously and in parallel but also intersecting at numerous points across the historical timeline of the United States. There is no way to extricate one movement from the other. Additionally, there are those who fought for the rights of all citizens at the intersection of race and disability status (Disability Rights Michigan, 2021). Although the civil rights and disability rights movements found successes in making progress for African Americans and citizens with disabilities, these should not be taken for granted. Additional progress is most definitely needed to ensure equitable treatment for all in all aspects of society.

REFERENCES

American National Standards Institute (ANSI). (1961). *ANSI specifications for making buildings and facilities accessible to, and usable by, the physically handicapped (A117.1)*. New York. https://education.ohio.gov/getattachment/Topics/Career-Tech/Civil-Rights-Methods-of-Administration-Program/ANSI.pdf.aspx?lang=en-US

American Psychological Association. (2005). Researching Roosevelt's disability rights. *Monitor on Psychology, 36*(2), 42. https://www.apa.org/monitor/feb05/roosevelt

Anderson, J. H., & Philips, J. P. M. (2012). *Disability and universal human rights: Legal, ethical, and conceptual implications of the Convention on the Rights of Persons with Disabilities* (No. 35). Netherlands Institute of Human Rights (SIM).

Anti-Defamation League. (2017). *A brief history of the Disability Rights Movement.* https://www.adl.org/education/resources/backgrounders/disability-rights-movement

Architectural Barriers Act of 1968, 42 U.S.C. § 4151 et seq.

Arkansas State University. (2016). *The history of special education in the U.S.* https://degree.astate.edu/articles/k-12-education/the-history-of-special-education-in-the-u-s.aspx

Beukelman, D. B., & Light, J. (2020). *Augmentative and Alternative Communication: Supporting children and adults with complex communication needs.* 5th ed. Paul H. Brookes.

Bright Hub Education. (2022). The advantages and benefits of inclusion in special education. https://www.brighthubeducation.com/special-ed-inclusion-strategies/66128-advantages-and-benefits-of-inclusion/#social-advantages

Brown, S. (2002). What is Disability Culture? *Disability Studies Quarterly, 22*(2). https://doi.org/10.18061/dsq.v22i2.343

Brown v. Board of Education, 347 U.S. 483 (1954).

Carter, E. W., Brock, M. E., & Trainor, A. A. (2014). Transition assessment and planning for youth with severe intellectual and developmental disabilities. *Journal of Special Education, 47*(4), 245–55.

CAST. (2018). The UDL guidelines. https://udlguidelines.cast.org/

Center for Parent Information & Resources. (2017). IDEA—the Individuals with Disabilities Education Act. Individuals with Disabilities Education Act. https://www.parentcenterhub.org/idea/

Civil Rights Act of 1964, Title VII, 42 U.S.C. § 2000e et seq. (1964).

Congress.gov. (1975). H.R.7217—Education for All Handicapped Children Act. 94th Congress (1975–1976). https://www.congress.gov/bill/94th-congress/house-bill/7217

Disability Rights Michigan. (2021). *Civil rights and disability rights: A celebration of intersectionality.* Lansing, MI. https://ddi.wayne.edu/possibilitiespodcast/civil_rights_disability_rights_drm.pdf

Disabled World. (2022). *Disability statistics: Information, charts, graphs and tables.* https://www.disabled-world.com/disability/statistics/

Dunn, D. S. (2021). *Understanding ableism and negative reactions to disability.* American Psychological Association. https://www.apa.org/ed/precollege/psychology-teacher-network/introductory-psychology/ableism-negative-reactions-disability

Encyclopedia.com. (2019). Education of Handicapped Children Acts 84 Stat. 175, 88 Stat. 579, 89 Stat. 773, 91 Stat. 230. https://www.encyclopedia.com/politics/encyclopedias-almanacs-transcripts-and-maps/education-handicapped-children-acts-84-stat-175-88-stat-579-89-stat-773-91-stat-230

Frieden, L. (2004). *Improving educational outcomes for students with disabilities.* National Council on Disability. https://ncd.gov/publications/2004/Mar172004

Friend, M., Cook, L., Hurley-Chamberlain, D., & Shamberger, C. (2010). Co-teaching: An illustration of the complexity of collaboration in special education. *Journal of Educational and Psychological Consultation, 20*(1), 9–27. https://doi.org/10.1080/10474410903535380

FXB Center for Health and Human Rights. (2014). Harvard University. https://fxb.harvard.edu/

Garland-Thomson, R. (2020). Integrating disability, transforming feminist theory. In *Feminist theory reader* (pp. 181–191). Routledge.

Gill, C. J. (2009). A new social perspective on disability and its implications for rehabilitation. *Occupational Therapy In Health Care, 4*(1), 49–55. https://doi.org/10.1080/J003v04n01_05

Gordon, J.-S., Põder, J.-C., & Burckhart, H. (2017). *Human rights and disability: Interdisciplinary perspectives.* Taylor & Francis.

GT Independence. (2020). *A quick history of disability rights.* https://gtindependence.com/a-quick-history-of-disability-treatment/

Herman, E. (2019). Hans Asperger, 1906–1980. The Autism History Project. https://blogs.uoregon.edu/autismhistoryproject/people/hans-asperger/

History.com. (2019). *Eugenics: Genetic engineering.* https://www.history.com/topics/european-history/eugenics#genetic-engineering

———. (2020). *Americans with Disabilities Act (ADA) signed into law.* https://www.history.com/this-day-in-history/americans-with-disabilities-act-ada-signed-into-law-george-bush

Historic England. (2022). *A history of disability: From 1050 to the present day.* https://historicengland.org.uk/research/inclusive-heritage/disability-history/

Jenkinson, J. C. (1997). *Mainstream or special? Educating students with disabilities.* Routledge.

Karcher, M. J. (2014). Cross-age peer mentoring. *Handbook of youth mentoring.* https://doi.org/10.4135/9781412996907

Ko, L. (2016). Reproductive rights: Unwanted sterilization and eugenics programs in the United States. *Independent Lens.* Public Broadcasting Service: KCTS. https://www.pbs.org/independentlens/blog/unwanted-sterilization-and-eugenics-programs-in-the-united-states/

Krings, K. (2015). It's time to end segregation of special education students, professors say. KU News Service. University of Kansas. https://today.ku.edu/2015/01/27/professors-argue-time-has-finally-come-fullyend-segregation-special-education-students

Lawson, A. (2011). Disability and employment in the Equality Act 2010: Opportunities seized, lost and generated. *Industrial Law Journal, 40*(4), 359–83. https://doi.org/10.1093/indlaw/dwr021

Lindsay, S., & Edwards, A. (2013). A systematic review of disability awareness interventions for children and youth. *Disability Rehabilitation, 35*(8), 623–46.

Makamure, C. (2017). Religion and disability: A reflection on the role of Pentecostal churches in curbing marginalisation of people with disability in Zimbabwe. *Boleswa Journal of Theology, Religion and Philosophy, 4*(3).

Meldon, P. (2017). *Disability history: Early and shifting attitudes of treatment.* National Park Service. https://www.nps.gov/articles/disabilityhistoryearlytreatment.htm

———. (2019). *Disability history: The Disability Rights Movement.* National Park Service. https://www.nps.gov/articles/disabilityhistoryrightsmovement.htm

McNaughton, D., Light, J., Beukelman, D. R., Klein, C., Nieder, D., & Nazareth, G. (2019). Building capacity in AAC: A person-centred approach to supporting participation by people with complex communication needs. *Augmentative and Alternative Communication, 35*(1), 56–68. https://doi.org/10.1080/07434618.2018.1556731

National Center for Education Statistics. (2022). *Students with disabilities: Condition of education.* US Department of Education, Institute of Education Sciences. https://nces.ed.gov/programs/coe/indicator/cgg#suggested-citation

National Museum of American History. (2017). *Exhibitions: Access! Everyone! Everywhere! Elaine Ostroff and the universal design movement.* Washington, DC. https://americanhistory.si.edu/exhibitions/access-everyone-everywhere

National Park Service. (n.d.) *Disability history series introduction.* https://www.nps.gov/articles/disability-history-series-introduction.htm

National Rehabilitation Information Center. (2017). *People with disabilities face barriers to employment, but accommodations may help.* https://www.naric.com/?q=en/rif/people-disabilities-face-barriers-employment-accommodations-may-help

Onion, A., Sullivan, M., & Mullen, M. (2019). Eugenics: Forced sterilizations. History.com. https://www.history.com/topics/european-history/eugenics#forced-sterilizations

Parrott-Sheffer, C. (2023). Americans with Disabilities Act: United States [1990]. *Britanica.* https://www.britannica.com/topic/Americans-with-Disabilities-Act

Plessy v. Ferguson, 163 U.S. 537 (1896).

Raghavendra, P., Hutchinson, C., Grace, E., Wood, D., & Newman, L. (2018). "I like talking to people on the computer": Outcomes of a home-based intervention to develop social media skills in youth with disabilities living in rural communities. *Research in Developmental Disabilities, 76,* 110–23. https://doi.org/10.1016/j.ridd.2018.02.012

Ravassard, M. (2022). *Persons with disabilities.* Right to Education. https://www.right-to-education.org/issue-page/marginalised-groups/persons-disabilities

ScienceDirect. (2017). Linguistic competence. From *The role of information professional in the knowledge economy.* https://www.sciencedirect.com/topics/social-sciences/linguistic-competence

———. (2019). Relativity. From *Encyclopedia of ecology.* 2nd ed. https://www.sciencedirect.com/topics/social-sciences/relativity

Shakespeare, T. (1994). Cultural representation of disabled people: Dustbins for disavowal? *Disability & Society, 9*(3), 283–99.

Shogren, K. A., Gross, J. M. S., Forber-Pratt, A. J., Francis, G. L., Satter, A. L., Blue-Banning, M., & Hill, C. (2015). The perspectives of students with and without disabilities on inclusive schools. *Research and Practice for Persons with Severe Disabilities, 40*(4), 243–60. https://doi.org/10.1177/1540796915583493

Slee, R. (2018). Defining the scope of inclusive education. Ministerio de Educación del Perú. https://repositorio.minedu.gob.pe/handle/20.500.12799/5977

Steinfeld, E. (1975). *Barrier-free access to the man-made environment: A review of current literature.* Department of Housing and Urban Development. Washington, DC.

Stewart, M., Letourneau, N., Masuda, J. R., Anderson, S., & McGhan, S. (2013). Impacts of online peer support for children with asthma and allergies: "It just helps you every time you can't breathe well." *Journal of Pediatric Nursing, 28*(5), 439–52. https://doi.org/10.1016/j.pedn.2013.01.003

Sweet, J. (2021). Research finds new reasons for unemployment among people with disabilities. Verywell Mind. https://www.verywellmind.com/what-stops-some-people-with-disabilities-from-working-5193854

Tajfel, H. (1978). The achievement of inter-group differentiation. In H. Tajfel (Ed.), *Differentiation between social groups* (pp. 77–100). Academic.

Tajfel, H., & Turner, J. C. (1979). An integrative theory of intergroup conflict. In W. G. Austin & S. Worchel (Eds.), *The social psychology of inter-group relations* (pp. 33–47). Brooks/Cole.

Theisen-Womersley, G. (2021). *Trauma and resilience among displaced populations: A sociocultural exploration.* Springer International. https://doi.org/10.1007/978-3-030-67712-1

Therrien, M. C. S., Light, J., & Pope, L. (2016). Systematic review of the effects of interventions to promote peer interactions for children who use aided AAC. *Augmentative and Alternative Communication, 32*(2), 81–93. https://doi.org/10.3109/07434618.2016.1146331

United Nations Children's Fund (UNICEF). (2021). Inclusive education: Every child has the right to quality education and learning. UNICEF: For Every Child: Education. https://www.unicef.org/education/inclusive-education

United Nations Department of Public Information. (2007). Fact sheet 1: Employment of persons with disabilities. *United Nations Enable Newsletter.* https://www.un.org/disabilities/documents/toolaction/employmentfs.pdf#:~:text=In%20developing%20countries%2C%2080%25%20to%2090%25%20of%20persons,countries%20the%20figure%20is%20between%2050%25%20and%2070%25

US Department of Justice. (2022). Justice department launches new Americans with Disabilities Act website (blog post). Office of Public Affairs. https://www.justice.gov/opa/blog/justice-department-launches-new-americans-disabilities-act-website

US Government Accountability Office. (2020). K–12 education: School districts need better information to help improve access for people with disabilities. GAO-20-448. https://www.gao.gov/products/gao-20-448

University of Technology Sydney. (2018). Improving communication for people with disabilities. https://www.uts.edu.au/about/graduate-school-health/speech-pathology/news/improving-communication-people-disabilities

University of Waikato. (2019). Research looks into "belonging" for disabled people. https://www.waikato.ac.nz/news-opinion/media/2019/research-looks-into-belonging-for-disabled-people

University of Washington. (2022). What is the Individuals with Disabilities Education Act? DO-IT: Disabilities, Opportunities, Internetworking, and Technology. https://www.washington.edu/doit/what-individuals-disabilities-education-act

US Department of Education. (2022). Statute and regulations: Individuals with Disabilities Education Act (IDEA). https://sites.ed.gov/idea/statuteregulations/

Vester, H. G. (2009). *Kompendium der Soziologie I: Grundbegriffe.* Verlag.

Waldschmidt, A. (2018). Disability–Culture–Society: Strengths and weaknesses of a cultural model of dis/ability / Handicap–Culture–Société: forces et faiblesse d'un modèle culturel des dis/abilities. *Alter, 12*(2), 65–78. https://doi.org/10.1016/j.alter.2018.04.003

Whole Building Design Guide (WBDG) Accessible Committee. (2022). History of accessible facility design. Washington, DC. https://www.wbdg.org/design-objectives/accessible/history-accessible-facility-design

World Health Organization (WHO). (n.d.). Health topics: Disability. https://www.who.int/health-topics/disability#tab=tab_2

CHAPTER 11

The Push and Pull of the Litigation-Legislation-Litigation Cycle

Chapter authors: *Jacquelyn Chovanes, David Bateman, Ruth Eyres, and Catherine Constable*

Vignette author: *Bob Eyres*

Editor: *L. Lynn Stansberry Brusnahan*

ABSTRACT

It is important to examine where we have been to ensure we have a clear vision of where we want to be. The purpose of this chapter is to provide the historical context of special education and examine how legislation and our language has evolved relating to students with disabilities and the services provided. Moving into a contemporary perspective, the chapter explores current educational access, unaddressed needs, and evolving attitudes toward evidence-based practices and intervention outcomes including integrated multi-tiered systems of support (I-MTSS) (Response to Intervention [RTI] and Positive Behavioral Interventions and Supports [PBIS]), evidence-based practices (EBP), universal design for learning (UDL), and assistive technology (AT) from a sociocultural perspective.

GUIDING QUESTIONS

- What is the history of special education in the United States?
- What legislation and litigation have impacted the education of disabled students and the services provided?
- How has language evolved?
- What are some of the current educational practices in schools and how do these meet the needs of students with disabilities?

KEY TERMS

Accommodations
Adaptations
Assistive Technology
Augmentative
  and Alternative
  Communication
Disproportionality
Evidence-Based Practice
Free Appropriate Public
  Education
Individualized
  Education Program
Least Restrictive
  Environment
Modifications
Multi-Tiered Systems of
  Support
Positive Behavioral
  Interventions and
  Supports
Response to
  Intervention
Schoolwide Positive
  Behavioral
  Interventions and
  Supports
Universal Design for
  Learning

There have always been individuals with disabilities, but educational services have not always been accessible to them. In fact, as recently as 1970 it was legal to prevent students with disabilities from attending school (Johnson, 1986). The history of educational services for disabled individuals is filled with stories and examples of wholesale exclusion and legal denials. Often, the best that could be hoped for was some form of educational service in a state-run institution (Scheerenberger, 1983).

This chapter describes the history of the education of disabled students. It provides descriptions of the legal cases that paved the way for the education of students with disabilities, along with descriptions of the litigation. Often lacking in the history of special education is the emphasis, or push and pull, of the litigation-legislation-litigation cycle and how that changes the services for students with disabilities. This chapter discusses the constitutional groundwork, which was the initial drive for special education. It displays how the cycle of case law works, which includes Congress passing laws and issuing regulations to the states, and states enacting laws by putting in place their own regulations. This chapter highlights the reauthorization of Individuals with Disabilities Education Act (IDEA) and the history of the law itself. This law includes evidence of the impact of litigation on legislation. Following the history of special education laws, this chapter describes the evolution of language used by the educational community in regard to special education. Finally, the chapter presents current issues and recommended practices related to equitable access to education for socioculturally diverse students with disabilities. Topics include disproportionality and educational frameworks such as integrated multi-tiered systems of support (I-MTSS), which includes both Response to Intervention (RTI) and Positive Behavioral Supports and Interventions (PBIS). Additionally, the chapter covers the adoption of socioculturally sustaining pedagogy, least restrictive environment (LRE), and inclusion. It describes evidence-based practices and universal design for learning (UDL) with a focus on how UDL contributes to socioculturally sustaining pedagogy. Lastly, the chapter discusses assistive technology (AT) and more specifically augmentative and alternative communication (AAC).

US SPECIAL EDUCATION LAW

Legislation has laid the foundation for special education today. This section presents the most prominent legislation and court cases that led to the passage of the Education for All Handicapped Children Act (EAHCA), frequently referred to as PL 94-142, and the Individuals with Disabilities Education Act (IDEA).

Brown v. Board of Education

Often forgotten is that the rights of students with disabilities in schools is a direct result of *Brown v. Board of Education of Topeka, Kansas.* There are several important reasons why we need to trace the education of disabled students back to this case. Even though *Brown* related to the education of students who were African American, students with disabilities were still being legally segregated from schools. As a result of *Brown*, there were increasing questions about the rationale and reasoning of continually segregating students with disabilities (Yell, 2017). The rationale for including students and the opportunity for them to receive an individualized education is one that is part of the services they now receive.

We discuss *Brown* as a part of the history of the education of students with disabilities in that it was the first time that the federal government ever said anything about a local educational matter; such issues had been historically reserved to the states. Without *Brown*, there would have been no federal changes to local educational policies and, almost certainly, it would have been much later than 1975 before Congress acted on national legislation for students with disabilities.

In the *Brown* decision, issued in 1954, Justice Warren wrote that "in the field of public education the doctrine of 'separate but equal' has no place," as segregated schools are "inherently unequal." As a result, the Court ruled that the plaintiffs were being "deprived of the equal protection of the laws guaranteed by the 14th Amendment" (*Brown v. Board of Education*, 1954).

Special education is a field influenced by the litigation-legislation cycle and defined by law. It relies heavily on the involvement of the court system. The impact of change is evident in the evolution of IDEA as well as across all aspects of special education. Decisions are made daily that continue to define the laws of special education. More information on *Brown*, including the effects on racialized students, can be found in chapters 4, 5, and 10.

Impact of Court Cases on Law

Special education has evolved throughout the years. Beginning in the 1970s, the litigation-legislation cycle that defines the field of special education started with a series of court cases. This was a defining moment that mapped out the future of the field and how it would develop from where it was to where it is today. Those changes were mainly the result of litigation. Multiple landmark decisions have occurred that further defined the laws of special education. As the result of several court cases and pressure from parents, Congress investigated educational services for students with disabilities. Two notable statements from their findings stand out.

> The long-range implications of these statistics are that public agencies and taxpayers will spend billions of dollars over the lifetimes of these individuals to maintain such persons as dependents and in a minimally acceptable lifestyle. With proper education services, many would be able to become productive citizens, contributing to society instead of being forced to remain burdens. Others, through such services, would increase their independence, thus reducing their dependence on society. (US Code Congressional and Administrative News [USCCAN], 1975, p. 1433)

> Providing educational services will ensure against persons needlessly being forced into institutional settings. One need only look at public residential institutions to find thousands of persons whose families are no longer able to care for them and who themselves have received no educational services. Billions of dollars are expended each year to maintain persons in these subhuman conditions. (USCCAN, 1975, p. 1433)

Congress realized that standard guidelines had to be developed to ensure some uniformity among the states in identification of need and provision of educational services for students with disabilities. The USCCAN report helped with this, as did several court cases at the local level. These court cases (a) clarified that specific procedures needed to be followed when determining that a student has a disability, (b) established the need for enforcement of compulsory attendance laws, and (c) helped alleviate biases against certain students (e.g., *Diana v. State Board of Education of California*, 1970; *Mills v. Board of Education of the District of Columbia*, 1972; *Pennsylvania Association for Retarded Children (PARC) v. Commonwealth of Pennsylvania*, 1972). In 1975, Congress passed special education legislation to address these issues being brought to the courts.

Education for All Handicapped Children Act (PL 94-142)

Referred to as PL 94-142, the passage of the Education for All Handicapped Children Act (EAHCA) provided guidance to states for allowing students with disabilities to access public education as well as providing financial assistance to states in order to provide special education and related services. This special education law, which began as PL 94-142, was the result of two landmark cases: *Pennsylvania Association for Retarded Children (PARC) v. Pennsylvania* and *Mills v. Board of Education.*

In the *PARC* case, parents were sending nondisabled children to local elementary schools that would not accept disabled students. The schools made excuses for why students with disabilities could not attend and did not follow due process procedures. This resulted in the courts approving consent decree, which affirmed that the states could not deny education to students with disabilities. The state had the responsibility to not only educate the students with disabilities but to also seek out students who needed assistance, provide a free appropriate public education (FAPE), and ensure due process rights.

In the *Mills* case, schools were denying students services and due process rights. This resulted in a detailed framework for due process procedures. These cases, like the *Brown* case, were based on the constitutional rights granted in the Fourteenth Amendment. This law did not answer all the questions; however, it was the first step that led the way for further special education law. This act mandated that in order for states to receive federal funding for special education, they had to comply with the law (Yell, 2017). Specifically:

> The intent when Congress passed PL 94-142 was to ensure that all students with disabilities will be assured that they in fact have a right to education, and to establish a process by which state and local education agencies may be held accountable for providing educational services for all handicapped children. (USCCAN, 1975)

The impact of this act is special education as you know it. This is the main law regarding the educational services for students with disabilities. The law and its specific components are important to the education of students with disabilities. Prior to 1975, education for students with disabilities existed in only a few locations across the country. As noted earlier it was legal to prevent disabled students from receiving an education. This law changed everything for students with disabilities, and public education became education for all.

Congress passing PL 94-142 provided for procedural safeguards, integration, and appropriate testing and evaluation materials and procedures. EAHCA guaranteed individual rights and provided funding to states to educate disabled students. The basic principles follow:

- Education must be given to all children with disabilities
- Education should be provided in the least restrictive environment (LRE)
- Education needs to be individualized and appropriate for the child
- Education must be free
- Procedural protections are to be in place

EAHCA was to be revised every five years. Major changes to the law have occurred during these reauthorization periods; changes also continue to take place because of litigation.

VIGNETTE 1: *MEET BOB*

I am a nineteen-year-old who has benefited from a public education. I sometimes identify as male and cisgender but other times identify as a transgender female. I typically use he/him pronouns but want to explore using she/her or they/them. I am multiracial but prefer the term mixed. Others usually label me as Black. During my early developmental years, I experienced many adverse childhood experiences affecting the way I view others and interact with most people.

I was born prematurely at twenty-five weeks weighing only one pound, eight ounces. My first medical diagnosis was cerebral palsy along with prenatal exposure to drugs and alcohol. Physical abuse at twenty months old resulted in my foster care system placement along with another medical diagnosis, traumatic brain injury. Medical exams during foster care resulted in adding speech, vision, and hearing impairments to my disability portfolio.

Losing my biological family and then living with four different families in just two years while in foster care still fuels my anxiety and fear of losing people important to me. It also hinders my friendship development and making social connections. This fear and anxiety affects my ability to trust others. I am shy in new situations and reluctant to participate in new activities or challenges.

My biological mother eventually lost her parental rights, which made me "available for adoption." I joined my forever-family two weeks before I turned four years old. Being in a loving and permanent family helped me to make progress toward developmental milestones. Although I did receive early intervention services (speech therapy-ST, occupational therapy-OT, and physical therapy-PT) at a state-funded center while in foster care, I did not start receiving these services until after I was two years old. I met most typical developmental milestones but at a delayed pace. Due to how cerebral palsy affects my legs, I walk with the accommodation of a walker or use a wheelchair to navigate longer distances.

Once my current family adopted me, an inclusion preschool was the place for me. From an early age, I did not want my differences or disabilities to be how others defined me. Until middle school, I would often tell people "I don't have cerebral palsy. I'm just like the other kids." I started attending my IEP conferences in middle school and hated them with a passion. I did not like to hear about my disabilities and weaknesses. I even told peers and school staff not to talk about me having cerebral palsy. By high school, I started to realize I could not escape my disabilities being a huge part of who I am. Receiving support staff to help me navigate my daily life post–high school required acknowledging and discussing my disabilities. I still am not thrilled about times when my disabilities are a focal point but I am more comfortable with it now.

From kindergarten through graduation, I attended local public schools. In elementary school, I received what they called "resource." The special education teacher would give me extra support in reading and math in her classroom. I also received school OT, PT, and ST services along with paraeducator support for safety and personal care assistance. I attended regular before and after school care. I recall not being comfortable with special treatment if it was different than what other kids in the class or care program received. My walker, helmet (to protect me if I fell), leg device (to keep my legs from scissoring), ankle foot orthoses (AFOs), and glasses screamed disability and difference! Entering the public school system added another label to my list, learning disabilities. I was also medically diagnosed with attention deficit hyperactive disorder (ADHD). Two memories stand out about elementary school. First, the teachers thought I could not read because I refused to read for them and did not show what I knew during tests. At home, I was reading chapter books but the teachers did not believe my mom when she told them. Second, I remember being included in general education and all-school activities, even climbing to the top of the jungle gym!

Additional Litigation That Impacted Special Education

Litigation brings about changes. Litigation such as *Board of Education v. Rowley* and *Smith v. Robinson* has contributed to improvements in special education. With litigation comes clarification and more detailed definitions related to special education.

The *Rowley* standard was the result of further litigation on special education laws. In *Rowley*, the definition of a free appropriate public education (FAPE) was in question. The case resulted in a detailed definition of an individualized education program (IEP), which includes related services, present levels of performance, annual goals/short-term objectives, dates and duration of services, and procedures for evaluating the student's progress. This IEP is to be developed at a meeting which includes, at a minimum, a public agency representative, the teacher, and the parents. This was the first Supreme Court case to address what "appropriate" means. The definition of appropriate continues to be the burden of the courts and hearing officers due to the vagueness of FAPE in the law.

In 1985, the EAHCA underwent changes due to the *Smith v. Robinson* case, which questioned the awards of attorney's fees in cases of FAPE. The result of the case was the Handicapped Children's Protection Act (PL 99-372, 1986), which stated if parents sue and win the case, they can be reimbursed by the school district for attorney's fees. Another aspect of this case was the ten-day letter. This letter is sent to parents with a settlement and if the decision is not close to that, they may not get reimbursed for fees. Another change was in the age requirements. Originally EAHCA was for students five to eighteen years old. It was changed to encompass a larger population including all children from birth to twenty-one years old in most states, with the exceptions of the states of Maine and Montana which provide education until the age of nineteen and Michigan which provides services until age twenty-six.

This age requirement was followed by a challenge of a "severity" requirement in the case of *Timothy v. Rochester School District* (1989). This case concluded that all children are to be educated regardless of the "severity" of their disability (we recognize this terminology is deficit-based). This is known as "zero reject." The goals of this were to increase a child's capacity, reduce the cost of special education, minimize the use of institutions, and help families by integrating many types of intervention.

Individuals with Disabilities Education Act

As discussed in chapter 10, in 1990, EAHCA was changed to the Individuals with Disabilities Education Act (IDEA). The purpose of this title change was twofold. It not only changed the identification of the law but also changed the terminology of the law itself. It used the term disability rather than handicapped and also utilized person-first terminology. In addition, it added the categories of autism and traumatic brain injury (TBI), which were being served under other categories until this time. Under IDEA, students with disabilities must be identified as having one of a set of thirteen categories of disability to such an extent that the disability interferes with their ability to learn in order to receive special education services (IDEA, 2004). The thirteen federal disability categories include autism, deaf-blindness, emotional disturbance, hearing impairment (including deafness), intellectual disability, multiple disabilities, orthopedic impairment, other health impairment, serious emotional disturbance, specific learning disability, speech or language impairment, traumatic brain injury, visual impairment (including blindness) (IDEA, 2004). Despite these changes, the basic principles of the law were not changed. These principles mandate that all children who meet the requirements are provided an education, LRE, IEP, and FAPE.

VIGNETTE 2: *BOB'S INCLUSION*

The terms inclusion and least restrictive environment did not have any meaning to me until I was at least fourteen. I think the first time I heard these terms was at one of my IEP meetings. Such terms may be part of why I hated to attend the meetings. Memories of middle school are hard for me. The school's use (or maybe misuse) of LRE and inclusion negatively impacted me academically, socially, and emotionally. My LRE changed, which resulted in less inclusion and I felt isolated without the peers I knew around me. Except for PE, communications, and art classes, a special education teacher in what they called a "learning lab class" provided the rest of my instruction. Many of the other students had behavior disabilities and interrupted class continually. I remember countless worksheets with very little instruction from the teacher. Class was not interesting and I believe I missed appropriate academic instruction. I also believe that my emotional health issues, including depression, link directly to a lack of social opportunities. A sad memory for me is meeting the requirements to go on two field trips, both of which I missed because an accessible bus did not arrive for me. This was after my mom talked to the principal ahead of time with him confirming that a bus to meet my needs would be available. My experiences with an inappropriate LRE resulted in limited general education and participation in school activities and demonstrates the importance of inclusion.

Surgery and the COVID pandemic altered my high school years in various ways. Following a major orthopedic surgery, I received homebound instruction for about eight weeks. One of my special education teachers would come to my house to work with me three times per week. The teacher helped me with all subject areas. Just as I was ready and able to return to school in-person, the school closed due to COVID. The remainder of that year and my entire 11th grade year, I attended school virtually but with more general education classes than in middle school. Although I have heard that many students suffered during virtual instruction, I thrived. I met with all my teachers and classmates daily using a school-provided computer with a conferencing app and learning management system. Because my disabilities were not visible during virtual instruction, my classmates did not perceive me as different. I had to have my camera

(continued)

VIGNETTE 2: *Continued*

on but it only showed my face and upper torso which is not affected as much as my legs from cerebral palsy. My classmates did not see my walker, wheelchair, or ankle foot orthoses (AFOs). If something was hard for me to say due to my speech articulation impairment, I could type it in the chat. If I needed something in larger print because of my vision impairment, I could enlarge it on my own. If I could not hear clearly, I could manipulate the computer volume on my own. When I needed one-on-one help from any of my teachers, I could set up a virtual chat with them without my peers knowing I needed extra assistance. Using the computer to generate and submit my work also worked in my favor since I had access to spell check, text-to-speech software, a word processing program, and the internet. I could use these built-in accommodations whenever I desired. My favorite was being able to type everything and not having to do anything handwritten since my cerebral palsy makes handwriting difficult.

The results of virtual instruction for me included all of the following:

- *Increased self-confidence*
- *Increased interaction with peers (via the phone, texts, and during class)*
- *Increased reading scores*
- *Increased self-determination*
- *Increased participation in classes*
- *Increased social connections with peers*
- *Signed up for classes out of my comfort zone for 12th grade*
- *Experienced a setting where my disability was not visible and did not matter*
- *Explored my gender identities with classmates who were not judgmental*

In 2002, the next major change to IDEA was made as a result of the *Arlington Central School District v. D.K. and K.K.* decision. Other changes to IDEA in 2004 included appropriate services to support participation in statewide assessments, with all supplementary aids and services to be reported in the second page of the IEP. There are multiple cases and decisions which still seek to answer the questions of what is "appropriate" and LRE. Since the last reauthorization, there have been many proposals for changes to IDEA. Some of these changes suggest:

- Removing objectives, leaving only annual goals on IEPs
- Establishing tri-annual reevaluations for all students
- Introducing pre-referral services
- Changing due process to give school district time to rectify situations
- Providing options for binding arbitration
- Providing guidance in cases of absence of consent
- Providing criteria for determination of eligibility
- Providing more guidance on functional behavioral assessments
- Changing discrepancy formula
- Changing the manifestation determination review process
- Changing requirements for behavioral intervention plans

Many of these proposed changes are in response to activism by individuals with disabilities, parents, and other stakeholders. Following is a discussion of the impact of activism on the language used to describe and refer to disabilities.

IMPACT OF ACTIVISM ON LANGUAGE

Language affects opportunities and outcomes for individuals with disabilities. Disability rights activists have long advocated for the use of respectful and inclusive language. It is critical that we describe characteristics of disabled students for the purposes of evaluation and treatment, but it is equally important that we do so in ways that promote the dignity and competence of every individual. Language reflects cultural norms for sociocultural identity, beliefs, and attitudes. Language choices also impact attitudes, beliefs, and the presumption of competency. For example, students with emotional and behavioral disorders now receive services in "emotional support" classrooms, reflecting a growing realization that these students are not "deviants" or "delinquents" who simply choose to engage in problematic behaviors and are therefore deserving of harsh punishments and exclusion from school; rather, they are students who may have experienced trauma or might have an underlying condition that makes regulating their emotions and actions more difficult.

The meaning of "inclusion" when referring to participation in the general education setting has evolved over time. Initially, the term mainstreaming was used. However, "mainstreaming" became associated with a connotation that students with disabilities had to meet certain criteria to *earn* access to general education classrooms. The term inclusion, on the other hand, implies that the student's right to participate in the general education setting with a sense of belonging does not depend upon any criteria; it is simply conferred as a *right* under IDEA.

As discussed in chapter 6, person-first language and identity-first language refer to the syntax used when referring to people with disabilities. In the past, terms like "physically disabled person" or "learning disabled student" were utilized. As a result of activism by the disability rights community with the American Psychological Association in the early 1990s (Crocker & Smith, 2019), it became more acceptable to use person-first language, in which the person was placed before the disability, to emphasize the humanity of the individual and to indicate that the disability was but one aspect of the whole person. Some examples of person-first language include "person with a physical disability" and "student with a learning disability." Adopting person-first language principles removed pejorative terms such as "crippled," "mongoloid," "idiot," "retarded," and others from professional discourse. For example, in the United States, "mentally retarded" went from being used as a medical term to describe an individual with an intellectual disability to entering the general discourse as a pejorative. In 2010, "intellectual disability" officially replaced references to "mental retardation" in all federal health, education, and labor statutes with the passage of Rosa's Law. (See more about Rosa's Law in chapter 6.)

Additionally, phrases that impart a negative connotation to having a disability are also no longer considered appropriate. For example, to say that a person is "wheelchair bound" implies that the person is helpless without their wheelchair. A person-first phrasing is to say "person who uses a wheelchair" because this language frames the person as active and capable of using the wheelchair as a tool or device, without implying dependence or frailty. Other terms such as "suffering" or "suffers from" have been replaced with terms such as "experiences" (e.g., suffers from a mental illness versus experiences a mental illness). Saying a person "suffers" is making assumptions about another's experiences.

Many people with disabilities prefer to use what is called identity-first language. Identity-first language syntax puts the disability first—disabled person, Deaf person—or uses the condition as a stand-alone descriptor: Autistic. Individuals who prefer identity-first language are clear that their disability is an important part of their identity—it is an integral part of who they are, and they want to acknowledge that part of themselves. Because people differ in their preferences, it is best to ask how an individual prefers to be addressed, and to honor their responses when interacting with, discussing, and writing about them (e.g., in an IEP or other professional report, as well as in informal communications). Parent, caregiver, or educator preferences should not take precedence over a disabled individual's choice, although many times professionals will utilize person-first language when an individual with a disability's preference is not available. Many disabled activists advocate that the default should be identity-first language.

INCLUSION AND LEAST RESTRICTIVE ENVIRONMENT

As noted earlier, legislation codified into law the right of all children with disabilities to receive a free and appropriate education provided by their local public school district in the least restrictive environment (LRE). However, this did not guarantee that disabled students are educated in the general education classroom or have access to the general education curriculum with their nondisabled peers. Between 1975 and 1990, most students with disabilities were placed in segregated classrooms with other students with disabilities (Blackorby et al., 2006). This could be due to the language used in PL 94-142 and its subsequent reauthorizations, IDEA (1997, 2004), in which LRE is described as:

> To the maximum extent appropriate, children with disabilities, including children in public or private institutions or other care facilities, are educated with children who are not disabled, and special classes, separate schooling, or other removal of children with disabilities from the regular educational environment occurs only when the nature or severity of the disability of a child is such that education in

regular classes with the use of supplementary aids and services cannot be achieved satisfactorily. 20 U.S.C. § 1412(a)(5)(A)

This language leaves much open to the interpretation of members of the IEP team. It can be inferred that if a student with a disability cannot be adequately served in the general education setting with supplemental aids and services, the recourse is to place them in a more segregated setting, rather than adapting the general education environment by intensifying aids and services to ensure accessibility to the student with a disability. **Adaptations** can include **accommodations** (i.e., adaptations that do not change the rigor or expected outcomes) and **modifications** (i.e., adaptations that do change the rigor or expected outcomes).

There is a continuum of placements available for students with disabilities to receive an education. Table 11.1 outlines a continuum of placement options.

Table 11.1. Continuum of Educational Placements from Least to Most Restrictive

Educational Placement	Description
General Education Classroom	Student attends the general education classroom for the entire school day without special education support; student may receive related services (e.g., speech, occupational or physical therapy)
General Education Classroom with Consultative Special Education Support	Student attends the general education classroom for the entire school day; a special education professional consults with the general education teacher; no direct special education services provided; student may receive related services
General Education Classroom with Collaborative Special Education Support (e.g., co-teach, paraprofessional)	Student attends the general education classroom for the entire school day; a special education professional provides direct service to the student in the general education classroom; student may receive related services
Resource Room Support	Student attends the special education classroom for some part of the school day; a special education professional provides direct service to the student in the special education classroom; student may receive related services
Self-Contained Special Education Classroom	Student attends the special education classroom for the entire school day; a special education professional provides direct service to the student in the special education classroom; student may receive related services; student may participate in some activities in the general education setting, often special classes such as gym, music or art
Segregated Special Day Program	Student attends an educational placement outside of the neighborhood school, continues to live at home with caregivers
Homebound Instruction	Student receives instruction at home from an itinerant teacher
Residential Treatment Program	Student attends a residential educational and therapeutic program
Hospital-Based Instructional Program	Student receives instruction from a hospital-based program while admitted as a patient

In the 1990s, parents and other disability rights advocates began to push for **inclusion** in the general education setting. Some individuals argue that nothing less than full inclusion (i.e., all students with disabilities receive all of their instruction in the general education setting) is fair and appropriate (Artiles et al., 2006). Proponents of full inclusion see segregation of students with disabilities as a social justice issue and believe that schools are responsible for providing the accommodations necessary to provide FAPE in the general education setting. On the other hand, advocates of a continuum of educational placements, which includes instruction in self-contained special education classrooms for at least some part of the school day, believe that for some students, the LRE is an alternative to the general education setting because it is in the least restrictive setting in which the student is best able to benefit from the educational program described in the student's IEP (Artiles et al., 2006). According to the advocates of a continuum of placements, students with any type of disability may benefit from services delivered in the special education setting.

In particular, students with complex instructional needs and students with significant communication or behavioral needs are often seen as requiring more restrictive educational placements.

Pause and Reflect

- When might full inclusion be beneficial?
- When might other placements be beneficial?
- How can disability as a sociocultural identity be centered across the continuum of educational placements?

VIGNETTE 3: *BOB'S JOURNEY*

Returning to in-person school for my senior year was nerve wracking since my virtual school experience was so positive. My senior year turned out wonderful largely because of my LRE requiring increased inclusion in academics and school activities. My accommodations included peer supports and continued use of accessibility options on the computer. Many of my classmates were the same students who I had virtual classes with the previous two years. My special education time centered on pre-employment skills, English, and math. I also was able to work for five hours a week at the school with a salary paid by the state's rehabilitation program for high school students. For theater, Spanish, dance, and financial literacy classes, I was fully included in general education. I made new friends in my theater and dance classes. My new friends identified socially in many different ways and had no problems accepting that sometimes I identify as a female.

My classes spanned across three different buildings, making it necessary for me to use my wheelchair. I was surprised that this visibility of my disability did not seem to bother anyone.

Unlike in middle school, I felt like an equal peer. I think my feelings of social acceptance were due to inclusion being a focus of everyone on my team, including me advocating for a LRE that correlated to inclusive settings and practices. Inclusion helped me stay busy with social and extracurricular activities. I joined the afterschool archery club, tried out for and got parts in two school plays, participated in three public dance performances, went to prom, and socialized after school and on the weekends with some of my new friends. I also participated in many fun events during the school day (like Homecoming dress-up days) and in all the senior special events! My favorite senior event was the award ceremony. I received awards for archery, English, theater, and Spanish!

Throughout my K–12 schooling and currently, I have had the privilege of strong family support. My family advocated on my behalf and was regularly involved with my school activities. My mom always attended my special education conferences. My privilege also is apparent in the fact that in addition to school therapies, I also have received outpatient therapy services since I was four years old. We live near an award-winning children's hospital so I receive regular access to excellent medical services to address all of my disabilities. These privileges correlate with me learning to be a self-advocate for my own educational experiences.

I graduated in the spring and took a gap year for another major orthopedic surgery and rehabilitation. I am currently doing daily PT and starting to apply for job-training programs. The application process includes piles of paperwork and staying connected with the state's rehabilitation services. Unfortunately, I am finding myself back in a situation where my disability is front and center on each application. It makes me feel like the system is more interested in what I cannot do than what I can. I have been discouraged while filling out the applications but at the same time need the program to gain the skills I need for competitive employment. I wonder what being part of one of the job-training programs will be like. Will it be more like my middle school or high school experiences? Will I be able to be seen for who I am or will there be more of a focus on my disabilities?

DISPROPORTIONALITY

In our education system, there is documented disproportionality in both special education identification and discipline. In this section, we define disproportionality, discuss patterns of disproportionality, describe why disproportionality is a problem, and why it persists despite efforts to reduce it. We also discuss disproportionality in discipline and offer suggestions to reduce disproportionality and provide alternatives to aversive disciplinary strategies.

Disproportionality in special education happens when there is a difference between the proportion of a given demographic group (e.g., race, ethnicity, gender, and other sociocultural identities) identified for special education in general or within specific categories, and the proportion of that group in the school-age population. For example, 2020–2021 school year figures from the National Center on Educational Statistics report that 17.7 percent of [cisgender] boys ages five to twenty-one were identified as having a disability, compared to 9.6 percent of [cisgender] girls, even though the populations of cis boys and girls in US schools are roughly equal (US Census Bureau, 2019). In the IDEA disability category of Intellectual Disability (ID), 5 percent of white students with a disability were identified as ID, while 8.8 percent of Black students were served under the ID label (NCES, 2021). To be clear, this does not mean that 8.8 percent of Black students have been identified with an ID; rather, out of the total number of Black students identified with any disability, 8.8 percent of them were identified as ID. This is larger than the rate of white students with disabilities who were identified as ID (5 percent), hence the term "disproportionality." More on this topic can be found in chapter 2.

Patterns of disproportionality exist and have persisted for decades (Hosp & Reschly, 2004; NCES, 2021). In general, students who are male and Black tend to be overrepresented in high-incidence disability categories (i.e., categories with large numbers of identified students relative to other disability categories) including mild intellectual disabilities (ID) and emotional disturbance (ED). Native Alaskan and Indigenous students are overrepresented in the category of specific learning disability (SLD). Black, Hispanic, and Indigenous students are underrepresented in the gifted and talented category, whereas Asian and Pacific Islander students are underrepresented in almost every category (Hosp & Reschly, 2004; NCES, 2021).

For decades, disproportionality has been considered a significant problem, beginning with Lloyd Dunn's seminal article identifying the problem in 1968. Numerous studies have been conducted in the intervening years to study the causes and effects of disproportionality (Donovan & Cross, 2002). The primary concern is that disproportionality in special education identification leads to limited access to the general education curriculum and more restrictive placements for students (Skiba et al., 2006). Disabled students are entitled by IDEA to be educated with their nondisabled peers to the greatest extent possible, however, the nature of special education services may require some differences in service delivery from the instruction typically developing students receive in the general education classroom and curriculum. Erroneously identifying students leads to labels and services the students do not need, in a setting that is more restrictive than they require. Additionally, the stigma of a special education label may be acceptable as a necessary component of the IEP process for a student with a disability but will be an undue burden for a student who is mislabeled. Consider the case of a Black male student who is underperforming in reading due to a language processing disorder, but who is given the label of ID instead of speech language impairment (SLI) or specific learning disability (SLD). This student, had he been properly identified, might have received services from a speech and language clinician and/or a special education teacher, provided in the general education setting, with perhaps a short period of time spent in a special education classroom. However, the ID label might result in the student being segregated into a special education classroom for a majority of the school day.

Chapter 2 discussed the overrepresentation of gender and racial disparities in special education, but we suggest it is also possible that some students who require services may not be receiving them. For example, Asian and Pacific Islander students are underrepresented in all categories. Consider a preschool Asian American autistic student whose culturally determined behaviors are assumed to be the reason they struggle socially, and who therefore is not referred for special education evaluation and misses out on important early intervention services. Reducing disproportionality in special education identification to the greatest extent possible ensures equitable access to needed special education services and also prevents racist and ableist identification and segregation into unnecessarily restrictive environments.

Disproportionality in Discipline

An important concern with disproportionality has been that some students with disabilities may be at increased risk of exclusionary discipline, such as out-of-school suspension (Skiba et al., 2011; 2014). The trend in higher rates of suspensions for disabled students begins as early as preschool (Garro et al., 2021). This is problematic because students who are suspended from school show lower academic achievement (Rausch & Skiba, 2005), higher dropout rates (Pesta, 2018), and higher likelihood of involvement in the juvenile justice system (Hughes et al., 2020). Researchers have found disproportionality in discipline on the basis of race to be mostly attributable to school-level variables, including building principals' attitudes toward discipline (Skiba et al., 2014). Other factors identified through research are that being male, experiencing poverty, and attending a lower-resourced school increase an individual student's chance of being suspended, with disability status as an insignificant factor (Morgan et al., 2019). This suggests that students whose disabilities intersect with other minoritized sociocultural identities are more likely to attend low-resourced schools where administrators follow zero tolerance policies and use exclusionary discipline practices, and that may be the reason they experience higher rates of suspension than their white peers and students who have more financial resources available to them. For more examples of this kind of intersectional disproportionality, see chapter 2.

Disproportionality in discipline also exists with respect to aversive procedures, including seclusion and restraint (Gage et al., 2020; Whitaker & Losen, 2019). Seclusion refers to the practice of segregating a student in a solitary space (e.g., a separate room with no furnishings, sometimes with carpeted or padded walls and floor). Physical restraint refers to school personnel physically holding a student so that the student cannot move freely, whereas mechanical restraint involves using devices such as straps or handcuffs to immobilize students (US Department of Education OCR, 2019). Students who traditionally experience oppression are more likely than other students to experience seclusion and restraint (Katsiyannis et al., 2020). In 2019, 15 percent of all students in US public schools were Black, and yet Black youth made up 27 percent of students restrained and 23 percent of students secluded. Also in 2019, 14 percent of all students were identified as having a disability, yet disabled students made up 71 percent of students who were restrained and 66 percent of students who were secluded (US Department of Education OCR, 2019). This is even more troubling when you consider that seclusion and restraint have been shown to be ineffective in preventing problem behavior, as well as having harmful effects including physical injury to students and increased aggression (Katsiyannis et al., 2020).

Reasons for Disproportionality

Some researchers attribute disproportionality to bias, including gender (Oswald et al., 2006) and racial bias (Harry & Klingner, 2014). As discussed throughout this text, racial bias may be due to a cultural mismatch between the student's sociocultural identities and those of practitioners and school leaders (Gay, 2002). While racial bias among teachers is a difficult subject to confront, it must be acknowledged. Bias can be either *explicit*, in which individuals are aware of their racial attitudes and knowingly act upon them, or *implicit*, in which individuals are not aware of their racial attitudes and do not understand the ways in which these attitudes impact their treatment of socioculturally diverse students. Studies have shown that white teachers interpret the behavior of Black children, particularly Black male children, more negatively than similar behaviors of white children (Halberstadt et al., 2018; Jarvis & Okonofua, 2019).

Since teachers are most often the first persons to initiate referral for special education evaluation, implicit bias is most likely a significant factor in disproportionality. Other researchers point to factors such as low socioeconomic status (SES), which tends to affect some groups of students in greater numbers, and school factors such as overall achievement and access to resources, both of which are depressed in schools with lower socioeconomic status (Hibel et al., 2010; Shifrer et al., 2011). While the link between low SES and disability cannot be clearly defined, we discussed in chapters 2 and 4 how students who grow up in lower socioeconomic environments have reduced access to high-quality prenatal care, adequate nutrition, and early intervention programs, and a greater chance of exposure to environmental hazards, such as lead and air pollution, all of which are noted to be risk factors for high-incidence disabilities (Kauffman et al., 2017). Research has shown underrepresentation of students with specific sociocultural identities in high-incidence categories when socioeconomic status (SES) and school variables have been controlled for (Morgan et al., 2015), suggesting that students attending under-resourced schools may in fact be less likely to have access to special education services. These contradictory findings suggest that more research is needed to determine the causes of disproportionality and the ways in which inequitable access to services impact students with and without identified disabilities.

Reducing Disproportionality

When teachers do not use culturally and linguistically sustaining pedagogy (CLSP), it negatively impacts diverse students' learning and behavior (Ladson-Billings, 1995). We suggest taking CLSP further and consider what sociocultural sustaining pedagogy may look like. In order to reduce disproportionality in special education identification, we recommend increasing training in intersectional sociocultural competence and socioculturally sustaining practices for pre- and in-service general and special education teachers. This can be accomplished through strategies such as improving teacher quality through better teacher preparation, reducing income inequities, and promoting equitable access to culturally relevant, evidence-based instructional practices (Anastasiou et al., 2017; Boveda & Aronson, 2019; Whitford & Carrero, 2019.) To reduce disproportionality in discipline, it is necessary for schools to collect and analyze data to determine where disparities and inequities exist.

> **Pause and Reflect**
>
> - What kinds of data have school districts historically collected to define demographics? Disparities? Inequities?
> - What kinds of data could school districts collect to identify sociocultural identities and experiences?

Then school leaders need to educate school personnel about historical patterns of disproportionality in discipline as well as contributing factors, such as implicit bias (Carter et al., 2017). Practitioners should implement alternatives to exclusionary discipline, including using a problem-solving approach and restorative practices rather than exclusionary or aversive disciplinary procedures.

Disproportionality exists where assessment, instruction, and disciplinary procedures are not responsive to the individual needs of diverse students. Following is a description of current academic and behavioral service delivery frameworks designed to increase responsiveness to intersectional student needs.

EDUCATIONAL FRAMEWORKS

In this section, we discuss the educational frameworks represented in this book: Integrated Multi-Tiered Systems of Support (I-MTSS), including Response to

Intervention (RTI) and Positive Behavioral Interventions and Supports (PBIS), and Universal Design for Learning (UDL). We also introduce Assistive Technology (AT), specifically Augmentative and Alternative Communication (AAC).

In order for any of these to effectively reduce disproportionality, practitioners must center socioculturally sustaining instructional, behavioral, and assessment practices (Sailor et al., 2021). This means practitioners are actively (a) valuing students' sociocultural identities; (b) incorporating students' interests and using instructional materials that are representative of students' sociocultural identities; (c) scaffolding and supporting student learning by meeting students where they are academically; and (d) using modeling and guided practice to help students master increasingly challenging material. Some specific examples of ways in which teachers incorporate students' sociocultural identities into their classrooms include (Morrison et al., 2008):

- using manipulatives (e.g., shells, dominoes) that are representative of students' cultures
- using students' home language or dialect along with Standard English in classroom labeling and discourse
- using songs, stories, games, and activities drawn from students' cultural expressions and traditions
- seeking input from diverse families and community members
- using socioculturally representative classroom signage, materials, and decorations
- attending local cultural events as class field trips
- inviting students to share socioculturally significant objects from home in class (e.g., class museum)
- encouraging students to share their families' cultural traditions and experiences during classroom activities (e.g., morning circle time and relevant class discussions)
- analyzing classroom materials and literature for bias

Socioculturally sustaining practice in schools involves practitioners being (a) willing to examine their own sociocultural identities and biases regarding students; (b) making classroom expectations clear, explicit, and socioculturally relevant; (c) teaching students the skills needed to meet expectations; (d) reinforcing students for meeting expectations; and (e) using problem-solving and restorative practices when needed (Childs et al., 2016; Sugai & Horner, 2020). Other chapters in this text can help you become a socioculturally sustaining practitioner.

Integrated Multi-Tiered Systems of Support

Integrated Multi-Tiered Systems of Support (I-MTSS) is a model of educational assessment and instructional service delivery designed to prevent several problems with traditional approaches to disability identification, including disproportionality in special education identification and discipline (Hoover & Soltero-Gonzalez, 2018). I-MTSS combines academic and behavioral supports into a three-tiered system of evidence-based core instruction, universal screening, and graduated levels of academic and behavioral intervention. It is imperative that educators using I-MTSS employ what are known as evidence-based practices (EBP). An evidence-based practice has been examined by researchers through multiple high-quality empirical studies and has been demonstrated to have had positive effects on the target skill or behavior without negative effects on the participants (Gersten et al., 2005; Horner et al., 2005). Teachers should verify that an evidence-based practice has been evaluated using participants who are similar to the student who will be using the intervention to make sure that the practice is socioculturally sustaining and appropriate.

A critical feature of MTSS is data-based decision making. The goal of data-based decision making is to increase diagnostic and prescriptive accuracy by (a) providing students with high-quality instruction; (b) using frequent progress monitoring to measure students' response to the instruction; and (c) making subsequent instructional and special education eligibility decisions based upon the data collected (Fuchs & Fuchs, 2006). Theoretically, this process will help to eliminate bias in these decisions and will therefore reduce disproportionality. Historically, academics were addressed through a three-tiered system known as response to intervention (RTI), while behavioral supports are provided through a tiered system known as positive behavioral interventions and support (PBIS).

Response to Intervention

Response to Intervention (RTI) is a three-tiered model of instructional delivery and assessment of student need for instructional support. Since the reauthorization of IDEA in 2004, RTI has become part of evaluation for special education services in the specific learning disability (SLD) category. At Tier 1, all students receive high-quality, research-based instruction in core subjects, including reading, writing, and math. All students in Tier 1 are universally screened to ensure they are meeting academic progress benchmarks, typically twice per school year. Students who score below what is considered a benchmark are moved to the Tier 2 level and provided with supplemental instruction targeted to their instructional needs. Assessment at Tier 2 involves more frequent **progress monitoring**, in which skills in reading, writing and math are monitored on a regular (e.g., weekly or biweekly) basis using alternate forms of the same curriculum-based measure (e.g., short reading passages or sets of math problems that reflect the specific skills and content the student has been taught) to track growth. This growth is used to determine the student's response to intervention—that is, how much the student's skill improved as a result of the supplemental instruction the student received. Students who show what is perceived to be "adequate growth" are determined to have responded well to the intervention and are returned to Tier 1. Students who show what is perceived as "slow or insignificant growth" are moved to Tier 3, where they are provided with more intensive, individualized instruction, and more frequent progress monitoring. Students who do not show what is perceived as "adequate growth" at Tier 3 are referred to special education.

RTI was created to address issues of diagnostic unreliability and alarmingly rapid growth in the number of students identified with disabilities, especially specific learning disabilities (SLD; Fletcher & Navarette, 2003; Vaughn & Fuchs, 2003). Prior to RTI, the ability-achievement discrepancy model used a comparison of scores on intelligence (IQ) tests and standardized measures of achievement to determine the presence of a learning disability. If a student scored in the average range on a standardized intelligence test but scored below average on achievement measures, the discrepancy was considered evidence of a learning disability. The main criticisms of this model are (a) IQ tests are not reliable measures of intellectual ability; (b) cut-off points for determining below-average performance on achievement measures are arbitrary and fail to meaningfully distinguish students whose scores fall close to the cut score; and (c) students must spend years in school without remediation before their achievement falls below the score needed to be considered eligible for services. The ability-achievement discrepancy approach became known as the "wait to fail" model (Vaughn & Fuchs, 2003).

A further criticism of the ability-achievement discrepancy model of special education identification is that it contributes to the overrepresentation of socioculturally diverse learners in the category of SLD (Fuchs et al., 2003). This is attributed to two reasons: (a) practitioners who are not familiar with or sensitive to a student's sociocultural identities may misinterpret behaviors and be less skilled at selecting appropriate evidence-based practices to address learning, leading to increased referral for special education services (Klingner & Edwards, 2006); and (b) research has shown that IQ tests contain biases that cause the overrepresentation of socioculturally diverse students in the disability categories SLD, ID, and ED (Proctor et al., 2012). In addition to these biases, socioculturally diverse students, particularly those still learning English, tend to score higher on nonverbal and performance-based assessments and lower on language-based assessments, including reading and writing, when assessed in English rather than their first language and therefore are overidentified as SLD by schools using the discrepancy model (Fletcher & Navarette, 2003).

Current best practice recommendations for RTI implementation for the purpose of SLD identification include the necessity for all practitioners to receive training in culturally sustaining pedagogy, including socioculturally sustaining assessment practices (Montalvo et al., 2014). Practitioners should be trained to use socioculturally sustaining instructional practices at Tier 1 to ensure all students are receiving core instruction that is sensitive to their instructional, sociocultural, and social-emotional needs (Montalvo et al., 2014).

Positive Behavioral Interventions and Supports

Whereas RTI focuses on academics, **Schoolwide Positive Behavioral Interventions and Supports** (SWPBIS) is a multi-tiered system that utilizes a positive approach to teach and support ALL students behaviorally. When creating a PBIS system, the first step is to draft a set (e.g., approximately three to seven) of positively stated expectations for behaviors in different contexts. Typically, these expectations are short and describe general principles (e.g., Be Safe, Be Responsible, Be Respectful). Under each general expectation, different sets of specific expectations for various environments are created using a behavioral matrix. Then there are procedures for preventing "inappropriate" behaviors; teaching the expectations; reinforcing the expectations; providing adaptations, reminders, and corrective feedback to meet expectations; and establishing consequences. To ensure the expectations and procedures are socioculturally sustaining, families and caregivers, students, and community stakeholders should be an integral part of the PBIS team.

All the expectations in a matrix should proactively include accommodations to meet intersectional student needs. For example, "Carry your tray and other items" in the cafeteria could be an expectation of all students, but an accommodation may be that the student asks for help carrying their tray. For an expectation such as "Follow directions," the practitioner could provide visuals with verbal directions and provide additional supports when necessary. When teaching about the social norms about voice volume, strategies could include a visual support scale and examples of different levels of voice volume. Best practices call for involving students in the creation of behavioral expectations to foster a sense of belonging and gain collaborative buy-in. Table 11.2 is a behavioral matrix that would be created by a teacher for use in a specific classroom.

There are three PBIS tiers, which include universal, secondary, and tertiary tiers. At Tier 1, all students receive universal training in the expectations and, ideally, the school provides universal instruction in social skills and emotional

Table 11.2. Behavioral Matrix

Expectation	Classroom	Playground	Cafeteria	Bathroom	Bus
Be Safe	Move safely around room	Follow safety expectations when using playground equipment	Eat your food safely	Wash your hands with soap after using the toilet	Stay in your seat while the bus is moving
Be Responsible	Ask for help				
Be Respectful	Listen when others are talking				

and behavioral regulation using a research-based social and emotional curriculum. Universal screening (e.g., tracking office disciplinary referrals [ODR]; Grasley-Boy et al., 2022) identifies students who need additional support. Given the bias discussed earlier in this chapter and volume, universal screening is flawed, but research shows that PBIS has the potential to reduce disproportionality in discipline (Childs et al., 2016; Sugai & Horner, 2020; Vincent et al., 2011). Universal screening is one way to identify students who need to be moved to Tier 2, where they are provided with targeted social and behavioral instruction and provided with evidence-based interventions, such as Check In–Check Out (Hawken & Horner, 2003). With Check In–Check Out, the student and a preferred adult meet in the morning, and they discuss the student's goals for the day. At the end of the day, they meet again and the student shares how the day went. The adult provides reinforcement for the goals that are met, and they work together to determine how to help the student work toward meeting all their goals. More intensive support is offered at Tier 3, where the interventions may include functional behavior assessments (FBA), individualized behavior support plans, and strategies such as daily data sheets, family involvement with specific reinforcement strategies, and sometimes referral for wraparound services involving service providers in the community.

Universal Design for Learning

One key instructional design practice that can promote equitable access to instruction for diverse learners is **Universal Design for Learning** (UDL). According to CAST, "Universal Design for Learning (UDL) is a framework to improve and optimize teaching and learning based on scientific insights into how humans learn" (CAST, 2022, para 1). UDL follows three principles for differentiating instruction (Rose & Meyer, 2002), which include providing multiple means of (a) representation, (b) engagement, and (c) action and expression. An overarching approach, UDL focuses at the outset of planning on the inclusive design of the whole learning environment to ensure all students have full and equitable access in the classroom with these principles embedded into all three tiers of RTI and PBIS. See chapter 10 for the history of universal design and the barrier-free movement.

The UDL method of universally planning and delivering instruction also provides differentiated instruction to students who require this level of support. **Differentiated instruction** is a teaching strategy that is individualized to address the needs and preferences of each student by modifying content and processes. Students with disabilities can achieve greater access to the general education curriculum when instruction is differentiated according to their specific learning strengths and needs (Kieran & Anderson, 2019).

Previous criticism has been raised in regard to UDL not including a sociocultural lens, and so we recommend adopting this lens when planning and

Table 11.3. Universal Design for Learning

Means	Description
Multiple Means of Representation	How teachers present information, skills, and concepts.
	Differentiation of representation might include presenting information visually as well as through lecturing.
	This might include using students' home language(s) along with English and using socioculturally relevant examples and manipulatives that capitalize on students' existing background knowledge and lived experiences.
Multiple Means of Engagement	How students interact with instructional materials and content.
	Differentiation of means of engagement might include varying the instructional grouping—using small groups instead of whole group instruction—or using choral responding so all students have an opportunity to respond and receive feedback instead of calling on one student at a time while everyone else sits passively listening.
	Honoring sociocultural preferences for cooperative versus individual learning and incorporating student choice of authentic learning activities may help them master complex material and increase their sense of belonging.
Multiple Means of Expression	How students demonstrate what they learned.
	Differentiation of expression might include allowing students to recite orally rather than provide answers in writing, or to write a poem or song instead of answering multiple choice questions.
	Frequent checks for comprehension and supportive feedback can support mastery of skills and concepts.

implementing UDL. Differentiation should also address intersecting sociocultural identities as well as individual characteristics. Table 11.3 shows examples of how UDL's three principles can infuse socioculturally sustaining practices:

Assistive Technology: Augmentative and Alternative Communication

Augmentative and Alternative Communication (AAC) is a type of assistive technology (AT) designed to help individuals better communicate with others. AAC can include the use of gestures, manual signs, drawings, picture/symbol boards, letter boards, and speech-generating devices (SGDs), or a combination of several of these. **Augmentative communication** refers to a system which *enhances* (augments) a person's use of existing speech. **Alternative communication** refers to a system that is *used in place of* nonexisting speech or nonfunctional speech. Alternative communication systems can be temporary in the case of stroke, head trauma, or as part of postoperative treatment (Elsahar et al., 2019). Language and communication skills can improve when well-organized, evidence- and research-based AAC interventions take place. For more information about alternative communication, see chapter 10.

The field of AAC is relatively young. Prior to the late 1970s, there were no academic courses offered on the topic in the United States. In part this was due to the myth that if persons were trained to use manual signs or any other alternative to speech in order to communicate, such persons would never learn to speak (Lloyd & Pufpaff, 1999). During this time, it is not known how many nonspeaking individuals were living in residential institutions, attending special education classes, or staying at home having no access to AAC intervention. Therefore these individuals had reduced human interaction and lacked the opportunity to develop social cognition.

In 1977–1978, the most significant advancement in services to persons without functional speech occurred. During that academic year, three midwestern US universities, with graduate and doctoral programs in speech language pathology and special education, offered the first courses in AAC as electives or seminars. In the forty years since those first AAC courses were offered, there has been slow but systematic growth in academic preparation for evaluation and treatment in AAC. The lack of widespread and in-depth preservice professional training, such as speech pathology and special education students receiving no clinical practicum in AAC (Johnson & Prebor, 2019), remains a barrier to the early and sustained intervention and education of persons with complex communication needs (CCN).

As awareness of persons with CCN increased (in part due to deinstitutionalization), many support groups and professional organizations formed. In 1983, the International Society for Augmentative and Alternative Communication (ISAAC) was founded to promote the best possible communication for persons with CCN and to promote the value of AAC across the world. This organization brings families, AAC users, therapists, practitioners, researchers, device producers, and politicians together to enhance the lives of AAC users, provide education, and promote international awareness. ISAAC is credited with increasing the linguistic and cultural diversity of persons who seek AAC across the globe. In 1991, the United States Society for Augmentative and Alternative Communication (USSAAC) was established as a chapter of ISAAC. USSAAC works to motivate and work with AAC users to become leaders in their respective fields, to affect public policy and work with the offices of Medicaid and Medicare to promote funding for AAC users to obtain devices.

In 2004, the Individuals with Disabilities Education Act was amended to provide for children's use of assistive technology for communication in all places where the student is communicating. Prior to this amendment, communication devices purchased by a school for a student had to remain in the school. However, it is essential that individualized education programs (IEPs) specify that students who are using/learning to use such devices have access to that device in all contexts of communication. This access is essential for individuals to develop communication in a variety of social contexts.

AAC systems can be divided into unaided or aided. Unaided systems are those which rely on the individual's use of their body (i.e., manual signs).

Aided systems include those which require special tools and equipment, and are divided into nontechnological, low technological, and high technological (Dukhovny & Kelly, 2015). Nontechnological systems include static picture or symbol communication boards. Low technological devices can be preset with different symbols on a grid and voice recordings can be programmed for each symbol. These devices can have anywhere from one to fifty symbols, can be used for particular contexts (i.e., a shopping trip or baseball game), and are easily portable. High technology devices require computerized software (Lloyd et al., 1997). Most of these systems are speech-generating devices. These systems work well for users who are literate or becoming literate. The user can begin to spell and a word prediction program can complete the word or add a phrase that is pragmatically and semantically appropriate, thereby increasing the speed of display and voice. Likewise, messages and phrases, even speeches or reports, can be preprogrammed by the user for communication in different contexts. Different pages can be accessed for particular subjects, classes, or social contexts. High technology devices have been revolutionized in the past decade with the rise of relatively low-cost AAC applications for touch-screen tablets, or advanced systems costing thousands of dollars. AAC systems have been found effective in improving communication (Schlosser, 2003).

There are an estimated five million people in America and ninety-seven million persons across the globe who would benefit from an AAC program (Beukelman & Light, 2020). Approximately 12 percent of preschoolers who receive special education need some form of AAC (Beukelman & Light, 2020). This is especially important because these children are at a disadvantage—most speaking children develop language in the very early preschool years, but children who are nonspeaking may not receive their devices until they are four to five years of age, if not later. These children are faced with acquiring language skills alongside learning academic content, which is very difficult.

Several challenges exist for AAC users from a sociocultural, economical, and educational standpoint. For starters, some might see the use of a device as stigmatizing, and therefore not want to use it. Multilingual people need to decide what language and what form of symbols are to be used. Family and student sociocultural needs may not match the practitioners' or professionals' expertise in programming. Professionals who work in this field and families require training on AAC device usage too, which means there needs to be funding for that training. Sometimes training can be covered as part of a student's IEP or it could be privately covered by some insurance companies. Some families and caregivers do not have the time to take away from work to meet such demands, but it is crucial that families are a part of the evaluation process and receive training. Additionally, AAC devices can vary in cost and the means of funding acquisition differs among states and school districts as well. While it is a school's responsibility to assist a family in purchasing an AAC device and other necessary devices (e.g., keyboard, joystick, head pointer), families may also need to explore other means of funding including Medicaid, Medicare, private insurance, or charitable resources. Negotiating and researching these options is complex and often serves as a barrier for people. Finally, it is not uncommon to have as many as thirty different professionals working with one individual, including but not limited to teachers (e.g., special and general education), therapists (e.g., speech and language, occupational, physical, music), paraprofessionals, rehabilitation engineers, assistive technology professionals, vision specialists, and respite care workers. This number of people involves a lot of coordination and team meetings. At least one professional should act as the liaison between service providers and the families of AAC users.

SUMMARY

This chapter described the history of the legislation of special education, including the legal cases that paved the way for the education of students with disabilities. The chapter introduced important, relevant litigation, including the push and pull of the litigation-legislation-litigation cycle and how that changes services for students with disabilities. This chapter highlighted the cycle of case law: Congress passing laws—regulations issued to the states—states enacting laws through regulations. Also highlighted was the reauthorization of the Individuals with Disabilities Education Act (IDEA), the evolution of language as a result of this activism, and recommended practices related to equitable access to education for socioculturally diverse students. Topics covered include disproportionality and multiple educational frameworks that have the potential to reduce disproportionality by centering socioculturally sustaining practices: Multi-Tiered Systems of Support (MTSS), Response to Intervention (RTI), Positive Behavioral Interventions and Supports (PBIS), Universal Design for Learning (UDL), and Augmentative and Alternative Communication (AAC).

REFERENCES

Anastasiou, D., Morgan, P., Farkas, G., & Wiley, A. (2017). Minority disproportionate representation: Politics and evidence, issues and implications. In J. Kauffman, J., D. Hallahan, & P. Pullen (Eds.), *Handbook of special education*. Pearson.

Artiles, A. J., Kozleski, E., Dorn, S., & Christensen, C. (2006). Learning in inclusive education research: Re-mediating theory and methods with a transformative agenda. *Review of Research in Education*, 30(1), 65–108. http://doi.org/10.3102/0091732X030001065

Artiles, A. J., Trent, S. C., & Kuan, L. A. (1997). Learning disabilities empirical research on ethnic minority students: An analysis of 22 years of studies published in selected refereed journals. *Learning Disabilities Research & Practice*, 12(2), 82–91.

Beukelman, D., & Light, J. (2020). *Augmentative and Alternative Communication*. Brookes.

Blackorby, J., Wagner, M., Cameto, R., Davies, E., Levine, P., Newman, L., . . . Sumi, C. (2006). *Engagement, academics, social adjustment, and independence: The achievements of elementary and middle school students with disabilities*. SRI International.

Boveda, M., & Aronson, B. (2019). Special education preservice teachers, intersectional diversity, and the privileging of emerging professional identities. *Remedial and Special Education, 40*(4), 248–60. https://doi.org/10.1177/0741932519838621

Brown v. Board of Education, 347 U.S. 483 (1954).

Carter, P. L., Skiba, R., Arredondo, M. I., & Pollock, M. (2017). You can't fix what you don't look at: Acknowledging race in addressing racial discipline disparities. *Urban Education, 52*(2), 207–35. http://doi.org/10.1177/0042085916660350

CAST. (2022). Universal Design for Learning guidelines. https://www.cast.org/impact/universal-design-for-learning-udl

Childs, K. E., Kincaid, D., George, H. P., & Gage, N. A. (2016). The relationship between school-wide implementation of positive behavior intervention and supports and student discipline outcomes. *Journal of Positive Behavior Interventions, 18*(2), 89–99. http://doi.org/10.1177/1098300715590398

Crocker, A. F., & Smith, S. N. (2019). Person-first language: Are we practicing what we preach? *Journal of Multidisciplinary Healthcare, 12*, 125–29. https://doi.org/10.2147/JMDH.S140067

Donovan, S. M., & Cross, C. T. (2002). *Minority students in special and gifted education.* National Academies Press.

Dukhovny, E., & Kelly, E. B. (2015). Practical resources for provision of services to culturally and linguistically diverse users of AAC. *Perspectives on Communication Disorders and Sciences in and Culturally and Linguistically Diverse Populations, 22*(1), 25–31. https://doi.org/10.1044/cds22.1.25

Dunn, L. M. (1968). Special education for the mildly retarded—Is much of it justifiable? *Exceptional Children, 35*(1), 5–22. https://doi.org/10.1177/001440296803500101

Elsahar, Y., Hu, S., Bouazza-Marouf, K., Kerr, D., & Mansor, A. (2019). Augmentative and alternative communication (AAC) advances: A review of configurations for individuals with a speech disability. *Sensors, 19*(8), 1911. https://doi.org/10.3390/s19081911

Fletcher, J. M., Denton, C., & Francis, D. J. (2005). Validity of alternative approaches for the identification of learning disabilities: Operationalizing unexpected underachievement. *Journal of Learning Disabilities, 38*(6), 545–52. https://doi.org/10.1177/00222194050380061101

Fletcher, T. V., & Navarrete, L. A. (2003). Learning disabilities or difference: A critical look at issues associated with the misidentification and placement of Hispanic students in special education programs. *Rural Special Education Quarterly, 22*(4), 37–46. https://doi.org/10.1177/875687050302200406

Fuchs, D., & Fuchs, L. S. (2006). Introduction to response to intervention: What, why, and how valid is it? *Reading Research Quarterly, 41*(1), 93–99. http://doi.org/10.1598/RRQ.41.1.4

Fuchs, D., Mock, D., Morgan, P. L., & Young, C. L. (2003). Responsiveness-to-intervention: Definitions, evidence, and implications for the learning disabilities construct. *Learning Disabilities Research & Practice, 18*(3), 57–171. https://doi.org/10.1111/1540-5826.00072

Gage, N. A., Pico, D. L., & Evanovich, L. (2020). National trends and school-level predictors of restraint and seclusion for students with disabilities. *Exceptionality, 30*(1). https://doi.org/10.1080/09362835.2020.1727327

Garro, A., Giordano, K., Gubi, A., & Shortway, K. (2021). A consultation approach to target exclusionary discipline of students of color in early childhood education. *Contemporary School Psychology, 25*(1), 124–35. http://doi.org/10.1007/s40688-019-00258-9

Gay, G. (2002). Culturally responsive teaching in special education for ethnically diverse students: Setting the stage. *Qualitative Studies in Education, 15*(6), 613–29. http://doi.org/10.1080/0951839022000014349

Gersten, R., Fuchs, L. S., Compton, D., Coyne, M., Greenwood, C., & Innocenti, M. S. (2005). Quality indicators for group experimental and quasi-experimental research in special education. *Exceptional Children, 71*(2), 149–64. http://doi.org/10.1177/001440290507100202

Grasley-Boy, N., Gage, N., Lombardo, M., & Anderson, L. (2022). The additive effects of implementing advanced tiers of SWPBIS with fidelity on disciplinary exclusions. *Journal of Positive Behavior Interventions, 24*(3), 183–95. http://doi.org/10.1177/10983007211011767

Halberstadt, A. G., Castro, V. L., Chu, Q., Lozada, F. T., & Sims, C. M. (2018). Preservice teachers' racialized emotion recognition, anger bias, and hostility attributions. *Contemporary Educational Psychology, 54*, 125–38. http://doi.org/10.1016/j.cedpsych.2018.06.004

Handicapped Children's Protection Act of 1986, Public Law 99-372, 20 U.S.C. § 1415 (1986).

Harry, B., & Klingner, J. (2014). *Why are so many minority students in special education? Understanding race and disability in schools.* Teachers College Press.

Hawken, L. S., & Horner, R. H. (2003). Evaluation of a targeted intervention within a schoolwide system of behavior support. *Journal of Behavioral Education, 12*(3), 225–40.

Hibel, J., Farkas, G., & Morgan, P. L. (2010). Who is placed into special education? *Sociology of Education, 83*(4), 312–32. https://doi.org/10.1177/0038040710383518

Hoover, J. J., & Soltero-Gonzalez, L. (2018). Educator preparation for developing culturally and linguistically responsive MTSS in rural community elementary schools. *Teacher Education and Special Education, 41*(3), 188–202. http://dx.doi.org/10.1177/0888406417753689

Horner, R. H., Carr, E. G., Halle, J., McGee, G., Odom, S., & Wolery, M. (2005). The use of single-subject research to identify evidence-based practice in special education. *Exceptional Children, 71*(2), 165–79. http://dx.doi.org/10.1177/001440290507100203

Hosp, J. L., & Reschly, D. J. (2004). Disproportionate representation of minority students in special education: Academic, demographic, and economic predictors. *Exceptional Children, 70*(2), 185–199. https://doi.org/10.1177/001440290407000020

Hughes, T., Raines, T., & Malone, C. (2020). School pathways to the juvenile justice system. *Policy Insights from the Behavioral and Brain Sciences, 7*(1), 72–79. http://dx.doi.org/10.1177/2372732219897093

Individuals with Disabilities Education Act (IDEA), 20 U.S.C. § 1400 (2004).

Jarvis, S. N., & Okonofua, J. A. (2019). School deferred: When bias affects school leaders. *Social Psychological and Personality Science, 11*(4). https://doi.org/10.1177/1948550619875150

Johnson, K., & Prebor, J., (2019). Update on preservice training in augmentative and alternative communication for speech-language pathologists. *American Journal of Speech-Language Pathology, 28*(2), 536–41. https://doi.org/10.1044/2018_AJSLP-18-0004

Johnson, T. P. (1986). *The principal's guide to the educational rights of handicapped students.* Reston, VA: National Association of Secondary School Principals.

Katsiyannis, A., Gage, N. A., Rapa, L. J., & MacSuga-Gage, A. S. (2020). Exploring the disproportionate use of restraint and seclusion among students with disabilities, boys, and students of color. *Advances in Neurodevelopmental Disorders, 4*, 271–78. https://doi.org/10.1007/s41252-020-00160-z

Kauffman, J., Hallahan, D., & Pullen, P. (2017). *Handbook of special education*. Pearson.

Kieran, L., & Anderson, C. (2019). Connecting universal design for learning with culturally responsive teaching. *Education and Urban Society, 51*(9), 1202–16. http://dx.doi.org/10.1177/0013124518785012

Klingner, J. K., & Edwards, P. A. (2006). Cultural considerations with response to intervention models. *Reading Research Quarterly, 41*(1), 108–17. https://doi:10.1598/RRQ.41.1.6

Krasnoff, B. (2016). *Culturally responsive teaching A guide to evidence-based practices for teaching all students equitably*. Region X Equity Assistance Center at Education Northwest. https://educationnorthwest.org/sites/default/files/resources/culturally-responsive-teaching-508.pdf

Ladson-Billings, G. (1995). Toward a theory of culturally relevant pedagogy. *American Educational Research Journal, 32*(3), 465–91. http://dx.doi.org/10.3102/00028312032003465

Linan-Thompson, S., Vaughn, S., Prater, K., & Cirino, P. T. (2006). The response to intervention of English language learners at risk for reading problems. *Journal of Learning Disabilities, 39*(5), 390–98. https://doi.org/10.1177/00222194060390050201

Lloyd, L., Fuller, D. , & Arvidson, H. (1997). *Augmentative and Alternative Communication: Handbook of principles and practices* (p. 108). Pearson.

Lloyd, L. L., & Pufpaff, L. (1999). They said it couldn't be done, but we did it anyway. *American Speech-Language-Hearing Association Augmentative and Alternative Communication: Special Interest Division 12 Newsletter, 8*, 8–11.

Montalvo, R., Combes, B. H., & Kea, C. D. (2014). Perspectives on culturally and linguistically responsive RTI pedagogics through a cultural and linguistic lens. *Interdisciplinary Journal of Teaching and Learning, 4*(3), 203–19.

Morgan, P. L., Farkas, G., Hillemeier, M. M., Mattison, R., Maczuga, S., Li, H., & Cook, M. (2015). Minorities are disproportionately underrepresented in special education: Longitudinal evidence across five disability conditions. *Educational Researcher, 44*(5), 278–92. https://doi:10.3102/0013189X15591157

Morgan, P. L., Farkas, G., Hillemeier, M. M., Wang, Y., Mandel, Z., DeJarnett, C., & Maczuga, S. (2019). Are students with disabilities suspended more frequently than otherwise similar students without disabilities? *Journal of School Psychology, 72*, 1–13. https://doi.org/10.1016/j.jsp.2018.11.001

Morrison, K. A., Robbins, H. H., & Rose, D. G. (2008). Operationalizing culturally relevant pedagogy: A synthesis of classroom-based research. *Equity & Excellence in Education, 41*(4), 433–52. https://doi.10.1080/10665680802400006

National Center for Education Statistics (NCES). (2021). *Digest of education statistics*. https://nces.ed.gov/programs/digest/2021menu_tables.asp

Orosco, M. J. (2010). A sociocultural examination of response to intervention with Latino English language learners. *Theory into Practice, 49*(4), 265–72. https://doi:10.1080/00405841.2010.510703

Oswald, D. P., Best, A. M., & Coutinho, M. J. (2006). Individual, family, and school factors associated with the identification of female and male students for special education. *International Journal of Special Education, 21*(3), 120–37.

Pesta, R. (2018). Labeling and the differential impact of school discipline on negative life outcomes: Assessing ethno-racial variation in the school-to-prison pipeline. *Crime & Delinquency, 64*(11), 1489–1512. https://doi.org/10.1177/0011128717749223

Proctor, S. L., Graves, S. L., & Esch, R. C. (2012). Assessing African American students for specific learning disabilities: The promises and perils of response to intervention. *Journal of Negro Education, 81*(3), 268–82.

Rausch, M. K., & Skiba, R. J. (2005, April). *The academic cost of discipline: The contribution of school discipline to achievement.* Paper presented at the Annual Meeting of the American Educational Research Association. Montreal, Canada.

Rose, D. H., & Meyer, A. (2002). *Teaching every student in the digital age: Universal Design for Learning.* Association for Supervision and Curriculum Development.

Sabnis, S., Castillo, J. M., & Wolgemuth, J. R. (2019). RTI, equity, and the return to the status quo: Implications for consultants. *Journal of Educational and Psychological Consultation, 30*(3), 285–313. https://doi.org/10.1080/10474412.2019.1674152

Sailor, W., Skrtic, T. M., Cohn, M., & Olmstead, M. (2021). Preparing teacher educators for statewide scale-up of multi-tiered systems of support (MTSS). *Teacher Education and Special Education, 44*(1), 24–41. http://doi.org/10.1177/0888406420938035

Scheerenberger, R. (1983). *A history of mental retardation: A quarter century of promise.* Paul H. Brookes.

Schlosser, R. (2003). Roles of speech output in augmentative and alternative communication: Narrative review. *Augmentative and Alternative Communication, 19*(1), 5–27. http://dx.doi.org/10.1080/0743461032000056450

Shifrer, D., Muller, C., & Callahan, R. (2011). Disproportionality and learning disabilities: Parsing apart race, socioeconomic status, and language. *Journal of Learning Disabilities, 44*(3), 246–57. https://doi:10.1177/0022219410374236

Skiba, R. J., Chung, C.-G., Trachok, M., Baker, T. L., Sheya, A., & Hughes, R. L. (2014). Parsing disciplinary disproportionality: Contributions of infraction, student, and school characteristics to out-of-school suspension and expulsion. *American Educational Research Journal, 51*(4), 640–70. https://doi.org/10.3102/0002831214541670

Skiba, R. J., Horner, R. H., Chung, C.-G., Rausch, M. K., May, S. L., & Tobin, T. (2011). Race is not neutral: A national investigation of African American and Latino disproportionality in school discipline. *School Psychology Review, 40*(1), 85–107. http://doi.org/10.1080/02796015.2011.12087730

Skiba, R. J., Poloni-Staudinger, L., Gallini, S., Simmons, A. B., & Feggins-Azziz, R. (2006). Disparate access: The disproportionality of African American students with disabilities across educational environments. *Exceptional Children, 72*(4), 411–24. https://doi.org/10.1177/001440290607200402

Sugai, G., & Horner, R. H. (2020). Sustaining and scaling positive behavioral interventions and supports: Implementation drivers, outcomes, and considerations. *Exceptional Children, 86*(2), 120–36. https://doi.org/10.1177/0014402919855331

US Census Bureau. (2019). *Age and sex composition in the United States: 2019.* https://www.census.gov/data/tables/2019/demo/age-and-sex/2019-age-sex-composition.html

US Code Congressional and Administrative News (USCCAN). (1975). https://search.usa.gov/search?affiliate=usagov_all_gov&query=United+States+Code+Congressional+and+Administrative+News+%28USCCAN%29.+

US Department of Education. (2004). Individuals with Disabilities Education Improvement Act of 2004, Public Law 108-466. Federal Register, vol. 70, no. 118, 35802–3.

US Department of Education, Office for Civil Rights (OCR). (2019). *Annual report to the Secretary, the President, and the Congress: Fiscal Years 2017–2018*. Washington, DC.
Vaughn, S., & Fuchs, L. (2003). Redefining learning disabilities as inadequate response to instruction: The promise and potential problems. *Learning Disabilities Research & Practice, 18*(3), 137–46. http://doi.org/10.1111/1540-5826.00070
Vaughn, S., Linan-Thompson, S., & Hickman, P. (2003). Response to instruction as a means of identifying students with reading/learning disabilities. *Exceptional Children, 69*(4), 391–409. http://dx.doi.org/10.1177/001440290306900401
Vincent, C. G., Swain-Bradway, J., Tobin, T. J., & May, S. (2011). Disciplinary referrals for culturally and linguistically diverse students with and without disabilities: Patterns resulting from school-wide positive behavior support. *Exceptionality, 19*(3), 175–90. https://doi.org/10.1080/09362835.2011.579936
Whitaker, A., & Losen, D. J. (2019). *The striking outlier: The persistent, painful and problematic practice of corporal punishment in schools*. UCLA: Civil Rights Project/Proyecto Derechos Civiles. https://escholarship.org/uc/item/9d19p8wt
Whitford, D. K., & Carrero, K. M. (2019). Divergent discourse in disproportionality research: A response to Kauffman and Anastasiou (2019). *Journal of Disability Policy Studies, 30*(2), 91–104. https://doi.org/10.1177/1044207318822264
Yell, M. L. (2017). *The law and special education*. 5th ed. Pearson.

CHAPTER 12

Intersectional Belonging in Special Education

Chapter authors: *Michelle Kalos, Elizabeth Finnegan, Shelley Neilsen Gatti, Salita Callicutt, Emily O'Brien Rank, and L. Lynn Stansberry Brusnahan*

Vignette authors: *T. Collin Brusnahan, Olivia Parry, Nathaniel Lentz, and Yokasta Urena*

Editor: *L. Lynn Stansberry Brusnahan*

ABSTRACT

The purpose of this chapter is to provide an explanation of influences on and influences of special education that help educators create a sense of belonging in education. In this chapter, we discuss the unique characteristics of special education within a school community. We highlight how special education includes shared beliefs and values shaped by federal legislation such as free appropriate public education (FAPE) and least restrictive environment (LRE). The chapter emphasizes the continued evolution of special education and disability rights movements that are rooted in the value of belonging and the work of advocacy for and with students, families, and educators.

GUIDING QUESTIONS

- What influences have shaped special education?
- How does special education influence assessment practices?
- How does special education influence the larger school community?

KEY TERMS

Advocacy	Culture	Inclusion
Belonging	Dominant Culture	

To create a sense of **belonging** in our schools for all students, it is imperative for practitioners to shape their practices through a socioculturally sustaining lens. Since the inception of the Individuals with Education Act (IDEA), special education has evolved to embrace inclusive models of instruction that comprise established practices and beliefs to provide a free appropriate public education (FAPE) to students with disabilities. Though the need for teachers prepared to meet the needs of diverse classrooms is increasingly recognized, many educators feel ill-prepared to teach students who are socioculturally diverse (Banerjee & Luckner, 2014; Michel & Kuiken, 2014; Mitchell, 2019; Slot et al., 2019). This chapter discusses factors that have influenced and shaped special education shared beliefs, values, and expectations and highlights the unique characteristics of special education influences, educational practices, and the larger school community for students in special education.

FACTORS THAT IMPACT SPECIAL EDUCATION

Previous chapters describe legislation leading up to the passing of IDEA. This chapter examines this history through the influences that have shaped special education expectations. These factors include federal legislation, advocacy, dominant cultural values, classification, sociocultural identities, parent participation, and media.

Federal Legislation

We can learn a great deal about special education "by understanding (its) values, . . . and by understanding the ways in which values are built into policy" (Marshall et al., 1989, p. 6). It is estimated that prior to the enactment of IDEA, only one in five students with disabilities received a public-school education (Gerber, 2017; Katsiyannis et al., 2001). Although states across the United States had instituted compulsory attendance laws in their statutes, public schools refused to educate disabled students, especially those with intellectual disabilities (Spaulding & Pratt, 2015). The exclusion of students with disabilities from schools led parents across the United States to use legal means to advocate for their children's education. As mentioned in chapter 11, *Pennsylvania Association for Retarded Citizens (PARC) v. Commonwealth of Pennsylvania* and *Mills v. Board of Education* (1972), established the right of disabled students across the United States to receive a free appropriate public education. In both of these cases, the courts found that the schools violated state and district regulations to provide a free appropriate public education, thereby denying the students' Fourteenth Amendment constitutional right to equal protection of the law. Subsequent lawsuits and court rulings across the United States pressured Congress to establish federal guidelines for special education (Katsiyannis et al., 2001).

Federal legislation, such as free appropriate public education (FAPE) and least restrictive environment (LRE), has shaped expectations for special education. Enacted in 1975, the passing of the Education for All Handicapped Children Act (EAHCA, 1975) demonstrated bipartisan recognition that it was in the best national interest to ensure that students with disabilities had equal protection of the law regarding schooling. The passage of the federally enacted EAHCA, now the Individuals with Disabilities Education Act (IDEA), marked the culmination of a number of societal trends and changing attitudes toward individuals with disabilities. These trends included advocating to secure the rights of disabled children to education and expanding public schooling to include them.

Recognizing that disability is part of the human experience, the IDEA aims to improve educational outcomes for students with disabilities (20 U.S.C. § 1400). Part A of the IDEA clearly delineates Congress' intended purpose is to provide a FAPE, which prepares students for "further education, employment, and independent living" (20 U.S.C. § 1400). In addition, the intention of IDEA is to (a) protect the rights of students with disabilities and their parents; (b) assist states and educational authorities in the provision of services; (c) provide technical assistance to parents and schools, which in turn aims to improve the provision of those services; and (d) ensure the effectiveness of those services. Federal legislation has been enacted, much in part, due to the advocacy efforts of organizations, disabled individuals, and their parents and caregivers.

Advocacy

Advocacy is defined as the act or process of supporting a cause or proposal (Merriam-Webster.com, 2023). It is essential to recognize the extent to which advocacy played a role in the realization of the IDEA. In the early 1900s, progressive social reformers sought to alleviate the hardships the large influx of immigrants entering major cities endured, which led to the expansion of public schooling (Gerber, 2017). Elizabeth Farrell's work at the Henry Street Settlement House in New York City exemplifies how these reform efforts could extend to students who needed individualized instruction. Farrell taught classes for students who had difficulty learning in American public schools (Gerber, 2017). Her work with students then deemed "defective" was probably "one of the most important and humanitarian activities of the Board of Education" (1908, as cited Gerber, 2017, p. 8).

Throughout the twentieth century, discrimination and exclusion of individuals with disabilities, especially those with intellectual disabilities, continued to be sanctioned. Increasing public awareness and legal advocacy (Katsiyannis et al., 2001), led by organizations and groups, such as families and parents of disabled children and disabled communities, created an advocacy movement (Rivera, 1972; Spaulding & Pratt, 2015) that led to the passage of the IDEA. As discussed in chapter 5, the disability movement has historically excluded Black voices and perspectives, and it has also failed to acknowledge the activism among Black disabled advocates. There are good outcomes too, however; this advocacy movement established parent participation in decision making regarding a child's educational services and placement, as well as the expectation that parents would advocate for their students in the Individualized Education Program (IEP) process and, if necessary, through due process. For more information on advocacy movements, see chapters 5, 10, and 11.

> **VIGNETTE 1: *YOKASTA'S STORY: ADVOCACY***
>
> *Looking back, I have to thank my mother as she was my biggest advocate; Mom was feisty and argued with anyone whom she felt was discriminating or ignoring my visual needs. I was often her translator and would have to remind her that the person could not understand what she was saying. This would not faze her. She would simply reply, "They know they are not being invited for dinner!"*
>
> *I became a teacher when Liam was born and diagnosed with Leber's congenital amaurosis (LCA). I wanted to be his advocate in the journey that awaited us. Over the past twenty years, and to my surprise, I have fallen in love with teaching! I have had the pleasure of wearing many hats, including Advocate, Parent Coordinator, Teacher Assistant, Lead Teacher, Program Manager, Special Education Evaluator, and more. As a Teacher of the Blind and Visually Impaired, I feel a shared sense of comradery and relationality with my students. I especially know the challenges students who are Blind/Visually Impaired (BVI) face in a sighted world; we, as a community, experience day-to-day unrealistic and ill-supported societal expectations. I understand my students' endless self-questioning, the fear of "doing it wrong," not fitting in, or simply not applying for a job due to a lack of experience or skill. In time, I learned to recognize my own inability (or unwillingness) to assimilate, to quiet the inner critique, and to gain skills that would make me a qualified candidate for the desired role. I am comfortable with my "normal" and no longer obsess over societal expectations. In the end, I am a Humanist; the ultimate goal is to have freedom, dignity, and fulfillment.*

Dominant Values

Societal shifts in how individuals with disabilities are viewed and the advocacy that ensued have also been shaped by American beliefs in individual rights and autonomy. Subsequently, the overarching values and ideals of the dominant culture are reiterated throughout schools. The field of special education has traditionally upheld deficit-framed views and norms toward a cure-oriented rather than care-oriented ethic. As discussed in chapter 5, current special education programs are often steeped in racism and ableism: (a) special education systems and policies largely minimize, erase, and exclude the experiences of Black individuals with disabilities and their families; and (b) children are expected to mask their disability and their disabled identities and therefore, culture, while upholding white and ableist norms. This kind of ableism is evident in legislation too, such as IDEA. Table 12.1 shows how the IDEA embodies many values that characterize special education today. The purpose of the IDEA echoes dominant (e.g., Westernized) values of individualism, inclusion, and self-determination.

Table 12.1. Values Embodied in the Individuals with Disabilities Education Act

Value	IDEA
Advocacy	Widespread advocacy led to the enactment of the IDEA. Parental participation is a required part of the IEP process. Children and their parents are "guaranteed procedural safeguards with respect to the provision of a free appropriate public education (20 U.S.C. § 1415). Parents have the right to ask questions, and appeal decisions they feel were made improperly.
Independence and Self-Sufficiency	Independence and self-sufficiency are embedded in IDEA's general provisions (20 U.S.C. § 1400), which state "educational results for children with disabilities is an essential element of our national policy of ensuring equality of opportunity, full participation, independent living, and economic self-sufficiency for individuals with disabilities." The provisions also indicate that the education students with disabilities receive should prepare them "to lead productive and independent adult lives, to the maximum extent possible" (20 U.S.C. § 1400).
Classification	Classification is utilized to determine whether or not a student is eligible for special educational services, as the child must meet the criteria established by IDEA for one of thirteen different categories (20 U.S.C. § 1414).
Individualization	A student eligible for special education receives an "individualized education program" or "IEP," which is a written program plan (U.S.C. § 1414).
Inclusion	Inclusion is based on the principle of least restrictive environment (LRE), which is designed to ensure that, "to the maximum extent appropriate, children with disabilities, including children in public or private institutions or other care facilities, are educated with children who are not disabled" (20 U.S.C. § 1412). Inclusion is when students with disabilities are included in a continuum of educational placements, including full time in general education classes in their neighborhood schools (Anastasiou & Kauffmann, 2012).
Protection	The IDEA was challenged with both protecting the rights of children with disabilities but also determining whom it was protecting. The law requires that disabled students receive a FAPE but also that nondisabled students are not inappropriately identified. This created a paradox. In order to include students with disabilities in the public school system, they had to be set apart by the classification system used to identify them. To do this, the IDEA adopted a model established in the medical field.
Parent Participation	State agencies are required to assist parents with their role in the process of providing services to their children (20 U.S.C. § 1417). This can range from helping parents understand the nature of their child's disability to providing tools to communicate with school personnel; information about the range, type, and quality of available services; and resources to help parents participate in the decision-making process regarding their child's education.
Self-Determination	Self-determination is embedded in IDEA. Postsecondary goals and transition services must be in effect by the time a student with an IEP turns sixteen years of age (20 U.S.C. § 1414). Students are invited to participate in their IEP meetings so that they can participate in the development of those goals.

Classification: Medical and Educational

In Western cultures, the biomedical model has held a long and authoritative perspective on disability and guides much legislation pertaining to government and insurance benefits (Smart & Smart, 2006). This means the purpose of diagnosing medically is to treat conditions effectively, ameliorate symptoms, or cure or make the symptoms disappear. Classification or the placement of a disability label on an individual occurs through two pathways: medical and educational. Medically, doctors evaluate and classify their patients utilizing the American Psychiatric Association (APA) Diagnostic and Statistical Manual (DSM; medical model) or they could use the World Health Organization (WHO; human rights model) diagnostic criteria. See chapter 6 for more information on the models of disability. Educationally, school personnel use psychometric testing (medical model) to evaluate and determine if a child or student has educational needs utilizing IDEA categories of disability criteria. In the United States, diagnoses are typically determined by the DSM and psychometric testing (medical model).

In order to receive educational services under the IDEA, an eligibility determination must be made through an evaluation process that determines whether the child has characteristics that meet the criteria under one of the IDEA's disability categories. The process of determining which category a student fits in is known as classification. There are many issues with bias in the classification system, as discussed throughout this text. Standardized testing (e.g., IQ tests) and other assessments play a determinate role in evaluating eligibility for some disability categories of special education (Gerber, 2017).

Special education services require "proof of an intrinsic deficit" (p. 17) to demonstrate that a child is eligible for special education (Harry & Klinger, 2007). For example, sometimes a discrepancy model is still applied when the difference between actual achievement and expected achievement is used to identify a student's disability (as opposed to an opportunity gap), which is usually determined by the scores on standardized tests. Furthermore, once deficits have been identified, practitioners are required to report a student's progress in meeting their IEP goals, which are influenced by dominant cultural values, preparing students "to lead productive and independent lives, to the maximum extent possible" (20 U.S.C. § 1400). This view reinforces the biomedical model that disability is a problem to be identified, treated, and fixed rather than accepting it and then adjusting the environment and instruction.

Sociocultural Identities

First, we want to remind you that intersectionality is not the same as multiculturalism and that sociocultural identities go beyond culturally and linguistically diverse identities. As introduced in chapter 8, families who are culturally and linguistically diverse are those whose primary language is not English or who are not of European American descent (Rossetti et al., 2017), but sociocultural identities are broader and—we cannot emphasize this enough—should be viewed through an intersectional lens. See chapters 1 and 2 for how intersectional sociocultural identities are conceptualized. We suggest these nuances are a major contributor to why significant equity challenges still persist in special education.

While there is no legislative language that considers intersectional impact, IDEA acknowledges the persistent overrepresentation of Black and African American students in the categories of intellectual disabilities and emotional disturbance and acknowledges students who are learning English as a new language are often misidentified and placed within special education programs (20 U.S.C. § 1400). Figure 12.1 shows a snapshot of the racial/ethnic makeup of school-age students in the United States.

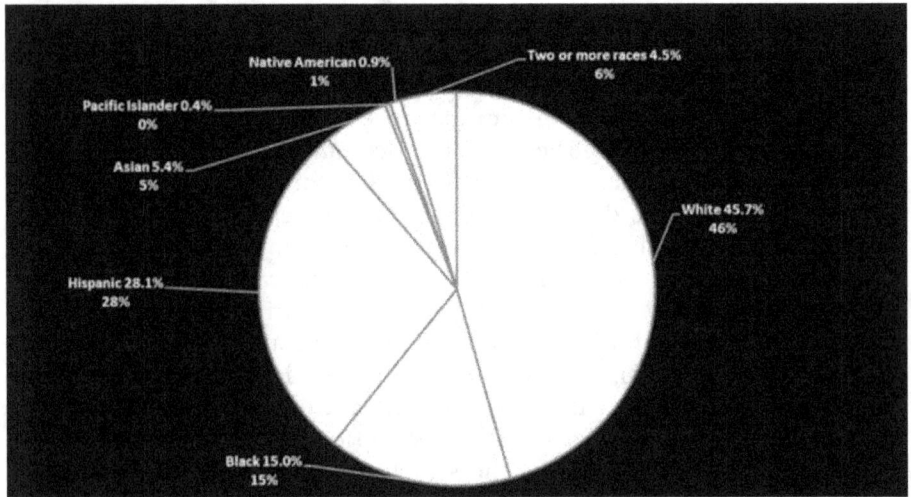

Figure 12.1. Total Enrollment in Public Schools in the United States 2020 (n = 49,375,000)

Source: Digest of Educational Statistics. Table 203.50 Enrollment and percentage distribution of enrollment in public elementary and secondary schools, by race/ethnicity and region: Selected years: fall 1995 through fall 2030.

Regional differences are also essential to note. In the west, 43 percent of public school students are classified as Hispanic, and in the south, 22 percent of students are Black (National Center for Educational Statistics [NCES], 2022). It is important that practitioners are aware of the sociocultural makeup of the students they serve and work with families to understand and align practices within special education with the values families themselves uphold. These values may not always align with those of the dominant culture.

There is a lot of evidence that shows discrimination and racism as pervasive and constant elements in schools (Castagno & Brayboy, 2008; Deyhle & Swisher, 1997). Historically, families and their students have faced many oppressions rooted in systemic inequality in US schools (Darling-Hammond, 2000; Pearson et al., 2021). As discussed in chapters 4 and 5, many race- and disability-evasive approaches in the classroom are decontextualized and do not account for the ways in which special education contributes to the othering and harm inflicted upon children of the global majority. One example is Hmong families' unfamiliarity with special education, which could be a result of differences in expectations and cultural beliefs (Wathum-Ocama & Rose, 2002). These families may feel disconnected from schools, which can result in estrangement, alienation, and discrimination when interacting with practitioners and attempting to access services (Adelman, 1994; Bempechat, 1992; Comer & Haynes, 1991; Lovelace et al., 2018). These experiences may also lead to caregivers feeling suspicious and distrustful of the educational institution (Brandon et al., 2010). Families from the global majority report they are viewed negatively, even being asked about their own personal medical history including speculation on substance abuse (Reiman et al., 2010). A study found that African American parents reported that teachers blamed parents and their community environments for their students' poor performances in school (Gatlin & Wilson, 2016).

The IEP process is often primarily influenced by society's racialized conceptions of disability and dominant cultural norms, which impact decisions about areas such as special education eligibility, IEP goals, LRE, and placement decisions. While there have been decades of research and debate on disproportionate representation in identification for special education, this book discusses how the disproportionality in access to general education classrooms has received less attention, yet it has significant implications for educational equity, bias, and segregation within schools (Cooc, 2022).

Once identified as eligible for special education services, students of the global majority are more likely to be segregated than their white peers with the same label into special education classrooms (Fierros & Conroy, 2002). According to a Report to Congress on the implementation of IDEA (2021), the percentage of school-age students ages five through twenty-one served under IDEA, Part B, who were educated inside the general class 80 percent or more of the day increased (US Department of Education, 2021). However, studies and national reports consistently document that, among students with disabilities, students of the global majority are less likely to spend time in general education settings than white disabled peers (Fierros & Conroy, 2002; Grindal et al., 2019; McFarland et al., 2018; Skiba et al., 2006). A longitudinal study examined inclusion across race and ethnicity, disability, and grade levels and found students' participation in general education declines as students progress through school (Cooc, 2022). Black students experienced the least access to inclusion. Asian American and Pacific Islander students were included more than Latine and white students with disabilities. Furthermore, even though Black and Hispanic students with disabilities had similarly low test scores relative to their white disabled peers, this difference was not observed for Hispanic students. When Asian American and Pacific Islander students with disabilities had lower academic test scores than their white peers with disabilities, they had higher inclusion rates. This highlights how decisions about inclusion using test score data differ by race and ethnicity and how bias and racialized stereotypes of groups show up in LRE decisions. Furthermore, these results illustrate how decisions about placement are socially situated and result from (unconscious) bias (Kendi, 2019).

Parents and Caregivers

The influence of families on special education is seen in the transformative outcomes of political legislative advocacy, improved educational services, and better quality of life for the family (Balcazar et al., 1996; Black & Baker, 2011; Conley Wright & Taylor, 2014; Kalyanpur & Harry, 2012; Vincent, 2000; Zaretsky, 2004). Parent participation can lead to more positive achievement outcomes for students. For example, there are differences in long-term outcomes for students when parents participated in IEP meetings as opposed to when parents did not participate (Poponi, 2009). Nevertheless, there are many reasons why families do not participate in the special education process.

Some barriers to familial participation are a lack of understanding of special education, the IEP process, and the structure of special education delivery (Buren et al., 2020; Wolfe & Durán, 2013). A study looking specifically at the experiences of Latine mothers trying to navigate the special education process for their children with disabilities (i.e., autism, intellectual disabilities, multiple disabilities, learning disabilities, and ADHD) who were being educated in either separate or inclusive settings found that these parents reported they lacked information, leading to feelings of isolation and vulnerability; additionally, they felt they did not have a way to communicate directly to teachers or administrators or that they had received either no responses or negative responses for their efforts (Mortier & Arias, 2023). This serves as a reminder to positively discuss students' strengths and not focus on deficits (Buren et al., 2020).

Parents from linguistically diverse families may have more difficulty due to language and cultural differences. They may be reluctant to ask questions or advocate for their children simply because they are not accustomed to giving opinions and/or believe they should not question the authority of the school (Burke & Goldman, 2018). Legal mandates designed to support socioculturally diverse families may do little to enhance the sharing of information and the development of shared goals (Wolfe & Durán, 2013). Much of the educational jargon and the concepts behind them, such as IEP, FAPE, and LRE, are unfamiliar to families, and may not even translate in other languages. Furthermore, translators are reported to be inadequate or to speak in a way that is difficult to understand (Burke & Goldman, 2018). Collectively, these issues create barriers for families to access resources, advocate for their children, and understand special education services, which has resulted in disproportionate practices. Specifically, there is a continued system of segregation and lack of equitable access to education (Cooc, 2022). While laws, such as IDEA, have been amended to improve services for students with disabilities and emphasize that all students should receive access to education and be educated alongside nondisabled students, there continue to be barriers.

Parent and Caregiver Advocacy

In regard to advocacy, parents may not know how or what to advocate for. How do you advocate when you don't understand what is happening in your child's education? How do you advocate when your expectations don't match the expectations of the school system? How can you advocate and encourage your child's education when you can't communicate with the professionals sitting across the table from you? For parents from nondominant sociocultural identities, this is the reality (Burke & Goldman, 2018).

Pause and Reflect

- How can you bridge sociocultural perspectives in your classroom? In your school? In special education?
- How can you align yourself outside of your own sociocultural norms to better work with and for families?

Advocacy is seen to both increase access to services as well as increase the power that parents feel to support their child's education (Buren et al., 2020). Parents who feel empowered are more optimistic and more likely to advocate for their students, even in difficult situations (Burke et al., 2019). By helping parents understand their roles in the special education process and sharing key terms, they (advocates in schools) support and empower parents (Burke et al., 2019). Yet parents of nondominant sociocultural identities often feel conflicted about their child's education (Burke et al., 2019).

Advocacy has played a key role in establishing the rights of disabled students in education, however, many families feel ill-prepared to advocate for their students (Wakelin, 2008). Advocacy requires familiarity with the law and the education system. Many families from historically oppressed groups often feel dismissed or excluded from the decision-making process regarding their students (Burke & Goldman, 2018). Furthermore, the IDEA requires that school districts support families and caregivers in the IEP process. At a minimum,

(a) a legal guardian must provide informed consent before evaluation or a change in placement; (b) an interpreter must be provided during the IEP meeting; and (c) schools must notify parents of their rights. These measures are to ensure that parents and guardians are treated as full participating partners in determining services for their child (Harry, 2008). Nevertheless, studies have shown that translation services are not always effective and language difficulties continue to present a barrier to effective collaboration (Reiman et al., 2010). Professional insensitivity can also lead to culturally inappropriate recommendations or hinder parental participation (Harry, 2008). Other issues include (a) conflicting views of disability, (b) deficit views, and (c) different expectations of the role of families in the educational system (Harry, 2008).

Parent and Caregiver Views of Disability

Not all communities view disabilities through the same lens (Hamilton et al., 2021) and various cultures may have very different understandings of what disability is. See chapter 1 for more information. In the United States, the widespread acceptance of the biomedical and deficit models used to determine a student's eligibility for special education often leads practitioners to assume that disabilities are universally understood factual phenomena (Kalyanpur & Harry, 2012). Education professionals may never have encountered perspectives of disability other than those they have learned from the culture they grew up in or from their teacher preparation courses. As introduced in chapter 3, the Deaf community has long taken the perspective that children born deaf should be accepted and celebrated as part of their community, but 90 percent of children with hearing loss are born to parents without a hearing loss or a family history of hearing loss. These kinds of differences in acceptance challenge professionals to (a) consider their personal perspectives of disabilities and (b) combat their own personal biases.

While a family from a white, middle-income background may view a young child who doesn't talk as a child with "speech delays," a parent of Asian descent may view a child with this profile as "quiet" (Pearson et al., 2021). These families may not understand why educators refer to their child as having a speech delay when their child is well-behaved, speaks two languages, reads, and writes (Harry, 2008). Many different languages do not have clear translations or words for disability or specific disability categories. For example, the Navajo lack a word for disability, viewing all human beings at different places in their development on the spectrum of human diversity (Kapp, 2011). The Somali language did not originally include a word for "autism." Thus, the American Somali community created a new term as a part of a larger community effort to destigmatize autism (Crann & Bui, 2022).

As discussed in chapters 1, 2, and 6, beliefs regarding disability may be linked to religious beliefs and shape how families view and interpret disability (Hamilton et al., 2021). Some may view the disability as a blessing from God while others view it as a punishment for sins (Hebert & Koulouglioti, 2010). For example, Islamic families may feel that they are blessed to be chosen by Allah to raise a "special" child and include the child in daily life and faith-based activities (Jegatheesan et al., 2010). Eastern religions of Hinduism and Buddhism point to regeneration and paying for the defects of past lives with this belief leading to a greater tolerance and acceptance of disabilities (Miles, 2002). Some Chinese American families may think that autism is punishment from a previous life (Hebert & Koulouglioti, 2010). The Ultra-Orthodox Jewish community living in Israel may view a child with the same diagnosis as having high spiritual status (Hebert & Koulouglioti, 2010). Hispanic immigrant families who had autistic children were found to think that autism was a temporary condition cured through divine intervention (Ijalba, 2016).

Pause and Reflect

Legally, "church and state" are separate in the United States, but consider:

- How does religion or spirituality affect your personal views on disability?
- How does religion or spirituality affect families' views on disability?
- Why is it important to develop an understanding of religious or spiritual influences on disabled individuals and their value systems?

Media

It is important not to overlook the role the media plays in changing public opinion about the education of individuals with disabilities by establishing values, beliefs, and expectations. Before the 1970s, it was not uncommon for parents to place their students with intellectual disabilities in residential institutions. Roy Rogers, a famous singer and television personality, and his wife Dale Evans had a daughter with Down syndrome who sadly died soon after her second birthday. Dale Evans Rogers wrote a best-selling book *Angel Unaware* (1953), in which she describes how the family was encouraged to have their daughter institutionalized but decided to raise her at home. The book profoundly influenced public attitudes regarding developmental disabilities, serving as a role model for other families who elected to raise their children at home.

Popular political leaders, the Kennedys, were another influential family who did much to shape attitudes toward individuals with disabilities. President John Kennedy's sister Rosemary had a disability. Initially, her parents considered keeping Rosemary from public view but later published family photographs where Rosemary poses alongside her siblings. Two years after John Kennedy became president, another one of his sisters, Eunice Kennedy Shriver, published an article describing the family's story. Shriver strongly believed that disabled children could learn and lobbied for better services for individuals with developmental disabilities (Spaulding & Pratt, 2015). Kennedy's rhetoric regarding the reforms needed in the treatment of individuals with intellectual disabilities echoed the Declaration of Independence in its reference to life, liberty, and the pursuit of happiness. When President Kennedy signed the Mental Health and Mental Retardation Reform Act of 1963, he stated,

> This approach is designed, in large measure, to use Federal resources to stimulate state, local and private action. When carried out, reliance on the cold mercy of custodial isolation will be supplanted by the open warmth of community concern and capability. Emphasis on prevention, treatment and rehabilitation will be substituted for a desultory interest in confining patients in an institution to wither away.

Kennedy condemned the institutions for disabled people as deniers of liberty. Without liberty, individuals with disabilities lack choice and are condemned "to wither away." In essence, they are denied life itself (Turnbull, 2012).

Kennedy was referencing the practice of institutionalization stemming from ideology established by Henry H. Goddard (1866–1957), a psychologist who used standardized testing tools to categorize and segregate. He believed that children deemed to be "defective" should be institutionalized and placed under medical supervision and that it was "unacceptable" to mix students with subaverage scores on mental testing with other children (Gerber, 2017). Over time, financial cutbacks and poor management led to the demise of institutions. They became what Robert Kennedy described as "a situation that borders on a snake pit, and that the children live in filth, that many of our fellow citizens are suffering tremendously because of lack of attention, lack of imagination, lack of adequate manpower" (Rivera, 1972, p. 57).

In 1965, two reporters, Burton Blatt and Fred Kaplan, carried a miniature camera and secretly snapped pictures as they toured five state institutional facilities for individuals with developmental disabilities in four states. They were moved to despair over what they had seen, so they published a photographic essay titled "Christmas in Purgatory" and distributed it to legislators, university professors, and advocacy groups (Blatt & Kaplan, 1974). It was the first time many had seen the conditions within institutions.

In 1972, Geraldo Rivera, a news reporter, did a groundbreaking television expose on Willowbrook State School. In Rivera's news reports, millions of television viewers saw neglected, naked, and semi-clothed people in overcrowded and filthy conditions left to huddle up for warmth, with nothing to occupy them (Reimann, 2017; Rivera, 1972). Public reaction was swift and advocated for real change. Government officials were inundated with telephone calls, and parents took to the streets to protest the conditions in the institutions. Rivera vowed to keep reporting on the issue until Willowbrook State School was closed, forcing local officials to concede that the conditions were deplorable in many large institutions.

The combination of public outcry in response to reporting, public empathy and support in response to families sharing their own stories, and legal actions instigated by the parents of students with disabilities created the conditions under which major changes needed to be made. The IDEA was one of those major changes. This advocacy, which provided the impetus for the IDEA, also significantly influenced the shaping of values embedded within it. In addition to parent participation, the IDEA also mandates IEPs, FAPE, and the rights of individuals with disabilities to pursue independent lives.

SPECIAL EDUCATION'S IMPACT

One of the most significant ways special education influences the larger school community is through inclusion when disabled students are educated alongside their nondisabled peers. This section discusses the influence of special education and sociocultural diversity on factors such as the eligibility and identification processes, diverse representation in schools, inclusion policies, and the benefits of special education.

Pause and Reflect

- Does inclusion automatically create a sense of belonging? Why or why not?

Eligibility and Identification Process

Until a student gets to the I-MTSS Tier 3 and special education is considered, there may be no communication of concerns to parents. Schools start to involve parents when they need to gain permission to conduct an evaluation for special education, however, this does not mean that parents fully understand what assessments are being used or why. Schools must provide parents a role in the referral and initial eligibility process. The school eligibility team needs to break down the testing expectations, the reasons for each test, and what information would be beneficial to gain in order to better understand the student and their educational strengths and weaknesses. During the assessment results meeting for eligibility, parents can be overwhelmed by the number of assessments and data presented to them. This questions I-MTSS in a different way. "Are there ways to provide parents the opportunity to learn more about the curriculum their students are participating in and the amount of time that they are spending receiving Tier 2 intervention?"

Schools could look at interventions that involve parents. For parents to be involved in their child's education and progress, they need the school to explicitly share how to do so (Quiocho & Daoud, 2006). Other researchers have looked at culturally and linguistically appropriate interventions that could be better provided. One example is the Dong et al. (2020) study that found when schools work with community partners and parents to overcome the stigma typically associated with mental health in the Latine community, Latine students with attention deficit hyperactivity disorder (ADHD) had increased access to psychiatric/medical supports.

As discussed in chapter 1, schools are microcosms of society and therefore should be considered diverse across sociocultural identities. Schools should consider socioculturally competent assessments, which include culture-specific styles of service delivery, the primary language, and an evaluation of the student as a sociocultural being prior to test administration using cultural orientation categories (Dana, 1996). A question we need to ask in the educational setting is "Are socioculturally relevant assessments being used during the eligibility process?" To ensure socioculturally relevant assessments, consider factors such as bias, language, and respect.

Bias

Bias during assessments is "a longstanding and persistent debate regarding the equitable use of tests and assessment strategies with diverse populations" (Ford, 2005, p. 1). For example, presenting a test question to a student that demonstrates something that they have never experienced puts them at a sociocultural disadvantage—for instance, using an assessment that requires a child to label something "cap" when the terminology they typically utilize is "hat" or asking the child to pretend to "make a cup of tea" when they have never seen this nor do they know what "tea" is. Another example is the student who is asked to participate in a "birthday party" scenario based on the dominant cultural idea of what this party should look like. There are also disadvantages when what would be appropriate based on the student's sociocultural identity is not what is deemed appropriate by the test creator. For example, the expectation that a student will look at the test administrator (to determine whether they will hold eye contact with another person) may be problematic as, in some cultures, direct eye contact with a stranger, a person in authority, or an elder might be viewed as disrespectful. In the autistic culture, this can be considered uncomfortable or painful.

Each school, each special education department, and each practitioner needs to take the time to examine their own explicit or conscious and implicit or unconscious biases to determine if biases are impacting instructional practice and student learning outcomes. Bias is discussed in more detail in chapters 2 and 7, but it's important to remember that when meeting with families, practitioners may experience blind spots and engage in unintended microaggressions. Families may have past trauma or be experiencing a cultural disconnect and therefore struggle to be present in the meeting because of these experiences.

As discussed, practitioners tend to rely on psychometric testing as their evaluation tools, but are the tests socioculturally responsive, appropriate, sustaining, and truly multifaceted? Educators should ask, "Have they engaged in best practices by ensuring a multifaceted evaluation approach has taken place, have they tested in multiple languages when needed, have they taken sociocultural factors into consideration when interpreting results?"

Research indicates that training on sociocultural competence and understanding bias is beneficial for all professionals (NeMoyer et al., 2020). Educational practitioners are encouraged to examine and rule out their own biases as part of the evaluation process (Ford, 2005). Fighting stigmas and supporting holistic aid for students should be a role fulfilled by educators, administrators, and support staff (NeMoyer et al., 2020), but this cannot be done unless we first understand our own sociocultural identities, perspectives, and how they benefit and/or hurt students.

Language Differences

Language differences constitute another common area of struggle for students for whom English is not their primary language. It has long been established that testing should be provided in a student's native language and that any language differences need to be taken into account when determining eligibility for services (US Department of Education, 2016). In other words, students who are English language learners must be assessed in their native language as well as in English to accurately evaluate whether learning differences occur in both languages.

In light of biased tests still being used within districts, table 12.2 provides some viable options that educators should consider when working to assess students from nondominant cultures and backgrounds (Ford, 2005).

Table 12.2. Assessing Students from Nondominant Cultures and Backgrounds

- Ensure test users (e.g., psychologist, practitioners, administrators, speech-language pathologists) gain experience in working with diverse groups in order to improve their ability to interpret and effectively use test scores.
- Select tests suitable for the characteristics and background of the test taker.
- Make every effort to eliminate inequities and to provide accurate and meaningful scores linked to appropriate intervention strategies. Essentially, use test scores to help students, not to hurt them.
- Use comprehensive assessments that gather a wide range of information about test takers.
- Place test scores into a sociocultural context and consider how an examinee's performance is influenced by acculturation, social identities, and culture.

Sociocultural Respect

Respect is another theme that continues to rise repeatedly throughout the literature. For families with nondominant sociocultural identities, respect can be both helpful and hurtful. Studies found that sociocultural respect for professionals kept many parents from feeling they could speak up in meetings (Wolfe & Durán, 2013). Other parents reported that they felt disrespected by professionals (Wolfe & Durán, 2013) based on their sociocultural background. Parents report that they do not feel welcomed by professionals to share information about their child's needs or desires and cited the limited time provided for meetings as another barrier (Burke et al., 2019).

Parent and Caregiver Participation

Schools are the entities responsible for providing education to parents about the special education process (Burke & Goldman, 2018), but community agencies also play a major role in the dissemination of special education information to families (Buren et al., 2020). Ideally, schools and community partners should work together to create opportunities to educate in disability advocacy, the jargon, roles, and expectations of the special education process and meetings. This would aid parents in being better prepared to navigate the special education system.

Advocacy organizations advise parents not to attend special education meetings alone (Rios et al., 2020), and to seek out special education advocates. Ideally, these advocates are people who have gone through training to learn how to support others on their journey through the educational process. Some benefits of working with advocates are that they (a) encourage parents to ask questions; (b) suggest communication with the school; (c) attend meetings with parents; (d) review IEPs to ensure understanding; and (e) educate parents about their rights (Burke et al., 2019). Advocates should be encouraged to aid in building relationships between families, students, and schools.

Parents can be empowered through the development of positive relationships with teachers and administrators. In addition to offering to provide an interpreter for parents who speak multiple languages, educators can communicate with parents through strategies such as (a) speaking using limited English; (b) utilizing online translation services for emails; (c) asking for help from older children; and (d) requesting help from an adult who speaks their first language (Mortier & Arias, 2023).

Diverse Representation in Schools

As mentioned in chapter 9, research suggests that preK–12 school diversity benefits all students including white and middle-class students (Chang, 2006; Page, 2008). Special education has broadened diverse student representation in schools and, in doing so, has influenced the greater school community affecting the academic and social experiences of both students with disabilities and their peers' (Stuart Wells et al., 2016). Centering sociocultural diversity in school settings enriches educational experiences because everyone is given opportunities to learn from people with different experiences, perspectives, backgrounds, beliefs, and abilities, which leads to greater awareness, understanding, and acceptance of differences. This provides opportunities to challenge predisposed stereotypes, developed due to a lack of exposure to diverse sociocultural characteristics, and presents opportunities to critically explore these norms to become more accepting, tolerant, and thoughtful. Studies show that students' exposure to other students who are different from themselves, and the novel ideas and challenges that such exposure brings, leads to improved cognitive skills, intellectual engagement, self-motivation, citizenship, cultural engagement, and academic skills (Stuart Wells et al., 2016). In socioculturally diverse classrooms, students can learn cooperatively alongside peers whose perspectives and backgrounds are different from their own. These kinds of environments promote creativity, motivation, deeper learning, critical thinking, and problem-solving skills (Chang, 2006; Page, 2008). The educational expectations for student performance from school staff in integrated schools are higher than those in segregated schools (Massey & Fischer, 2006). However, the benefits of diverse classrooms aren't always realized for students.

The closer students are to the dominant social identities (e.g., white, male, cisgender, heterosexual, nondisabled), the more likely they are to be perceived as capable (Broderick & Leonardo, 2016). Thus, schooling practices position some as deserving and therefore worth supporting in general education classrooms, while situating others as problematic and thus in need of remediation or segregation (Walton et al., 2016). This results in different educational experiences for students of the global majority who receive special education services—specifically, they have limited opportunities and inequitable access to effective teachers and rigorous coursework. One way to examine these outcomes and the intersectionality of racism and ableism is through Disability Critical Race Theory (DisCrit). As noted in chapters 4, 5, and 6, a further perspective is offered by the emerging interdisciplinary field of Disability Studies in Education (DSE), which posits that there are both intrinsic and extrinsic challenges that exist for disabled people, and that negative social perceptions create substantial barriers.

Students, who are positioned as "less desirable" are often barred access to (a) engaging and accurate curriculum; (b) responsive and ingenuous pedagogy; and (c) authentic and hopeful relationships (Annamma & Morrison, 2018). Categorical processes that sort students into different disability categories and classrooms also create and reinforce racialized categories of disability and racial inequity (Domina et al., 2017; Fish, 2019). Even before IDEA was originally passed, special education researchers cautioned against relying heavily on labeling and sorting students for fear that the system would create segregation and disparities for certain groups (Dunn, 1968).

Inclusion Policies

As discussed throughout this chapter, there are policies that shape the curriculum and the educational framework of schools. A school's administration may choose to implement "full inclusion" for all students with disabilities while other school administrators may continue to provide the full continuum of services where placement in the LRE is impacted by formal assessments. These decisions impact how a specific school will interpret IDEA, how assessments are utilized, and how professionals will collaborate with families to access special education.

Whether inclusion is accepted or expected in schools impacts the planning of every teacher, grade level, and schoolwide initiative. If schools are built on a culture of inclusion, teachers are more likely to be aware of a variety of students' needs. There are many frameworks in schools that can support creating a sense of belonging for students who receive special education services in inclusive environments. As mentioned in previous chapters, current educational frameworks that address the needs of all students are Universal Design for Learning (UDL), the Integrated Multi-Tiered Systems of Support (I-MTSS) approach, which includes Response to Intervention (RTI) for academic support and Positive Behavioral Interventions and Supports (PBIS) for behavioral and social-emotional (SEL) support. These frameworks support the learning of all students by meeting their unique needs. When UDL is planned through a socioculturally sustaining lens, it can accommodate the needs of individual learners and their inclusion while honoring their unique needs by building flexibility in the ways learners can access information and in the ways students can demonstrate their knowledge. I-MTSS relies on the use of data to make decisions about students, instructional practices, prevention efforts, and schoolwide programs to improve academic, behavioral, and social-emotional outcomes for all students (Wexler, 2018). I-MTSS provides multiple opportunities for students to access research-based instruction and curriculum. Each portion of the framework involves additional support and more exposure and opportunities to demonstrate students' learning and progress in a variety of ways. In some ways, this meets the goals of looking holistically at students to determine educational needs (Ford & Russo, 2014) because I-MTSS offers increased support in order to prevent inappropriate referrals to special education. Barrio (2017) discussed the positive impact that I-MTSS has on the reduction of non-native English speakers being labeled with a disability, for example, when English language learners receive sufficient support for their language needs.

The IEP

One of the final decisions the IEP team makes is where and how special education services are provided for a student who meets eligibility criteria. This placement decision, referred to as the LRE, is a long-standing, guiding principle of IDEA. The belief that all students should receive access to education and be educated alongside students without disabilities to the maximum extent possible guides the LRE principle. Defined in chapter 11, this principle was mandated in the first passing of EAHCA in 1975. When IEP teams are making decisions for a student with regard to LRE, they are required to consider both the student's access to the general education curriculum and the individual learning needs of the student, what services and supports a student requires to be successful, and where and how those services and supports can be provided effectively (Stone, 2019). The IEP team must make sure that the child has the appropriate opportunity to learn with students who do not have disabilities in academic, nonacademic, and extracurricular activities, while still making progress toward their own educational goals. If students move to more restrictive educational placements, the programming and services should become even more specialized and individualized, and include increased application of evidence-based special education practices (Gargiulo & Bouck, 2021; Stone, 2019) that are socioculturally informed.

Legally the IEP team must annually (a) assess to determine present levels; (b) write goals based on education needs; (c) identify services and supports; (d) determine placement and remember that a student may receive services and supports in different settings throughout the day based on what is needed to achieve each annual goal; and (e) document the reasons in the LRE statement in the IEP if the team decides that any services need to be delivered outside of the general education classroom (IRIS Information Brief, 2022). Reasons such as insufficient resources or the child not being able to cope with the general education curriculum, thus needing an individualized one, are not sufficient to justify removing a student from the general education classroom (Francisco et al., 2020; Yell & Katsiyannis, 2004). Placement decisions have proven problematic as evidenced by the considerable amount of litigation related to the procedural and substantive errors made by IEP teams regarding placement (Yell et al., 2020) and the differences in placement for students with diverse sociocultural identities, particularly students of the global majority.

Least Restrictive Environment

As teams are making decisions about where and how to provide special education services, they may consider a range of educational placements to meet the individual needs of students with disabilities. IDEA maintains that all districts must provide a full continuum of placement options that range from the least restrictive (e.g., general education classroom) to the most restrictive setting (e.g., residential facility) (Deno, 1970). Traditionally, IEP teams have interpreted LRE as meaning the team must first make an effort to provide services in the general education setting and when the nature or severity of the student needs is such that satisfactory progress cannot be achieved in the LRE, even with supplementary aids and services, placement in a more restrictive setting is considered to meet the principle of appropriate education. More recent interpretations of LRE emphasize the importance of FAPE and, while still considering the full continuum of placements, IEP teams select a placement that prioritizes a student's educational progress (Stone, 2019).

The History of LRE. Advocacy groups and public figures fought long and hard to bring students with disabilities out of institutions with newfound access to public schools. Access to public school was the first step but, unfortunately, it led to dual and separate education systems for disabled students through segregated special programs and classes within the school (Kavale & Forness, 2000). The clear divide between general and special education classes resulted in students with and without disabilities learning near one another, but not with one another. Special education researchers challenged the field to look forward and reimagine special education beyond just access. In the 1960s and 1970s, educational researchers (e.g., Maynord Reynolds, 1962) called for more integrated educational systems for students, recommending service delivery frameworks (e.g., Evelyn Deno, 1970) that continue to be used today. These systems were intended to bring together general education and special education systems, not separate them further (Deno, 1994). In 1968, Lloyd Dunn, the president of the Council for Exceptional Children (CEC), published an article in the *Exceptional Children* journal, which ignited the half-century debate on special education services. Specifically, he said, "we cannot ignore the evidence that removing a handicapped child from the regular grades for special education probably contributes significantly to his feelings of inferiority and problems of acceptance" (p. 9). While the debate continued, publications and subsequent conversations about where and how special education should be provided influenced language in the EAHCA with a presumption for inclusion as well as requiring a range of placement options.

Since 1975, districts have been required to provide a continuum of placement options (e.g., originally outlined by Reynolds and exemplified in Deno's cascade mode). Deno (1970) first defined this system as

> The cascade system is designed to make available whatever different-from-the-mainstream kind of setting is required to control the learning variables deemed critical for the individual case. It is a system which facilitates tailoring of treatment to individual needs rather than a system for sorting out children so they will fit conditions designed according to group standards not necessarily suitable for the particular case. (p. 235)

The cascade or continuum of services became the norm with the resource room model as the primary placement option. Originally referred to as mainstreaming, students would spend part of the school day in the general education setting and part of the day in the resource room rather than a full-time, separate special education placement.

Originally Deno's cascade system addressed individualized services and access to general education services, but in a 1970 seminal article, Deno recommended getting away from the application of the student's disability label (medical model) to determine placement in special education and recommended instead to plan services around specific educational needs. The rationale was that by focusing on these educational needs rather than the "deficit," the focus would be on the variables educators can change rather than sending students out to be "fixed or cured." In addition, around this same time, scholars recommended examining the effects of segregated education for students with disabilities and looking more systematically at the race and language status of students being identified and placed in special education (Deno, 1970).

IDEA's mandates of FAPE, LRE, shared decision making, and teamwork frame the interactions of the stakeholders in special education. Armed with these understandings, special education practitioners must strive to create effective learning environments by teaching colleagues and administrators as much as they teach students. This necessitates collaboration among special education and general education teachers, as well as parent and student participation. Each interaction embodies the values from IDEA (see table 12.1) and reinforces the importance of considering intersectional social identities and cultural expectations.

Counternarratives to Inclusion

Since its earliest days, the IDEA has included a strong preference for inclusion and for students with disabilities to be educated alongside their peers without disabilities. LRE is the entrance to general education classrooms for students with disabilities. While IDEA describes the necessity for placement planning decisions based on the impact on the student's IEP goals and objectives, it does not address the inevitable influence of students with disabilities and special education practitioners in general education classrooms. Inclusion can be considered a social reform perpetuating respect and tolerance for disabled people and greater inclusion in society outside of the school environment (Lipsky & Gartner, 1996). This is not always viewed as the best approach, however. Most notably (as discussed in chapter 3), the Deaf community does not prefer educational settings that rely on oral communication provided by FAPE (Stone, 2019). This raises questions regarding other disability cultures and where and how they are represented in current special education programs, or in inclusion.

Pause and Reflect

- How do you honor disability in your classroom? School?

The practice of LRE has been a controversial topic in the field (Kavale & Forness, 2000). One factor is the wide variety of needs of students across disability areas, but the debate centers around two factors: (a) specially designed instruction and (b) individualization versus access to general education peers, classrooms, and curriculum. General education teachers are often not trained in the needs and effective interventions and teaching techniques for students with disabilities (Crispel & Kasperski, 2021). Researchers have found that teachers embrace teaching in inclusive classrooms, but they lack confidence in their ability to teach and meet the needs of their disabled students (Chiner & Cardona, 2013). General education teachers need comprehensive training in special education, but in general, they rely on their special education colleagues and related professional development. Collaboration among experienced special education practitioners and general education teachers can promote or prohibit effective teaching in the inclusive classroom (Abegglen & Hessels, 2018; Schwab et al., 2017).

Various studies show that inclusion does not adversely impact the academic outcomes of students with or without disabilities and in fact may be beneficial (Cole et al., 2004; Cosier et al., 2013; Oh-Young & Filler, 2015; Ryndak et al., 2013; Salend & Duhaney, 2007; Tremblay, 2013). In fact, inclusion results in higher academic achievement for disabled students and nondisabled students, and higher graduation rates for nondisabled students (Westling, 2019). Research has demonstrated that when nondisabled students are educated with disabled students, it positively affects the interpersonal skills of nondisabled students by increasing their awareness of individual differences, including gaining friendships through the development of appreciation and acceptance of other students and a greater understanding of disability-related issues (McLeskey et al., 2018; Oh-Young & Filler, 2015). Classes with students with disabilities also often receive additional resources, such as additional qualified adults, which can positively affect all students' performance (Cipani, 1995; Dalcin, 2022; Hanushek et al., 2009; Williams & Downing, 1998). It benefits students with disabilities, too. Students in well-designed inclusive programs demonstrate greater academic achievement, increased self-confidence, and more on-task behaviors (McLeskey et al., 2018). Social and emotional improvements include greater self-esteem, more interactions with other students, richer and more long-lasting friendships, and improved social status within school communities (McLeskey et al., 2018).

Research has demonstrated that teaching styles become more caring and sensitive toward all students after general education teachers receive instruction in special education techniques (Crispel & Kasperski, 2021). Considering the ongoing disparities in educational settings, ongoing teaching is necessary for truly inclusive and culturally sensitive schools.

VIGNETTE 2: YOKASTA'S STORY ABOUT LEAST RESTRICTIVE ENVIRONMENT

Both Liam and I are legally blind as a result of Leber's congenital amaurosis (LCA), a diagnosis that affects the rods and cones found in the retina. As a result, we have low visual acuity and are unable to drive. It is difficult to see fine detail and color perception due to photophobia (sensitivity to light). Some of our accommodations include wearing prescription distance/reading/sunglasses as needed. We also benefit from assistive technology and accommodations (in order to access print materials) such as inverted contrast, zoom and/or voiceover on our devices in addition to other daily visual accommodations. We both use a long white cane for domestic and international travel as needed.

The 1980s and 1990s were a time of educational reform in Westernized nations that focused on placing students with disabilities in the least restrictive environment, spearheaded by the push for integration. The United States served as a model for third-world countries, so naturally, the Dominican Republic followed suit. Since I did not fit the stereotypical social ideologies of what children with low vision looked like, I grew up with minimal to no accommodations and was fully mainstreamed in both countries; but integration without support is segregation . . . so, in a sense, I grew up in the most restrictive environment.

My educational experience was abysmal. The only accommodations I received were extended time on tests, a monocular to copy the blackboard, and a peer notetaker. If my peer was out, I was out of luck and had to find a way to get notes from someone else. This system was incredibly flawed as it put all of the responsibility on me to provide for my own accommodations. There was no forethought on service provision, just the unrealistic assumption that since I did not "look blind," I should be able to keep up. As a result, I missed valuable opportunities for incidental learning as I could not experience the world in the same manner as my sighted peers. I became great at cutting corners and worked double time to fill the gaps I knew I was missing in a class by conducting my own research after school; if students were looking at a live butterfly in science class, I'd go home, take out my magnifier and Encyclopedia and look at a picture of one. In the end, and despite all of the challenges along the way, I was a good student and learned ways to compensate for my sensory "deficit."

VIGNETTE 3: *MEET NATHANIEL LENTZ*

When I was seven years old, I saw my mom receive her master's degree. Seeing my mom walk onto the stage and get her degree gave me the desire and goal to go to college.

During my school years, I was able to achieve academically with accommodations, but it was very difficult for me to make friends. My classmates were put off by my inability to control my left arm and the difficulty I had in expressing myself.

During my elementary years, I was in general education classes. I did the same work, worked on the same homework, and worked with the same study guides, but there was a catch: I needed to study more than anyone else to learn the material. When I was in first grade, my parents arranged for an expert in accommodations for students with disabilities to visit the school. She looked over the classrooms and my disabilities. Then she made suggestions to the school principal and teachers about what I needed to do my best.

(continued)

VIGNETTE 3: *Continued*

When I was in middle school, the teachers wanted to make my classes easy for me. At one meeting, the teachers suggested that I take a particular teacher's class because she did not ask her students to write a lot. My mom said writing was exactly what I needed, so I was put in a class where the teacher had a lot of writing assignments.

When I was in high school, I had a test reader and would take my tests in a room in the Learning Disabilities Department. I also had teacher and aide support to help me understand the lessons and the assignments. When I was a freshman, I said that I wanted to be in the college-prep program. I could tell that the special education teachers did not think that was a good idea. But my parents supported my decision so I was able to complete the required classes needed for the university system.

During school, I volunteered to be an assistant manager of the basketball team. After the practice, the players would get together. One day, right in front of me, one of the players said someone should invite Nathaniel. The star player said, "Well, you invite him, then." Nobody did. When it was time for the team photo, I was sick, so I am not in the team photo. I bet if one the players were sick, they would have rescheduled the photo.

I also volunteered to help with the props for the school musical. There was a party for anyone who worked on the musical. A friend of mine, who was one of the actors, drove us to the party. The others who worked on the musical said that I couldn't be at the party because I hadn't worked enough on the musical. It was January and the temperature was ten degrees, but they wouldn't let me in, so I sat in my friend's car while he was at the party. He did not stay very long because he knew that it was too cold for me to sit in his car.

During school, I decided to join the Capital Sound Drum and Bugle Corps. I learned how to act professionally and be a team player. The drum corps was very challenging for me because the left side of my body was not strong enough to hold up a soprano horn for eight hours a session. Also, the weakness in my left leg made it impossible for me to march in the precise way necessary for drum corps. I worked with the staff, one-on-one, to try to overcome the challenges I faced because of my disability. I was offered a position in the pit because the staff saw how hard I worked trying to march. The pit is where the shaker, triangle, cymbals, bass drum, windchimes, and marimbas are set up. The players in the pit do not march during the performances. I participated for three years with the drum corps playing shows all over the country.

When I started my college career, the Center for Students with Disabilities assigned tutors to help me. Before I met with my tutor, I would complete the assignment on my own. The tutor would check my work, make suggestions, and set new goals for the following week. The tutor would not do my work for me. Every week I would meet with my professor, one-on-one, to review my notes, homework assignments, and study materials to make sure I was on the right track. I would also meet with my professor if there was something I did not understand. I was permitted to take my exams in a private room with a test reader or in professors' offices. I used a computer program that would speak the text as I was reading it. I used an iPad for taking notes because I type faster than I write, and my writing is often difficult to read afterward, even for me. I also used technology to take photos of what the professor had written on the board. One of my accommodations was permission to record lectures. I met my goal. I graduated from college and received my bachelor's degree.

CREATING A SENSE OF BELONGING

All models of inclusion are aimed at providing a restructured and unified system of special and general education to meet the needs of all students (Skrtic, 1991). Inclusion alone is not the destination but a process of reimagining education for all students and meeting the aspirations of IDEA. While IDEA requires inclusion, the movement has been an incremental, multifaceted evolutionary process as school systems adapted to the changing needs of learners and societal changes in values and beliefs (Francisco et al., 2020). In light of these changing values and beliefs, we suggest an expanded definition that centers racial equity and sociocultural intersectionality that moves us to the concept of **belonging** as "engagement within a community where the equal worth and inherent dignity of each person is honored. An inclusive community promotes and sustains a sense of belonging; it affirms the talents, beliefs, backgrounds and ways of living of its members" (Cobb & Krownapple, 2019, p. 33). As illustrated in figure 12.2, researchers have identified ten essential dimensions of belonging for students with disabilities.

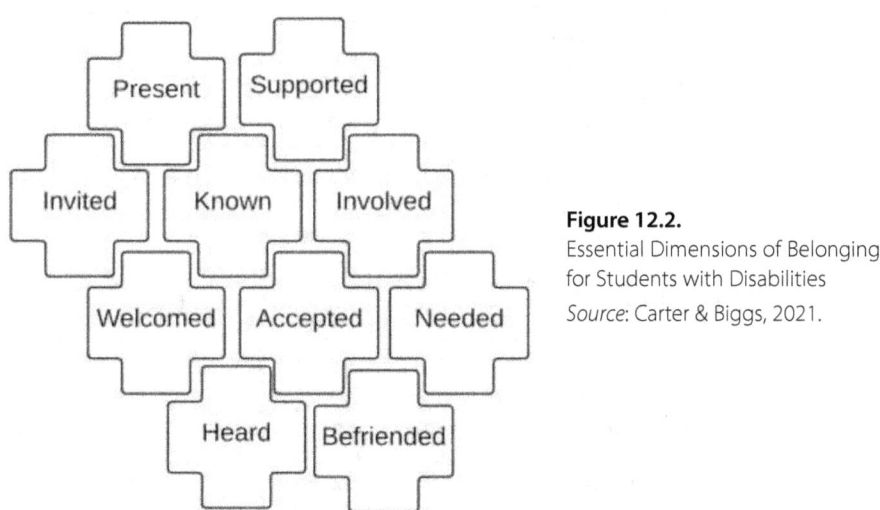

Figure 12.2.
Essential Dimensions of Belonging for Students with Disabilities
Source: Carter & Biggs, 2021.

When each of these areas is addressed well, schools become learning environments in which students thrive and are seen as valued and indispensable members of the school community. This is perhaps special education's greatest influence on general education—years of advocating for all students to belong and benefit from an integrated, intersectional educational system. As the field has evolved and we strive to create a more inclusive, integrated, and effective system for all students, the next set of practices to aspire to are outlined in table 12.3.

Table 12.3. Move to More Inclusive Values Influencing Education

Component	Description, Examples, and Resources
Mindsets/ Beliefs	Mindsets and beliefs can drive practices. We want to change the mindset of "These are my students, and those are your students." Special education influences general education through the following beliefs and mindsets.
	• We treat each student as a valued member and contributor to the community. • We take mutual responsibility for this work because we believe EACH student is OUR student and the responsibility of the whole team (i.e., both general and special education). • We do not label our students or our work with them and avoid labels that limit beliefs, add barriers, or stereotype. • We support each child collectively because this is much better than we can individually. • Resource: https://publications.ici.umn.edu/ties/peer-engagement/belonging/introduction#Dimensions-of-Belonging
Leadership	Administrator support and vision is an important predictor of educators' beliefs toward inclusion (Villa et al., 1996). Effective leadership vision and practices benefit all students when . . .
	• We approach every single policy, practice, and decision through a socioculturally sustaining lens of inclusion and belonging. • We design the structures and scheduling within the school to support the reduction of barriers for student access and to allow for engagement in general education learning, including professional development, extra planning time, collaboration, and communication. • We create systems for collecting and regularly analyzing student learning data to guide instructional decisions and groupings that are not based on educational labels but on student needs; these groups change based on the data and needs of the students. • Resource: https://ccssoinclusiveprincipalsguide.org/
Collaboration	Collaboration is considered a high-leverage practice in special education and a critical dimension to the planning, delivery, and evaluation of special education and related services (Friend & Cook, 2017, p. 20; McLeskey et al., 2017). Due to the emphasis on collaboration, special educators can support this collaboration through their preparation, experience, and beliefs.
	• We collaborate with every member of the school community as they are needed to ensure EACH student is given the right support to be successful. • We create classroom placements and groupings with attention to the needs of students to maximize the support available within the general education setting through co-teaching partnerships and collaboration.
Redefined Roles	One collaborative model used in special education is transdisciplinary collaboration. The application of transdisciplinary practice can help schools become more inclusive.
	• We share responsibility for student learning by expanding and exchanging knowledge within and between team members. • We all (each team member) assume the role of teacher, learner, and implementer (Rainforth & England, 1997). • We share the education of individuals with disabilities with all school personnel, whether they are general education teachers or specialized service providers. • We change silo thinking and practices and even professional labels to a more general job description for all licensed staff that articulates collaboration and shared responsibility.

VIGNETTE 4: *MEET COLLIN AND OLIVIA*

Inclusive School Experiences

Collin: When I started elementary school, my district wanted to bus me to a school with other kids with special needs in another district because I have autism. My parents advocated for me to remain in my neighborhood school. Around 3rd grade, the school was doing a good job with including me and started including other kids with special needs in our district. When I graduated in 6th grade, the principal said I had changed the inclusive mindset of the school.

Olivia: I have Down syndrome. I went to small schools. There were eighty students in my high school. The school figured out how to include me.

Collin: I have an example of my participation in classes from my high school literature class. When the class was reading *The Secret Life of Bees*, I read the book but also listened to an audio version of the book and watched the movie. Instead of writing a paper, I created a label for a jar of honey about what I read in the book to show what I learned.

Olivia: In my literature classes, the teacher required students to work on twenty new vocabulary words per lesson. My teacher would choose ten of the most meaningful terms to my life from the list of twenty to focus on for each lesson.

Collin: In history class, I really liked learning US presidential facts. For the final project, I completed a timeline of when US presidents served instead of a critical analysis paper focused on a political cartoon related to American humorists.

Olivia: In science, I had a paraprofessional aide as an accommodation to assist with note taking. I participated in the same science experiments as the other students.

Collin: I was in the band and played the cymbals for four years in high school. With the band, I went to all the home football and basketball games. We also marched in the homecoming parade. When the high school band traveled to other states for performances in St. Louis and New York, I and my special education teacher visited the menus of restaurants the band would eat in and planned my order, the cost, and the tips. We put the required amount of money into envelopes, and I wrote the date and the name of the restaurant on the envelope.

Olivia: I was in choir during the first period of all four years of high school. With the choir, there were a lot of concerts. One of the last concerts during my senior year, the music teacher talked about each senior. He said such positive things about me that his words brought tears to my and my parents' eyes. I had a lot of friends in choir.

Extracurriculars

Collin: The summer before high school, my elementary school physical education teacher asked me if I would like to join the cross-country team. During practices, I did my best to stay with the rest of the team during runs and never quit when I was tired. Every Friday night, our team got together for pasta dinners and would state our personal goals. I had goals like "keep my laces tied" and "try to pass everyone in front of me." When I met my personal best one week, I got the jersey given to the runner who gave the best effort the previous week. In my fourth year, I received the "most improved" award. Our team won our division state championship three out of four years I was running. It has been twelve years since I graduated from high school, and sometimes I still go up to the high school and run with the team to maintain my personal health.

(continued)

VIGNETTE 4: *Continued*

Olivia: *My speech and language teacher coached the girls' volleyball team and asked me to be the student manager. I was a member of the team who helped run drills, maintained the water bottles, and collected balls. I did such a good job in the fall volleyball role, the school asked me to participate on the girls' basketball team. These activities required me to stay after school for practices and attend home and away games. I helped with fundraising for the teams, such as painting pumpkins pink for breast cancer awareness. Some of the students from the volleyball team asked me to go out to eat, take pictures, and go to the homecoming dance with the group.*

Postsecondary
Collin: *I went to Edgewood College's Cutting Edge program for four years. In college, my favorite classes were Spanish. I volunteered in a multicultural center, drove students to classes in a golf cart, and worked in a pet spa to gain some work experience during college. I met Olivia in college. I asked her out by giving her a card for her birthday. On our first date, we went to a movie. Olivia is sweet and we like to travel together. We have been dating for seven years.*

Olivia: *I also went to Edgewood College. I had no clue Collin was going to ask me out and when he did, I was excited. Collin had been my workout buddy going to the fitness center. I love spending time with him.*

Adulthood
Collin: *I am working at an urban farm. I travel a lot and like to attend sporting events. I enjoy watching* Wheel of Fortune *and* The Good Doctor.

Olivia: *I am living my dream of working in retail and participating in the church choir. I live in my own home and have a dog I care for. I also have my own business where I sell my art.*

SUMMARY

The path to a free appropriate public education has been long and arduous, but it is important that we continue to evolve as a field. Understanding our own and our students' sociocultural identities is vital to self-discovery and personal growth. Not only that, when we infuse intersectional socioculturally sustaining practices in inclusive whole-school processes—that is, evaluation, placement, learning, and discipline—we can increase a sense of belonging for all. These processes require reflection and action. They are ongoing and have the capacity to impact equity by helping educators avoid "othering" students. This text aims to help us create belonging and community for *all* of our students by (a) conceptualizing disability and race in an intersectional way; and (b) centering sociocultural identities and values to drive daily decisions in our daily practices, in our classrooms and schools, and in our advocacy.

REFERENCES

Abegglen, H. J., & Hessels, M. G. (2018). Measures of individual, collaborative and environmental characteristics predict Swiss school principals', teachers' and student teachers' attitudes towards inclusive education. *Psychoeducational Assessment, Intervention and Rehabilitation, 1*(1), 1–24.

Adelman, H. S. (1994). Intervening to enhance home involvement in schooling. *Intervention in School and Clinic, 29*(5), 276–87.

Anastasiou, D., & Kauffman, J. M. (2012). Disability as cultural difference: Implications for special education. *Remedial and Special Education, 33*(3), 139–49.

Annamma, S. A., & Morrison, D. (2018). DisCrit classroom ecology: Using praxis to dismantle dysfunctional education ecologies. *Teaching and Teacher Education, 73*, 70–80.

Balcazar, F. E., Keys, C. B., Bertram, J. F., & Rizzo, T. (1996). Advocate development in the field of developmental disabilities: A data-based conceptual model. *Mental Retardation, 34*(6), 341–51.

Banerjee, R., & Luckner, J. (2014). Training needs of early childhood professionals who work with children and families who are culturally and linguistically diverse. *Infants & Young Children, 27*(1), 43–59. https://www.researchgate.net/publication/271683178_Training_Needs_of_Early_Childhood_Professionals_Who_Work_With_Children_and_Families_Who_Are_Culturally_and_Linguistically_Diverse

Barrio, B. L. (2017). Special education policy change: Addressing the disproportionality of English language learners in special education programs in rural communities. *Rural Special Education Quarterly, 36*(2), 64–72.

Bempechat, J. (1992). The role of parent involvement in children's academic achievement. *School Community Journal, 2*(2), 31–41.

Black, A. P., & Baker, M. (2011). The impact of parent advocacy groups, the internet, and social networking on rare diseases: The IDEA League and the IDEA League United Kingdom example. *Epilepsia, 52*(2), 102–4.

Blatt, B., & Kaplan, F. (1974). *Christmas in purgatory*. Human Policy.

Brandon, R. R., Higgins, K., Pierce, T., Tandy, R., & Sileo, N. (2010). An exploration of the alienation experienced by African American parents from their children's educational environment. *Remedial and Special Education, 31*(3), 208–22.

Broderick, A., & Leonardo, Z. (2016). What a good boy: The deployment and distribution of "goodness" as ideological property in schools. In D. J. Connor, B. A. Ferri, & S. A. Annamma (Eds.), *DisCrit: Disability Studies and Critical Race Theory in education* (pp. 55–67). Teachers College Press.

Buren, M. K., Maggin, D. M., & Brown, C. (2020). Meta-synthesis on the experiences of families from nondominant communities and special education collaboration. *Exceptionality, 28*(4), 259–78.

Burke, M. M., & Goldman, S. E. (2018). Special education advocacy among culturally and linguistically diverse families. *Journal of Research in Special Educational Needs, 18*(51), 3–14. https://doi.org/10.1111/1471-3802.12413

Burke, M. M., Rios, K., & Lee, C. E. (2019). Exploring the special education advocacy process according to families and advocates. *Journal of Special Education, 53*(3), 131–41.

Carter, E. W., & Biggs, E. E. (2021). *Creating communities of belonging for students with significant cognitive disabilities*. University of Minnesota, TIES Center, Belonging Series.

Castagno, A. E., & Brayboy, B. M. J. (2008). Culturally responsive schooling for Indigenous youth: A review of the literature. *Review of Educational Research, 78*(4), 941–93.

Chang, M. (2006). The educational benefits of sustaining cross-racial interaction among undergraduates. *Journal of Higher Education, 77*(3), 430. http://muse.jhu.edu/journals/jhe/summary/v077/77.3chang.html

Chiner, E., & Cardona, M. C. (2013). Inclusive education in Spain: How do skills, resources, and supports affect regular education teachers' perceptions of inclusion? *International Journal of Inclusive Education, 17*(5), 526–41.

Cipani, E. (1995). Inclusive education: What do we know and what do we still have to learn? *Exceptional Children, 61*(5), 498–500.

Cobb, F., & Krownapple, J. J. (2019). *Belonging through a culture of dignity: The keys to successful equity implementation.* Mimi and Todd.

Cole, C. M., Waldron, N., & Majd, M. (2004). Academic progress of students across inclusive and traditional settings. *Mental Retardation, 42*(2), 136–44.

Comer, J. P., & Haynes, N. M. (1991). Parent involvement in schools: An ecological approach. *Elementary School Journal, 91*(3), 271–77.

Conley Wright, A., & Taylor, S. (2014). Advocacy by parents of young children with special needs: Activities, processes, and perceived effectiveness. *Journal of Social Service Research, 40*(5), 591–605.

Cooc, N. (2022). Disparities in general education inclusion for students of color with disabilities: Understanding when and why. *Journal of School Psychology, 90*, 43–59. https://doi.org/10.1016/j.jsp.2021.10.002

Cosier, M., Causton-Theoharis, J., & Theoharis, G. (2013). Does access matter? Time in general education and achievement for students with disabilities. *Remedial and Special Education, 34*(6), 323–32. https://doi:10.1177/0741932513485448

Crann, T., & Bui, N. (2022). "It means everything": Somali community creates word for autism. https://www.mprnews.org/story/2022/06/07/it-means-everything-somali-community-creates-word-for-autism.

Crispel, O., & Kasperski, R. (2021). The impact of teacher training in special education on the implementation of inclusion in mainstream classrooms. *International Journal of Inclusive Education, 25*(9), 1079–90.

Dalcin, A. K. (2022), Learning together: The effects of inclusion of students with disabilities in mainstream schools. *EconomiA, 23*(1), 1–24. https://doi.org/10.1108/ECON-05-2022-0005

Dana, R. H. (1996). Culturally competent assessment practice in the United States. *Journal of Personality Assessment, 66*(3), 472–87.

Darling-Hammond, L. (2000). *Solving the dilemmas of teacher supply, demand, and standards: How we can ensure a competent, caring, and qualified teacher for every child.* National Commission on Teaching & America's Future.

Deno, E. (1970). Special education as developmental capital. *Exceptional Children, 37*(3), 229–37.

———. (1994). Special education as developmental capital revisited: A quarter-century appraisal of means versus ends. *Journal of Special Education, 27*(4), 375–92.

Deyhle, D., & Swisher, K. (1997). Research in American Indian and Alaska Native education: From assimilation to self-determination. *Review of Research in Education, 22*(1), 113–94.

Domina, T., Penner, A., & Penner, E. (2017). Categorical inequality: Schools as sorting machines. *Annual Review of Sociology, 43*, 311–30. https://doi:10.1146/annurev-soc-060116-053354

Dong, Q., Garcia, B., Pham, A. V., & Cumming, M. (2020). Culturally responsive approaches for addressing ADHD within multi-tiered systems of support. *Current Psychiatry Reports, 22*(6), 1–10.

Dunn, L. (1968). Special education for the mildly retarded—Is much of it justifiable? *Exceptional Children, 35*(1), 5–22.

Education for All Handicapped Children Act (EAHCA), Public Law 94-142 (1975).

Evans, D. (1953). *Angel unaware.* Revell.

Fierros, E. G., & Conroy, J. W. (2002). Double jeopardy: An exploration of restrictiveness and race in special education. In D. J. Losen & G. Orfield (Eds.), *Racial inequity in special education* (pp. 39–70). Harvard Education Press.

Fish, R. E. (2019). Standing out and sorting in: Exploring the role of racial composition in racial disparities in special education. *American Educational Research Journal, 56*(6), 2573–2608.

Ford, D. Y. (2005, Winter). *Intelligence testing and cultural diversity: Pitfalls and promises.* University of Connecticut. Newsletter of National Research Center on Gifted and Talented.

Ford, D. Y., & Russo, C. J. (2014). No Child Left Behind, unless student is gifted and of color: Reflections on the need to meet the educational needs of the gifted. *Journal of Law and Society, 15*(2), 213–40.

———. (2016). Historical and legal overview of special education overrepresentation: Access and equity denied. *Multiple Voices for Ethnically Diverse Exceptional Learners, 16*(1), 50–57.

Francisco, M. P. B., Hartman, M., & Wang, Y. (2020). Inclusion and special education. *Education Sciences, 10*(9), 238.

Friend, M., & Cook, L. (2017). *Interactions: Collaboration skills for school professionals.* 8th ed. Pearson.

Gargiulo, R. M., & Bouck, E. C. (2021). *Special education in contemporary society: An introduction to exceptionality.* 7th ed. Sage.

Gatlin, B. T., & Wilson, C. L. (2016). Overcoming obstacles: African American students with disabilities achieving academic success. *Journal of Negro Education, 85*(2), 129–42. https://www.jstor.org/stable/10.7709/jnegroeducation.85.2.0129

Gerber, M. M. (2017). A history of special education. In J. M. Kauffman, D. P. Hallahan, & P. C. Pullen (Eds.), *Handbook of special education* (pp. 3–15). Routledge.

Grindal, T., Schifter, L., Schwartz, G., & Hehir, T., (2019). Racial differences in special education identification and placement: Evidence across three states. *Harvard Educational Review, 89*(4), 525–53. https://doi.org/10.17763/1943-5045-89.4.525

Hamilton, M-B., Stansberry Brusnahan, L. L., & Pearson, J. N. (2021). Culturally competent educational practices: Supporting students with disabilities and their families. *Division on Autism and Developmental Disabilities Online Journal, 8*(1), 114–28.

Hanushek, E. A., Kain, J. F., & Rivkin, S. G. (2009). New evidence about *Brown v. Board of Education*: The complex effects of school racial composition on achievement. *Journal of Labour Economics, 27*(3), 349–83.

Harry, B. (2008). Collaboration with culturally and linguistically diverse families: Ideal versus reality. *Exceptional Children, 74*(3), 372–88. https://doi.org/10.1177/001440290807400306

Harry, B., & Klingner, J. (2007). Discarding the deficit model. *Educational Leadership, 64*(5), 16–21. https://eric.ed.gov/?id=EJ766321

Hebert, E. B., & Koulouglioti, C. (2010). Parental beliefs about cause and course of their child's autism and outcomes of their beliefs: A review of the literature. *Issues in Comprehensive Pediatric Nursing, 33*(3), 149–63.

Ijalba, E. (2016). Hispanic immigrant mothers of young children with autism spectrum disorders: How do they understand and cope with autism? *American Journal of Speech-Language Pathology, 25*(2), 200–13. https://doi: 10.1044/2015_AJSLP-13-0017

Individuals with Disabilities Education Act (IDEA), 20 U.S.C. § 300.114 (2004).

Individuals with Disabilities Education Act (IDEA), 20 U.S.C. § 1400 (2004).

Individuals with Disabilities Education Act (IDEA). (2022, January 21). *43rd Annual report to Congress on the implementation of the Individuals with Disabilities Education Act, 2021.* IDEA. https://sites.ed.gov/idea/department-submits-the-43rd-annual-report-to-congress-idea

IRIS. (2022). *Information brief on Least Restrictive Environment (LRE).* University of Florida College of Education. https://udl4cs.education.ufl.edu/resources/iris-information-brief-on-least-restrictive-environment-lre/

Jegatheesan, B., Miller, P. J., & Fowler, S. A. (2010). Autism from a religious perspective: A study of parental beliefs in South Asian Muslim immigrant families. *Focus on Autism and Other Developmental Disabilities, 25*(2), 98–109. https://psycnet.apa.org/doi/10.1177/1088357610361344

Kalyanpur, M., & Harry, B. (2012). *Cultural reciprocity in special education: Building family–professional relationships.* Paul H. Brookes.

Kapp, S. K. (2011). Navajo and autism: The beauty of harmony. *Disability & Society, 26*(5), 583–95. https://doi.org/10.1080/09687599.2011.589192

Katsiyannis, A., Yell, M. L., & Bradley, R. (2001). Reflections on the 25th anniversary of the Individuals with Disabilities Education Act. *Remedial and Special Education, 22*(6), 324–34. https://doi.org/10.1177/074193250102200602

Kavale, K., & Forness, S. (2000). History, rhetoric and reality: Analysis of the inclusion debate. *Remedial and Special Education, 21*(5), 279–96.

Kendi, I. (2019). *How to be an antiracist.* One World.

Lipsky, D. K., & Gartner, A. (1996). Inclusion, school restructuring, and the remaking of American society. *Harvard Educational Review, 66*(4), 762–97.

Lovelace, T. S., Robertson, R. E., & Tamayo, S. (2018). Experiences of African American mothers of sons with autism spectrum disorder: Lessons for improving service delivery. *Education and Training in Autism and Developmental Disabilities, 53*(1), 3–16.

Marshall, C., Mitchell, D., & Wirt, F. (1989). *Culture and education policy in the American states.* Falmer.

Massey, D., & Fischer, M. (2006). The effect of childhood segregation on minority academic performance at selective colleges. *Ethnic and Racial Studies, 29*(1), 1–26. http://www.tandfonline.com/doi/abs/10.1080/01419870500351159

McFarland, J., Hussar, B., Wang, X., Zhang, J., Wang, K., Rathbun, A., . . . Bullock Mann, F. (2018). *The condition of education 2018* (NCES 2018-144). US Department of Education. National Center for Education Statistics. https://nces.ed.gov/pubsearch/pubsinfo. asp?pubid=2018144

McLeskey, J., Barringer, M-D., Billingsley, B., Brownell, M., Jackson, D., Kennedy, M., . . . Ziegler, D. (2017). *High-leverage practices in special education.* Council for Exceptional Children & CEEDAR Center.

McLeskey, J. L., Rosenberg, M. S., & Westling, D. L. (2018). *Inclusion: Effective practices for all students.* 3rd ed. Pearson.

Merriam-Webster.com. (2023). Advocacy. https://www.merriam-webster.com/dictionary/advocacy

Michel, M. C., & Kuiken, F. (2014). Language at preschool in Europe: Early years professionals in the spotlight. *European Journal of Applied Linguistics, 2*(1), 1–26. https://doi.org/10.1515/eujal-2014-0005

Miles, M. (2002). Disability in an Eastern religious context: Historical perspectives. *Journal of Religion, Disability & Health, 6*(2–3), 53–76.

Mitchell, C. (2019). Most classroom teachers feel unprepared to support students with disabilities. *Education Week*. https://www.edweek.org/teaching-learning/most-classroom-teachers-feel-unprepared-to-support-students-with-disabilities/2019/05

Mortier, K., & Arias, E. (2023). "The Latino community is not accustomed to arguing for the rights of their children": How Latina mothers navigate special education. *Journal of Latinos and Education, 22*(2), 642–53.

National Center for Education Statistics (NCES). (2022). *State nonfiscal survey of public elementary/secondary education*. US Department of Education, National Center for Education Statistics, Common Core of Data (CCD), https://nces.ed.gov/programs/digest/d22/tables/dt22_203.70.asp?current=yes

NeMoyer, A., Nakash, O., Fukuda, M., Rosenthal, J., Mention, N., Chambers, V. A., . . . Alegría, M. (2020). Gathering diverse perspectives to tackle "wicked problems": Racial/ethnic disproportionality in educational placement. *American Journal of Community Psychology, 65*(1–2), 44–62.

Oh-Young, C., & Filler, J. (2015). A meta-analysis of the effects of placement on academic and social skill outcome measures of students with disabilities. *Research in Developmental Disabilities, 47*, 80–92.

Page, S. E. (2008). *The difference: How the power of diversity creates better groups, firms, schools, and societies.* Princeton University Press. http://press.princeton.edu/titles/8757.html

Pearson, J. N., Hamilton, M. B., Stansberry, L., & Hussein, D. (2021). Empowering families by utilizing culturally responsive strategies in the education of children with multi-layered identities. In E. A. Harkins Monaco, M. C. Fuller, & L. L. Stansberry Brusnahan (Eds.), *Diversity, autism, and developmental disabilities: Guidance for the culturally sustaining educator* (pp. 131–56). Prism Series, 13. CEC-DADD.

Poponi, D. M. (2009). The relationship between student outcomes and parental involvement in multidisciplinary IEP team meetings. *PCOM Psychology Dissertations*. 116. https://digitalcommons.pcom.edu/psychology_dissertations/116

Quiocho, A., & Daoud, A. (2006). Dispelling myths about Latino parent participation in schools. *Educational Forum, 7*(3), 255–67.

Rainforth, B., & England, J. (1997). Collaborations for inclusion. *Education and Treatment of Children, 20*(1), 85–104. http://www.jstor.org/stable/42940553

Reiman, J. W., Beck, L., Coppola, T., & Engiles, A. (2010). Parents' experiences with the IEP process: Considerations for improving practice. *Center for Appropriate Dispute Resolution in Special Education (CADRE)*. https://files.eric.ed.gov/fulltext/ED512611.pdf

Reimann, M. (2017). Willowbrook, the institution that shocked a nation into changing its laws. *Timeline*. https://timeline.com/willowbrook-the-institution-that-shocked-a-nation-into-changing-its-laws-c847acb44e0d

Reynolds, M. C. (1962). A framework for considering some issues in special education. *Exceptional Children, 28*(7), 367–70.

Rios, K., Aleman-Tovar, J., & Burke, M. M. (2020). Special education experiences and stress among Latina mothers of children with autism spectrum disorder (ASD). *Research in Autism Spectrum Disorders, 73*(2), 101534.

Rivera, G. (1972). *Willowbrook: A report on how it is and why it doesn't have to be that way*. Random House.

Rossetti, Z., Sauer, J. S., Bui, O., & Ou, S. (2017). Developing collaborative partnerships with culturally and linguistically diverse families during the IEP process. *TEACHING Exceptional Children, 49*(5), 328–38.

Ryndak, D., Jackson, L., & White, J. (2013). Involvement and progress in the general curriculum for students with extensive support needs: K–12 inclusive education research and implications for the future. *Inclusion, 1*(1), 28–49.

Salend, S., & Duhaney, L. (2007). Research related to inclusion and program effectiveness. In J. McLeskey (Ed.), *Reflections on inclusion: Classic articles that shaped our thinking* (pp. 127–59). Council for Exceptional Children.

Schwab, S., Hellmich, F., & Görel, G. (2017). Self-efficacy of prospective Austrian and German primary school teachers regarding the implementation of inclusive education. *Journal of Research in Special Educational Needs, 17*(3), 205–17.

Skiba, R. J., Poloni-Staudinger, L., Gallini, S., Simmons, A. B., & Feggins-Azziz, R. (2006). Disparate access: The disproportionality of African American students with disabilities across educational environments. *Exceptional Children, 72*(4), 411–24. https://doi.org/10.1177/001440290607200402

Skrtic, T. M. (1991). The special education paradox: Equity as the way to excellence. *Harvard Educational Review, 61*(2), 148–207. https://doi.org/10.17763/haer.61.2.0q702751580h0617

Slot, P. L., Romijn, B. R., & Nata, G. (2019). *A virtual learning environment model of professional development aimed at enhancing diversity and inclusiveness*. ISOTIS.

Smart, J. F., & Smart, D. W. (2006). Models of disability: Implications for the counseling profession. *Journal of Counseling & Development, 84*(1), 29–40. https://psycnet.apa.org/doi/10.1002/j.1556-6678.2006.tb00377

Spaulding, L. S., & Pratt, S. M. (2015). A review and analysis of the history of special education and disability advocacy in the United States. *American Educational History Journal, 42*(1), 91–109. https://eric.ed.gov/?id=EJ1143593

Stone, D. H. (2019). The least restrictive environment for providing education, treatment, and community services for persons with disabilities: Rethinking the concept. *Touro Law Review, 35*(1), 523–90.

Stuart Wells, A., Fox, L., & Cordova-Cobo, D. (2016). *How racially diverse schools and classrooms can benefit all students*. Century Foundation. https://tcf.org/content/report/how-racially-diverse-schools-and-classrooms-can-benefit-all-students/

Toldson, I. A., & Ford, D. Y. (2015, July 5). Study on Black, Hispanic children in special ed wrong, regressive. *Diverse Issues in Higher Education*. http://diverseeducation.com/article/76088/

Tremblay, P. (2013). Comparative outcomes of two instructional models for students with learning disabilities: Inclusion with co-teaching and solo-taught special education. *Journal of Research in Special Educational Needs, 13*(4), 251–58.

Turnbull, H. R. (2012). "Free at last": Kennedy, King, and the meaning of liberty in the Disability Rights Movement. *Research and Practice for Persons with Severe Disabilities, 37*(3), 210–16. https://doi.org/10.2511/027494812804153543

US Department of Education. (2016). Tools and resources for addressing English learners with disabilities. *English learner toolkit,* chapter 6. https://www2.ed.gov/about/offices/list/oela/english-learner-toolkit/chap6.pdf

US Department of Education. (2021). *43rd annual report to Congress on the Implementation of the Individuals with Disabilities Education Act, 2021.* US Department of Education, Office of Special Education and Rehabilitative Services, Office of Special Education Programs. https://sites.ed.gov/idea/files/43rd-arc-for-idea.pdf

Villa, R. A., Thousand, J. S., Meyers, H., & Nevin, A. (1996). Teacher and administrator perceptions of heterogeneous education. *Exceptional Children, 63*(1), 29–45. https://doi.org/10.1177/001440299606300103

Vincent, C. (2000). *Including parents?: Education, citizenship and parental agency.* Open University Press.

Wakelin, M. M. (2008). Challenging disparities in special education: Moving parents from disempowered team members to ardent advocates. *Northwestern Journal of Law and Social Policy, 3*(2), 263–88.

Walton, J., Priest, N., Kowal, E., White, F., Fox, B., & Paradies, Y. (2016). Whiteness and national identity: Teacher discourses in Australian primary schools. *Race, Ethnicity and Education, 21*(1), 132–47.

Wathum-Ocama, J. C., & Rose, S. (2002). Hmong immigrants' views on the education of their deaf and hard of hearing children. *American Annals of The Deaf, 147*(3), 44–53.

Westling, D. L. (2019). Inclusion in the United States: Correlations between key state variables. *International Journal of Inclusive Education, 23*(6), 575–93.

Wexler, D. (2018). School-based multi-tiered systems of support (MTSS): An introduction to MTSS for neuropsychologists. *Applied Neuropsychology: Child, 7*(4), 306–16.

Williams, L. J., & Downing, J. E. (1998). Membership and belonging in inclusive classrooms: What do middle school students have to say? *Research and Practice for Persons with Severe Disabilities, 23*(2), 98–110.

Wolfe, K., & Durán, L. K. (2013). Culturally and linguistically diverse parents' perceptions of the IEP process: A review of current research. *Multiple Voices for Ethnically Diverse Exceptional Learners, 13*(2), 4–18. https://eric.ed.gov/?id=EJ1034651

Yell, M. L., Collins, J., Kumpiene, G., & Bateman, D. (2020). The individualized education program: Procedural and substantive requirements. *TEACHING Exceptional Children, 52*(5), 304–18. https://doi.org/10.1177/0040059920906592

Yell, M. L., & Katsiyannis, A. (2004). Placing students with disabilities in inclusive settings: Legal guidelines and preferred practices. *Preventing School Failure, 49*(1), 28–35. https://doi.org/10.3200/PSFL.49.1.28-35

Zaretsky, L. (2004). Advocacy and administration: From conflict to collaboration. *Journal of Educational Administration, 42*(2), 270–86.

Glossary

Keyword: Chapters: Definition

Ableism: 5: Ableism is defined as a system that places values and asserts oppression upon people's bodies and minds based on a constructed ideology of functionality, normalcy, and intelligence. This fuels society's determination of who is valuable and worthy or able to produce based on societal standards.

Access: 5: Access is a concept that signifies the right, privileges, opportunities, and sense of belonging available within various aspects of society including housing, education, employment, transportation, public and commercial buildings, communal spaces, entertainment venues.

Accommodations: 11: Accommodations are adaptations that do not change the rigor or expected outcomes.

Active Listening: 9: Active listening is a strategy that requires individuals to restate or paraphrase what each party has said, check understanding, and let the individuals involved know that they have been heard.

Adaptations: 11: Adaptations include both accommodations and modifications.

Advocacy: 12: Advocacy is defined as the act or process of supporting a cause or proposal.

American National Standards Institute (ANSI): 10: ANSI published standards on building accessibility for individuals with disabilities, which became the private sector model for accessibility.

American Sign Language (ASL): 3: ASL is one of the signed languages that is commonly used among Deaf people in the United States; ASL is a full and natural language with its own structure and does not represent English or any other spoken language.

Glossary

Americans with Disabilities Act (ADA): 6, 10: The ADA is a civil rights law that guarantees that disabled persons have the same opportunities as everyone else to enjoy employment opportunities, purchase goods and services, and to participate in state and local government programs.

Architectural Barriers Act: 10: The Architectural Barriers Act was passed by Congress in 1968; the act requires facilities receiving federal funds to be accessible to disabled individuals in design, construction, and alteration.

Art: 1: Art is the expression of ideas or emotions through creative outlets and products, such as literature, music, sculpture, and acting.

Artificial Intelligence (AI): 9: AI is a powerful machine-based technology that utilizes algorithms to make predictions, diagnoses, recommendations, and decisions.

Assistive Technology: 9: Assistive technology is the use of any equipment, tool, or strategy to improve functional or daily living in individuals with disabilities or limitations.

Audism: 3: Audism is the notion that being able to hear is superior.

Augmentative and Alternative Communication (AAC): 1, 10, 11: AAC refers to any method to share thoughts, ideas, feelings, and needs that ranges from unaided (body language, facial expressions, use of sign language) to low-tech (communication boards, picture exchange communication systems) to high-tech (speech-generating devices, communication applications on tablets).

Autism: 3: Autism is a widely recognized, lifelong neurodevelopmental disability described as a spectrum of conditions with heterogeneous characteristics.

Autistic Identity: 3: Autistic identity embraces a sense of identity and sees autism as a different way of thinking and functioning rather than as an illness or deficit to be cured.

Autistic Self-Advocacy Network: 3: Formed in 2004 the United States, the Autistic Self-Advocacy Network advocates for the rights of Autistic people so that Autistic people have equal access, rights, and opportunities and to make their voices heard in the conversations that affect them.

Barrier-Free Access Movement: 10: Barrier-Free Access Movement offered total independence to those who would otherwise need to be dependent upon an institution, a family, or an aide.

Behavior-Specific Praise (BSP): 9: BSP is a behavior management strategy that involves providing targeted positive feedback to students. This feedback explicitly identifies and praises specific malleable factors within the student's locus of control, empowering them to take ownership of their behavior and its outcomes.

Belonging: 1, 12: Belonging is considered an essential human need; the feeling of connection to and engagement with a larger social community where the equal worth and inherent dignity of each person is honored by affirming the talents, beliefs, backgrounds, and ways of living of its members.

Bias: 2, 7: Bias is a tendency to prefer one thing over another, which can be conscious or unconscious, that prevents objectivity.

Black Disability Studies: 5: Black Disability Studies emerged from Disability Studies. This field explores the relationship between disability and racism throughout history, centering the experiences among Black disabled people and communities, and how disability theories, movements, and fields have excluded Black disabled voices and fail to recognize their modes of activism.

Charity Model of Disability: 6: According to the Charity Model, disabled people are viewed as victims worthy of "pity" and without the capacity to think and live independently or with people without disabilities. Moreover, disabled people are expected to live in separate facilities with other people with similar "problems" because they aren't able to make independent decisions.

Cisgender: 2: Cisgender is used by people whose gender identity aligns with the sex they were assigned at birth.

Civil Rights Act of 1964: 10: The Civil Rights Act of 1964 is one of the most substantial wins in the civil rights movement; the passage of this act made it illegal to discriminate against any person in the United States based on race, color, religion, sex, or national origin.

Civil Rights Movement: 10: The civil rights movement pushed for basic human rights for African American citizens of the United States and is traced back to the days of slavery and abolitionist movements; this refers to the social and cultural progress.

Cognitive Grouping: 1: Cognitive grouping refers to cognitive categories leading to the increased salience of distinguishing features between categories, exaggerating category differences.

Colorblindness: 4: Colorblindness is a racial ideology that aims to treat all students equally, regardless of their race, thus negating parts of some students' identities.

Communicative Competence: 1: Communicative competence is having linguistic knowledge and a functional means of purposeful communication in one's native or studied language. Three main competencies are: (1) linguistic, (2) sociolinguistic, and (3) pragmatic.

Complex Communication Needs (CCN): 10: CCN include having limited or no oral speech, having speech not adequate for daily use, having speech only intelligible for familiar partners, or having communication breakdowns when in distress.

Co-Navigation: 8: Co-Navigation is a key feature of CSP. Schools are accountable to the community—school professionals are in conversation with all members of the broader school community about what they desire and want to sustain through schooling. The purposes, norms, and functions of schooling are considered, discussed, and established *with* rather than *for* students, families, and community members.

Convention on the Rights of Persons with Disabilities (CRPD): 10: In 2006, the United Nations General Assembly adopted the CRPD as a treaty to promote, protect, respect, support, and celebrate human diversity by creating the conditions that allow meaningful participation of all persons with disability. It is predicated on the belief that a physical or mental impairment should not diminish human dignity or access to opportunity.

Critical Consciousness: 7: Critical consciousness is the ability to recognize oppressive social forces shaping society and to take action against them.

Critical Disability Theory: 5: Critical Disability Theory views disability as a cultural, historical, relative, social, and political phenomenon through an interdisciplinary array of theoretical approaches. What unites these approaches is a common interest in how power operates in society via histories, systems, structures, and cultural practices that sustain or challenge social inequities.

Critical Race Theory: 4: Critical Race Theory is a cross-disciplinary framework to explore how laws, social and political movements, and media shape and are shaped by social conceptions of race and ethnicity.

Critical Theory: 4: Critical Theory is an approach to social philosophy that focuses on the assumptions and ideologies of society and culture to reveal and challenge power structures.

Cultural Adaption: 9: Cultural adaptation is a purposeful and collaborative process that entails adjusting materials to ensure their relevance for individuals within a specific population. It involves modifying an evidence-based intervention protocol by taking into account language, culture, and context to ensure alignment with the cultural patterns, meanings, and values of the intended audience.

Cultural Discontinuity: 9: Cultural discontinuity refers to a mismatch between a student's culture and the teacher's culture. The condition exists when there are significant differences in styles and language of communication between diverse students and teachers who are Eurocentrically oriented, resulting in misinterpretations on the part of both groups.

Cultural Identity: 10: A cultural identity forms when we subconsciously interpret and incorporate signals from the world around us into our own identity so we can belong.

Cultural Mismatch: 9: In the context of a classroom, cultural mismatch occurs when teachers and students are unaware of the different ways they approach tactics, rules, nuances, and unique aspects of their cultures. This lack of awareness can lead to a disconnect between school staff and students, creating a cultural mismatch.

Cultural Model of Disability: 6: The Cultural Model of Disability has the same tenants as the Social Model, and adds value to disability as a part of overall human diversity. Within this perspective, the belief is that society's views on disability can be changed by understanding that disability is a culture unto itself and is not a "problem" to be solved.

Culturally and Linguistically Diverse Families: 12: Culturally and linguistically diverse families are those whose primary language is not English or who are not from European American descent.

Culturally and Linguistically Sustaining Practices: 2, 4, 7, 8, 12: Culturally and Linguistically Sustaining Practices extend on culturally responsive practices in moving beyond respecting or valuing diverse languages, cultures, ways of being. An explicitly anti-colonialist and anti-deficit stance, culturally and linguistically sustaining practice seeks to center and sustain the diverse linguistic, literate, and cultural practices of our students.

Culturally Sustaining Pedagogy: 12: Culturally sustaining pedagogy maintains heritage, values, and cultural and linguistic pluralism. It has the explicit goal of sustaining and supporting bi-/multilingualism and multiculturalism.

Culture: 1, 2, 7, 10, 12: Culture is our shared understanding and meaning within which we live and includes the customs and interactions of the socially constructed groups with which we identify. Culture also refers to the values, practices, habits and patterns, customs, beliefs, and expressions shared by a group of people; (a) shared history, (b) expression of identity and meaning, and (c) pride.

De Facto Segregation: 4: De facto segregation describes instances where segregation in fact (de facto) exists, but it's not from legislation overtly segregating students by race.

Deaf-Centric and ASL-Centric Spaces: 3: Deaf-centric and ASL-centric spaces make it possible for signing Deaf students to learn and build their signed language skills, Deaf cultural identity, and Deaf epistemologies by interacting with signing Deaf instructors and peers in their signed language on a daily basis.

Deaf Culture: 3: Deaf culture refers to a group of Deaf people who share similar experiences of being Deaf, signed languages, beliefs, values, norms, histories, and arts; culturally Deaf people embrace and celebrate their Deaf identity.

Deaf Gain: 3: Deaf gain challenges the ideology of normalcy and argues that being Deaf has intrinsic and extrinsic values.

Deaf Space or DEAF-WORLD: 3: Deaf space or DEAF-WORLD refers to Deaf people getting together in certain places, such as social clubs, political associations, and deaf schools, not to a specific geographic location.

Deafhood: 3: Deafhood was introduced in the United Kingdom in 2003; this is the journey that each Deaf individual has to find their Deaf identity.

Deafness: 3: Deafness refers to (1) the biomedical perspective—being deaf is biologically defective and needs to be corrected, and (2) the sociocultural and biocultural perspective—being Deaf is a gain and offers a rich language, culture, and community.

Demystification: 8: The act of making something less complicated and easier to understand by explaining it in a clear and simple way.

Direct Instruction (DI): 9: DI refers to teacher-led, explicit instruction characterized by structured presentation of academic content, frequent practice of learned material, and scaffolding during skill acquisition.

Disability: 6: In the 1980s, sociologists in the United States and United Kingdom started to contextualize disability as an intersectional difference of (or combination of) four domains: health, functioning, achievement, and physical appearance.

Disability Critical Race Theory (DisCrit): 5: DisCrit views disability as a cultural, historical, relative, social, and political phenomenon through an interdisciplinary array of theoretical approaches. What unites these approaches is a common interest in how power operates in society via histories, systems, structures, and cultural practices that sustain or challenge social inequities.

Disability Justice Movement: 5: Disability Justice Movement is a movement originated and led by disabled Black, Indigenous, other people of the global majority, and queer/trans people to amplify collective access and collective liberation and prioritize the voices of the most impacted.

Disability Studies: 5: Disability Studies is an interdisciplinary academic discipline that focuses on all aspects of disability from the perspective of a minoritized group in society that is subjected to ableism while also able to generate specific, valuable knowledge about the human experience.

Discrimination: 7: Discrimination is the unequal treatment of members of various groups based on race, gender, social class, sexual orientation, physical ability, religion, and other categories.

Disproportionality: 2, 11: Disproportionality is when the proportion of a particular group identified for general special education eligibility, or within specific categories of disability, differs from the group's proportion in the general population.

Domains of School Engagement: Attendance, Attachment, and Achievement: 8: The National Center for School Engagement (NCSE) has identified domains of school engagement as crucial in improving the outcomes for youth who are at greater risk of dropping out of school. The goal of school engagement is to ensure school success for children and their families by promoting (a) Attendance—implementing evidence-based strategies to reduce excused and unexcused absences; (b) Attachment—building meaningful connections between students, families, and schools through cultural awareness, mutually defined expectations, and positive school climates; and (c) Achievement—providing the tools and resources necessary to complete high school courses and graduate well-prepared for the future.

Dominant Culture: 12: Dominant culture in a society where multiple cultures and subcultures exist is one which, through economic or political clout, is able to assert its values on subordinate groups, thereby making its values and customs the norm.

Dysconscious Audism: 3: Dysconscious audism is when deaf children/adults internalize a form of audism or they accept dominant hearing privileges and norms.

Dysphoria: 2: Dysphoria is when a gender variance causes discomfort or distress. Another name for this is "incongruence."

Economic Model of Disability: 6: The Economic Model of Disability defines disability completely based on a disabled person's ability to participate, contribute, and be productive in society. The degree of impairment of the disabled person is related to the economic consequences for the actual individual (loss of earnings), the employer (lower productivity and profit margins), and the government (welfare to support the disabled person).

Education for All Handicapped Children Act: 6, 10: Education for All Handicapped Children Act of 1975 was the first to guarantee a free appropriate public education (FAPE) for all children with disabilities in the least restrictive environment (LRE).

Emic Perspective: 6: Emic perspectives are characterized by their nature as internal to a given situation, individual, etc. They often take into account the external circumstances acting on the subject, as well as personal testimony and more in-depth and personal analysis and observation. They also often result in better outcomes for the subject.

Equity: 7: Equity is to treat everyone fairly. An equity emphasis seeks to render justice by deeply considering structural factors that benefit some social groups/communities and harm other social groups/communities. Sometimes justice demands, for the purpose of equity, an unequal response.

Equity Literacy (EL): 3: EL is a framework that is centered on one's understanding of equity/inequity and justice/injustice; EL is different from cultural literacy and helps educational practitioners build knowledge and skills to threaten inequity in their spheres of influence.

Etic Perspective: 6: Etic perspectives are characterized by a more analytic and external view of a given situation, individual, etc. Such a perspective has often been considered more objective and scientific, even when that is far from the truth, and can also tend to pathologize its subject(s).

Eugenics: 5, 10: Eugenics refers to the belief that humanity can be improved by controlling genetics; managing reproduction within a human population to increase the occurrence of heritable characteristics regarded as desirable.

Evidence-Based Practice: 11: Evidence-based practice is methods, interventions, and strategies that have been validated by empirical research as effective and not harmful.

Extended Attachment Theory: 9: Extended attachment theory applies to a child's sense of emotional stability, fostered by a warm and caring connection between them and their teacher.

Formulated Experiences: 3: Formulated experiences refer to when practitioners engage in an environment where aural/oral is not the primary orientation.

Free Appropriate Public Education (FAPE): 9, 11, 12: FAPE: free (at no cost), appropriate (IEPs outline a program for students to meet their individualized needs), public (students have the same right to attend public schools as all children), education.

Gender: 2: Gender is a social construct of what it means to be female or male; often conflated with the sex assigned at birth based on a person's biological status as determined by external anatomy.

Gender Expression: 2: Gender expression is outwardly visible to others and is how people present gender, through behavior, clothing, haircuts, or other characteristics. Society identifies cues as masculine or feminine, although what is considered masculine or feminine varies.

Gender Identity: 2: Gender identity is not outwardly visible to others and is people's own internal sense of self and their gender (e.g., man, woman, neither. both). Gender identity can correlate with people's assigned sex at birth or not.

Gender Variance: 2: Gender variance is the difference between the sex a person was assigned at birth and the gender a person identifies with and experiences, which exists across all races, ethnicities, cultures, and socioeconomic statuses, for example.

Gestalt Phenomena: 1: Gestalt phenomena is where the whole is greater than the parts.

Handicap: 6: The term handicap refers to a disadvantage for a given individual that limits or prevents the fulfillment of a role that is "normal." This is not currently viewed as a positive term.

Human Rights Model of Disability: 6: The Human Rights Model has some connections to the Social Model approach, but it underscores the idea that people with disabilities have rights and that the government (and by extension all of society) must recognize and respect those rights, such as the right to equal opportunities and participation in society. Furthermore, all of society should take ownership in promoting, protecting, and ensuring that these rights materialize.

Identity-First Language (IFL): 6, 11: IFL emphasizes the disability before the person and the disability is listed first in the description, for example "autistic person" or "deaf person."

Identity Model of Disability: 6: The Identity Model of Disability holds many of the same beliefs as the Social Model but goes beyond the model by truly affirming a disabled identity in the same way as racial, gender, sexuality, or special interest categories. In this model, "person-first" language would be discouraged.

Impairment: 6: Impairment is defined as something that occurs in a person's body structure or function, or mental functioning.

Implicit Bias: 2: Implicit bias is the unconscious bias one may have against another that is dependent on stereotypes and includes unconscious reactions and attitudes to other individuals or groups of individuals.

Inclusion: 12: Inclusion is students with disabilities being including in a continuum of educational placements, including full time in general education classes in their neighborhood schools.

Independence: 3: Independence refers to a valuable part of disability culture as it involves centering voices and capacity, for instance, by using equipment and devices (i.e., wheelchairs, prosthetics) and taking care of personal hygiene independently.

Individualized Education Program (IEP): 11, 12: An IEP provides the special education instruction, supports, and services a student needs to thrive in school and includes related services, present levels of performance, annual goals/short-term objectives, dates and duration of services, and procedures for evaluating the student's progress.

Individuals with Disabilities Education Act (IDEA): 6, 10: Renamed in 1990, the IDEA is a federal law that supports the rights of disabled students and their parents by defining special education and related services programming for children with disabilities—birth to twenty-one years old.

Integrated Multi-Tiered Systems of Support (I-MTSS): 2, 6, 8, 9: I-MTSS is a comprehensive and equitable prevention framework for improving the outcomes of all students, including students with or at-risk for disabilities, through integrated academic and behavioral support.

Intercultural Competence: 2, 7: Intercultural competence prepares educators to identify how sociocultural identity markers impact students within the educational system in complex ways, such as teacher bias, educational access, and federal policies.

Interest Convergence: 4: Interest Convergence is a theory by Derrick Bell that the majority group allows advances for justice, equity, diversity, and inclusion only when these advances also benefit the majority.

Intersectionality: 1, 2, 4, 7, 8: Intersectionality is a framework created by Kimberlé Crenshaw used to understand how systemic oppressions (e.g., racism, sexism, ableism, classism, and other forms of discrimination) intertwine and intersect within individuals' experiences due to their identification with multiple [historically disenfranchised] sociocultural groups (e.g., race, socioeconomic status, gender identity, sexuality, disability).

Intersex: 2: Intersex is variations in exterior and/or interior genitals such as a person that has both male and female sex organs or other sexual characteristics.

Joint Committee on Human Rights: 10: Established in 2012, the Joint Committee on Human Rights monitors compliance with laws and policies around the world that support the human rights of disabled persons.

Language (ethnography): 1: Language (ethnography) references speaking techniques within individual cultures that center the traditions of oral literature and subsequent social norms.

Learning Partnerships: 9: Learning partnerships require the educator to learn about who the students are, how they think, how they learn, and their perceptions of self. This is not just about positive interactions; it is the consideration of the students' learning and development of critical skills for life-long success.

Least Restrictive Environment (LRE): 9, 11, 12: LRE is a federal regulation that stipulates that a child with a disability must be educated within the same classroom as typical mainstreamed nondisabled peers to the fullest extent possible in order to ensure that a disabled child is receiving a free appropriate public education.

Linguicism: 3: Linguicism is a form of systemic oppression on the basis of language. Linguicism occurs often in those phenomena where signed languages such as American Sign Language are intentionally denied and are treated unfairly.

Marginalization: 2, 7: Marginalization is a social process by which individuals or groups are (intentionally or unintentionally) distanced from access to power and resources and constructed as insignificant, peripheral, or less valuable/privileged than another community or "mainstream" society.

Mass Culture/Dominant Culture: 1, 12: The mass culture, dominant culture, or popular culture sets the standards, beliefs, values, and norms for a society. Mass culture is often dictated by those with demographic privileges, resources, and access to power.

Material Determinism: 4: Material determinism refers to how one's choice is influenced by power and materialistic factors.

Medical Model of Disability: 3, 5, 6: The Medical Model of Disability indicates that disabled people need to be changed, "cured," or treated through medical intervention before they can be fully included in society. This is a deficit-based model with a focus on the body alone that ignores the surrounding social issues that contribute to disability.

Model: 6: Model refers to the perceptions or ideas that define constructs that may be difficult to understand. For the purposes of this textbook, a model explores how to define the disability experience and the attitudes of nondisabled people toward disabled people.

Modifications: 11: Modifications are adaptations that do change the rigor or expected outcomes.

Multiculturalism: 4: Multiculturalism is the state of a society or the world in which there exists numerous distinct ethnic and cultural groups seen to be politically relevant. Also called pluralism, cross-culturalism.

Multi-Tiered Systems of Support (MTSS): 8, 11: Inspired by a medical model of prevention, MTSS is a continuum, generally illustrated as a three-tiered pyramid of support for education. Primary prevention (Tier 1) involves strategies provided to all and is designed to prevent or limit the emergence of problems. Secondary prevention (Tier 2) incorporates more intensive supports, but only for those who need a modest level of increased assistance to be successful. Tertiary prevention (Tier 3) is more intensive and more individualized.

Neurodiversity: 3, 5: Neurodiversity refers to a movement by and for disabled people to redefine themselves not as sick, in need of a cure, deficient, or disordered, but rather as being reflective of natural human variation. Neurodiversity is a framework for people with diverse neurological conditions; it acknowledges the fundamental identity of autistic people alongside others who are neurodivergent; and it calls for efforts to improve the oppressive nature of accessibility and social attitudes.

Nonbinary: 2: Nonbinary is used by people who do not describe their genders as exclusively fitting into the categories of man or woman. Nonbinary can identify as both a man and a woman, somewhere in between, or fall outside of these categories.

Norming: 8: The process of constructing what is considered typical within a particular context or for a particular group.

Opportunities to Respond (OTR): 9: OTR is a teaching practice that creates a learning environment where students are actively engaged with academic material or assignments. This can include asking questions, reading aloud, or writing answers to a problem. The teacher can modify the lesson's pace, demands, and content based on student feedback.

Oppression: 7: Oppression is the systematic subjugation of one social group by a more powerful social group for the social, economic, and political benefit of the more powerful social group. Oppression exists when: (a) the oppressor group has the power to define reality for themselves and others, (b) the target groups take in and internalize the negative messages about them and end up cooperating with the oppressors (thinking and acting like them), (c) genocide, harassment, and discrimination are systematic and institutionalized, so that individuals are not necessary to keep it going, and (d) members of both the oppressor and target groups are socialized to play their roles as normal and correct.

People of the Global Majority (PGM): 4: PGM is an alternative term to BIPOC or people of color. This term is inclusive of all non-white people around the world. It does not center the American or Eurocentric experience or the white experience against the rest of the world.

Person-First Language (PFL): 6, 11: PFL emphasizes the person before the disability and the person is listed first in the description, for example "person with deafness" or "person with a seizure disorder."

Philosophical Chairs: 9: Philosophical Chairs is an academic activity that proposes a controversial idea or topic to students. Students gather in groups according to their topic and perspective and present arguments supporting their viewpoints. After presenting their opinions, students have a choice to switch groups. This activity encourages students to listen to each other and share their thoughts.

Positive Behavioral Interventions and Supports (PBIS): 2, 6, 8, 9, 11: PBIS is an evidenced-based three-tiered system supporting students' behavioral, academic, social, emotional, and mental health, with increasingly intensive assessment and intervention at higher levels. Sometimes used as a method of identifying students with behavioral disabilities; based on proactive instruction and positive reinforcement.

PreCorrection (PC): 9: PC is a proactive approach to managing behavior in the classroom that aims to eliminate predictable undesired behaviors before they occur. This technique involves identifying potential issues early and intervening with strategies such as providing clear instructions, positive reinforcement, and setting rules and expectations. The goal of PC is to enable teachers to spend more time creating positive classroom climates and opportunities to reinforce appropriate behaviors with praise, while preventing students from repeating undesired behaviors.

Prejudice: 7: Prejudice is a prejudgment or unjustifiable, and usually negative, attitude of one type of individual or group toward another group and its members. Such negative attitudes are typically based on unsupported generalizations (or stereotypes) that deny the rights of individual members of certain groups to be recognized and treated as individuals with individual characteristics.

Privilege/White Privilege: 4: Privilege consists of any right or immunity granted as a peculiar benefit, advantage, or favor. It is a set of unearned benefits that apply to those that meet specific social criteria. It is often used in the phrase "white privilege" to describe the advantages white Americans have over minoritized populations—for example, American history lessons written as interpreted by white men while other American cultural perspectives are only taught as electives.

Progress Monitoring: 9: Progress monitoring assessments are specifically designed to assist educators in tailoring instruction and providing individualized support based on their students' levels and specific needs.

Race: 4, 7: Race refers to a socially constructed grouping of people based on the physical characteristics they share (e.g., skin color, facial features, hair texture). Every human being can be categorized into one or more races and for hundreds of years, race has been used as a way to discriminate and treat people unfairly.

Race-Evasiveness: 4: Race-evasiveness refers to the refusal to discuss or examine race or racism and the impact it has on institutions and society.

Racism: 4, 7: Racism is different from racial prejudice, hatred, or discrimination. Racism is the attitude or action that can be deliberate or unintended and is based on the belief of white superiority and oppression of nonwhites. Racism involves one group having the power to carry out systematic discrimination through the institutional policies and practices of the society and by shaping the cultural beliefs and values that support those racist policies and practices.

Rehabilitation Act of 1973: 6: The Rehabilitation Act of 1973 provided protections related to affirmative action and nondiscrimination in federal employment within the executive branch and government contractors/subcontractors, opportunities for access to support for education, employment, and other settings, and funding to make more aspects of the government accessible through technology for disabled people.

Response to Intervention (RTI): 2, 6, 8, 9, 11: RTI is the three-tiered process used to identify and support students who are at risk for academic and behavioral difficulties that uses a problem-solving model to determine the type and intensity of support needed and to evaluate its effectiveness over time. RTI using data-based decision-making based on universal screening and progress monitoring of evidence-based interventions.

Restorative Practices: 8: Restorative practices refer to methods of addressing conflict constructively with an emphasis on community building; an alternative to zero-tolerance discipline policies which have historically been harmful and counterproductive. Rooted in Native and Indigenous communities, the method provides safe spaces for students and educators to connect through understanding accountability, practicing empathy, and self-reflection. This method is also known as restorative discipline or restorative circles.

Ritual: 1: A ritual is the sustained reproduction of a practice/series of acts.

Schoolwide Positive Behavioral Interventions and Supports (SWPBIS): 11: SWPBIS is a three-tiered system of behavioral support, with increasingly intensive assessment and intervention at higher levels; used as a framework to ensure accountability for implementation of PBIS within a school community.

Section 504 of the Rehabilitation Act: 10: Section 504 of the Rehabilitation Act marked the first time in history that disabled people were legally protected. Section 504 offered three main protections: (1) banned discriminatory practices for disabled people in federal agencies and other public institutions receiving federal funds; (2) mandated equal access to public services, e.g., public housing and public transportation services; and (3) allocated funding for vocational training.

Self-Determination: 3: Self-determination refers to being autonomous, such as when one makes choices, develops goals, and advocates for oneself; common in countries of the Western Hemisphere that value individualistic pursuits over collective pursuits; has been found as one of the predictors of success in adult life.

Semantics: 6: Semantics is the branch of linguistics and logic concerned with meaning. In terms of disability language, this often manifests in how we refer to disability.

Sexual Identity: 2: Sexual identity is how one thinks about their own sexuality and how one expresses that sexuality.

Sexuality: 2: Sexuality can be defined as a multitude of thoughts, fantasies, desires, beliefs, attitudes, values, behaviors, practices, alongside interest in intimate roles and relationships. It is influenced by the interaction of biological, physiological, social, economic, political, cultural, legal, historical, religious, and spiritual factors.

Social Capital: 1: Social capital is associated with demographic-based privileges which also lends itself to influence but not exclusively or predominantly in a political way.

Social Emotional Learning (SEL): 9: SEL is the process that promotes students' development of the knowledge and skills to establish healthy identities, manage emotions, foster empathy, and establish and maintain positive relationships.

Social Identity Theory (SIT): 1: SIT is a framework that defines how groups of people identify themselves into social groups of "us" versus "them" by connecting with others who have similar beliefs, behaviors, and lived experiences.

Social Model of Disability: 3, 5, 6: The Social Model of Disability frames disability as a consequence of the interaction of the individual with an ableist society which constricts the disabled individual from having full societal participation. Under this model, the focus is on removing barriers so that people with disabilities can contribute. Additionally, disability is not considered "bad" but is rather a strength of a diverse society.

Social Power: 1: Social power is associated with politics and means of influence.

Sociocultural Consciousness: 7: Sociocultural or sociopolitical consciousness is an awareness and desire to act against societal inequities that disadvantage individuals.

Sociocultural Constructs/Social Construct/Social Identity: 1, 7: A sociocultural construct or identity refers to the attributes of someone within the groups they belong to and is often characterized by social norms of linguistic or behavioral attributes. Examples include but are not limited to race, ethnicity, gender identity, sexual orientation, ability, socioeconomic status, spiritual affiliation, nationality, and other physical, social, cognitive, and emotional characteristics.

Socioculturally Sustaining Practices: 7: Socioculturally sustaining practices extend from culturally responsive practices and culturally and linguistically sustaining practices in moving beyond respecting or valuing diverse languages, cultures, ways of being. An explicitly anti-colonialist and anti-deficit stance, socioculturally sustaining practices seek to center and sustain the diverse linguistic, literate, and cultural practices of our learners.

Socioeconomic Status: 2: Socioeconomic status is a social standing or classification that is typically measured in terms of income, education, where one lives, and occupation.

Sociolinguistics: 1: Sociolinguistics is the study of language in the context of society and demographic groups and their proximity to power; the scholarship of language use in culture.

Socratic Seminar: 8: The purpose of a Socratic Seminar is to achieve a deeper understanding of the ideas and values in a text. In the seminar, participants systematically question and examine issues and principles related to particular content and articulate different points of view. The group conversation assists participants in constructing meaning through disciplined analysis, interpretation, listening, and participation.

Special Education: 9: Special education refers to an educational system designed to create specially designed instruction to meet the unique need of a child with a disability at no cost to the parent. Specially designed instruction is a systematic approach that is aligned to a student's needs.

Strengths-Based Approach: 3: A strengths-based approach helps improve the social validity and acceptability of practice; this looks like listening to and centering disabled voices, supporting a disabled person's identity and allowing them to be themselves rather than trying to make them camouflage any traits related to their disability, and constantly examining perspectives of stakeholders, i.e., autistic people, on the perceived ethicality and benefits of practices on enhancing their quality of life.

Textured Teaching: 9: Textured teaching is a pedagogical approach that integrates the cultural and linguistic backgrounds of students into the teaching and learning process. It recognizes the diversity of students' experiences and uses these experiences to inform and enrich the educational experience. This approach seeks to create a classroom environment that is inclusive, culturally sustaining, and engaging for all students.

Transdisciplinary Teams: 9: Transdisciplinary teams are groups of professionals who perform related tasks interactively by sharing not only information but also roles. The team members accept and accentuate each other's knowledge and strengths to benefit both the team and the child.

Transgender: 2: Transgender is a term used by people whose gender identity differs from their sex assigned at birth.

Universal Design (UD): 5: UD is an approach which considers and modifies the built environment in order to ensure that it can be "accessed, understood and used" as freely, widely, and independently as possible by any person. UD includes the removal of structural barriers, replacing them with any type of accessible support, so that as few modifications and accommodations as possible are needed for people to access what they need.

Universal Design for Learning (UDL): 5, 6, 10, 11: UDL is an educational framework which combines the concepts of Universal Design and learning science to promote accessibility in the classroom curricula and environment by incorporating three core principles: Multiple Means of Engagement, Multiple Means of Representation, and Multiple Means of Action and Expression.

Whiteness: 4: Whiteness refers to the way that white people, their customs, culture, and beliefs operate as the standard by which all other groups are compared. This white-dominant culture also operates as a social mechanism that grants advantages to white people, since they can navigate society both by feeling normal and by being viewed as normal.

Index

AAC. *See* Augmentative and Alternative Communication
ableism: ableist messages and, 132; COVID-19 and, 135; definition of, 291, 381; disability rights and, 291–92; DisCrit and, 138–40, 143; in lived experience, 15
abolitionist movements, 296
acceptance, *201–2, 206*
access, 381; barrier-free access movement and, 295–96, 382; building standards and accessibility, 295–96, 297–98, 382, 395
accommodations, 381
achievement gap, 110–11
action, *204–5, 207*; goals action plan and, 208–11, *209–10*
active listening, 270, 381
ADA. *See* Americans with Disabilities Act
adaptation, 323, 381; cultural, 264, 384
ADHD. *See* Attention Deficit Hyperactivity Disorder
adoption, 317
advocacy: belonging and, 347; by caregivers, 353–54; definition of, 381; LRE and, 364; in media, 355–57; parents and family, 133–35, 353–54, 360; self-advocacy, 68, 80, 382; special education and, 346–47, 353–54

AI. *See* artificial intelligence
allergies, 12–13
alternative communication, 335
alternative narratives, 125
American National Standards Institute (ANSI), 296, 381
American Sign Language (ASL), 66, 67, 74–76, 381; ASL-centered spaces, 78–79, 385
Americans with Disabilities Act (ADA), 135, 153–54, 299, 382; Titles of, *299*
Angel Unaware (Rogers), 355
Annamma, S. A., 137
ANSI. *See* American National Standards Institute
anti-racism, 103–4, 115
appreciation, *203, 207*
architectural barriers, 295–96, 297–98, 382
Architectural Barriers Act, 296, 382
Arlington Central School District v. D.K. and K.K. (2002), 320
art: culture and, 17–19; definition of, 382

397

artificial intelligence (AI), 280–81, 382
ASAN. *See* Autistic Self-Advocacy Network
Ashby, C., 170
ASL. *See* American Sign Language
Asperger, Hans, 294–95
assessment: CBM and, 279; FBA, 334; flexibility in, 279; of intersectional sociocultural competence, 197–208; language and, 282; nondiscriminatory, 281–82; progress monitoring and, 279; sociocultural differences and, 282; of students from nondominant cultures and backgrounds, *359*
assistive technology, 382; AAC and, 335–38
Attention Deficit Hyperactivity Disorder (ADHD), 70, 168, 358
attitudinal bias, 304–5
audism, 67, 382; as oppression, 76
Augmentative and Alternative Communication (AAC), 9, 306, 382; CCN and, 336–37; history of, 336; socioculturally sustaining practices for, 335–38
authentic relationships, 242–43
autism, 168, 318–19, 355; characteristics of, 68; defining, 68, 382; diagnosing, 69–70, 165; DisCrit and, 138–40; gender and, 40, 41–42; IFL and, 69, 82, 388; inequities in education for, 63–65, 77–81; key terms relating to, 64–65; stereotypes about, 71; student perspective on, 172–73, 371–72
autistic communities, 63; disability culture in educational contexts and, 72–77; inequities in education for, 77–81; sociocultural identity and, 65–71
autistic identity, 64, 382; constructing, 69–70; culture and, 68–71; Dylan's school experiences with, 70, 71; embracing, 69; intersectionality of, 70; learning about, 69; in schools, 70–71, 172–73
Autistic Self-Advocacy Network (ASAN), 68, 382

autoimmune disorder, 13, 14
aversion, 199, *205*
aversive procedures, 327–28
awareness: of bias, 233, 238–39; in intersectional sociocultural competence, *200*, *206*; of marginalization, 233; social, 131–32

barrier-free access movement, 295–96, 382
Barrio, B. L., 362
behavioral matrix, *333*
behaviorism, 133
Behavior-Specific Praise (BSP), 266–67, 382
beliefs: education and, 227; marginalization and, 227; values and, 347, *370*
Bell, Derrick, 89–90, 91, 96–97, 131, 135, 389
belonging: advocacy and, 347; capitalism and, 21; communication and, 306; creating sense of, 369–72; cross-age peer mentoring and, 307; culture and, 3–4, 15–17; definition of, 3, 382; disability rights and, 292, 305–7, 369–72; equity and, 182; essential dimensions of, *369*; inclusion and, 305–7, 362–72; intersectional, 344–45, 369–72; lived experience and, 371–72; in special education, 344–45
bias, 34, 382; action planning steps for, 211–13; attitudinal, 304–5; B.I.A.S. self-reflection tool, *195*; CDT and, 131–32; critical consciousness and, 194–95; equity and, 183, 193–96, 211–13; examination of, 193–96, 358–59; fighting against, 304–5; gender, 39–40; implicit, 39–40, 193, 388; journey map and, 196, *196*; nondiscriminatory assessment and, 281–82; racial, 257; self-reflection of, 194–96, *195*, *196*; special education and, 358–59; stereotypes and, 193–94; understanding and awareness of, 233, 238–39
Black Americans: Black Disability Studies and, 383; Black women, 98, 129;

Index

human rights and, 296–98; racial segregation and, 96–97, 296, 385; slavery, abolition, and, 296. *See also* civil rights; Critical Race Theory; race; racism
Blatt, Burton, 356
blindness, 319
body shaming, 12
book bans, 100, 112
"brave" conversations, 237–38
Broadwell, M. M., 197–98
Bronfenbrenner, U., 128
Brown v. Board of Education (1954), 96, 130, 153, 295, 296; special education and, 314–15
BSP. *See* Behavior-Specific Praise
building standards and accessibility, 295–96, 297–98, 382, 395

capitalism, 21
"Capitol Crawl Protest," 153
caregivers, 352–55, 360. *See also* family; parents
CBM. *See* curriculum-based measurement
CCN. *See* complex communication needs
CDC. *See* Centers for Disease Control and Prevention
CDSE. *See* Critical Disability Studies in Education
CDT. *See* Critical Disability Theory
CEC. *See* Council for Exceptional Children
celiac disease, 12–14
center disability culture, 81
Centers for Disease Control and Prevention (CDC), 155
cerebral palsy (CP), 8–10, 166–67, 317
charity, 95–96
Charity Model of Disability, 158, 383
Check In-Check Out intervention, 334
childhood lead poisoning (CLP), 165
Christianity, 17, 152
Christmas in Purgatory (Blatt and Kaplan), 356
churches, 152
cisgender, 39, 40, 383
civil rights, 270; CDT and, 121–22, 130–36; CRT and, 96–98, 130–31; disability rights and, 295, 296–98; grassroots social movements and, 130–31, 133–34; human rights and, 296–98; Supreme Court and, 97–98, 295; voting and, 297
Civil Rights Act (1964), 296–97, 383
classroom environment: creating flexibility in, 274–78; critical thinking activities and, 272–73; furniture and, 275; graphic organization and, 279; higher-order thinking in, 273–74; innovation in, 274–81; lesson plan example, 276–78; meaningful and relevant learning environments, 271–74; REMIXed education and, 271–81; special education and, 271–81, 304; student media and content in, 271–72, *272*
climate change, 273
CLP. *See* childhood lead poisoning
CLSP. *See* Culturally and Linguistically Sustaining Practices
cognitive grouping, 21, 383
collaboration, 270; co-teaching and, 274
collectivism, 248–49
collectivist practices, 248
Collins, Patricia Hill, 129, 143
colorblindness, 94–95, 109–10, 182, 383
Commitment to Equity Statement, 214, *214*
The Common Law (Holmes), 90
communication: AAC, 9, 306, 335–38, 382; active listening and, 270, 381; alternative, 335; belonging and, 306; CCN and, 306, 336–37, 383; in C.U.L.T.U.R.E. framework, 237–38; deafness and, 66–68, 74–76; disability rights and, 306; empowerment and, 270; IDEA and, 336; inclusion in opportunities for, 306; interactive activities for, 307; language, culture, and, 4–11; language barriers and, 50, 352–53, 354, 359; language disabilities and, as culture, 10–11; language-related disabilities and, 7, 7–10; speech and, 8–9; technology and, 335–38

communicative competence, 4–5, 221, 383
complex communication needs (CCN), 306, 383; AAC and, 336–37
co-navigation, 226, 383
conflict, student, 250
Connor, D., 137
Convention on the Rights of Persons with Disabilities (CRPD), 301, 383–84
Cosier, M., 170
co-teaching, 274
Council for Exceptional Children (CEC), 364
counternarratives: counter-storytelling and, 99–100; to inclusion, 365
"courageous" conversations, 237–38
COVID-19, 3, 14, 141, 319–20; ableism, racism, and, 135
CP. *See* cerebral palsy
Crenshaw, Kimberlé, 23, 89, 98–99, 389; "Race, Reform, and Retrenchment" by, 91
criminal justice system, 37
critical consciousness, 186–88, 384; bias and, 194–95
Critical Disability Studies in Education (CDSE), 127–28
Critical Disability Theory (CDT), 120; bias and, 131–32; civil rights and, 121–22, 130–36; definition of, 384; disability justice in education, 133–34; disability justice in lived experience, 134–36; DisCrit and, 137–44, 386; identity and, 129; improvements needed in, 131–32; intersectionality and, 128–30; key terms relating to, 121–22; LGBTQIA+ and, 121–22; looking forward, 142–43; need for, 127–30; PSP and, 126–27; race, racial justice, and, 130–42; on redefining normality, 132–33; reframing research and shifting paradigm, 136–37; transformative change for, 132; valuing critical theoretical perspective and, 126–27
critical learning, 239–40
Critical Legal Studies, 90–91

Critical Race Theory (CRT): "already dones" in, 104–7; anti-racism and social justice work in, 103–4, 115; barriers to teaching, 108–16; being an agent of race and, 109–10; checklist of CRT framework and student activities, *105–6*; civil rights and, 96–98, 130–31; CLSP and, 103–4; colorblindness and, 94–95, 109–10; defining, 89–90, 384; DisCrit and, 137–44, 386; don'ts and what CRT is not, 100–104; dos and what CRT is, 93–100; in education, 91–93, 101, 104–16; on education as racist institution, 110–16; in higher education, 108–15; history of, 90–93; history teaching and, 100; institutional racism and, 110–16; interest convergence and, 89–90, 91, 96–97, 135, 389; intersectionality and, 89–92, 98–99; in K-12 curriculum, 101, 104–7; key terms, 89–90; law and, 90–91; PSP and, 95, 108, 114–16; race as social construct and, 97–98; on race-evasiveness in professional development, 111–15; racism as "normal" and, 93, 94–96; sociocultural identity mismatch and, 108–9; states that have banned, 89; stop doings in, 108–16; storytelling, narratives, and, 91–92, 99–100; Supreme Court and, 90; tenets of, *93*, 93–100; themes within scholarship of, *92*; white demoralization and, 101–2; white people pitted against PGM and, 102–3; white privilege and, 102–3. *See also* Disability Critical Race Theory
Critical Theory, 126, 384
critical thinking activities, 272–73
cross-age peer mentoring, 307
cross-cultural affirming practices, 47
Cross et al., 197–98
"crosswalks," 246
CRPD. *See* Convention on the Rights of Persons with Disabilities
CRT. *See* Critical Race Theory
cultural adaptation, 264, 384

cultural discontinuity, 260, 384
cultural identity, 21, 73–74, 384. *See also* sociocultural identity
cultural learning, 233
culturally and linguistically diverse families, 384
Culturally and Linguistically Sustaining Practices (CLSP), 46–47, 81, 385; C.L.S.P. continuum, *229–232*; competencies, 224, *224*; CRT and, 103–4; culturally relevant pedagogy and, 221, *222*; disproportionality and, 329; genesis of, 221; pedagogy and, 220–35; shared understanding in, 228. *See also* socioculturally sustaining practices
culturally relevant pedagogy, 221, *222*
culturally relevant teaching, 222
culturally responsive teaching, 221, 222, *223*
culturally sustaining pedagogy, 222, 385. *See also* socioculturally sustaining practices
cultural mismatch, 108–9, 260, 384
Cultural Model of Disability, 157, 302, 384; four pillars of, *303*
cultural pluralism, 224
culture: art and, 17–19; autistic identity and, 68–71; belonging and, 3–4, 15–17; collectivism and, 248; communication, language, and, 4–11; communication and language disabilities as, 10–11; communication and language-related disabilities and, 7, *7*–10; cultural perspectives of disability, 354–55; deaf, 64–68, 73–74, 385; deaf identity and, 65–68; definition of, 4, 185, 385; disability as, 304–5; disability rights as cultural phenomenon, 301–5; dominant, 4, 22, 102–3, 183–84, 361, 386, 389; educators and, 47, 236, 259; expressions of, 4–15, 24; family and, 270; flags and, 24; food and, 11–15; individualism and, 248; intersectionality and, 23; key terms relating to, 3; marriage and, 16–17; mass, 4, 22, 390; modern view of, 21–24; multiculturalism and, 349–50, 390; multidimensionality of disability and, 23–24; reframing sociocultural construct of disability and, 19–21; religion and, 17; schools and, 24–25, 259–60; self-determination and, 72–73; SIT and, 20–23; social capital and, 22–23; stigma and, 261; summary of, 26. *See also* disability culture
C.U.L.T.U.R.E. framework: communication in, 237–38; empowerment in, 243–44; learning in, 239–40; reflection in, 242–43; socioculturally sustaining practices in, 236–44, *237*; teaching in, 240–41; understanding in, 238–39; utilizing knowledge in, 241–42
curriculum-based measurement (CBM), 279

Danforth, Scot, 169–70, 173
Day, T. L., 104
deaf-centric spaces, 78, 385
deaf communities, 63, 157, 354; disability culture in educational contexts and, 72–77; inequities in education for, 77–81; key terms relating to, 64–65; sociocultural identity and, 65–71
deaf culture, 64, 385; deaf identity and, 65–68; IDEA and, 73–74
deaf gain, 67, 385
deafhood, 67, 385
deaf identity, 64; culture and, 65–68
deafness, 65–66, 319, 385; communication and, 66–68, 74–76; dysconscious audism and, 67, 386; home environment and, 68; sign language and, 66, 67, 74–79, 381; World Federation of the Deaf and, 67
deaf schools, 73–76, 78–79
deaf space, 66, 67, 78, 385
DEAF-WORLD, 66, 385
de-escalation, 214
de facto segregation, 96–97, 385
Delgado, Richard, 91–93
demystification, 228, 385
Deno, Evelyn, 364–65

Derrida, Jacques, 93
De Valck et al., 137
DI. *See* direct instruction
diagnosis, 69–70, 165; medical classifications and, 349
DiAngelo, Robin, 95, 111, 114–15
dilemma of difference, 133
direct instruction (DI), 266–67, 385
disability: cultural perspectives of, 354–55; as culture, 304–5; defining, 123, 164–65, 386; equity and, 183–84; etymology of, 164–66; food and, 12–15; four domains for contextualizing, 302; how we view, 151–52, 154–56.161–162; inclusion and, 169–73, 301, 319–24; intersectionality of gender and, 39–43; intersectionality of race, ethnicity, and, 35–37, 297, 349–52; intersectionality of sexual identity and, 43–46; intersectionality of socioeconomic status and, 37–38, 165; language of, 162–66, 173, 321–22; learning about disabilities, 167–68; LGBTQIA+ community and, 45–46; in media, 162–63, 166–68, 302; models, in education, 169–73; models of, 154–62, *159–60*, 169–73; multidimensionality of, 23–24; parenting and, 133–35, 140–41, 167–68, 352–55; parent perspectives of, 124, 140–41, 354–55; police violence and, 98–99, 172; race and, in schools, 170–73; racialization of, 37; reframing sociocultural construct of, 19–21; religion and, 17, 152, 292; segregation of disabled students and, 298, 302–4; sexuality and, 45–46; sociocultural identity and, 65–71, *190*, 302–4, 354–55; term differences, 154–56, *155*, 164–65, 322; visible and non-visible, 18. *See also specific disabilities; specific topics*
disability-as-deviance, 133–34
Disability Critical Race Theory (DisCrit): ableism and, 139–40, 143; autism and, 139–40; defining, 386; future of, 142–44; IBPA and, 143–44; impacts of, 137–42; intersectionality of, 139–40; narratives of, 139; pedagogy and, 142; resources and information about normalcy, *144*; social justice work and, 143–44; tenets of, 137–39, *138*
disability culture, 65; center, 81; in educational contexts, 72–77; honoring, 81; IDEA and, 73–74; in schools, 73–77; self-determination and, 72–73
disability justice: Disability Justice Movement, 386; DisCrit and, 143–44; in education, 133–34; in lived experience, 134–36
disability rights, 290; in 1900s through 1940s, 293–95; in 1950s through 1960s, 295–98; in 1970s, 298; in 1990s, 298–300; in 2000s to now, 300–301; ableism and, 291–92; ADA and, 135, 153–54, 299, *299*, 382; barrier-free access movement and, 295–96, 382; belonging and, 292, 305–7, 369–72; civil rights and, 295, 296–98; communication and, 306; CRPD and, 301; as cultural phenomenon, 301–5; Disability Rights Movement and, 134–35, 154, 296–98, 386; Economic Model of Disability and, 158; effective interventions for, 305–7; history of, 151–54, 293–301; housing and, 292; human rights and, 157–58, 297–98, 356–57, 388; IDEA and, 299–300; inclusive practices for, 305–7; key terms relating to, 291; language and, 321–22; law and, 152–54, 294–95, 298–301, 356–57; LRE and, 322–25; oppression and, 291–92, 295; religion and, 292; in schools, 292; Social Model of Disability and, 156–57, 304; stigma and, 291–92; universal design and, 295–96, 395; WHO on, 291–92; in workforce, 292
Disability Rights Education and Defense Fund, 298–99
disability studies, 120; Black, 383; CDSE and, 127–28; critical reflection questions for, 124; definition of, 122–

23, 386; future of, 142–44; key terms relating to, 121–22; Medical Model of Disability and, 123, 390; race and, 124; Social Model of Disability and, 123, 394; valuing critical theoretical perspective and, 126–27. *See also* Critical Disability Theory
Disability Studies in Education (DSE), 125–26
#DisabilityTooWhite, 135
disabled couples, 158
discipline: aversive procedures in, 327–28; BSP and, 266–67; disproportionality in, 327–29; expectations and, 333–34; PBIS, SWPBIS, and, 333–34; PC strategies and, 267, 392; restraint and, 327–28; in schools, 212–13, 259, 265–68, 327–28, 333–34, 392; seclusion as, 327–28; suspension as, 327; unintended consequences of, 259
discrimination, 143; Civil Rights Act and, 297; equity and, 183; xenophobia and, 36, 99. *See also* racism
disproportionality: CLSP and, 329; definition of, 325, 386; in discipline, 326–28; gender and, 327, 328; race, ethnicity, and, 327, 328; reasons for, 328–29; reducing, 329–30; socioeconomic status and, 328–29; in special education, 325–30
disruptive technology, 280–81
diversity: in culturally and linguistically diverse families, 224–25, 384; representation and, 360–61; in special education, 360–61; training, 211–12
divine judgement, 292
domains of school engagement, 386
dominant culture, 4, 22, 102–3, 386, 389; diversity and, 361; equity and, 182–83
dominant values, 347–48
Dong et al., 358
double standards, 41–42
Down syndrome, 124, 140–41, 154, 355, 371; Goode and emic perspective on, 161–62
The Dreamkeepers (Ladson-Billings), 211

Dred Scott v. Sandford (1857), 97–98
DSE. *See* Disability Studies in Education
Du Bois, W. E. B., 93
Dunn, Lloyd, 326, 364
dysconscious audism, 67, 386
dysphoria, 39, 387

EAHCA. *See* Education for All Handicapped Children Act
EBD. *See* emotional and behavioral disorders
EBPs. *See* evidence-based practices
Ecological Systems Theory, 128–30
Economic Model of Disability, 158, 387
education: achievement gap in, 110–11; beliefs and, 227; CDSE and, 127–28; CRT in, 91–93, 101, 104–16; CRT in, K-12 curriculum, 101, 104–7; disability culture in educational contexts, 72–77; disability justice in education, 133–34; disability models in, 169–73; extracurricular activities and, 10, 73, 368, 371–72; GPA and, 113; inequities in, 77–81; more inclusive values influencing, 370; parental involvement in, 225–26, 360; as racist institution, 110–16; socioeconomic status and, 110–11; spaces of educational hegemony, 226–27. *See also* schools; special education
Education for All Handicapped Children Act (1975) (EAHCA), 122, 134, 152, 298, 387; litigation relating to, 318; overview of, 315–16, 318. *See also* Individuals with Disabilities Education Act
educators: CRT and barriers for, 108–16; culture and, 47, 236, 259; diversity training for, 211–12; history teaching for, 100; intersectional sociocultural competence for, 196–214; race and, 47, 259; racial identity of, 259, 260; supporting professional learning for, 234; textured teaching by, 262
EL. *See* equity literacy
ELLs. *See* English Language Learners
emic perspectives, 161–62, 169, 387

emotional and behavioral disorders (EBD), 133–34, 264–65, 325; IEP and, 269
empowerment: activities for, 243–44; communication and, 270; in C.U.L.T.U.R.E. framework, 243–44; IEP and, 268–69; for parents and family, 360; through relationship building and collaboration, 270; in REMIXed education, 268–70; student-led meetings and, 269, *269*
English Language Learners (ELLs), 246
Enlightenment, 133
epilepsy, 152, 168
Equality of Opportunity Project, 40
equity, 180; belonging and, 182; bias and, 183, 193–96, 211–13; Commitment to Equity Statement, 214, *214*; critical consciousness and, 186–88; definition of, 387; disability and, 183–84; discrimination and, 183; dominant culture and, 182–83; equitable foundation for growth and success, 183–85, *184*; inclusion and, 182; intersectional consciousness and, 185; intersectional sociocultural competence and, 185, 196–214; key terms relating to, 181; opportunity and, 183–85; oppression and, 183, 187–88; overview of, 181–85; race and, 182–83, 211–13; social justice work and, 181–85; sociocultural identity and, 185–93; trust and, 213; white privilege and, 187–88, 211–13
equity literacy (EL), 77, 387; DSE and, 125–26
ESN. *See* extensive support needs
essentialism, 99
ethnicity: assessing students from nondominant cultures and backgrounds, 359; disproportionality and, 327, 328; intersectionality of disability, race, and, 35–37, 297, 349–52; self-determination and, 72–73; sociocultural identity and, 36–37, 187–92, *190*, 349–52. *See also* race
ethnography, 389

etic perspectives, 161–62, 172, 387
eugenics, 293–95, 387
euthanasia, 294–95
Evans, Dale, 355
evidence-based practices (EBPs): BSP and, 266–67, 328; definition of, 387; lesson plan example and, *276–78*; OTRs, 264–66, 391; PC strategies and, 267; REMIXed education and, 263–67; strategies for, 264–70; using caution when selecting, 263–64
Exceptional Children (journal), 364
expectations, 48, 169–70, 333
exploitation, 21
extended attachment theory, 258, 387
extensive support needs (ESN), 305–6
extracurricular activities, 10, 73, 368, 371–72

Faces at the Bottom of the Well (Bell), 97
family: advocacy of parents and, 133–35, 353–54, 360; barriers to, 352–53; culture and, 270; empowerment for, 360; engagement and participation, 225–26, *226*, 360; IDEA and, 353–54; influence of caregivers and, 352–55; socioculturally sustaining practices and, 225–26, *226*; systems, 72–73; teacher-family solidarity framework, *226*; themes, 270, *270*
FAPE. *See* free appropriate public education
FBA. *See* functional behavior assessment
feminism, 98, 129
Ferri, B., 137
flags, 24
flexibility: in assessments, 279, *280*; in classroom, 274–78; in progress monitoring, 279
Floyd, George, 49
food: allergies to, 12–13; autoimmune disorder and, 13, 14; culture and, 11–15; disability and, 12–15; rituals, 11–12
forced sterilization, 293–94
formulated experiences, 78, 387
foster care, 317
Frederick-Clarke, 224

free appropriate public education (FAPE), 122, 153, 270, 316, 318, 387–88
Freeman, Alan, 91
Freudian psychology, 133
functional behavior assessment (FBA), 334
Fundamental Principles of Disability (UPIAS), 156–57
furniture, classroom, 275

Game of Thrones (television show), 166
Gay, G., 222
gender: autism and, 40, 41–42; bias, 39–40; cisgender and, 39, 40, 383; definition of, 388; disproportionality and, 327, 328; double standards and, 41–42; dysphoria, 39, 387; expression, 39, 388; gender-neutral bathrooms and, 40–41; impact of gender mismatches, 39–43; intersectionality of disability and, 39–43; intersex and, 39, 389; malnutrition and, 15; nonbinary, 39, 391; perspectives on, 41–43; race and, 40; social capital and, 22–23; as social construct, 39; transgender, 39, 42–43, 395; variance, 388
gender identity: definition of, 388; parent perspective on, 42–43; sociocultural identity and, 39, 189, *191*
gestalt phenomena, 21, 388
gifted and talented learning disabled (GTLD), 70
gluten, 12–13
goals: goals action plan, 208–11, *209–10*; SMART, 266
Goddard, Henry H., 356
Goldstein, T., 95
The Good Doctor (television show), 166
Goode, David, 161–62
Goodley, 127
grade point average (GPA), 113
Gramsci, Antonio, 93
Grant, C. A., 96
graphic organization, 279
grassroots social movements, 129–30; civil rights and, 130–31, 133–34; Disability Rights Movement and, 134–35
Greeks, 151–52
group success, 248
GTLD. *See* gifted and talented learning disabled

Haller, Beth, 162–63
handicap, 154, *155*, 164, 388
Handicapped Children's Protection Act (1986), 318
Hankivsky et al., 136, 143
hegemony, 227–28
Hernández-Saca, D. I., 140
higher-order thinking, 273–74
hiring practices, 292
history: of AAC, 336; of CRT, 90–93; of disability rights, 151–54, 293–301; of IDEA, 313; of LRE, 364–65; of special education, 313–21; teaching, in schools, 100
Hitler, Adolf, 293, 294
Holmes, Oliver, 90
housing: disability rights and, 292; redlining and, 97
Hughes, Charles, 90
human rights: civil rights and, 296–98; disability rights and, 157–58, 297–98, 356–57, 388; Joint Committee on Human Rights and, 301, 389; labor rights and, 297. *See also* civil rights; disability rights; social justice work
Human Rights Model of Disability, 157–58, 388

IBPA. *See* Intersectionality-Based Policy Analysis
IC. *See* interest convergence
IDD. *See* intellectual and developmental disabilities
IDEA. *See* Individuals with Disabilities Education Act
IDEIA. *See* Individuals with Disabilities Education Improvement Act
identity: autistic, 64, 68–71, 172–73, 382; CDT and, 129; cultural, 21, 73–74, 384; deaf, 64–68; having multiple identities, 129, *189*; intersectionality

and, 129, 224–25; language and, 157, 163–64; names and, 107; oppression and, 187–88; racial, 94–96, 259, 260; self-identity activity, 272; sexual, 43–46, 393; socioculturally sustaining practices and, 224–25. *See also* gender identity; Social Identity Theory; sociocultural identity

identity-first language (IFL), 69, 82, 163, 187–88, 321–22, 388

Identity Model of Disability, 157, 388

IEP. *See* individualized education program

IFL. *See* identity-first language

IGD. *See* intergroup dialogue

impairment, 154, *155*, 388

implicit bias, 39–40, 193, 388

I-MTSS. *See* Integrated Multi-tiered Systems of Support

inclusion: barriers to, 170; belonging and, 305–7, 362–72; in communication opportunities, 306; counternarratives to, 365; definition of, 169–70, 321, 388; disability and, 169–73, 301, 319–24; equity and, 182; in IEP, 362–63; I-MTSS and, 362; inclusive practices for disability rights, 305–7; lived experience and, 371–72; LRE and, 319–20, 322–25, 363–67; more inclusive values influencing education, *370*; pedagogy and, 171; policies, 362–68; positive impacts and benefits of, 366; race and, 170–73; in schools, 170–73, 362–68; socioculturally sustaining practices and, 225; student perspectives on, 367–68; UDL and, 362

independence, 248, 389; self-determination and, 72–73

independent living, 294, 300–301

individualism, 248–49

individualistic practices, 248

individualized education program (IEP), 8, 122, 389; barriers to, 48; empowerment and, 268–69; inclusion in, 362–63; language in, 268–69; litigation relating to, 318; LRE and, 323–24, 363–67; placement decisions, 363; race and, 359; sociocultural factors and, 282–83; socioculturally sustaining practices and, 225–26; student-led IEP meetings, 269, *269*

Individuals with Disabilities Education Act (IDEA), 33, 130, 154, 389; communication and, 336; deaf schools and, 73–74; disability culture and, 73–74; disability rights and, 299–300; family and, 353–54; history of, 313; inclusion policies and, 362–68; legislation and, 299–300, *300*, 313–15, 318–21, 356; LRE and, 322–23, 363–67; Statute, *300*; values embedded in, *348*

Individuals with Disabilities Education Improvement Act (IDEIA), 122

inequities, 181; in education, 77–81; intersectional, 79–81; language and, 79; strengths-based approach for addressing, 80, 395. *See also* equity

infantilization, 20

innovation: in classroom environment, 274–81; flexibility and, 274–78; graphic organization and, 279; in REMIXed education, 274–81; student self-monitoring and flexible assessments, 279, *280*; technology and, 280–81

institutional racism, 110–16. *See also* Critical Race Theory

Integrated Multi-tiered Systems of Support (I-MTSS), 169, 389; ELLs and, 246; impact of, 362; inclusion and, 362; PBIS and, 247–49, 333–34; RTI and, 246–47, 331–32; socioculturally sustaining practices in, 245–49, 330–34; special education and, 51–52, *53*, 357–58; Tier 1 Universal Supports, 52, *53*; Tier 2 Secondary Supports, 52, *53*; Tier 3 Individual Supports, 52, *53*, 357

intellectual and developmental disabilities (IDD), 133–34, 153, 304, 319, 325–26

intercultural competence, 74, 197, 389

interdependence, 248

interest convergence (IC), 89–90, 91, 96–97, 135, 389
intergroup dialogue (IGD), 250
International Society for Augmentative and Alternative Communication (ISAAC), 336
intersectional belonging: key terms relating to, 344–45; in special education, 344–45, 369–72. *See also* belonging
intersectional consciousness, 185
intersectional inequities, 79–81
intersectionality, 32; of autistic identity, 70; CDT and, 128–30; CRT and, 89–92, 98–99; culture and, 23; definition of, 389; of disability, race, and ethnicity, 35–37, 297, 349–52; of disability and gender, 39–43; of disability and sexual identity, 43–46; of disability and socioeconomic status, 37–38, 165; of DisCrit, 139–40; identity and, 129, 224–25; intersectional competence in special education, 46–56, 181; key terms, 33–34; marginalization and, 224–25; of race and special education, 98–99, 297, 350–52; SIT and, 34; sociocultural identity and, 34–46, *36*, 349–52; socioculturally sustaining practices and, 224–25; socioeconomic status and, 23, 49–50; special education and, 262; summary of, 54–56
Intersectionality-Based Policy Analysis (IBPA), 143–44
intersectional sociocultural competence: acceptance in, *201–2, 206*; action in, *204–5, 207*; appreciation in, *203, 207*; assessment tool, 197–206; aversion in, 199, *205*; awareness in, *200, 206*; equity and, 185, 196–214; 5As of, 197–208, *198*; goals action plan, 208–11, *209–10*; perspective on understanding, 211–13; scoring assessment results, 205–8; socioculturally sustaining practices and, 197; trust and, 213

intersex, 39, 389
ISAAC. *See* International Society for Augmentative and Alternative Communication
Islam, 17

Johnson, Lyndon B., 297
Joint Committee on Human Rights, 301, 389
journey map, 196, *196*
Judaism, 17

Kaplan, Fred, 356
Kauffman et al., 125
Kennedy family, 355–56
King, Martin Luther, Jr., 93; Martin Luther King Day and, 97
King Thorius, K., 137

labeling, 163–66, 349, 364–65
labor rights, 297
Ladson-Billings, Gloria, 92, 96, 170–71; culturally relevant pedagogy and, 221; culturally sustaining pedagogy and, 222; *The Dreamkeepers* by, 211
language: ASL, 66, 67, 74–76, 78–79, 381, 385; assessment and, 282; communication, culture, and, 4–11; communication and language disabilities as culture, 10–11; communication language-related disabilities, 7, 7–10; definitions and, 228; demystification of, 228; of disability, 162–66, 173, 321–22; disability rights and, 321–22; ethnography, 389; identity and, 157, 163–64; in IEP, 268–69; IFL, 69, 82, 163, 187–88, 321–22, 388; impact of activism on, 321–22; importance of, 163–65; inequities and, 79; labeling and, 163–66, 349, 364–65; linguicism and, 390; linguistics and, 5–6, 394; norming and, 228; oppression and, 187–88; PFL, 69, 82, 163, 187–88, 321–22; semantics and, 163, 393; sign, 66, 67, 74–79, 381; sociocultural identity and, 349–50;

Spanish-only speakers and, 50, 79; special education and barriers in, 50, 352–53, 354, 359
law: Critical Legal Studies and, 90–91; CRT and, 90–91; disability rights and, 152–54, 294–95, 298–301, 356–57; impact of court cases on, 314–15; legislation and, 313–14; sociological jurisprudence and, 91; special education and, 314–21. *See also* legislation; Supreme Court
Law for the Prevention of Hereditarily Diseased Offspring, 294
LCA. *See* Leber's congenital amaurosis
learning: about autistic identity, 69; critical, 239–40; cultural, 233; in C.U.L.T.U.R.E. framework, 239–40; about disabilities, 167–68; partnerships, 271–75, 389; professional, *234*; SEL, 249–50, 394; about sexuality, 44–45. *See also* Universal Design for Learning
least restrictive environment (LRE), 50, 122, 153, 390; advocacy and, 364; continuum of educational placements from least to most restrictive, *323*; controversy around, 366; disability rights, legislation, and, 322–25; history of, 364–65; IDEA and, 322–23, 363–67; inclusion and, 319–20, 322–25, 363–67; special education and, 319–20, 322–25, 363–67
Leber's congenital amaurosis (LCA), 367
legislation: Americans with Disabilities Act and, 135, 153–54, 299, *299*, 382; Architectural Barriers Act and, 296, 382; Civil Rights Act and, 296–97; EAHCA and, 122, 134, 152, 298, 315–16, 318, 387; Handicapped Children's Protection Act and, 318; IDEA and, 299–300, *300*, 313–15, 318–21, 356; key terms relating to, 313; law and, 313–14; litigation and, 312–14, 318; LRE and, 322–25; Mental Health and Mental Retardation Reform Act and, 356; for Rehabilitation Act, 153, 158, 392; for Section 504 of Rehabilitation Act, 298, 393; for Social Security Act, 152–53, 294; special education and impacts of, 345–46; "Stop WOKE Act" and, 113
lesson plan example, *276–78*
LGBTQIA+ community, 42–43; CDT and, 121–22; disability and, 45–46
liberty, 356
linguicism, 76, 390
linguistic pluralism, 224
linguistics, 5–6, 394
listening, 270, 381
litigation, 312–14, 318. *See also* Supreme Court
lived experience: ableism in, 15; disability justice in, 134–36; inclusion and belonging in, 371–72; sociocultural identity and, 256–57
lived "truths," 122
lobotomies, 293
LRE. *See* least restrictive environment

Malcolm X, 93
malnutrition, 13, 15
Mansfield, Gregory, 26
Marcellino, Rosa, 154
marginalization, 34, 390; awareness of, 233; beliefs and, 227; intersectionality and, 224–25; oppression and, 224–25; "othering" and, 91, 129, 139, 351; stigma and, 48, 136, 170, 260–61, 291–92, 326
marriage: culture and, 16–17; disabled couples and, 158; as ritual, 16
Martin Luther King Day, 97
mass culture, 4, 22, 390. *See also* dominant culture
master status, 187–88
material determinism, 96, 390
Mayfield, V., 197–98
media: advocacy in, 355–57; disability in, 162–63, 166–68, 302; representation in, 166–68, 355–57; social, 274; special education and, 355–57; student media and content, 271–72, *272*
mediation, 250

Medical Model of Disability, 123, 155–56, 158, 390; labeling in, 165–66, 349; medical classifications and, 349; special education and, 349
Mental Health and Mental Retardation Reform Act (1963), 356
mentoring, 307
meritocracy, white, 95–96
Mills v. Board of Education (1972), 315–16
models: Charity Model of Disability, 158, 383; Cultural Model of Disability, 157, 302, *303*, 384; definition of a model, 151–52, 390; different approaches to, 155–56; of disability, 154–62, *159–60*, 169–73; disability models in education, 169–73; Economic Model of Disability, 158, 387; Human Rights Model of Disability, 157–58, 388; Identity Model of Disability, 157, 388; importance of, 155; key terms and types of, 151–52; Medical Model of Disability, 123, 155–56, 158, 165–66, 349, 390; relationships between models, *159–60*; Social Model of Disability, 123, 155–57, 169, 304, 394
modifications, 168, 323, 390
Mosen, J., 169
MTSS. *See* Multi-tiered Systems of Support
multiculturalism, 349–50, 390
Multicultural Reflective Behavior Analytic Practice (Broadwell), 197–98
multidimensionality, 23–24
Multi-tiered Systems of Support (MTSS), 34, 152, 169; description of, 390; restorative practices and, 250; special education and, 52, *53*, 357–58. *See also* Integrated Multi-tiered Systems of Support

names, 107
narratives: alternative, 125; counternarratives to inclusion, 365; counter-storytelling and, 99–100; CRT and, 91–92, 99–100; DisCrit, 139
National Center for School Engagement (NCSE), 74, 249, 325–26, 386
Nazi Germany, 293, 294–95
NCSE. *See* National Center for School Engagement
neurodiversity, 64–65, *65*, 390–91
nicknames, 107
nonbinary, 39, 391
nondiscriminatory assessment, 281–82
normality: DisCrit resources and information about normalcy and, *144*; redefining, 132–33
norming, 228, 391
"nothing about us without us" mantra, 68, 135

Ocasio-Stoutenburg, L., 140
Oliver, Michael, 137, 143, 156
opportunities to respond (OTRs), 264–66, 391
opportunity: equitable, 183–85; gap, 111
oppression: acknowledging, 157; audism as, 76; definition of, 391; disability rights and, 291–92, 295; equity and, 183, 187–88; forms of, 76; identity and, 187–88; language and, 187–88; linguicism as, 76; marginalization and systems of, 224–25; "oppressed" and "oppressor," 102–3; "othering" and, 91, 129, 139, 351; privilege and, 187–88; in schools, 76–77. *See also* ableism
"othering," 91, 129, 139, 351
OTRs. *See* opportunities to respond

Padia, D., 140
parents: advocacy and, 133–35, 353–54, 360; barriers to, 352–53; disability and parenting, 133–35, 140–41, 167–68, 352–55; education and involvement of, 225–26, 360; empowerment for, 360; on gender identity, 42–43; influence of family and, 352–55; parent perspectives of disability, 124, 140–41, 354–55; special education and, 352–55, 360
paternalism, 227–28
PBIS. *See* positive behavioral interventions and supports
PC. *See* PreCorrection

PCP. *See* person-centered planning
pedagogy, 113; CLSP, socioculturally sustaining practices and, 220–35; culturally relevant, 221, *222*; culturally sustaining pedagogy, 222, 385; DisCrit and, 142; inclusion and, 171
Pennsylvania Association for Retarded Children (PARC) v. Pennsylvania (1971), 315–16
people of the global majority (PGM), 94, 96–97, 391; diversity and, 361; inclusion and, 170–73; white people "pitted" against, 102–3
people with stuttering (PWS), 11–12
person-centered planning (PCP), 53–54, *54*, *55*
person-first language (PFL), 69, 82, 163, 187–88, 321–22
PGM. *See* people of the global majority
Philosophical Chairs, 273, 391
physical activities, 267
Plessy v. Ferguson (1896), 296
police violence, 49, 98–99, 172
polio, 294
politics, 227
positive behavioral interventions and supports (PBIS), 52, 169, 362, 391; behavioral matrix and, *333*; socioculturally sustaining practices and, 247–49, 333–34; SWPBIS, 333–34, 393
positive feedback, 266–67, 271
poverty, 37–38. *See also* socioeconomic status
power structures: engagement and, in schools, 124; transformative change and, 132
practitioner training, 113
pragmatic competence, 5–6
pragmatics, 5–6
PreCorrection (PC), 267, 392
prejudice, 183, 392
preservice practitioners (PSP), 73; CDT and, 126–27; CRT and, 95, 108, 114–16
privilege, 392; oppression and, 187–88. *See also* white privilege

professional development: practitioner training and, 113; race-evasiveness in, 111–15
professional learning, 234
progress monitoring, 392; flexibility in, 279
prosthetics, 152
PSP. *See* preservice practitioners
PWS. *See* people with stuttering

race: being an agent of, 109–10; CDT, racial justice, and, 130–42; colorblindness and, 94–95, 109–10, 182, 383; definition of, 98, 392; disability and, in schools, 170–73; disability studies and, 124; disproportionality and, 327, 328; educator perspective on, 47; educators and, 259; equity and, 182–83, 211–13; gender and, 40; IEP and, 359; inclusion and, 170–73; intersectionality of disability, ethnicity, and, 35–37, 297, 349–52; intersectionality of special education and, 98–99, 297, 350–52; neutrality, 100; police violence and, 49, 98–99, 172; racialization of disability and, 37; as social construct, 97–98; sociocultural identity and, 94–95, 187–89, *191*, 350–52; socioeconomic status and, 49; in total enrollment in public schools during 2020, in the United States, *350*. *See also* civil rights; Critical Race Theory
"Race, Reform, and Retrenchment" (Crenshaw), 91
race-evasiveness (RE), 111–15, 392
racial affirming practices, 47
racial bias, 257
racial identity, 94–96; of educators, 259, 260
racial segregation: de facto segregation and, 96–97, 385; redlining and, 97; Supreme Court and, 96–97, 296
racism, 183; anti-racism, 103–4, 115; COVID-19 and, 135; CRT and racism as "normal," 93, 94–96; definition of,

392; discomfort discussing, 111–12; education as racist institution and, 110–16; in schools, 36–37; "white flight" and, 134; xenophobia and, 36, 99. *See also* Critical Race Theory

RE. *See* race-evasiveness

Reasonable Doubts (television show), 167

redlining, 97

reflection, 124, 192–93; B.I.A.S. self-reflection tool, *195*; in C.U.L.T.U.R.E. framework, 242–43; self-reflection, 194–96, *195*, *196*, 228

Rehabilitation Act (1973), 153, 158, 392; Section 504 of, 298, 393

relationship building, 233; for authentic relationships, 242–43; empowerment through, 270; relationship transformation and, 225–26, *226*

religion: Christianity and, 17, 152; churches and, 152; culture and, 17; disability and, 17, 152, 292; disability rights and, 292; divine judgement in, 292; Islam and, 17; Judaism and, 17

REMIXed education: classroom environment and, 271–81; EBPs and, 263–67; empowerment in, 268–70; examination strategies in, 281–83; framework, *263*; innovation in, 274–81; learning partnerships and, 271–74; nondiscriminatory assessment and, 281–82; sociocultural factors and IEP process in, 282–83; sociocultural identity and, 262–83; socioculturally sustaining practices and, 262–63; textured teaching and, 262

Renaissance, 152

representation: critical thinking activities and, 273; diversity and, 360–61; lack of, in special education, 258–60; in media, 166–68, 355–57

reproduction, 293–94

respect, 242–43, 247–48, 333; sociocultural, 359–60; in special education, 359–60

Response to Intervention (RTI), 51–52, 169, 246–47, 331–32, 393

restorative practices, 250, 393

restraint, 327–28

ritual, 152, 393; food as, 11–12; marriage as, 16

Rivera, Geraldo, 356

Rogers, Roy, 355

Roosevelt, Franklin Delano, 152, 294

Rosa's Law, 154, 321–22

Rose, C., 224

RTI. *See* Response to Intervention

"Say Their Names" campaign, 98

Schalk, Sami, 139

schools: autistic identity in, 70–71, 172–73; book bans in, 100, 112; culture and, 24–25, 259–60; deaf, 73–76, 78–79; disability and oppression in, 76–77; disability culture in, 73–77; disability rights in, 292; disabled student segregation in, 298, 302–4; discipline in, 212–13, 259, 266–69, 327–28, 333–34, 392; domains of school engagement and, 386; as equalizer, 25; hegemony and, 227–28; history in, 100; inclusion in, 170–73, 362–68; power structures and engagement in, 124; race and disability in, 170–73; race-evasiveness in, 112; race in total enrollment in public schools during 2020, in the United States, *350*; racial segregation in, 96–97, 296, 385; racism in, 36–37; whiteness and, 25

Schoolwide Positive Behavioral Interventions and Supports (SWPBIS), 333–34, 393

scientific standard measurements, 133

seclusion, 327–28

Section 504 of Rehabilitation Act (1973), 298, 393

segregation: de facto, 96–97, 385; of disabled students, 298, 302–4; racial, 96–97, 296, 385

SEL. *See* social emotional learning

self-advocacy, 68, 80, 382

self-determination, 72–73, 393

self-identity activity, 272
self-reflection, 194–96, *195*, *196*, 228
semantics, 163, 393
SES. *See* socioeconomic status
sexual development, 44
sexual identity, 393; intersectionality of disability and, 43–46; terms associated with, 44
sexuality, 43–44; definition of, 393; disability and, 45–46; learning about, 44–45; models of, 44
SGDs. *See* speech-generating devices
shared understanding, 228
Shrek (film), 187
Shriver, Eunice Kennedy, 355–56
sign language, 66, 67, 74–79, 381
SIT. *See* Social Identity Theory
Skinner, B. F., 133
slavery, 296
SLD. *See* specific learning disabilities
Sleeter, Christine, 113
SMART goals, 266
Smith, Will, 102
Smith v. Robinson (1985), 319
Smith v. Timothy v. Rochester School District (1989), 318
social awareness, 131–32
social capital, 22–23, 393
social categorization, 34–35
social comparison, 34, 35
social emotional learning (SEL), 394; socioculturally sustaining practices in, 249–50
social identification, 34–35
Social Identity Theory (SIT): culture and, 20–23; definition of, 394; intersectionality and, 34; three ideas behind, 34–35
social isolation, 18–19; seclusion and, 326–27
social justice work: CDT, racial justice, and, 130–42; in CRT, 103–4, 115; disability justice, in education, 133–34; disability justice, in lived experience, 134–36; DisCrit and, 143–44; equity and, 181–85
social media, 274

Social Model of Disability, 123, 155, 394; disability rights and, 156–57, 304; UDL and, 169
social power, 394
Social Security Act (1935), 152–53, 294
sociocultural competency, 213; developing, 233–34. *See also* intersectional sociocultural competence
sociocultural consciousness, 394; critical consciousness and, 186–88; intersectional sociocultural competence assessment and, 197–214
sociocultural construct: culture and, 19–21; definition of, 394
sociocultural identity, 33–34; conflict and, 250; deaf and autistic communities and, 65–71; disability and, 65–71, *190*, 302–4, 354–55; equity and, 185–93; ethnicity and, 36–37, 187–92, *190*, 349–52; exploration of, *190–91*; gender identity and, 39, 189, *191*; intersectionality and, 34–46, *36*, 349–52; language and, 349–50; layers of, 36, 189, *189*; lived experience and, 256–57; personal identification of, 188–93; race and, 94–95, 187–89, *191*, 350–52; reflection questions on, 192–93; REMIXed education and, 262–83; self-examination of, 187–88; socioculturally sustaining practices and, 224–25, 330; sociocultural mismatch and, 108–9; special education and, 257–62, 349–52; utilizing, 241–42; whiteness and, 95
socioculturally sustaining practices, 46–47, 219; for AAC, 335–38; CLSP and pedagogy in, 220–35; C.L.S.P. continuum and, *229–232*; competencies, 229, 233–35; culturally relevant pedagogy and, 221, *222*; culturally relevant teaching and, *222*; culturally responsive teaching and, 221, *222*, *223*; culturally sustaining pedagogy, *222*, 385; in C.U.L.T.U.R.E. framework, 236–44, *237*; defining,

394; developing competency in, 233–35; embedding practices into special education, 235–36; family and, 225–26, 226; IEP and, 225–26; implementation of, 226–35; in I-MTSS, 245–49, 330–34; inclusion and, 225; intersectionality and, 224–25; intersectional sociocultural competence and, 197; key terms related to, 220; lesson plan example and, 276–78; overview of, 224–25; PBIS and, 247–49, 333–34; policy and practice recommendations, 234; practicality of, 227–28; relationship transformation and, 225–26, 226; REMIXed education and, 262–63; RTI and, 246–47, 331–32; in SEL, 249–50; shared understanding in, 228; sociocultural identity and, 224–25, 330; socioculturally sustaining person-centered planning, 53–54, 54, 55; in special education teaching frameworks, 244–51; in UDL, 244–45, 334–35, 335
sociocultural respect, 359–60
socioeconomic status (SES), 170–71, 354, 394; disproportionality and, 328–29; education and, 110–11; intersectionality and, 23, 49–50; intersectionality of disability and, 37–38, 165; race and, 49; school administrator perspective on, 49–50
sociolinguistics, 5, 394
sociological jurisprudence, 91
sociology, 162–63; values and, 347
Socratic Seminars, 273, 394
spaces of educational hegemony, 226–27
Spanish-only speakers, 50, 79. *See also* language
Special (television show), 166–67
special education: advocacy and, 346–47, 353–54; assessing students from nondominant cultures and backgrounds, 359; barriers in, 48–51; belonging in, 344–45; bias and, 358–59; *Brown v. Board of Education* relating to, 314–15; challenges in, 258–62; classroom environment and, 271–81, 304; definition of, 395; disproportionality in, 325–30; diversity in, 360–61; dominant values relating to, 347–48; DSE and, 125–26; EAHCA and, 315–16; eligibility for, 349, 357–60; factors impacting, 345–57; frameworks, 329–38, 362; history of, 313–21; impact of, 357–68; intersectional belonging in, 344–45, 369–72; intersectional competence in, 46–56, 181; intersectionality and, 262; intersectionality of race and, 98–99, 297, 350–52; labeling and, 349, 364–65; lack of representation in, 258–60; lack of strong relationships in, 258; language barriers and, 50, 352–53, 354, 359; law and, 314–21; legislative impacts on, 345–46; LRE and, 319–20, 322–25, 363–67; media and, 355–57; Medical Model of Disability and, 349; MTSS, I-MTSS, and, 52, 53, 357–58; overview of, 257–58; parents and, 352–55, 360; poverty and, 37–38; REMIXed education and, 262–83; respect in, 359–60; sociocultural identity and, 257–62, 349–52; socioculturally sustaining practices embedded into, 235–36; socioculturally sustaining practices in frameworks of, 244–51; stigma relating to, 260–61, 326
specific learning disabilities (SLD), 8, 38
speech, 8–9; stuttering and, 10–11. *See also* communication; language
speech-generating devices (SGDs), 335
standards, redefining, 133
Stefancic, J., 91–93
stereotypes, 10, 38, 122, 140; about autism, 71; bias and, 193–94
sterilization, 293–94
stigma, 48, 136, 170; culture and, 261; disability rights and, 291–92; shame and, 261; special education relating to, 260–61, 326
"Stop WOKE Act," 113
storytelling: counter-storytelling and, 99–100; CRT and, 91–92, 99–100
strengths-based approach, 80, 395

student conflict, 250
student engagement: SEL and, 249; UDL and, 245
student-led meetings, 269, *269*
student media and content, 271–72, *272*
student self-monitoring, 279, *280*
stuttering, 10–11
subordination, 227–28
success, 25; equity and, 183–85, *184*; group, 248
Supreme Court: *Arlington Central School District v. D.K. and K.K.* and, 320; *Brown v. Board of Education* and, 96, 130, 153, 295, 296, 314–15; civil rights and, 97–98, 295; CRT and, 90; forced sterilization and, 294; impact of court cases on law, 314–15; *Mills v. Board of Education* and, 315–16; *Pennsylvania Association for Retarded Children (PARC) v. Pennsylvania*, 315–16; *Plessy v. Ferguson* and, 296; racial segregation and, 96–97, 296; *Smith v. Robinson* and, 318; *Smith v. Timothy v. Rochester School District* and, 318
suspension, 327
SWPBIS. *See* Schoolwide Positive Behavioral Interventions and Supports

Tajfel, Henri, 21
Tate, W. F., 92, 96
taxes, 315
TBI. *See* traumatic brain injury
teaching: co-teaching, 274; CRT and, 100, 108–16; culturally relevant, 222; culturally responsive, 221, 222, *223*; in C.U.L.T.U.R.E. framework, 240–41; history, 100; special education teaching frameworks, 244–51; teacher-family solidarity framework, *226*; textured, 262, 395
technology: AAC, 335–38; AI and, 281–82, 382; assistive, 382; communication and, 335–38; innovation and, 281–82
textured teaching, 262, 395
Thompson, Vilissa, 135
transdisciplinary teams, 282, 395

transgender, 39, 395; parent perspective on, 42–43
trauma, 162
traumatic brain injury (TBI), 318–19
Traxler, E., 140
trust, 50, 136, 236; equity and, 213
Truth, Sojourner, 93

UD. *See* universal design
UDL. *See* Universal Design for Learning
understanding: in C.U.L.T.U.R.E. framework, 238–39
UNICEF. *See* United Nations Children's Fund
Union of the Physically Impaired Against Segregation (UPIAS), 135; *Fundamental Principles of Disability* by, 156–57
United Kingdom, 135
United Nations Children's Fund (UNICEF), 292
United Nations General Assembly, 301
universal design (UD), 295–96, 297–98, 395
Universal Design for Learning (UDL), 126, 142, 152; benefits of, 169; "crosswalks" in, 245; framework, 334–35; higher-order thinking and, 273–74; inclusion and, 362; lesson plan example, *276–78*; overview of, 169–70, 395; socioculturally sustaining practices in, 244–45, 334–35, *335*; student engagement and, 245
UPIAS. *See* Union of the Physically Impaired Against Segregation
US Code Congressional and Administrative News (USCCAN), 315–16

values: beliefs and, 347, *370*; dominant, 347–48; in IDEA, *348*; more inclusive values influencing education, *370*
victimization, 158, 383
visual impairments, 319, 367. *See also* colorblindness
voting, 297

Waitoller, F., 137
Waldschmidt, A., 301–2, *303*
Ware, Linda, 132
wealth, 95–96. *See also* socioeconomic status
"white flight," 134
white fragility, 111–12
White Fragility (DiAngelo), 111
whiteness, 395; CRT and white demoralization, 101–2; CRT and white people "pitted" against PGM, 102–3; schools and, 25; sociocultural identity and, 95; wealth and, 95–96; white meritocracy and, 95–96
white privilege, 392; charity and, 95–96; CRT and, 102–3; equity and, 187–88, 211–13; interest convergence and, 96–97; master status and, 187–88; oppression and, 187–88
WHO. *See* World Health Organization
Willowbrook State School, 356
women, Black, 98, 129
workforce: CRT and, 108, *108*; labor rights and, 297
World Federation of the Deaf, 67
World Health Organization (WHO), 151, 154; on disability rights, 291–92
World War II, 294

xenophobia, 36, 99

"zero reject" policy, 318

About the Contributors

EDITORS

Elizabeth A. Harkins Monaco, EdD, (she/her/disabled), is a white scholar who studies social justice in special education, intersectional pedagogy, and disability studies in education. A former special education administrator, classroom teacher, and family advocate, she has worked with autistic students and students with developmental disabilities in a variety of settings. Trained in Intergroup Relations, she is now an assistant professor of Disability Studies and Special Education in the Department of Special Education, Professional Counseling, and Disability Studies at William Paterson University. Dr. Harkins is on the Board of Directors of the Council for Exceptional Children's (CEC) Division on Autism and Developmental Disabilities (DADD) and is on the Fulbright Specialist Roster. In her free time, she is fueled by live theater, music, her dogs, and plants.

L. Lynn Stansberry Brusnahan, PhD, is a white, cisgender female who is the parent of an adult with autism. Dr. Stansberry Brusnahan is a professor in the School of Education at the University of St. Thomas in Minnesota where she coordinates the autism spectrum and developmental cognitive disabilities programs. Dr. Stansberry Brusnahan's scholarly focus is on the autism spectrum, the intersection of disability and diversity, and the utilization of socioculturally sustaining practices that promote justice, equity, diversity, and inclusion. Dr. Stansberry Brusnahan is coauthor of *Do-Watch-Listen-Say: Social and Communication Intervention for Autism Spectrum Disorder*. She is a former recipient of the Autism Society of America's Professional of the Year award. Dr. Stansberry Brusnahan serves on the Council for Exceptional Children's (CEC) Division on Autism and Developmental Disabilities (DADD) executive board.

Marcus Charles Fuller, PhD, is a Black, pansexual heteroromantic, cisgender, educated, male originally from the city of Harrisburg, Pennsylvania. Marcus has many years of experience as a practitioner, as well as an intervention coach, within the preK–12 classrooms across several geographical areas including Pennsylvania; Texas; Louisiana; Washington, DC; Vermont; and Maryland. Currently, Marcus is an assistant professor of special education at the University of Maryland Eastern Shore, a land-grant 1890 Historically Black University. His research focuses on disability and diversity by helping practitioners increase their use of culturally and linguistically sustaining pedagogies, the understanding of intersectionality in the classroom, and creating a classroom environment that promotes justice, equity, diversity, and inclusion (JEDI). He is also an active member of the Council for Exceptional Children and other subdivisions such as DADD, and DEBH. In his free time, Marcus enjoys running, catching up on his streaming shows, and playing with his dog and pet clients.

Martin Odima Jr., MA, is a Black, cisgender, male from St. Paul, Minnesota. Martin is a Special Education Teacher Coach in the Saint Paul Public School (SPPS) District in Minnesota. Martin is also an adjunct faculty in the Department of Special Education at the University of St. Thomas where he teaches undergraduate and graduate students the history, policies, and practices of special education. He studied psychology at the University of Minnesota and completed his master's in special education at the University of St. Thomas. His scholarly interests focus on educational equity, inclusive practices for students with disabilities, and retention of teachers of color. His publications include a focus on teaching strategies for special education teachers to thrive and persist in the field. Martin is currently pursuing a PhD in special education at the University of Minnesota.

CHAPTER AUTHORS

Kenyon Andrews, MS and doctoral candidate, is an African American, cisgender, husband, father, mental health champion, and K–12 educator. Kenyon's advocacy work promotes teacher leadership within Teach Plus Texas, the Texas State Teachers Association, and the National Education Association. Kenyon's expertise lies in instructing learners with exceptional needs and neurodiversity, as well as gifted and talented learners, while providing professionals with the necessary tools to better understand and value diverse cultures within the classroom setting. His advocacy work focuses on addressing cultural bias, the stigmas experienced by learners with disabilities, and the retention of educators of color. Kenyon is dedicated to policing for equity, fostering a sense of belonging within educational culture, promoting collaboration and accountability among teachers, and shifting perspectives on behavioral challenges. He serves in various roles within the National Council for Mental Wellbeing, 100 Black Men of America, Kappa Delta Phi, and the Council for Exceptional Children.

Kara B. Ayers, PhD, is a white, disabled, cisgender woman who is an associate professor at Cincinnati Children's Hospital Medical Center. She is the associate director of the University of Cincinnati Center for Excellence in Developmental Disabilities, where she researches and teaches about a wide range of disability-related topics. Kara is trained in clinical psychology and applies a disability justice framework to many of her pursuits, including efforts to transform public policy. Her scholarly interests focus on disabled parenting, health equity, and disability ethics. Kara lives near Cincinnati, Ohio, with her family.

David F. Bateman, PhD, is a principal researcher at AIR (American Institutes for Research), and the project director for the Massachusetts IEP project. He is a former professor at Shippensburg University of Pennsylvania in the Department of Educational Leadership and Special Education. He is a former state due process hearing officer using his knowledge of special education litigation to assist school districts in providing appropriate supports for students with disabilities. Dr. Bateman has been a classroom teacher of students with learning disabilities, behavior disorders, intellectual disability, and hearing impairments. He has recently coauthored the following books: *A Principal's Guide to Special Education; A Teacher's Guide to Special Education; Special Education Law Case Studies; Special Education Leadership: Building Effective Programming in Schools; Developing Educationally Meaningful and Legally Sound IEPs*; and *Current Trends and Issues in Special Education*. He was recently coeditor of a special issue of *TEACHING Exceptional Children* focusing on legally proficient IEPs. He is also coeditor of the Special Education Law, Policy, and Practice series for Rowman & Littlefield.

Amy Eelkema Baxter is a white, cisgender female from St. Paul, Minnesota. She earned her bachelor's degree from Augsburg University in elementary education and did her graduate work in special education at Bethel University. Amy started her teaching career in the Republic of the Marshall Islands and has spent over twenty years as a special education teacher for St. Paul Public Schools working in a multitude of settings including day treatment, residential, self-contained classrooms, and resource rooms as well as co-teaching in general education classrooms. She is an advocate for equity in education and has lobbied and testified for eliminating school suspensions in the primary grades. Amy works as adjunct faculty for the University of St. Thomas St. Paul Residency Program, supervising residents working on their special education licensure.

Cindy Bentley is an African American female activist who is the executive director of People First Wisconsin. Born with an intellectual disability as the result of fetal alcohol syndrome, Cindy Bentley spent much of her childhood at the Southern Wisconsin Center for the Developmentally Disabled. No one expected her to learn the skills necessary to live on her own, but she did and then accomplished so much more. Cindy is coauthor of the book *Spirit of a Champion*, which is the story of Cindy's life, from her childhood in the institution, to her adventures with Special Olympics to meeting presidents. Chosen as a Global Messenger for the Special Olympics International in 2000, Cindy had dinner at the White House with two different American presidents, traveled around the world, and gave speeches in front of thousands of people.

Susannah (Suz) Boyle, (she/they), is a white, queer, nonbinary person who is a former special education PK–5 teacher and a current associate professor at Millersville University in the Department of Special Education. Dr. Boyle's research interests include preparing teachers to serve *all* students in inclusive settings, designing high-quality communication and literacy interventions for children with developmental delays and disabilities, and creating frameworks to understand the experiences of LGBTQIA+ children and youth in the US educational system. As part of their community outreach, they present on the use of alternative and augmentative communication to educators and parents as well as presenting on the needs of LGBTQIA+ students in the current shifting political landscape. She is also on the executive board of the President's Commission on Gender and Sexuality Diversity at Millersville University, where she has advocated for LGBTQIA+-inclusive policies and helped put on events celebrating that community such as PrideFest and Rainbow Graduation. Dr. Boyle's teaching includes courses on early literacy, inclusion, LGBTQIA+ issues in education, and special education methods.

T. Collin Brusnahan is a white male who is on the autism spectrum. Collin was included in general education through his preK–12 public school experiences. He exited high school at age twenty-one and attended Minnesota Independence College and Community (MICC). Afterward, he attended Edgewood College's postsecondary Cutting Edge program to gain additional life skills. Collin works at an urban farm where he grows and harvests produce as well as makes and packages spices, teas, and other herbs. Collin has presented at numerous state and national conferences about his experiences as an individual with a disability.

Salita Callicutt, EdD in educational leadership, is a white, cisgender, heterosexual female from the Piedmont of North Carolina. She is a teacher of the Deaf and Hard of Hearing in North Carolina. She also works as a World Languages Teacher instructing students in American Sign Language. Her research focuses on the practice of inclusive education and the impact of teacher perspectives on those practices. As a parent of children with disabilities, Salita is passionate in understanding inclusive education and how successful this framework of education is for student success academically, socially, and emotionally.

Aaron Campbell, PhD, (she/her), is a cisgender Black female and assistant professor of special education at University of Missouri (Mizzou). Dr. Campbell's teaching and research focuses on culturally responsive intervention delivery within a multi-tiered behavior support framework with a specific emphasis on supporting historically marginalized children and youth in schools and communities. She is particularly interested in (1) culturally responsive Positive Behavioral Interventions and Supports (PBIS), (2) culturally responsive social emotional learning (SEL), (3) alternatives to exclusionary discipline, (4) addressing the impact of implicit biases on racial disproportionality and school discipline, and (5) implementation and sustainability of evidence-based practices. Prior to joining Mizzou, she served as an assistant professor of special education at Pennsylvania State University in the College of Education. Dr. Campbell is a current Institute of Education science fellow in the Research Institute for Implementation Science in Education at University of Washington. Dr. Campbell earned her doctorate in educational psychology with an emphasis in special education from the School of Education and Human Development at Texas A&M University (TAMU). She earned her master's degree in clinical psychology from North Carolina Central University and her bachelor's degree in psychology from Florida A&M University.

Jacquelyn Chovanes, PhD, is a white, cisgender, heteroromantic woman who was born in Pennsylvania. She was a K–12 special education teacher and consultant in Pennsylvania, Alaska, Michigan, and Maine. She earned her MEd in special education from the University of Pittsburgh, and her PhD in special education from Lehigh University. She currently teaches in the Department of Educational Leadership and Special Education at Shippensburg University, where she directs the Ship SAILS program, which affords on-campus social, vocational, and academic opportunities to students with autism and intellectual disabilities. Her research interests cover a variety of topics but converge around the idea of educational equity for students with disabilities.

Liza E. Citron is a disabled, autistic, Ashkenazi Jewish, queer woman originally from Rochester, New York, but who grew up all over the northeastern United States. Her experiences as an autistic woman, including the issues she faced in school (and currently faces in society), have motivated her to work as an advocate and organizer for a disability advocacy group, and she is also an avid disability researcher. She is continuing her studies at SUNY Cortland. Her advocacy and research particularly focuses on developmental disability in elementary education and during children's formative years, with a special emphasis on sociology, psychology, and history as they relate to disability. Specific contemporary topics of interest include intersectionality, confronting and combating inequity in education, inclusive pedagogy, psychology and neuroscience of developmental disability, and applications of disability history. In addition to her professional pursuits, she is a musician and artist, and is interested in tiny home/RV living, anthropology, and natural candlemaking. She currently resides in the Berkshires in Massachusetts near her family, with significant amounts of time also spent in central New York.

David J. Connor, EdD, is Professor Emeritus, Department of Special Education, Hunter College (Learning Disabilities and Instructional Leadership Programs), and the Graduate Center (Urban Education Program), City University of New York. David is a white, gay male of Anglo-Irish descent and working-class origin, born in the Northeast of England, who immigrated to New York City in his early twenties. He taught there for thirty-five years in public schools and universities. Throughout his career, he has always been interested in issues of equality, particularly in regard to dis/ability, race, and social class. He is the author/editor of articles, book chapters, and books, including: *DisCrit: Disability Studies and Critical Race Theory* (2016) and *DisCrit Expanded: Inquiries, Reverberations and Ruptures* (2022), coedited with Subini Annamma and Beth Ferri. He also writes fiction. For more information, see https://hunter-cuny.academia.edu/DavidJConnor.

Catherine M. Constable, PhD, CCC-SP, is a life member of the American Speech-Language-Hearing Association. Her areas of scholarly concentration are Language Learning and Literacy and Language in Social Context. Dr. Constable spent nine years teaching in higher education before and during her codirection and direction of the Rye Learning Center in Rye, New York. Her clinical work involves emergent literacy and language and literacy in school-age children. She has been the literacy consultant and demonstration language and literacy teacher/therapist at the Parkside School in Manhattan, New York, for twenty-three years. She served six years on the Coordinating Committee of the ASHA Special Interest Group 1, Language Learning and Education. Likewise Dr. Constable has been a reviewer for articles submitted to the journal, *Perspectives of the ASHA Special Interest Groups*. Her publications relate to language intervention context and collaboration with teachers. In 1980, Dr. Constable took one of the first Augmentative and Alternative Communication (AAC) courses ever offered in the United States which was from the Department of Communication Sciences and Disorders at the University of Wisconsin–Madison.

Joseph Cremona, MAT, MEd, is a homosexual, white, disabled, cisgender male who is currently in his ninth year of teaching science. For the majority of his career, Joseph has been teaching 7th grade science in the Nutley Public School District, including most recently in the out-of-classroom resource and replacement setting. As of the 2022–2023 school year, Joseph will teach general and honors Forensic Science to juniors and seniors at Nutley High School. Joseph considers himself a lifelong learner, as he is currently working on his fourth college degree. Joseph is a two-time graduate of Fairleigh Dickinson University (FDU) in Teaneck, where he earned his Bachelor of Science (concentration in biology) in 2013 and his Master of Arts in Teaching in 2014, as part of FDU's QUEST practitioner preparation program. Joseph earned his Master's in Education in Special Education from Montclair State University in 2019. Joseph is currently a candidate for a Doctor of Education degree in Special Education at Rutgers University. At Rutgers, his research focus is on inquiry-based science instruction for students with disabilities. Joseph is an active member of multiple educational organizations, including the Council for Exceptional Children, the National Science Teaching Association, and the Association for Middle Level Education (AMLE).

Eric Elmore, ABD, is an African American male from Aurora, Colorado. Eric currently attends University of Colorado Denver where he is obtaining a Doctor of Education in Leadership for Educational Equity, in Early Childhood Education. Eric was an Office of Special Education Program (OSEP) Scholar. Eric has worked as an early childhood educator, early childhood special educator, special education director, culturally responsive specialist, and a K–12 principal. Eric works as a lecturer at Metropolitan State University of Denver, a Hispanic-Serving Institution. His research focuses on culturally responsive pedagogy, instructional pedagogy, professional development, educational leadership, and early literacy.

Bob Eyres is a self-described gamer and aspiring social media influencer. Bob is multigender, multiracial, and questioning. A lifelong lover of books (especially comic books) and a foodie, Bob loves libraries, bookstores, trying new restaurants, and both chocolate and lemon desserts! Although several disabilities are part of his identity, Bob prefers being defined by his witty sense of humor and charm. A recent high school graduate, Bob is exploring job training options and plans to be a voice actor.

Ruth M. Eyres, EdD, NBCT, is a white, hearing impaired, cisgender female who lives in Arkansas with her wife and children. They are parents of two children both with disabilities including cerebral palsy, learning disability, intellectual disability, autism, traumatic brain injury, and seizure disorder. Ruth's work in special education spans over twenty-four years including serving as a K–12 public school special education teacher and as an education consultant meeting the needs of students with complex learning needs. Ruth is a National Board Certified Teacher and is currently an assistant professor of special education at Henderson State University. Ruth completed her doctorate degree in Instruction and Curriculum Leadership at the University of Memphis and received her MSE in special education from the University of Central Arkansas. Her research focuses on sexuality education for students with intellectual disabilities and autism. Ruth is active on the boards of the Center for Exceptional Families, the Arkansas branch of the Division on Autism and Developmental Disabilities (DADD), and the Arkansas Council for Exceptional Children (CEC).

Erin Fitzgerald Farrell, EdD, BCBA, is a white, cisgender female. Erin is an adjunct faculty at the University of St. Thomas in Minnesota in addition to supporting educators and families across the state in other roles. Erin's research interests include examining the roles of behavior analytic support for individuals and systems across settings. Erin is a wife and mother of three whose children have given her parental experience with autism spectrum disorder, anxiety, depression, ADHD, gender identity, sexual orientation, behavioral needs, special education support needs, and intersecting identities across disability and gender and sexual identity.

Elizabeth G. (Liz) Finnegan is a heteronormative, cisgender woman with a facial difference, who grew up in rural Buckinghamshire, England. She is a former special education teacher and early interventionist. Dr. Finnegan is currently a professor of special education in the School of Education at St. Thomas Aquinas College in New York, teaching graduate and undergraduate classes in special education. Her research interests focus on literacy for individuals with autism, with a special focus on applying findings to classroom teaching. Dr. Finnegan has served on the membership and advocacy committees of the New Jersey Unit of the Council for Exceptional Children, the board of the American Educational Research Association's Autism Spectrum Research Committee, and on a regional advisory board for Today's Students, Tomorrow's Teachers.

Jasmine Fleming, MSEd, is a Black American cishet woman born and raised in the heart of Philadelphia, Pennsylvania. Jasmine has several years of experience in education, including early childhood education, civic education, and secondary education. She is the executive director and founder of Prosperity Prep, a nonprofit organization serving teen girls in Philadelphia. She earned her Master of Science in Education from the University of Pennsylvania Graduate School of Education, specializing in educational anthropology. She serves as an adjunct professor and student teaching supervisor at La Salle University's Education Department. Her teaching centers on teaching preservice teachers to use culturally sustaining pedagogy that is liberative racially, politically, economically, and culturally. Heavily influenced by her upbringing in resource-starved Philadelphia, her research focuses on the intersection of education and urban life and, specifically, on the ways in which education can empower youth to overcome the ills of urban education such as poverty, racism, and oppression. Jasmine also serves as president of the Academic Discovery Program advisory board, an Act 101 program advancing college access and retention in low-income, first-generation, or at-risk college students.

Miles Forma is a thirty-five-year-old white Jewish male from the New York Metropolitan Area. Miles was born with cerebral palsy. He is a member of the International Society for Augmentative and Alternative Communication. He is an advocate for people who use or need AAC devices. Presently Miles is a lecturer, presenter, and educator who presents to college and university classes across the United States. Additionally, he has developed PowerPoint lectures which he delivers to various elementary schools in Westchester County, New York. Prior to this work and since high school, Miles was engaged in fundraising work for the American Jewish Committee and the AFYA Foundation.

Shelley Neilsen Gatti, PhD, is a white, cisgender, female, mother, daughter, sister, and educator who grew up in Montana before moving to Minnesota to further her education. She is an associate professor in the Special Education Department at the University of St. Thomas in Minnesota. She coordinates the license program in emotional and behavioral disorders and St. Thomas's Teacher Residency Programs. She started her teaching career in Montana before completing her PhD at the University of Minnesota in educational psychology. While finishing up her PhD, Dr. Gatti worked as a teacher on special assignment in the special education department at Minneapolis Public Schools. Throughout her career, she has studied assessment and intervention for students with social emotional behavioral needs and most recently teacher preparation pathways. She has served on various CEC-DEBH boards at the national and state level. Dr. Neilsen Gatti's scholarly interests focus on embedding culturally sustaining pedagogy across all sectors of education and teacher preparation and evaluation.

Ambra L. Green, PhD, is an African American female associate professor of special education in the Department of Curriculum and Instruction within the College of Education at the University of Texas at Arlington. Dr. Green is a national scholar with publications and research focused on students of color with and at-risk for disabilities, issues related to inequitable school practices (i.e., disproportionality in special education and exclusionary practices), behavior disorders, positive behavioral interventions and supports, and teacher use of evidence-based practices. She is the primary investigator on a US Department of Education Office of Special Education Programs (OSEP) personnel preparation grant which provides rigorous training for master's special education and social work students to support K–12 students with disabilities and high-intensity needs. In addition to providing technical assistance at the school, district, and state levels, Dr. Green has provided professional special education consultation in a number of capacities, including for offices of former US senators and the Texas Education Agency. Prior to her work in higher education, Dr. Green was a middle school special education teacher and PBIS coach.

Lindsay M. Griendling, PhD, is a white, cisgender female with a dis/ability (attention deficit hyperactivity disorder), and an assistant professor of special education at Appalachian State University in North Carolina. Dr. Griendling's research interests are twofold: (1) understanding how ambiguity in education policy may perpetuate inequities for students with dis/abilities from marginalized racial/ethnic backgrounds; and (2) centering student and family voices in educational spaces to effectively inform and improve classroom practice and, thereby, the schooling experiences of multiply marginalized youth. Prior to entering her role in academia, Dr. Griendling served as a middle school special educator for seven years across urban, suburban, and rural public school systems in the northeastern and southeastern United States.

Michelle Kalos, MA, is a homosexual, cisgender female from northern California. She has worked as a teacher of Deaf and Hard of Hearing students and a generalist special education teacher with students of all ages and disabilities for sixteen years. Michelle is a PhD student at the University of Northern Colorado in the School of Special Education. Her research focuses on transition practices for youth with disabilities and how those practices increase inclusivity and equality in our society for those with disabilities. Michelle's interests include special education practices internationally and collaboration among countries for positive outcomes for people with disabilities. She is an active member of the Council for Exceptional Children in the DCDT, TED, and DISES divisions.

Veronica Y. Kang, PhD, is an Asian cisgender female who has spent most of her life in Korea, Seattle, and Chicago. Dr. Kang has collaborated with students with autism and developmental disabilities as an educator in families' homes and preschool and kindergarten classrooms. Dr. Kang is now an assistant professor of special education in the Department of Counseling, Higher Education, and Special Education at the University of Maryland at College Park. Her research focuses on naturalistic early language and communication instruction and collaborating with culturally and linguistically diverse students and families in early intervention and early childhood education. Dr. Kang is an active member of the Division for Early Childhood (DEC) of the Council for Exceptional Children and serves as the cochair of the DEC's Consortium for Innovations in Doctoral Excellence.

Dylan Kapit, MA, (they/them), is a white, queer, transmasculine, nonbinary, Jewish, autistic individual living on Lenape land in New York City. Their life mission is to make the world a better, safer, and more inclusive place for LGBTQ+ folks and autistic individuals through their work as a LGBTQ+ and autism–focused special educator, sex educator, consultant, speaker, and advocate. Dylan is currently a doctoral student in Special Education and Equity and Justice Scholar at the School of Education at the University of Pittsburgh, where their doctoral work focuses on creating a queer- and trans-inclusive, autistic-focused sex education curriculum. They are also the program coordinator for LGBTQ+ Outreach at Barnard College of Columbia University, their alma mater, where they meet the needs of LGBTQ+ students through programming, and provide competency training to faculty, staff, and administrators around best practices for supporting that student population. Dylan has also presented at several national conferences, including the Division of Autism and Developmental Disabilities Conference and the National Sex Ed Conference, and leads professional development for educators all across the country.

Chelda Smith Kondo, PhD, (she/her/hers), identifies as a cisgender, able-bodied, Americanized Haitian woman. Chelda is an associate professor specializing in Culturally Sustaining Pedagogy at the University of St. Thomas (UST). Her scholarly articles have been published in leading education journals and interdisciplinary journals, and her scholarship has been honored for excellence in three different subfields: intersectional justice in education, qualitative research, and culturally relevant pedagogy. Chelda currently sits on the governing board of InterAction Inc., a nonprofit committed to activating and advancing Young Black, Indigenous, People of Color and their counternarratives to build a more just, inclusive, and equitable society. In 2021–2022, she was a visiting scholar at the Opportunity & Inclusive Growth Institute (OIGI) at the Federal Reserve Bank of Minneapolis where she edited and cowrote a forthcoming book exploring the application of critical pedagogy in teacher preparation.

Nathaniel Lentz is a white male from Reedsburg, Wisconsin. Nathaniel was born with cerebral palsy and a learning disability. He has presented at numerous state and national conferences about how people with disabilities can achieve success in education and employment. Nathaniel was a member of the Wisconsin Board for People with Developmental Disabilities for eight years. He served on the Think College Steering Committee to help students with disabilities succeed in college. Nathaniel advocated for people with disabilities at the Wisconsin Legislature and the US Congress in Washington, DC. He advocated before the Wisconsin State Joint Committee on Finance for more financial support for people with disabilities. He served as a mentor for the Cutting Edge Program at Edgewood College. He is an advocate for the Living Well Grant and for People First Wisconsin. Nathaniel has been in the Social Isolation coalition, Technology coalition, and the Voting coalition. Nathaniel is a self-advocate on the National Council of Self-Advocates with the Arc. Nathaniel earned his bachelor's degree from the University of Wisconsin–Whitewater in 2014.

Meaghan McCollow, PhD, BCBA-D, is a white, queer, cisgender female who has lived and worked in a variety of areas across the United States including Arizona, New York, Washington, California, and Michigan. Dr. McCollow has many years of experience as an educator. Currently, Dr. McCollow is an associate professor of special education at California State University East Bay. Dr. McCollow's scholarly interests focus on the professional development and training of education specialists, the diversity of participants included in research-based practices, and sexuality education for individuals with intellectual and developmental disabilities.

Paul I. McGill, MA, CCC-SLP, is a Korean cisgender male originally from Gunsan, South Korea, and adopted into an interracial Irish-Filipino family. He is a licensed speech-language pathologist working in Orange County, California, in the high school setting and private practice. Mr. McGill's clinical expertise is in the areas of pragmatic language, executive functioning skills, and speech sound disorders. He is trained in several evidence-based methodologies including the Kaufman Speech to Language Protocol (K-SLP), Prompts for Restructuring Oral Muscular Phonetic Targets (PROMPT), and Program for the Education and Enrichment of Relational Skills (PEERS). He is interested in how intersectionality, current cultural trends, and environmental variables can influence positive therapy outcomes and increase generalization opportunities for students. He is a member of the American Speech-Language-Hearing Association (ASHA), the California Speech-Language-Hearing Association (CSHA), and the Corporate Speech Pathology Network (CORSPAN).

Michelle Eastey Mercado earned her BS in occupational therapy in 1997 from the College of St. Catherine. Shortly after graduation, she returned to the College of St. Catherine and earned her MA in occupational therapy in 2001, while working as an pediatric outpatient occupational therapist. She is a heterosexual, cisgender woman, and an occupational therapist-educator serving children and families across a variety of settings, including early intervention, schools, hospitals, and outpatient clinics. Michelle returned to college after working for fourteen years in healthcare and schools and earned her doctorate in occupational therapy from St. Catherine University in 2014. Michelle has a long-standing interest in disability, equity, and inclusion and she is now the Lead for Occupational Therapy, Physical Therapy, Music Therapy, Art Therapy, Physical/Health Disabilities Teachers and Developmental Adapted Physical Education Teachers for St. Paul Public Schools. She is also an adjunct professor in the Occupational Therapy Department at the Henrietta Schmoll School of Health Sciences at St. Catherine University and is the president of the Sotos Syndrome Support Association and sits on its medical advisory board. In addition to her professional interests, the most rewarding is her lived experience as the parent of four multiracial children, one of whom has a rare genetic condition, autism, and complex developmental/healthcare needs. She resides in Minneapolis, Minnesota, with her husband and children, where they enjoy spending time working out and traveling.

Emily O'Brien, MEd in special education, is a white, cisgender, female, mother, daughter, sister, and educator from the Twin Cities in Minnesota. Emily has a master's of education specializing in autism spectrum disorder. After spending four years as a general education teacher, Emily found a passion for working with students with disabilities in inclusive classrooms as an elementary school resource special education teacher. Throughout her experiences in teaching, she has developed a strong interest in early child development, and social emotional learning and how it relates to children with disabilities. This interest has sparked a drive to research and implement evidence-based practices for both academic and social skills. Emily is invested in collaborating with her students and their families in supporting their academic, social-emotional, and behavioral learning which allows them to be successful in an inclusive school environment.

Lydia Ocasio-Stoutenburg, PhD, is an assistant professor of special education at Pennsylvania State University. She is a Black woman with Afro-Indigenous roots and Puerto Rican ethnicity. She is a wife and mother to five children, one of whom happens to be a young man with Down syndrome. Her scholarship, teaching, and service focus on equity, responding to the unceasing need to advocate for systems to better support people who hold multiple marginalized identities, as well as their families. Some of her work includes caregiver advocacy, experience addressing intersectionality among Black and Brown families of children and adults labeled with intellectual and developmental disabilities (IDD), using critical ethnography to uplift family-disability counternarratives, and empowering teachers to support students through holistic and asset-based approaches. Lydia uses qualitative inquiry through critical, intersectional, and emancipatory frameworks, drawing from Black feminist theory. Lydia remains a lifelong activist for both disability, family, and community justice. She has also coauthored two books on family advocacy across racialized identities, ethnicities, cultures, languages, disabilities, and other social identities.

Olivia Parry is a white female who has Down syndrome. Olivia was fully included through her preK–12 public school experiences. After high school, she attended Edgewood College's postsecondary Cutting Edge program to continue her education. Olivia works in fashion and art, which are passions of hers. She owns her own business and lives independently. Olivia is an active member of her church and choirs. Olivia has presented at numerous state and national conferences about her experiences as an individual with a disability.

Dana Patenaude, MEd, BCBA, LBS, is a white cisgender woman doctoral candidate at the Pennsylvania State University. Previously, Dana worked as a board-certified behavior analyst in an applied behavior analysis (ABA) clinic in Pittsburgh, Pennsylvania. During this time, she created and supervised verbal behavior-based programs for children on the autism spectrum as well as working closely with their families to create socially significant goals and objectives. Dana currently serves as a diversity and inclusion consultant for an ABA clinic, ensuring their practices and protocols are inclusive for both staff and clients. Dana is currently working on an AAC Leadership Project in which professionals in the Special Education and Communication Sciences and Disorders fields work to advance knowledge and increase community engagement in AAC. In her free time, Dana enjoys walking her dog and spending time with her family.

John Pirone, EdD, identifies as a white, straight, and cisgender man. Dr. Pirone currently coordinates an American Sign Language (ASL) program and teaches ASL and Deaf Culture courses at the University of Vermont. His research interests include ASL education in postsecondary settings and equity in education for Deaf children. Dr. Pirone is an author of several articles and a book chapter on equity in public education and ASL education. He has offered numerous presentations and workshops on a range of topics such as equity in education; access/inclusion; best practices for ASL pedagogy, curriculum, and assessments; and advocacy at local, state, and international levels. Dr. Pirone has been teaching ASL, Deaf Culture, and Deaf Studies at colleges and universities in Vermont, New Hampshire, and Massachusetts for over eighteen years. In addition to teaching, Dr. Pirone actively engages in community advocacy through several organizations in Vermont. He cofounded and serves on the Association of Sign Language Vermonters whose mission is to protect, promote, and advance the linguistic human rights—signed languages—of Vermonters. Dr. Pirone previously served on numerous boards for organizations such as The Learning Center for the Deaf, Massachusetts Commission for the Deaf and Hard of Hearing, Disability Policy Consortium, and National Research Center for Parents with Disabilities.

Colin Rose, EdD, is a Black, cisgender male and is the founder and CEO of Perennial Education Consulting where he supports state, district, and nonprofit leaders to create coherence and operationalize improvement for excellence and equity. Prior to his consulting work, Dr. Rose was an assistant superintendent at the Boston Public Schools wherein he was able to build a legacy of effective policies, systemic initiatives and professional development, meaningful programming, and innovative school models. Dr. Rose's leadership and equity innovations have been featured in multiple journals and media outlets and he has been part of many national initiatives focused on educational improvement including the Aspen Institute Education & Society Program and the AERA (American Educational Research Association) Equity Working Group. Dr. Rose's foundation in education was formed as a teacher, fostering some of the highest student growth scores in Massachusetts.

Kendra V. Saunders, PhD, NCSP, is a Black, Christian, heterosexual, nondisabled woman originally from Fort Lauderdale/Miami, Florida, and now living in Dallas, Texas. Kendra's teaching experience includes working with students from prekindergarten through graduate school. Additionally, she has provided psychological services in both school and clinical settings. Her passion for disability rights, history, and the dismantling of ableism is connected to her personal experience as the sister of a disabled woman. She is currently an assistant professor of school psychology at Texas A&M University–Commerce. Her primary research interests are in the multiple facets of school-based mental health services, including the delivery of services through MTSS (Multi-Tiered

Systems of Support), which includes community-based support. Additionally, she is interested in how the mental health attitudes of students, teachers, and parents impact access to mental health services. Her hope is that her research will provide better access to mental health services for all students, which often begins with addressing negative attitudes about mental health and mental illness. In her free time, she enjoys reading, watching vintage TV shows, listening to entertainment and political/legal podcasts, and baking.

Sandy Smith, PhD, is an assistant professor in the Department of Elementary, Early, and Special Education at Southeast Missouri State University and a member of the LGBTQIA+ community. She earned her doctorate in educational psychology with an emphasis in special education from Texas A&M University. Dr. Smith began her career in education as a paraprofessional for children with emotional and behavioral disorders (EBD). After supporting students with EBD at both the elementary and secondary levels, Dr. Smith began coaching teachers on classroom and behavior management. She continues to serve as an educational consultant in general and special education settings. Dr. Smith's research interests include Positive Behavioral Interventions and Supports (PBIS), coaching classroom management, and interventions for students with EBD.

Jonte' C. Taylor (JT), PhD, is a cisgender, Black male and an associate professor of special education at Pennsylvania State University (Penn State). His research includes examining effective strategies for inclusive STEAM education for students with disabilities and improving school/classroom climates for students, families, and teachers. His STEAM scholarship focuses on supporting inquiry-based science instruction and using the arts in research and evidence-based interventions and practices. His school/classroom scholarship emphasizes student/classroom motivation, student/teacher relationships, followership/leadership dynamics, and using hip-hop in the classroom across educational settings. Prior to being at Penn State, Dr. Taylor did his postdoctoral work as an Institute of Education Sciences (IES) scholar at the University of Iowa investigating science education for students with disabilities. He earned his bachelor's degree in special education from Tuskegee University and his master's and doctorate from Auburn University in collaborative education and special education with an emphasis in autism and emotional/behavioral disorders, respectively. His classroom instructional experiences have included a variety of settings including juvenile justice, preK–12 grade schools, and group home environments, with a variety of students including adults with moderate to severe intellectual disabilities and students with autism spectrum disorder and/or emotional/behavioral disorders.

Elizabeth Thao, MEd, is an Asian, Hmong, pansexual female who works as a special education teacher and autism specialist based out of St. Paul, Minnesota. She has worked in various roles in special education, including as a teaching assistant/para, a self-contained classroom teacher, a co-teacher, and a teacher on special assignment (TOSA) on district-level teams, serving students across multiple disability areas and ability levels. She received a Bachelor of Individualized Studies with concentrations in Asian American Studies, Asian Languages and Literature, and Teaching English as a Second Language from the University of Minnesota, and she received her master's in special education and autism licensure from the University of St. Thomas. Her scholarly interests focus on equity, training, and advocacy in regard to teachers of color in the field and students of color in special education. She is an alumnus of the Institute for Teachers of Color Committed to Racial Justice, and has been an active member of several racial equity teams and affinity groups focused on the support and retention of educators of color.

Sharde Theodore, MSEd, EdS, is a Black, cisgender female who has had five years of experience as an elementary special education teacher in Miami-Dade county. Currently, she is a doctoral candidate studying special education at Florida International University. Her research is focused on culturally responsive and sustaining practices and social and emotional supports for diverse students with or at risk for emotional and behavioral disorders.

Yokasta Urena is a forty-three-year-old Latina from Queens, New York. Her parents immigrated from the Dominican Republic in the early 1960s. Yokasta and her nineteen-year-old son are legally blind due to a retinal condition known as Leber's congenital amaurosis. Yokasta is currently a doctoral candidate at New England College focusing on educational leadership. The focus of her dissertation is on the lived experiences of transition-age youth with visual impairments in inclusive, self-initiated internship programs. Over the past twenty years, Yokasta has held many positions in the field of special education, including parent coordinator, advocate, teacher of the Blind and Visually Impaired, integrated preschool classroom teacher, direct service provider/evaluator in early childhood, and youth program manager. Yokasta is an adjunct instructor for Illinois State University's Special Education and Low Vision and Blindness programs.

Rebecca Wade, EdS, MA, is a white, cisgender female from St. Paul, Minnesota. Rebecca is an elementary school principal and former special education teacher in the Roseville Area Schools and an adjunct faculty at the University of St. Thomas in the Department of Special Education and at Metropolitan State University in the Department of Urban Education. Rebecca is committed to interrupting and interrogating practices and policies that perpetuate white supremacist ideologies and predictably lead to disproportionate outcomes for learners who have been historically marginalized.

Sara E. Wildman, MEd, is a white, cisgender female who has twenty years of experience as a special education practitioner. Sara has served students within special education in a variety of settings including as a paraprofessional, special education teacher, teacher on special assignment within a due process office, special education program manager, and special education academy principal serving students with emotional and behavioral challenges. Mrs. Wildman is currently a special education coordinator with San Diego County Office of Education as part of a grant from California Department of Education to support districts throughout California on timeliness compliance and the writing of high-quality IEPs. Mrs. Wildman's professional interests focus on supporting students and families from marginalized communities in understanding the special education process.

James Williams is a white, autistic, asexual, cisgender male adult. His sexual orientation has often intersected with his autistic identity as he has lived a lifetime of struggling to understand social rules in a society that were based on interests and attractions that he has never fully experienced before in his lifetime. He was diagnosed with autism at the age of three in 1991. He graduated from Glenbrook North High School in Northbrook, Illinois, in 2010. Today, he travels the United States lecturing on autism, and is the author of several autism-related books. He is also a recorderist who has performed at numerous conventions. He is a member of the SPARK Community Advisory Committee, and Wisconsin's Community of Practice on Autism Spectrum and other Developmental Disabilities.

Gulnoza Yakubova, PhD, is an associate professor in Special Education in the College of Education at the University of Maryland, College Park. She is a cisgender female who grew up in a rural area of Kazakhstan. She has expertise in working with autistic children and those with developmental disabilities to teach them independent living skills and support them in an academic environment. Her research interests focus on examining technology-based interventions to teach autistic students the skills they need to have a successful life after school. She is an active member of the Council for Exceptional Children, the Cultural Diversity Committee of the International Society for Autism Research, and the International Association for Special Education.

www.ingramcontent.com/pod-product-compliance
Lightning Source LLC
Chambersburg PA
CBHW051553230426
43668CB00013B/1836